A History of Swedish Literature

A History of Scandinavian Literatures

Sven H. Rossel, General Editor

VOLUME 3

A History of
Swedish Literature

Edited by Lars G. Warme

Published by
the University of
Nebraska Press,
Lincoln & London,
in cooperation
with The American-
Scandinavian
Foundation

Publication of this book was
assisted by a grant from the
National Endowment for the
Humanities.

Library of Congress
Cataloging-in-
Publication Data
A history of Swedish
literature / edited by Lars
G. Warme.
p.   cm. —
(A History of Scandinavian
literatures; v. 3)
Includes
bibliographical references
and index.
ISBN 0-8032-4750-8 (cl:
alk. paper)
1. Swedish
literature—History and
criticism.   I. Warme, Lars G.
II. Series.
PT9263.H57   1996
839.709—dc20
95-43124 CIP

Contents

6. Into the Twentieth Century: 1890–1950

Susan Brantly

7. Literature after 1950

Rochelle Wright

8. Women Writers
Cheri Register

9. Literature for Children and Young People
Maria Nikolajeva

Acknowledgments

I owe a debt of gratitude to a number of people on both sides of the Atlantic for providing valuable information, suggestions, and constructive criticism. Among them is the late Yvonne Sandstrom, whose death is a great loss to the community of Scandinavists; she is fondly remembered. My very special thanks go to Robert Bjork, who generously shared his expertise and critical acumen. Other scholars readily responded to requests for general assessments or specific elucidations: Monica Asztalos, Synnöve Claesson, Vivi Edström, Sverker Göransson, Joseph Harris, Sven-Bertil Jansson, Kurt Johannesson, Torborg Lundell, Börje Räftegård, Birgit Sawyer, Ross Shideler, Barbro Söderberg, and Alan Swanson.

To Sven H. Rossel, general editor of *A History of Scandinavian Literatures*, and to the nine contributors to this volume, my heartfelt thanks. In addition to their professional excellence, they have proved to possess the virtues of kindness and patience to an exceptional degree.

Introduction

"Beyond the Suiones is another sea . . . so far (and here rumor speaks the truth), and so far only does the world reach." In his *Germania*, Tacitus (ca. A.D. 55–120) provides this early literary reference to the Swedes (*Suiones*). For the next millennium, the countries of the North continued to exist for the civilized world as a nebulous region inhabited by peoples reputed to indulge in wild and barbaric customs, an *Ultima Thule* at the end of the world. Occasional visits from the northerners in the form of Viking raids lent substance to the rumors and did little to dispel the popular view.

The introduction of Christianity in Scandinavia around the year 1000 gave Sweden membership in the Catholic community, the "European Union" of the Middle Ages. With Latin serving as a lingua franca, occasional voices could now be heard, at great time intervals, from within this region. There was Birgitta, in the fourteenth century, recording her revelations or upbraiding kings and popes, and there were the brothers Magnus, Johannes and Olaus, in the sixteenth century, presenting histories in Latin of the Nordic peoples and their kings as well as descriptions of local customs. The brothers became casualties of the Reformation, leaving their country rather than abandon the faith of their fathers. The effect of the Reformation on letters and culture in general in Sweden was critical: the severance from the Roman Catholic Church meant cutting off a cultural taproot. Left on its own, Swedish culture was too feeble to produce even a semblance of the Renaissance and humanist culture that flourished in other parts of Europe. The Reformation's emphasis on the use of the vernacular, on the other hand, strengthened the position of the Swedish language and laid the foundation for a national culture and literature. By the same token, it made this culture and literature less accessible to the rest of the world. Latin remained for at least another two centuries the language of international exchange through which a Swedenborg or a Linné, in the eighteenth century, made his voice heard outside Sweden. In the previous century, Queen Christina had chosen to write her aphorisms in French.

It was not until the early nineteenth century that Swedish literature attracted enough attention or curiosity to tempt translators to bring it out of its linguistic isolation. This happened during the romantic era, when there was a great deal of interest in the manifestations of some real or imagined "national soul" or "national character." Posterity may not share the contemporaries' enthusiasm for Esaias Tegnér's viking verse epic *Frithiofs saga*, but in its own time the poem enjoyed unprecedented popularity, and translations appeared in several languages, Longfellow presenting one of the English versions. By midcentury, Fredrika Bremer's travelogues from both the Old and the New World as well as her prose fiction found avid readers outside Sweden, not least in the United States. In the last couple of decades of the nineteenth century, August Strindberg made his presence felt on the international stage, where the Norwegian Ibsen and the Dane Brandes had already caused the literary world to take note of new and revolutionary signals issuing from Scandinavia.

In the twentieth century, thanks to the efforts of dedicated translators, many more Swedish authors can be read outside the sphere of their original language; some of them have reached considerable audiences— Selma Lagerlöf, Pär Lagerkvist, Vilhelm Moberg, Astrid Lindgren, and the Finland-Swedish author Tove Jansson, to mention a few. In the English-speaking world, renditions from the rich treasures of Swedish poetry have been offered by translators who, like Longfellow, are poets in their own right—among them W. S. Auden, May Swenson, and Robert Bly. Their renditions have made the worlds of such twentieth-century poets as Gunnar Ekelöf, Harry Martinson, and Tomas Tranströmer accessible to modern readers, while others, such as Judith Moffett, have salvaged poems of previously untranslated "classics" from earlier centuries. Almost two hundred years after Carl Michael Bellman (1740–95) captured scenes and impressions in words and music from Stockholm during the Gustavian Age, English readers could begin to appreciate the unique genius of Sweden's most popular poet of all time. Translations of works by prose writers such as C.J.L. Almqvist (1793–1866) are also giving belated recognition to the originality of these authors and the boldness of their ideas. Ultimately, the translations constitute previously missing pieces in the larger cultural mosaic of civilization, as they add to our awareness of the richness and complexity of a common past and a shared present.

Invaluable as these translations are, they cover but a fraction of the total national literature of Sweden, offering tantalizing samplings of treasures locked in a "small" language. The question could be raised whether these relatively few translations are truly representative of Swedish literature as a whole, a question that in turn leads to reflections on what is specifically "Swedish" about Swedish literature.

The present volume, *A History of Swedish Literature*, may not directly address the elusive notion of Swedishness, but the nine separate chapters tracing the history of Swedish letters from the earliest runic inscriptions to the literature of the 1990s nevertheless give the reader a sense of both what is particular about Swedish culture and what makes it an integral part in a larger European cultural context. It is not unreasonable to claim that Sweden's relative isolation in a remote corner of Europe, its small and homogeneous population with its own set of traditions, customs, and beliefs, as well as social and political institutions and a shared fate through the vagaries of history, all combined to produce a common outlook different from that of other countries subject to their particular conditions. The importance of language to define national identity is as obvious as it is often overlooked. It is the repository of a collective experience, and—as repeatedly pointed out by Lars Gyllensten, for example—it contains a description of the world and is our chief instrument for experiencing and exploring the world. On the most immediate level, translators can testify to the occasional frustration when they attempt to find equivalents for certain expressions and turns of phrase that remain stubbornly and unyieldingly "Swedish." In the course of history, the Swedish language has absorbed elements from other languages, proving itself either flexible enough to incorporate these elements or not strong enough to resist them; important in this respect are the "invasions" from Low German in the Middle Ages, from French during the Age of the Enlightenment, and from English in the twentieth century, especially after the Second World War. Voices have been raised to criticize and deplore this loss of Swedishness, this propensity of the language to succumb to foreign influences, most vociferously perhaps by Georg Stiernhielm in the seventeenth century and Olof von Dalin in the eighteenth. But the language simply reflects the general phenomenon of a smaller culture's adapting itself to influences from more powerful ones. Such assimilation is not necessarily synonymous with slavish imitation; enough of the native character remains to lend a particular color, a special flavor to the end result. The phenomenon is clearly manifested in Swedish literature as impulses from the main currents of European thought revitalized a more native tradition; thus we are justified in prefixing with a qualifying "Swedish" the major aesthetic, philosophical, or ideological movements—whether baroque, enlightenment, romanticism, naturalism, or modernism.

The present volume is the work of nine contributors. Guided by the ideal of an impossible objectivity, they have been faced with difficult choices regarding what to include and what to omit in the rich material at their disposal. True to its title, *A History of Swedish Literature* uses a traditional chronological approach, confident that Schlegel's pronouncement in 1812 still holds true, that "the best theory of art is its history." By the same token, the development of Swedish literature is viewed as inseparable from its historical and social context and its receptiveness to the international cross-fertilizations mentioned above. Each new history has the advantage of drawing on and adding to the achievements of its predecessors while revising their findings in the light of more recent scholarship. Impressive works have been produced in Sweden in the past one hundred years to record the history of the nation's literature. The first edition of the pioneering volumes by Henrik Schück and Karl Warburg appeared in 1895 with later editions by E. N. Tigerstedt and new chapters added by E. Hj. Linder, and the monumental six-volume *Den svenska litteraturen* (The Swedish literature), edited by Lars Lönnroth and Sven Delblanc with a seventh bibliographical volume, saw completion in 1990.

In the English-speaking world, Alrik Gustafson's *A History of Swedish Literature* has been the standard work in English since its publication in 1961. It remains a remarkable achievement with all the strengths and only few of the inevitable shortcomings due to the single perspective of one author. It brings Swedish literature up to the early years of the 1950s in the wake of the Second World War. With some justification Gustafson can still refer to Sweden as a model of "the middle way," an epithet of enduring sticking power from the book by Marquis W. Childs published in 1936. The epithet is hardly applicable in the 1990s; Childs himself felt compelled to write a sequel in 1980, *Sweden: The Middle Way on Trial.* The present volume records the changes that have taken place since Gustafson's history appeared, changes that we find reflected in the documentary literature of the 1960s and the radical politicizing of large segments of the cultural life in the early 1970s, but also in the growth and development above the fray of such remarkable authorships as those of Pär Lagerkvist, Gunnar Ekelöf, Eyvind Johnson, Lars Gyllensten, and Tomas Tranströmer. A more recent survey of Swedish literature is Ingemar Algulin's *A History of Swedish Literature*, published in Stockholm in 1989.

Considerably more circumscribed than Gustafson's work or the present volume and designed, perhaps, for a more general audience, it provides a useful introduction to Swedish literature.

It could be argued that offering a separate chapter on women's literature is counterproductive, vitiating the idea of equality by making a special case for women writers who in the process will be "ghettoized" according to gender. Even from this brief introduction it should be eminently clear that some of the most remarkable and most successful writers through the ages happened to be women, foremost among them Birgitta, Queen Christina, Fredrika Bremer, Selma Lagerlöf, and Astrid Lindgren. Along with other women writers they are dealt with in their respective chapters, not primarily as women but as outstanding contributors to Swedish culture and literature. A chapter on women's literature is, however, justified, as it provides a salutary view of the gender issue in Swedish literature and focuses on an often overlooked female perspective and on the development of a feminist awareness.

In recent decades literature for children and young people has attracted special attention. The readers of the last chapter in the present volume will note the great number of Swedish children's books that have been translated into English, making this literature a major Swedish export. It is tempting to see a correlation between a flourishing children's literature of high quality and the proud statistics for book consumption in Sweden and the rest of Scandinavia (with Iceland topping the list). A similar connection could be made between Stockholm's having more theaters in relation to its population than any other capital in the world and Sweden's long tradition of an intensely active children's theater.

In the preface to his literary history Gustafson regrets the fact that he has not had the space to deal with "Swedo-Finnish" literature except in the case of a few portal figures, such as Johan Ludvig Runeberg and the "poetic moderns" of the 1920s. Readers of the present volume will find the same selectivity regarding the important literature produced by the Swedish-speaking minority in Finland with the inclusion of a few writers such as Runeberg, Zacharias Topelius, Edith Södergran, Tove Jansson, and Märta Tikkanen. The seemingly arbitrary exclusion of a large number of others, however, is emphatically not the result of neglect but simply a matter of avoiding duplication: these writers along with the ones mentioned above are given the full treatment they amply deserve in the companion volume of the present one, *A History of Finnish Literature*.

What is the future of Swedish literature? The question is justified on the eve of a new millennium with Sweden's membership in a larger European community. The political-economic nature of this "European Union" may have an even greater impact on the culture of smaller nations than did the spiritual European community of the Middle Ages and may entail greater sacrifices in terms of national identity for all nations. In addition, forces within Sweden are having an impact on its culture. In 1975, Sweden adopted a new official cultural policy involving among other things government support for literature. Notwithstanding its impressive book consumption, Sweden is a small nation with a proportionately modest readership, which in combination with high production costs makes book publishing unprofitable. Few authors in Sweden are able to support themselves solely from the results of their creative writing. There is also strong competition from literature in translation and from readily available sources of entertainment in the electronic media age. The government support of literature had as its aim the safeguarding of the diversity and the quality of Swedish literature (it is worth noting that the government was given only a minority voice in determining the ultimate worthiness of recipients of support). It is uncertain to what extent such measures will be able to protect the continued growth and health of national literatures. In a global perspective, the larger and seemingly irresistible forces of ecological diminution and destruction of the diversity of species have their disturbing counterpart on the cultural level.

The present volume is offered as a contribution to the knowledge and preservation of Swedish literature. It is hoped that the references in the text to English translations of works under discussion and the bibliographies will open doors to further explorations and discoveries.

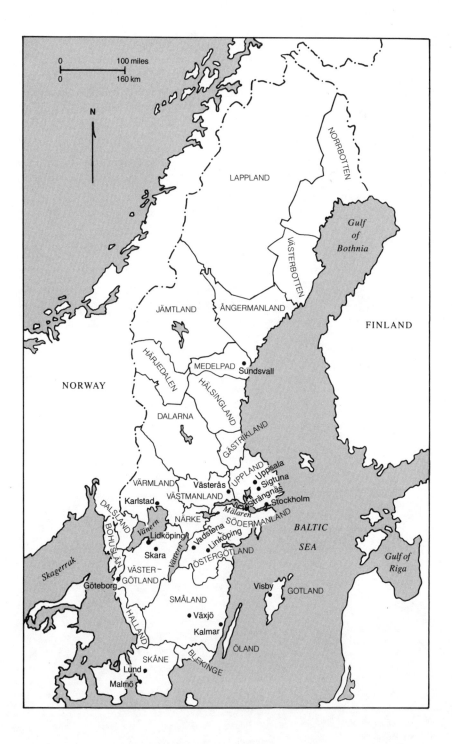

The Middle Ages

Stephen A. Mitchell

1

Little can be said with certainty about spiritual culture in Sweden in the earliest periods, yet it can at least be partially inferred from pictorial and commemorative inscriptions in rock and other nonperishable materials. Although the precise interpretation the carvers themselves would have placed on their works remains an enigma, the earliest rock carvings, the so-called *hällristningar*, provide a tantalizing glimpse into cult activities and other religious preoccupations of the Nordic Bronze Age (1800–400 B.C.). In the north of Sweden, such carvings tend to be of simple, naturalistically shaped animal forms, presumably connected with hunting rituals, whereas those to the south more often present ships, armed warriors, abstractions generally interpreted as sun signs, and other figures associated with an agrarian society. Study of these carvings has suggested to some that the inhabitants of Sweden in this early period worshiped a sky god, whose occasionally phallic figure is a common participant in the busy scenes portrayed in the *hällristningar*. The concatenation of men (typically armed with spears and axes), ships, sun signs, and horses in these carvings, together with such finds as a small horse-drawn cart laden with a gilded sun disk discovered in neighboring Denmark, has been read by some scholars as testimony to a belief system in which the central myth concerned the movement of the sun across the sky. Others have connected the carvings to fertility rituals, legal rituals, and hunting rituals, as well as to cults of the dead, of the moon, and of wagons, and to the Norse deities known from much later written materials. The numerous small figurines of naked females wearing necklaces from the Bronze Age have been interpreted, in conjunction with the later mythological materials, as a sign that female deities played an important, perhaps key, role in the religious life of the early periods.

The Swedish Iron Age (400 B.C.–A.D. 1050) is typically divided into Pre-Roman (400 B.C.–A.D. 50) and Roman (50–400) periods, the Migration Era (400–550), the Vendel Era (550–800), and the Viking Age (800–1050). The archaeological record of these centuries reflects periodic restlessness and anxiety, if we may judge from such criteria as the numerous fortifications that were erected (e.g., the late Iron Age fortress Eketorp on the island of Öland in the Baltic). The archaeological testimony has also sometimes been interpreted as indicating large-scale population movements; certainly contemporary authorities regarded the Nordic area as the homeland of many of the barbarian peoples with whom the classical world had contact. Writing in the sixth century, for example, the Gothic historian Jordanes refers in his *Getica* (Eng. tr. *Gothic History)* to the region (*Scandza insula*) as an *officina gentium* ("factory of races") and a *vagina nationum* ("womb of peoples"). With respect to native aesthetic monuments (in addition to the runic inscriptions), of special interest from these early periods are the Gotlandic picture stones, the erection of which flourished in the fifth, eighth, and eleventh centuries; of particular note are those stones bearing scenes that complement heroic and mythological tales known from later Nordic tradition.

The centuries before the conversion of Sweden to Christianity, but roughly proximate with missionary activities there, are so dominated by the voyages of various Swedish traders and pirates, known collectively as vikings, that the period is named the Viking Age after them. Memorials that mention expeditions to England, together with the archaeological record (which has yielded, for example, tens of thousands of Anglo-Saxon coins), amply confirm that some Swedish adventurers journeyed to the west, although Swedish "viking" activity was predominantly oriented to the east. In addition to creating settlements along coastal Finland, Poland, Estonia, and Russia, the Swedes of the ninth to eleventh centuries traveled through the Slavic areas to the east, especially along various Russian rivers, such as the Dnieper. For the most part, the "viking" presence was probably one in which control of the waterways and trade was maintained. According to Russian chronicles, however, the "calling of Rurik," in which Scandinavians (Varangian Rus') under the leadership of Rurik were supposedly invited to rule over the area, began the establishment of a state in the East Slav area (Eng. tr. *POS*, 298 [see p. 515 for a list of the abbreviations used in this chapter]). Certainly the legendary works of later Nordic tradition accept the idea of large Scandinavian settlements in Russia, but whatever the actual numbers, by the twelfth and thirteenth centuries the Scandinavian community had presumably been absorbed into the Slavic population, leaving little more than a variety of place- and proper names as their legacy (e.g., Igor from Yngvarr; Olga from Helga). Perhaps the most interesting document concerning the Rus' resulted from the encounter of an Arab emissary, Ibn Fadlān, with a group of them on the Volga in the year 922: his description of their habits, including the spectacular cremation of their dead chieftain, provides an astonishingly detailed glimpse into the world of the pagan Rus' with many parallels to later Nordic literary sources (Eng. tr. *POS*, 299–301).

The establishment in the thirteenth century of the Svear (Swedes) from the area of Lake Mälaren-Uppland as the preeminent political power in Sweden, at the expense of the Goths and Ostrogoths (who occupied areas roughly equivalent to the modern provinces of Västergötland and Östergötland), may have begun in the Vendel period; this point of view has been argued by those who see in the events of the Anglo-Saxon epic *Beowulf* a reflection of such activities. If indeed something along those lines did transpire, the results were not long-lasting; ninth-century commentaries, such as Rimbert's *Vita Anskarii* (Eng. tr. *Ansgar*) and the account in *King Alfred's Orosius* (Eng. tr. *Two Voyagers*), still tend to identify the Swedish region with the Baltic coastal areas and islands. Östergötland and Västergötland did not consistently come under the rule of a Swedish monarch for many centuries; in general, despite the occasional hegemony of the Svear over the other groups, Sweden appears to have consisted of a loose federation of Goths, Ostrogoths, and Swedes until the thirteenth century.

Still, it is not surprising that when Ansgar, the first Christian missionary, came to Sweden in A.D. 829 from Rheims, he went to King Björn in Birka. His work there, and a subsequent visit in 855 when he returned as bishop of Hamburg, are unusually well documented, for his companion on his second trip—and his successor as spiritual leader to the Swedish Christian community—also became his biographer. Unlike earlier commentators, such as Tacitus, Procopius, and Jordanes, whose information was often based on secondhand reports, Rimbert in his *Vita Anskarii* provides us with the first really reliable information we have of life in Sweden at this early date. The early Christianizing activities he records failed to take hold, however, partly because of pagan uprisings, a reaction that lasted many centuries: according to Icelandic sources, King Inge the Elder was driven from Old Uppsala (and the throne) in the late eleventh century by the Swedes for refusing to "observe the ancient laws" concerning sacrifice.

The king's brother-in-law was then elected to fulfill the joint duties of king and priest. In this capacity Blót-Sveinn ("Sacrifice-Sveinn") presided over the sacrifice of a horse, its dismemberment and ritual consumption, and the reddening of the sacrificial tree with its blood (*Saga Heiðreks*, 62–63; Eng. tr. *The Saga of King Heidrek*).

Unfortunately, we know with certainty all too little about the magicoreligious world of the heathen Swedes. The reports of foreign observers, the rich but often enigmatic archaeological record, later mythological texts from West Norse sources, and inferences drawn from comparative Indo-European linguistics are the eclectic and shadowy sources of our knowledge. Yet, there are indications that Nordic methology and religion as it has been interpreted by modern scholarship applies in broad terms to Sweden as well, although there can be no question of an organized or monolithic religion ever having held sway throughout the area or with all members of society. Regional and possibly social differences were no doubt manifested in religious beliefs. Cult practices about which there is general agreement include sacrifice, perhaps even human sacrifice, which seems to have played an important role in the rituals of the religion. The key deities were probably much the same as those known from thirteenth-century Icelandic sources: Óðinn, who was particularly associated with poetic composition, death, battle and magic; Þórr, the robust and nearly indestructible warrior; and Freyr, the god of fertility and generation whose worship seems to have been especially popular in Sweden. Contemporary authors support this view: writing in about 1070 and using the Danish king as his informant, Adam of Bremen describes a cult site at Uppsala in his *Gesta Hammaburgensis ecclesiae pontificum* (Eng. tr. *History of the Archbishops of Hamburg-Bremen*) at which the bodies of sacrificed animals and men were hung in trees; little more than a century later, Saxo Grammaticus claims in his *Gesta Danorum* (Eng. tr. *The History of the Danes*) that the Swedes worshiped Freyr at Uppsala with sacrifices and with lewd dancing and singing; and in Snorri Sturluson's early-thirteenth-century *Ynglingasaga* (Eng. tr. *The Saga of the Ynglings*), based on a skaldic poem from ca. 900 by Þjóðólfr of Hvin, Freyr is called the "lord of the Swedes" and credited with having built the great temple at Uppsala (Snorri, 1:23). There is, however, evidence to suggest that some other deities, such as Ullr, although fairly obscure figures in West Norse literary sources, may have enjoyed great popularity at one time in Sweden.

If pagan worship in pre-Christian Sweden was variegated—and it surely was—so too were the directions from which the conversion to Christianity came. The English and German churches, for example, vied for this honor.

Thus, although Hamburg-Bremen had begun its missionary activities in Sweden a century and a half earlier, the reign of Olof Skötkonung, the first monarch who can be documented as the king of both the Svear and the Götar and the first Swedish king to become a Christian, shows evidence of Anglo-Saxon influence (in minting coins and in the architecture of stone churches, for example). The career of the "archbishop" at the court of King Edmund the Old—the English-born, German-trained, and possibly Orthodox-consecrated Osmund—whose pretenses to being Sweden's archbishop and whose false teachings caused Adam of Bremen such great concern (3, chap. 14), is indicative of the many faces of Christianity at work in Sweden.

On the whole, the missionaries made their appeals to the ruling elite, and though nominally Christian heads of state can be traced back to the conversion of Olof Skötkonung at about the millennium, it is not until the eleventh and even early twelfth centuries that the population as a whole began to embrace the new faith. The support of the secular powers was fundamental to the growth of the church, and the missionaries were highly successful in acquiring it: one of the first cloisters in Scandinavia, for example, was founded by the Cistercians in 1143 at Alvastra in Östergötland at the request of King Sverker the Elder. Some years earlier (ca. 1130), the Sigtuna bishopric had been moved to the pagan cult site of Old Uppsala, a date that is often used for marking the triumph of Christianity over paganism. Yet the Christianization of the more remote areas of the land took even longer, perhaps well into the Middle Ages. Crusades, practiced in the Baltic as much as in the Holy Land, were often little more than an excuse for piracy, and we should therefore be reluctant to place too much weight on their testimony, but the fact that the Norwegian king Sigurðr the Crusader led an expedition in the 1120s against the Swedes of Småland, who were said to be heathens and bad Christians (Snorri, 3, 263; Eng. tr. *The Saga of the Sons of Magnus*), probably reflects well-entrenched resistance in certain areas and among some populations to the church's teachings. Within only a few decades (ca. 1156) the Swedes themselves launched the so-called first Finland crusade, reportedly under the leadership of King Erik the Saint and the English-born Bishop Henry, worshiped in the following century as the patron saints of Sweden and Finland, respectively.

When Sweden became a Christian nation, the results were mixed as far as the native spiritual culture is concerned. Seats of learning soon sprang up around the country, and the use of Latin, rather than the vernacular, within ecclesiastical and secular scriptoria was the norm. An example of the excellence a Swedish student might achieve in the language is to be found in the case of Gísli Finnsson, who was brought to Iceland in the early twelfth century by Bishop Jón of the Hólar See to teach Latin at the newly founded cathedral school (*Jóns saga helga* [The saga of St. Jón], 36). Yet the introduction of the Latin alphabet with the conversion was not the country's first encounter with writing, which was known in Sweden by the second century A.D., as documented by a spearhead found at Mos on Gotland with the (possibly fragmentary) runic inscription *gaois*. Whether it is part of the spear's name or had some other function is not clear, but it bears early testimony to one of the most important aspects of pre-Christian, but obviously not entirely preliterate, Sweden—the use of symbols to write down words and thoughts. Debate rages over the origins of this Germanic epigraphic system: Etruscan, Roman, and Greek alphabets have been suggested as possible forebears of the runes, an angular set of characters for carving in wood and stone which consisted of twenty-four letters in the older so-called *fuþark* and sixteen in the younger. It is probable that those who used runes regarded them as coming "from the gods," one interpretation postulated for the *rAki-ukutu* (from *ræginkundr*) on the ninth-century Sparlösa stone (Västergötland), a view also reflected in later Nordic mythological tradition (i.e., the eddic poem *Hávamál*; Eng. tr. "The Sayings of Hár," 80). Whatever the beginnings of the system, its effect has been to provide a rich legacy of material concerning early Swedish culture and language, for although runes were used throughout Scandinavia and the rest of the Germanic world, the harvest has been especially great in Sweden, which can boast of approximately thirty-five hundred inscriptions on stones, primarily from the eleventh century and often invoking the Christian god.

Among early runestones, the Rök inscription (ca. A.D. 800 [Eng. tr., *POS*, 296–97]) from Östergötland deserves special attention, for whereas the vast majority of runestones briefly commemorate dead friends and relatives or important events in the community, such as the erection of bridges, this ninth-century lithic document is a work with literary dimensions, including elaborate poetic diction, a structure that is strongly riddle-like, and a wide spectrum of heroic materials, partially in verse. In fact, it is frequently cited as representing the beginning of Swedish literature. Central to the inscription is the strophe:

> Theodoric the bold,
> king of sea-warriors,
> ruled over
> Reid-sea shores.

Now he sits armed
on his Gothic horse,
shield strapped,
protector of Mærings.
(Jansson 1962, 14)

A nearly ubiquitous figure in Germanic legendary texts, this Theodoric (also known as Þiðrikr and Dietrich, and as Didrik in later Old Swedish texts) demonstrates the connectedness of Swedish popular tradition to the rest of the Teutonic world, although the source of this reference has been the subject of much debate.

A number of petroglyphs likewise portray aspects of widely known heroic and mythological materials, the dominant story among which is, not surprisingly, that of Sigurðr the Dragon-slayer. Portions of his career are portrayed in the carvings on the Gök stone (Södermanland), the Drävle stone (Uppland), the Stora Ramsjö stone (Uppland), the Ock-elbo stone (Gästrikland), and the recently discovered Västerljung stone (Södermanland), but nowhere is the legend better presented, or executed with a greater appreciation for the tradition as a whole, than at Ramsund in Södermanland. Here the carver has placed a runic message, the celebration of a bridge construction by a certain Sigrid in honor of her father-in-law's death ("for Holmger's soul"), within the body of a highly stylized dragon, which Sigurðr is killing from below. In the middle, the viewer is provided with representations of the most dramatic moments in the legend: while roasting the dragon's heart, Sigurðr burns his finger on the meat and sticks his thumb into his mouth, only to find that he now understands the language of the birds sitting in the tree to which his horse Grani is tied; they warn him of Reginn's baleful designs, and the young hero beheads the treacherous smith, the symbols of whose trade— a bellows, a hammer, tongs, an anvil—are strewn about. The church was quick to exploit this popular legend, and several baptismal fonts from Bohus (Norums kyrka) and Jämtland (Näs kyrka) prominently display another part of the Sigurðr legend, Gunnar in the snake pit, presumably to be interpreted as representing the evils of a dangerous world which threaten mortal man. It is worth noting that the distribution of plastic representa-tions of the Sigurðr materials is especially rich in areas where the English church appears to have played an important role (e.g. Norway, which was Christianized from England; areas along the Swedish-Norwegian border; Södermanland, where the Anglo-Saxon missionary Eskil was martyred; and Uppland, where Anglo-Saxon influence in both secular and religious issues was present in the early eleventh century). This fact suggests that the church itself may have had a hand in promoting such artistic displays as the carvings from Norwegian stave-churches (such as Hylestad church in Setesdal), the baptismal fonts from Jämtland and Bohus, the carvings with their Christian rune messages in Södermanland and Uppland, and the Andreas Cross from the Isle of Man, just as it surely did in the case of such works as the Halton Cross in Lancashire.

Similar portrayals of surviving narratives about Vǫlundr the smith (the Gotlandic Ardre stone 8), Þórr and the World Serpent (the Upplandic Altuna stone), and Óðinn at Ragnarǫk (the Ledberg stone in Östergötland) indicate that these stories too—preserved in prose and poetry in Iceland during the Middle Ages—were known in Sweden as well. That exactly these tales should be found in the East Norse area is hardly surprising, since they belong to the most widely attested stock of legends in the Germanic world; from the Weland panel of the Anglo-Saxon Franks Casket to the Velent of German tradition, from the use of the Sigurðr story to celebrate Beowulf's victory over Grendel (*Beowulf*, ll.875–900) to the introductory matter of the German *Nibelungenlied* and the nineteenth-century Faroese *Sjúrðarkvæði*, stories of this sort enjoyed amazing longevity and popularity in northern Europe. But although we may know what tales are portrayed on a dozen or so of these magnificent cultural documents, there remain many more about which almost nothing is known.

It is, however, possible to winnow fascinating historical data and even hints of nascent legendary materials from the runic inscriptions. The Gripsholm stone (Södermanland), for example, after declaring that the monument has been raised by Tola in memory of her son Haraldr, Ingvarr's brother, bears the following inscriptions:

> They fared like men
> far after gold
> and in the east
> gave the eagle food.
> They died southward
> in Serkland.
> (Jansson 1962, 41)

More than twenty stones dealing with this same expedition were raised during the eleventh century in the area around Lake Mälaren. Typically, they mention the journey through Russia under Ingvarr and the death of one of the group's members in foreign lands. There is nothing unusual about the messages themselves—numerous Swedish inscriptions mention expeditions west to the British Isles and east to Russia and Constantinople—but the scale on which Ingvarr's journey is commemorated is unprecedented. Well known elsewhere in Scandinavia (it stands, for example, as the entry for A.D. 1041 in the Icelandic *Annals*), the story became a fully developed saga about "Yngvarr the wide-traveled" three centuries later in Iceland (*Yngvars saga víðförla*; Eng. tr. *The Vikings in Russia*) and circulated in a number of manuscripts. In a colophon, the saga writer claims that the tale was known from several oral sources, including a rendition heard in the Swedish king's retinue; though the story itself is fantasy, it is not unthinkable that the foundation in oral tradition the saga presents may be accurate. In this case, as is so often true concerning literature in early Sweden, the extent and nature of the tradition can unfortunately be only inferred, not substantiated.

A further indication of literary activity is reflected in the versified inscriptions of runic monuments, for though runic texts are typically highly prosaic in every sense, poetry also occurs. The two verses cited above from Rök and Gripsholm are in a meter known from learned Icelandic works as *fornyrðislag*, an eight-line strophe in which couplets are bound together by alliteration, the initial rhyme of like consonant with like consonant (with special treatment of *sp-*, *st-*, and *sk-*) and of any vowel with any vowel. *Fornyrðislag* is one of the simplest forms of poetry found in Scandinavia, roughly analogous to the meters of the Old English *Beowulf* and the Old High German *Hildebrandslied*. The much more complex skaldic meter known in Icelandic as *dróttkvætt*, with greater fixity of syllables per line, more elaborate rules governing initial and internal rhyme, and a greater propensity toward metaphoric language, is also preserved in Sweden; indeed, the *only* complete skaldic verse actually from the Viking Age is on a runestone from Öland (Karlevi), although debate continues concerning the poet's origins, which are likely to have been Norway or Iceland. A small container dating to the early eleventh century from the trading center of Sigtuna, however, secures the place of this elaborate poetry for the East, as well as West, Norse cultural region: it is inscribed with two lines in *dróttkvætt*, apparently consisting of a warning against theft.

THE EARLY MIDDLE AGES

As the case of Inge the Elder and Sacrifice-Sveinn demonstrates, the battle between Christianity and paganism continued until the late eleventh and even early twelfth centuries; by the time that conflict was finally being resolved, a dynastic rivalry had developed that would direct the course of Swedish history for some time to come. For more than one hundred years (ca. 1135–1249), factions associated with Sverker the Elder and St. Erik vied with each other. The conflict included such famous engagements as the Battle of Lena (1208) and only came to an end in the middle of the thirteenth century with the accession of Birger Jarl to power: Birger had connections through his mother to the Sverker line but had married the sister of King Erik "the lame and halt," who was a descendant in the line of St. Erik. King Erik died without issue, and the next year (1250), Birger's young son Valdemar, heir to both lines in the rivalry, was elected king. It was in his name that Birger ruled for the next sixteen years, establishing what has come to be called (erroneously) the Folkung dynasty. Although never himself king, Birger was undoubtedly one of the most effective rulers of premodern Sweden, consolidating central authority, establishing important ties with both Norway and Denmark, and initiating new relations with the German cities, including the treaty with Lübeck that resulted in the beginnings of modern Stockholm.

In this period Sweden began to take shape as a nation and to make significant contacts with the rest of Europe on many fronts. In addition to increased trade with the other nations, education in Sweden blossomed as cathedral schools (*domskolor*) were opened in Linköping (1230s), Uppsala (1247–48), and Skara (1257). Swedes began to study in other countries as well. As early as 1219, a Simon of Sweden was studying in Bologna, and by 1225 "magister Stenarus" (later bishop of Skara) is mentioned in a document, his title ("master") presumably having been earned in Paris. By the end of the century, large numbers of Swedish students traveled to Paris and Cologne to augment their educations.

Among the first items written in the vernacular were the provincial laws (*landskapslagar*). Provincial laws exist for Västergötland (in older and younger versions), Östergötland, Västmanland, Gotland, Dalarna, Hälsingland (which also applied to Norrland), Småland, Uppland, and Södermanland (*SGL*); those for Närke and Värmland, although mentioned in other sources, have not survived. In addition, a text known as *Hednala-gen* (The law of heathens) is concerned with ritual insult and single combat. The oldest codex of all, *Äldre Västgötalagen* (*SGL* I, 3–74; The older West Gautish law), dates to the 1280s in a complete manuscript, and to ca. 1240 in fragments: it was probably written in the 1220s by the West Gautish law man Eskil Magnusson, brother of Birger Jarl and host for a time to the Icelander Snorri Sturluson.

Before the codified provincial laws of the extant manuscripts, the laws had evidently been recited orally at assemblies on an annual basis, or at least that is the understanding of Pope Innocent III in a bull he sends to the archbishop of Uppsala in 1206 (*SD* 1, 156–57). This convention of *laghsagha* (law recitation; Modern Swedish *lagsaga*) eventually came to refer to the district over which the law had authority, but in some texts the original sense is still quite clear, for example, *Smålandslagen*: "Now men should go to the assembly and hear our *lagsaga*" (*SGL* 6, 97). The idea of the "law man" has its counterparts in the legal traditions of the other Nordic countries. In Sweden the law man was frequently of high birth, and in at least some instances the institution appears to have moved within lineages: in a later appendix to the laws of Västergötland, the so-called *Vidhemsprästens anteckningar* (*SGL* 1, 285–347; "The Annotations of the Vidhem Priest") from ca. 1325, some of the law men are listed. Several sets of male relatives are to be found among the names, for example, "The eleventh was Karle from Edsvära. . . . The twelfth was his son Algot" (*SGL* 1, 296). Likewise, the law man responsible for the laws of Östergötland, Magnus Bengtsson, was probably the nephew of Birger Jarl and Eskil Magnusson. At once repositories and interpreters of the laws, these men wielded great power, and when the time came for the laws to be codified, it was the law men who generally undertook the task, especially in the early period of recording. *Vidhemsprästens anteckningar* maintains that Eskil Magnusson, for example, ransacked the laws of his predecessors and from them crafted with genius and cleverness the West Gautish Laws (*SGL* 1, 297). Since Eskil was not himself a native of Västergötland, if we are to believe this passage, we must assume that he either interviewed those knowledgeable about the legal tradition or perhaps had access to the private notes of families that had an interest in the laws. Eventually, the king established commissions that took over the function of codifying the laws and whose work he would approve (e.g., *Upplandslagen* 1296). In general, the reasons for recording the laws can only be inferred, although in the case of the laws of Gotland (*SGL* 7) the source of inspiration was undoubtedly a visit in 1207 from the Danish archbishop Andreas Suneson, who encouraged the Gotlanders to reduce strife by writing down their laws. It is worth noting that the laws were written down first in Gotland and Västergötland, following, in both cases, visits by prominent men from other Scandinavian countries where the practice had already been established.

Parallel to the provincial laws, there existed legal codices concerned with conduct in the cities, which had substantial foreign populations, especially from north German cities that made up the Hanseatic League. *Bjärkorätten* (*SGL* 6, 113–34; The law of Birka) was the main such city law; the name itself is of uncertain origin and may or may not have to do with the city of Birka.

What is clear is that the law was used in several cities, including Stockholm, Lödöse, and various locations in Södermanland and Östergötland. Visby was governed by *Visby stadslag* (SGL 8; The city law of Visby) from the early 1340s. By the middle of the fourteenth century, the use of local laws was replaced by *Magnus Erikssons landslag* (SGL 10; Magnus Eriksson's national law), a work that drew heavily on *Upplandslagen* (SGL 3) and, to a lesser degree, *Östgötalagen* (SGL 2). This work was soon followed by *Magnus Eriksson stadslag* (SGL 11; Magnus Eriksson's city law). The *landslag* was reworked again in the reign of King Kristoffer (1442; SGL 12).

The provincial laws are filled with fascinating cultural revelations, although they are not nearly so archaic a source of information as some previous generations of scholars thought—*Upplandslagen*, for example, was once rendered into verse in the belief that the text would have come down in this way from pre-Christian times. There can be no doubt that some versification occurs in the provincial laws, but this fact need not imply that they ever existed in their entirety as versified works. Alliteration, for example, occurs more frequently in the younger laws than the older ones. Cases such as "baþi j kirkiu rætt oc kiæsæræ laghum" (SGL 3, 31; both in Christian justice and royal laws) can easily be dismissed as incidental or as imitations of the prose alliteration popular in Latin writing of the times. On the other hand, a phrase such as "Engin ma haita a huathci a hult eþa hauga eþa haþin guþ" (SGL 7, 141; No one may pray to grove or mound or heathen god) may well go back to a traditional formulation, especially since it has analogues elsewhere in Nordic literature. Although the concept of the fully poetic legal text is no longer accepted, the prosimetrical character of the extant works remains beyond dispute, as when the laws state that after a thief has been found guilty, he should be judged:

til hogs ok til hangæ.	to blow and to hanging,
til draps ok til döþæ	to loss of life and to death,
til torfs ok til tiæru.	to turf and to tar.
(SGL 1, 53)	

Here the law combines alliteration with rhythm and displays a marked poetic quality. These formal properties are often quite pronounced in the provincial laws, as in the following passage, which echoes the Germanic tradition of wisdom poetry, exemplified in Scandinavia in the Icelandic *Edda* (e.g., *Hávamál*; Eng. tr. "The Sayings of Hár"):

þæn a hæræ, ær hændir	A rabbit belongs to the one who catches it

þæn a ræf ær reser.	A fox belongs to the one who puts it up
þæn a vargh ær vinþær.	A wolf belongs to the one who defeats it
þæn a biorn ær betir.	A bear belongs to the one who hunts it. *(SGL 1, 65)*

By the time of the late-thirteenth-century *Upplandslagen* (and those laws influenced by it), rhymed verses tend to conclude the various sections dealing with the powers and obligations of the church and crown, with inheritance, with property, with administration, and so on. Thus, the section devoted to personal injury ends:

| Nu æru tald manhælghis mal. | Now the cases of personal safety have been enumerated. |
| Guþ giömi os baþi liff ok sial. | May God keep our lives and souls safe. *(SGL 3, 178)* |

There are simply no other documents like the provincial laws, for they project a panorama of daily life during the early Middle Ages. Though their concerns are by no means exhaustive, the texts suggest legal preoccupation with the larger ecclesiastical and political issues of the times (e.g., the status of the clergy, the duties of the king) as well as with questions pertinent to life in a community: infractions against community standards (e.g., sexual misconduct: adultery, incest, bestiality, rape) and the details of social order (e.g., the rules governing inheritance). The provincial laws can be quite specific with respect to penalties (e.g., the fines for assaults against men of different regions and status), and occasionally they rise to cleverness in their regulations (e.g., a rule concerning collecting evidence, in which a home can be searched only by someone whose belt has been removed, thus keeping his hands busy holding his pants up and preventing him from planting evidence). Moreover, they can project the fears of society, as when the laws declare: "Now a woman is charged with witchcraft and is taken in its practice and [the charge] is accompanied by reliable witnesses; now she has forfeited her life; and she shall be stoned to death" (*SGL* 2, 85). No other group of documents so fully captures the range of ideas, customs, and concerns current in the Swedish Middle Ages as do the provincial laws.

It has been noted that in some manuscripts, *Västgötalagen* concludes with the historical annotations of the Vidhem Priest. It is not the only legal text concerned with historical developments: the laws of Gotland, preserved in an early-fourteenth-century manuscript, end with a legendary history, often called *Gutasagan* (*SFSS* 64). It is a fascinating document that traces the development of the island from its earliest settlement to more recent times, when it came under the jurisdiction of the Swedish king and under the ecclesiastical authority of the bishop of Linköping. It is a tale filled with traditional lore—how the island was prevented from sinking during the day, how it was forced to drive some of its inhabitants away because of ecological pressures, how it was converted to Christianity by St. Óláfr. Everywhere the text promotes the notion of the Gotlanders' traditional independence and the idea that all the island's foreign relations were taken on willingly. *Gutasagan* is intended as a commentary on the laws, and its mission is clearly propagandistic. The legendary history of Gotland may be the first text of this sort from the Swedish Middle Ages, but it is only an indication of what will become the greatest literary achievement of Catholic Sweden, the historical chronicle.

Not all surviving thirteenth-century texts are secular, of course. Among the important religious works from Sweden at this time are those relating to saints, local saints in particular, in the form of hymns and other aspects of the *officia divina* (a term that includes a multitude of liturgical works), in collections of miracles, or in biographies. The oldest such text relates to Botvid, known as "the apostle of Södermanland." Still a pagan, Botvid had gone on a trading expedition to England, where he was converted to Christianity. After his return to Sweden, he championed his new faith widely. Botvid met his death (ca. 1120) when a slave he had freed (in the hope that the man would help spread the Christian message in his Slavic homeland) killed him in his sleep. Botvid's feast day is recorded in the oldest surviving Swedish calendar, *Vallentunakalendariet* (The Vallentuna calendar, ca. 1198), and to this feast day should be tied the prosimetrical Latin *officium* written in honor of Botvid (*SRS* 2, 383–88). Likewise, the story of Sigfrid, the English missionary, is the inspiration for an *officium* called *Celebremus*, after its first word, also recounted in Latin and Swedish prose versions (*SRS* 2, 344–76). The legend tells how the English cleric Sigfrid comes to Sweden at the request of Olof Skötkonung and works in Småland. While Sigfrid is away, his three nephews, Unaman, Sunaman, and Vinaman, are killed and their heads deposited in a lake. Through a miracle, Sigfrid is able to recover the heads, which speak to him.

The best-known author of liturgical poetry in thirteenth-century and early-fourteenth-century Sweden was Brynolf Algotsson. A member of a powerful family from Västergötland that sported many law men, Brynolf was born ca. 1240. He studied in Paris during the 1260s and 1270s and returned to his homeland, where he soon became bishop of Skara (1278–1317). Fairly soon after his death a cult began to grow around him; part of its power derived from a vision Birgitta (see below) had while on a visit to the church at Skara. The popularity of Brynolf was substantial, as evidenced by the fifteenth-century *Vita Brynolphi* and the fact that he underwent at least part of the beatification process, the so-called translation, in which the individual's bones are ceremoniously transferred to a special location in the church or placed in a reliquary. To Brynolf are attributed four prominent religious works: the stories of Helena (or Elin) of Skövde (*Helenaofficiet*) and of St. Eskil (*Den helige Eskils officium*), an *officium* in honor of the Virgin Mary (*Officiet till Jungfru Marias ära*), and *Historia de spinea corona* (*Törnekroneofficiet*). The last work apparently derives from a gift made to Skara Cathedral by Håkon Magnusson. Håkon's father, King Magnus Håkonsson of Norway, had been presented with part of the relic of Christ's crown of thorns from La Sainte Chapelle in Paris by King Philip III of France. The fact that some part of this relic was to be given to the cathedral evidently inspired Brynolf to write the following for its reception on 2 September 1304:

Dies est leticie,	It is a joyful day,
dies gloriosa,	a glorious day,
qua datur Westgocie	when to Västergötland
spinea preciosa.	is given the valuable thorn.
(Hymni 2, 94)	

Other major works from this period include biographies of, and *officia* for, the patron saints of Finland and Sweden: *Vita et miracula Sancti Henrici* (SRS 2, 331–43); *Vita Sancti Erici* and *Miracula Sancti Erici* (SRS 2, 270–316). Both the life and miracles of St. Erik appeared in Old Swedish versions as well (SFSS 7, 343–84; Eng. tr. POS, 307–09). These vernacular treatments of St. Erik constitute a small portion of *Fornsvenska legendariet*, an Old Swedish legendary, which builds on a number of well-known European texts (e.g., the *Legenda aurea* of Jacobus de Voragine, the *Chronicon pontificum et imperatorum* of Martinus Oppaviensis). It is, however, in no sense a slavish translation of preexisting materials. Although the author draws from a wealth of texts of both foreign and local provenance, he has also added annotations and, perhaps most significant, his own chronological order to the whole. The result is something far different from a simple compilation of saints' lives; it is a religious history of the world, beginning with such biblical figures as the Virgin Mary and John the Baptist, and working its way up to such contemporary thirteenth-century figures as St. Francis, St. Dominic, and Elizabeth of Hungary. Although we do not know for certain the identity of the author, we do know that he was a well-educated Dominican, knowledgeable in German as well as Latin. He was from one of the Götaland provinces and wrote the legendary sometime between 1276 and 1307. There are reasons for believing that he may have worked at the Dominican cloister in Skänninge, although the evidence is not conclusive. If Skänninge was the site for the work, we would also have a potential explanation for the project, for there existed in the town a large community of Beguines (lay sisters who tended the poor and sick but who did not take vows and who could leave in order to marry) and other female orders, such as the Dominican sisters. It is possible that the translation was for the use of such women, who generally lacked the training necessary for using Latin texts. In 1267, for example, Pope Clement IV calls on the Dominicans to care for the spiritual education of the female members of the order. The background to and an explanation for such a large hagiographic work in the vernacular may reside in these facts, although still unexplained is the author's elaborate organization.

One figure known to have been associated with the Dominican cloister at Skänninge (indeed, the same writer from whom we learn of his female core-ligionists), was Petrus de Dacia (Dacia was the term used by the religious orders for the entire Scandinavian area). He was born on Gotland ca. 1230 but spent much of his life at the various ecclesiastical and educational centers of northern Europe. He no doubt began as a novitiate at the relatively new Dominican cloister in Visby, after which he continued his education at the "Studium generale" in Cologne (1266–69). In 1269 he went to Paris to study and after a year returned to Sweden. Back in his homeland, he was lector at the Dominican convents in Skänninge, Västerås, and finally Visby. Eventually, Petrus became the prior in Visby, where he died in 1289. The careful attention given his biography provides an excellent window on the ecclesiastical world of the thirteenth century, but what sets the career of Petrus de Dacia apart from those of his fellow clerics is his encounter and lengthy association with a German mystic, Christina. She had run away from home to join the Cologne Beguines as a youth, but at the time Petrus met her she resided once again in her nearby village of Stommeln. Christina underwent a variety of mystical religious experiences, including demonic possessions that would cause her to be thrown against the walls and furniture, visions of Christ, and stigmatization on her hands and feet. Petrus had ample opportunity to witness such events: in addition to the twelve times he visited her during his student days in Cologne, he saw her on his way to and from Paris and on a special trip he made to Stommeln from Sweden in 1279; he may also have met her in 1287 on his return trip from Bordeaux.

Petrus was clearly attracted to the ecstatic form of piety he saw in Christina, and between them a deep and profound love grew, as reflected in their correspondence (she dictated her letters to the village priest and others). The importance of this association for the history of literature in Sweden derives from the new level to which Petrus raises the hagiographer's art: he takes the form of the saint's life and imbues it with a deeply personal artistic design. When, for example, Petrus describes an occasion on which Christina pulled from her body an iron spike wet with her blood and supernaturally warm with demonic heat, he tells how she placed it "in manu mea" (in my hand [*SFSS*, ser. 2:2, 5]). The interiority of the texts derives not from the pronoun employed, that is, from the fact that Petrus is a participant in events, but rather from the way in which he reflects on the things he has witnessed: when he returns to Cologne from his first meeting with Christina, he is a changed man, and his ruminations on this and other occasions sometimes distinguish this *vita* from other medieval saints' lives with their endless accumulations of reports of miracles and good deeds. Petrus preceded Christina in death by more than twenty years, and it would be left to others to complete his work of documenting her life and the miracles associated with it (she was finally declared a saint by the church on 12 August 1908). Although Petrus was unable to finish his work, his efforts on behalf of winning recognition for Christina's piety have been widely acknowledged as one of the most important contributions to literature in medieval Sweden, and he is often cited as Sweden's first named author.

THE HIGH MIDDLE AGES

The literature of Sweden in the High Middle Ages was in many important ways shaped by political events. In 1275, one of Earl Birger's sons, Magnus Ladulås, became king of Sweden after deposing his brother, King Valdemar. On the death of King Magnus in 1290, Torgils Knutsson began a regency that lasted until Magnus's oldest son, Birger—who had been elected king in his infancy (1284)—was crowned king in 1302. The king's brothers, Erik and Valdemar, were then established as the dukes of Södermanland and Finland, respectively. A long series of intrigues characterized the relations of the siblings, which concluded when King Birger treacherously invited his brothers to a banquet in 1317 (the so-called *Nyköpings gästabud* [feast of Nyköping]) during which he had them taken prisoner and killed (or starved to death) early the next year. King Birger was eventually deposed by the followers of the two brothers, and ultimately Duke Erik's son Magnus became king (1319–64). The events from ca. 1230 to 1319 form the basis for *Erikskrönikan* (The chronicle of Erik), named after Duke Erik and written by one of his admirers. This text forms much of our knowledge of the period and is one of the landmark literary works of the era.

Important as domestic politics were in the development of Sweden at this point, it was the foreign component that was crucial. German influence was especially great, as increasing numbers of Hansa merchants settled on Gotland and in mainland Sweden. For the most part, the German residents were involved in commerce or in specific industries such as mining. Their numbers were substantial in such key centers as Stockholm and Visby, and their influence in these towns corresponded to their numbers: the first known mayor of Stockholm, for example, was a German. By the time of *Magnus Erikssons stadslag* (*SGL* 2; Magnus Eriksson's city law, ca. 1350), it was necessary to specify that cities have six burghers, three Swedish and three German, and that city councils consist of thirty members, half from each community. Smaller cities might have lower total numbers, but the ethnic ratio was to be maintained. The German presence would be felt in a variety of ways, most notably through its impact on the development of the Swedish language. As could be expected, lexical terms fitting particular activities (e.g., *borghmæstare* 'mayor' from Middle Low German *borgemester*; *hantverk* 'handicraft, trade' from MLG *hantwerk*) were introduced, but of more profound influence was the adoption by Swedish of such fundamental parts of speech as prefixes (e.g., *be-*) and suffixes (e.g., *-het*). It has also been suggested that the presence of such a large foreign population contributed to the simplification of the Swedish inflectional system.

The German contributions, that is to say, the contributions of such north German cities as Lübeck, to all aspects of Swedish culture, language, and technology were significant, but on the whole, the surviving literary and historical sources focus on the activities of a small elite that was receptive to foreign influence. The interactions of this group were most often with ethnic Germans, but it was especially French cultural norms, received either directly or through these German intermediaries, that were eagerly imitated by the budding aristocracy. Some aspects of knighthood (e.g., the title *herra* 'sir') were already in use by the early thirteenth century, although only the most enthusiastic researchers feel that anything like knighthood in its accepted sense existed in Sweden before the third quarter of the thirteenth century. By the 1280s, however, activities associated with the institution, such as the *riddara slagh* (the act of dubbing a knight), were well known in Sweden. The oldest use of the term "knight" (*riddare*) preserved in a contemporary document is in the *Alsnö stadga* (The Alsnö statute), from ca. 1280. It is fairly certain that the idea of knighthood in something like its European sense had taken hold by the end of the thirteenth century. *Erikskrönikan* (SFSS 47), for example, presents its eponymous hero as the very embodiment of this chivalric ideal at his brother Birger's wedding in 1298. So gallant an affair was the ceremony, the poet employs the images of both Gawain and Parceval to praise those in attendance (l.1395). Among all the great feats at the wedding, none outshone those of Duke Erik: his mildness and gentleness (l.1431) serve to enhance his brave deeds, and he is dubbed a knight at the festivities. The polemical writer leaves little doubt but that Duke Erik is, indeed, the perfect union of Germanic heroism and Christian temperament, and he even goes so far as to compare Erik favorably to "an angel of heaven" (l.1442). Continental notions of courtly behavior and chivalric institutions had a perceptible influence on the world of the Swedish upper classes—in their social organization (e.g., use of titles), amusements (e.g., tournaments), and literary tastes (e.g., chivalric romances). It is important to bear in mind, however, that despite the popularity of such preoccupations among the elite, these attempts to mimic Continental tastes had essentially no effect on the circumstances of the great bulk of the population in Sweden, as no feudal system of the sort known in western Europe ever developed there.

The means by which Sweden acquired three of its most important documents of spiritual culture from this period is instructive, especially as regards the questions of foreign influence and the increasingly international character of the elite sector of society. In 1299, the same year in which he succeeded to the Norwegian throne, Håkon V Magnusson of Norway married Eufemia. According to Icelandic sources, Eufemia was the daughter of Count Günther of Ruppin, the maternal granddaughter of Prince Vitslav of Rügen, and the great-granddaughter of Duke Otto of Braunschweig (d. 1252), although other sources make her the daughter and granddaughter of Vitslav and Otto, respectively. Princess Ingeborg was born to King Håkon and Queen Eufemia in 1301, and arrangements for her marriage to Duke Erik of Sweden were begun the next year; the plans were periodically broken off and revived until the actual wedding took place in 1312. Since King Håkon and Queen Eufemia had no other children, it was agreed that if Håkon were to die without male issue, Duke Erik was to be given "filiam nostram Ingeburg cum regno Norvegie" (our daughter Ingeborg and the Norwegian realm [*Sverges traktater* 1, 361]). In essence, the marriage arrangements represented a search for King Håkon's successor, and the suitor needed attributes that extended beyond mere political expediency: Duke Erik was regarded as just such a man. In fact, he was widely viewed as the most outstanding figure of the early fourteenth century.

It was during the many years in which Erik's marriage to Ingeborg was being arranged, called off, and arranged again that the three parts of the so-called *Eufemiavisor* (Eufemia poems) were apparently translated. At one level they represent a grand gesture from the future mother-in-law to her future son-in-law; at another they represent an innovation in Swedish literature that would revolutionize it. The three texts that make up the Eufemia group—translations concerning "Yvain, le chevalier au lion," "Floire et Blancheflor," and Duke Fredrik—are remarkable first for the fact that they are metrical romances, the first texts of this sort anywhere in Scandinavia. *Herr Ivan Lejonriddare* (SFSS 50; Eng. tr. *John, the Knight of the Lion* [MS, 58–119]) is, of course, an Arthurian romance built on Celtic materials that were taken up in French by Chrétien de Troyes; his works in turn inspired Hartmann von Aue to rework them into German. The story concerns one of Arthur's knights, Ivan, who sets out to avenge an offense against one of the other members of the Round Table. He is victorious but falls in love with his enemy's widow, whom he marries. When Ivan departs to seek new honor, he neglects to return within the allotted time frame of one year. His wife rejects him for his inconstancy, and he must then undergo further adventures, including a bout of madness, to atone for his failure. During his wanderings, Ivan saves a lion, who thereafter follows and aids him, hence his cognomen, "Knight of the Lion." Through his prodigious brave deeds, and a clever ruse, Ivan and his wife are reconciled.

Hertig Fredrik av Normandie (SFSS 49; Eng. tr. *Duke Frederick* [MS, 25–57]) also asserts a connection to Arthur and the Round Table, although this claim has no foundation. Like *Herr Ivan*, much of the story centers on the theme of the bridal quest. The adventures begin when Duke Fredrik gets lost while hunting and assists a dwarf-king in putting down a revolt by his rebellious subjects. The duke then encounters a fellow knight and his lady, who are being abused by a giant, whom he defeats. With his newfound friends Duke Fredrik then goes to Ireland, where he "steals" his bride from her overprotective father, although not without a long series of mishaps and adventures. Finally, the wedding takes place, forming the basis for a reunion of all the characters of the preceding sections.

Flores och Blanzeflor (SFSS 46; Eng. tr. *Flores and Blancheflor* [MS, 1–26]) ultimately derives from a medieval Greek romance concerning two lovers. A heathen prince, Flores, and the daughter of a captive Christian woman of noble birth, Blanzeflor, are reared together and greatly love each other. They are parted when Flores's parents tell him that she is dead; in fact, she has been sold to merchants who convey her to Babylon. Flores's parents finally reveal what has transpired when Flores prepares to kill himself in the belief that his companion is dead. He sets off in search of her and eventually locates Blanzeflor in the caliph's harem. Their devotion to each other, together with Flores's martial skills in single combat, result in Blanzeflor's being freed. The reunited couple returns home to find Flores's parents dead, and the married Flores and Blanzeflor rule as king and queen for several years. They go to Paris, where Flores is baptized, and end their days living separate, cloistered, but holy lives.

The three texts are at some pains to tell their audiences about their patroness, and there is little doubt but that Eufemia exercised considerable control over the selection of the materials, with their emphasis on bride quests, on young lovers who are in each case parted and reunited, on fidelity, and on knightly virtues. In concluding *Hertig Fredrik*, for example, the author-translator writes:

> The book which you hear here,
> Kaiser Otto had translated
> from French into the German tongue,
> God bless that noble's princely soul!
> Now it's been turned once again into rhyme
> recently in a short time,
> from German into the Swedish tongue;
> everyone old and young understands
> that Queen Eufemia had it translated
> into our language
> (SFSS *49, 3279–88*)

Similar statements concerning Eufemia's role conclude *Herr Ivan* and *Flores och Blanzeflor*. The actual dates for the translation of the poems are in some doubt; the manuscripts themselves say that *Herr Ivan* was translated in 1303, *Hertig Fredrik* in 1308 (although one manuscript says 1301), and *Flores och Blanzeflor* in 1312. Considerable debate has raged over the chronology of *Hertig Fredrik* and *Herr Ivan* in particular; it is fairly certain that these two were written during the first decade of the 1300s, whereas *Flores och Blanzeflor* was probably rendered into Swedish as a result of the wedding itself in 1312.

The question of authorship has been addressed repeatedly. It has, for example, been argued that the texts may have been translated by more than one person. Although opinions continue to vary, it seems probable that only one individual was responsible for all three works; moreover, he was almost certainly from a western and southern part of Sweden, and it is more than likely that he had a clerical background. One possibility is that he was a cleric, or someone with similar training, in the retinue of men who accompanied Duke Erik to Oslo at Christmas 1302. An attractive candidate, although he was not a member of the duke's retinue, and despite some conflicting evidence, is Peter Algotsson, the brother of Brynolf Algotsson, bishop of Skara. He came from the area that would generally fit the linguistic evidence and was from a powerful law-man family in Västergötland. Moreover, he had studied in Paris and had served as King Magnus Ladulås's chancellor before going into exile. He had also been sent on diplomatic missions by the Norwegian king to the English and Scottish courts.

Much debate has also been devoted to whether or not the Swedish versions were made from Old Norwegian prose translations or directly from the Continental versions. *Flores och Blanzeflor* does not detail the nature of its model, but since it seems to have so few points of contact with the French version, it is assumed on this negative evidence to be a reworking of an Old Norwegian translation. *Herr Ivan*, on the other hand, expressly states that it was translated from a French original:

> One thousand winters, three hundred years
> had passed since God's birth,
> plus three more, at that time
> this book was turned into rhyme,
> Queen Eufemia, you may believe,
> had this book translated
> from the French tongue into our language—
> may God bless the noble lady's soul
> (*SFSS 50, 6431–38*)

There is undoubtedly some truth in this picture of the translation of *Herr Ivan*, for at some junctures the Old Swedish poem reflects exactly the text of Chrétien de Troyes's *Ivain*, although at other points it is apparent that the West Norse prose translation has also been consulted. *Hertig Fredrik* also claims to have originated as a French work, although the translator says that he was using a German version, a statement supported by investigations of the text's language. No corresponding Fredrik poem is known in these languages, however, making the Old Swedish *Hertig Fredrik* (and the Old Danish text derived from it) unique literary monuments. Moreover, it has been cogently argued that the attribution of *Hertig Fredrik* to a French original is an amiable fiction designed to lend it authenticity and acceptability and that instead the romance was commissioned by Duke Otto of Braunschweig. This possibility provides a valuable perspective on the transfer of literary texts between various linguistic and cultural regions. Whether or not the text was originally composed for, or simply translated at the behest of, Duke Otto, it would have been intimately tied to Queen Eufemia's own family (i.e., sponsored by either her grandfather or her great-grandfather), and this connection enhances the possibility that she had a copy of it in her possession. Furthermore, it is not unthinkable that by having this German text translated, Eufemia sought to underscore the parallel between the Norwegian and Swedish royal families: Ingeborg was the daughter of a Scandinavian monarch and a German aristocrat, just as Erik and his brothers were the sons of King Magnus Ladulås and the German-born Helvig, daughter of Count Gerhard of Holstein.

Erik's connection with the German nobility appears to have been quite strong. In the Icelandic annals, the entry for 1302 mentions that when Duke Erik had been engaged to Ingeborg (now just one year old), he went to Oslo to celebrate Christmas with King Håkon and Queen Eufemia. Eufemia's father (or grandfather), Vitslav, apparently accompanied him in his retinue and therefore had presumably been in Erik's company since the summer. When Vitslav died during the festivities, Duke Erik is mentioned in Vitslav's will as one of its executors. This point is supported by *Eriks-krönikan* (SFSS 47), which makes much of the death of Vitslav and of Duke Erik's relationship to his future mother-in-law. Some of the descriptions of their meetings must be ascribed to the poet's desire to paint Erik in the best chivalric light, but even allowing for such propagandistic designs, perhaps a kernel of truth remains in such scenes as those that describe his arrival in Oslo for Christmas 1302, in which she is said to receive him well, with heartfelt "sweet words and a red mouth" (ll.1886–88). And as Duke Erik departed after the burial of her father (or grandfather), the poet writes, "She held him dear in her heart / without any falseness" (ll.1925–26). When the engagement ran afoul of Duke Erik's and King Håkon's disagreement over the disposition of Kungahälla in 1308, the poet of *Erikskrönikan* tells us that its disruption—temporary, as it turned out—happened without the queen's permission and that "the Queen regretted it most of all" (l.3107).

The Norwegian royal family clearly had a great stake in Erik's position, and this fact has led to the suggestion that the Eufemia poems were intended to have a pedagogical function. *Hertig Fredrik*, for example, has occasionally been likened to the tradition of the *Fürstenspiegel* (princes' mirror), and certainly aspects of the poem support this analogy: one cannot escape the thought that Queen Eufemia (and King Håkon) would have hoped it to have a salubrious effect on their future son-in-law when, for example, the poem describes its hero as clever, very powerful, possessing great piety, true, honorable, gentle, steadfast, merry, and cheerful, and that "who would praise him rightfully / he might well say with honor / he finds few who can match him now" (*SFSS* 49, 30–38). Of course, these attributes are clichés in the chivalric epic, but the poet goes on to point out that "he was an honor to all his kinsmen" (*SFSS* 49, 40). Likewise, the poem closes with a necrologue reflecting on what a good ruler, *miild ok bliidh* (1.3133), exactly the words used to describe Duke Erik in *Erikskrönikan*, should do during his reign: dispense justice, support Christianity through the construction of cloisters, leave a new generation to take over the kingdom, and so on. In addition, some broad aspects of the poem's themes and events may have been meaningful to Duke Erik's, and Queen Eufemia's, situations, such as the separation of Duke Fredrik and Floria vis-à-vis the wait facing Duke Erik and the youthful Ingeborg. And one cannot avoid speculating on whether the burlesque episode in which Duke Fredrik helps the dwarf-king Malnrit against his rebellious subjects led by the king's *own kinsman, Duke Yrrik* [Erik], is not intended as a commentary on the historical Duke Erik's situation: he seems to have been the most talented of Magnus Ladulås's sons and the one with the greatest ambition, a desire for distinction that would lead him to the so-called *Håtunalek*, or Håtuna game (when in 1306 Erik and his brother Valdemar took King Birger prisoner and ruled in his stead for several years), to something like a separate kingdom in the west of Sweden, and ultimately to *Nyköpings gästabud* (the feast of Nyköping). Indeed, if the manuscript's own date of 1308 is correct, the events surrounding *Håtunaleken* would have been in full swing as the piece was being written, and the parallel between the rebellious Duke Erik of fact and the rebellious Duke "Yrrik" of fiction would scarcely fail to be noticed.

The purpose behind the project is Eufemia's intent to honor her future son-in-law and the political union his marriage to Ingeborg represented. The *Eufemiavisor* thus functioned as an elaborate social contract between the queen and the duke; the tales project behavioral expectations and express idealized ways of conducting oneself. To the degree that the stories of the *Eufemiavisor* were at any stage more than mere diversion, they required public ventilation. They were part of a ceremony. The social and political matrix within which the selection and translation of the Eufemia poems occurred thus provides us with one means for understanding their place in Swedish literary history, but they were surely meant to entertain as well, and in this context the question how such manuscripts were employed is inevitable. Certainly there is no likelihood of Duke Erik's sitting down and leafing through the texts, reading silently to himself. After all, the translations were part of a set of publicly displayed negotiations. Moreover, the texts themselves indicate that as entertainment they were probably read aloud to gatherings of the aristocracy: the narrator of *Herr Ivan*, for example, opens the poem by saying that he intends "to relate old tales for the enjoyment of those who will listen" (*SFSS* 50, 3–4) and closes the text by wishing the joy of the Lord on "all those who heard the book" (*SFSS* 50, 6444). Phrases of this sort are common in romances and should be interpreted cautiously, but there is no reason to doubt that the Eufemia poems were, as one commentator has said of medieval manuscripts, read with the ear rather than the eye.

The subject matter of the *Eufemiavisor*, chivalric romance, is alone sufficient to secure the poems an important place in the history of Swedish literature and culture, but there is another way in which they mark an important development in Nordic literature. It will be recalled that the dominant poetic principle of Swedish verse before the fourteenth century or so was alliteration. In the period in which the Eufemia poems are translated, the tendency toward end-rhymed poetry increases: Brynolf Algotsson's Latin poetry is partly based on this principle. A verse of the oldest surviving religious poem in Swedish, *Kristi lidande* (or *pina*, Christ's suffering), from ca. 1300 (in a manuscript dated to 1350–70), combines the two principles of alliteration (*g-g*; *b-b*; *p-p*; *h-h*) and end rhyme in a manner reminiscent of the Icelandic *rímur* (metrical romances), although whether intentionally or by remarkable accident is unclear:

> ihesu guz son ihesu goþe
> Bløt mit hiærta mæþ þino bloþe
> at þænkia mz þakom þina pino
> af allom hugh ok hiærta mino.
> [Jesus, God's son, Jesus good,
> soften my heart with your blood
> that I may gratefully think of your suffering
> with all my thought and all my heart.]
> (*SFSS* 25, 4–7)

The increased popularity of versification built on end rhyme at just this moment is significant, for the point is frequently made that in the history of Scandinavian literature, the thirteenth century evinces a need for a form of poetry capable of sustaining lengthy narration. Such does not seem to have been the case with the indigenous eddic and skaldic strophic meters. Hence when Continental *poetry* is translated at the Norwegian court during the 1200s, it is turned into West Norse *prose* (e.g., *Tristrams saga, Alexanders saga, Karlamagnús saga*). The translation of the *Eufemiavisor* for this same court in the early fourteenth century is evidently the first transfer of Continental metrical romances into Nordic *metrical* romances. The tales of the *Eufemiavisor* are not the first end-rhymed texts in Scandinavia: it has been pointed out that the tradition of end-rhymed couplets in Nordic verse goes back at least as far as Egill Skallagrímsson's tenth-century *Hǫfuðlausn*, with periodic, if not general, use over the next four centuries. Religious poetry in Latin undoubtedly played a key role in the increased popularity of this convention. There is thus no reason to believe that the concept of end-rhymed poetry was quite so revolutionary at the time of the *Eufemiavisor* as is sometimes suggested. On the other hand, the execution of the idea, the use of end rhyming as the key poetic mechanism for lengthy narration, is unprecedented in Nordic poetry before the *Eufemiavisor*.

With these three texts the so-called *knittel* verse makes its important entrance into Swedish literature. The rules governing *knittel* are not strict; in general, it consists of end-rhymed couplets, normally with four stressed syllables and a varying number of unstressed syllables per line. In Swedish literature before the Reformation, lengthy end-rhymed poetry is generally used for writing historical works (e.g., *Erikskrönikan, Karlskrönikan*) and for translating foreign texts (e.g., *Historia Sancti Olai, Konung Alexander*)—in other words, about the same sorts of purposes to which the Icelandic *rímur* are put, although many prose texts are recast as *rímur* in Iceland. About the earliest history of the *rímur* little is known, but in the late fourteenth century the Icelandic metrical romances appear as a fully developed genre, suggesting that their origins may be roughly contemporary with the introduction of *knittel* verse in Sweden.

The man in whose honor the *Eufemiavisor* project was undertaken, Erik Magnusson, is also intimately tied to what might be called the greatest original work of medieval Swedish literature, *Erikskrönikan* (SFSS 47; The chronicle of Erik). A poem of about forty-five hundred lines, it encompasses the history of Sweden from the time of King Erik Eriksson "the lame and the halt" (ca. 1230) to the election of Duke Erik's three-year-old son, Magnus Eriksson, as king in 1319; the poem focuses on events surrounding Duke Erik and with only slight exaggeration might be thought of as an encomium in his honor. *Erikskrönikan* can be dated only with difficulty, since the three main manuscripts of it are all fifteenth-century copies. Details in the text, such as the death of Sir Bo Nilsson, suggest that it could not have been composed before late 1322, and the proximity the poem portrays to the later events in it suggests that it may have come into existence not long thereafter. There is no corresponding indication of the date before which it must have been composed, and this fact has led to the suggestion that since Magnus Eriksson reached his majority in 1332, the poem may be connected with the celebration of this event. The gap for the years 1314–17 in the chronicle has led to numerous speculations, including everything from the possibility that the section is missing on purely mechanical grounds (i.e., that a manuscript gathering was lost) to the suggestion that the missing portion may be related to details of the text's composition.

Little is known about the author of *Erikskrönikan*, although it can be surmised that he was affiliated with the Erik faction (perhaps particularly with Ingeborg, whose son had been elected king) and that he treats certain figures, such as Mats Kettilmundsson, with special respect and warmth. That he was a professional minstrel or troubadour has generally been ruled out. In fact, it is likely that he was a member of the aristocratic circles of which he wrote but unlikely that he was one of the central figures that dominate the epic. Based on the review of the chronicle for various points of view, it has been suggested that the author had a special relationship with Uppland or, alternatively, with Västergötland. He was, in any event, an individual of learning and of great native talent, as demonstrated by his ability to cobble together annalistic writings and oral accounts and from this synthesis forge a new literary form in Swedish, the rhymed chronicle (Sw. *rimkrönika*), that is, the presentation of historical matter in verse.

Although *Erikskrönikan* represents an important innovation in Swedish learned culture, it is not without precedent in other European literatures. Already known in the traditions of Germany (*Reimchronik*), France (*chronique metrée*), and England (metrical chronicle), the genre of the rhymed chronicle had been extensively developed. In the two centuries before *Erikskrönikan*, the rhymed chronicle had been very popular, first in the Anglo-Norman tradition and then in the German sphere. It was presumably under the influence of the flourishing German tradition of rhymed chronicles (e.g., *Livländische Reimchronik*, *Braunschweigische Reimchronik*) that the author of *Erikskrönikan* transferred the practice to native materials presented in his own tongue, a possibility undoubtedly facilitated by the presence of large numbers of Germans within Swedish borders at this time. The extent to which *Erikskrönikan* drew its inspiration directly from the German chronicle tradition, however, has been much debated, and the results suggest that although it is possible that such a direct filiation existed, nothing in the surviving materials demands it. More apparent is the degree to which the chronicle author employed Swedish annals and death notices (*dödsnotiser*), which were often incorporated into the annals, as source materials. The historical data in these works provided the author of *Erikskrönikan* with his chronological skeleton. Occasionally, death notices are employed directly, as in "Sigge Loke was killed there; God grant his soul a heavenly fate" (*SFSS* 47, 1378–79), for which there is a corresponding annals entry. The question of influences is a tricky one, however: it has been pointed out that correspondences between *Erikskrönikan* and the annals can have gone in either direction. Especially in the case of later annalistic works, such as the so-called *Chronologia anonymi* of the fifteenth century, where there is substantial similarity between the texts, the parallels are open to either interpretation.

Erikskrönikan is the first of what became in the fifteenth century the major form of Old Swedish literature, the rhymed chronicle. The writer himself no doubt thought that his creation had much in common with the French national epics, the chansons de geste (historical songs) such as the *Chanson de Roland*, which were connected with historical figures. The particular contribution of the author of *Erikskrönikan* was to take the form of the *Reimchronik*, imbue it with the passion of the chansons de geste, and turn it to native themes. An example of this emotional treatment, laced with heroic and antiheroic precedents, comes when King Birger takes his two brothers prisoner at Nyköping. After a slight resistance, they are captured; before he has them locked up in a tower, the king reminds them of his shame when they took control of the kingdom after the Håtuna game. When the dukes' men are also captured, King Birger is shown in a mad moment, drunk with his triumph yet prophetically reminded that his fall cannot be far away. He claps his hands together, laughs heartily, makes merry, and is compared by the poet to a fool (*amblodhe*, i.e., Hamlet) and a buffoon (*gäk*) (*SFSS* 47, 3914–23). Moreover, when the king is finally able to crow proudly that "now I have Sweden in my hand," one of his chancellors tells him that he believes the situation to be very different. This passage is filled with heroic allusions: to the legend of Gunnar and Högni (i.e., the treacherous taking of two brothers attending a feast in good faith); to the story of Hamlet; and to the fall of King Óláfr Tryggvason when Einarr Þambarskelfir breaks his bow and the king asks, "What broke there so loudly?" to which Einarr responds, "Norway out of your hand, king" (Snorri, 1.363).

The poet's object at one level was to create a Swedish national epic based on historical personages, for which the so-called Folkung dynasty was eminently suited, but *Erikskrönikan* is also a tendentious work, a text with a political program of sorts. Everything in the poem leads up to the point when the son of Duke Erik, Magnus, is elected king. Thus, the brothers Valdemar and Magnus Birgersson in one generation squabble over the throne and are paralleled in the next generation by Birger, Erik, and Valdemar Magnusson likewise fighting over the crown, decades that threaten the security of the nation from within, just as the Russian peril threatens the country from without. Bloodshed, cruelty, and anarchy result, and it is not without reason that the author, near the end of his poem, carefully inverts the sequence of events: although King Birger's son, also Magnus, was executed on 2 June 1320, nearly a year after the three-year-old Magnus Eriksson had been elected king, in *Erikskrönikan* the death of Magnus Birgersson is placed before the election, a final bloody event before the peaceful reign of Magnus Eriksson begins. In fact, Magnus Birgersson goes to the block asking why he must die. He receives no answer, but soon thereafter at the election of Magnus Eriksson, a spokesman for the author provides the response:

> This I've heard said all my life
> if a king is legally elected
> at Mora-stone by the "people,"
> he'll be good throughout his days
> and bring good luck to the populace
> and be mild and bring prosperity
> and provide good peace to farmers;
> that king we well need.
> (*SFSS 47, 4456–63*)

Not surprisingly, Magnus is elected king of Sweden and is soon, according to the poem, elected king of Norway as well. In fact, by virtue of his grandfather's death a few months earlier, Magnus had already inherited the Norwegian crown, but the author's purpose here is to underscore the concept of the elected, rather than inherited, kingship.

It has been suggested that the ascension of Magnus Eriksson to the throne in 1332 (i.e., his coming of age) is connected with *Erikskrönikan*. The same suggestion has been made of *Konungastyrelsen* (*SFSS* 69:1; Royal rule). On linguistic and other grounds, the text can be dated to the early fourteenth century (1319–50). Despite the high regard in which the work is widely held today, it was long suspected of being a seventeenth-century forgery. It was first published by the antiquarian Johannes Bureus in 1634, but no medieval text of *Konungastyrelsen* was known until several leaves of a manuscript turned up in Finland in 1867. This discovery finally validated the authenticity of the work. *Konungastyrelsen* belongs to the well-established tradition of the *Fürstenspiegel*, didactic texts intended to help train young rulers. The best-known such work from Scandinavia, the Norwegian *Kounungs skuggsjá* (Eng. tr. *The King's Mirror*), had been written in the previous century and has a different scope and nature. Much more eclectic than *Konungastyrelsen*, *Kounungs skuggsjá* includes large sections on geography and the wonders of the world. The Swedish text may, however, be connected with *Kounungs skuggsjá*, as the Norwegian compendium had been written for one of Magnus Eriksson's forefathers on his mother's side. As Magnus was to rule both Sweden and Norway, and was required by treaty to spend alternate periods in the two kingdoms as a youth, knowledge of the older Norwegian text may have inspired the composition of *Konungastyrelsen* as a corresponding Swedish training manual. A great many names have been promoted as the possible author of this work, two of which merit serious attention. Filip Ragvaldsson, the deacon of Linköping, had studied many years in France, came from an area of Sweden (Östergötland) consistent with the language of the text, and was a member of the regency during Magnus's minority. Another possibility is Master Matthias (Övidsson), canon at Linköping and later confessor to St. Birgitta. Like Filip Ragvaldsson, Matthias had studied at length in France and came from Östergötland. He enjoyed the favor of the king, accompanying him as preacher during the Russian war in 1348. Matthias was the most learned Swede of the century and is known to have authored several other works, including *Testa nucis*, *Poetria*, and *Homo conditus*, and he may have paraphrased the Pentateuch. Like *Konungastyrelsen*, Matthias's own works display a strong sense of Aristotelianism. If Matthias (ca. 1300–1350) was the author, then *Konungastyrelsen* would presumably have been written for Magnus's sons, Håkon and Erik, and the date would be closer to 1340 than 1330.

Konungastyrelsen makes no pretense about its compositional history: the first line informs the reader that it consists of excerpts from the books of wise men, and certainly the Old Swedish text offers testimony to its author's familiarity with earlier works relevant to his project, especially the *De regimine principum* of Aegidius of Colonna (ca. 1280), as well as *De regno* of Thomas Aquinas and the Old Testament. Yet although straightforward translation plays a role in some parts of *Konungastyrelsen*, the work bears the stamp of its author, its milieu, and its sponsor. Thus, native terminology, particularly legal terminology, is employed throughout; likewise, philosophical concepts are turned into Swedish equivalents (e.g., *animal politicum* becomes *samwistelikt diur*). *Konungastyrelsen* is divided into four parts, concerning the justification for kings, how rulers should conduct themselves, how they should control the conduct of their households, and how they should govern. It is not hard to imagine that the preceding Folkung experiences are very much in the author's mind: the text asks rhetorically if it would not be better to have several kings rule instead of a single powerful monarch. Not surprisingly, it answers firmly in the negative and asserts that one strong ruler is better than many. Similarly, the bitter experiences of that divisive dynasty, together with the theological learning of a Filip or a Matthias, may have inspired the wisdom of the statement that it is a great and honorable act to forgive one's enemies their crimes, even though one possesses the power to take revenge.

The rule of Magnus Eriksson as king of Sweden (1319–64) marks the high point of the Swedish Middle Ages: during the early years of his reign, peace was maintained, national laws codified, political ambitions realized, national boundaries extended, and the life of the mind expanded. In addition to such figures as Master Matthias, the activities of Laurentius of Vaksala (author of the theological handbooks *Suffragium curatorum* and *Summula de minstris et sacramentis*) gives evidence of Sweden's increased foreign contacts and growing participation in intellectual issues. A list of materials to be given to Ingemar Ragvaldsson from the royal treasury indicates too that this was a period of marked interest in literature: besides referring to legal codices, a paraphrase of the Bible in Swedish, and other religious texts, the inventory specifically names *Hertig Fredrik av Normandie* and *Herr Ivan Lejonriddare* (SD 4, 709).

That Sweden finally emerged from obscurity to a place of greater prominence on the European scene during the Folkung era is indicated by the marriage of Magnus in 1335 to Blanche of Namur, daughter of Count Jean of Namur (in Flanders) and Maria of Artois. At the same time, the country's standing in Nordic affairs grew: Skåne and Blekinge were purchased from a much weakened Denmark, and control of Copenhagen fell to Sweden as well. Denmark was soon rekindled under Valdemar Atterdag and regained possession of Copenhagen, but Swedish control of Blekinge, Halland, and Skåne was recognized by Denmark in the Treaty of Varberg (1343). With his hold on the entire Scandinavian peninsula thus consolidated, Magnus turned his attention to the east, ordering a blockade against Novgorod and undertaking a military crusade against it in 1348. From this zenith in the 1340s, things soon began to unravel. The arrival of the Black Death in 1349, injudicious handling of the eastern campaign, the jealousy and ambitions of the Hanseatic cities, Birgitta's attacks on the life of the court (below), and the taxes necessary to support Sweden's various foreign entanglements all played a role in the decline that followed, but none more so than a renewal of the dynastic infighting that had so characterized the Folkungs.

The advice of *Konungastyrelsen* notwithstanding, the two sons of Magnus and Blanche, Håkon and Erik, had been proclaimed the future kings of Norway and of Sweden and Skåne, respectively. Håkon was to ascend to the Norwegian throne when he reached his majority in 1355, and Erik was to become king following his father's death.

Dissatisfaction among the aristocracy had been growing, and Denmark and the Hanseatic cities were quick to take advantage of the opportunities Swedish discord offered. After Håkon became king of Norway, Erik joined the rebellious faction in the hopes of gaining his inheritance, but like others, he was probably opposed as much to the court favorite, Bengt Algotsson, as to his father. Nevertheless, the threat forced Magnus into an alliance with Valdemar of Denmark, who proceeded to wrest Skåne and Gotland away when a subsequent reconciliation between Magnus and the rebels caused Magnus to break off the Danish alliance. After Erik's death in 1359, Håkon joined the rebels against his father, but this alliance broke down when Håkon was pressured into marrying Valdemar's daughter, Margareta. Magnus Eriksson's reign was effectively over at this point, and the Swedes turned to his nephew, Albrekt of Mecklenburg (son of Magnus's sister Eufemia). He was offered, and accepted, the crown and arrived in Sweden with a sizable army of his own.

The Mecklenburg forces were able to seize many estates and castles, but Albrekt's reign was neither peaceful nor popular. Magnus and Håkon were reconciled in the face of the German presence, and Håkon's forces fought their way to the outskirts of Stockholm. A compromise was eventually reached in 1371, with Bo Jonsson Grip playing a leading role in the agreement: Albrekt was allowed to keep the title of king, but all strongholds were to be turned over and manned by native Swedes. Magnus Eriksson, who had been held captive for some years, was released and allowed to govern several provinces. With grim regularity, however, all three males died: Magnus Eriksson in 1374, Håkon Magnusson in 1380, and Olav Håkonsson in 1387. With them died not only the Swedish Folkung dynasty but also the Norwegian line that stretched back to the founding of a national kingdom under Haraldr inn hárfagri ("the Fair-Haired") in the ninth century. Bo Jonsson Grip, who had managed to consolidate his personal power and possessions during the interim, died in 1386, and the stage was set for a renewal of conflict between the Germans and the Swedes.

The preeminent figure throughout this period is Birgitta Birgersdotter (ca. 1303–73), whose role in medieval Swedish literary and cultural history is without parallel. She was the daughter of Birger Persson of Finsta and Ingeborg Bengtsdotter, and it should be noted that Birgitta's genealogy provides interesting testimony to how written cultural developments in Sweden in the Middle Ages were frequently the result of a small number of elite families. Her father was a powerful figure: law man for the province of Uppland, involved in the codification of its influential laws, and an active opponent of King Birger after the feast of Nyköping (indeed, the quotation cited above at the election of Magnus Eriksson is often attributed to him). Through her mother, Birgitta descended from the Folkungs: her maternal grandfather, Bengt Magnusson, was also a law man (the redactor of the laws of Östergötland), as was his father (Magnus Bengtsson, who may have codified the so-called Older East Gautish Laws), whose father (Bengt Magnusson) had been bishop of Linköping and one of the brothers of Earl Birger. In fact, Birgitta's family was the subject of a separate fifteenth-century chronicle by Margareta Clausdotter (SRS 3, 207–16).

Even as a young girl Birgitta reported having visions. It has often been noted that she was reared in a spiritually charged atmosphere, that is, in the proximity of St. Erik's relics, with which accounts of miracles were frequently associated, as well as within the context of Sweden's only medieval heresy trial and execution (i.e., Botulf of Gottröra, d. 1310), the prosecution of which intimately involved her family. At an early age Birgitta was married to Ulf Gudmarsson (1298–1344), who was to become a law man (Närke), a knight, and a royal councillor. Together they had eight children, and when King Magnus's Flemish bride, Blanche of Namur, came to Sweden, Birgitta was given a prominent role among the ladies at court. Her personal observations of life at court would later inform her attacks on King Magnus and Queen Blanche. Birgitta led a pious life, and she and her husband went on several pilgrimages, including the long journey to Santiago de Compostella. She was soon thereafter widowed, and two major events took place at the Cistercian cloister at Alvastra: Birgitta had her great vision in which she was revealed as *sponsa Christi* ("the bride [betrothed] of Christ"), and she became acquainted with Petrus Olai, who was to become her confessor, secretary, and follower and who accompanied her to Rome and the Holy Land (not to be confused with Petrus Olai of Skänninge, who also filled these roles in Birgitta's life). In 1349, Birgitta and her party departed for Rome; she would not return to Sweden until her body was brought back after her death in 1373.

From Rome, Birgitta attempted to exercise her power not only with regard to religious affairs but also concerning secular issues such as Swedish politics, the Hundred Years' War, and the pope's "Babylonian captivity." The focal point of her energies, however, was always papal approval for her new religious order, Ordo Sanctissimi Salvatoris, which she received in 1370. Birgitta's plan called for religious communities consisting of both nuns and monks, under the administration of an abbess. Her organization was detailed: sixty nuns were to live in proximity to (but separate from) a community of thirteen priests, four deacons, and eight lay brothers. The general confessor would have ultimate responsibility for the community's spiritual welfare, the abbess for its secular affairs. Birgitta herself planned the realization of the new order at Vadstena, Östergötland. Work began there in the late 1360s, and the cloister was dedicated in 1384. A major feature of the complex was the centrally located cloister church, which had a separate entrance on an upper level from the nuns' cloister, a former royal residence. Vadstena, especially with St. Birgitta's relics, became a major pilgrimage site, and the cloister functioned as the mother institution for dozens of (perhaps as many as eighty) other Birgittine cloisters in Denmark, Norway, Germany, Poland, England, Estonia, Italy, and the Netherlands. Direct knowledge about life at Vadstena is best preserved in two documents, *Vita Katherine* and *Diarium Vadstenense*. *Vita Katherine* was written in the early 1400s by the general confessor at Vadstena, Ulf Birgersson (d. 1433), in fulfillment of a prayer for the improvement of Bengta Gunnarsdotter (d. 1451), the abbess at Vadstena. Katarina was the fourth of Birgitta's eight children, had accompanied her mother to Rome, and had been the first abbess at Vadstena. She died in 1381, and the *vita* is apparently built on oral tales about her that circulated in the cloister. The text became so popular that it was one of the first printed Swedish books (1487). *Diarium Vadstenense* has annotations for the years 1344–1545. There are other surviving Swedish "diaries" (*Diarium fratrum minorum Stockholmiensium* [SRS I, 67–83], *Diarium minoritarum Wisbyensium* [SRS I, 32–39]), but the one for Vadstena contains especially rich biographical and historical notices. The cloister became the center of a lively intellectual community that included a scriptorium and a library of well over a thousand volumes, while the surrounding town (granted city privileges in 1400) grew rich from the pilgrim trade. As a token of the important position the cloister at Vadstena held (and of the influential families represented by the nuns who were members of it), it was not until some seventy years after the Reformation that the last nuns were driven away.

Birgitta's ecstatic experiences may be compared with those of other female mystics such as Hildegard of Bingen and Catherine of Siena, but her idiosyncratic style, as well as her themes and intentions, distinguish her from this broader tradition. Her "revelations" numbered upward of seven hundred at her death, and it was left to her acquaintance, the former Spanish bishop Alfonso de Jaen, to assemble the visions as part of the canonization process, which began immediately after Birgitta's death. By 1377, he had edited them into eight books, which were turned over to a papal committee; Birgitta's canonization was quickly made official (1391). *Revelaciones celestes* was printed in Lübeck in 1492. Not all the visions were employed by Alfonso, and these unused texts were returned to Alvastra by Petrus Olai and have come to be known as the *Reuelaciones extrauagantes* (*SFSS*, ser. 2:5). The Birgittine texts exist in both Latin and Old Swedish variants. In general, Birgitta wrote out her revelations and then had them translated into Latin, although on some occasions her amanuenses translated them directly from her oral dictation. Questions have inevitably arisen concerning the Old Swedish texts, especially as to whether or not they are Birgitta's originals. Although at least one manuscript is believed to be in Birgitta's own hand, they are mostly translations from the Latin texts made for the use of the nuns at Vadstena perhaps as early as the 1380s.

Birgitta's authority for her visions, her order, and her new rule (which was not accepted) was that Christ had revealed himself to her and taken her as his bride: "Ego elegi te et assumpsi te michi in sponsam, ut ostendam tibi secreta mea, quia michi sic placet" (*SFSS*, ser. 2:7, 245), or, as the Old Swedish text states, "I chose you and I took you as my bride that I should show you and make known to the world through you my heavenly secrets as it pleases me" (*SFSS* 14:1, 7). Heavenly inspiration is a regular feature of Birgitta's visions. Phrases of the sort "St. Peter spoke to God's bride, saying" (*SFSS* 14:2, 8) and "Christus loquitur sponse sue dicens" (Christ spoke to his bride, saying [*SFSS*, ser. 2:7, 145]) are common. These "spoken" words are converted through Birgitta into written words, texts that form the source of her power. Indeed, the parallel between Christ and the saints speaking to Birgitta and making divine revelations to her, which she then writes down, and Birgitta speaking to her assistants and making divine revelations to them, which they then write down in Latin, is striking. In fact, the entire range of images associated with composition and delivery—words, texts, books—are frequently equated with power and divine judgment in Birgitta's works: in a vision of three kings (including Magnus Eriksson) before the judgment seat of God, for example, the Lord's celestial throne is presented as a pulpit or writing desk (*bokastol*). Birgitta sees a building in heaven of wondrous beauty and size and in it a pulpit and on the pulpit a book. The *bokastol* is of magnificent size and radiance; the book is open and each word in it "was living and spoke by itself," and it was as if someone said, "do this or that, and immediately it was done with the word's delivery" (*SFSS* 14:3, 425). Small wonder that medieval representations of Birgitta often picture her hard at work, listening to voices from heaven, pen in hand, poised to write down those "living words," and seated at just such a *bokastol*, which, of course, functions as her own judgment seat.

And judge Birgitta certainly did, for in addition to her visions of a mixed religious community of men and women and other strictly spiritual matters, she was greatly concerned with secular issues, especially those of Sweden. Thus, she frequently wrote warnings about contemporary events and allegorized individuals she believed the nation's enemies: Bengt Algotsson becomes a fearful dragon (*SFSS* 14:3, 365); Albrekt the Elder of Mecklenburg and his wife, Eufemia (sister of King Magnus), a poisonous snake and its mate (*SFSS* 14:3, 332); and so on. No topic was too delicate for Birgitta to take up in this public way. After Håkon and Erik were born to Queen Blanche and King Magnus, Birgitta wrote a "parable" (ca. 1341, before the birth of their daughters) about a king and queen who had had two sons and had then sworn to live a chaste life, the king because of a volatile and unsteady spirit (among other reasons), and the queen (again, among many other reasons) so "that she should not experience the pain of childbirth" (*SFSS* 14:3, 318). And when King Magnus considers undertaking a military crusade in the eastern Baltic, Birgitta is ready to give him some very specific advice about how it should be carried out (*SFSS* 14:3, 406–16). Ecclesiastics were equally within her reach: in a vision of a cardinal being punished in the afterlife, Birgitta relates how his soul is forced to wander through four rooms, one filled with beautiful clothes, one with vessels of gold and silver, one with food and other sensuous items, and one with horses and other animals by which he had been conveyed in life. As his soul passes through the rooms, it is chilled in the first chamber by cold, since he had loved what was beautiful over what was nourishing; in the second room it is singed by flames, since he had drunk to excess and sought lovely material possessions; in the third room it experiences a vile stench and burning snakes, since he had loved the servant girls; and in the fourth room it hears a terrible sound like thunder and cries out that his retribution is well deserved. Christ then reminds him that priests, bishops, and cardinals will also be held accountable for their deeds (*SFSS* 14:3, 190–92).

Birgitta's personal role in fourteenth-century culture, politics, and theology was enormous, and the founding at Vadstena of a Birgittine cloister strongly influenced spiritual and literary matters in all subsequent periods of the Swedish Middle Ages. A *legenda* and an *officium* in her honor were written by Birger Gregerson, but it was perhaps best left to Birgitta herself to write her epitaph—as always in her writings, in veiled terms. In the context of a deeply personal vision concerning the fact that her daughter has left the cloister at Skänninge, Christ suggests three examples of good women: Susanna, Judith, and Thecla of Iconium. The first was married, the second a widow, the third a virgin; "these had different lives and purposes, yet they are alike in the worthiness and reward of their achievements" (*SFSS* 14:2, 138). It is not hard to believe that in these three figures Birgitta could see the three phases of her own life: her devout childhood, her years as a pious wife and mother, and her victorious widowhood in which she was armed not with Holofernes's sword but with the still mightier quill.

From the high point Swedish spiritual culture reached during the reign of King Magnus, it moved into a period largely dominated by translations of one sort and another. Perhaps the most impressive is the rhymed Old Swedish *Konung Alexander* (*SFSS* 12; King Alexander), a work of more than ten thousand *knittel* verses. The unique manuscript in which it is preserved is from the middle of the fifteenth century, but the project itself can be dated to a narrow range at the end of the fourteenth century. The poem states that it was translated for Bo Jonsson Grip, who died in 1386 and who is referred to as *drots* (deputy), a title he held as of 1375. *Konung Alexander* as a Swedish poem based on the Latin prose text *Historii de preliis Alexandri Magni* must have been created in the years between these dates. The translator used the so-called Orosius redaction of the *Historii de preliis*, which was itself based on a late Greek work, *Pseudo-Kallistenes*. Despite suggestions that the Old Swedish *Konung Alexander* might go back to an Old Danish or Middle Low German text, it seems certain that the Swedish version was translated directly from the Latin, possibly by a native from the area around Kalmar. The translator was an individual of considerable learning, knowledgeable about foreign literature and about native Swedish literary traditions (e.g., the *Eufemiavisor, Erikskrönikan*).

Yet despite the continuity the text exhibits with various Continental and Swedish traditions, *Konung Alexander* is imbued with an entirely different spirit. The poem opens by suggesting in polemical terms that such heroic figures as Gawain, Parceval, and Dietrich of Bern accomplish only meaningless deeds, whereas Alexander set himself a much more practical sort of goal, that is, to conquer the world. Gone from this work are the chivalric ideals that had flowed into the country so prominently at the beginning of the century, and the victory of pragmatism over courtliness in *Konung Alexander*, together with the poem's politically significant sponsor, has led to speculation that the work may be a tendentious roman à clef in which, for example, Alexander could be equated with Bo Jonsson and the weak Darius with Albrekt. Such an allegorical interpretation of the work has been almost uniformly rejected, however, if only because much of the "allegory" was present in the Latin original. Yet the rejection of this idea should not suggest that the translator did not place his own stamp on the material. Much of the celebrated vividness of the text derives from the quality of the translator's rhymes and his lively sense of detailed imagery, and the language of the text compares well with *Alexanders saga*, a West Norse prose translation of Gautier de Châtillon's Latin poem *Alexandreis*. The Alexander legend was extremely popular in Scandinavia, and in addition to *Konung Alexander*, this figure is known in Swedish tradition from artistic representations (e.g., Fardhem Church, Gotland) and from a prose version of his life in *Siælinna thrøst* (translated directly from the Middle Low German *Seelentrost*).

Konung Alexander may not provide an allegorical treatment of King Albrekt, but just the opposite is true of *Om konung Albrekt* (SFSS 25, 177–84; Concerning King Albrekt). Probably composed in the 1390s, shortly after the conclusion of Albrekt's disastrous Swedish adventure, the poem is an elaborate allegory of his rule. A beautiful grove (Sweden), filled with fruits and gems, is harassed by various wild beasts (Albrekt's advisers) through the inattention and ineffectiveness, at best, of its owner (Albrekt). The piece is elaborately contrived, and the degree to which relations with the German prince had been strained is evident throughout, not least in the poet's presentation of the German troops as marauding brigands. The poet does not leave the interpretation of his meaning to the audience but devotes much of his poem to its own interpretation: "and now I will interpret this for you" (1.69).

As an original composition *Konung Albrekt* is an exception to the trend in the late 1300s; much more common are the various translations of religious works, such as *Kroppens och Själens träta* (The quarrel between the body and the soul), *Julen och Fastan* (Christmas and Lent), and *Riddar Sankt Göran* (Saint George). *Kroppens och Själens träta* (SFSS 25, 92–107) is a moralizing dialogue between a body and soul just at the moment after death. The introduction to the long poem (482 verses) makes it a piece of vision literature as well as a debate poem (*conflictus*). The narrator, a master of "book learning," is convinced that one winter night he witnessed a body and its soul engage in a wrangle filled with recriminations, characterized by questions of the sort, "Where are now your costly clothes?" (1.23 and passim). The soul has been condemned to eternal damnation, and the poem concludes with two devils taking it away. *Kroppens och Själens träta* is a serious work, at its most startling when the soul asks rhetorically why God created it when He must have known what its fate would be. Quite different with respect to both tone and length (482 lines as opposed to 46) is the fragmentary *Julen och Fastan* (SFSS 25, 382–84), also a debate poem but not in the serious moralizing vein of *Kroppens och Själens träta*. In *Julen och Fastan*, the two holidays stand as representatives of gluttony and abstinence, and to Lent's call for greater piety, Christmas responds, "That's your purpose, to listen to confession, sit in church, and do nothing else" (ll.37–38). Also from the late 1300s (or possibly the early 1400s) is the rhymed *Riddar Sankt Göran* (SFSS 25, 185–99). The legend of St. George and the dragon was well known in Sweden: the theme inspired a ballad, and prose versions of it make up part of *Fornsvenska legendariet* (SFSS 7) and *Siælinna thrøst* (The consolation of the soul), for example, and a day in his honor is included in *Calendarium Vallentunense* (1198). The legend's most famous artistic realization in medieval Sweden is the sculpture of the maiden, the dragon, and St. George by Bernt Notke in Storkyrkan, Stockholm. The rhymed *Riddar Sankt Göran*, a text of 460 lines, focuses on the image of St. George as both knight and Christian, a man who can defeat a dragon in one line and almost literally in the next be preaching to the townsfolk about Christ. There is a controlled pace to the poem, and though still very much a religious work with a didactic, moralizing purpose, it is also an excellent example of chivalric literature.

At the close of the fourteenth century, one of the truly remarkable figures of the Nordic Middle Ages dominates developments: Margareta. Daughter of King Valdemar Atterdag of Denmark, wife of King Håkon of Norway, and mother of Olav, heir to both the Swedish and Norwegian crowns, Margareta had been married to Håkon at a tender age and reared in the household of one of St. Birgitta's daughters. By shrewd machinations and careful politics after Olav's death, Margareta managed to have herself declared ruler of Denmark, Norway, and Sweden in turn. Two years later (1389), she was essentially in control of Sweden, with Albrekt and his son Erik captured and his army defeated. In 1397, a meeting was held at the Swedish castle in Kalmar, with delegates from the three Nordic kingdoms (although Norway was only poorly represented). The participants agreed that henceforth there would be a single Scandinavian monarch, to be selected unanimously by the three kingdoms (later dubbed the Kalmar Union). This federation was to be Sweden's fate, controlling Swedish history from 1397 to the Reformation. In essence, the union was valid only as long as the indomitable will of Margareta was alive to sustain it. Cracks appeared in the alliance soon after the meeting at Kalmar and widened to a chasm with Margareta's death in 1412. If dissolution was inevitable, it was also inevitably bloody.

From Margareta's death (1412) to the establishment of an independent Swedish kingdom under Gustav Vasa in the 1520s, Sweden was part of what is usually referred to as the Kalmar Union. The concept of a union is misleading, however. It is true that one of the documents associated with this pan-Nordic treaty envisions a single sovereign with the power, if not the right, to name his successor and make foreign and military policy, but a second document places important strictures on the pact. Not least among them was the agreement that the three kingdoms were to continue as separate entities and that they were to retain their individual rights in matters of law and administration. Although an oversimplification, the history of fifteenth-century Sweden can be characterized as the history of the tension between these two interpretations of the Nordic federation. Certainly the image of conflict dominates original Swedish literary works of the period.

As her successor, Margareta selected her grand-nephew, Erik of Pomerania (son of her sister's daughter and thus a great-grandson of Valdemar Atterdag). He had been duly elected by the three countries as their new monarch and possessed many attributes that should have strengthened his position, including an advantageous marriage to Philippa, the daughter of Henry IV of England. Nevertheless, Erik ran afoul of the aristocracy through his appointments of foreigners as castellans and through his ever greater need for revenue. Moreover, outside Sweden he aroused the ire of the Hanseatic cities through his trade policies and of the noblemen along the Dano-German border through his claims to the province of Schleswig. By 1432, Erik's position as king of Sweden was effectively over, and a peasant revolt in the Swedish mining province of Dalarna broke out under the capable leadership of Engelbrekt Engelbrektsson. Differences were resolved for a while, only to be followed by renewed hostilities. In 1436, a council of Swedish noblemen renounced their allegiance to Erik and elected Karl Knutsson commander, with Engelbrekt appointed cocommander by popular demand. Engelbrekt was murdered a few months later by a personal enemy; although the aristocracy had little use for him alive, it was quite willing to exploit him in death for his value in rallying the country, as in the poem *Engelbrekt och Karl Knutsson* (below).

Karl Knutsson was initially appointed *rikis forstandare* (Modern Swedish *riksföreståndare*, lit. "director of the realm"), but in 1448, after the sudden death of Kristoffer of Bavaria (who had been elected in 1442 as king of the "union"), Karl was elected king by both Sweden and Norway. He was king of Sweden until 1457, again in 1464–65, and again from 1467 to 1470. In 1457, he was driven from office by a revolt led by some of the country's most prominent aristocratic families, which had both economic and personal reasons to dislike him. For a few years (1457–64), the Swedes accepted the rule of King Christian I of Denmark, but economic distress brought on under him led the same aristocratic forces to bring Karl back. Never able to reestablish his authority, Karl retreated to Finland, and Sweden was governed by various constellations of noblemen. Karl retained the title of king, however, and his death in 1470 provided the opportunity for Denmark to press its claims once again. Karl's nephew, Sten Sture (the Elder), was appointed *riksföreståndare*, and the stage was set for confrontation: it came in 1471, when the Danes and Swedes met at the Battle of Brunkeberg, celebrated in the work of the same name, *Slaget vid Brunkeberg* (below). The battle was also commemorated by the St. George sculpture in Stockholm's Storkyrka (above): in it, St. George represents Sten Sture; the dragon, Denmark; and the maiden, Sweden.

Sten Sture continued as regent for nearly three decades (1470–97, 1501–3), but during that narrow window of 1497–1501, the possibility of Danish suzerainty reemerged under King Hans, who was recognized as king of a reunified federation. With Hans weakened by a terrible defeat on his southern border in 1500, Sten rallied support for a revolt against him. When Hans retaliated by attacking Swedish coastal regions, the Swedes renounced him as king and reaffirmed Sten as *riksföreståndare*. Sten had very nearly liberated all of Sweden when he died (1503), and Svante Nilsson (Sture), one of Sten's most implacable enemies, was elected *riksföreståndare* (1504–12). Although arrangements had been made to reconcile the two countries, the deaths of Svante in 1512 and Hans in 1513 opened the door for the next generation to resolve the conflict. Through some clever arranging, Svante Nilsson's son, Sten, who came to be called Sten Sture the Younger, was elected *riksföreståndare*; in Denmark, Christian II, the son of King Hans, became king. When negotiations failed, King Christian launched several unsuccessful invasions of Sweden, taking with him six hostages after the last attempt, including the man who would eventually become the founder of the modern Swedish state, the youthful Gustav Eriksson (Vasa).

In 1520, King Christian returned to Sweden with French, German, and Scottish mercenaries: Sten Sture the Younger was killed in battle, and Christian managed to take Stockholm, which surrendered after certain guarantees were made, including a general amnesty. A Danish bishop declared Christian king of Sweden by virtue of inheritance, intentionally ignoring the Swedish practice of electing monarchs. Some members of the Swedish clergy, who had their own axes to grind (Archbishop Gustav Trolle's father had been outmaneuvered by Sten Sture for the position of *riksföreståndare*), produced a charge of heresy against the Swedish leaders. Heresy was not covered by the amnesty, and through it, Christian and his Swedish allies were able to rid themselves of their leading enemies. Eighty-two Swedes were beheaded on 8 November 1520 and later their bodies were burned on a funeral pyre; the frenzied atmosphere of what has come to be known as "Stockholm's Bloodbath" was so great that the corpses of Sten Sture and one of his sons were even exhumed and burned on the pyre. By the time the man known in Swedish as "Christian the Tyrant" returned to Denmark, as many as six hundred people had been executed. Christian possessed an unusual personality, and insofar as this rampage was politically (as opposed to personally) motivated, he no doubt sought to put an end to the troublesome Swedish uprisings. What he did not foresee was the galvanizing effect the outrage would have on the country as a whole and on Gustav Eriksson Vasa in particular. Beyond his personal loss at the Bloodbath (his father and several other relatives were executed there), Gustav would turn the act into a rallying point for the nation, for he was the man who would soon become king of an independent Sweden, which he ruled for nearly forty years.

Interest in historical matters is manifested early and often in Sweden (e.g., the runic inscriptions, *Vidhemsprästens anteckningar*, *Erikskrönikan*), and frequently history and politics are key components in understanding medieval Swedish literature. For no period is this concept more true than the fifteenth century. This interest, now fostered by propagandistic goals and official support, resulted in a series of historical works outlining Sweden's past (listed here without respect to the date of composition and with the years they cover): *Förbindelsedikten* (The connecting poem, 1319–89); *Engelbrektskrönikan* (The chronicle of Engelbrekt, 1389–1436); *Karlskrönikan* (The chronicle of Karl, 1436–52); *Sturekrönikan* (The Sture chronicle, 1452–96); *Lilla rimkrönikan* (The little rhymed chronicle, from the first king [Erik] to 1448, with later additions to 1520); *Yngsta rimkrönikan* (The youngest rhymed chronicle, from Erik to 1520); and *Prosaiska krönikan* (The prosaic chronicle, from the Goths to 1449). *Om ett gyllene år* (SFSS part 243; Concerning a golden year), a translation made in 1503, celebrates King Hans's defeat in Dithmarschen. The *Chronica regni Gothorum* of Ericus Olai details both the secular and religious history of the kingdom. In addition, *Skara biskopskrönika* (SFSS 25, 432–42; The chronicle of the bishops of Skara) and *Linköpings biskopskrönika* (SFSS 25, 483–508; The chronicle of the bishops of Linköping), from the late fourteenth and early fifteenth centuries, represent the growth of bishops' tables into historical poetry of a sort very similar to the rhymed chronicles.

Förbindelsedikten (*SFSS* 17:1, 171–92), a poem of 632 verses, takes up events directly after *Erikskrönikan*, which is not to say that this poem possesses its predecessor's literary merits. A number of works appear to have been used for source materials, including St. Birgitta's revelations. The writer has great respect for Birgitta and maintains that it was through her that God told King Magnus how he should reign (ll.123–25), but he did not heed the advice. A xenophobic outlook permeates the text, and when Margareta and King Albrekt contend for the country, the period is painted in eschatological terms that seem to hark back to Nordic mythological tradition as represented in the eddic *Vǫluspá*:

> The realm was in a bad way without reason,
> brother killed brother,
> and son worked against father,
> no one asked about the law or justice
> (*SFSS 17:1, 573–75*)

The poem is believed to have been written in the 1450s, specifically for the purpose of filling the chronological gap between *Erikskrönikan* and *Karlskrönikan* (also known as *Nya krönikan* [The new chronicle]), as well as for providing legitimacy to Karl Knutsson's claims to descent from St. Erik.

Karlskrönikan (*SFSS* 17:2) is now generally regarded as consisting of two parts, an original *Engelbrektskrönikan* and a subjoined *Karlskrönikan*, written at the behest of Karl Knutsson. The entire text consists of 9,628 lines and is preserved in a contemporary manuscript. There can be little doubt but that the work is the product of a chancellory and represents a sort of "official" poetry with clearly tendentious overtones. The mission of *Engelbrektskrönikan* is to justify the Swedish revolt in the 1430s, and again and again the text tries to portray Eric as a faithless oath breaker; the mission of its sequel (*Karlskrönikan*) is to display Karl in the best possible light, in particular as the legitimate heir to Engelbrekt's popular status as folk hero. Following Engelbrekt's murder, for example, the poet maintains that Karl is loved by the populace and that he treats them well (ll.2767–68). *Karlskrönikan* echoes, or at least wants to echo, *Erikskrönikan* in many respects, but certainly not with regard to chivalric tone, which finds no place in the later chronicle.

Sturekrönikan (*SFSS* 17:3, 1–144) follows the course of Swedish events from 1452 to 1496 in 4,198 lines. Earlier scholarship on the chronicle tended to see in it three separate texts by three different authors (1452–70, 1470–87, 1488–96); more recently, the view has emerged that *Sturekrönikan* consists of two sections, one covering the years 1452–87, sponsored by Sten Sture the Elder, and the second treating the period 1488–96 and probably sponsored by Archbishop Jacob Ulfsson. Like *Karlskrönikan*, *Sturekrönikan* is a tendentious work, with the added anomaly that its political point of view shifts from a pro-Sten stance in the first section to a pronounced anti-Sten position in the second section. In general, scholarship on *Sturekrönikan* has tended to be atomistic, searching for the "original" texts within the preserved work, and as yet no synthetic view of the work as a whole exists; given its origins in two opposing political ideologies, it may well be that none is possible.

One of the most interesting of the rhymed chronicles appeared in the mid-fifteenth century, *Lilla rimkrönikan* (SFSS 17:1, 215–88). This text follows Swedish history from the nation's mythological beginning to King Kristoffer (with lengthy continuations added in the 1500s that take the chronicle all the way to Sten Sture the Younger). What sets this chronicle apart is its format of monologues by each of Sweden's regents, in which they relate aspects of their reigns and deaths. The form parallels the Danish rhymed chronicle and is widely believed to derive from pictorial presentations of the "Dance of Death," such as those attested from fifteenth-century Lübeck. Among the considerable number of nonhistorical monarchs are such figures as King Frode and King Domalder (ll.110–16), known from earlier Nordic historical works such as *Ynglingasaga* and *Historia Norvegiæ* with which the author was familiar. Similar traditions are common to the texts—that Frode's reign was peaceful, that Domalder was sacrificed to alleviate terrible conditions in Sweden (both *Lilla rimkrönikan* and *Historia Norvegiæ* say that he is offered to Ceres), and so on. Like so much else that was created in this century, the poem has a political slant, namely, to deprecate foreign rulers: Albrekt gives away land and castles to Germans and holds the Swedes in contempt; Margareta gloats over conquering the country through her counsel alone (ll.414–19); Erik of Pomerania admits that he had always planned to ruin the three Nordic countries (ll.426–34); and Kristoffer says that he is prevented from placing the country in great distress only by his sudden death (ll.446–47). The poem is preserved in several manuscript "books" belonging to aristocratic families, and its popularity among such circles must have been quite high. The monologues of the sixty-two regents in the original *Lilla rimkrönikan* are brief, usually on the order of about a dozen lines, and display a structure not unlike that of a guessing game. It is not difficult to imagine that the "speaker" tags that introduce each statement in the manuscript are solutions to a parlor game of the "Who am I?" variety in a read-aloud performance. Thus, for example,

> I starved my brothers to death,
> therefore I was driven from the realm,
> and forced to flee to Denmark
> and died there in Ringsted.
> (answer, Birger Magnusson)
> (*LL.379–82, 378*)

Politics aside, if *Lilla rimkrönikan* had a use other than entertainment, it was pedagogy, and its riddle-like character would certainly lend itself to such a purpose. A fourteenth-century Swedish riddle collection (in Latin) combines these same elements: the riddles concern learned topics and are set up as a conversation between student and teacher (Wahlgren).

Yngsta rimkrönikan (*SFSS* 17:1, 254–88) was written in the early sixteenth-century (1523–25) by a cleric from Östergötland and follows Swedish history from its beginnings in Gothic tradition to Stockholm's Bloodbath; the period from 1452 to 1520 was added later. Although the author is largely reliant on songs, annals, and earlier chronicles, especially *Lilla rimkrönikan*, he did not draw on *Sturekrönikan*. His project resembles *Lilla rimkrönikan* in chronology and in form, with each monarch telling something of his reign, and the text is notable for its strongly pro-Swedish, anti-Danish sentiments. These views are most pronounced in the 140-line prologue, which details the natural bounty of Sweden and praises the country's heroic deeds.

Like *Lilla rimkrönikan*, *Prosaiska krönikan* (*Småstycken*, 217–57) was written in the 1450s. The two texts bear a resemblance on other fronts as well: they appear to be products of Karl Knutsson's propaganda machine, they outline Swedish history from its mythological beginnings, and they represent early attempts to create a national history. *Prosaiska krönikan* draws on a vast array of resources, including Jordanes, Adam of Bremen, and various West Norse sources dealing with the Ynglings and Dietrich of Bern. The chronicle's most notable contribution is its interweaving of traditional wisdom concerning the Goths with Swedish history; certainly as a form of pro-Swedish propaganda, *Prosaiska krönikan* served its purpose well, although perhaps more so in the seventeenth than in the fifteenth century.

As part of an emerging sense of nationalism, a university was founded in Uppsala in 1477, and it was a man who would become one of this institution's first professors, Ericus Olai, who took the sentiments of *Lilla rimkrönikan* and *Prosaiska krönikan* and from them created in the late 1460s an international version of Swedish history, *Chronica regni Gothorum* (*SRS* 2, 1–166). It should be noted that the "Gothic" identification that informs these texts was not original with the chronicles: in 1434, Nicolaus Ragvaldi, bishop of Växjö, attended a church council at Basel and delivered an oration concerning the identification of the conquering Goths of antiquity with the *götar* of Sweden. He, in turn, could find support for this identification in both "native" tradition (e.g., *Fornsvenska legendariet*) and learned tradition (e.g., Jordanes, Isidore of Seville, Rodrigo Jiménez). By using the earlier chronicles (especially *Prosaiska krönikan*) and the learned sources, including Saxo Grammaticus and Adam of Bremen, Ericus Olai created a work whose "Gothicism" would have great significance for such later authors as Johannes Magnus and Olof Rudbeck.

Propaganda and nationalism clearly played a role in the composition of the rhymed chronicles; indeed, the same thing may be said about much of the activity surrounding the creation and translation of literature in the Swedish fifteenth century. In some instances even the selection of materials translated into Swedish (e.g., *Sagan om Didrik af Bern, Historia Sancti Olai*) appears to have been influenced by such considerations. One text for which that was probably not true is *Karl Magnus* (*SFSS* 63; Eng. tr. "The Journey to Constantinople," "Roland" [*MS*, 175–211]), a translation of ca. 1400 from a thirteenth-century West Norse compilation of French chansons de geste treating the career of Charlemagne and his paladins. Four manuscripts of the Swedish *Karl Magnus* exist (earliest ca. 1420); these codices tend to be large anthologies containing works from various genres, including secular translations, rhymed chronicles, chivalric romances, and religious and didactic works. Only two of the dozen texts that make up the extant West Norse cycle (*Karlamagnús saga*) exist in Swedish translation, although scholars have speculated (based on a closely related Old Danish translation) that there once was a much fuller Swedish version. This view was widely accepted for some time but has been left in question since the manuscript filiation on which the theory rested was rejected. The Swedish versions closely follow the Old Norse (and display frequent Norwegianisms) and, though the stories are entertaining enough in themselves, show little originality.

Of much greater moment is *Sagan om Didrik af Bern* (*SFSS* 10; The saga of Dietrich of Bern), also a translation of a West Norse text (*Þiðreks saga af Bern*). Although legendary material about Dietrich (or Theodoric) was known in Sweden as early as ca. 800 (the Rök stone), there is no demonstrable continuity between the two; nevertheless, this most famous of Germanic heroes is frequently mentioned in Old Swedish texts (e.g., *Fornsvenska legendariet*, *Herr Ivan*, *Erikskrönikan*). The manuscript on which *Didrik af Bern* is based probably came back to Sweden with Karl Knutsson in 1449 after he had gone to Norway to be crowned king. As with most projects connected with Karl Knutsson, *Didrik af Bern* can be interpreted politically, for the text mentions Sweden as an ancient kingdom and the home of powerful monarchs and thus fits well with the growing nationalistic and "Gothic" sentiments of the aristocracy. Although not an independent source of information on the heroes whose deeds it relates (e.g., Hillebrand, Sigord [= Hildebrandr, Sigurðr]), *Didrik af Bern* is an entertaining example of the translator's art at its best.

From the same period, and quite possibly carried out for the same propaganda purposes, is *Historia Sancti Olai* (SFSS 25, 313–76), a much reduced translation of the massive Icelandic work *Óláfs saga helga* (Snorri, 2, 3–451; Eng. tr. *St. Óláf's Saga*) by Snorri Sturluson, which the Swedish translator incorrectly attributes to Ari the Wise (1.13). Obviously, a condensation of this magnitude, together with the fact that the translator has turned his prose model into 2,003 lines of Swedish *knittel* verse, makes *Historia Sancti Olai* a very different translation project from *Karl Magnus*, for example, which closely parallels its model. The Swedish editor-translator has focused primarily on cobbling from his original the story of Swedo-Norwegian cooperation against the Danes, of how in spite of original enmity, the Norwegian and Swedish thrones had joined in common cause against the hegemony of King Knut the Great (cf. ll.875–83). It is not difficult to imagine that such a work came about in connection with Karl Knutsson's attempts to maintain just such an alliance against Christian I of Denmark.

A very different sort of mission inspired *Siælinna thrøst* (SFSS 59; The consolation of the soul), the Swedish translation of a compilation of narrative materials shaped as edifying literature. This pedagogical distinction is underscored in the introduction, which says that there are those in the world who enjoy reading and hearing "books about bygone worldly things and deeds" and "books about heroes," such as Dietrich of Bern and Parceval. This work, on the other hand, is intended for *siælinna helsa* (the health of the soul). *Siælinna thrøst* is largely based on the Middle Low German *Seelentrost*, although the editor has also used miscellaneous Latin and native materials. The work was done at Vadstena sometime in the second quarter of the 1400s and is organized around the Ten Commandments, each of which is given and then expounded by dozens of exempla, short moralizing tales often used in sermons. In the context of the Eighth Commandment (against bearing false witness), for example, comes a tale known throughout Europe and Scandinavia, "aff amelio oc amico" (*SFSS* 59, 331–45; Eng. tr. "Amicus and Amelius" [*MS*, 299–321]). It is a tale of deceit in the service of love and has numerous analogues (e.g., Tristan, *Grettis saga*, Sigurðr and Gunnar). The story has the unusual dimension of interiority: the character actually questions the morality of his conduct. Moreover, his deception does not go unpunished, as the character is stricken with leprosy and must undergo numerous trials before his friend's faithfulness (and trust in God) saves him. A similar sort of edifying work is *Barlaam och Josaphat*, an abbreviated version of which appears in *Fornsvenska legendariet* but which is translated anew in a much longer version (*SFSS* 28, 3–107) at Vadstena. It is roughly contemporary with *Siælinna thrøst*, which it was probably intended to supplement.

At about the same time (ca. 1420), *Sju vise mästare* (*SFSS* 28, 113–245; Eng. tr. "The Seven Wise Masters" [*MS*, 212–98]) was first translated into Swedish. Known in English tradition as *The Seven Sages*, this collection of tales was enormously popular throughout Europe (about two hundred fifty manuscripts of it exist), although its roots are ultimately to be derived from the Orient and the tradition of works such as *The Thousand and One Nights*. Its acclaim in Sweden is attested by the fact that it was translated into Swedish on three separate occasions, twice from Latin and once from Middle Low German. *Sju vise mästare* has remained popular in Sweden into modern times as a chapbook (*folkbok*). The anthology is held together by a framing device in which the emperor's son is accused by his stepmother of attempting to seduce her; in fact, the opposite is true. The prince is unable to speak on his own behalf, and with his life hanging in the balance, each of his seven teachers takes a turn delaying his execution by telling the emperor a story. The empress responds to their narratives with her own tales. Finally, the prince is able to speak for himself and relate the truth. The fourteen stories contained in *Sju vise mästare* are populated by scorned lovers, faithful dogs, deceived husbands, avaricious rulers, and a host of other familiar characters whose adventures and misdeeds are intended to edify and entertain the emperor and the audience. The three versions differ considerably with respect to style, the German-based text (*C*) lacking the lightness and pace of the others (*A*, *B*). Thus, for example, when the empress fabricates the prince's attack in *A*, she gives the emperor this lively report: "This one who you say is your son, he seems to me to be a devil in a man's shape, and if you had not come, I would be dead, or he would have done his will with me" (p.116). In *C*, on the other hand, even the beginning of the corresponding section (which is quite long) gives an impression of how much more ponderous and forced the text sounds: "Oh Lord, have mercy on me and behold the great dishonor which has been done to me" (p.230).

One of the most entertaining translation projects of the period is a brief satire that introduces itself as *Hær sigx aff abbotum allum skemptan myklæ* ("Here is related a great jest about all abbots," also known as *Skämtan om abboten*, "The jest about the abbot" [*SFSS* 28, 353–55]). It is preserved in several manuscripts from the middle of the 1400s and was probably rendered in Swedish in the earlier part of the century. There is no known foreign original, although the work is similar in spirit and subject matter to some of the so-called Goliard poems. This parody, or as the text calls itself in one manuscript, *fabula* (p.355), uses elevated language and style to poke fun at the excesses of abbots, especially their fondness for victuals. Overindulgence competes with gluttony in the scene, which is given in humorous detail and followed by the order's pious limit on what the abbot can consume. When, for example, the abbot has gorged himself on dozens and dozens of eggs prepared in every conceivable manner (five fried, five poached, and so on), the text says, "It is forbidden for him to eat more" (p.354)!

Although the chivalric tone had largely disappeared from native Swedish literature by the fifteenth century, it was still present in some imported works, perhaps most prominently *Namnlös och Valentin* (*SFSS* 52; Eng. tr. "Nameless and Valentine" [*MS*, 120–61]). Translated from a Middle Low German poem ca. 1450, the Swedish prose story tells of twins who are separated at birth: one, like Moses, is found by the king's daughter, who rears him, while the other is reared by a she-wolf. The rest of the tale concerns their reunification, the rescue of their mother, the winning of their respective brides, and their ascension to the thrones of France and Hungary. The style of *Namnlös och Valentin* is informed by the fact that the translator, who was well read in the tradition of earlier Swedish *knittel* poetry, used a versified original.

A text of a very different sort is *Schacktavels lek* (*SFSS* 25, 200–309; The chess game), an allegory of society, its hierarchy, and its members: kings, queens, knights, farmers, and tradesmen, all segments of society are represented on the chess table. This particular kind of allegory has its beginnings in the thirteenth century with Jacobus de Cesselis's *De ludo scaccorum*. The Swedish translator and editor has used both Latin and Middle Low German materials, as well as his own original contributions, in creating his *knittel* text of 3,322 lines. Written ca. 1460, the poem displays surprisingly little anti-Danish sentiment, although the author has some pointed views: that an inherited throne is superior to an elected one (l.461), that native rule is better than foreign rule (ll.291, 469), and so on. *Schacktavels lek* is a difficult work to identify generically: it is at once allegory, exemplum, and *Fürstenspiegel*, and although part of a broader European tradition, it has its own peculiarly Swedish character. Of particular note in this regard is the so-called *Äktenskapsvisan* (The marriage song [ll.643–732]), an original Swedish contribution to the work that treats marriage humorously yet in a starkly realistic tone.

The secular translations that so characterize the later Middle Ages in Sweden come to an end only after an independent Swedish kingdom had been established, that is, with *Riddar Paris och jungfru Vienna* (Sir Paris and Maid Vienna, ca. 1520) and *Historia Troiana* (1529). *Riddar Paris och jungfru Vienna* (*SFSS* 25, 443–50) is preserved in a manuscript from 1523 and is assumed to have been translated a few years earlier, but whether there ever existed more than the extant fragmentary poem of 208 lines is uncertain. It is the last attempt at chivalric verse of the period, and although the story of two young lovers divided by differing social statuses would find a natural audience as a chapbook (*folkbok*) in a later era, the most remarkable aspect of this poem is its poetic form, unique for the Swedish Middle Ages: cross-rhymed four-line strophes. It is surprising that although the story of the Trojan War was well known elsewhere in Scandinavia as early as the thirteenth century (and may have been known in Sweden as well), it was not translated before the rather tortured rendering of 1529. It is perhaps an appropriate comment on the end of the Middle Ages that *Historia Troiana* was translated from a version *printed* in Strassburg in 1494.

In addition to literary works, religious and didactic texts continued to be translated into Swedish at a rapid pace throughout the fifteenth and early sixteenth centuries: among the most important and prolific of the translators were Jöns Budde (fl. 1475), a monk at the Birgittine cloister at Nådendal, Finland, and Peder Månsson (d. 1534). Among Budde's contributions were the visions of St. Mechtild (as *Heliga Mechtilds Uppenbarelser* [*SFSS* 32]), Henrik Suso's *Horologium Sapientiae* (as *Gudeliga snilles väckare* [*SFSS* 18; Call to pious genius]), the allegorical *Claustrum animae* (as *Själens kloster* [The soul's cloister]), and the *Elucidarius*. Peder Månsson, a monk at Vadstena, was sent on an important mission to Rome (namely, to ensure that the Birgittine quarters there, an important pilgrimage site and hostel to numerous visiting Swedes, remain in the order's hands), where he stayed from 1508 to 1524. He was called back to Sweden in 1524 to become bishop of Västerås. Månsson translated into Swedish an incredible number and array of technical works from Italian and Latin. These texts included such diverse topics as warfare, agriculture, gemology, and art and drew on the works of both contemporary (e.g., Erasmus) and ancient (e.g., Flavius Vegetius) writers. Månsson's project appeared in print only in modern times, although at least one of his works (on mining) was used in the seventeenth century. On the whole, their greatest contribution is to supplement our knowledge of this period in the history of technology, although Månsson often wrote poetic introductions of some note to his translations.

One of the most significant literary developments of the Swedish Middle Ages—the introduction of the ballad—cannot be dated with anything like precision. Questions of when and how the ballads came to Scandinavia have a long and complex history in scholarly debate, but the data suggest an established ballad tradition in Sweden as early as about 1300; how extensive, well known, and diverse, and what the processes of composition and performance were like, and so on, are all issues without certain answers. Many of these questions can be addressed only within the context of Nordic balladry in general or, even more broadly, of the entire North Sea ballad community (i.e., Scandinavia, Scotland, England). The discussion here focuses on the history and development of the extant Swedish ballad tradition, signs of which are well attested by the fifteenth century.

The medieval ballad is an orally transmitted song with two- or four-line stanzas coupled by end rhyme or assonance and whose content is distinguished by the use of commonplaces and traditional themes and a stylized narrative objectivity. Each stanza is syntactically complete. Refrains, frequently exhibiting a less restrained meter and more lyrical character than the stanzas, accompany each strophe, typically following it, although in the case of the two-line stanza, a shorter additional refrain may come between the two lines. Several of these features are exhibited in the following stanza from *Den förtrollade riddaren* (The bewitched knight [*smb* 5A]), collected from Ingierd Gunnarsdotter, a peasant from Västergötland, in the 1670s. It is from a ballad that relates how a stepmother transforms her stepson into various objects and finally into a wolf that cannot regain its shape until it has drunk its brother's blood (in the end, the stepson drinks the blood of its unborn sibling):

And said I'd never be cured
—*my paths are laid so wide*
Before I'd drunk my brother's blood
—*she must herself await sorrow*

Somewhat uncharacteristic, however, is the first-person narrative style; typically, ballads are dispassionate. The "intrusive" shorter refrain between the lines does not occur in all two-line ballads; it never occurs in the four-line Swedish ballads, which always have refrains at the end of the stanza, as in the following verse from *Herr Mårten* (Sir Mårten [*SMB* 35]) by the same singer. It tells of a dead knight whose soul cannot rest until his wife has righted a wrong he committed in life:

> Thanks to Sir Mårten's wife
> she wished Sir Mårten well,
> she had seventy masses said
> for Sir Mårten's soul.
> —*Thus dead, Mårten rides through Fouglesångh.*

This stanza also underscores the archaic nature of the ballads: having a mass said for someone's soul is a distinctly un-Lutheran activity, and, indeed, the ballads were often eschewed after the Reformation for their "popishness." The language in the ballads frequently points to their historical origins as well: in *Jungfrun i hindhamn* (The maid transformed into hind [*SMB* 10B]), this same woman, Ingierd Gunnarsdotter, sings that the mother teaches the son "Huru han skall beta en hind" (how he should hunt a hind). The native word *beta* in the sense "hunt (with a dog)" had been largely replaced by the German loanword *jaga* in normal speech, yet the ballad appears to have preserved the older word. Despite the fact that they were untranscribed and in some instances existed for many centuries only in their oral forms, the texts display remarkable "stability" in their reflection of the culture and language of earlier periods.

Precisely because the ballad was orally transmitted, the Swedish evidence for it in the earliest periods comes primarily from the "echoes" of ballad commonplaces and phraseology (e.g., *arla om morghin*, "early in the morning") found in such fourteenth- and fifteenth-century texts as *Herr Ivan*, *Hertig Fredrik*, *Flores och Blanzeflor*, *Erikskrönikan*, *Konung Alexander*, *Sagan om Didrik af Bern*, and the fifteenth-century historical chronicles. In addition to such literary testimony, the activities surrounding ballad performance may give some indication of their earliest presence in Sweden. The ballad was often associated with chain and ring dances, and early texts sometimes mention dances. In describing the wedding of Valdemar Birgersson, for example, the author of *Erikskrönikan* says that the ceremony was accompanied by dancing, jousting, games, and lovely words (*SFSS* 47, 448–49). The scene purports to treat events that took place in 1260, but it is highly unlikely that it tells us anything about the mid-thirteenth century. On the other hand, it does surely indicate that dancing and "lovely words" were a normal part of the world in which the fourteenth-century writer moved. Similarly, a little later St. Birgitta has a vision in which the Virgin Mary talks to her using the dance—and its "loud voices"—as a metaphor for what is useless in the world (*SFSS* 14:1, 83). Of course, there is nothing that demands that references to dancing of this sort necessarily indicate ballad dancing, although it is likely; as late as the 1730s, Carl von Linné (Linnaeus) described seeing such a ring dance in Dalarna. Still, the evidence is much firmer if we turn to pictorial representations of the ballad. The church at Dädesjö, Småland, for example, contains thirty paintings from the 1260s; one of them shows a scene that could easily be from *Sankte Staffan* (*SMB* 39; Saint Staffan). More decisive still is the ceiling painting by Albertus Pictor from Floda kyrka, Södermanland (ca. 1480), which graphically portrays the hero Holger Dansk dispatching the giant Burman (*SMB* 216); moreover, the painting bears a line from the ballad as an inscription.

There are also some fifteenth-century textual references that clearly indicate ballad activity in Sweden. In one manuscript of *Fornsvenska legendariet* (Cod. Ups. C 528) from the early 1400s, the text relates a miracle ascribed to St. Magnus of Orkney, on which islands the events are said to have taken place. The concepts of singing and dancing are mentioned several times, as is the refrain: "to dance and sing the same songs, 'why are we standing, why aren't we moving?' " (*SFSS* 7:2, 877–78). The most pointed textual testimony to ballad singing in Sweden itself comes just before the account of the Battle of Brunkeberg in *Sturekrönikan*:

> therefore they all began to sing
> and greatly comforted themselves
> and sang "The Ballad of St. George"
> (*SFSS* 17:3, 2215–17)

Unfortunately, no full Swedish ballad text exists from the Middle Ages, and the first preserved ballad, the same one sung by the Swedish army in 1471 (*Sankt Göran och draken* [*SMB* 49]), dates from the middle of the sixteenth century. From that point to modern times, however, a large number of Swedish-language ballads have been transcribed. The earliest recordings were by members of aristocratic circles who were mimicking German and Danish fashions. Later, ballads were collected because of their presumed value in bolstering Swedish nationalism, and finally, in the modern period, collections have been made with a more scientific goal. The melodies for the ballads were recorded primarily in the nineteenth and twentieth centuries. It has been estimated that 224 types of the traditional Swedish ballad have been collected in about four thousand different recordings. As early as the late sixteenth century, ballads began to be printed as broadsheets (*skillingtryck*), a practice that flourished in the eighteenth and nineteenth centuries.

Modern scholarly interest in the Swedish ballad was inspired by nineteenth-century romanticism, and the legacy of this movement is still felt in the nomenclature used (e.g., *folkvisor*, lit. "folk songs", and *kämpavisor*, lit. "songs of heroes") and in the divisions into which the ballads are typically articulated (i.e., in that they are grouped according to narrative, as opposed to singer, community, or other criteria). Six broad categories are used in the definitive edition of the Swedish ballads (*SMB*) (the examples cited are by no means exhaustive): ballads of the supernatural (*naturmytiska visor*), legendary ballads (*legendvisor*), jocular ballads (*skämtvisor*), chivalric ballads (*riddarvisor*), heroic ballads (*kämpavisor*), and historical ballads (*historiska visor*).

The ballads of the supernatural treat otherworldly creatures well attested through Europe (e.g., werewolves, *SMB* 6; elves, *SMB* 29), as well as some specifically Nordic characters (e.g., the "water spirit" [Näcken], *SMB* 20). The legendary ballads comprise a group of religious ballads, such as the still popular *Sankte Staffan* (*SMB* 39), although the category is surprisingly small, consisting of only eighteen types. The jocular ballads consist of variations on the familiar "numbskull" themes: farmers who trade away their possessions unwisely (*SMB* 244), maidens fooled by angry suitors into marrying beggars who pretend to be rich (*SMB* 236). The chivalric ballads make up a large group (130 types), ranging widely from those dealing with last-minute rescues from forced marriages (*SMB* 71) to family mayhem on a grand scale (*SMB* 82), from faithfulness (*SMB* 109) to adultery (*SMB* 113), from fratricide (*SMB* 153) to false witchcraft accusations (*SMB* 166). The heroic ballads, although not especially numerous (23 types), have received a great deal of attention because of their filiations with the Icelandic eddas and sagas and West Norse balladry, although in some instances they derive from other traditions (e.g., *SMB* 200, which is based on the biblical theme of David and Goliath). Others unquestionably evince some sort of connection with Icelandic materials, such as the eddic story of Þórr's retrieval of his hammer from the giants (*Þrymskviða* [Eng. tr. "The Lay of Thrym"], *SMB* 212), but the nature of the relationship is very much open to interpretations of various sorts. Still others, such as *Stolt Herr Alf* (Proud Sir Alf [*SMB* 206]), ultimately derive from the late Icelandic *fornaldarsögur*, or legendary sagas, in this case *Hálfssaga*, although this ballad has come to Sweden by way of the Faroese ballad tradition. Finally, a tiny but nevertheless important group of texts belongs to the category of historical ballads. Numbering a mere eleven types, these ballads have also played a significant role in discussions of Nordic balladry. In the early period of ballad scholarship this fact derived from the belief held by some students of the ballad (e.g., Svend Grundtvig) that the texts would have been composed at a time proximate to the events involved. *Slaget vid Lena* (The battle at Lena [*SMB* 56]) is based on a confrontation between the warring Erik and Sverker parties in 1208 and could thus be used to bolster the notion of a very early ballad tradition in Scandinavia. Interest in such ballads has increasingly come to focus, at least in some quarters, on their political character and use as propaganda by the various factions involved in the conflicts of the later Swedish Middle Ages.

A similar point has been made concerning not only the historical ballads but almost all original Swedish lyric poetry of this period. The earliest of these works, *Trohetsvisan* (*SFSS* 25, 393–97; The song of loyalty) and *Frihetsvisan* (*SFSS* 25, 391–92; The song of freedom), are associated with Bishop Thomas Simonsson of Strängnäs (d. 1443). He is a likely author, insofar as he had studied in Paris and Leipzig and is believed to have written documents containing verbal echoes to the poems. Moreover, the poems are preserved in a legal codex from ca. 1470 that claims in a colophon that they were composed by Bishop Thomas. Still, the question of authorship has been hotly debated. Usually, the poems are interpreted by contextualizing them, that is, by reading them against the period of intense political activity of the 1430s and 1440s: *Trohetsvisan*, for example, is thus understood as a comment on the treacherous murder of Engelbrekt in 1436 (or possibly of Erik Puke in 1437). Such readings are less certain if, in fact, Bishop Thomas is removed from the equation and the poems simply become Swedish manifestations of a widespread genre of moral lamentation with stereotyped subjects. That the issue has occasioned such debate is no doubt connected with the status *Frihetsvisan* in particular holds in modern Swedish society, where it is something of an unofficial national anthem. It owes its place in the national consciousness to stirring lines of the sort "Freedom is the best thing / which can be sought throughout the world" (*SFSS* 25, 391). Whether or not Bishop Thomas was the author, two facts remain: the poem continues to be susceptible to tendentious interpretation and, more important, in its fast-paced and imagery-rich eight stanzas, it represents one of the best original lyric poems of the Swedish Middle Ages.

Works of a corresponding quality are few but include such hymns and psalms as *Then signadhe dag* (SFSS 25, 172c–e; The blessed day) and *Een rikir man* (SFSS 25, 167–71; A rich man).

The political character of other lyrical works from the fourteenth and fifteenth centuries is easily seen; *Engelbrekt och Karl Knutsson* (SFSS 25, 385–90; Engelbrekt and Karl Knutsson), *Striden om Visby 1449* (SFSS 25, 403–11; The Battle for Visby 1449), *Tord Bondes mord 1456* (SFSS 25, 412–13; Tord Bonde's murder 1456), *Slaget vid Brunkeberg 1471* (SFSS 25, 414–18; The battle at Brunkeberg 1471), and *Slaget vid Brännkyrka 1518* (SFSS 25, 471–73; The battle at Brännkyrka 1518) all treat events that are in and of themselves political. Perhaps less obvious, however, is the extent to which these texts represent propaganda produced by the various political factions in Sweden. *Striden om Visby*, for example, has been shown to be remarkably similar to a report by Karl Knutsson on the unsuccessful attempt to wrest the island of Gotland from the control of Erik of Pomerania, in which the failure is ascribed to treachery. In a period before inexpensive printing, the political song was a useful means of broadcasting propaganda; moreover, the tradition of the sung ballad lent such songs acceptability, appeal, and vitality.

Few Scandinavian politicians would understand the use of propaganda better than Gustav Vasa, especially when it was combined with the flourishing art of printing. But printing was hardly new in Sweden when he took up the struggle for independence in 1520: by the close of the fifteenth century, some presses had existed in Sweden. In fact, in the 1470s Gotmannus von Ravensburg, an agent for Peter Schöffer's press in Mainz, was sent as a representative to Sweden. Although many of the first books connected with Sweden were actually printed in Lübeck and other German cities (e.g., Bartholomaeus Ghotan's Lübeck editions of *Vita beati Brynolphi* [1491] and of St. Birgitta's *Revelaciones* [1492], G. Stuck's Nürnberg *brevarium* for the Linköping diocese [1493]), very early presses existed in Sweden itself, including Johann Snell's, which produced *Missale Uppsalense vetus* (1484) and had earlier printed the schoolbook *Remigius, Magister que pars*. Also published at Snell's Stockholm press was the fable collection *Dialogus creaturarum moralisatus* (1483), the first book actually printed in Sweden. In 1486, Ghotan relocated his Lübeck operation to the Franciscan cloister in Stockholm, where he began producing liturgical texts as well as *Vita Katherine* (1487). Presses were set up at Vadstena (which burned shortly after printing *Horae de domina* in 1495) and at a cloister in Mariefred that in 1498 printed Alanus de Rupe's *De psalterio b. Marie virginis*. The first Swedish-language book to be published in Sweden was, appropriately enough, a translation—Jean Gerson's *Tractatus de diuersis diaboli tempta-tionibus, Aff dyäffwulens frästilse* (On the devil's temptation), printed by Johan Fabri (1495).

Dating the close of the Swedish Middle Ages with precision is difficult, as the criteria fail to cluster neatly: book printing was already well established in Sweden by the beginning of the sixteenth century; the Reformation process began in the 1520s and is widely associated with the meeting at Västerås Cathedral in 1527, but the Lutheran creed was not proclaimed for the nation until the late sixteenth century; the transition from one period of Swedish-language history to another (Younger Old Swedish to Older New Swedish) is marked by the publication of the New Testament in the vernacular (1526), yet the linguistic realities (e.g., development of velar palatalization, simplification of the case system) on which the distinction is based had been under way for many years. Although it is true that cultural as well as political authority was consolidated increasingly around Stockholm in the sixteenth century, Vadstena, for example, continued to be active throughout much of the century. The most tangible events marking the beginning of a new era are those surrounding the rise of Gustav Vasa to power, and it is convenient to use this period (1520–23) as a focal point for all the changes that mark the end of the Middle Ages in Sweden. That the new nation Gustav Vasa was building had little use for the cultural legacy of the Middle Ages is typified one hundred years later when a shipment of books taken from the Vadstena library is turned over to the authorities, who comment that they have received twenty-five vellum books (*pergementtz böcker*) that they used for binding other materials, since they were useless for anything else.

The Reformation and Sweden's Century as a Great Power: 1523–1718

James Larson

2

THE REFORMATION

In June 1523, the Swedish estates elected Gustav Vasa their king. He in turn appointed a reform-minded archdeacon from Strängnäs, Laurentius Andreae, his chancellor. Another reformer from Strängnäs, Olaus Petri, or Master Olof, as he was familiarly known, was summoned to Stockholm in 1524 as town secretary and preacher in Storkyrkan. The New Testament appeared in Swedish in 1526, and a Riksdag at Västerås in 1527 completed the first stage of the Reformation: the Word of God was to be preached "purely and clearly." The crown gradually assumed control of church property. In four short years Sweden had pulled free from Rome.

With the clarity of hindsight and on the basis of our own secular and skeptical outlook, it is customary to say that the Reformation was primarily a political and economic event. Certainly there were political and economic reasons for the termination of the financial hegemony of the old church and for the dependency of the new church that grew up out of the confusion of the early years of the Reformation. But it is also clear that the spiritual break with the past was the most violent Sweden has ever experienced; the realignment of the populace's minds with the new realities consumed at least three generations. Anyone who hopes to understand this old culture should admit the possibility that the Reformation was as much a spiritual, religious movement as a political and economic event.

Over the next two centuries Swedish learning and letters drew heavily on Lutheran doctrine. Less obviously, but of equal importance, the reformers were indebted to humanism. Although the traditions of Lutheranism and humanism were apparently opposed, theologians and humanists concluded an alliance that affected Swedish cultural life for centuries.

Lutheran doctrine depended, to a surprising degree, on one man's conception of faith. Under the old dispensation, grace, mediated by the church and the clergy, was tied to laws, penances, and tests that measured the seriousness of the believer. Martin Luther's conception of grace was radical by comparison. Grace communicated itself to the individual through the Word of God. Redemption was a drama with two actors, God and the believer. The measure of grace was the believer's disposition of mind. What was miraculous about grace was that an individual, in his or her fallen state, could appropriate the conviction communicated by Christ.

For all the centrifugal tendencies in this conception—its pronounced individualism; its location of redemption in personal, inward piety; its appeal to the private interpretation of Scripture—Luther did not, perhaps could not, conceive religion without a church. But it was to be a reformed church that would preach the Word of God correctly and intelligibly; after close scrutiny, two of the seven sacraments, baptism and communion, would again become the means of salvation; the church would confine itself to the spiritual activity of proclaiming absolute truth. How, though, to secure the integrity of this one, unchanging truth?

Readers of the late twentieth century are quick to turn this institutional question into the central problem of the Lutheran cult. The question concerned the reformers as well. The Lutheran solution, a temporary compromise that endured, was to ally the church with the lords of the German and Scandinavian principalities. The church would keep the Word pure, while the worldly powers would protect the church and punish the ungodly. This division of power within the social order involved many difficulties from the beginning and quickly outgrew the impractical ideal.

In the opening phase of the Reformation, however, the interests of the reformers were simpler and more innocent. They instructed believers in the evangelical view of the path to redemption and conducted polemics on a broad front against the old faith. The New Testament and the Bible, published in the vernacular, were the sources for a flood of sermons, hymns, catechisms, and prayer books that engulfed northern Europe. As the reform movement matured, there was a marked shift toward institutional and political concerns. The reformers modified the faith and the offices of the church and attempted—this time in vain—to redefine the powers of this world with respect to the church.

Humanism was apparently the antithesis of Lutheranism, and the nascent reform movement had shown scant respect for classical authority. Cicero and Virgil, raged Luther, knew nothing of sin and grace, and Aristotle was a godless heathen; the only wisdom for which man had need was biblical. Erasmus, the oracle of humanism in northern Europe, warned that where Lutheranism came in, learning went out.

Humanism had deep roots in learned culture, however, and humanists controlled access to the languages of the Bible and the arts of interpretation. Within the reform movement Melanchthon was the first to recognize the need for an alliance. Under his leadership the University of Wittenberg became a model for learning in the Lutheran world. Theologians, philosophers, and classicists found it possible to live together with no more than the usual bickering. Melanchthon himself published Greek and Latin grammars and textbooks in logic, lectured on the rules of eloquence, and indoctrinated students in the formal arts of poetry.

Text-oriented cultures are notoriously resistant to change, and the learned basis for the Reformation was no exception. The practical effects of religious reform were revolutionary, but the reformers' ideas turned toward the past. Lutherans respected authorities quite as much as any medieval scholastic. The seven liberal arts continued to serve as the cognitive landscape for all learning and teaching, and men continued to interpret the structure of the world and the laws of nature with the help of classical and medieval authors. Aristotle was as powerful as ever: his logic was the basic instrument of thought, and his doctrine furnished physics and theology with their fundamental concepts.

This, then, was the general background of Swedish learning and letters during the Reformation. From Germany, chiefly the Wittenberg of Martin Luther and Philip Melanchthon, Swedes brought home Lutheran theology and the spoils of humanism. Sweden had long been a German cultural province. The Reich was the source of as much science, technology, and learning as Sweden could claim. Just as the Hanseatic League dominated Swedish trade, so German universities dominated Swedish education. The Reformation confirmed this state of affairs. But there is one significant difference between the Reich and her Scandinavian client. The Reformation coincides in Germany with what is justly called a renaissance; in Swedish history it ranks as an iron age. Men poured their energy and passion into religious and political conflict, with no occasion for the dispassionate pursuit of culture.

The Reform and the Reformers

Wherever the reform won a foothold, the reformers were confronted with the task of making the Bible accessible to ordinary folk. Translations were nothing new in Sweden; during the Middle Ages there had been translations of various books into Swedish, but for the reformers translation was an immediate and central task.

In the summer of 1525, the king, prompted by Laurentius Andreae, ordered his Roman Catholic archbishop, Johannes Magnus, to undertake a translation of the New Testament. Within a year *Thet nyia Testament på swensko* (1526; The New Testament in Swedish) was printed by the royal press in Stockholm.

Andreae was responsible for the final editing and spoke of "our translation," but there is little information about the translation or the translators. Specialists have discussed the question for more than a century and have arrived at no certain results. Their controversy, which can never be resolved finally, is one indication of the importance Swedes attribute to the translation: linguistically, literarily, and religiously, it is an achievement of a very high order. The Latin translation of Erasmus (1516) is the basis for the Swedish text; reference has also been made to Erasmus's Greek version (1522). Luther's German has left its mark, but on many points the Swedish version takes an independent line. The language, an unusually simple and up-to-date Swedish, has been influenced by medieval Vadstena; it is free on the other hand from the Danicisms that had infiltrated learned language. The spelling and grammatical forms are simple, the word order is natural to Swedish, and the participial constructions of medieval Latin have been all but eliminated.

The success of the translation more than answered the hopes of the reformers. In his foreword Olaus Petri mentioned only the most immediate audience: "The priest's foremost office is to teach the Word of God to his commons. For this reason the New Testament is now set out in Swedish . . . that poor, simple priests, who know little Latin and are inexperienced in the scriptures, and likewise other Christian persons, who are able to read in books, might at least have the simple text, as written by the Evangelists and the Apostles."

We do not know how many Christians living in Sweden in 1526 were able to read. Probably, there were not many. But as time went on, their numbers grew. In the end, the life of Jesus, the acts of the Apostles, and the revelations of St. John permeated the national consciousness.

The martial vigor and moral severity of the Old Testament had an even greater effect on Swedish minds. During the 1530s, the reformers published translations of some books from the Old Testament for use in church services, but the entire Bible appeared only in 1541, *Biblia, thet är, all then helgha scrifft på swensko* (The Bible, that is, all the Holy Scripture in Swedish). Gustav Vasa's Bible, as it is called, was the work of many men; Olaus Petri was certainly among them, but it was his brother, now Archbishop Laurentius Petri, who led the committee. For the sake of consistency, the New Testament was reworked and differed significantly from the version of 1526. The spoken language of the Mälar provinces established itself as the norm. The translators tried to find good Swedish expressions for God's holy Word, and the Bible is strikingly free of loanwords. In their search for a lofty, dignified language, the reformers favored archaic forms and inflections, one important point on which the Bible differed from the earlier New Testament. In the choice of pithy words and expressions, Luther's Bible exercised an increased influence, and as a consequence the Bible grew in severity and solemnity.

Even at the very high price of a good saddle horse, Gustav Vasa's Bible spread far and wide. "It has exercised," says Elias Wessén, "greater influence on written Swedish than any other book in our literature." The translation became the linguistic norm for the Swedish language, and it remained the basis for all revisions of the Lutheran Bible. Gustav Adolf's Bible, 1618, offered only a superficial revision of the text; Karl XII's Bible, the Bible of the Swedish church until 1917, offered no new or independent interpretations; the changes were of spelling and modernized forms.

The sincerity of devout feeling and grave diction formed by reading the Bible found a natural outlet in the hymnals that accompanied the Bible translations. The first German hymnal, the *Erfurt Enchiridion*, had appeared in 1524. The Swedish reformers were not far behind; the first Swedish hymnal, now lost, may have been produced as early as 1526, the same year as the New Testament. A new collection appeared in 1530; of this a large fragment has been preserved. New collections followed in 1536, 1543, 1549, 1567, 1572, and so on into the next century.

The oldest Swedish hymns breathe a vigorous, simple piety. They appeared anonymously, although it is probable that Olaus Petri was responsible for many of them. As music and verse, these hymns had already stood the test of time. The verses were translations or adaptations of German and Latin hymns; only a few were original creations. The provenance of the melodies was even more diverse: Latin hymns, to be sure, but also street songs, tavern songs, and love songs. The devil, said Martin Luther, did not need all the good tunes for himself. The reformers used the same principles with regard to the tunes as they did with regard to the texts: they took old melodies that suited their purpose and "improved" them. The improvement was often drastic. The reformers' first concern was to see that the psalms were singable and easily grasped. They were not content just to borrow the simple, naive vitality of the old tunes and texts: they converted it into a powerful religious force.

The hymns were intended for individual devotion and secular gatherings, not for the church. Congregational singing found a place in the

Lutheran service only after the church ordinance of 1571. In Sweden, as in Germany, congregations had had the right to join in the Kyrie and the Alleluia. Gustav Vasa reminded the Dalesmen in 1527 that "it is accepted all around the kingdom in all parish churches, that one is in the habit of singing in Swedish, and praising God"; and Laurentius Petri mentioned the singing in church at Christmas and Easter. But Olaus Petri praised the primitive church for celebrating mass "without ceremonies, vestments, songs, and readings," and his Swedish mass was spoken, not sung; the introitus calls for "some psalm or other song of praise," and in one other place, "one reads or sings the song of God's commandments"—both probably performed by the clergy. The Lutheran reform was above all a triumph of the Word, and the Lutheran service made no provision for sacred song.

The man who more than any other worked for this triumph, Olaus Petri (ca. 1493–1552), was born the son of a smith in Örebro. Nothing is known of his childhood. His career as a student was that of a man destined for the church. The obligatory visit to a German university was in his case decisive: he matriculated at Wittenberg in the fall of 1516. The two years spent there coincided with Martin Luther's reform movement. We do not know whether the young Swede had any personal contact with Luther, but he was a warm adherent of the Protestant cause when he returned to Sweden in 1518. At the cathedral in Strängnäs Master Olof became the center of an admiring circle of students and clergy, among them Laurentius Andreae, to whom he expounded the reform. In spite of attacks by powerful defenders of the old faith, Bishop Brask and others, the reform movement prospered. When Andreae followed Gustav Vasa to Stockholm, Master Olof was not far behind. His appointment as town secretary and preacher at Storkyrkan increased his activity and, if possible, his zeal. Under the auspices of the state, he championed the reform movement. He married not for love but to demonstrate that God's law must come before all human laws. With the royal press at his disposal he turned out a flood of pamphlets, polemics, and instructions.

Olaus Petri's reform work falls under four headings. The core of his early writing addressed all Christians pondering the meaning of the redemption offered by Christ. A related set of pamphlets polemicized on subjects on which evangelical and papist doctrine did not pull together. A third set explained the duties of various human offices—priest, king, husband, and so on. And finally, a series of handbooks codified the services of the Swedish church.

The earliest works on evangelical doctrine, *Een nyttwgh wnderwijsning* (1526; A useful instruction) and *Een skön nyttugh vnderwisningh* (1526; A beautiful, useful instruction), both issued anonymously, are loosely composed and quite incoherent. The first mixes a translation and paraphrase of Luther's *Betbuchlein* with independent composition; the latter is a reworking of a Hussite catechism, *Kinderfragen*. A far better introduction to Petri's expository skill is his *Hwar igenom menneskian får then ewiga saligheterna* (1535; How man attains eternal blessedness). The question how is man justified, by deeds or by faith, was one often touched on by Petri but never with greater seriousness or consistency than here. His basic texts are Paul's letters to the Romans and Galatians; justification comes not from any deed but from faith alone. Petri opens with a discussion of the requirements of God's law and shows that man cannot be justified by deeds that accord with the law. Man attains blessedness by belief in Christ, who revealed God's grace and mercy. This faith, if living and inward, results in good deeds, but human deeds are never perfect, and man can only trust that they are acceptable to God. Petri then summarizes the essential points of his argument in fifty-seven short theses that are the best brief introduction to the new faith.

The polemics are occasional pieces, none fully comprehensible without some notion of the actual situation. Typical of these is *Swar påå tolf spörsmål* (1528; Answers to twelve questions). In 1526, Gustav Vasa issued some questions on contested theological points, hoping, he claimed, that a public debate would clear the air. The composition of the king's questions betrayed, however, his evangelical leanings. A copy was sent to Peder Galle, a canon at Uppsala Cathedral, with a request for a reply by Christmas. Olaus Petri also answered the questions and journeyed twice to Uppsala in hope of a public debate. He had to be satisfied with developing his position before the king, the council, and other good men. A discussion does seem to have taken place between Galle and Petri after the Riksdag at Västerås in 1527, too late to affect the issue of the Reformation. The polemic gives a clear picture of the collision of the old and new faith. Galle, the learned scholastic, is erudite but ponderous; he appeals to the immemorial tradition of the church, the guarantee of sixteen centuries, the authority of the fathers. Petri boldly casts all tradition overboard and insists that in spiritual matters the Bible is the sole authority.

The works in which Petri lays out the functions of social callings or offices contain few surprises. Lutheranism placed the idea of a personal calling at the very center of Christian morality and subordinated the entire system of callings to the need for social order. The most interesting of Petri's analyses concerns the office of the prince, his coronation sermon, *En Christelighen formaning til Sweriges inbyggiare* . . . (1528; A Christian exhortation to the inhabitants of Sweden). Petri's text is Deuteronomy 17:15–20. A king is a man chosen by God for the sake of the people, and not the people for the sake of the king. A king does not seek his own good; if so, he is no true Christian but a tyrant over God's commons. The people owe obedience to the king and his officers. They are not obliged, though, to go against the commandments of God. They are to be more obedient to God than to man. A king, to the degree that he wishes to be a Christian king, must above all preserve the purity of his subjects' souls, risking life and neck therefor. The sermon is a plainspoken summary of early Lutheran views on the relation of church and state. We may suppose that it was received with reservations by the high and mighty King Gustav.

Petri's church handbooks are the province of church history. I mention them only to point out that they contain devotions of surprising sensitivity and beauty. Petri's *Een handbock påå Swensko* (1529; A handbook in Swedish) contains rituals for the common occasions of baptism, marriage, and the like. One frequent occurrence in old Lutheran society was the public execution of criminals. The ritual Petri provides is sensitive and compassionate. He reminds the victim that Christ, too, was condemned and that a human court is not the last judgment. Before the final act he asks the victim "to think of nothing but upon Jesum Christum, who has suffered death for you: doubt nothing, He is certainly with you."

The man we meet in Petri's reform works is not an individual in the modern sense, not even a forerunner. He is a man who believes that by accepting the irksome necessities to which God has called him, he has transformed his situation into freedom. And so he has, in the Lutheran sense. At this point in his career, Petri has no doubts and few scruples; he is wholly at the service of the inspiration he received in Wittenberg. And though he is not a fanatic, he is not capable of more than one perspective.

On the retirement of old Master Laurentius in 1531, Olaus Petri became the chancellor, a task for which he was as ill-suited, said one of his successors in office, Conrad von Pyhy, "as a Frisian cow at spinning silk." Petri wanted, said the king, "to reform my regiment, which his office did not allow." Petri openly disapproved of the royal policy of confiscation and the royal practice of swearing; it was rumored that in private he had gone much further. At the end of 1539, Olaus Petri and Laurentius Andreae were arrested, accused of treason, tried, and sentenced to death. The trial demonstrated to all and sundry just who was the master of Sweden. The king commuted the sentences and allowed the reformers to buy their freedom. Shortly thereafter, Gustav Vasa tried to persuade Master Olof to write a chronicle of his reign.

The aging reformer is a changed man. A note of bitterness recurs in the later work: "faith has burnt out, and love has turned to ashes"; "this world is always like herself, she is noisy and troublesome to be in." Petri, who remained active, became a pastor in Stockholm. He wrote several legal pamphlets; the most important, *Domareglerna* (ca. 1540; Rules for judges), is still printed at the beginning of the law of Sweden. He also wrote a school drama, *Tobiae comedia* (1550; The comedy of Tobiah), the oldest preserved Swedish drama. His most original work, however, *En swensk cröneka* (1530s? A Swedish chronicle), went unpublished.

The chronicle has been overpraised by Swedish historians, largely because Petri's method and point of view foreshadow their own. It remains one of the few works from the Swedish sixteenth century that can be read for pleasure. Petri gave the work the form of a medieval chronicle, and he based his facts on the information of the old chroniclers; his most important source was the chronicle of Ericus Olai (ca. 1470). In his introduction he denied the truth in "old rumors, songs, and other embroidered inventions"; he himself tried to eliminate all that was fabulous, sycophantic, partisan, and trivial, the better to illuminate God's truth: the vanity of this world, the wiles of the devil, God's punishment of tyrants, and the like.

Petri's prose is, as always, terse, sober, and simple, wonderfully adapted to the telling of tales. His version of Stockholm's Bloodbath is the best of the many sixteenth-century reports that have come down to us; his King Christian is the very pattern of a sixteenth-century Herod.

Petri was at his best, in fact, in telling the misdeeds of Sweden's lords, and one of them was keenly aware of it. Master Olof, Gustav Vasa wrote his sons, "is said to have written a secret chronicle of our regiment. And since one will not let it see the light of day while we yet live, it is easily believable that not everything is laid out to our best." The suspicious, querulous tone is typical of the letters of Gustav Vasa. The register for King Gustav covers the range of Swedish history over forty years, always with an engaged and personal point of view. The kingdom of Sweden was, in the mind of Gustav Vasa, a private estate, and there was not a detail in its management that did not interest him. The king was a choleric man and his moods were various; in his letters he adopted whatever attitude he deemed effective—rage, sarcasm, benevolence, even resignation—for all of which he found a language easily comprehensible to the unfortunate recipient.

Like all the rulers of the early sixteenth century, Gustav Vasa had experienced the anarchy characteristic of the final phase of feudalism. By way of reaction, he tended to stress the need for social order and to equate the creation of that order with himself. He had led the struggle for independence, and for the rest of his reign he lived off the moral capital. In his letters he always contrasted the bad old days of King Christian with his golden age. One proof of Gustav Vasa's ability as a writer is that the legend survived.

Among contemporaries, though, there was another side to the matter. Even for a sixteenth-century prince, Gustav Vasa was remarkably self-sufficient. Only he understood everything. He blamed others—enemies, partisans, kinsmen, the Swedish people—for his mistakes and encroachments, and sooner or later he broke with all his collaborators. Cooperation was impossible for the loneliest wolf in the forest. Toward servants of the crown he was capricious and unreliable. His reputation abroad was bad. Certainly he was a treacherous patron of the Swedish Reformation. Or, to put it another way, he viewed the reform movement from a political vantage. All values were relative to the social order guaranteed by himself. Clergy who advocated a Lutheran theocracy were seditious. Master Olof, for example, had openly promoted disaffection. One solution, beyond the royal monopoly on justice, was a strict censorship. "No book," the king wrote his archbishop, "can be published or come into general use unless that takes place *cum regis gratia et privilegio*." Books that undermined his authority were to be corrected "and set forth on a sounder basis." Foreign books suffered the same fate. In 1550, Doctor Andreas was ordered "to deal with booksellers on the books they bring into the country."

Roman Catholic books, that is, the libraries of cloisters and cathedrals, represented papist error. With the exception of Vadstena and Grayfriars in Stockholm, these were almost entirely destroyed. The paper went for waste; the parchment was used to bind royal accounts. Not even the buildings escaped; bricks and stones went to build the royal castles. If the buildings remained standing, they were used for profane purposes: Åbo cloister became a salt magazine; St. Nicolai in Sigtuna, a stable.

Education, the province of the old church, was laid waste. Only the burghers' town schools and a few cathedral schools remained open. At Uppsala University study lapsed altogether sometime between 1515 and 1520, and activity remained in abeyance until 1593. The reformers took no interest in a general, secular education; their goal was to spread the new faith and to save souls. To all this Gustav Vasa remained indifferent, as long as his subjects obeyed. Sweden, complained Göran Gylta a year before the king's death, had descended into "vile barbarism."

The Sweden of Gustav Vasa and his sons lacked almost everything essential to the cultivation of letters and learning. The educated public was limited to a tiny elite. Intellectual impulses came from two or three universities in the Reich. The kingdom of Sweden possessed a single, ill-equipped press, whose products were severely censored. Printed work always served some immediate practical goal and consisted entirely of religious, political, and panegyric products.

Humanism and the Humanists

Humanism was an international phenomenon at the beginning of the sixteenth century, not easily suppressed by the partisan spirit or cultural decline of a single nation. Humanism had entered Sweden in the fifteenth century. Theologians who studied at German and Italian universities, virtually the entire upper clergy, could not ignore the new learning. Bishop Kort Rogge of Strängnäs, for example, had studied in Italy, where he read Petrarch and Aeneas Sylvius—to which a dissertation by him still testifies—and he cultivated an elegant Latin. Other humanists reformed or enriched Swedish with translations. For example, Peder Månsson's *Barnabok* (15   ? Child's book) was a translation of Erasmus's *Institutio principis christiani* (1516; The education of a Christian prince). There were other instances of this hothouse culture in Sweden. But with the triumph of the Reformation, the humanist elite was dispersed and church education ended.

Archbishop Laurentius Petri's school ordinance in 1571, based on Melanchthon's regulations for Saxon schools, reestablished Latin in a dominant position in the curriculum. Swedish students drilled year after year in grammar and syntax; they grew up reciting Cicero, Virgil, Terence, Plautus, and Erasmus. The goal was eloquence, oral expression based on Latin models.

Greek came later, again by way of Melanchthon's Wittenberg. The Swedes who studied in the Reich in the 1550s learned Greek, which, as the language of the New Testament, had established itself as a requirement for Lutheran theologians. Erasmus Nicolai praised Greek and Hebrew as the "sources of divine teaching," but Greek, he added, had its own pleasures. Greek entered the Swedish theological curriculum in 1571, and by the 1580s the language was taught in Kalmar, Åbo, Söderköping, Nyköping, and Stockholm.

Hebrew was the last and remained the least of the three languages expected of the trained humanist. Archbishop Petri had known enough Hebrew to check the translation of the Old Testament, but the subject was slow to enter the theological curriculum. At the Collegium in Stockholm in the 1580s, Nicolaus Olai Bothniensis taught Hebrew and even wrote a key to the Oriental languages that included Chaldaic, Arabic, and Syriac. On the restoration of Uppsala University, Greek and Hebrew were offered regularly, but Hebrew had not become a normal part of clerical education at the end of the sixteenth century.

History ranked first among the branches of learning cultivated by European humanists. Every court employed a man of learning to celebrate the princely house and honor the national past. This was not the artless history of the medieval chronicles. Medieval perspectives and forms survived, of course; Protestants found it impossible to eliminate the old metaphysical framework. Melanchthon approached the past as a theologian: history taught moral wisdom and proved God's omnipotence. But in the new princely courts Caesar, Tacitus, and Livy became stylistic models, both in Latin and in the vernacular. Interests broadened; new sources and new perspectives established themselves; wars and negotiations were no longer the whole story. One's own country and people became legitimate objects of history; cultural history, illuminated by laws, church documents, and traditions, came into its own.

In the Reich, historical orientation was inspired by patriotic self-assertion. With Tacitus in hand, Konrad Peutinger (1465–1547) and others rediscovered a long-forgotten Germany. Parallels to the concerns of these German humanists are easily found in two Latin works written by the brothers Magnus, Johannes and Olaus. Both works are national histories inspired by the spirit of Gothicism, a myth originating in late antiquity that described Sweden as the womb of nations from whence, since early times, the Goths had gone forth to conquer the south. During the reign of Gustav Vasa, the myth was widespread, an expression of strong national feeling.

The monumental and definitive expression of these ideas was Johannes Magnus's *Historia de omnibus gothorum sveonumque regibus* (1554; History of all the Gothic and Swedish kings). The work was written in exile as an assertion of Catholic policy, as a criticism of Gustav Vasa, and as a competitor of Saxo's Danish chronicle. Published in Rome, where in 1544 Johannes Magnus had died the consecrated Catholic archbishop of Sweden, his work gave the fatherland a past extending back to the Deluge and included the deeds of the Goths from Asia Minor to Spain. Johannes honorably cited the whole of recorded tradition but supplemented what was missing with his own invention, a practice allowed by contemporary historiography. The archbishop's great vanity was his mastery of Ciceronian eloquence, another sin forgiven by contemporaries. Throughout the Vasa dynasty the chronicle of Johannes Magnus was treated with wary respect, an inspiration to research and political action.

Olaus Magnus, who succeeded his brother as the last Roman Catholic archbishop of Sweden, shared Johannes's exile, policies, and projects. Sten Lindroth has suggested that the brothers' treatises, taken together, also formed a unity, a monumental *Svecia illustrata*; Johannes answered for the political chronicle, whereas Olaus was responsible for a description of the land and the folk. This project, too, had its parallel in Continental historiography. In the manner of Pliny, the twenty-two books of the *Historia de gentibus septentrionalibus* (1555; History of the Nordic peoples), illustrated by woodcuts, treat Scandinavian geography, climate, nature, peoples, customs, and beliefs. Olaus's accounts are remarkable for their unpretentious and brisk style. Published in Rome, the folio was an international success and for more than a century determined the learned European's view of the North and its people.

The brothers Magnus, though active in Continental literary circles, remained outside the cultural life of Sweden—if not as far outside as some historians have imagined: Gothicism was to have a potent effect on the Swedish imagination.

Histories written inside Sweden, with the exception of Petri's Swedish chronicle, were less interesting. Peder Swart, the Lutheran bishop of Västerås and a pliable tool in the hands of Gustav Vasa, wrote a chronicle about his master's youth and early deeds, a princely biography according to the taste of the age. Swart is too much a partisan to be reliable, but he is also a fresh and entertaining purveyor of gossip and teller of tales. Others, royal secretaries chiefly, assembled documents and wrote royal chronicles, but these were dry, derivative, and without much literary value.

The Latin poetry that began to be written at midcentury was not, at least in its initial phase, so very different from the historical subject matter of the humanists. Again, the source was Philip Melanchthon. A member of Melanchthon's circle, Henricus Mollerus, introduced the fashion to Sweden, where he served as a court poet to Gustav Vasa.

The first well-known Swedish practitioner of Latin verse was Magister Laurentius Petri Gothus (ca. 1530–79), whose *Stratagema gothici exercitus adversus Darium* (1559; Stratagem exercised by the Goths against Darius) celebrated a Scythian victory, a tale from Herodotus by way of Johannes Magnus. To this Laurentius added two poems in Greek, the earliest known by a Swedish poet. On his return to Sweden, Laurentius published a book of shorter lyrics, *Aliquot elegiae* (1561; A number of elegies), and in time became a fluent composer of hymns in his own tongue.

The line of Swedish court poets extended from Master Laurentius through Ericus Jacobi Skinnerus, whose *Epithalamium* (1585) celebrated the marriage of Johan III to Gunilla Bielke, to Sylvester Johannis Phrygius, whose *Threnologia dramatica* (1620; Dramatic threnody) lamented the death of Johan III in the reign of Gustav II Adolf. Throughout these same decades Swedish students and teachers at home and abroad wrote countless Latin panegyrics, epithalamia, threnodies, and elegies. This flood of Latin verse has been forgotten, a literature, as Kurt Johannesson has remarked, that has no place in literary history. And perhaps it was the sixteenth century's insistence on classical Latin that ultimately made it a dead language. The humanists revived a language whose value was purely aesthetic and could be used without difficulty only for classical studies and rhetoric. But the world of classical antiquity, which is very different from the world of Lutheran piety, served as an alternative inspiration for Swedish men of letters over the next two centuries. The concerns of a small educated elite for aesthetic form and elegant expression gradually began to raise the vernacular to a European standard of literary excellence.

Literature and the Four Orders of Society
During the reigns of Gustav Vasa's sons, an upper stratum of Swedish society began to respond to international culture. A small court nobility—the Geras, Gyltas, Bielkes, and Sparres—had traveled abroad; they learned Latin and read and spoke French, German, and Italian. Their interests were not limited to theology; worldly learning took a central place in their educations, as Per Brahe's *Oeconomia* (ca. 1580) still testifies. Their ideal was the perfect courtier found in Castiglione's *Cortegiano*. Their libraries contained not only shelves of classical authors but also Boccaccio and Rabelais. As great men of affairs it is doubtful whether they spent much time puzzling over Latin poetry, but their aesthetic and literary culture was solid, a harbinger of things to come half a century later and in much broader circles of the Swedish nobility.

As for the lower orders, it is difficult to speak of popular culture in the sixteenth century. Commoners, *allmogen*, could not read; the printed or written word was a world closed to all but a few of them. A secular literature of broad appeal survives, but it was obviously intended for educated folk, the small minority in the society who knew how to read.

Songs, the antithesis of learned Latin poetry, found an audience among the burghers and the nobility, above all among young ladies. Many song collections survive from the sixteenth and seventeenth centuries, such as *Harald Oluffsons visbok* (ca. 1575; The songbook of Harald Oluffson), and *Bröms Gyllemars visbok* (ca. 1670; The songbook of Bröms Gyllemar). Individuals wrote down and pieced together what struck their fancies; love songs, obviously, constituted one important kind; complaints of life's inconstancy, another; nature lyrics, perhaps the least affected by time, were a third. In age and origin the material was various; some songs were original compositions, some were found abroad, some were medieval. The persistence of medieval forms is striking. Many medieval ballads are known through versions found in the songbooks. And new ballads continued to be written in a more or less medieval style throughout the seventeenth century.

Narratives in verse or prose consisted mainly of beasts' fables, proverbs, and tales, for which Swedish editions began to be printed early in the seventeenth century. A Swedish Aesop appeared in 1603, followed by the anti-Catholic *Gåås-Kong* (1619; Goose king) and *Reyncke Fosz* (1621; Reynard the fox). Prose tales from *The Decameron* were published in the 1620s; the adventures of Til Eulenspiegel, known in Sweden since the late Middle Ages, first appeared in print in 1661: *Ett hundrade twå underliga, sällsamma och mycket lustige historier om Thil Ulspegel* (One hundred and two wonderful, rare, and very pleasurable stories of Til Eulenspiegel). But with this popular literature my own story has been carried beyond the limits of the sixteenth century, into a new and very different era.

SWEDEN'S CENTURY AS A GREAT POWER

The Later Vasas, 1611–1654
During the reign of Gustav Adolf (1611–32), Sweden rose from obscurity to establish itself among the great powers of Europe. The move had long been meditated. The national goal was dominion in the Baltic. Sweden did not achieve absolute dominion, but it remained the greatest power in northern Europe for almost a century.

Reformation Sweden had been a provincial backwater. The situation now changed; the nation entered the great world politically and culturally. Throughout the Thirty Years' War, large numbers of Swedes—warriors, of course, but also diplomats, bureaucrats, and students—lived on the Continent, learned to know the great world, and experienced new customs and ideas. At the same time, a horde of French, Dutch, Germans, Balts, and Scots poured into Sweden to take service with the new empire. Many stayed on and won a place alongside the native nobility. The enormous expansion of Swedish industry and commerce was largely the doing of foreigners. Uppsala University, restored by Gustav Adolf for the express purpose of meeting state needs, attracted famous men of learning from abroad. The House of Nobles in Stockholm became positively cosmopolitan; more than a third of the new nobility was of foreign origin.

The pace of Swedish society had quickened by 1620, but no new elements entered the culture; Lutheranism and humanism remained vital forces. Seventeenth-century Lutheranism gradually hardened into a rigid orthodoxy; dogmatic theology required absolute submission. Humanism, too, tended toward slavish obedience to classical authority. To these a third body of ideas was added, a Gothicism nourished by the fortunes of war; Gothicism provided Sweden with an imperial ideology. These constituted the three essential elements of the official culture of Sweden in the first half of the seventeenth century. Aristotelianism, which had emerged victorious from the conflict with Ramism at the newly restored Uppsala, belatedly became a fourth element of official culture—and like the rest, conservative, authoritarian, and absolute in its claims.

At midcentury there were signs that this ponderous culture had been fatally undermined. The pressures of war changed Swedish society radically. Gustav Adolf transformed the old nobility into a military and administrative elite. Chancellor Oxenstierna saw to it that the highest offices in the state went to men of his own order. During the long minorities of Queen Christina and Karl XI, the council aristocracy not only ruled the country but aspired to limit the power of the crown. The war on the Continent brought the expected wealth and territory. The nobles built great town and country houses and launched themselves on a boisterous and extravagant way of life without a counterpart in Swedish history.

Among the other social orders, only the burghers experienced a prosperity at all comparable to that of the Swedish nobility. The forced pace for industry and trade during Sweden's century as a great power meant, at least for wealthy townsmen, a way of life analogous to that of Dutch merchants. Stockholm became the undisputed center of a Baltic empire; by the reign of Queen Christina, the insignificant town had become a city, even by European standards. And around the shores of the Baltic and along the west coast new towns were founded and granted trading privileges. For the first time in modern history, Swedish burghers looked beyond the borders of the kingdom.

Contrasts among the four orders of society, exaggerated by war and the acquisition of great new territories, led to serious conflicts between nobles and commons, aired in a succession of Riksdags after 1650. The conflict ended only with the declaration of absolutism in 1680, when at last the Swedish nobility understood what the authority of the crown meant.

To say that social differences were sharp does not imply, however, that they could not be bridged. Talent—military, financial, political, and bureaucratic—always found a place for itself in seventeenth-century

Sweden. Social mobility also belongs to the picture of that expansive age. The sons of burghers and the clergy occupied high office and were often rewarded with noble status.

The power of the nobility and the prosperity of the burghers not only characterized seventeenth-century Swedish society but eventually determined the conditions under which a new and more worldly culture replaced the old. Young aristocrats and the sons of rich burghers questioned the continued dominance of Latin, learned to speak and write modern languages, and sought practical, worldly educations. Experimental science, brought from Holland by young scholars, won a place for itself at the university. Aristotle was set aside, to the consternation of the faculty of theology. The grip of Lutheranism loosened. Christianity was never openly attacked, and the state religion ended the century apparently as powerful as ever. But in influential intellectual and economic circles the tone had changed; Sweden began to take the first steps toward a secularized, utilitarian society.

The situation of literature remained precarious. To be sure, many more books were printed. The number of printers increased; from the lone press of Gutterwitz at the beginning of the century, there were eventually six in Stockholm alone. The entire kingdom boasted seventeen printers. The best of these craftsmen, Ignatius Meurer and Henrik Keyser, served as booksellers as well; using their keen sense of the market, they sold almanacs, Bibles, hymnals, and textbooks but not much poetry, drama, or criticism. Men of learning and the clergy kept to what was by now a well-established literature in Latin. A somewhat larger reading public preferred the genres of the previous century: fables, hymns, proverbs, and songs. Sten Lindroth once imagined a Swedish library around 1630, a short shelf that included history, politics, and proverbs, a little law and medicine for household use, and rhymed prayers for the woman of the house. Under these conditions, the art of literature survived only among students and noble amateurs and as a pastime for learned men.

Conditions improved during the reign of Queen Christina (1644–54). The Thirty Years' War came to an end. A social transformation had created a new public seriously interested in learning and letters. Small elites, burghers' sons, young nobles, and administrative officials, provided an appreciative audience for literature in the vernacular. Over the course of two or three generations, these small elites established a canon and a secure tradition of evaluation. As in so many other spheres of public life, Sweden discovered itself literarily by integrating itself with the Continent— something made possible only because of changes in the structure of society, the aims of education, and relations abroad, all established during the Thirty Years' War.

Two Portal Figures

Two minatory figures flank the entry to seventeenth-century literature, emblematic of the unbending religious and social rigidity of the older Protestant culture.

Johannes Messenius (ca. 1579–1636) spent a controversial and restless life colored by the religious conflict of the age. At fifteen he entered the Jesuit seminary at Braunsberg where, like many other young Swedes, he acquired a fine humanist education. He first took service in Catholic Poland; in 1608, he changed sides and sought preferment with Karl IX. His education brought him a chair in law at Uppsala University. His febrile activity as professor, dramatist, and historian won only the envy and hatred of his colleagues, and in short order Messenius departed for Stockholm to become royal antiquary. There, too, his difficult personality brought him enemies. The enemies conspired, accusing Messenius of being a crypto-Catholic and of sending messages to Danzig and the court of King Sigismund. As a precaution, Messenius was sentenced to Kajaneborg in northeast Finland, a seventeenth-century predecessor of the Gulag. He was allowed to take his books and documents, and there, under harsh conditions, he wrote a grandiose history of Sweden, *Schondia illustrata* (1700–1705; Illustrious Sweden). In the preface he prophesied the glorious deeds of the young Gustav Adolf. When all hope of liberation died, Messenius openly confessed his Roman Catholic faith: "In this Church I will live, and in her I wish to die." Nevertheless, he was freed shortly before his death. The inflammatory and dangerous *Schondia* could be published only in the next century.

The same year that Messenius emerged from two decades of imprisonment, another captive arrived at Kajaneborg, Lars Wivallius (1605–69). The son of a sheriff, plain Lars Svensson entered the Latin school at Örebro; following a well-marked path to preferment, he enrolled at Uppsala as Laurentius Svenonius Wivallius. At twenty he threw over his prospects in Sweden for life as a wandering studiosus on the Continent. Attracted to the entourages of young nobles, Wivallius adopted their speech and mannerisms. At some point he conferred on himself the title *Friherre* and took the name Erik Gyllenstierna; his motto was "Not to seem, but to be." A title brought easy credit at inns and hostelries, although he was exposed from time to time. He spent a year in jail in Nuremberg; another time he fell into the hands of Wallenstein. On his way home Wivallius drifted through the Catholic and Protestant fronts in north Germany, making his way to north Skåne where, as Erik Gyllenstierna, he married the noble lady Gertrud Grijp. Wivallius was again unmasked, escaped, and was finally arrested in Stockholm. After an interminable trial, he ended in a windowless cell in the fortress of Kajaneborg. There he sat for five long years, unbroken and unrepentant. In the spring of 1641 he was freed. Wivallius returned to Stockholm, where he practiced as an advocate and rose to the rank of auditor. A hardened and cynical fraud had replaced the charming and deceitful youth. Wivallius lived on in a netherworld of dubious clients, shady lawyers, and shabby intrigues, shunned and feared by respectable folk.

This sad wretch was undoubtedly the greatest poet in Sweden during the reign of Gustav Adolf. All his poetry was written in the shadow of prison; his poetic gift related directly to his central flaw, the appropriation of the ethos of others. He could capture the essence of a broadside, the Bible, a ballad, in a phrase; over the course of a few lines he might allude to the medieval *Frihetsvisan*, Gustav Vasa's Bible, and Renaissance *consonantia*. All this he held in place and harmonized, not with his overweening self-assurance but with the pathos appropriate to an innocent. When he petitioned his betters, Wivallius also offered them a suitable context to guide their responses. "See," he wrote, "in this night I lay on my bed and meditated David's third psalm and made upon it a song that I now send for your favor."

The poetry that speaks directly to a modern reader has to do with Wivallius's personal experience. The poet moved over a full range of reactions. In one song he might adopt the stance of a contrite sinner; in the next he was a betrayed innocent; his enemies, he imagined, stood with hands uplifted, rejoicing in his fall. From his cell he identified with birds and beasts moving freely in nature. He himself was a caged bird:

> han sjunger väl av sin natur,
> > men hjärtat är bedrövat,
> när han hörer de fåglar skön,
> > som uti luften sjunga,
> sig glädja över marken grön
> > efter sin art och tunga.

> [He sings well from his very nature,
> but his heart is desolate,
> when he hears the beautiful birds,
> that sing in the air,
> taking joy over the green earth
> according to their kind and tongue.]

The intense personal feeling for freedom in nature in this song, "Ack Libertas" (Ah freedom), and in "En torr och kall vår" (A dry and cold spring) has no counterpart in the public, impersonal literature of seventeenth-century Sweden.

No seventeenth-century poet can be completely understood on the basis of personal reference, however, certainly not Lars Wivallius. He was a great concocter of schemes revolving around his "studies" on the Continent. He placed his knowledge of languages and manners at the service of the state, either to awaken a new piety among the folk or to justify Swedish policies to the subject peoples of Europe. In Kajaneborg, Wivallius began a Latin epic whose fourth book survives. The dying Gustav Adolf struggles with fearsome images of Satan; the king finds peace in prayer to God, a paraphrase of a hymn by Prudentius, remembered, suggests Kurt Johannesson, from Latin school. Another project, *Sweriges Rijkes Ringmur* (The ring wall of the kingdom of Sweden), alternating between Latin and Swedish, exhorts the Swedish people to unite, trust in God, and obey authority. These projects were intended to unlock the gates of prison and transform Wivallius into a salaried hack.

Metrical Reform

In one respect, Wivallius was to be a transitional figure in the history of Swedish poetry. During the first half of the seventeenth century, Swedish poets learned to adapt classical meters to the Swedish language. In this stylistic mutation the syllabic verse favored by Wivallius belonged to the past; in less than a generation his prosody may have seemed old-fashioned. This is a complicated story whose gist is the following.

Sixteenth-century ballads, hymns, and songs offer variations on the principle of *knittelvers*, or doggerel. A line may contain any number of syllables as long as the number of stressed syllables is fixed: in the case of *knittel*, four. Ballads, hymns, and songs might build on two, three, or four stresses per line.

Hymns are interesting because they lead to another stage of formality. Hymns were often translated from medieval Latin, which not only counted unstressed syllables but regularized their occurrence; and hymns were sung to established melodies. This regularity passed insensibly into Swedish as syllabic verse, a pattern in which the number of syllables in a line was fixed, usually at eight or nine, but in which the alternation of stressed and unstressed syllables was free. Syllabic verse spread from hymns to other poetry and in the early seventeenth century became the dominant metrical pattern.

As early as the 1620s there were impulses toward greater regularity. Poets and theorists hoped to enrich and beautify literary language by adapting quantitative classical meters to the Germanic pattern of stress and tone. Verse, wrote Swedish poet Samuel Columbus, becomes "so much the more perfect" when it observes the classical rules. The principles that led to metrical reform were formulated by the German Martin Opitz in his *Buch von der deutschen Poeterey* (1624; Book of German poetry). A Dane, Anders Arrebo, adopted this reform as early as 1627. In Sweden individual poets, including Wivallius, experimented with classical meters during the 1620s and 1630s. For many, the results did not justify the labor: "the beauty," wrote Columbus, "does not answer to the difficulty."

These experiments were not lost on the poet who actually carried out the reform in the 1640s. As early as 1643 Georg Stiernhielm wrote a birthday song for Princess Christina, "Heroisch fägne-sång" (Heroic song of rejoicing), in what he called "iambic-heroic alexandrine verse"; in many positions he used a stressed syllable in place of a long syllable, a practice he repeated the next year in his "Heroisch jubel-sång" (Heroic song of jubilation). Alexandrines had by this time established themselves in Continental prosody; they were regarded as a modern equivalent to hexameters and, like them, especially apt for heroic subjects. As far as we know, Stiernhielm first used hexameters in his program poem, *Hercules*, 1648. His solution to the problem of quantity versus stress is not clear. He believed that verse should build on quantity and strove to observe the classical rules for position; but again, he often substituted a stressed syllable for a long syllable. Whether Stiernhielm built on quantity or stress, he believed he was writing classical verse in Swedish, and in later works he offered examples of pentameter, sapphic and adonic verse, iambic and trochaic dimeter, catalechticus, and so on.

When Andreas Arvidi published his poetics, *Manductio ad Poesin Sue-canam, Thet är, En kort Handledning til thet Swenske Poeterij* (1651; A short guide to Swedish poetry), the metrical reform he advocated was an accomplished fact. "All those syllables," he wrote, "pronounced slowly with a sharp or loud tone are long, and, on the contrary, all syllables executed abruptly and with a lowered tone, those are short." Brilliant examples of two quantities advocated less brilliantly by Arvidi, unrhymed hexameters and alexandrines, already existed, models for formal patterns that came to dominate seventeenth-century Swedish poetry.

Peace and the Muses

Although metrical reform was obviously the product of many minds, credit has always been given to one man, Georg Stiernhielm, who regarded prosody as only a single element in the instauration of literature in Sweden.

Georg Stiernhielm (1598–1672), the son of well-to-do burghers in

Dalarna, entered Uppsala in 1611, where he read Aristotle and classical poetry under Johannes Rudbeckius. Stiernhielm apparently left Uppsala when Rudbeckius was banished for his part in demonstrations against Messenius. An unusually long sojourn as a wandering scholar included a year at Greifswald, where Stiernhielm defended a dissertation on the Scholastic doctrine of nature. He returned to Sweden to become a lector at Rudbeckius's secondary school in Västerås. In short order he was appointed to a new academy for nobles in Stockholm, Collegium Illustre. There his patron, Johan Skytte, turned Stiernhielm's attention to the expanding state bureaucracy, in which the poet was to spend the rest of his life as an administrator. In 1630, Stiernhielm became assessor at the court of appeals in Dorpat, Estonia; the following year he was ennobled. During the two decades he spent in this Baltic province, he lived for extended periods in Stockholm, where his rank and learning earned him a place in the very highest circles. After 1660, he returned to Stockholm permanently, first as a member of the war council, then as head of the new Collegium Antiquitatum.

Throughout his long career, Stiernhielm believed his true vocation was learning. "How sweet it is to know," he once exclaimed, and he meant it. Like many another intellectual educated in the early seventeenth century, Stiernhielm focused on the symbolic and esoteric functions of language. To this obscure and fantastic compound he added a Gothic element: more than any other language, Gothic had preserved the purity of the language spoken in the Garden of Eden. He meditated a great project, *Runa-Suethica*, and published a fragment of it, *Gamble Swea- och Götha måles fatebur* (1643; Treasury of the language of the old Svear and Goths), a lexicon of "Gothic" words. Over the years his private meditations carried Stiernhielm far from his Aristotelian beginnings; he ended a Platonist of the purest water.

Stiernhielm's literary career was, by comparison, almost accidental. The scholar began as a humanist Latin poet; his oldest known poem, "Carmen iambicum" (1624; Iambic song), depicts the separate paths of virtue and pleasure. He continued to write occasional poems in Latin for patrons and colleagues. Stiernhielm's first poems in Swedish date from his stay in Stockholm, 1642–45, obviously a part of his attempt to insinuate himself at court. The birthday song "Heroisch Fägne-Sång" praises fulsomely the gifts conferred on Princess Christina by classical deities:

Konst, Lärdom, Slögd och Dygd, och måål af många Tungor,
Ther i hon öfwergår i werlden alle Kunger.

[Art, learning, craft and virtue, and speech in many tongues,
Therein she surpasses all kings in the world.]

"Heroisch Jubel-Sång" greeted the queen's accession to majority: the Swedish ship of state, without her captain, had made port. The conceit became a staple in Swedish panegyrics, adapted by both Israel Holmström and Gunno Dahlstierna to later accessions. During this year, Stiernhielm wrote what many consider his most beautiful shorter lyric, the sonnet "Emblema authoris" (1644; Emblem of the author), in which he found a symbolic expression for his belief that what is eternal and immortal emerges from earthly toil and trouble.

During a second stay in Stockholm, 1649–50, Stiernhielm came into his own as a court poet, providing masques and ballets for court celebrations. The allegorical court ballet united music, dance, poetry, and spectacle. The action was pantomimed; the text was a kind of program to be read as the action proceeded. It was usually available in Swedish, German, and French, as in the case of Stiernhielm's ballets. *Then fångne Cupido* (performed 1649; The captive Cupid) offers a sampler of classical meters embroidered on a charming mythological theme, a fine expression of classicist *Schwärmerei* in mid-seventeenth-century Sweden. *Parnassus triumphans* (performed 1651; Parnassus triumphant) celebrates Queen Christina as a patroness of letters and learning; the muses, long silenced by war, return to her court. The ballet contains the glorious arioso "Hjertans lust! sij hafwet huru stilla" (Heart's joy! how still the sea), and wonderful examples of Stiernhielm's orotund and ponderous conceits. The dawn of peace, for example, begins:

Then gull hårige Phoebus, klar vpstijger i högden
　　Liuflig, och vppenbar; glimmand' i gyllene wagn.
Hafuet, och brusande flod sig sachta; the berg-höge böllier
　　Lägga sitt ifrige raas, bullra nu icke som förr. . . .

[Golden-haired Phoebus, rises clearly on high
Lovely and revealed; gleaming in golden chariot.
The sea, and rushing flood grow still; the mountain-high waves
Cease their eager race, do not thunder as before. . . .]

And so on for another fourteen lines. Stiernhielm needed ample space to develop the simplest effect. The last and oddest of these occasional pieces, the macaronic *Discursus astro-poeticus* (ca. 1660; Astro-poetic discourse), celebrates Karl X's Danish war and the Peace of Roskilde. Since Stiernhielm's program, peace and the muses, opposed royal policy, the *Discursus* probably circulated only among like-minded patrons.

This is, perhaps, the place to mention the epithalamium *Bröllopsbeswärs ihugkommelse* (Remembrance of the difficulties of wedding). The poem, first published in 1818, had been attributed to Stiernhielm since the seventeenth century. As long as the attribution remained unquestioned, the poem was highly valued. Without a doubt the prosody and some of the scenes are directly indebted to *Hercules*. The grotesque description of wedding drunkenness, for example, amplifies a similar scene in *Hercules*. Johan Nordström was the first to dispute the attribution: the poem, in tone and thought, was too banal to be attributed to the master. But Nordström's criticism ignored generic conventions respected by Stiernhielm. An epithalamium, argues a recent historian, was a publicly recognized genre with determinate rules expressing received ideas. If Stiernhielm had written an epithalamium, it might very well have resembled *Bröllopsbeswärs ihugkommelse*.

During his first stay in Stockholm, in the early 1640s, Stiernhielm planned his greatest poem, *Hercules*. He finished a first short version in 1648, filed and polished for another decade, and published in 1658. The germ of the poem, Hercules at the crossroads, came from Xenophon's *Memorabilia*. In the Protestant North, Hercules had become a humanist ideal, the pattern of honor and virtue, often cited and commented on. He had already appeared several times in seventeenth-century Swedish, in poems and academic orations. Stiernhielm's Hercules incarnates this humanist cult. More important, though, he provides an occasion for a confrontation between pleasure and virtue, an old concern of the poet's. The hero never speaks directly; the poem develops from the conflict of the two women who represent alternative ways of life. Fru Lusta and her motley crew preach the gospel of pleasure. Fru Dygd intervenes with the stern morality of duty and honor. A speculative element in her sermon was a late addition; Dygd describes the human soul as the spark in flint; wisdom is the steel that alone can strike the spark, dispersing darkness and mist.

The opposing voices of pleasure and virtue speak for themselves; the reader never learns whether Hercules chooses one or the other. The alternatives continue to confront each other and, as Kierkegaard wrote of a similar confrontation, "await no finite decision in particular personalities." This static *pro et contra* conforms to seventeenth-century definitions of the genre. The epic, wrote Le Bossu in his *Traité du poème épique* (1675), "is a discourse invented with art in order to form manners by instructions disguised under allegories." Stiernhielm observed, as far as possible, other seventeenth-century requirements for the genre. He wrote in hexameters, adapting antitheses, compound epithets, learned allusions, and sententia not only from Virgil and Silius Italicus but from Trissino and Jacob Cats.

But *Hercules* was a Swedish poem as well, meant to reveal the strength, richness, and beauty of the vernacular. Swedish, Stiernhielm wrote, in *Gamble Swea- och Götha måles fatebur,* "is full of all kinds of remarkable, meaningful words and ways of speech that, for the most part, could be taken up, renewed, and set in use again, making our language not only fluent and rich but soft, beauteous, and decorous." Poetry was one way in which old words could again be set in motion. Accordingly, Stiernhielm added a lexicon to his poem, "old and seldom-used words," taken from provincial laws, old sagas, and other medieval texts.

Cumbersome and contradictory as this moralistic epic seems to us, it was admired and imitated as soon as it appeared in manuscript. *Hercules* was a Swedish poem, filled with Gothic patriotism, yet it followed classical prescriptions and observed the decorum appropriate to its kind. When Stiernhielm collected his verse in 1668, he explained his title, *Musae Suethizantes,* with well-founded pride: "That is, the muses now first learning to write and play in Swedish."

In the same year *Hercules* appeared in print, 1658, another poem with the same linguistic program, *Thet Swenska Språkets Klagemål* (Lament of the Swedish language), was published by the pseudonymous Skogekär Bergbo. Like *Hercules, Klagemål* was appreciably older, perhaps written as early as 1632. Many years later two smaller collections appeared under the same pseudonym, *Wenerid* (1680; Venerid) and *Fyratijo små vijsor* (1682; Forty small songs), both written thirty years earlier. Much ingenuity has been spent in unmasking the man behind the pseudonyms; two brothers, Schering and Gustav Rosenhane, have often been mentioned. The question of authorship is unanswerable, and either brother will do as a candidate. Of noble descent, they traveled widely, absorbed the courtly worldliness of the Continent, and were adepts in foreign literature.

Klagemål is a plea for the dignity of the Swedish language. Again, the old Goths prop up fragile Swedish self-esteem. Gothic feats of arms were known throughout the world. Now their language is despised even in its homeland, where German and French corrupt speech, and books are written in Latin. The poet urges contemporaries to drop their swords, grasp their pens, and create a culture that does honor to the nation. Seemingly a poem of national glorification, *Klagemål* is in fact a part of the international movement toward linguistic purism, with counterparts in Spain, France, Holland, and Germany.

Wenerid is a different kind of book, an experiment in the Continental vogue for sonnet sequences. These hundred sonnets, the author explains, were "pieced together to show the proficiency of Swedish in rhyme"; almost incidentally, they also run through the stereotyped cycle of sonnet romance. This work, the first psychological study in Swedish, as Henrik Schück once called it, is more obviously an attempt to annex a new sophisticated worldliness through the complexity of form.

It is worth considering this aristocratic ambition a little more closely, since it goes to the heart of seventeenth-century culture. Linguistic purism, literary classicism, and the aspiration to formal sophistication are manifestations in the cultural sphere of a single process unfolding everywhere in Swedish national life during the seventeenth century. Norbert Elias, in his *Über den Prozess der Zivilisation* (1939), has called it the civilizing process. The national state of Sweden, in centralizing and differentiating social functions, carried out a complex transformation of society and culture peculiar to itself yet analogous to the transformation of society in Holland, France, Germany, and Denmark. In the literary life of all these countries the vernacular became an object of solicitude and study during the seventeenth century. Sooner or later—in Sweden's case, relatively late—an aristocratic coterie insisted that the native language was, or might become, the fairest of them all triggering in every case the impulse to transpose classical achievement into the vernacular. This is, of course, only a small part of a process that embraced all elite culture and the upper reaches of society. But it is entirely correct to speak of national integration in an international process, even though one of the most obvious external consequences was a sharper individuation of each nation.

Obviously, the process unfolded at different rates in different countries. In Sweden, it was accelerated by involvement in the Thirty Years' War. The results were apparent during the reign of Queen Christina (1644–54). Under her supervision, the court became the center of cultural and intellectual life. Several factors favored Christina's achievement. The kingdom's responsibilities as a great power justified a certain amount of representative pomp, and for the first time in modern history, an economic basis for conspicuous display was in place. Again for the first time in Swedish history, the court resided more or less permanently at the castle in Stockholm, now an important European capital. And finally, the kingdom had almost unlimited access to highly cultivated men and women who asked for nothing more than to go to court and exhibit their merits. But first and last, court culture expressed the unquiet spirit who ruled the stage, the queen herself.

Queen Christina made a dazzling impression. Even Chancellor Oxenstierna admitted that she was almost as intelligent as a man. No one pretended to understand her, of course. She was insufferably haughty, secretive, and capricious; yet no one could deny her strength of character and intellectual gifts. No expense had been spared on her education. She spoke, as Stiernhielm said, many tongues. She was a connoisseur of Latin literature, a passionate admirer of Roman historians, moralists, and rhetoricians. At enormous cost she assembled a library filled with Latin, Greek, and Eastern manuscripts. She collected men of learning, too: the philologist Isaak Vossius; the Ovid specialist Nicolaus Heinsius; the Pliny commentator Claudius Salmasius; the expert on biblical geography Samuel Bochart; Cardinal Mazarin's librarian, Gabriel Naudé; and Christina's instructor in Roman politics, Johann Freinsheimius. Descartes came to Stockholm in 1649; before his premature death he drew up a plan for a court academy that met in the queen's library once a week. Her agents acquired, either by honest purchase or as war booty, innumerable statues, paintings, medals, and objects of art, including the entire Kunstkammer of Rudolf II from Prague. Learned Europe was, as intended, astonished. A myth grew up around the Nordic Minerva; she had transformed her rustic court into a center of European humanism.

If Christina's passion for learning went beyond what was expected of a seventeenth-century monarch, the queen was, in the management of her court, entirely the creature of her age. As a young woman she had already acquired the secret of controlling a complex and explosive court society with a relatively small expenditure of personal energy. Ceremonies, banquets, receptions, balls, tourneys, masques, and ballets followed one another at a hectic pace, simultaneously enhancing her prestige and promoting the inequities, jealousies, and hatreds that surrounded her. "The court," wrote Johan Ekeblad in 1653, "now begins to take shape beautifully with Frenchmen and Italians."

This perpetuum mobile was not without its significance for the arts. Birthdays, victories, treaties, and ceremonies all provided occasions for a spate of celebratory poems and pompous orations. Painters, architects, composers, dancers, and actors, not to mention tailors, jewelers, wig makers, and cooks, found ready employment at court and with the court nobility.

One significant literary innovation of Christina's reign was the introduction of sophisticated theater. As early as the mid-sixteenth century, schools had presented dramas based on biblical narratives, and these pieces had grown more secular over the years; Messenius, for example, had written and staged plays on Sweden's legendary past at Uppsala. And troupes from Holland, Germany, and France toured Sweden throughout the seventeenth century. But when Queen Christina established a court theater, it had nothing to do with school drama or foreign troupes; her models were rather French and Italian. The court ballet, a child of the Italian Renaissance, was a favored diversion in the perpetual round of masquerades, tableaux, and divertissements. Christina's dancing master, Beaulieu, trained her courtiers in the various steps; then, while an Italian *machinista* operated the cumbersome machinery, the nobility of Sweden skipped and mimed on stage, attired as classical gods and allegorical virtues.

During the last years of her short reign, Queen Christina's devotion to these entertainments grew more intense. She seemed utterly frivolous; she abandoned the pursuit of truth and virtue and mocked learned pedantry and religious bigotry. The queen had apparently been captured by the libertine party. Out of the public eye, however, she underwent a spiritual crisis that led her by obscure paths to abdication, exile, and Rome.

In Rome during the 1680s, Queen Christina came to terms with her destiny and human nature. She wrote two collections of aphorisms, *L'ouvrage de loisir* (The work of leisure) and *Les sentiments héroiques* (Heroic sentiments). She began her memoirs as well but abandoned them out of ennui. Her literary master was Rochefoucauld, whose *Maximes* she had read and annotated. Her work lacked the disabused poignancy of the master, and she was never driven as far as his disillusioned aestheticism. Since she had never known any other existence, she continued to think and feel as a superior, chosen being. She took pleasure in the spectacle of the militant order of warriors and heroes. The natural element of the great spirit was, she claimed, solitude. Her twentieth-century reader will substitute the word *isolation*, an impression that grows as she distills her experience of the lower orders. Man, she implies, is born in sin as a sinner and is made to be ruled. She discerned in man "a secret sorrow that instills a disgust with everything and makes him insatiable." A Christian paradox, in fact, and not so very distant from the *Pensées de M. Pascal* published in the preceding decade. The combination of Stoic heroism and Christian pessimism is characteristic not only of Christina but of the entire Swedish noble order. This is the authentic voice of the austere, aristocratic seventeenth century confronting the fact of human existence—abstract, rational, and implacable. Queen Christina's maxims, like so much else in seventeenth-century literature, are now chiefly read by specialists.

The immediate beneficiaries of the new spirit prevalent at Christina's court were the Swedish nobles. Close ties with the Continent, established during the war, made nobles receptive to foreign fashion and behavior. The desire for luxury in Sweden, wrote the French ambassador Chanut, was, in relation to the resources of the country, greater than in any other kingdom. The political alliance with France, a condition for Sweden's existence as a great power, had enormous consequences for Swedish culture. French ideals dominated Swedish society. Young nobles who would have visited Lutheran Germany a century earlier now traveled to Paris and, if we are to believe Stiernhielm, returned to Sweden dissolute fops. In Sweden, French ways had a trickle-down effect; burghers' sons aped their betters, thus initiating their own gentrification. Their elders and the Lutheran clergy protested in vain.

The French ideal is to be found most readily in Swedish imitations of Georges de Scudéry and Honoré d'Urfé and in the private correspondence of young nobles. The vogue for bucolic sensibility invaded Sweden around 1630. French pastoral novels, including d'Urfé's *Astrée* and Vincent Voiture's *Alcidales et Zélide* and *Lysandre et Caliste*, were translated and studied. The earliest known Swedish creation in the genre, the fragmentary *Herrestadsromanen* (ca. 1650; The novel of Herrestad), treats the chaste love of Tyrsis and Amorilla. The best-known Swedish creation in this precious form is Urban Hiärne's *Stratonice* (1665). The shepherd Celadon seeks the favor of Stratonice; his friend Sophronius praises his love as divine, the gate to all good manners, "teaching us to scorn that which is impure."

Johan Ekeblad (1629–96), who essayed something along these lines after his marriage and retirement to Stola, is better known for the letters he wrote his father and brother from the Stockholm of Queen Christina. Ekeblad had accompanied Magnus de la Gardie to the French court in 1646 and remained in Paris three years. He returned to Sweden a complete worldling; he had read Montaigne and Balzac and was an adept in the jargon of refined sensibility. His fresh and lively correspondence from his years at court, the most remarkable in seventeenth-century literature, is a revelation of an entire generation of young Swedish nobles.

The reign of Queen Christina lasted only a decade. Many historians treat Christina's achievement as the equivalent of opening Pandora's box. During her ten hectic years as queen, so the argument goes, she released all kinds of alien and unwanted fads and fancies, poisoning the minds of the innocent and unsuspecting Swedish people. In many ways the judgment passed by Henrik Schück in 1926 still stands: "Queen Christina may well be said to be the century's most complete cosmopolitan. In the history of Swedish literature she has not found a place, and the oversight is fully justified to this degree, that she wrote nothing in Swedish, nor did she have any appreciable influence upon literary development in our country." Readers who know a little Swedish history, even after they acknowledge all that was precious, affected, and worst of all, foreign in the culture of Christina's court, will still find themselves unwilling to accept Schück's summary judgment. Queen Christina's reputation has suffered, more than that of any other Swedish monarch, from the national ambiguity over the great world. Christina did not confuse the irksome necessities of her position with the highest good. She aspired to the sovereign freedom of a great spirit, a condition that seemed to require her absolute and public submission to God and the Roman Catholic Church. Her countrymen have not yet forgiven her. But while she was the queen of Sweden, she sacrificed herself willingly to the needs of the state. "I have nothing for which to reproach myself in this rule," she wrote Chanut. Throughout her life she exercised an enormous influence as a knowing patroness of learning and the arts. By insisting on the very highest standards for scholarship, judgment, and taste, she not only raised the level of achievement, but released many new impulses that survived and grew in the harsh and intolerant environment of seventeenth-century Europe.

Caroline Sweden, 1654–1718

After the abdication of Queen Christina, the Pfalz kings, Karl X, Karl XI, and Karl XII, resumed the policy of war and conquest that had made Sweden a great power. It is a difficult task simply to enumerate the wars fought by the kingdom between 1654 and 1718. Finally, in the reign of Karl XII, Sweden entered a maelstrom of unending war without a prospect of resolution. A combination of territorial overextension, slender resources, limited manpower, and an exhausted population ended Sweden's policy of aggression and dominion in the Baltic. As one would expect, while the energies of the state were directed outward toward expanded power, the conservative elements of religion and social authority reasserted themselves at home.

Led by powerful and dogmatic Lutheran bishops, the Swedish church dominated the lives of the faithful from the cradle to the grave. The clergy strove, by means of the catechism, the Bible, the hymnal, and the pulpit, to make the Swedes a people obedient to God and to His regents on earth. "To examine, judge, and command," was, according to one bishop, the task of the Swedish priest. As the century wore on, there was more than a suspicion that the worldly authority of the church was an empty show, and thoughtful individuals attempted to reestablish a more inward relation with Christian teaching. Officially, though, no one could follow his own imagination or new ideas that might contradict received truth. "And if anyone does so," warned Archbishop Lenaeus, "we shall punish him severely."

The Swedish universities—Uppsala, Åbo, Dorpat, and Greifswald— established an orthodoxy of their own. Under the watchful eyes of the professors of rhetoric and poetics, Latin antiquity dominated instruction.

Swedish students, noble and common, became citizens of ancient Rome; the university libraries still contain a rich harvest of Latin academic orations on steadfastness, honor, and the dignity of the liberal arts, all according to Ciceronian formula. Since few students went beyond the required humanist studies, they became Romans for life. Inevitably, law, politics, and preaching followed the prescriptions of Roman eloquence. The public life of Caroline Sweden was played out against a heroic backdrop of Roman pomp.

Gothicism constituted a kind of homegrown classicism. In Caroline Sweden the state regarded this national fantasy as a legitimation of Sweden's role as a great power; in 1622, the state established a chair in antiquities at Uppsala; in 1667, an office in Stockholm, the Collegium Antiquitatum. Antiquarian research had many important results; specialists collected runic inscriptions, undertook excavations, initiated a topographical survey, and edited old manuscripts. Of these, the most important were the sagas of Old Iceland. Scholars equated the language with Gothic and believed that the manuscripts from Iceland offered information about the old Gothic kingdom and religion. Chancellor de la Gardie used his enormous resources to support this research and in 1669 presented Uppsala with a collection that included the most valuable manuscript of Snorri's *Edda* and the *Codex Argenteus*. Under the impact of the new information, Gothicism changed shape. Sweden was not just the home of warlike heroes; it was also the cradle of culture.

The most important political shift in Caroline Sweden was the abrupt transformation of the old mixed monarchy into an absolute monarchy in 1680. Long in the making, absolutism proved a cruel shock to the old nobility, financially and politically. The king, according to the declaration of sovereignty, was "absolute, all-commanding," not responsible for his actions to anyone on earth. With the complicity of the clergy and lawyers, an appropriate ideology was hammered out, university instruction was changed, and the people submitted obediently. A whole continuum of social, religious, and cultural opportunities accrued to the monarchy.

These are, or would seem to be, the distinguishing characteristics of a totalitarian society that shunned heterodoxy and looked on foreign cultures and ideologies with a mixture of ignorance and fear. That is true in part, and many horrifying details—witchcraft trials, legal barbarities, and social tyrannies—could be added to the picture. But the picture itself is actually a product of an old prejudice that regards absolutism as the unqualified opposite of individual freedom. The misconception continues to occupy a central position in cultural history. Literary histories written in the heyday of nineteenth-century liberalism are unanimous in dispraise of absolutism.

The poverty of Swedish culture is treated, at least implicitly, as a product of the straitened unity imposed from above. "If we except a few writers," writes Henrik Schück, "seventeenth-century literature seems to lack culture not only in expression, but also in the conception of life that lies behind it." The criticism has only grown louder in the century of the common man. The latest history of Swedish literature, *Den svenska litteraturen* (completed 1990), labels seventeenth-century society "totalitarian"; the literature is said to be "humiliatingly poor."

Those who hope to make contact with this old society will have to free themselves from this prejudice. Measured by today's standards, the absolute power attained by the crown in seventeenth-century Sweden was far from all-embracing; on the contrary, it was restricted to a narrow area of sovereignty, hemmed in by different forms of legality, tradition, and political considerations and equipped with extremely modest instruments of power. Royal authority was absolute only by comparison with the old mixed monarchy that it replaced.

This precaution needs to be kept in mind in making any generalizations about culture. In spite of the explicit instruments of control placed in the hands of the crown bureaucracy—sumptuary laws, censorship, and patronage—the elements of late-seventeenth-century Swedish culture were surprisingly heteronomous, as anyone who has tried to come to terms with the production of the period can testify. The very historians who have complained most bitterly of the stultifying nature of absolutism have also been the first to discover that Caroline literature has many voices. Kurt Johannesson, who knows this literature as well as anyone, has argued that the period is more complex than has usually been believed. He maintains that the increasing differences among the social orders enhanced the importance of distinctive external symbols and signs, the marks of social status. "Perhaps," writes Johannesson, in 1987, "this heightened consciousness of the unique expressive forms and styles is what finally characterizes the art and literature of the period—a perpetual investigation of the possibilities of style."

Let me begin with as unpromising a cultural sphere as can be imagined for this particular investigation of the possibilities of style. Among ordinary folk of Stockholm, an older, artless poetry not only survived alongside imported Continental fashions but prospered among the many anonymous practitioners who wrote for the unlettered. A funeral poem, for example, included reflections on mutability, an inventory of the merits of the deceased, and consolation for the survivors; the poet's honorarium was one of the ordinary expenses of the funeral, along with bell ringing, carrying the coffin, and a sermon. In Stockholm an informal guild of craftsmen lived by celebrating every solemn occasion in the lives of merchants and craftsmen. These poets were so importunate that in 1664 the regency forbade the composition of grave poems, bridal poems, New Year's poems, and "other forms of mendicant writing," unless the poet had been invited to do so. The fine was twelve daler silver, a vast sum.

The foremost practitioner of this poetry is known to posterity as Lasse Lucidor, born plain Lars Johansson (1638–74). His is one of the most fascinating lives in seventeenth-century literature. Orphaned at an early age, he was raised by his mother's stepfather. He studied briefly at Uppsala, then wandered about on the Continent. By 1667, he was back at Uppsala teaching modern languages. By 1669, he settled in the netherworld of Stockholm, where he eked out an existence as a language teacher and poet until 1674, when a tavern brawl ended his life at the age of thirty-six.

Lucidor did not share Stiernhielm's estimation of the poet's calling; he printed his epithalamia and eulogies because they brought a modest income, but once he had been paid, he was not interested in the poem or its subject. Along with these professional efforts, Lucidor wrote songs for his own pleasure. He did not have them printed and does not seem to have circulated copies. After his death the printer Andersin found them in his room, jotted down on scraps of paper, often in such haste that they could not be deciphered. Along with the wedding and funeral poems, a few of these were published in 1668 in *Helicons blomster* (The flowers of Helicon).

Judged by the highest standards of his own age, Lucidor was a careless and old-fashioned poet. He estimated the value of his occasional poems correctly. They are often interesting as mirrors of the age or as revelations of the poetics of Grub Street. But Lucidor is at his best in the few bacchanalian and religious poems retrieved for us by Andersin. Here Lucidor is the founder of one authentic and enduring strain in Swedish poetry:

Kom, käre broder kom
Och lät oss denna dag
Dricka friskt i detta lag.
Uti lust och behag
Driva bort hjärtegnag,
Så! Låt glasen gå rundom!

[Come, dear brother, come
And let us this day
Drink deep in this company.
In pleasure and delight

Drive away gnawing of heart,
So! Let the glass go 'round!]

Like his great successors, Runius and Bellman, Lucidor reached an underlying stratum of melancholy and despair in these apparently careless moods,
and that gave rise to the legend of a surly misanthrope. Samuel Columbus,
who created this legend, called the poet Diogenes and described Lucidor
as walking the streets of Stockholm, singing to himself. When asked why,
Lucidor replied, Why not? "Wind and weather belonged to all and everyone
had a right to use them freely. . . . His tongue was his own and the song he
sang he had composed himself." Columbus advised him to find a patron
to spare him indigence and dishonor. Lucidor exclaimed "that it was crazy
to sell his freedom for some hundred riksdaler a year. And the honor was
pure imagination . . . if you sit at the head of the table and I at the bottom,
dear fellow, what advantage in felicity do you have over me?"

Samuel Columbus (1642–79) was no very sympathetic audience for this
sort of talk, which, if it did take place, must have left him incredulous.
He was not the sort of man to question an orthodoxy that had been
good to him. Columbus was born and bred in a traditional world; both
his father and his brother were recognized Latin poets, and Columbus
himself wrote poetry in Latin until he entered Stiernhielm's circle. At
Uppsala, where he committed his only known offense against public order,
Columbus belonged to a sophisticated literary coterie. Following the path
of least resistance, he took service as a tutor to the brothers Blixencron,
thereby gaining entrée into the upper orders. He met Stiernhielm, who
valued literary talent and made Columbus his amanuensis at the Collegium
Antiquitatem. When a ballet based on *Hercules* was to be performed
before Karl XI in 1669, Columbus wrote some new parts, among them
a gavotte for the five senses that contrasts wonderfully with the master's
more ponderous style.

Känslen [Touch]
Ingen må mig däd förneka / at jag kärligt älska må:
Kärlig Leek / och kärlig Skämtan / sicktar all Natur uppå:
        Lärcke-kirr och Dufweputter
        Tuppenknorr och Orrekutter
        Går dock äntlig ut därpå
        At Hahnan Hönan nalkas må.

[None can deny me this, that I may love tenderly:
Loving play and loving jest, all Nature aims at this:

Chirping lark and cooing dove
Cock's crow and grouse's chuckle
Finally come down to this
That the cock may approach the hen.]

At Christmas in 1670, Columbus again took service as a tutor with the sons of a wealthy Dutch merchant, Momma. In 1674, he began the obligatory grand tour with his charges. Before Columbus left Sweden, he published two volumes of poetry. *Den bibliske Werlden* (1674; The biblical world), dedicated to Archbishop Stigzelius, depicted human history from the Creation to the Last Judgment. These were not subjects suited to the light, worldly manner of Columbus, and his poems are notably lacking in grandeur. Fortunately for the survival of his reputation, Columbus published simultaneously *Odae Sveticae* (1674; Swedish odes), dedicated to Chancellor de la Gardie. The lyrics are short reflections on the vanity of this world and the consolations of God and death. Here Columbus's ambition matched his talent perfectly. His verse has the lightness and musicality that "moves the heart inwardly." Columbus probably thought of these poems as a manifesto for a new and more elegant lyric poetry.

After two years in Leipzig, Holland, and England, Columbus and his charges entered Paris, that "school of all civility," where they spent another two years in the company of young Swedish nobles and their preceptors. Columbus wrote, among many other things, *Mål-Roo eller Roo-mål* (Table pleasures or pleasurable talk), a charming book of sketches and anecdotes focused on the most transient of arts.

When Columbus returned to Sweden in 1679, he approached Chancellor de la Gardie. He described "the glorious taste I have found in French comedies, especially in Molière's and Corneille's." He offered to translate them, along with Ovid's *Metamorphoses*. But he needed a position. He had begun an epic on Karl XI's Danish war when he mentioned "an incipient illness"; he died within two months.

In 1679, the same year young Samuel Columbus died and was buried at Uppsala, a bizarre but remarkable work was published there by Olaus Rudbeck (1630–1702), the professor of medicine. Two further volumes of *Atland eller Manheim* (Atlantica or Sweden) appeared in 1689 and 1698; a fourth remained incomplete after the fire that burned Uppsala in 1702. Olaus Rudbeck's monumental *Atland* was the culmination of the national Gothic fantasy. Rudbeck's thesis was that Sweden was the world's oldest kingdom and the light of the world; all religion and culture were Gothic in origin.

The professor of antiquities at Uppsala, Olof Verelius, had been publishing editions of Icelandic manuscripts since his appointment, and in 1672 he had asked his colleague Rudbeck to draw a map of Sweden for an edition of *Hervarar Saga*. Rudbeck himself wrote of this fateful encounter: "In the *Saga* there were some old words, which I, as in a dream, seemed to have read in the writings of the old Greeks and Latins, and so was daily given more light on the deeds of our forefathers, that I began (for the sake of a little amusement) to set down my thoughts on paper." Rudbeck propped up these ideas with the most recent results from antiquarian and linguistic research. Like his colleagues, he did not, perhaps could not, distinguish history from tradition, myth, and hearsay—a method that transformed the utopias of antiquity into historical entities. His approach to language was equally uncritical; from the likeness of *king*, *König*, and *konung* he concluded that all vowels were interchangeable, a rule he later extended to consonants of an almost like nature. His method could be used to prove, after suitable circumduction, almost anything.

He took his title from Plato; fabled Atlantis, situated far out in the ocean, had been rediscovered. Plato had actually been describing Sweden. Sweden, moreover, was actually intended in all the utopias of classical literature—the gardens of the Hesperides, the isle of the Hyperboreans, the Elysian Fields, and so on. Rudbeck carried out the idea with a crazy inventiveness and patriotic fervor that in time became a religious faith. During his lifetime, "Rudbeckianism" was a Swedish state religion, and every attempt to cast doubt on the thesis of *Atland* was regarded as heresy. The work was published with state support, and Johan Peringskjöld planned new folios showing that every district and parish in Sweden contained marvels from the old Gothic kingdom. Rudbeckians survived into the middle of the next century, but Rudbeck's dream did not survive Caroline absolutism and the end of the Swedish empire around the Baltic.

University professors such as Rudbeck were not the only supporters of the Swedish state. Throughout the seventeenth century, Swedish clerics reiterated that the king was king by the grace of God. The idea did not take root in the first half of the century, when the council aristocracy was actively engaged in limiting the power of the crown. But the theocratic view of the king's omnipotence persisted in clerical circles. Mathias Hafenreffer's compendium, used by the theological faculties at all universities, taught that authority was ordained by God. The king was God's representative on earth, His *vicarius*, His "living image." The Caroline clergy regarded the description of a king in 1 Samuel 8:16, as eternally valid: "And he will take your menservants, and your maidservants, and your goodliest young men, and your asses, and put them to his work."

Thus, when all the instruments of spiritual authority were placed in the king's hands in 1686, it was only in fulfillment of tendencies that went back to the earliest days of the Reformation. Independent members of the clergy protested the loss of spiritual freedom. J. Boethius, an outspoken priest in Dalarna, declared that the king had become a pope and an Antichrist. His colleagues, however, not only acquiesced, but cooperated with the Crown bureaucracy in the creation of strict uniformity. In quick succession, state commissions worked out a new church ordinance, a school ordinance, a catechism, a hymnal, and a translation of the Bible.

The most interesting of the new creations was the official hymnal. The idea came from Jesper Svedberg (1653–1735), who had begun to revise the semiofficial hymnal of 1645. He and his friend Urban Hiärne sifted out old-fashioned hymns; reworked, corrected, and translated others; and wrote new hymns on their own. On Svedberg's initiative, Karl XI appointed a commission of bishops and professors to recommend a new hymnal. The commission worked quickly, and in 1693 the Uppsala faculty in theology scrutinized its work. The faculty approved, the archbishop appended his signature, and Svedberg received the king's permission to print the so-called Svedberg hymnal containing four hundred and eighty-two hymns.

A violent storm broke out when a quarrelsome clerical party questioned the orthodoxy of some hymns and pointed out that others were "composed in too lofty a style, little suited to devotion." The verse "gave birth to Thee of Thy force" was inauthentic; the Father gave birth to the Son not out of force but from His nature. The expression "took the shape of man" denied the true human nature of Christ and revived Gnostic and Manichean docetism (*Den svenska litteraturen*, 1:256–61). In other hymns the fashionable antitheses and astonishing metaphors—darkness became clarity, cool moonlight burned in praise of the Lamb—were incomprehensible. Contemporary poetry and the church had collided.

The quarrel was so violent that the king appointed a new commission, including Svedberg's critics. Their accusations were exposed as an unnecessary wrangle, but the assembled bishops of Sweden and Finland then complained that Svedberg's creation contained too many incomprehensible novelties. A new hymnal, actually a revised version of Svedberg's, appeared in 1695. After all the changes and exclusions recommended by the bishops, the new publication contained four hundred and thirteen hymns; it held its official position in the Swedish church until 1819. In its way the hymnal was the most remarkable collection of poetry published in the seventeenth century.

This was poetry for daily use, a kind of *Gebrauchspoesie*, with a short devotion for every possible stage on life's way. Israel Kolmodin's "Then Blomstertijd nu kommer" (The season of flowers now arrives), for example, opens with an invocation of the loveliness of the short Nordic summer. In the third stanza the tone changes; when even the birds praise God, shall man alone dwell on earthly things? Suddenly, the believer is in another landscape with the lily that alone can save his soul. The hymn ends with a prayer for good harvests and accordingly found a place in the section on earth's fertility. Perhaps the theologians approved Kolmodin's hymn because it used biblical tradition. But "Blomstertijd" went on to a life of its own and promises to survive the church that gave it birth. The hymn is now sung in celebration of the end of the school year and has established a firm association with the joys of summer vacation.

Other hymns are intimately tied to seventeenth-century devotion. One identifiable group, influenced by the revival of earlier forms of meditation, focused on the visual detail of Christ's passion. "Jesus," wrote Haquin Spegel, "wants us to look upon his sorrow." By reliving Christ's death, the believer acquired an insight into his meaning. Hymn 158 by Spegel opens:

Jesu, lär mig rätt betänka
din tänkvärda svåra död
och din bittra pinas nöd:
Hjälp att jag mig nu må sänka
i din helga djupa sår
där jag liv och hälsa får.

[Jesu, teach me rightly to ponder
your thoughtworthy hard death
and bitter suffering's distress:
Help that I may now sink
in your holy deep wounds
where I shall find life and health.]

Hymn writing engaged all of literary Sweden in the seventeenth century. Contributors to the hymnal included bishops, professors, laymen, poets, and even a chancellor of Sweden, Magnus Gabriel de la Gardie. Among the most prolific contributors was Haquin Spegel (1645–1714), superintendent of the church on Gotland, then bishop at Skara, and finally archbishop during the last three years of his life. He is now remembered for his fifty-eight hymns in the 1695 hymnal and his long poem in the hexaemeron tradition, *Gudz werk och hwila* (1685; God's work and rest).

It was a maxim of the Stiernhielm school that a poet ought to be a learned man, and on this barren reef Spegel's poetic enterprise stranded.

Gudz werk och hwila is a compendium of contemporary learning; the poem has by turns the character of a theological treatise, a text in geography, and a system of natural history, with lists of plants, mammals, birds, minerals, and heavenly bodies. Learning had, however, a definite limit. When Spegel came to Copernican theory, he turned back.

Men hellre vill jag dock med Moses' brillor skåda,
Hur himmelen är byggd, om eljes jag får råda.

[And yet I would prefer to look through Moses' spectacles,
How heaven is built, if indeed I may choose.]

Spegel saw the whole of creation through the spectacles of Moses and concluded, quite predictably, that it was good. Spegel was not a poet by nature and did not aspire to that honor. He wished to give his countrymen an edifying, useful work, an ambition in which he succeeded beyond his modest expectations: new editions of *Gudz werk och hwila* appeared in 1705, 1725, 1745, and 1857.

The only other figure in the Lutheran clergy during the Caroline period of comparable literary interest is Bishop Jesper Svedberg (1653–1735). Toward the end of his long life he wrote *Lefvernesbeskrifning* (1729; Description of his life), a book that guaranteed him a place in the long line of Swedish visionaries. In spite of a sound theological education and the orthodoxy of his day, Svedberg remained a tolerant visionary, convinced that religion was essentially life, not doctrine. Among colleagues he was always suspect, but that did not impede his climb up the rungs of the hierarchy. He began his career as a court preacher; he became a professor at Uppsala, where he led the royal commissions revising the hymnal and the Bible; and he ended as the bishop of Skara. His literary ideal, not a particularly orthodox choice in that bombastic age, was the simple and pure Swedish prose of the Bible. At his best he was a pithy, concise, but disorganized writer. Much that is merely edifying, credulous, and naive in his *Lefvernesbeskrifning* is no longer of great interest, but his anecdotes and glimpses of everyday life satisfy our hunger for telling detail and novelistic verisimilitude.

As the obedient instrument of state authority, the Lutheran Church gradually lost touch with religious life. Among ordinary folk this was acceptable; they adjusted to clerical supervision and made no undue spiritual demands. They were not disturbed by dogmatic questions and found it as natural to obey the prescriptions of the clergy as the regulations of worldly authority. Orthodoxy's lack of feeling and imagination did not satisfy everyone, of course. Among the lower orders, an epidemic of witchcraft and trolldom broke out; among the educated, indifferentism took hold; and among the middling kind we find the beginnings of a new religious movement, pietism. The first edict against pietism appeared in 1702; a similar ordinance from 1713 stated that "it is His Royal Majesty's most serious wish and exhortation that no one hold in his house or permit an assembly of few or many persons who come from other houses, and undertake with them any devotion, much less dare to lay out and explain Holy Scripture." This defense of spiritual monopoly failed; the new movement could not be stopped. When the Caroline wars were over, pietism won the support of the men who returned from Siberia with a more inward understanding of spirituality. A pietist hymnal, *Mose och Lambses wisor* (Songs of Moses and the Lamb), appeared in 1717 and was being reprinted as late as 1877.

The first significant Swedish poet to work within this movement was Jacob Frese (1690–1729). At the age of twenty-two, Frese fled to Stockholm from a Finland harried by Peter the Great. He established himself in literary circles and wrote fashionable occasional verse like that of his friend Johan Runius. After a severe illness, he emerged as a serious religious poet, temperamentally opposed to fashion and frivolity. Frese was never a pietist in any strict sense, but he caught something of the personal warmth and feeling that characterized the spirituality of the members of the movement. *Passionstankar* (1728; Thoughts on the Passion), his greatest work, was written in order that "I and all distressed souls might taste the consolation of Jesus' suffering, and rest my head on the opening of His blessed wounds and propitious side." Frese's favorite subject was the consolation of death.

Hur vilar sig min Kropp i kyla sanden
    Och i sitt rum en ljuvlig svalka får!
Hur gläder sig hos Gud den sälla anden!
    O huru väl mig dock på slutet går.

[How my body rests in cool sand
And in its place receives soothing relief!
How the blessed soul delights in God!
Oh, how well my end suits me.]

These are tastes more easily understood than shared. It is natural that the voice of subjectivity, a voice seldom heard in the sixteenth and seventeenth centuries, should make itself heard in religious poetry. No believer could hide his thoughts and feelings from God, after all, and every wavering and anxious soul found consolation and strength in an honest report of the struggles of another for peace and reconciliation.

But this personal, emotional consolation never touched more than a minority in Caroline Sweden. The pietists' insistence on rebirth and authenticity was incomprehensible to most orthodox Lutherans. The state church, like the old church it had replaced, created a purely public, external faith that required assent and conformity but little more. If public interests and tastes can be judged on the basis of literary production, then it is clear that Caroline Sweden vastly preferred pompous orations, clerical exhortations, joyous occasional verse, and drastic realism to the personalist piety of *Mose och Lambsens wisor*.

One poet whose work seems to reflect Caroline interests more accurately is Johan Runius (1679–1713). Among contemporaries his popularity was enormous; his collected work appeared in two editions during the eighteenth century, and innumerable copies of individual pieces by him passed from hand to hand. One explanation of his unusual popularity seems to be that he wrote for a broader public than any other contemporary.

Johan Runius was born in Västergötland, the son of a Lutheran pastor; his father died early and Johan supported himself as a tutor. After study at Uppsala he became a secretary for Count Stromberg and lived in the count's household until shortly before his death in 1713. His poems first appeared in 1714–15 under the title *Dudaim*; a third volume was added later.

Runius wrote his share of poems on church texts and the royal house, but he was never a member of the church, the university, or the court. As a humble secretary he supplemented his modest salary with occasional verse of all kinds, a situation about which he joked in more than one poem. Runius was a virtuoso in rhyme, and he enlivened the stiff conventions of occasional verse with imagination and irreverence. His verse contains many impulses—light melodies, elegant compliments, and impressionistic bagatelles—that point toward the eighteenth century. Better than any other contemporary he could transform trifles into a celebration of ephemeral sensations and thoughts:

> Nu är en fröjdetid, nu börjar fiskar spritta,
> Nu börjar gräset fram ur dystra dvalan titta.
> Evart ur örat hör, evart ur ögat ser,
> Allting i glädje mys och ganska ljuvligt ser.
>
> [Now is a season of joy, now fish begin to wriggle,
> Now the grass begins to peep from gloomy slumber.
> Wherever the ear hears, wherever the eye sees,
> everything in joy seems smiling and quite sweet.]

For all their broad public appeal, neither the fugitive verse of Runius nor the private meditations of Frese are representative of Caroline elite culture at the end of the seventeenth century. Absolutism required and initiated a new art and literature that gave a heroic and metaphysical justification to an often arbitrary royal power. This became one of the main themes in the Latin orations of Johannes Columbus (1640–84) and Andreas Stobaeus (1642–1714), professors of poetry and eloquence at Uppsala and Lund, respectively. For their students, panegyric poetry seemed the high road to honor and office. Olof Hermelin (1658–1709), professor of eloquence at Dorpat, later administered propaganda and diplomacy from the field chancery of Karl XII. Torsten Rudeen (1661–1729), professor of poetry at Åbo, wrote odes in praise of the royal house and became the Lutheran bishop in Karlstad and Linköping.

By general agreement, the greatest of these political poets was Gunno Eurelius Dahlstierna (1661–1709). The son of a Lutheran pastor in Dalsland, plain Gunno Eurelius was ennobled Dahlstierna in 1702. While he was a student at Uppsala, Olaus Rudbeck had recommended Dahlstierna for the land survey commission in Livonia, then Swedish Livland. As a surveyor and administrator Dahlstierna spent most of his life in Sweden's Baltic provinces. Like many officials in the state bureaucracy, he had literary ambitions and had mastered the striking metaphors, mythological scenes, and rhetorical pathos that were all the fashion in Latin panegyric poetry. Dahlstierna found other sources of inspiration as well, the new baroque poetry in Germany and Italy and Professor Rudbeck's antiquarian research on the old Goths.

The results can be puzzling. Take, for example, the eulogy of Secretary Carl Liedemann, 1691. The poem is written in ottava rima but depicts the native province of the poet and Secretary Liedemann, Dalsland. In the Stoicism of that period, simple country contentment was treated as the basis for true happiness. Dahlstierna attributed this exemplary virtue to the natives of the province:

> Där bor ett stille folk, enfaldighetens venner:
>> ett folk i armod svår sin egen rikedom:
> ett folk som är förnöjt, i trohet, brör och fränder.

> [There lives a quiet folk, the friends of simplicity:
> a folk whose deep poverty is their wealth:
> a folk content with fidelity, fraternity, and kin.]

Older commentators were so puzzled by the absence of bombast in this and other poems that they took it as a sign that the foreign baroque style was alien to Dahlstierna. But the poem is rather a finger exercise in the plain style. In this corner of the kingdom, the folk respect authority and obey commands; behind the herdsmen of Dalsland move the old Goths with their heroic songs and virtuous ways.

It may seem strange that a political poet would write a poem of this kind and even stranger that he would translate Guarini's *Il pastor fido*, which he described as admirable above all for its instruction in ordinary life. These are the same literary and patriotic motives that induced Haquin Spegel to write in the hexaemeron tradition. Moral values were an essential element of seventeenth-century poetics.

On 5 April 1697, Karl XI died. The king's death and the famine that year were taken as signs of God's wrath. The king was buried months later, on 24 November, and on that day an official description of his bravery and patient suffering was read aloud from every pulpit in the kingdom. Lutheran bishops instructed the clergy in the correct explication of the set texts. State and church cooperated to confirm poor, simple folk in their belief in the blessings of absolutism. On that same day poets and orators offered their most profound thoughts on the blessings of the royal house at universities, council houses, and the House of Nobles in Stockholm. This single occasion was the high water mark of the baroque in Caroline Sweden.

Dahlstierna's contribution to the occasion, *Kunga skald* (1697; The king's skald), depicts the sorrow of all kinds and conditions by playing over the full range of styles from high to low. Since the poem is long and resists translation, I summarize. A humble shepherd living in the German forests—Dahlstierna was then posted to Swedish Pomerania—declares himself unfit to praise the dead king:

Men hur man kungars död för riken skall beklaga
det måste stora män, med lärdan mun framdraga.

[But how is one to lament the death of kings to the kingdoms
Great men must do so, with learned mouth.]

The muse Thalia appears and in the high style describes how the old Goths chose their kings for protection after evil had destroyed the happiness of the golden age: the death of kings had always been the Goths' greatest sorrow. When Karl XI became king, a golden age began anew. Thalia is interrupted by the clamor of funeral bells. She describes the deathbed of Karl XI and his last words to his son.

The goddess Svea enters with the spokesmen of the four estates. The scene that follows is based on Giambattista Marini's *Adone*; in place of

Bacchus, Apollo, Ceres, and Thetis's consoling of Venus, Dahlstierna's spokesmen console Svea. The nobleman and the cleric use the high style to depict the heroic deeds of Karl XI; the burgher uses the middle style, the farmer the low style.

To this stylistic principle Dahlstierna adds an allegorical element, also drawn from Marini, with biblical, classical, Gothic, and official allusions. The burgher, for example, tells of a shipwreck whose survivors see the polar star appear in the heavens—"a dream-puzzle none could interpret," adds Dahlstierna. But of course, the interpretation was obvious. The pole star had become the symbol of the royal house, with the motto, "It knows no decline." Its appearance after the shipwreck could only allude to the national catastrophe, followed by Karl XII's accession as the new star. Again, the antiphony related by the spokesman for the farmers is a paraphrase of Virgil's Fifth Eclogue, in which Mopsus and Menalcas sing of the death of Daphnis and his ascent into heaven, itself an allusion to the apotheosis of Julius Caesar. Dahlstierna's shepherds sing of Hialmar Herda-Hiälm and his ascent, with Gothic and Christian overtones. To this elaborate confection, in which Karl XI exchanges "the earthly Stockholm for the heavenly Jerusalem," Dahlstierna added eight sonnets based on the texts set for the clergy on the day of mourning.

Dahlstierna lived to celebrate Karl XII's fateful victories at Narva and in Saxony. For these joyous celebrations the poet concocted a ballad pastiche. In *Giöta kämpa wisa* (1701; Battle song of the Goths), Herr Peter courts the proud young Narva in vain; she has plighted her troth to a victorious young hero, Karl XII.

Fortunately, Dahlstierna did not live through the disasters of this reign and the end of the Sweden he had served. Literary judgment was reserved not for the loyal servants of absolutism but for a man whose mind was already attuned to the new century, as C. G. Cederhielm wrote in 1720:

> Alt hwad sin period til högsta punkten sedt,
> Måst åter strax igen sitt sidsta Inte röna.
> Kung Carl man nyss begrof, Kung Fredrich wi nu kröna,
> Så har wårt Swenska Ur gått rätt från Tolf til Ett.

> [All that has seen its period to an apex
> Must immediately experience again its final nullity.
> King Carl we just buried, now we crown King Fredrich,
> Thus our Swedish clock has gone from Twelve to One.]

The Enlightenment and the Gustavian Age

James Massengale

3

SWEDEN'S AGE OF LIBERTY

It is usual and convenient for European literary historians to equate the eighteenth century with that period known as the Enlightenment. This truism could be more narrowly defined in the case of Sweden as that period in its intellectual development corresponding historically to the Age of Liberty and the Gustavian Age, that is, from the death of Karl XII (1718) until the death of Gustav III (1792). This leaves the century short by twenty-six years and excludes, on both ends, some matters of interest; but it is not entirely misleading as a generality. A greater problem with the truism may arise in the application of the term "Enlightenment" in general. Although it is clear to us today that what we call the "modern world" or the concept of "modern man" was formulated on Enlightenment principles, we cannot assume that the average eighteenth-century Swede was fully cognizant of the implications of such a change, even though he or she may have been fascinated—or horrified—by the new trends that were sweeping Europe. Furthermore, the Enlightenment did not spring forth all at once, not even in Sweden, where its trends were assimilated largely from abroad. The whole century might be looked on as a gradually developing movement, the characteristics of which were only fully realized and understood toward the end. Nonetheless, the period that for all western Europe was the "most vigorous phase in the transition from the medieval to the modern world" (Robert Anchor) clearly had a powerful effect on the development of Swedish literature. In many cases, it precipitated a reevaluation of traditional forms; in others, it gave rise to forms that Sweden had previously not seen at all.

Literary works until well into the eighteenth century in Sweden may be classified according to a hierarchical system ultimately derived from Aristotle's *Poetics*, as adapted by various Renaissance and baroque authorities. In practice, it set a strict code for the aspiring poet regarding subjects worthy of poetic and dramatic treatment and for the metrics involved in such works. Among the "high" genres were the heroic poem, the tragedy, and the ode. The preferred meter used for such higher poetry was the alexandrine, or rhymed iambic hexameter (not to be confused with the earlier, more complex hexameter meter of Stiernhielm, which was based on a direct imitation of Greek meter). To the "lower" genres were relegated satires, epigrams, pastoral poems, and comedies. A common meter for satirical poetry was trochaic tetrameter or trimeter. But many of the poems, especially those lyrics written to melodies, fell into no classification at all, and the dichotomy between poetic theory and the actual composition of poetry led gradually to a reevaluation of the art as a whole by the end of the century.

At the beginning of the period, the concept of the writer bore little resemblance to the one we know today. Because of the expense of printing, the lack of copyright protection, and a relatively small reading audience, authors could not expect to live by sales of their works. They could, however, use their talents to gain royal favor or direct or indirect financial patronage. "The function of the author in this older society was not to express his own feelings and opinions, but to place his gift at the service of a patron or the civil service" (Gunnar Sahlin). Moreover, in the beginning of the century, there was no theater for which to write. Some of what we may consider the best works of the early eighteenth century were produced not as central activities of the authors but as personal, noncommercial commentaries on their experiences. It is not certain that such personal opinions were held in the same sort of esteem at the time they were written as they are today. The development in the eighteenth century may be seen as a fairly rapid shift from the older patronage system to the threshold of a modern, market-oriented basis for the production of literature. That in turn precipitated a radical change in literary style and even in the types of literary products that have come down to us.

Swedish writers in the beginning of the century came generally from the upper levels of society, and most were university educated. Only in the publication of broadside pamphlets can one find examples of literature produced by members of the lower social orders. Among the educated poets, even if they were sons and daughters of the nobility, the clergy, or burghers, however, few were independently wealthy, and none could depend on writing skills to put bread on the table. For university students, who often obtained employment in the houses of the nobility as private tutors to the children, the production of poetry was looked on as a social skill. Boarded tutors would often write pompous laudatory poems in honor of a family birthday, wedding, or funeral. Drinking songs and satires were also in demand. Poets early in the century did not experiment in any radical sense—not, at least, by modern standards—or mix forms. But from the very beginning, they found ways of expressing the hopes and fears of a new and troubling time. The literary personalities depicted in this brief overview tend to be the innovators, the experimenters, or those who took an oppositional position. Behind them may be found, if one wishes to take the trouble to search through the dusty shelves of larger libraries, some modestly talented, sometimes charming, but usually plodding types, who fill out the profile of the Enlightenment century without adding greatly to its distinction.

The eighteenth century began with a war that shook the foundations of the kingdom. Sweden had enjoyed years of prosperity under the absolute monarchy of Karl XI, who had shown himself to be both an astute leader in war and a clever economist in peace, although his seizure of property belonging to the nobility had both weakened and estranged that estate. His son, Karl XII, was only fifteen when he was crowned. The young king was compelled to take the reins of absolute monarchy during a time of military unrest. Responding to incursions in Sweden's Baltic possessions with a stunning victory at Narva at the turn of the century in 1700, the eighteen-year-old commander-king then began a series of campaigns that gradually deteriorated into an extensive exile, sapping the country's resources, decimating its armies, and leading the nation ever further from its position as one of the dominant powers in Europe. Seen from the literary point of view, the writers' natural inclination to contribute to court life or seek patronage from it was impossible to maintain: Karl XII left Stockholm in 1700, and when he returned in 1718 he lay in his casket. The nobility, also traditional protectors of literary efforts, were in disarray: some were left impoverished by the seizure of their property; some followed their king into battle and ended up dead or in a foreign prison; some more fortunate ones simply moved out of the capital city to their country estates.

Everything about the development of Sweden between 1700 and 1718 reflects the central, negative fact that literary production had been Stockholm-oriented and largely court-oriented. Without a resident king or a reliable group of patrons, the demand for literary products was greatly diminished. A theatrical troupe from France had arrived in 1699, with Racine and Molière in its repertoire, but it stayed only until 1706. Karl XII's relationship to Nikodemus Tessin the Younger (designer of the Royal Palace in Stockholm) and to the practical scientist Christofer Polhem may be used to demonstrate the continuing royal support of art and science. It must be noted, however, that many of the projects of both these resourceful men were left in abeyance during the king's wars or after his death. From having been a land that exported grain, wood, iron, and other metals in the mid-1600s, Sweden rapidly became an impoverished backwater during the first two decades of the 1700s, experiencing famine, agricultural underproduction, and a lack of capital for investment. In this unstable period, the progress of literature suffered most of all. Painters and musicians could leave the country, since their art was truly international. The Swedish literati, who could produce works understandable only to a Scandinavian audience, were left behind to languish.

The Early Years of the Age of Liberty

Certain of the events that hamstrung Sweden politically during the following reign of Fredrik I (1720–51) ultimately contributed to a revival of the arts. Since there was no direct heir to the Swedish throne in 1718, Karl XII's sister was placed there, at least nominally. But the nobility secured guarantees that the autocratic rule of the Caroline period would not be extended. Queen Ulrika Eleonora showed her displeasure with the new balance of power by abdicating in favor of her husband, Fredrik of Hessen. The ensuing "Age of Liberty" (1720–72) refers to that period in Swedish history when the four estates experimented with an alternative ruling system, forcing the king and queen to function almost as mere figureheads—a precursor, as it were, of the modern-day system. Two political parties, the "Hats" and "Caps," vied for power from the late 1730s until the return of absolute monarchy in 1772. The parliament became the forum for political discussion, and its leaders were the source of power in the country. At the same time, the central bureaucracy was expanded. Seizing on a new opportunity for political influence, foreign countries began to lobby at the highest levels of Swedish government. Foreign diplomats exerted influence directly through bribery and intimate contact with the members of parliament, and many high-ranking Swedes sought out such contact, both on the cultural level and in the political arena. They accepted readily the notion of the cultural superiority of France and England and with it the correlate that Swedish culture—even the Swedish language itself—was gravely deficient. The emulation of what was perceived as the grace and nobility of classical French poetry and drama remained a major concern of some of the more conservative writers for the greater part of the eighteenth century.

By the beginning of the reign of Fredrik I, it was clear to many leaders that new cultural currents—the Enlightenment—had begun. The period of Fredrik I marks a time in Sweden when conscious efforts were initially made to assimilate these new currents. Central to them was a humanistic, optimistic belief in the power of scientific and intellectual reason, and a skepticism regarding those values perceived as antiquated: religious dogma, absolute monarchy, or societal control by a minority of any sort. Some of the tenets of Enlightenment thought were ultimately recast into revolutionary ideas. But many other precepts that emerged during the same time were not revolutionary in the political sense. They were scientific and philosophical principles that have guided much of Western thought ever since, adapting themselves to an increasingly complex world situation. In looking back on the eighteenth-century formulation of Enlightenment precepts, we may find some of them naive, but we will recognize in them the initial expression of many of our present beliefs and democratic ideas. Among them may be mentioned the following:

- Experimental science was recognized as part of the cutting edge of intellectual thought, changing our conception of the world around us (Newton). That led to the Enlightenment thinkers' fascination with scientific experiment and scientists in general and to popular science as a means of spreading scientific discoveries to a broader audience (Fontenelle).

- Empiricism was seen as a means of arriving at scientific or intellectual conclusions (Locke). The supposed superiority of empiricism contributed to a skepticism about metaphysical ideas and traditional educational principles. It led to later Enlightenment theories of natural education and a return to nature (Rousseau). A general dislike of superstition and religious intolerance and a belief in humanistic values (Voltaire) was expressed in its most radical form as atheism (La Mettrie).

- Utilitarianism, growing out of two contrasting points of view (an egocentric one from Hobbes and an altruistic one from Shaftesbury) and coalescing at a middle point with the notion of "the best possible good for the most possible people" (Bentham), had subsequent implications for economic theory regarding both the individual and the nation (Adam Smith).

- Optimism, a keynote of the period, expressed itself in the concept that we live in the "best of all possible worlds" (Leibniz). By midcentury, the dogma of infinite human progress had given way to some extent to a stoic, reduced goal to "cultivate one's garden" (Voltaire).

- Literary criticism, based on principles of reason (Boileau), with "taste" as supreme arbiter rather than the formal rhetorical principles that guided the literature of the 1600s, and a concept of original "genius" (Dubos) eventually led the thought of critics and creative writers to appreciate the rule breakers (Diderot) and ultimately to the threshold of romanticism.

Such new principles of scientific and artistic criticism, however, would have had little impact during the eighteenth century had it not been for the explosive increase of printed materials: books, pamphlets, and newspapers or journals. The various threads of the century of Enlightenment were gradually woven together to make a new fabric of literary creation and to redefine the working principles of the writers as well.

Positioned just behind the dominant trends of Enlightenment thought was an emotional, mystical attitude toward life that stands in marked contrast to the prevalent materialistic, practical theories. This attitude is clearly perceivable in pietist and Moravian (Sw. *herrnhutiska*) circles, which were widespread alternatives to the orthodox Lutheran Church. But such sentimentality was not restricted to the religious milieu; it found its expression even in the works of nonsectarian and secular writers. Elements of mystical, Neoplatonic thought may also be found in literary and theoretical works long before they congealed into the philosophical foundations of the romantic movement that reached Sweden at the turn of the nineteenth century. At times explicitly formulated (as in Swedenborg), at times seen only as a passing or indistinct influence (as in Nordenflycht) or an emotional outburst (as in Lidner), the mystical-sentimental attitude may be followed as a secondary trend throughout the century.

Enlightenment tendencies did not enter Sweden simultaneously and were not all fully assimilated or unconditionally accepted. It would be impossible to mark any specific years as the beginning and end of the period in Sweden. It could even be argued that Sweden's most characteristic "Enlightenment" man was the now little-known Nils von Rosenstein, whose *Försök till en afhandling om upplysningen* (Essay concerning the Enlightenment) was printed in 1793. Rosenstein certainly assimilated and described the Enlightenment, but his writings appeared too late to exert any noteworthy influence on it. By the 1790s, younger writers had fully absorbed the basic precepts, but many had also turned away from the authorities that had fostered them.

As must be evident from this sketch of Enlightenment trends, few if any of the age's many impulses actually had their intellectual bases in Sweden. But a "hidden hand" (one of Adam Smith's metaphorical concepts) seemed to guide the development of the period: just as the death of Louis XIV (1715) precipitated new relations between royalty, aristocracy, and burghers in France, the death of Karl XII had a similar effect in Sweden only three years later. Just as the French Revolution marked the end of the Enlightenment there in 1789, a small but deadly "revolution" in Sweden in 1792 had the same effect. It was not as easy to reform Sweden's cultural contour, however, as it was to reorganize its system of government. The transition from a great European power to a small, somewhat backward European country meant a loss of the optimism and the pride in the nation that had marked the literature of Sweden's century as a great power. As has often been pointed out, the Age of Liberty was not noticeably free, from the point of view of the common citizen. Those first hard, prosaic years following the death of Karl XII produced no literary spokesmen in the traditional sense, but the period did foster the careers of two extraordinary men whose works lie at the periphery of literary endeavor.

The Scientific Muse: Swedenborg and Linné

For the English-speaking public, probably the best known of the Swedish Enlightenment thinkers is the remarkable scientist and religious writer Emanuel Swedenborg (1688–1772). He was born in Stockholm, the son of Jesper Svedberg, who was one of the most creative and important of the Caroline bishops. The family took up residence in Uppsala in 1692, and when his father moved to Skara in 1702, Emanuel remained at the university town to continue his education. After writing a dissertation on classical philology at Uppsala University (1709), Swedenborg traveled to England and was soon engaged in research based on a Newtonian and Cartesian mechanistic view of the world, which he then gradually codified as a philosophical system (*Opera philosophica et mineralia*, 1734). His studies in natural science during the first forty years of his life are largely unknown to an international audience but have earned him a place of respect in the history of Swedish geology, anatomy, and metallurgy. It has been pointed out (Henrik Schück) that Swedenborg was not an experimenter or an empiricist. He was rather a comprehensive theoretician whose talent lay in combining others' experiments into a broad framework. At the same time, he was a true Enlightenment scientist in the sense that he was deeply concerned with the practical applications of his theories. He threw himself with great energy into utilitarian projects; edited Sweden's first scientific journal, *Dædalus hyperboreus*; and was appointed a member of the Academy of Sciences. Then on a fateful day in August 1736, while on a trip to Holland, Swedenborg was seized by a fit of fainting, during which he reportedly experienced an overpowering light. He interpreted the incident mystically, as an act of divine intervention. This, perhaps combined with his frustration in his search for the source for the human soul (a goal he had set himself), gradually brought about a drastic shift in his thought, from a materialistic view of the world to an animistic one, in which matter and mechanics were of the least possible consequence. By 1744, Swedenborg had become a theosophist, a spiritist, a dedicated religious thinker, and—in the opinion of some of his distinguished contemporaries—a complete lunatic.

Swedenborg's highly individual religious system, as presented in his compendious *Arcana coelestia* (1749–56) and *De coelo et de inferno* (1758), has its roots in Neoplatonic thought. Each thing in the natural world around us may be conceived of as a shadow of a spiritual reality, which in turn may be a representation of a divine quality: that is the basis for his "theory of correspondences." Swedenborg was convinced that earthly objects and events contained mystical significance understandable only to the initiated. Earthly life he envisioned as a preparation for the life of the spirit, into which one would be transformed at death. The good person would gradually become an angel; the bad one would soon be drawn to hell by his or her own predilection. The spirits with which Swedenborg claimed to communicate resembled earthly beings exactly: they were clothed and lived in towns in lands with mountains and lakes. Such civilized units were representative of *spiritual* states, however, not political states. The religiously inspired scientist described his visions, as Martin Lamm has pointed out, with all the objectivity and exactitude that he had previously devoted to his scientific deductions. Swedenborg thus turned his world inside out, yet he never changed his scientific method. To the end of his life, he continued to work diligently (diligence was the attribute of an angel, according to his own system) and to converse with his spirits. His teaching was dismissed out of hand by a majority of his Swedish contemporaries, but it gained a following in Holland and England, where his writings were printed. It was on a trip to England that he died in 1772.

By the time of his death, Swedenborg had become a legendary figure, and numerous stories were circulated about the accuracy of his prophecies. Those who had contact with him were often bewildered by his ideas, but no one considered him a charlatan, and he kept himself aloof from fake spiritists and Rosicrucians. Although he did not claim to start a "church," his radically original religious system has since exerted considerable influence, especially in England and the United States. Years later, when the Neoplatonic romanticists had won the day in Europe, some outstanding writers (including Goethe, Balzac, Baudelaire, and two of Sweden's leading authors, Almqvist and Strindberg) found themselves singularly attracted to that particular combination of Enlightenment logic and arcane biblical interpretation that Swedenborg fashioned into a system. In the United States, Ralph Waldo Emerson and other transcendentalists were profoundly influenced by Swedenborg, and toward the end of the nineteenth century the symbolist movement would acknowledge its debt to the Swedish visionary.

Like Swedenborg, the natural scientist Carl von Linné (1707–78) represents an area that lies outside "pure literature." Nonetheless, he and Olof von Dalin have been pronounced the greatest Swedish prose writers of the Age of Liberty. Linné's life represents the epitome of what one would be inclined to picture as the Enlightenment personality: optimistic, creative, poetic, and yet rigorously scientific, Linné combined his idealistic and deeply humanistic values with a surprisingly down-to-earth sense of publicity and the practical progress toward his life goals. Born the son of a poor minister in the southern Swedish province of Småland, Linné developed his love for botany only gradually, as he resisted those school subjects that would have led him to the calling of a minister. Resolved instead to be a medical doctor, he found his way to Lund University at the age of twenty and then continued his botanical studies, mostly without help, in Uppsala. In spite of this (or even *because* of this lack of inhibiting academic diversion from his systematic observations), Linné developed his original theories in a remarkably short time. While grounding his comprehensive theory about the categorization system for the plant world, Linné also took part in his first important naturalist's journeys, to Lapland (1732) and to Dalarna and Norway (1734). Then he went to Holland to publish his dissertation (1735) and establish his international reputation in order to obtain a Swedish professorship (1741).

Even as a twenty-year-old student, Linné had been one of Uppsala's most popular lecturers, and in his three decades of university service, he built up single-handedly an entire school of naturalists, who then tested his theories at the ends of the earth. His day-long "herbations" out in nature ordinarily drew two hundred to three hundred students, who brought their specimens to him for scrutiny and received minilectures for their pains in

Linné's engaging scientific style. After a long and rewarding career as a professor, Linné was raised to the nobility in 1761. On his death, he was mourned as a national hero.

Linné's penchant for natural and ethnological observation is astonishing. Equally important to his particular method, however, is an underlying belief in the well-ordered structure of the world, based on his conception of God's own rationalistic behavior. Linné was apparently never bothered by seeming discrepancies between the natural reality he studied and the Old Testament faith of his childhood. System builder though he was, he was totally unlike Swedenborg in personality. Swedenborg built up fantastic systems on the basis of limited empirical or experimental evidence. Linné built his comprehensive systems in a provisional way, without attempting to derive any ultimate conclusions from them. The final truth he preferred to leave to his childhood Bible—or to a later generation.

Linné's legacy is primarily his epoch-making classification system, first sketched out in the brief *Systema naturae* (1735), with its botanical component expanded in various books, and culminating in the final edition of *Genera plantarum* (1771). For the literary Scandinavianist, however, and for many of his contemporary readers, Linné is best known for his travel books: *Öländska och Gothländska resan* (1745; Journeys to Öland and Gotland), *Västgötaresan* (1747; Journey to Västergötland), and *Skånska resan* (1751; Journey to Skåne). Perhaps better known today are the *Iter lapponicum* (Journey to Lapland) and *Dalaresan* (Journey to Dalarna), which were published posthumously in 1888–89.

The question may well be asked if strictly nonfictional travel descriptions constitute "literature." In one sense, the lyrical passages that abound in Linné's travel books do not in and of themselves warrant a reevaluation of the genre as a pure literary art. On the other hand, the power of Linné's prose and its influence must not be underestimated. Partly because of the enormous popularity and impact of Linné's writings, the tradition of collecting scientific and ethnographic information from specific geographical areas was strengthened and financially supported on a permanent basis in Sweden. And partly because Linné showed himself to be a natural stylist, not only a natural scientist, other writers began to respect his chosen genre and to try to imitate his deceptively simple prose style. Schück compares his naive, joyous empirical observations to the convoluted periodic sentences of the otherwise highly regarded C. G. Tessin. For the cognoscenti of the earlier eighteenth century, Tessin would have been the exemplary rhetorician. But as the times changed—and they did so rapidly during this period—the terse, precise style of Linné quickly became the more popular one for the general public. That of Tessin never returned to prominence. Linné's style mixes critical observation with an inborn poetic flair that cannot be found to the same degree in other works of this type:

> The autumn had displayed itself before our eyes continuously from Fällingsbro. To be sure, the forest was green, but with a more serious mien than in the summer. Pastures and meadows were green enough, but without flowers, for the cattle had swept up the former and the scythe the latter. The fields were full of golden shocks, and the yellowish stubble from the grain was interspersed with green weeds. The ditches were full of water after the wet summer, and the multitude of burr marigold turned them yellow. The sides of the roads were covered with *persicaria acri* that began now to turn red and hang on their stems. The farmers were out everywhere, hard at work . . . while young shepherds sang and blew their horns to the animals that were grazing in the mowed fields, until the chilled evening wind began to whistle and the clear sun sink down under the horizon, as we came into Uppsala's garden. *(From Västgötaresan)*

If there had been a novelist of merit during Sweden's Age of Liberty, one might have seen Linné's talent for precise natural description borrowed to advantage in fictional prose. But Sweden boasted no novelist during the entire century who could emulate either this style or that of imported British masters such as Fielding and Sterne. Jacob Mörk and Anders Törngren's *Adalriks och Giöthildas äfventyr* (1742–44; The adventures of Adalrik and Götilda) marks the beginning of the art of the novel. In the Enlightenment period it stands as an isolated curiosity.

The Culmination of the Age of Liberty

Fredrik I and Ulrika Eleonora had no children, and at the queen's death in 1741 Sweden once again found itself searching for a crown prince. The lot fell to Adolf Fredrik, the prince-bishop of Lübeck, who happened to be a great-great-grandson of Karl IX as well as a relative of the crown prince of Russia. The Swedes had been waging a useless war with Russia since 1738, a result of the Hat party's inept political posturing. When the luck of war turned against Sweden, the Russians threatened to take Karelia, or even the whole of Finland, if an heir to the Swedish throne were chosen who was incompatible with their own political ends. An uneasy peace treaty was eventually signed in 1743, and the "Russian candidate," Adolf Fredrik, was designated heir. He became king in 1751. His marriage to Lovisa Ulrika, sister of Frederick the Great of Prussia, strengthened the image of the royal family and added a great deal of cultural prestige to the court. But the Hats and Caps continued their seesaw battle for political dominance, and an attempt by the royal pair to seize power for themselves in 1756 backfired miserably. Their function in government was reduced to that of a rubber stamp (quite literally) wielded by the Hat party, and for a few days in December 1768 the king refused to reign at all. The last decade of the Age of Liberty was marked by almost unbridled corruption in government, economic disaster, and the constant fear of foreign intervention. Sweden's political connections with France and England, disruptive though they often were in the political arena, at least helped further the trends of the Enlightenment, which by now were setting the literary tone. Another ray of hope in all the political unrest was the Freedom of the Press Act of 1766, which accompanied the Caps' assumption of power after a bitter parliamentary struggle. The Freedom of the Press Act, the second oldest law of its kind in Europe, provided a strong impetus for literary production. Censorship had exerted an inhibiting influence on the book and newspaper market, and the removal of certain restrictions can be linked to remarkable advances in numbers of book printers, booksellers, and newspapers. This window of increased publishing activity was to some extent closed by Gustav III in 1774, but the pressure by writers and publishers to expand the literary market and the role of the printed word continued for the rest of the century.

The Swedish Comedy, 1737–1754

Swedish theater as late as 1730 may be accurately characterized by a single word: nonexistent. The lack of general governmental support and the disinterest of King Fredrik I, combined with the Lutheran Church's distrust of actors and the pietists' open hatred of anything resembling theater, made drama an art form that was slow to take hold. Nonetheless, private playacting had been in fashion among both aristocrats and students for some time, when, as C. G. Tessin has related, a group of students produced a part of the story of Tobias for a larger public. It was no stirring production, but the spectators liked it because it was in a language they could understand, and the young people were encouraged by those of both higher and lower estates to continue. The leaders of the Hat party seemed particularly interested in the establishment of a Swedish theater that might be a forum for their political ideas, and they managed to convince the students that they would not be regarded as vagabonds—a common stigma placed on acting troupes. Under royal protection, the Swedish Comedy (Swenska Comedien) was founded in October 1737. The repertoire was largely translated, but the members had received promises of scripts from the more talented literati of or closely aligned with the Hat party: Carl Gyllenborg, Erik Wrangel, Olof Dalin, and R. G. Modée.

The best of the original Swedish plays for the budding theater came from Carl Gyllenborg (1679–1746), a leader of the Hat party from the time of its inception in 1734. He had been a diplomat in England in his youth and had married an Englishwoman before returning to Sweden. He had tried his hand at playwriting long before the Swedish Comedy was conceived but had not had a forum for production. His contribution to the theater was *Den Swenska sprätthöken* (1738; The Swedish coxcomb). Though loosely based on a one-act French play, *Le François à Londres*, by Louis de Boissy, Gyllenborg's play has a more complex plot, more psychological depth, and a good measure of Swedish politics as well. It premiered on 11 October 1737 and continued for a number of performances in 1738. It may be somewhat too wordy to rank as a true classic, but its characters are rather well constructed, and with some careful cutting, it could undoubtedly entertain a modern audience.

Gyllenborg was lost to the theater troupe as early as 1739, when the opposing Cap party was overthrown and he became president of the chancellery. Soon afterward, the Swedish Comedy itself lost momentum, and after being shut down for more than a year because of public mourning at the death of Ulrika Eleonora in 1741, it failed to regain its high-level support and internal enthusiasm. It lingered on under the leadership of one of its actors, Petter Stenborg, playing under increasingly demeaning circumstances, until it officially folded in 1754. The tradition of using foreign traveling companies for Sweden's aristocratic entertainment was reinstated, and the permanent establishment of a Swedish theater had to await the Gustavian Age almost twenty years later. The writers of the Age of Liberty were forced to seek other outlets for their artistic talents.

Olof von Dalin

Olof von Dalin (1708–63), described as that most mysterious of Swedish poets, was not one who produced mysterious poetry or even pondered obscure ideas. Indeed, what has proven elusive for researchers is to fathom how a poet could be so conscientious in revealing inner foibles of others, so sharp-witted and explosively talented, and yet, through a long career, never tell us what he *really* thought. In Dalin, we find another important aspect of the burgeoning Enlightenment: that of the upwardly mobile virtuoso whose virtuosity itself gradually hardens into an impenetrable mask. Dalin has been called by some "the Voltaire of the North," and his talent might indeed be compared with that of Voltaire—that is, with that of a collector and expert formulator of eighteenth-century ideas that were not necessarily his own. Dalin's career could also be likened to Linné's, were it not for the radical difference in personality: the worldly-wise cynical dissector of society versus the wide-eyed, pious dissector of plants. Like Linné a son of a minister and from a provincial area of southern Sweden (Halland), Dalin was sent as a thirteen-year-old to Lund University, where he stayed for six years, even studying medicine for a brief period with Stobaeus, who was later to be the young Linné's mentor. A more important instructor for Dalin, however, was the professor of logic and metaphysics, Anders Rydelius, whose open and liberal views on the new Enlightenment thinkers are found in a book called *Nödiga förnuftsövningar* (1718–20; Exercises in reason). Dalin never attained an academic degree at Lund but stayed with his moral guide until he was called to assume the position of private tutor with one of Stockholm's leading noble families, that of Claes Rålamb. Between 1727 and 1732, Dalin polished his poetic skills as he moved in the aristocratic circles that gave his writing its peculiar mixture of improvisational adeptness, moralizing satire, and impersonal servility.

Dalin's work came into prominence at almost exactly the same time as that of Linné, but his name was not generally known to the public for several years. His famous journal, *Then Swänska Argus* (1732–34; The Swedish Argus), was published anonymously. The Greek name refers to a many-eyed giant, that is, a journal that sees everything everywhere. "Argus" appears in the articles themselves, however, as a neutral, reasonable Enlightenment man. It has been said, and not without reason, that the birth of newer Swedish literature corresponds to the day of the first issue of *Then Swänska Argus*, 13 December 1732. What is equally true is that the Swedish reading public had become sufficiently aware of the newer European trends in literature that they were ready to appreciate Dalin's works as soon as they appeared. Dalin had the foresight to anticipate the needs of his reading audience, but he also had the talent to produce the sort of prose that was necessary for the new journalism—a light, gentle, satirical, orally based style that turned his borrowings into miniature masterpieces of Swedish description. Here for the first time in Swedish literary history a work was authored not for a literary minority but rather for the "common good." This excerpt from his satirical journal of a dandy can serve as a stylistic tidbit:

> *Monday.* 8 A.M. I threw on my robe and stood at the window. Autumn weather much too cold, the wind out of the north. 9 A.M. I had Bengt put the tea on. Smoked a pipe Virginia tobacco—much too bitter on

the tongue. 10 A.M. drank tea, washed and dressed. One shoe-buckle broke; Bengt's fault. N.B. when he comes back, he's going to get it. 11 A.M. I put my other buckles on and the little wig. N.B. I think a dark wig would give me a braver appearance. 11:30 I went out into the Riddarhus market. At noon Brother Snoppstiern wanted me to go to Roussels, not Guillemots. Two schnappses. The King of Prussia's sickness needs to be confirmed. N.B. Brother Bouteille's thoughts re: the Brandy-tax. 1 P.M. Lunch. No meatballs in the soup. Since the cook fell in love with Berthel, she has been crazy.

The reading public took *Then Swänska Argus* to its heart; the identity of the anonymous author was a matter of speculation; it was difficult to believe, as rumor had it, that a twenty-four-year-old unsalaried clerk was behind all those original pieces. Later researchers have dispelled the mystery. Virtually the whole paper was undoubtedly conceived and written by Dalin himself. He based his idea to some degree on Sweden's first major journalistic paper of the Age of Liberty, the *Sedolärande Mercurius* (1730–31; The moralistic Mercury) of Carl Carlsson, but he went far beyond that publication, both stylistically and with respect to his sources. *Then Swänska Argus* was not original in the modern sense of the word. Most of its articles are clever rewritings of material from other journals, notably Addison and Steele's *Spectator* and the Hollander Justus van Effen's *Le Misanthrope*. The innovations in the Swedish version lie in Dalin's eye and ear for Swedish detail and personal psychology, which often raise his articles above the borrowed sources and make them into a compendious picture of everyday life—satirically twisted, of course—and of the bourgeois households of the capital city.

One might not wish to peruse *Then Swänska Argus* from cover to cover today, but to dip into its funniest parts is one of the most pleasurable ways to get a contemporary picture of the Age of Liberty. The intellectual backbone of *Argus* is a morality based on reason, and the carefully composed implicit criticism of his society's faults made it read, in the words of Henrik Schück, like an open "window to the cultural world of Europe." Dalin was compelled to tread a narrow path between the political power brokers in Sweden and the censor of publications, which is one reason why he stopped his journal after two years, despite an overwhelming expression of regret by its readers. Another reason is that he had never intended to end up as the editor of a journal. His sights were set higher.

Once he had been acknowledged as the author of *Argus*, Dalin swung himself into a central position in Swedish letters, a position he would hold for the rest of his life. In 1737, he was appointed royal librarian and was tapped, as noted above, as one of three notable authors to write plays for the newly formed Swedish Comedy. Dalin contributed two plays, the comedy *Den afvundsiuke* (1738; The envious man) and the tragedy *Brynhilda* (1738). The comedy is the more successful of the two. Written in the spirit of Molière and Ludvig Holberg, although with a moralizing, rather bitter tone, it contains some scenes marked by an excellent sense of comic timing and repartee. In *Brynhilda*, Dalin tries to form the dramatic events of the Norse *Vǫlsunga saga* into a sort of classic French drama, with a notably weaker result.

Dalin's little prose allegory, *Sagan om hästen* (1740; The story of a horse), is only a bagatelle, but it is a particularly well turned piece of work, the story of Sweden's history from Gustav Vasa to Fredrik I in terms of a series of farmers (i.e., rulers) in their relationship to their trustworthy horse, Grålle (i.e., Sweden itself, or the Swedish people). Although Dalin himself expressed no particular regard for the tale and expended a great deal more energy on the composition of *Swenska friheten* (1742; Swedish liberty), an epically conceived elegy on the death of Queen Ulrika Eleonora, his unpretentious horse allegory has contributed more to his lasting fame.

The work Dalin produced in his later years bears the stamp of his position as entrusted court poet and educator. On commission from the Swedish parliament, he began a voluminous history of Sweden in 1747, working on it nearly until the time of his death. Although not academically rigorous and never completed, it remained for many years a standard history book for Sweden. Dalin was made Crown Prince Gustav's private tutor in 1750, and he was raised to the nobility in 1751 (his name then became officially *von Dalin*), and his titles after that time followed apace: member of the chancellery, secretary of the newly established Academy of Letters, and so on. His solidarity with King Adolf Fredrik and Queen Lovisa Ulrika during their unsuccessful coup d'état in 1756 lost him his high post for a time and almost cost him his life. But when the affairs of state settled down again, he rose once more to a high position before his death in 1763.

It has been said that Dalin's best work lay in the light, attractive *poésie fugitive* that he strewed liberally to the families of the nobility and royalty. To say that anyone's *poésie fugitive* is his most memorable work implies, of course, a contradiction in terms. Occasional poems designed for immediate consumption were not—by definition—supposed to be memorable, and many of the verses that swelled the posthumous edition of his works to six volumes were never intended for publication. They should really be differentiated from those well-made "shepherd" songs and satirical pieces that show Dalin at his relaxed best. A measure of their popularity is their appearance in dozens of handwritten collections of poetry and broadsheets during the rest of the century. Among the best of them could be mentioned "En Celadon gav fröjderop" (A Celadon gave joyous cry); "Jag svär, sad' Malin, vid min hy" (I swear, said Malin, by my complexion); his "Spring song," "Bort med höga ting!" (Away with higher things!); a "Dance song," "Skatan sitter på kyrkotorn" (The magpie sits on the steeple); and the folk-song parody "Stolts Ingeborg hon var den fagraste mö" (Proud Ingeborg, she was the fairest of maids).

Drawing from a wide range of parody sources, Dalin's poems are both carefully and ingeniously constructed. Although many of his songs are translations or adaptations from French, the tradition behind them is a solidly Swedish one, stretching back through Johan Gabriel Werwing and Johan Runius to Lasse Lucidor. Dalin's own production, in turn, was clearly an inspiration to the young Bellman (below).

Was Dalin as happy a man as he was successful? No one seems to know. He certainly played the game of the eighteenth century correctly, using his own moralizing reason and satirical wit to further his career. Once at the top, he played the part of a highly intellectual court jester for Queen Lovisa Ulrika; at the same time, he was a moral mentor for her talented son, Prince Gustav. To contend, with Martin Lamm, that he was of a weak temperament or an underdeveloped personality is to underestimate his genuine accomplishments. It was no coward who held out for peace as a member of the (Hat) party that often opted for war or laid his life on the line for his king and queen when he felt it warranted. It was no idler who single-handedly published his own journal for two years, wrote a three-volume history of Sweden without having studied the subject academically, or produced hundreds of poems on demand. It was no intellectual weakling who kept himself up-to-date in the quickly changing intellectual climate of the Enlightenment and distilled some of its best ideas for the Swedish public. Some later critics have expressed disappointment over a perceived lack of creative genius. It would seem unfair to hold that against Olof von Dalin.

Nordenflycht and the Thought Builders
The position of women was anything but favorable for literary endeavor in the eighteenth century. Those talented women in the middle and upper echelons of society who sought a literary outlet were largely restricted to "lower," or nonliterary, forms of expression—letters, diaries and that *poésie fugitive* of which Dalin was the master. Once in a generation, however, a

woman rose above such a level. Sophia Elisabeth Brenner (1659–1730) was the first serious Swedish woman writer of the eighteenth century. But it was Hedvig Charlotta Nordenflycht (1718–63) who gave real substance to the identity of the Swedish female poet. She not only exemplified the concept; her identity, as expressed in her poetry, exhibited an acute awareness of her different status and goals specifically as a woman. Poet and critic Oscar Levertin stated that Nordenflycht's life can be seen in terms of the chronological logic of her choice of men. The statement is an ironic way of acknowledging the honesty with which she laid bare her heart and her passions. As a young girl, she had been intensely interested in "unfeminine" and bookish pursuits. She was soon reading the French philosopher Pierre Bayle and trying to reconcile Enlightenment skepticism with the Lutheran values of life on a small farm in Västmanland. Though her attempts at self-education were to some extent encouraged by her father, she was still caught, like the rest of her sex, in the patriarchal mores of the times. Her forced engagement to her hunchbacked tutor by her father on his deathbed should be sufficient to exemplify this point. Only by a remarkable happenstance was Hedvig Charlotta spared a physical relationship with the tutor, for he died before the wedding could take place.

Her duty as an engaged woman compelled her to sorrow over his early death, but a certain sense of relief can also be seen in her reaction to the turn of events. Her first real love dates from her return to Stockholm after about seven years in the country, in 1737 or 1738. Her French tutor in town was a mystic, Neoplatonic theologian, Jacob Fabricius, and their marriage, despite obstacles raised by Nordenflycht's callous family, was consummated in 1741. Only seven months later, Fabricius died of a fever. Nordenflycht moved to a little farmhouse on the island of Lidingö, outside Stockholm, and became, in her own words, the "sorrowing turtle-dove" of Swedish poetry.

Even before the occurrence of this tragic impetus to express her situation poetically, Nordenflycht had intended to support herself by her pen. It was a daring idea, but equally daring was her belief that she could win readers to her side by projecting a specifically feminine point of view. Numerous critics from Levertin on have analyzed Nordenflycht as a kind of "surrogate male" poet, dependent on her masculine mentors and wavering between the different Enlightenment trends that reached Sweden from the 1740s to the 1760s. What has not been sufficiently studied is Nordenflycht's particularly feminine answer to these waves of thought: her appeal for the betterment of female education in her *Qvinligit Tankespel af en Herdinna i Norden* (1744; Feminine thought play by a shepherdess from the north) and her response to Rousseau's male chauvinism in "Fruentimrets försvar" (1759; Woman's defense).

The literary society called Tankebyggarorden (the Order of Thought Builders) was not founded by Nordenflycht, but she became its soul and primus motor. It was begun in 1753, possibly as a conscious counterpart to the Academy of Letters, which started under the patronage of Queen Lovisa Ulrika that same year, with Dalin as its secretary. The Thought Builders could hardly be called a bourgeois counterpart to the Royal Academy, when its three most famous members—Nordenflycht, Gustaf Fredrik Gyllenborg, and Gustaf Philip Creutz—all were of the nobility. But with its public anonymity, its nod to Freemasonry, and its serious pretensions as a cohesive producer of published works, the order soon began to dominate the literary scene in those circles where royal patronage and the influence of Dalin himself were not all-prevalent. In its publications, *Våra försök* (1753–56; Our endeavors) and the later and more noteworthy *Vitterhetsarbeten* (1759–62; Literary works), the Swedish Enlightenment found some of its richest expression, although Nordenflycht herself, as many have pointed out, was never wholly at one with the more radical manifestations of the age. The last and most tragic of her inclinations was for the attractive but less inspired young poet Johan Fischerström. Out of this wrenching and denigrating relationship between 1760 and her death in 1763, Nordenflycht would write such classical small pieces as "Öfver en hyacint. Til . . ." (1763; Over a hyacinth. To: . . .), of which the famous final strophe is as follows:

But shall I chide a simple flower,
Or even blame the gentle being,
Her fate is to transform herself,
She has to be the way she can.
She is an herb, she must decay,
I feel no bitterness against her.
I see your heart grow cold as well,
It has to be the way it is.

Nordenflycht's legacy is an important one and has not been universally appreciated by the critics. A consistent part of her production lies in her adherence to a self-consciously feminine point of view, a woman's reply to the male-dominated literary scene of the eighteenth century.

Compared with Nordenflycht, her fellow Thought Builders and friends Gustaf Fredrik Gyllenborg (1731–1808) and Gustaf Philip Creutz (1731–85) present a much more traditional image. Count Gyllenborg was rather like a wordy, humorless version of Dalin. A nephew of Carl Gyllenborg (above), he had a modest career in the civil service as well as several years as cavalier to the young Crown Prince Gustav. For a decade starting in 1753, he produced some satirical and philosophical poems under the watchful and enthusiastic eye of Nordenflycht. His satire, *Om Fruntimret bör studera* (1756; If a lady should be educated), exhibits a dry and critical wit. At other times he takes the stance of a heavy, virtuous midcentury stoicism and a critic of the vanities and frivolities of his age: "Vinter-Qväde" (1759; Ode to winter) and "Människans elände" (1762; Miseries of man) are among the best-known poems in this spirit.

> Upon this darkened road, if you in peace would wander,
> Ask not, within your lifetime, of you or any other,
> For something of perfection that mankind cannot bear.
> But let your sorrow's night by glimpse of pleasure fade,
> And seek with steadfast virtue and downcast eyes to reach
> An unknown final goal.
> *("Människans Elände")*

After Nordenflycht's death and Creutz's removal abroad, Gyllenborg ceased all memorable production. Life's prosaic duties smothered his flickering poetic talent. It was not so much that he aged—even his early thoughts are hardly "youthful"—but rather that he lost the edge of his capacity to despise mankind in effective verse. His talent could not support itself without the intellectual nurturing provided by the literary society of the Thought Builders.

Creutz was born in Swedish Finland and came to Stockholm in 1751 after a short period of university study in Åbo. Like his best friend, Gyllenborg, Creutz was appointed cavalier to a royal child (Gustav's younger brother, Fredrik Adolf). He also joined the Thought Builders at the same time as Gyllenborg. Creutz's intellectual models were Voltaire and the Encyclopedists, and his special talent was a command of graceful verse, an epicurean point of view, and a thorough grounding in the poetry of Greece and Rome, on which his idylls drew. Creutz's *Daphne* and especially *Atis och Camilla* (1762; Atis and Camilla) have a stylistic quality that sets them apart from any previous Swedish poetry. For the first time, with Creutz, Swedish takes on a true Gallic charm and suppleness, those very qualities that many had feared were impossible to achieve in a Germanic language. An English translation cannot do justice to the delicacy of Creutz's verse, so the reader will have to imagine passages such as the following couched in perfect alexandrines:

In those Arcadian fields, far from the prideful cities,
Where pleasure's traded off for vacuous ambition;
Out in a lovely tract, where innocence draws fortune,
Where rapture, peace, and calm are seen to hold and keep her;
Where rivulets are bending through dales bedeck'd in flowers;
Where all is touched by love, and naught speaks but of loving:
In this contented place Camilla lived her life.
(*Atis och Camilla;* from "the first song")

Creutz's lasting poetic works, like Gyllenborg's, fall in the short period of the Thought Builders (1753–63). Creutz was sent to Madrid as
envoy in 1763 and continued as ambassador to France, where he became a central figure in the cultivated circles of Madame du Barry, Jean
François Marmontel, and other Enlightenment personalities. He was called
home to Sweden in 1783 to become president of the chancellery but died
shortly afterward, without having added to the remarkable legacy of his
youth.

THE GUSTAVIAN AGE

The Beginning of the Gustavian Age

Although the Age of Liberty had seemed a positive political experiment
at its inception, the problems it had engendered were evident by the
1760s. The two parties' brief periods of dominance (the Caps took over
in 1765 but lost again to the Hats in 1769, who then held power only until
1772) were characterized by violent shifts of policy and acts of retribution
against opponents. The Caps were ruling for a last brief time when Adolf
Fredrik died in 1771. From the moment Gustav III was crowned, he started
plotting to overthrow the warring parties and their constitution, which he
accomplished on 19 August 1772, to the relief of many who had tired of the
political bickering and the resulting economic instability. The new king was
well aware of the democratic progress that had been made during the Age
of Liberty, and attempted, at least in the beginning of his reign, to combine
populist Enlightenment ideas with firm central control. But he also had a
sweeping vision of Sweden as an intellectual and cultural center. It is this
vision, its surprising initial success and ultimate fall, that is meant when
one refers to the last quarter of the eighteenth century in Sweden as the
Gustavian Age. In a direct or indirect way, most of the cultural triumphs of
the Gustavian Age may be seen in terms of their relationship to the court
of Gustav III. The king played a surprisingly active role in many of these
achievements. He himself should be considered one of the central Swedish

authors of his own era, although his production was sporadic and nearly always collaborative.

Gustav III was a child of German blood: his father, Adolf Fredrik, was of the house of Holstein-Gottorp, and his mother was, as noted, the sister of Frederick the Great of Prussia. Nonetheless, Lovisa Ulrika had determined that his education should follow the leading trends of the time—meaning those of France. As a child, Gustav learned French better than Swedish, and his education was heavily weighted toward Enlightenment theory, with Voltaire (a favorite of both Dalin and Lovisa Ulrika) as the oracle. His youth cannot have been trouble-free, since the four estates attempted to steer his thought by appointing tutors acceptable to them, while the king and especially the queen, who was bitterly resentful of what she considered Sweden's underdeveloped culture, attempted to draw him to their own side. Gustav developed into an extremely complex person. Charming, theatrical, willful, effeminate, generous, tyrannical, and courageous by turns, he aspired to embody the eighteenth-century concept of the enlightened despot. Many Swedes came to worship his enlightened qualities. Others attempted to manipulate his weaknesses. Most of those in contact with him eventually felt the effects of his neurotic and despotic side.

Gustav III had been passionately interested in the theater all his life. But his first major project after his coup d'état was still a surprise to his advisers: he decided to create a national Swedish opera. Notwithstanding the apparent frivolity of the venture in such threatening times, and despite the fact that there was no functioning Swedish theater of any sort to build on, he assembled a staff of associates from the nobility, and they managed to compose and stage an opera, *Thetis och Pelée* (Thetis and Peleus), on 18 January 1773. The amazing success story of this production encouraged Gustav to venture more and more deeply into theatrical projects, scripting or outlining numerous plays and libretti, mostly on Swedish patriotic themes. Since his Swedish language was never adequate for polished poetry, he actively sought poets who were capable of filling out his scripts. His opera *Gustaf Wasa* (1786) was the most renowned of these collaborative efforts. It was enormously popular during the latter part of his reign and has been revived successfully.

The last several years of the reign of Gustav III were clouded by political misjudgments, increasing censorship, scandal in the court itself, unsuccessful economic policies, and an unpopular war. As Sweden entered the period in which other nations' Enlightenment ripened into open revolution against their monarchies, Gustav was warned about the possibility of uprising or assassination in his own country, but his attitude toward such threats was courageous—or, perhaps, simply negligent. He was shot at a masked ball at his beloved opera house on 16 March 1792, but he lived long enough to make the "event" a theatrical one as well, taking leave of his faithful followers and forgiving his adversaries from his deathbed. He ultimately made himself the central, martyred figure in a Swedish royal drama in real life. He died on 29 March 1792 of an infection from his wound.

Bellman, the Poet of Love and Wine

One poet rises above all the others of the eighteenth century in Sweden, to claim the name of real genius: Carl Michael Bellman (1740–95). But Bellman is a severely limited poet as well, and his genius by no means represents all that the latter half of the eighteenth century could offer. A word about the term *genius* itself may well be in order here. In describing certain writers such as Holberg and Strindberg as geniuses, one tends to note their apparent ease in moving from one literary form to another, as they imbue each with the stamp of an extraordinary personality. That could never be said of Bellman, whose literary range was small and whose faults, when he moved outside that narrow range, are easily observable. In describing others, one might note the universality of their creations or the "modernity" of their ideas, which open new vistas for a following generation. Neither of these attributes really clarifies Bellman's special talent. Ultimately, a workable attribute—one dare not say a definition— of literary genius is that something in the works created simply defies previous (and possibly subsequent) rules for our perception of an art form. In Bellman's case, the medium he chose was not regarded by literary authorities as an "art form" at all, before he transformed it into one that could not escape notice.

Sweden's most popular poet of all time was born in Stockholm to a rather well-to-do, middle-level bureaucrat and his wife, the daughter of a Lutheran minister. His education leading up to the university level was of good quality. His private tutor, Claes Ennes, was especially noteworthy in teaching Bellman to write poetry. Following in the footsteps of Dalin, the young Bellman produced moralizing satirical verses that matched the wit and style of the older master. Having shown no particular academic inclination during a short period at Uppsala University, the young poet was placed in a bank as supernumerary in 1759. Had he been diligent and patient, he might have matched his father's bureaucratic career. But Bellman never showed any great aptitude for either mathematics or civic work, and the company he kept led him further and further into the frivolous and debt-ridden life of the city.

He fled to Norway for a brief period—his only trip abroad—to avoid debtor's prison and was moved to another bureaucratic job on his return to Stockholm. The second position, at the Manufacturing Office, was closed in 1766, and he moved again, to the General Customs Office. He obtained the title of chancellery clerk but was let go when that office ceased to exist in 1772. During the period of this singularly undistinguished official career, Bellman emerged, in an apparently offhand way, as a most controversial and renowned poet. That in turn dictated the next series of events in his life, as his talent met with the rising star of King Gustav III.

The tradition of writing poems to popular melodies—vaudevilles, or parodies—was a very old one in Sweden. It had grown out of the bawdy Latin student songs of the Middle Ages and had continued after the Reformation in the vernacular. By the eighteenth century, it had become an indispensable component of private entertainment and was usually accompanied by serious drinking. Nicolas Boileau, the French poet, critic, and arbiter of eighteenth-century literary taste, had called the form the "Agréable Indiscret, qui conduit par le chant, / Passe de bouche en bouche, et s'accroît en marchant" ("That congenial rogue, who, accompanied by song, / passes from mouth to mouth and accumulates on the way"; from *L'Art poétique*). In Sweden such poetry was not considered part of the realm of literary endeavor, and the vaudeville or parody poet was not deemed "serious." Yet Lucidor, Runius, Werwing, Dalin, and Norden-flycht had all written such parodies, and Bellman, who would become the acknowledged master of the form, found in them his special quality. Unlike Dalin and Nordenflycht, Bellman also appears to have been a consummate entertainer. He apparently sang in a high baritone or tenor voice that was not of great carrying power but was supple, and he had a natural talent for imitative sounds. He accompanied himself on the lutelike *cister* and used his hands to produce other sounds as well. Given his abilities, Bellman found himself a welcome guest in the homes of the bourgeois and nobility. As his bureaucratic career headed toward its inevitable dead end, as the declining days of the Age of Liberty lurched from one economic disaster to another, his drinking songs increased by leaps and bounds in depth and complexity.

Many of his earliest songs from the mid-1760s later found their way into his collection called *Fredmans sånger* (1791; The songs of Fredman; a selection in English is translated by Paul Britten Austin in *Fredman's Epistles and Songs*). His biblical parodies, "Gubben Noach" (Old man Noah), "En Potifars hustru" (A Potiphar's wife), "Joachim uti Babylon" (Joachim in Babylon), and many others, have kept their place in the repertoire of modern-day Swedish troubadours.

A Potiphar's wife with beautiful ways
   Joseph to love is seducing,
Clutches his mantle and sighs, and says:
   Sit down, sit down.
Now under the bedclothes the prettiest rose
   Was there for our Joseph's taking,
But like a scoundrel away he goes,
   They say, they say.
Ah, had I been in Joseph's place,
Ah, had I been in Joseph's place
   I know what I'd have done!
(Fredmans sång 38)

The gentle spoofing of biblical figures implies no heretical thought by today's standards, but it caused a vehement reaction from the clergy of his time. In 1773, he was instructed by the Stockholm consistory to "use his cleverness on such works which were useful and civil, without coming into conflict with religion." But since the bourgeois circles in which Bellman moved were not particularly sympathetic to the clergy, the censure seems to have had little or no dampening effect on his popularity or production.

In 1767, a watchmaker from Stockholm named Jean Fredman died. The fact that Fredman's marital problems and drinking had precipitated his fall from the status of propertied alderman to abject poverty in the gutter offered Bellman an opportunity. The poet had been searching for a "mythical" figure who could be used as an alter ego and a central personage in a group of mock-biblical characters, and "Saint" Fredman (whose name was similar enough to that of the poet to draw attention to it) appeared to fit perfectly. *Fredmans epistlar* (1790; The epistles of Fredman) is in concept a fictional set of letters written by the "Saint" to his faithful group of followers. Around this "apostle of Bacchus" Bellman created other semifictional types: the prostitute Ulla Winblad (Maria Christina Kiellström in real life), the tavern musician Father Berg, the wigmaker and artillery constable-turned-musician Mowitz, Corporal Mollberg, and many others. The gallery of drunks and prostitutes is cheerfully admonished in the early poems to follow the teachings of the gods of wine and of love, forming a parallel, of course, to the performance situation of Bellman himself and his bourgeois audience. The distancing effect of the poetic ploy made it possible for Bellman to depict drastic and comic effects without directly implicating either himself or members of his audience.

Each of Fredman's "epistles" reflects a scene or an anecdotal experience by the troupe of faithful drinkers and lovemakers. The early ones had held on to the fiction of a leader (Fredman) who addressed himself to some bacchanalian situation, often making direct references to a kind of "teaching": "Tipple, drink, / and have one's wench / Is what St. Fredman teaches." But Bellman soon abandoned all pretense of preaching an alternative gospel and turned his attention instead to the interactions of his cast of characters. Catching them in the act of making love (even allowing Fredman to participate in it himself, accompanied solemnly by Father Berg and his cello), dancing or brawling in a local tavern, or parading about on the streets of Stockholm, Bellman began to amass a comprehensive picture of lower-class life in the city he loved.

His eye for detail is so sharp that he has been lauded as the first Swedish realist. On the other hand, it is clear that his particular brand of "realism" carries with it a heaping measure of pure fantasy, grotesque humor, and—not least—an elegant veneer of classical mythology. Bellman knew the tools of the literary trade and used his rhetoric and his classical Roman traditions to provide a theatrical backdrop for his tavern folk.

> Jupiter himself rocks
> 'Mid Gods and Kings
> On the peaks of the waves.
> Horses lift their tails;
> Neptune himself dances—
> With his trident on the Ocean

is part of the surprising depiction of a load of drunken sots in a boat, as the prostitute Ulla makes her way back to the town from the Deer Park. All this astonishing mixture of realism and wild mythological fantasy is set to complex musical patterns: marches and contradances, operatic ariettes, and graceful minuets. The result is related to the lowly drinking song only by derivation. As an artistic achievement it stands alone in the history of Swedish poetry.

> The brethren lose their way at times
> 'Mongst glasses, but never 'mongst taverns;
> All of them make it to wine-grapes' land.
> Drink, brethren, drink just a bit.
> Hear how they totter and scrape in the sand,
> Fumble at door latches, bang with their fists,
> Stagger and stumble with tankard in hand,
> Bleeding from biting their tongues.
> Father Movitz, top off my glass!
> My lass has forgotten me, I'll die faithful.

Night and day in a drunken daze
   My sorrow shall all fade away. . . .
   (Fredmans epistel 35)

Bellman had already written hundreds of poems in the bacchanalian genre and more than half the collection of Fredman's epistles when his song "Gustavs skål" (Gustav's skoal) stirred the king and his soldiers. It precipitated a brief turning point in Bellman's private life as well, for the king was convinced that the song had contributed to the solidification of support behind him on the day of his coup d'état. Gustav III gave Bellman the title of court secretary, allotted him a pension from royal private funds, and arranged for a sinecure for him in the lottery, in such a way that he could draw a reasonable salary without having to use his feeble bureaucratic talents, or indeed without having to show up to work on a regular basis. Bellman was instead invited to the palace on certain Wednesdays to amuse the king.

It has often been said that Bellman's good luck ran out when he was attacked by the critic Johan Henrik Kellgren (below) in 1778. The crux of the matter is that Bellman had already reached an impasse on his own. He had been unable to get his epistles into print. His economic situation had improved, but he was by no means well off. Although his entertainments at the palace brought him into direct contact with the king and the high nobility, that in itself did nothing to bring him the respect he deserved. When Bellman was encouraged to write longer theatrical pieces as part of Gustav's grand plan for the sublimation of Swedish language and culture, he found it a task that lay outside the range of his particular talent.

Bellman tried his hand at a number of dramatic pieces, some of which contributed to the entertainments of the inner circle of Gustav III but none of which became a public success. A mixed form involving a fictitious bacchanalian lodge, the so-called *Bacchi Orden* (Order of Bacchus) poems, begun as solo performance pieces for his friends during the 1760s, was also expanded dramatically. The largest of them, *Bacchi Tempel* (Bacchi temple), was published in book form in 1783. But the appeal of these longer pieces was largely limited to an "in group" of Stockholm's bourgeoisie who enjoyed the parody on the various "orders" of the day, such as the Freemasons. Readers from later generations tend to wonder why Bellman expended so much energy on a form that had so little real literary potential. The same could be said for Bellman's occasional poetry, much of which was composed to alleviate his sorely pressed financial situation.

Nevertheless, Bellman had not dried up as a poet of power. On the contrary, though his production of "epistles" and "songs" was greatly reduced during the late 1770s and early 1780s, those poems that were newly composed exhibited additional dimensions. When Olof Åhlström, owner of the Royal Music Publishing Company, introduced a relatively cheap method of printing music at the end of the 1780s, an edition of Bellman's poetry was immediately brought up for discussion, and hindrances to the project were quickly cleared away. The king's permission for printing was granted, Kellgren was contacted and promised to write an introduction to the book, and Bellman hurried to produce a few new poems to round out the collection of *Fredmans epistlar*, which had once been projected at one hundred but ultimately numbered eighty-two.

Fredmans epistlar, with Kellgren's subsequently famous legitimizing introduction and Åhlström's piano arrangements of the melodies, finally appeared in 1790. It is arguably the most important songbook in Swedish literary history and probably Sweden's most popular single collection of poems in general. It is rivaled only by its successor, *Fredmans sånger* (1791). Where *Fredmans epistlar* comprises a fairly coherent cycle of poems, all generally dealing with the vagaries of its long cast of characters from the lower levels of Stockholm's society, *Fredmans sånger* is a much more heterogeneous collection. Its name actually has little meaning, since Fredman does not have much to do with it and the songs include biblical parodies, drinking songs, a patriotic poem or two, and the lyrical ariettes that are characteristic of Bellman's final period:

> Step forth, thou god of night, the sun's flames now to soften,
> Bid a star upon your cloud the evening glow to rival,
>   And to cool the tepid wave.
> Draw a curtain o'er the eye, assuage our anguish and pain,
>   And the surging of our blood.
> *(Fredmans sång 32)*

Bellman realized little profit from the venture, although the Swedish Academy awarded him its Lundblad Prize and he was made a member of the Swedish Musical Academy (not of the literary one). He lived a few more years, increasingly pressed by financial worries and sickness. Imprisoned for a debt in 1794, he wrote there a fragmentary but charming autobiography. He regained his freedom after two and a half months, but his health was broken, and he died early in 1795. Stories about Bellman quickly became legends, but the "orphic" or "folk poet" epithets one often sees in connection with his name began to be circulated only during the romantic era. Because of the enormous difficulty in translating his complex rhythmic patterns and many-layered comic structures, Bellman has been slow to become known in countries outside Scandinavia. Selections of his poetry have finally been translated into English, French, German, Russian, Hungarian, and Italian. The interested reader, however, will inevitably be drawn back to the Swedish original to savor Bellman's inimitable style.

The Court Poets

The progressive development of the Enlightenment brought a gradual decentralization of literary endeavor, as growing attention was paid by the writers to new, bourgeois audiences as a source of income and to journals as a source of communication. In Sweden this trend was arrested in part by the special personality and enthusiasm of Gustav himself and, not least, by his sensitivity to and encouragement of young poets. The bourgeois media developed strongly during the 1770s and 1780s, but their domination of the literary scene became evident only during the last decade of the century. For the period that lasted until the end of Gustav's life, it is convenient to divide the poets and dramatists into two traditional groups: that of the "insiders" at court and that of the "outsiders," or potentially rebellious spirits whose ideas were (or were conceived of) as being in conflict with royal intentions. This division is naturally an oversimplification: the greatest poet of the age, Bellman, could be perceived sometimes as an insider enjoying royal support, sometimes as an outsider struggling on his own. But that does not in itself obviate the need for making this literary distinction between poetic careers when dealing with other writers of the time.

Johan Gabriel Oxenstierna (1750–1818) bore the family name of the great state chancellor of Gustav II Adolf and was a highly privileged, albeit destitute, son of the nobility. He was given a classical education worthy of his social station and had as his tutors both a respected critic (Olof Bergklint) and an important poet (his uncle, G. F. Gyllenborg). He spent a great deal of time at his family estate, Skenäs, in Södermanland, and although he showed little talent or inclination for a diplomatic career or any sort of political work, he was eventually made president of the chancellery, because Gustav III wanted to show that he, like Gustav II Adolph of Sweden's century as a great power, was accompanied in his triumphs by an Oxenstierna as his chancellor!

Oxenstierna produced several "thought poems," among which "Natten" (1769; Night) and "Morgonen" (1771; Morning) are undoubtedly the best. They are inspired by Creutz and by a brief love affair Oxenstierna had experienced at Skenäs. To these two poems he eventually added a weaker "Afternoon" and "Evening" by 1785, which were published in 1806. A longer cycle, *Skördarne* (The harvests), was begun in 1772 and was finally published in 1796. The cycle was highly regarded during the poet's own lifetime. Modern opinion, by contrast, is sharply divided. "No Swedish poet has handled alexandrines as naturally and supplely as Oxenstierna" (Sverker Ek, in *Illustrerad svensk litteraturhistoria*); although the "anemic erotic intrigue" (Sverker Göransson, in *Den svenska litteraturen*) of *Skördarne* recalls his youthful encounter with "Themire" of his diaries, it lacks both the charm and the intensity of the latter. The combination of Virgilian classicism and Linnean botanical interest appeared excessively conservative to the progressive literati of 1796. The critics seemed to have overlooked what was indeed novel about *Skördarne* and *Dagens stunder* (1785; The hours of the day), namely, a nature sensibility that, as the next chapter shows, could be labeled "preromantic."

It is perhaps Oxenstierna's diaries that most engage the interest of a modern reader. His French-language diary from 1766 to 1768, published in Swedish translation by Estrabaut, and the "Diary Notes, 1769–71," published by Stiernstedt, give a clear picture of the last years of the Age of Liberty, including a view of Stockholm with the fresh eyes of the young noble just arrived from his country estate. He provides a rare description of Bellman, whom he heard on 4 December 1769, in an oft-quoted passage: "His gestures, his voice, his playing, which are inimitable, lend added delight to the verses. Always beautiful, they contain thoughts sometimes ridiculous, sometimes sublime, but always strong, always unexpected, and at which no one can help his astonishment, being out of himself with amazement." But also in his less eventful discoveries, his amorous dalliance at his beloved estate, or his fretting over the drawbacks of city life, Oxenstierna provides us with a critical view of that one part of Sweden that Linné never covered—the urban part.

Oxenstierna's last poem of merit, "Disa," from 1795, is concerned with a legendary figure from Uppland and to some extent appears to anticipate the "Gothicists" of the Romantic Age. But his treatment is flippant, like that of French fable or *conte*, and his interest could be said to lie in the same vein as that of Dalin's pseudoballads. The amiable and mild-mannered Oxenstierna lived on well into a new age but remained a Gustavian, an erudite, correct, elegant gentleman who knew how to amuse and draw admiration from his equally erudite and elegant surroundings. As the Gustavians gradually disappeared, so did Oxenstierna's poetic reputation.

Johan Henrik Kellgren (1751–95) is, by way of contrast, a key figure of the

Gustavian Age. Indeed, he could be said to have risen and fallen with the age itself. His powerful critical position carries with it both the consolidation of later Enlightenment principles and the establishment of the Stockholm court as a center reflecting those principles. It would not be too much to say that Kellgren was the finest Swedish literary thinker of the period. He had considerable power as a poet as well, but not all his work is immediately accessible to the modern-day reader. He at times poses as an egocentric, erotomanic, sarcastic snob. At other times he becomes a sensitive, death-marked epicurean whose musings about the lies and fantasies of humankind have a compelling desperation. Seen from the point of view of his own time, his straightforward, undisguised thoughts rise above posing and rhetoric to heights of expression unique for his age. From the point of view of our time, the classical and topical references form a stumbling block that may cause the reader some difficulty before he or she comes to grips with the qualities that were so highly regarded by Kellgren's contemporaries.

Born the son of a rural clergyman in Västergötland, Kellgren had had an outbreak of tubercular fever before he traveled to the Swedish-Finnish University of Åbo for his education. He stayed in Åbo for eight years and, freeing himself from the shackles of the orthodox Lutheranism of his home, attained the title of lecturer in poetry and classical literature, thus thwarting his family's hopes that he become a minister. In early poems he shows the influence of Voltaire, who remained one of his intellectual ideals for the rest of his life. Some of the translations and poetic essays he produced were printed in the journal *Åbo Tidningar* (Åbo times), via the literary club Aurora. After attempting an ode to Gustav III in 1774, Kellgren turned away from the conservative meter of the Pindaric ode and cultivated a preference for a nonstrophic iambic tetrameter, which would soon become his stylistic trademark. He allowed this "lower" style to rise to heights of eloquence and thus undermine to some extent those stylistic boundaries between "high" and "low" poetry that were still being rigorously observed.

With his sights on Sweden's culturally developing royal court, Kellgren took up residence in Stockholm in 1777 as a tutor with the family of General Meijerfelt. His poetic attempt to be admitted to Queen Lovisa Ulrika's Academy of Letters, *En stadig man* (A steady man), was rejected for its radical (anticlerical) ideas. It was followed by Kellgren's first critical work, some harshly styled articles in the newspaper *Dagligt Allehanda*, which led to an indictment. Without retreating an inch, Kellgren continued with the poems "Sinnenas förening" (The unity of the senses) and "Mina löjen" (My ridicules) in 1778.

Among the trash with which my mind
Was filled in all my younger days
Is a thing I read, I don't know where,
That when you've lost one of your senses
An even greater strength you'll find
In those that you have left to use.

"Sinnenas förening" starts in this startlingly nonchalant way but presently develops into a "sensual union" that is so sexually explicit, given the standards of the times, that Kellgren himself later hesitated to include it in his *Collected Works*. "Mina löjen" is his critical attack on all the aristocratic, clerical, and poetical follies of the time; neither Nordenflycht nor Bellman escaped Kellgren's arrogant censure. Nordenflycht is a Swedish Sappho, only "a thousand times more ugly and more lovesick," and Bellman has "veins he's filled with double beer; / His muses kept at Spinning Houses [i.e., reform houses for prostitutes], / His Graces all have had the cure." Unfortunately, the poem is destructive as literary criticism—and if it is supposed to be a moral judgment, it is certainly a stone thrown by a dweller in a glass house. He ends the poem with the self-ironic lines: "And when I laugh out loud at others, / I laugh in silence at myself." But we are not apt to believe him.

By this time, Kellgren had nonetheless caught the attention of Gustav III, who found this new and radical voice potentially useful to his own plans. Kellgren's success with a little theatrical piece in honor of the queen's pregnancy brought him in direct contact with the king, who immediately set him to work in his theatrical productions, with a yearly salary. Kellgren also contributed to the newspaper *Stockholms Posten* from its inception in 1778. When the editorial policy of this leading newspaper displeased him, he managed to take over the editorship himself, together with his friend C. P. Lenngren. His critical work for the paper divides itself into several intensive periods, interspersed with silences marking those times when his attention was directed elsewhere. Kellgren was also made artistic director of the important literary society Utile Dulci (For utility and pleasure), with the responsibility of editing its upcoming volume of *Vitterhetsnöjen* (1781; Literary entertainments). Indeed, he had managed to place himself quickly at the very center of the Gustavian literary scene. Although his situation was financially precarious, he left the comfortable home of the Meijerfelts in the summer of 1780 to begin work as a free-lance writer. The best-known of his poems from this period is "Våra villor" (Our illusions), which calls to mind the thought poems of Gyllenborg, whom Kellgren admired. The difference between the two poets is striking, however. Gyllenborg's central thought in a poem such as "Människans elände" is simple and immediately understood. We may enjoy the older poet's consistent flow of images or we may be bored by them, but we are not likely to be surprised. Kellgren's thought in "Våra villor" is complex, and its poetic flow is quicker and more animated:

> And Love, of all the gifts of life
> The sweetest and the greatest;
> What would you be, if our desire
> Would look no further than the truth?
> A rutting, spread throughout the blood,
> A lust, awakened but by need,
> That died as soon as 'twas enjoyed.

This is part of Kellgren's *defense* of illusion, but it is clearly a fragile one, an eighteenth-century argument in favor of that "life lie" that supports our ideals, or our useful fantasies.

Kellgren's principal triumph at the Gustavian court was his collaboration with Gustav III on the opera *Gustaf Wasa*. The king had sketched out a lyrical drama in 1777–78 on the theme of Sweden's victory over "Christjern the Tyrant" (Christian II of Denmark). His French-language draft, influenced by Alexis Piron and Shakespeare (*Richard III*), was unquestionably vitalized by Kellgren's nuanced, clear Swedish, and in the moving choruses the poet managed to give the patriotic Swedish opera its most stirring expression at the same time that he cleverly bound it up with his own Enlightenment ideals of individual freedom.

Greatly inspired by the collaboration, Gustav III went on to write five more historical dramas while he and Kellgren waited for the composer, J. G. Naumann, to complete the score for *Gustaf Wasa*. The king would have had Kellgren turn all his prose dramas into poetry, and Kellgren tackled the problem at first with optimism, then gradually with increasing irritation and frustration. Returning to his work as a poet and journalist for *Stockholms Posten*, he also became embroiled in 1783 in a satirical polemic with the young poet Thomas Thorild. The bitterness of the attack from Thorild's side caused Kellgren to lay his pen aside for the better part of two years, or until the premiere of *Gustaf Wasa* on 19 January 1786. The overwhelming success of this most spectacular of all the Gustavian operas restored Kellgren's creative energies—but not with respect to collaborative libretti. After the completion of the libretto for *Gustaf Adolf och Ebba Brahe* (1786–87), Kellgren refused to continue with theatrical work.

The generosity of Gustav III toward his reluctant collaborator is indicative of the king's understanding for poets in general. He appointed Kellgren to his newly formed Swedish Academy in 1786 and maintained the poet's generous salary as dramatist even when Kellgren not only stopped working on the dramas but distanced himself from the court and the king's politics. Kellgren had meanwhile allied himself with the secretary of the Swedish Academy, Nils von Rosenstein, in an attempt to preserve the principles of the Enlightenment against what they saw as a backlash of superstition, alchemy, and Swedenborgianism that was condoned even to some degree by Gustav himself and his brother, Karl. Regarding other elements of these waning years of the Gustavian era—especially Gustav's foolish war with Russia in 1788–89 and the revolution in France in 1789—the king and Kellgren also found themselves on opposite sides of the fence. Gustav III had had contact with the king of France and had loose and dangerous plans to employ Swedish troops to protect Louis XVI and Marie Antoinette. Kellgren saw the outbreak of the French Revolution as an expression of that freedom of the people that he had always hailed. And in his "Cantat d. 1 jan. 1789" (Cantata on 1 Jan. 1789), Kellgren depicted his country's fate without mention of the king, a unique and daring omission in Gustavian literature.

During the last period of Kellgren's short life, a new lyricism suddenly appeared in his poetry, and an increasingly nuanced attitude toward other poets colored his journalism. The source of this lyricism and positive spirit has been much discussed; a brief love affair has been surmised, but the lady has never been definitively identified. Whatever the impulse for "Den nya Skapelsen" (1789; The new creation), which bears the subtitle, "The World of the Imagination," it marks a high point in Kellgren's oeuvre:

> You, who of beauty and of charm
> Project a pure and primal image!
> I saw you—and from that day forth,
> See naught but you in all the world.

The refrain strophe of the rondeau, the form that is the underlying structure of "Den nya Skapelsen," has become an often-quoted verse in Swedish poetry. The poem itself, with its rapturous discovery of the lover's image in all of nature, its Neoplatonic renouncement of temporal things and longing for a higher world, its animistic view of the world, and its intimation of a higher, idealistic world ("a godly race," "the harmony of the spheres," etc.), has justly been called preromantic. But Kellgren, as scholars have noticed, is not devoting himself uncritically to the rapture that would guide the later romantic poets. The "heavenly primal image" is, after all, a figment of the poet's imagination, as the subtitle suggests; so the message of the poem need not be regarded as diametrically opposed to that of the earlier "Våra villor."

"Dumboms lefverne" (1791; The life and times of Dumbo) is another complex thought poem. Encased in a shell of apparent stupidity, as the title indicates, it changes into an offbeat look at the Enlightenment principles of moderation, reason, and the rejection of theological excess. The poet concludes with the Delphic *gnothi seauton* ("know thyself"), which hardly sounds like the motto of a Dumbo.

Of Kellgren's later prose, the most famous piece is his introduction to the edition of Bellman's *Fredmans epistlar* (1790). The two poets had finally been reconciled, and Kellgren, who doubtless regretted his scathing attack on the gentle bacchanalian poet, agreed to help with a judicious selection of "epistles" and to show them to be the work of genius. The introduction, which indeed helped establish Bellman among the upper echelons of society as a poet of real worth, is nonetheless not a complete reversal of the critic's earlier points of view, although the perspective is enormously widened and the tone warmhearted. Bellman, according to Kellgren, is still not "the Swedish Anacreon." Kellgren plays with the idea of making him the "Swedish Pindar" and finally settles on a truism that is also a late-eighteenth-century acknowledgment of the individuality of genius: Anacreon is Anacreon, and Bellman is simply Bellman.

Meanwhile, his own creativity had reached a peak. Freed from the drudgery of libretto work but intuitively aware that his days were num- bered, Kellgren threw himself once more into his journalistic work at *Stockholms Posten*, which he and Lenngren now owned. His critical work of this final period is much more balanced and informative, and his chron- icles of Stockholm's theatrical activity for the years 1790 and 1791 are comprehensive and well worth studying. By December 1791, however, his tubercular condition had advanced to a life-threatening stage. His last important satirical poem, "Ljusets fiender" (The enemies of light), in the best Enlightenment tradition, was completed in 1792. He was preparing the edition of his collected works when he was silenced in 1795.

Kellgren is not as easy for an English-speaking audience to assimilate as Bellman. His best work is much more diverse in character, not confined to a single genre. Many of his references are topical and therefore obscure to today's reader. For this reason, the attention that has been paid him by Swedish literary historians may at first be hard to understand. The quickest way to gain access to Kellgren is through his "provocative" poetry—

"Sinnenas förening" or "Dumboms lefverne"—followed by his sensuous, lyrical "Den nya Skapelsen." But to understand his powerful position in Swedish letters from 1778 to 1792, one has to leave the anthologies behind and look into his work in *Stockholms Posten*, where his defense of Enlightenment principles was consistently and eloquently propounded.

Carl Gustaf Leopold (1756–1829) was the youngest of the poets connected with the Gustavian court. He came to the court rather late, in 1786, after having finished his academic studies in Greifswald four years earlier and having worked for a time as a librarian. His early attempts at writing odes in the higher style, of which the best known was written to celebrate the birth of the crown prince in 1778, brought him into Kellgren's critical line of fire, and the two were not on friendly terms for some time. But Leopold learned from his mistakes and showed considerable improvement with his *Erotiska oder* (Erotic odes) in 1785, the same year that he also emerged as a critic with his study of an epos by Gyllenborg. When called to the court to serve as playwright-adapter, he responded enthusiastically and soon had replaced Kellgren as Gustav III's principal librettist. At the same time, he filled the ancient function of official flatterer to the king, a position he occasionally found onerous but never relinquished. The king rewarded him richly, doubtless beyond his minor talent, for his faithfulness. Leopold moved into the Royal Palace, became a founding member of the Swedish Academy (1786), and was given the title of royal private secretary (1788). Eventually, he would become a member of the chancellery (1799) and be ennobled as "af Leopold" (1809).

More than the flexible and perceptive Kellgren, Leopold represented in his criticism a central Enlightenment view that closely corresponded to the opinions of Gustav III. His literary reviews, designed to preserve "good taste," may seem antiquated to a modern audience and were undoubtedly antithetical even to the younger writers of his time. His polemic in 1792 against Thomas Thorild, *Bref till den store och märkvärdige författaren Th——* (Letter to the great and remarkable writer Th——), served to protect the "national" literary interests against their most radical opponent. Leopold took over Kellgren's critical torch and held it, in his adept but conservative way, during the latter's last illness.

After the death of Gustav III and the collapse of the "Royal Parnassus," Leopold spent the years 1792–95 working for the paper *Extra Posten*. He opposed the liberal tendencies of the late nineties and the new developments in literature (Kantian philosophy and traits of what later historians would call preromanticism). Using his considerable skill as an essayist, he valiantly tried to hold back the dawn of romantic literature in the post-

Gustavian period. Generally hated by the romantics during their early development, he was ultimately accepted near the end of his life as a kind of Gustavian relic. Certain of his nonliterary activities benefited Swedish literature in an oblique way: he contributed to the law ensuring freedom of the press in 1809 and wrote *Afhandling om Svenska Stafsättet* (Treatise on Swedish spelling) in 1801. Among the younger generation, it was Esaias Tegnér who felt the most kinship with Leopold and praised him in the name of truth, by which he meant clearly defined rhetorical principles. But that great romantic poet was also aware of the older writer's severe limitations, and Tegnér's final dictum about Leopold, that he was "perhaps not foremost as a poet, but foremost as a genius," is ambiguous to the point of incomprehensibility.

Leopold's best-known poem, *Predikaren* (1794; The sermonizer), gives a sensible but certainly also a sobering picture of the requirements of the Gustavian courtier:

> Distinguish shell from kernel, the magnate from his medals;
> The two are often proved quite incompatible.
> Let never biased power, nor fool's coercion
> Find favor from your mouth, that should praise only virtue.
> Yet for the sake of order, to which all must defer,
> Bow before the high-born fool
> But deeply, son, so deeply that he can't see you smile.

Perhaps if Leopold had used even more the cynicism that informs *Predikaren*, he might have struck a richer vein of poetry. His works for the most part do not observe his cynical situation; they remain guarded products of it. As latter-day readers we share the difficulty of his noble superiors of detecting his smile.

The Role of the Parodists

Outside the court circle during the waning Age of Liberty and never a part of the Gustavian Parnassus, yet not in direct conflict with it either, lay the work of the Enlightenment parodists. Jacob Wallenberg (1746–78) is an early member of this group. He came from Östergötland and was taken in hand by the Latinist Samuel Älf, who led him through his secondary studies. Then he spent some time at Uppsala but left after two terms to become a tutor. The impoverished but witty young teacher was later employed by the Holterman family in Göteborg. Martin Holterman was one of the directors of the East India Company, and Wallenberg managed to obtain the post of ship's chaplain at age twenty-three, although he had not been ordained. The ship he sailed on, the *Finland*, was one of the finest in the East India Company's line, and Wallenberg's single renowned work is a description of the voyage of that vessel from 1769 to 1771: *Min son på galejan* (1781; My son on the galley). This masterpiece, often reprinted, is considered by some the only literary prose piece from the Swedish eighteenth century that is still a living work. On further journeys to the Far East, Wallenberg wrote a verse drama on the biblical story of Susanna. He was appointed to the pastorate of Mönsterås in Småland in 1777 but died of an illness in 1778, before his talents had been fully developed or tested.

"Every one has his style, and I follow mine," Wallenberg wrote to his old Latin teacher. Wallenberg's own idiom was a curious mixture of satire in the style of Dalin's *Then Swänska Argus*, Runius's drinking songs, Paul Scarron's *Roman comique*, and (some have suggested) Laurence Sterne's *Tristram Shandy*. But there is one overriding parodic element in the production of Wallenberg's rollicking travel book: it clearly mocks the Linneans. When Linné elevated himself to the rank of the world's prime botanist, he launched a project to classify and describe the natural elements not only of Sweden but of the entire world. For this purpose, he assembled a troupe of young scholars and encouraged, even cajoled, them into undertaking perilous journeys to the ends of the earth. His own travel books were to serve as a model, and the students were to spread the teachings of Linné as well as to assemble new materials that could be used to justify the Linnean system. Since Linné's scientific travel books also contained poetic observations, exaggerations, and loosely connected anecdotes, they lent themselves to parody, as Wallenberg was quick to discover. At times Wallenberg therefore becomes a quasi-Linnean, as in his scientific observations of prostitutes or flying fish. At times he simply shrugs off the Linnean mantle and tells the reader that he is not interested. On other occasions he takes on Linné's polar opposite—Swedenborg.

Stenborg's Theater, (1773–1799)

The Swenska Comedien, led by Petter Stenborg, had never managed to reestablish itself after it was dissolved in 1754, but Stenborg, working under economically distressing conditions, had moved about the country with a small traveling troupe. Finally, in 1773, his players were granted the use of a little pavilion in Humlegården (behind the present Royal Library, where the statue of Linné now stands) for summer productions. The new theater caught on and soon provided a venue for the works of two satirical dramatists, Olof Kexél (1748–96) and Carl Israel Hallman (1732–1800).

Kexél was a friend of Bellman's who had had some difficulties with the Hat party, and with his creditors as well. The latter conflict gave rise to *Mina Tidsfördrif på Gäldstugan* (1776–77; My pastimes in debtor's prison). But his farcical plays helped bring the Stenborg repertoire up-to-date, and his realistic character portrayal in *Capten Puff* (1789; Captain Puff) provided Lars Hjortsberg, a leading comic actor of the day, with one of his most successful roles.

Hallman, a minor bureaucratic functionary and also a friend of Bellman's, seized the opportunity to write opera parodies for the rejuvenated Stenborg theater: *Casper och Dorothea* (1775; Casper and Dorothea) made fun of the Royal Opera's production of *Acis och Galathea*, and *Petis och Telée* (1779; Petis and Teleus) parodied the triumphant opening of the Gustavian opera *Thetis och Pelée*. Hallman's burlesque style won its greatest triumph in a little vaudeville play, *Tillfälle gjör tiufven* (1783; Opportunity makes the thief), which has been revived down to the present day. It was the first real vaudeville (musical comedy using borrowed song melodies and excluding spoken dialogue) in Sweden. The period of greatest success for the Stenborg theater came after the transfer of its leadership from Petter Stenborg to his son Carl in 1781.

The talents of Carl Stenborg far overshadowed those of his father. He was a leading singer and actor at the Royal Opera. He composed music and had a refined sense of the theater. He enjoyed the support of Gustav III and was apparently a good leader and businessman for his troupe. He brought his theater over to Munkbron in the Old Town of Stockholm in 1784, where a loge was built for the king. The prolific translator and dramatist Carl Magnus Envallsson (1756–1806) provided French lyrical comedies (musical comedies with original or parody song melodies) with a Swedish flavor and added a sure touch of robust, rural coloring without falling to the rougher level of the Kexél and Hallman satires. His best-known musical play, *Slåtterölet eller kronofogdarne* (1787; The harvest feast, or The bailiffs), far exceeded in number of performances any of the Royal Opera's, even the enormously successful *Gustaf Wasa*. Well into the nineteenth century, it remained on the boards as the most-played Swedish comedy, until it was eventually surpassed by F. A. Dahlgren's *Wermlänningarne* (1846; The people of Värmland). All in all, Envallsson provided Stenborg with about eighty plays and libretti, and this productivity undoubtedly helped keep Stenborg's theater alive. It lost its favored status at the death of Gustav III in 1792, and it was regarded by Gustav IV Adolf as an unnecessary rival to the Royal Theater. When the doors of the Stenborg theater were shut in 1799, a most promising chapter in Swedish theater history had come to a close.

Outside the Court Circle

The work of Anna Maria Lenngren (1754–1817) lies close to that of the bourgeois satirists: Dalin, Bellman, Kexél, Hallman. She showed no evidence of wanting to be drawn into the magic circle of the royal court but preferred to maintain a critical distance to the establishment and to contemporary society from the vantage point of a comfortably bourgeois position. Her principal chosen medium became the newspaper *Stockholms Posten*. Unlike Hedvig Charlotta Nordenflycht, Lenngren showed little need of proving herself as a poetic representative of her sex. Rather than contribute thought poems and odes to the critical scrutiny of the male-oriented poetic establishment, she began with small satirical pieces and remained with this format all her life, only deepening and broadening her humor as she matured. Hers was a different temperament from Nordenflycht's. She was happily married and apparently convinced of the superiority of the married woman's status and of the dangers of being "free." She maintained her household with equanimity and wrote only when she wanted to. Yet she was no dilettante. There is a freshness in her style and an acumen that is immediately apparent to the reader. One finds in her writings a sharp wit and a good perception of psychology and manners. She is apt to give the impression that personal inner problems do not exist or are not relevant to her craft. She is a *professional* poet, in the sense that her private life is kept private. But the fictional privacies of the objects of her satires are treated with gusto.

Born Anna Maria Malmstedt in 1754 to a lecturer in Latin at Uppsala University, she grew up in an educated but impoverished home. Her father lost his place at the university for his Moravian views. More receptive to her father's Latin authors than to his sectarian religion, the young poet freed herself from Moravianism and began writing satires—notably *Theconseillen* (The tea party)—as a teenager. In a more intimate way than either Bellman or Dalin had been able to do, she exposed the foibles and prejudices of her own sex. In one especially noteworthy strophe of this slightly awkward but entertaining poem, an elderly matron speaks of the education "nowadays" of a young girl, with novels, French lessons, and encouragement to be creative:

> Then she gets a taste for literature,
> And off she goes to make her rhymes;
> It makes its mark upon the roast—
> The gravy is as tough as glue;
> I realize, you can boast of them,

But put your verses in a pot,
And see if the soup gets richer!

Though the poem on the whole makes it clear that it is the old matron who is mocked rather than the young girl, the problem of the pen versus the soup pot would never be entirely resolved in the poet's own life.

Turning to the theater, she quickly showed her talent at translating French operas into Swedish: *Lucile* (1776), *Zémire och Azor* (1778; Zémire and Azor), and *Arsène* (1779). These light, sentimental works were a welcome addition to the repertoire and established her as a dramaturge of value. At the same time, however, she began working at *Stockholms Posten*, and in 1780 she married Kellgren's friend and coeditor, Carl Petter Lenngren. Her literary stance from this time could be characterized as demure. It is doubtful that she was plagued by a lack of self-confidence regarding her talents as a serious writer, but she preferred the anonymity of *Stockholms Posten*, where she could develop her own style of ironic poetry and prose without being drawn into literary conflict. Another possibility that cannot entirely be discounted, although it may be a pose, is that she actually may have believed that an honorable married woman's duties were incompatible with the freer life of a poet.

Since Kellgren, C. P. Lenngren, and A. M. Lenngren clearly had a close working relationship during the 1780s, it may ultimately be impossible to determine definitively who wrote all the anonymous pieces in *Stockholms Posten*. The idea that A. M. Lenngren should have completely abandoned all literary work, devoting herself solely to her new household between 1780 and 1790, has been clearly refuted by several scholars, beginning with Warburg. Although she contributed numerous works to *Stockholms Posten*, however, she tried to maintain the outward appearance of the proper, nonliterary wife.

After *Stockholms Posten* was taken over economically by Kellgren and C. P. Lenngren in 1790, the acknowledged work of A. M. Lenngren became more evident. It also matured rapidly, possibly because of her closer contact with Kellgren and a deeper understanding of Bellman (*Fredmans epistlar*, with its music arranged by C. P. Lenngren's brother-in-law, Olof Åhlström, had appeared that same year). Kellgren's ill health also apparently provided A. M. Lenngren with an excuse to take over his satirical pen. But rather than direct her attention to generalized foibles or philosophical criticism in his style, she contributed a poetic gallery of satirical portraits, which to a much greater degree than Bellman's might be called Hogarthian. In quick succession were composed "Biographie," about a middle-aged failure; "Min salig man" (My dear departed), about a drunk; "Porträtterna" (The portraits), about an old countess and her maid; and "Rosalie," about a young lady who learned to lose her morals. These along with other delicious satires won her immediate public acclaim and have remained accessible to reading audiences ever since. A. M. Lenngren also became one of the foremost representatives of a new popular genre, the salon song. This lighter relative of the *romans* or lied began to replace the previous generation's parody song, and Stockholm's best composers—Åhlström, Johan Fredrik Palm, and others—vied to set her popular texts to music.

The winter of 1797–98 was one in which A. M. Lenngren seemed to be torn from the private bastion of her home and cast before the public eye. First Gyllenborg, who had long admired her work, read a poem in her honor at the Swedish Academy on 20 December. A few days later, her father, whose actions had become strange in his old age, visited the Lenngrens and then drowned on his way home from what had probably not been a pleasant conversation. Lenngren's reaction to the publicity surrounding these two events was characteristic: she withdrew into her home, responded to Gyllenborg in a poem ("Dröm" [Dream]) comparing herself unfavorably to Nordenflycht, and ultimately refused to be publicly honored or to allow her poems to be published as a collection during her lifetime. One of her most famous poems, "Några ord till min kära Dotter, i fall jag hade någon" (Some words to my dear daughter, if I had one), is another deliberation on the relative merits of poetry and supper, as she instructs her dear "Betti":

> Don't waste your time with reading books,
> Our sex has little need of that,
> And must you read, then make it quick,
> So that the gravy won't boil over!

The message has been taken seriously, but several scholars of this century have noted that the poem is yet another pose. The picture of the mother in the poem does not resemble Lenngren, even if one were willing to read the title of the poem without noting the irony. In truth, what she seemed to want most was to keep on writing as she had, maintaining the posture of the perfect wife while allowing the various levels of Stockholm's society to supply her with objects for her satirical wit. One of the finest of her scenes is found in "Grefvinnans besök" (1800; The visit of the countess), in which a parson's family is strained to its limits to host a noble lady in proper style. The mood is idyllic, in the sense that no catastrophe occurs throughout the visit, and every detail is in perfect order. But Lenngren's patience runs thin with the obsequious family, as she describes the departure of the countess:

> And the pastor then followed Her Grace to the linden—
> His well-mannered daughter and wife
> Then curtsied at the steps, at the door, at the gate
> And . . . are standing there curtsying still.

Lenngren's production gradually tapered off during the first years of the new century. At her own request, the first collection of her poetry, modestly entitled *Skaldeförsök* (Poetic attempts), was published posthumously in 1819. Among writers of the eighteenth century, only Bellman surpasses Lenngren in popularity today. Her sharp eye for realistic detail and her straightforward, colloquial style make her easily accessible to us. Like few other Swedish authors, she has the capacity to make the Enlightenment period spring into life.

Unlike Anna Maria Lenngren, Bengt Lidner (1757–93) and Thomas Thorild (1759–1808) both aspired to a "place in the sun," hoping to bask in royal favor. Although their creative careers largely coincided with the Gustavian period, they were temperamentally and intellectually too independent to fit the rigorous definition of the Swedish Academy's motto "snille och smak" (genius and good taste), the first part of which suggested an Enlightenment ideal of rational intellectualism, lucidity, and wit, and the second part, an adherence to a narrowly defined aesthetics of formal rules. In their refusal or inability to conform, they became transitional figures whose work ushered in a new era. They are dealt with at greater length in the next chapter as proponents of a preromantic sensibility. In their attempts to "court the court," however, they are typical representatives of a period when the surest way to artistic recognition and success was through royal approval.

It was therefore reasonable strategy when Bengt Lidner, after studying in Greifswald and fleeing from his creditors in Stralsund, appeared in Stockholm in 1779, carrying a book of fables he had written (mostly translations from French and German) as a present for the newly born crown prince and, more important, drafts of several musical dramas. It was common knowledge that Gustav III was looking for young talent for his theatrical projects. The strategy worked—the king became genuinely interested in Lidner—but since the poet was clearly in need of refinement, Gustav made the unusually generous move to provide him with a stipend for an educational journey, ostensibly to France and Italy. In Paris he was placed under the tutelage of the Swedish minister, Gustaf Philip Creutz.

Creutz made his literary knowledge, his apartment, his library, and his connections available to Lidner. He was himself initially inspired by the visit and began to write creatively again after nearly a decade of literary silence. He prepared a draft of an opera, *Rustan och Mirza* (Rustan and Mirza), for collaboration with the young poet. What happened at that point is not entirely clear. Lidner returned to Stockholm in 1782, and in 1784 Creutz accused him of stealing the best parts of the opera, changing the name to *Medea*, and calling it his own. Lidner's chances for continued support from Creutz were ruined. News of the deterioration of the relationship was conveyed to Gustav III, who would have nothing more to do with Lidner. The poet was forever banished from Gustav's inner circle. A patriotic "Ode till finska soldaten" (Ode to the Finnish soldier), concerning the unfortunate Finnish War of 1788, brought him a small royal pension, and he married and returned to Stockholm. He outlived Gustav III by less than a year. During the regency period he was actually given the title of royal secretary for a few months before his death. His economic situation was so desperate during his last years, however, that it is related that Bellman (who was soon to be imprisoned for his own debts) went from tavern to tavern in Stockholm to "sing in" the money needed for Lidner's burial.

When Thorild appeared in Stockholm at the beginning of 1781 with the intention of making a place for himself on the literary scene, his stated goal was "to be the friend of the king." After all, Kellgren had only recently risen to such prominence with great rapidity. One way of attracting royal attention was to enter one of the official literary contests of the period. Thorild hoped to win the accolades of the literary society Utile Dulci and establish himself as a rising poetic star. Utile Dulci, in which Kellgren was a leading member, had offered a prize for the best poem concerning "Passionerna" (The passions). Thorild's entry in the contest, while using this title, had little to do with what one ordinarily would call the passions, but it is at least consistently passionate in its formulation of a philosophical idea. Thorild's own exalted view of his entry ("as good as any poem in the whole world") was not entirely shared by Utile Dulci, but in awarding it an honorable mention, Kellgren was careful to extol the virtues of the 278-line tirade, only objecting to its "unrhymed dactylic verse," which he considered "against those principles of good taste commonly accepted in the area of belles-lettres." Thorild, who had of course expected to win, took issue with the judgment in an article in *Stockholms Posten* on 4 March 1782: "Rhymeless harmony has greater and more important difficulties than one knows," he wrote, "but I dare say that these are of a higher sort than those of rhymed poetry. Every genius is a born lawmaker, a self-creator in his field. The genius does not abide by laws; he makes them. He knows no other rules than those of nature, of the highest power and the highest beauty."

This rejoinder marks the point in Swedish literary history where the reasonable, law-bound Enlightenment and the romantic, lawmaking individual genius confronted each other. As pointed out in the next chapter, Thorild's position as an opponent to Kellgren, and soon to the entire Gustavian inner circle, was clearly stated here.

The Art of Literary Criticism

A profound change in the role of the literary critic occurred in the course of the eighteenth century. The classical Greek and Latin descriptions of the art, especially Aristotle's *Poetics* and Horace's *Ars poetica*, had been cited and imitated constantly since the early Renaissance. By the beginning of the Enlightenment, it was clear to numerous critics that other rules than those guiding classical literature would have to be formulated. The famous "querelle des anciens et des modernes" (quarrel between the old and the new writers) raged in France toward the end of the seventeenth century, and it was finally resolved in favor of newer trends in literature. At the same time, the guiding principles of the classical Greek and Roman authors were never rejected out of hand. The most influential literary critical work during the eighteenth century, Boileau's *L'Art poétique*, is a direct offspring of Horace, even though it points toward a new age of Enlightenment reason and includes descriptions of types of poetry unknown to the Roman poet.

In Sweden, critical works at the beginning of the new century were similar to those of Boileau, although they were less comprehensive in scope. Samuel Triewald (1688–1743) couched his satirical criticisms in verse, as Boileau had done, and aimed them at the poetasters and dilettantes of his age. He shared Boileau's concerns for "taste" and "reason" in literary work, which in practical terms meant that writers should not try to enter the field unless they had a broad educational background and had mastered both metrics and the vocabulary of their art, as well as a comprehensive knowledge of earlier poets' work. Dalin's critical works, "Tankar över criti-quer" (1736; Thoughts about critics) and "Korta påminnelser vid swenska skaldekonsten i vår tid" (1755; Short reminder regarding Swedish poetic art in our time), are small prose essays reflecting some of the same concerns as Triewald's but expanding the argument in a positivistic way, perhaps with a nod to Addison's critical thought. The poet "flies to the heavens and to new worlds; he descends into chasms and to the bottom of the sea / Only Nature is his guide, and Truth / shines from all his pronouncements." The critic must exercise care (except in special cases in which poets attack the church, the government, or any individual's honor) not to undermine the poets' work and must never attempt to destroy their personal integrity. At the same time, Dalin rails against preciosity and affected verse and against the concept of *licentia poëtica*, which is often used by inferior poets to cover their faults.

As book and newspaper publishing expanded in the middle of the century, and as French and English Enlightenment theory permeated the cultural scene, there arose an increased need for literary criticism in Sweden. Earlier critics had generally avoided naming specific works and authors, although the object of their negative remarks could often be identified. Individual book reviews that appeared in journals were frequently written by publishers or booksellers who wished to advertise the books as desirable products.

It is Olof Bergklint (1733–1805), mentioned above as Oxenstierna's tutor, who has been called Sweden's first review critic. But it was Kellgren who changed the face of Swedish criticism, starting with his articles in *Dagligt Allehanda*, Stockholm's first daily newspaper, and continuing in *Stockholms Posten*. It was as principal critic of the latter journal that Kellgren fought his witty and interesting polemic battle with Thorild over the latter's poem, *Passionerna*, from 1782 to 1784. As a Voltairean with a liberal measure of influence from La Mettrie and Helvétius, Kellgren maintained a skeptical view not only of excesses in literature but of passion in general, since it might reflect, as Helvétius believed, a propelling force based on the fundamental egotism of humankind. Thorild's polemic response in this, the first literary battle in Sweden, was that the true poet had a right to formulate his own rules: in other words, he used Edward Young's concept of the creative genius to answer Kellgren's appeal to taste and clarity. Kellgren broke off the quarrel in 1784 but took up his position as reviewer for *Stockholms Posten* once more in 1790, working in his last years very like a critic of today. By the end of the Gustavian Age, the theater and literature in general had become well established in Sweden, so there was no longer any need to encourage the general population to become poets, as Dalin had done. Furthermore, questions of the appropriateness of the Swedish language for the writing of odes had long been laid to rest by the work of Gyllenborg and Creutz, and the whole antiquated idea of poetic hierarchies seemed increasingly meaningless in the wake of Bellman's brilliant hybrid poems as well as Thorild's and Lidner's ecstatic fantasies. The groundwork had thus been laid for German idealistic philosophy and the arrival of the romantic era.

The End of the Gustavian Age

No period of literary activity in Scandinavia has ever ended as definitively and abruptly as that of the Gustavian Age in Sweden. Gustav III carried the literary aegis for the time and remained to the hour of his death the cultural focal point. That is not to say that he was loved by all his subjects: he was the recipient both of fawning adulation in the exaggerated rhetoric required by official applicants and well-wishers and of vulgar innuendo regarding his perceived homosexuality and his theatricality, as well as of more serious concerns about his high-handed political schemes. Regardless of their private opinions about their king, his people were stunned when he was killed. When the entertainment activities of the capital city resumed, the climate had changed and there was a notable decrease in literary activity on and around the Parnassus.

By 1795, Kellgren, Bellman, and Lidner were gone and Thorild was in exile. By 1800, the survivors—Lenngren, Leopold, and Oxenstierna—had passed their peaks. The intellectual ideas that made up Enlightenment thought had broken down the floodgates of convention and spilled over into a sea of revolution and cultural bewilderment. The complexity of modern politics and morals had become only too evident. Sweden's leaders, fearful of further revolution on the one hand and of absolute monarchy on the other, steered a middle course with the Reuterholm government until Gustav III's son came of age. A brief period of increased freedom of the press directly after the death of Gustav III was soon followed by severe censorship once more, and several budding new journals were driven out of business. Gustav IV Adolf became king at the age of eighteen in 1796. But he was cut of a singularly different cloth than Gustav III. He lacked the charisma and the cultural interests of his father, he had pietist leanings and manic tendencies, and worst of all, he lacked the strength and intelligence to steer Sweden through a period of major international change. When Sweden lost Finland in yet another disastrous war with Russia, a group of political and military leaders forced him into a humiliating abdication in 1809.

After 1792, the court lost its importance as a cultural generator and forum. Toward the last years of the century, it appeared that the universities would fill the gap left by the lack of intellectual stimulation in Stockholm, but not before a decade of the new century had passed were there clear indications of a budding new age in Uppsala and Lund. Looking back on the eighteenth century, the Swedish romantics respected the Gustavian Age, even though their own point of departure was a radically different one. The Enlightenment had given rise to progress as well as revolutionary turmoil, and Swedish literature under Gustav had built itself up on a broad and solid basis. The century had produced writers of international repute and of literary genius. Sweden's theaters, newspapers, and book publishers had come into their own. The country's artistic products were no longer dependent on foreign ideas. The literati of Sweden had learned from the Enlightenment, had assimilated its varied perspectives, and had responded in a creative way. The Gustavian Age in particular had left a legacy of remarkable value. Even the revolution that pulled the curtain down on the whole era could be seen as the last manifestation of that spirit of Enlightenment that would not tolerate a despot. In retrospect, Esaias Tegnér summed it up in a poem to Gustav's Swedish Academy on its fiftieth anniversary:

> For greater spirits lend the age their contour,
> So Gustav's epoch thus bears Gustav's features . . .
> There lay a luster o'er the days of Gustav,
> Fantastic, foreign, wanton, if you will,
> But there was sunshine there, and, whatever else is said,
> Where would we be, if they had not existed?

The Romantic Period

Bertil Nolin

Translated by
Yvonne Sandstrom

4

THE CONCEPT OF ROMANTICISM

The term "romanticism" and the possibility of using it to describe a period that covers all of European literature has been the subject of much debate, ever since Arthur Lovejoy started this discussion in the 1920s. Among other things, he contends that romanticism was too disparate ideologically, politically, and chronologically and that consequently the concept is meaningless. Lovejoy, however, viewed romanticism from the perspective of a historian of ideas. A literary scholar like René Wellek has a different and more constructive view of the usefulness of this concept. Wellek believes that a phenomenon such as a literary period must be based on common norms and conventions and that, to a certain extent, this is true in the case of romanticism.

Modern hermeneutics have questioned this reasoning, holding that the choice of criteria determines our construction of a period. The hermeneutic concept of period is open-ended. For those critics, romanticism is actually an intersubjective consciousness structure (Asbjorn Aarseth). Our image of romanticism is dependent on the "hermeneutic keys," that is, the concepts we use when approaching the texts. I concur in this view to some degree, primarily with regard to our interpretation of specific texts that fall inside the chronological framework of romanticism. In principle, this view is valid for the interpretation of older texts in general. It does not exclude the possibility of arriving at some characteristics both for romanticism as a literary-sociological phenomenon and for texts commonly classified as romantic.

It is hardly possible to escape the fact that even though romanticism does not break through at the same time all over Europe, it still exhibits certain common patterns: above all, it involved revolt against the aesthetics of classicism with its stylistic and genre ideals. Seen from a Scandinavian perspective, its dynamic centers were some rather small German university towns. The strong cultural pressure from France, which reached its peak in Sweden under the French-educated Gustav III, was succeeded by a German-English influence. Thus there are striking similarities between the romantic movement in Germany and in Sweden. In addition, German romanticism received some of its most important impulses from England, as for example, Shakespeare started to be translated and performed. The Swedish reception of Shakespeare comes in part via Germany. Kant's criticism of reason and of the evidence of the senses, of our inability to comprehend the core of reality, "das Ding an sich" (the thing-in-itself, or noumenon), prepared the way for a new philosophy of nature that would become central for Swedish romanticism as well. The formulation of this philosophy of nature, primarily as stated in the works of F. W. Schelling, not only had a decisive influence on writers of the romantic school, such as Atterbom and Hammarsköld, but also came to characterize some of the most prominent natural scientists of this period, among them Elias Fries and Carl Adolph Agardh. From today's perspective, it is easy to point out that this philosophy of nature in part was based on incorrect interpretations of phenomena such as magnetism, electricity, and gravity. For the romantics, nature was perceived as an organic whole, infused with life and power. "Is Nature itself anything but a large, unconscious poem, written by the World Poet, God?" asks the poet and bishop Esaias Tegnér in a letter to his friend, the prominent chemist Jacob Berzelius, the originator of atomic weight tables and of the theory of electrochemistry.

Modern Swedish scholars, primarily Horace Engdahl, have focused on the texts in a way quite different from that of earlier critics. For them, romanticism is first of all a family of texts with certain common stylistic traits that distinguish them clearly from those of classicism. That is especially true of the vague real-life references in the texts. The "space" in the text cannot be referred back to any particular reality but refers rather to fantasy, dream, or memory. This tendency began as early as the period that, in accordance with French and English usage, is called *förromantiken* (preromanticism). Quite a number of new genres and stylistic devices were put into operation, and the foundation was laid for what we can appreciate today as a literary language, a language of feeling, of inner experience, of dream and longing, rather than a tool for describing external reality.

Thomas Thorild: A Swedish Preromantic Figure

The revolt against classicism and its foremost proponents in Sweden—Johan Henrik Kellgren, Carl Gustaf Leopold, and Anna Maria Lenngren—began in the 1780s with the appearance of Thomas Thorild and Bengt Lidner. Of these two, Thorild is the man of ideas and the philosopher whereas Lidner is the more important poet. It may be no coincidence that both came from the west coast and got their schooling in Göteborg, with its excellent commercial and cultural connections to England. Afterward both studied at the University of Lund and were subsequently able to spend long periods abroad: Lidner in Germany and France, Thorild in England and later in Germany. Thus they were exposed to the Sturm und Drang (storm and stress) movement in Germany and to its moving spirits in different parts of Europe. Important works for Thorild and Lidner were Rousseau's *La nouvelle Héloïse*, Goethe's *Die Leiden des jungen Werthers* (The sorrows of young Werther), Macpherson's Ossian poems, and the works of Shakespeare, Milton, and Klopstock. Thorild translated the central fourth song from Edward Young's *The Complaint, or Night Thoughts* from a French edition. That he had studied another important preromantic text, Young's "Conjectures on Original Composition," is evident from the fact that Thorild chose a quotation from this poem as the motto of his poetic manifesto, *Passionerna* (The passions): "Born Originals, how comes it to pass that we die Copies?" In his essay, Young develops the doctrine of the original genius who makes his own laws, aesthetics that became very important for the break with French classicism. As a theorist, Thorild also received strong impressions from Spinoza, Shaftesbury, and Herder. The Swedish preromantics simply searched out a tradition quite different from the one adopted by the young Kellgren and Leopold.

The first confrontation between the new generation and the old was not long delayed. Thorild came to Stockholm in the beginning of the 1780s to make his fortune in literature. As was the custom, he submitted a competition poem to one of the literary societies, Utile Dulci. At that time, Kellgren was the leading light. Thorild had chosen to call his text *Passionerna* (1781: not published until 1785), which put an intricate problem of genre before the learned members. There was no narrative to follow as in Creutz's work, nor was there any landscape description with lyrical overtones as in Oxenstierna. Above all, the text lacked elegant versification in the obligatory alexandrine meter. It was neither satire nor idyll and hardly pure didactic poem either. Sometimes it has the character of an ode.

Thorild himself called it a "song of instruction." What is being celebrated is first of all Nature, a key word in Thorild's aesthetics and philosophy. The main current in his world of ideas is pantheistic with dynamic but also religious overtones. "Strength and harmony explain all of Nature," says the concluding line in the "Fourth Song" of the poem, and this line might also be seen as a summing up of the poem, if, that is, it is possible to view the work as a structured statement. Above all, it lives in its style, which is characterized by ellipses, exclamations, interrogatory phrases, and imperatives. Thorild's texts are also distinctive typographically, with some words in capitals and the frequent use of question marks and exclamation points.

Language such as this, so strongly emotional and in which coherent logical structure is obviously absent, had hardly any counterpart among the foreign authorities apostrophized in the poem: Homer, Shakespeare, Milton, Goethe, Voltaire, Rousseau, Helvétius, and Macpherson. In Thorild's text, a modernistic language is glimpsed for the first time in Swedish literature. It is possible that Thorild has been inspired by and tried to imitate musical expression in *Passionerna*. He was particularly fascinated by Gluck's music and was a close friend of one of the men in the forefront of Gustavian musical life, the composer Joseph Martin Kraus. Perhaps it is no coincidence that the great innovator and experimenter, Strindberg, felt a particular affinity for Thorild and makes him the one Gustavian author sympathetically portrayed in his play *Gustav III*. Thorild himself believed, as he would put it later, that "pathos" rather than "mythos" was the central feature of a poem. By "mythos" he supposedly means "narrative," and that is completely absent from *Passionerna*.

Thorild received no prize for his poem in Utile Dulci, only an honorable mention. He was not satisfied with this rebuff, and in a separate polemical essay he explains his rejection of Utile Dulci as a court of aesthetics. One of the reasons cited for refusing him the grand prix was that his poem was unrhymed. Consequently, Thorild attacks the constraints of rhyme and of French taste in general. Instead of French aesthetic hegemony, he postulates principles that he claims prevail in England, Germany, and Italy. Furthermore, he asserts: "But each genius is born a law-giver: a self-creator in his field. He does not receive but gives laws."

For the first time in Swedish literature, Thorild opposes the demand for originality to the French demand for rules, heralding the romantic movement proper. Leading theorists among the romantics perceived him as important. Erik Gustaf Geijer devoted an enlightening character sketch to him.

Thorild also speaks of the relationship between the sexes and expresses a modern viewpoint in his essay *Om qvinnokönets naturliga höghet* (1793; On the natural nobility of the female sex). He objects to the fact that women are early indoctrinated into accepting a conventional gender role and draws up some propositions that he feels should be valid for the female sex. The first is, "A *reasonable being*: with all the rights and nobility of such a being." Thorild also demands complete civil rights for women and stresses that they are first of all human beings, not sexual beings.

Evidently, Thorild saw himself very much as a social reformer and philosopher, more so than as a writer of literature. He frequently contributed to *Stockholms Posten* and in 1784 started his own paper, *Den nye Granskaren* (The new observer), in which he pleaded for complete freedom of the press. He was influenced by the liberal ideas of the French Revolution and worked for democratization of government.

Pioneering such thoughts, Thorild went to England in 1788. Here he published, among other things, the pamphlet *The Royal Moon, or On Insanity in Politics*. He saw Charles Fox as a political ally and fought against Pitt the Younger. Thorild was upset by the poverty he saw in London and lambasted the clergy and the wealthy. He was not particularly successful in England with his campaign, however, and did not make a name for himself there, as had probably been his intention. Instead, in 1790 he returned to Stockholm, where he published *En Critik öfver critiker* (A criticism of critics) the following year; it appeared in three small booklets in 1791–92. It is a new attempt to settle accounts with Kellgren and with the principles Kellgren applied as a journalist in *Stockholms Posten*. Thorild's scrutiny of the role of the critic was to become very important, since there had been a breakthrough in favor of a bourgeois public in Jürgen Habermas's sense and because papers and magazines that reviewed publications had become more common. Thorild established ground rules for critical practice, rules that have often been referred to in Sweden. His point of departure is what he calls a basic truth: to take each thing for what it is. Important rules are:

1. Know what you are supposed to judge.
2. Judge everything by its degree and kind.
3. Nothing is done for the sake of its flaws but for the sake of its value.

Among other things, Thorild believed that pieces offered without any literary pretensions, such as occasional poetry, should not be judged by the same principles as literature proper. That nothing is done for the sake of its flaws is, of course, a valid maxim in other contexts as well. In view of his criticisms of society, Thorild was not particularly appreciated by the administration that took charge after the death of Gustav III. He is one of the first in Sweden who can be termed an intellectual, in the sense of the word that became common much later on. He continued the best of the traditions of the French Enlightenment but was at the same time open to those new ideas that paved the way for romanticism. In 1795, Thorild was appointed librarian and professor at the University of Greifswald, in the part of Pomerania that still belonged to Sweden. Thus, Sweden rid itself of a troublesome critic of the administration. But the young romantics in Uppsala took him to their hearts. "With Thorild, the genius of our Poetry departed," V. F. Palmblad wrote.

Bengt Lidner: The Interpreter of Compassion

Bengt Lidner represents a different trend in preromanticism. Political controversy did not suit his gentler disposition. Compassion for the weak and unfortunate was an important ingredient in his oeuvre, as shown in his best-known work, *Grevinnan Spastaras död* (1783, 1786; The death of Countess Spastara). At that time, he had behind him a long sojourn abroad, with university studies in Greifswald and a period in Paris as secretary for the Swedish minister there, Gustav Philip Creutz, a prominent author known for his elegant versification. Among other things, Lidner wrote opera librettos with Creutz, something that was encouraged by the opera-loving Gustav III. Lidner was protected by the court in the beginning of his career. He ended up in disgrace, however, and had to resort to writing for money. He died in extreme poverty in 1793.

Lidner can be characterized as the interpreter of tender feelings and compassion and in this respect is of the same ilk as the Rousseau of *La nouvelle Héloïse* and the Goethe who created Werther. *Grevinnan Spastaras död* can be described as a hybrid of epic poem and ode. Its most distinctive trait is the manifest presence of the narrator in the text, a form of extreme empathy with what is being related. The poem is based on an item in *Stockholms Posten* about the Countess Spastara, who tried to save her child from the flames during an earthquake in Messina and perished in the attempt. Lidner depicts the pathos of Spastara's situation with great vividness. The setting is that of melodrama, which had a similar predilection for putting defenseless young women into spectacular and catastrophic situations. The only difference is that in Lidner there is no rescuing hero.

It is quite a new style that has succeeded the disciplined, couplet-rhymed alexandrine cultivated by Creutz and others. The strong emotional engagement is mirrored in the alternation of different meters, the numerous exclamation points and question marks, and a kind of syntactic staccato, which is supposed to imply that the narrator is so carried away by what he is relating that he is unable to express his feelings clearly. In some ways, Lidner is a typical representative of the culture of sentiment that now seems foreign, but for those who had read their Gessner and Rousseau, there was nothing unnatural about it. "In tears, joy" was one of Lidner's mottoes.

His penchant for spectacular catastrophe can be observed in other texts by Lidner, *Yttersta domen* (1788; The Last Judgment) and *Jerusalems förstöring* (1791; The destruction of Jerusalem). *Yttersta domen* belongs to a tradition of religious poetry from Dante to Milton and Klopstock, whose *Messiah* strongly influenced Lidner. The funeral poem was a fashionable genre at the time, and the burial vault was a common setting for plays of horror with which Lidner was probably familiar. The opening lines in *Yttersta domen* have an evocative power that does not suffer from comparison with Young and Gray: "The door of the grave is opened! The stiff hinges creak, / And the faint light of the lamp trembles on the black marble."

Lidner himself wrote a play, *Erik XIV* (not published until 1800), which demonstrates thorough knowledge of the new French theater; he also wrote several librettos, among them *Medea*, in which he does not eschew horror effects. Thus—in direct contradiction to the prescription of classical tragic theory—he lets Medea kill her children in front of the audience. "A single line able to squeeze forth tears means infinitely more than all Aristotelian rules," he wrote in his preface to the work.

Bengt Lidner is rather representative of the preromantic literary climate in Sweden. Logically constructed classical rhetoric has given way to fragmentary aesthetics without central perspective in which visions, voices, and imaginary space suffer continual displacement. The introduction of Macpherson's Ossian poetry and Young's *Night Thoughts* have left their mark. In Lidner, one can also discern a clear tendency to have nature convey the feeling of the narrator's persona, often religiously colored.

Kellgren and Preromanticism

Preromantic stylistic ideals finally affected the person who had been laboring most strenuously to preserve and confirm the rules of classicism in Swedish eighteenth-century literature, Johan Henrik Kellgren. Around 1790, he wrote two poems that show traces of the preromantic cult of emotion: "Til Christina" (1789; To Christina) and "Den nya Skapelsen eller Inbildningens Verld" (1790; The new creation, or The world of the imagination). In the former, the poem's speaker appears in the role of the misanthrope Timon, who has retired from the world to a remote cave but is pulled from his isolation by his meeting with a family, "a mother, two daughters, / One son." The poem has an obvious biographical background, but its most interesting aspect is that it introduces all the melancholy moods, the props, and the characters of preromanticism. Here are the moonlit landscape; the harp, the emblematic attribute of the Ossianic poet, "whistling in the wind without strings"; and "the sad recluse on the rock / stretching his arms in worship." These gestures, the tears, the broken voice, these vivid images, must have made a strong impression on Kellgren's contemporaries, because here a new literary language was made manifest, a palpable expression of deep and true feelings. The landscape is transformed from lonely and repellent into green and flourishing. In principle, it is the same poetic technique that comes into its own much later in literary history in the French symbolists. The meter is eleven-syllable blank verse. Rhyme, which Kellgren had defended so energetically in his fight with Thorild, he himself now renounces.

The liberating power of love is the subject of "Den nya Skapelsen." This time, Kellgren uses rhymed iambic meter, and the poem as a whole is an attempt to imitate a musical genre, the rondo. Above all, he has written a love poem, a celebration of his beloved, whose image he sees reflected everywhere. This experience is combined with a view of nature that is new to Kellgren, influenced by Rousseau and perhaps by Kellgren's antagonist Thorild. Paradoxically, the work is also a poem of creation. All of nature is being recreated in the gaze of the speaker, as once happened in the mythical account of divine creation:

> Nature lay dead before my eyes,
> Profoundly dead was she to my emotions—
> Then came a breeze from above,
> And bade light and life in the world.

The last phase of Kellgren's poetry, especially as far as the poems treated here are concerned, marks the beginning of romanticism proper, although the romantic style is not completely developed. The rhetorical figure he uses more than any other is personification: "In the field the mirth of peace was smiling" and "Revenge honed the darts of lightning, / Courage shook the arm of the hurricane," it says in "Den nya Skapelsen." In Kellgren's works, those poems are exactly the ones the romantics could appreciate.

Johan Gabriel Oxenstierna: A Gustavian Nature Romantic
The poetry of preromanticism paved the way for romanticism proper. In this new view of nature the landscape becomes a reflection of the emotions

and moods of the speaker in the poem. In addition to Kellgren, this approach was taken by Gabriel Oxenstierna. While he served as a diplomat in Vienna in 1772–73, he wrote his extensive landscape poem *Skördarne* (The Harvests), which, however, was not published until 1785, in revised form. Here Oxenstierna associates himself with the tradition of Virgil's *Georgics*, which had been continued by the Englishman James Thomson in *The Seasons*. Another long poem in the same genre, *Dagens stunder* (The hours of the day), is of greater interest as a precursor to the romantic view of nature. This work was finished as early as 1785 and circulated in handwritten copies, but it was not published until 1805. The poem focuses in turn on the different phases of the day: morning, noon, evening, and night. The opening section contains a magnificent description of sunrise, admired by contemporaries and posterity alike. His treatment has models in Milton and Thomson, but Oxenstierna has given it a personal and evocative form.

The influence of preromantic stylistic ideals is most evident in "Natten" (Night), which shows obvious traces of Oxenstierna's reading of Young's poem on the same topic. It is true that Oxenstierna's style retains much of the preference of French classicist aesthetics for personification and for the rhetorical figure called periphrasis. Instead of mentioning darkness directly, for example, he writes "the mantle of the night," which presupposes a person wearing this garment. At most, we are allowed to catch a glimpse of the reality behind a rhetorical game, often made concrete by means of tableaux in which mythological figures act as in a court masque. In the fourth song of *Dagens stunder*, the different constellations fulfill such an illustrative function.

Frans Michael Franzén

Frans Michael Franzén (1772–1847) was a transitional figure and a bridge to romanticism proper. He was born in Finland to Swedish-speaking parents and was educated at Åbo University, where he later became a professor. After the harsh peace of 1809, when Sweden lost Finland, he moved to Sweden and eventually became bishop in Härnösand, a small city in northern Sweden. Before he left Finland, Franzén had already attracted attention in Stockholm with his prize poems to the Swedish Academy. His "Sång öfver grefve Gustaf Philip Creutz" (Song on Count Gustaf Philip Creutz) is no conventional encomium on the older poet. The imagery in the poem bears witness to Franzén's familiarity with the stylistic ideals of preromanticism.

Franzén had a different and more positive attitude toward religious subject matter than did the Gustavians in general. He was no friend of philosophical materialism. In one of his early poems, "Människans anlete" (1793; The human face), which had a motto from Milton, "The human face divine," he writes:

You who cry: There is none,
No soul hidden within matter,
All is dust, nothing else;
Fools! Only walk to the spring
Regard your visage, and be still.

The leader of the romantic movement, Per Daniel Amadeus Atterbom, gave Franzén a positive review in the periodical *Phosphoros* in 1811. Particularly appreciated was the poem "Det nya Eden" (The new Eden), published in *Stockholms Posten* in 1795, which shocked the French classicist arbiters of taste with its visions and "confused images that have hovered before the fancy of my soul," as Franzén himself was later to describe his poem. His poetry has a broad register. As a hymn writer, Franzén is among the best of his generation. Perhaps influenced by Walter Scott, he early cultivated the verse narrative on historical topics. *Julie de St. Julien* (1824) deals to some extent with contemporary history that Franzén himself had experienced during a journey to revolutionary France in the 1790s.

Franzén was much esteemed among such different circles of his contemporaries as those of Atterbom and Tegnér. A contributing factor was his sure grasp of versification, which perhaps shows to best advantage in the almost epicurean attitude expressed in such convivial songs as "Champagnevinet" (1804; Champagne wine) and "Glädjens ögonblick" (1803; The moments of joy).

A CHANGE OF EPOCH

On 16 March 1792, when Gustav III was murdered by a pistol shot during a masked ball in the opera house he himself had built, it meant the end of an epoch. Gustav had gathered authors and other practitioners of the arts around him, partly as a conscious cultural policy to confer splendor and power on the person of the king. It was in the capital, under the protection of the king, that authors could have a career. There they could be active in the Swedish Academy the king had founded, participate in brilliant festivities, and contribute texts to spectacular theater performances. Now conditions changed, almost overnight. The regency that was formed under the leadership of G. A. Reuterholm and the young successor to the throne, Gustav IV Adolf, did not share Gustav's interest in the arts. On the contrary, the attitude toward intellectuals was initially characterized by great suspicion. Reuterholm, the man in power, issued a decree about freedom of the press, which facilitated the flow of information from revolutionary Paris, but it was soon rescinded. The philosopher Thorild seized this opportunity, however, and published the pamphlet *Om det allmänna förståndets frihet* (1792; On the freedom of general reason). His ultimate aims were freedom of thought, freedom of the press, and basic democratic rights. But he was arrested on the day the pamphlet was published, and when he was taken to the appeals court, the carriage was followed by a great throng of people. A situation similar to the one that had led to the storming of the Bastille was not unthinkable. Political clubs were prohibited, and troops were concentrated in the capital.

The period from the death of Gustav III to the overthrow of absolute rule has been called the iron age of Swedish cultural life following the golden age of Gustav's reign. The activities of the Swedish Academy were suspended from 7 March 1795 to 20 November 1796. Theaters were censored, and performances in the university towns were sometimes prohibited. French literature was banned in 1804.

In the years immediately following the death of Gustav III, the court and the capital lost something of the central role in cultural affairs they had enjoyed during Gustav's reign. Instead, the emerging bourgeoisie increasingly became the carriers of culture. The two university towns, Uppsala and Lund, which had contacts with new romantic ideas in Europe, evolved as the centers. A process of change began around the turn of the century, and an important ingredient was the introduction of a new, more democratic constitution in 1809, in which freedom of the press was guaranteed. Freedom of the press as a constitutional right had been introduced as early as 1766, but it had been rescinded or modified periodically. In 1810, a special press law, rewritten in 1812, was issued. It was a significant condition for the wave of new publications, literary calendars, periodicals, and newspapers that again started to vitalize cultural life around 1810.

In 1808, as a result of the turbulence stemming from the Napoleonic Wars, Sweden was attacked by Russia. When the war ended, Sweden had to surrender all of Finland, as well as Åland, in the Treaty of Fredrikshamn in 1809. A third of Sweden was lost and, with it, Swedish hegemony in the Baltic. It was no great help that the successor to the Swedish throne, the French marshal Jean Baptiste Bernadotte, guided the country into a union with Norway (1814). This move was no more than a half-measure, and after major dissensions, it was finally dissolved in 1905.

When Esaias Tegnér said in his extensive, national poem "Svea"—awarded a prize by the Swedish Academy—that the goal was to "recover Finland within the boundaries of Sweden," it was an expression of national compensatory thinking, prompted by the loss Sweden had suffered. The romantic movement in Sweden is marked by a struggle for national renaissance.

Industrialization proceeded slowly compared with the progress in the precursor country, England. Between 1810 and 1850 there was a hefty population increase, from 2.5 to 3.5 million. This dramatic growth prepared the way for the wave of emigration, primarily to America, that began in the 1840s. The countryside was proletarized by extensive division of homesteads. Only 10 percent of the population were city dwellers, and the self-sufficient agrarian economy was still dominant. Such figures as the poet and bishop Tegnér received salaries in kind. Literacy increased rapidly, however, especially after 1842, when obligatory schooling was introduced.

ROMANTICISM

Foreign Models

Swedish romanticism might appear somewhat delayed compared with the advent of the same movement in England, Germany, and Denmark. In international writings, there has been discussion about whether the romantic movement should be viewed as a *revolution* or as an *evolution*. From a Swedish perspective, it is quite possible to speak of a *cultural revolution*, and the same could be said for the breakthrough of the new school in the rest of Europe. Romanticism established itself very rapidly and presented a well-defined front against earlier aesthetic ideals. This circumstance, however, must not be allowed to obscure the fact that the movement, especially in Germany, had quite a protracted incubation period. This preparatory stage is marked by such works as Johann Gottfried Herder's *Stimmen der Völker in Liedern* (1778–79; Peoples' voices in songs), perhaps the most important impetus for the interest in medieval ballads and folk literature; Immanuel Kant's *Kritik der reinen Vernunft* (1781; Critique of pure reason), which delivered a fatal blow to the overconfidence in the rationalism and empiricism of the Enlightenment and classicism; and Friedrich Schelling's *Ideen zu einer Philosophie der Natur* (1797; Ideas for a philosophy of nature), which introduced the idea of animate nature.

Goethe's and Schiller's early works also belong in this picture. The true breakthrough of German romanticism is usually indicated by the publication of the periodical *Atheneum* (1798–1800), edited by the brothers

Schlegel. Here Friedrich Schlegel published perhaps his most important aesthetic tract, "Gespräch über die Poesie" (Dialogue on poetry). It should be pointed out that this beginning of German romanticism is simultaneous with Coleridge and Wordsworth's joint collection *Lyrical Ballads.*

Among the Nordic countries, Denmark was somewhat ahead of Sweden in picking up the new aesthetic signals. In 1802, the young Henrich Steffens gave lectures at the University of Copenhagen. He had studied in nearby Kiel, where he had come into contact with the new ideas in philosophy and literature during his studies of Herder and Fichte, among others. Steffens influenced the young Danish poet Adam Oehlenschläger, whose ballad "Hakon Jarls död" (The death of Hakon Jarl) and a poem stating his poetic program, "Guldhornerne" (The golden horns), mark the renaissance of Old Norse topics.

German romanticism was based in the German university towns of Jena and Heidelberg and in the Prussian capital Berlin. The Jena circle, with the Schlegel brothers, would be particularly important for Swedish romantics.

The philosopher Benjamin Höijer (1767–1812) was one of the links between German and Swedish romanticism. During the 1790s, he belonged to the radical discussion group Juntan in Uppsala, where he argued for constitutional change and for reform of the outmoded four-estate Riksdag. His radical views made him unpopular in both Stockholm and Uppsala. In the spring of 1798, Höijer made his first extensive foreign journey, coming into contact with Fichte in Jena. Another, longer sojourn abroad began in 1800; this time, he also went to France, whose cultural life he considered stagnant in comparison with that of Germany.

Höijer was one of the first Swedes to read and understand Kant's philosophy, and he became personally acquainted not only with Fichte but with Schelling as well. Although Kant's philosophy had already been introduced by Höijer's teacher, Daniel Boëthius (1751–1810), it had met with strong opposition from Leopold, among others.

On his return to Uppsala, Höijer gathered around him a group of young students who would later be the spokesmen of romanticism: Lorenzo Hammarsköld, Erik Gustaf Geijer, Vilhelm Fredrik Palmblad, Clas Livijn, and Per Daniel Amadeus Atterbom. Höijer's *Afhandling om den Philosophiska Constructionen* (1799; Treatise on philosophical structure) was translated into German and reviewed by Schelling. The transference of the aesthetics and philosophy of German romanticism started at about the same time in Denmark and in Sweden; Höijer played a role in Sweden similar to Steffens's in Denmark. He took an early interest in aesthetic problems and started working out systematic concepts of aesthetics. His investigation into the kinship between the sublime and the ridiculous, the tragic and the comic, bears witness that he took early notice of questions that would be central for the aesthetics of the nineteenth century.

Contrary to conditions in Denmark, where the romantic movement had a central position in Copenhagen, in Sweden there were three different centers for romanticism: Uppsala, Lund, and Stockholm. Lund had only one proponent, but he was a giant: Esaias Tegnér. In 1824, however, Tegnér moved to the scholastic town of Växjö in southern Sweden, where he became bishop. At different periods, Lorenzo Hammarsköld, Clas Livijn, Carl Jonas Love Almqvist, and Erik Johan Stagnelius were in Stockholm. The ideological center of Swedish romanticism, however, was Uppsala.

The Uppsala Romantics

It started when a few young men founded a literary society in the fall of 1803. Among them were Lorenzo Hammarsköld (1785–1827), the most prominent critic in the group, and Clas Livijn (1781–1844), best known for his bizarre, burlesque novel *Spader Dame* (1824; Queen of Spades). It became a truly dynamic group only after the fifteen-year-old Per Daniel Amadeus Atterbom was elected a member in 1805. The society was re-formed a few times, first as Musis Amici (1807) and shortly afterward as the Aurora League. The organizational forms are not unimportant, because in this group, with its regular meetings, presentation of programs, and united front against the old, Stockholm-based school, there was an awareness that it had been allotted an important, historical, and almost divine mission: to make a fundamental change in the literary climate and to return literature to its former greatness and dignity.

There are religious overtones in the proclamation of a new literary era in which poetry would become central. This ambition for cultural revolution is fittingly expressed in the names of the group's monthly journal, *Phosphoros* (1810–14), and the association behind it, the Aurora League. The source of the dawn metaphor might be Schlegel's "Gespräch über die Poesie," but in Atterbom's treatment it became a striking image of the recreative powers the new movement was supposed to convey. The first issue of the journal contains a manifesto poem called "Prolog" (Prologue), in which the new aesthetics is proclaimed in lofty tones. The poem is both retrospective and forward-looking. At the same time, the text expresses a striking self-awareness, the recognition of a new epoch about to be born.

The journal *Phosphoros* was an ambitious enterprise. Here the Uppsala romantics acquired a forum where new ideas about romantic literature could be presented. The group sought a different tradition from the one cultivated by authors inspired by French classicism. It turned directly to the Greeks, Aeschylus and Sophocles among them, as well as to Shakespeare and Schiller. New verse forms were introduced, and in this connection— as was the case with German romantics—the musical quality of the verse had great importance. It is difficult to understand the work of renewal the poetry of the romantics signified without some knowledge of the discussion on aesthetics carried on in *Phosphoros.*

The romantic school in Uppsala also issued other publications: in 1810–22, *Poetisk kalender* (Poetic calendar) and, in 1813–25, *Svensk Litteratur-Tidning* (Swedish literary journal). This activity was facilitated because two of the most prominent members of the group, Axel Stenhammar (1788–1826) and Vilhelm Fredrik Palmblad (1788–1852), were engaged in publishing and printing in Uppsala. There were many favorable factors working together to establish a creative literary setting in the old university town.

The New School and the Old

The romantics appeared as a rather firm group within Swedish literature, and with the aid of their journals, they carried on an aggressive debate directed at the representatives of classicism. The publishing organ of the old school was *Journal för Litteraturen och Theatern* (Journal for literature and theater), edited by Pehr Wallmark (1777–1858). By now, the romantics had established themselves in Stockholm as well, with Lorenzo Hammarsköld and Clas Livijn, and in the weekly journal *Polyfem* (1809–12), they acquired a forum for their literary-political campaign. The romantics wanted to rediscover a Swedish literary tradition beyond classicism, which they considered a trivialization of literature characterized by imitation and epigonic practice. For the first time in Swedish literary history, a dispute developed between two literary schools. It was much more extensive than the one carried on by Thorild and Kellgren, even though their controversy may be regarded as a preliminary skirmish. The young authors in *Polyfem* spoke for German romanticism, and Wallmark, who was the spokesman for the Swedish Academy, with its close ties to French culture, attempted to discredit German literature in his *Journal.* The fight was carried on with considerable polemic gusto, perhaps because it was now possible, for the first time, to have such a free, public discussion. The debate between the old and the new school culminated in a high-spirited pamphlet, a combined effort by some younger romantics, *Markalls sömnlösa nätter* (1820; Markall's sleepless nights), in which dead and living authors make their appearance behind easily penetrated fictitious names. A more serious result of this literary battle was Lorenzo Hammarsköld's *Svenska vitterheten: Historiskt-kritiska anteckningar* (2 vols.; 1818–19; Swedish literature: Historical-critical notes).

Gothicism and the Historical Horizon

Historical considerations were tremendously important to the romantics. Thus, an attempt to write the history of Swedish literature in earnest was made for the first time; Stiernhielm was held up as the great figure of past literature. Another result of the historical orientation was an interest in Old Norse literature and mythology. This movement was stimulated by Götiska förbundet (the Old Norse League), founded in Stockholm, where the historian Erik Gustaf Geijer (1783–1847) soon became the most influential member. The association published the journal *Iduna* (1811–24), which was an important organ for literature inspired by Old Norse themes. Here Geijer published his poems "Manhem," "Vikingen" (The viking), and "Odalbonden" (The yeoman farmer), which were to have the same importance for the Old Norse renaissance as Oehlenschläger's "Guldhornerne" in Denmark. Stagnelius also gravitated toward Gothic or medieval motifs in epic poems such as *Gunlög* (1814) and *Blenda* (1822).

Another contributor to *Iduna* was Esaias Tegnér, who published some poems in this journal, among them the first songs of *Frithiofs saga*. In this manner Geijer established a connection between the Uppsala and Stockholm groups and Tegnér, with his ties to Lund. Tegnér otherwise had a more positive attitude toward the Swedish Academy and the old school.

Yet another manifestation of historical interest, concentrated on the Middle Ages, was the desire to collect and publish folk songs and folktales. In this respect, there are links to the German Heidelberg school and to Achim von Arnim and Clemens Brentano's *Des Knaben Wunderhorn* (1806–8; Youth's magic horn), a collection of German folk songs, and to Jacob and Wilhelm Grimm's collection of fairy tales, *Kinder- und Hausmärchen* (1812–15; Children's and household tales). In both Denmark and Sweden, people started methodically collecting, writing down, and publishing folk songs and folktales. With Arvid August Afzelius (1785–1871), Geijer published *Svenska folk-wisor från forntiden* (1814–17; Swedish folk songs from ancient times) in three volumes. Gunnar Hyltén-Cavallius (1818–89) performed a similar pioneering effort with George Stephens (1813–89) in *Svenska folksagor och äfventyr* (1844–49; Swedish folktales and adventures) and *Sveriges historiska och politiska visor* (1853; The historical and political songs of Sweden). Geijer's extensive introduction to his and Afzelius's publication gives an idea of how the rediscovered cultural heritage was regarded. The folk songs differed from literary poetry in the respect that they incorporate the common memories of a people. It is only in art that some kind of property rights begin, Geijer asserts, and that is not the case with folk songs. In this work, the tunes were given in musical notation with the help of Friedrich Haeffner (1759–1833), a German-born composer who in 1808 had moved to Uppsala.

The Old Norse renaissance is part of this obvious attempt to return to sources, to the very foundations of national culture. The inspiration had partly come from abroad, with such works as Paul Henri Mallet's *Introduction à l'histoire du Dannemarc* (1755–56; Introduction to Denmark's history) and Thomas Percy's *Five Pieces of Runic Poetry* (1763). In Denmark, N.F.S. Grundtvig had already finished his *Nordens Mythologi* (Norse mythology) in 1808.

The wave of interest in Old Norse topics informed many of the romantic texts. The most devoted follower of this subject may have been Per Henrik Ling (1776–1839), best known as the father of Swedish gymnastics. He wrote a large number of plays that are hardly enjoyable today, such as *Agne* (1812) and *Den heliga Birgitta* (1818; St. Birgitta), and in epics, such as *Gylfe* (1813) and *Asarna* (1816–33; The Aesir). Old Norse motifs are represented, more or less, in the works of most Swedish romantics, but such texts are among the least vital. That the subject matter had the ability to engage contemporaries, however, is clear from the fact that Tegnér's *Frithiofs saga* (1820–25) was tremendously popular and was even set to music.

Inside as well as outside Scandinavia, the sphere of Ossianic myth was frequently confused with that of Old Norse. Both Atterbom's "Prolog" and Tegnér's "Epilog" (1820) also mix ancient Greek mythology with Norse and Christian; the latter work, however, is suffused with the subject matter of ancient Greek myth. There is a strain of neo-classicism in Swedish romanticism: both Tegnér and Palmblad were professors of Greek, and the latter translated Aeschylus, Sophocles, and Homer. Stagnelius's work is permeated by Neoplatonism and Greek mythology.

Swedish romanticism was a broad cultural movement that included most of the arts. The crossing of boundaries and breakup of genres were central features of romantic aesthetics. All-encompassing art, in which all art forms contribute to a single unity, was also a romantic idea. The interest in music, for example, was striking. Both Almqvist and Geijer set their own poems to music, and Geijer wrote independent tonal works.

The Swedish Academy and the Romantic School
The eighteen-member Swedish Academy, founded by Gustav III, had rapidly acquired great prestige as arbiter of taste and distributor of prizes. When the new century began, the most prominent of the members of the first generation, Kellgren, had died. The most influential man was now the gifted, smooth, and versatile Carl Gustaf Leopold. His words weighed

heavily when prizes were awarded, and he made important contributions to the academy's task of caring for and developing the Swedish tongue. In 1801, for example, he published *Afhandling om Svenska Stafsättet* (Treatise on Swedish spelling), which helped normalize Swedish orthography. Because of his ability to please the various powers-that-be, Leopold succeeded in obtaining a large number of bequests and stipends, not least by means of his writings on behalf of the academy. As a result, he was the best-paid official in the country during some periods. But he also became a target for the polemics of the young authors. They made fun of the texts, often quite weak, that were awarded prizes by the academy. This campaign was carried on in *Polyfem*, whose best-known contributors were Hammarsköld, Atterbom, and Palmblad, as well as in *Phosphoros* and *Svensk Literatur-Tidning* (1813–25), both edited by Atterbom. In an otherwise rather positive review of Leopold's work, Palmblad made an attempt to sum up Gustavian literature, regarded as largely dominated by Leopold. Palmblad wrote that poetry had "degenerated into a fashionable doll who knows nothing but catechism lessons, maxims, and bons mots that were new a hundred years ago." In this pronouncement, it is easy to see the great difference between the young romantics and the French classicist Leopold. Finally, in reaction to the young authors' attacks on his work, he tried to silence his critics in Uppsala through his government connections. Freedom of the press was still rather precarious in Sweden.

Gradually, however, the leading romantics conquered the Swedish Academy. Wallin and Franzén were the first elected; they were partly outside the militant faction. Then came Tegnér, Geijer, and finally—in 1839—Atterbom. But the two most singular and original geniuses, Stagnelius and Almqvist, remained beyond the pale of the academy.

In the Salon of Malla Silfverstolpe

Malla (actually Magdalena) Silfverstolpe (1782–1861) was a significant cultural presence in the Uppsala of the romantics. She kept a detailed diary and wrote her *Memoarer* (4 vols., 1908–11; Memoirs; edited posthumously). For several decades, starting in November 1820 but with some long interruptions, she held a literary salon in her Uppsala home. The better-known romantic writers—Atterbom, Geijer, Palmblad, later on Almqvist, and the composer Adolf Fredrik Lindblad (1801–78) as well—were frequent visitors. Music and singing were important features of these get-togethers. Musical settings of Geijer's poems, for example, were performed; the authors read their own texts; and tableaux vivants were presented. The point of departure for the latter was often an existing painting that was rendered as a theatrical and musical performance. The genre had become fashionable, not least because of Goethe's *Die Wahlverwandtschaften* (1809; Elective affinities), which was read and discussed at Malla Silfverstolpe's. An illuminating example of the basis for a "living picture" is Geijer's "Skärslipargossen" (1836; The knife-sharpener boy). In the first stanza, its potential for theatrical production becomes evident:

> Good people! I am a poor boy,
> Who sharpens knives and scissors.
> I am the knife-sharpener boy
> Who sharpens knives and scissors.
> Is there no work here?
> I only ask small recompense.

The subject of the knife sharpener, treated by Goya and others, was quite common in the pictorial art of the time. In the rest of the poem, a girl enters who wants something sharpened, and a small scene in an erotic key is played out between the two before the boy moves on. "Now I am done, thank you! / Now I will wander off again, alas!" The text is artless and naïve and can be viewed to advantage only at the moment of performance in an intimate group like that of the literary salon.

When C.J.L. Almqvist entered the scene, his *songes* (dreams), brief little poems he had set to music himself, were likewise given theatrical form as "living pictures," something which, incidentally, was also done in theaters. This literary salon expanded into the homes of Atterbom and Geijer. In 1829, Almqvist read his satirical fairy tale "Ormus och Ariman" at Malla Silfverstolpe's, ten years before its publication. Thus in this salon a way of providing public dissemination of literature had been created as a complement to the printed word, one that was not insignificant for the position of the writer, since he was able to reach key persons.

Several contemporary women authors also belonged to this circle, first of all Thekla Knös (1815–80), who produced works in different genres. In addition to lyrics and epics—*Ragnar Lodbrok* (1851) was given the Swedish Academy's grand prix—she wrote fairy tales. Another salon participant, Eleonora Charlotta d'Albedyll (1770–1835), published a hexameter poem on an Old Norse subject, *Gefion* (1814), which was praised by Atterbom in a detailed review in *Svensk Literatur-Tidning*. Unlike the masculine heroism of *Iduna* and Tegnér's writings, peace and everyday work are celebrated in *Gefion*. Another woman author whom Atterbom tried to rescue from oblivion was Ulrika Carolina Widström (1764–1841). She had earlier had contact with Kellgren and Thorild, and in 1799, she published the collection *Erotiska sånger* (Erotic songs), a rather slim volume of poems that bear witness to a sure stylistic grasp. Atterbom's encouragement led to her return with the collection *Höstaftnarne* (The autumn evenings), but her range of subject matter was narrow.

Malla Silfverstolpe's *Memoarer* is one of the most important documents for our knowledge of the attitudes among high society in the first part of the nineteenth century. Silfverstolpe relates her inner history, with Rousseau, Goethe, and Madame Roland as some of her models. Geijer's *Minnen* (1834; Reminiscences) may also have been an inspiration for her. She tells of her childhood, of the erotic games of her youth within the boundaries erected by the conventions of the period, of her (not particularly happy) marriage to an officer, of life in country manors, and, above all, of the circle of art practitioners that gathered in her Uppsala home. One of them, a German lady with literary ambitions, was Amalia von Helvig (1776–1831), who had associated with Goethe and Schiller in Weimar. She was married to a Swedish officer who served in Germany. Geijer, Atterbom, and Silfverstolpe visited her in her home country, and in this way she became an important link between German and Swedish romanticism. She was a close friend of Geijer's and translated some of his poems as well as poems by Atterbom and Tegnér (e.g., *Frithiofs saga*) into German.

There were no prominent women authors in the period of high romanticism (1810–30). Women still had no access to higher education, and the role for women cherished at the time constituted an obvious barrier to their emergence into public and cultural life. Their gifts were channeled into the literary salon and into the writing of letters and diaries. Among the aristocracy, diary writing was not uncommon. The diaries of Hedvig Elisabet Charlotta (1759–1818), written in French, are remarkable examples of this genre. They are actually so-called monthly letters, which provide informed descriptions of Gustav III's court. She was married to Gustav III's brother, who later became king under the name of Karl XIII. These diaries were published in 1902–42, in nine volumes, in Swedish.

Julia Christina Nyberg (1785–1854) had the courage to appear on the public stage. Under the pseudonym Euphrosyne, she contributed to *Poetisk kalender* and also published larger works such as *Dikter* (1822; Poems) and the dramatic poem *Vublina* (1823). Some of her poems that were set to music are still sung, such as the well-known "Vårvindar friska" (Fresh spring breezes). Both Thekla Knös and Christina Nyberg belonged to Malla Silfverstolpe's circle of friends and appear in her memoirs.

Religious Renaissance and the New Hymnal

That poetry and religion were closely related was a conviction shared by many romantics, not least Atterbom, who came from a clergy family.

Poetry offered a special way to knowledge of higher matters. The romantics broke radically with the rationalistic view of religion found in, for instance, Kellgren and Leopold, for whom Voltaire and Diderot were the great authorities. For several decades, efforts had been made to compile a modernized hymnal. It was a task that ultimately devolved on the government, since Sweden had a state church. The leader of the editorial committee established in 1811 was Johan Olof Wallin (1779–1839); he would become Sweden's most important hymn writer, not only because of the new hymns he wrote but also because of his reworkings of older texts. The hymnal of 1819 was to have a central position in Swedish cultural life: almost everyone came into contact with it when attending church, and in school, children often had to memorize hymns. The German-born composer Friedrich Haeffner, who for a long time was employed at Uppsala University, was responsible for the new hymnal's chorale.

The importance of *Den svenska psalmboken* (1819; The Swedish hymnal) can hardly be overestimated. Wallin's style has a rhetorical flair that is often emphasized by the tunes. Many of the hymns were translations or reworkings of older Swedish or German originals, with respect to text as well as music. Wallin also wrote new hymns, such as "Var hälsad sköna morgonstund" (Hail beauteous morning), an obligatory part of every Swedish Christmas service. Geijer put his signature on one of the most frequently sung Easter hymns, "Du bar ditt kors, o Jesu mild" (You carried your cross, gentle Jesus), and Frans Michael Franzén wrote the stately advent hymn "Bereden väg för Herran" (Prepare a way for the Lord).

Wallin's hymns are often characterized by gentle, quiet longing for the beyond, a kind of weariness of life. Humans are guests and strangers on earth, and their true home is on the other side of the grave. God's presence in nature is another theme treated by Wallin with great artistic sensitivity, as in Hymn 564, "Var är den Vän, som överallt jag söker?" (Where is the friend I seek everywhere?), which speaks of God's traces being visible "wherever a force reveals itself: / A flower puts forth its scent, an ear of grain is bending."

Wallin also wrote secular poetry. Two texts are in a class by themselves, imprinted with the same longing for the beyond and fixation on death as that found in the hymns: "Hemsjukan" (1821; Homesickness) and "Dödens Engel" (Eng. tr. "The Angel of Death"), written during the terrible cholera epidemic that struck Sweden in 1834. The "sickness" mentioned in "Hemsjukan" is weariness of life and its quotidian round, an intense longing for death. "I have seen how it happens on this earth, / But never have I seen anything new under the sun." Our brief earthly life is compared to "A dance of mosquitoes thronging / In the sunshine hours, / Until the night puts an end to both fight and union." "Dödens Engel" does not have the same artistic intensity, but it is still a magnificent monologue poem with an imagery rooted in medieval and baroque poetry. The Angel of Death is the speaker; stanza after stanza develops the message of the transience of earthly life and of how death might suddenly descend in the middle of life:

Then the dance will stop,
The noise turn quiet,
Then the wreath will wither,
The bride turn pale.

In 1837, Wallin was made archbishop. His contemporaries noticed him mostly for the eloquence he developed in his sermons. Like many others—one might compare him with Søren Kierkegaard—Wallin published his sermons, an important genre during the nineteenth century. One of these texts, "Quinnans ädla och stilla kallelse" (1827; The noble and quiet calling of woman), is a key document for our knowledge about the conservative view of women. In Wallin's sermon, the ideal figure is Mary, Mother of Christ. Taking the image of her that he considered conveyed by the Bible, Wallin concludes that the role of woman should be distinguished by piety, submission, the simple mind of a child, patience, self-denial, and a love that endures all. Her true and only sphere is the home; consequently, she should eschew public life. One can easily understand that Fredrika Bremer reacted against this view of women, which was particularly influential because it was preached by one of the most prominent and most rhetorically schooled orators of the age.

ATTERBOM AS POET AND PLAYWRIGHT

Per Daniel Amadeus Atterbom (1790–1855) was the most important theorist among the Swedish romantics. In many of his contemporaries, primarily Tegnér and Stagnelius, one can easily trace connections to the stylistic and genre patterns of classicism. For Atterbom, the break with the older school was more total. In his texts, we get only occasional glimpses of surrounding reality, such as in his "Minnes-Runor" (1812; Runes of memory), a nostalgic look at his childhood. In this poem, it is the imaginary world of the child that occupies the foreground. Atterbom constructs a textual world rooted in dream and imagination. It often has the character of metatext: poetry about poetry. Several of his poems are contributions to the quarrel between the old school and the new in which he engaged himself so fervently. That is the case in "Härskri" (1810; War cry), published in *Polyfem*, the journal that carried on the fight with a polemic sting. "To battle then! The insolent ones are arming themselves," the first line runs; typically for Atterbom, the poem is a sonnet.

Atterbom believed that poetry at the end of the eighteenth century had become trivialized. He wanted to create a special literary language, and he used every device imaginable to give his texts what the formalists would later call "literariness." He introduced and employed several new verse forms: canzone, ottava rima, blank verse. To enhance musical values, he played with assonance and alliteration. His texts were often written in symbolic or allegorical form, with characters taken from Greek or Norse mythology. In his striving for a poetic style different from everyday language, he seized on exotic color words. A stanza from "Den nya Blondel" (1815; The new Blondel), also more or less a metapoem—the point of departure is Richard the Lion-Hearted's favorite poet—illustrates this technique:

I became acquainted with a king,
His daughter gave me wine;
Blue eyes, golden hair,
Breasts like lilies, gait like the hind,
Cheeks of carmine—
Dressed in diamond.

Atterbom's poetic style may sometimes appear precious and elaborate, and when Geijer, his ally from the first breakthrough period, broke with romanticism, he pointed out such weaknesses in Atterbom's poetry in an influential review.

A suite of twelve poems that Atterbom called *Blommorna* (The flowers) was published in *Poetisk kalender* in 1812. The idea is that they symbolize both the different seasons and the different "individuations" (as Atterbom expresses it) of human beings. The spring life of the flowers, their brief summer, and their final autumn and withering are also applicable to human life. The sequence of the poems emphasizes this feature: it starts with spring flowers such as "Snödroppen" (The snowdrop) and "Sippan" (The anemone) and ends with flowers that allude to night and death such as "Nattviolen" (The butterfly orchid; in Swedish the name includes the word *night*) and "Vallmon" (The poppy). All these poems are dramatic monologues, and the flowers represent different temperaments or attitudes to life. The stately sunflower is a symbol of genius; the rose, of erotic love. To make a text carry several, in part divergent, symbolic functions entails certain dangers. No profound interpretation, however, is needed to understand a poem like "Rosen" (The rose), whose first stanza runs:

The lush splendor of living fullness,
The inebriating power of the fiery kiss,
The sweetness of the festive day of life,
Were given to me by the grace of benign Norns.

Later Atterbom expanded this suite of poems to about forty.

A genre more or less created by the romantics, with its point of departure in Shakespeare, was the fairy-tale play. The plays of the German Ludwig Tieck, such as *Der gestiefelte Kater* (1797; Puss-in-Boots), *Prinz Zerbino* (1799), and *Kaiser Octavianus* (1804), were predecessors. Oehlenschläger also cultivated this genre, in *Aladdin* (1805). Atterbom made two major attempts to write a Swedish fairy-tale play. The first was *Fågel Blå* (1818, 1839; Bird blue), which never amounted to more than a fragment. The main character, Deoletus, has been seen as a portrait of the romantic poet. In one of his long speeches, there is a frequently quoted passage that may be viewed as a summing up of an extreme romantic aesthetics: "And isn't poetry the true / Nature? The life and mother of matter?"

The contrast between life and reality, the foreignness in life that distinguishes the character of Deoletus was even more prominent in *Lycksalighetens ö* (1824–27; The isle of bliss), Atterbom's major work. Evidently, his impulse for writing this play came from the German romantic Novalis's novel *Heinrich von Ofterdingen* (1802), a celebration of the imagination and an attempt to write the history of poetry in symbolic form. Atterbom had similar ambitions; he also wanted to create a romantic tragedy incorporating an internal, not just external, determining force, or fate, as in Greek tragedy. The "remainder" from after the Fall, which, according to Neoplatonic views, exists in every human being, creates a premise for such an "inner fate." The main character, Astolf, the king in the Land of the Hyperboreans (a transparent circumlocution for Sweden), displays some similarities to Karl XII; the resemblance may, however, be misleading, since the events are supposed to start in the sixteenth century and to cover three hundred years.

Astolf likes to listen to the poet Florio's stories of "an eternal spring, of the world of poetry and beauty, of chivalric tales, premonitions and miracles." Influenced by these stories, Astolf develops into a visionary dreamer who longs to get away from his wintry country, where he is not understood. His long monologue at the beginning of the play presents the premise and ideational content of the drama in a nutshell.

—Oh! If there were some sorcery
that could drown all our naked reality
so deeply in the sea of the dream image world
that no bridge from our world might reach
the ever summer-green isle of poetry—
I would at once, and at whatever price,
exchange in favor of such dreams
my waking life, my empty hero's name.

This wish is fulfilled when Astolf loses his way during a hunt and arrives at the Cave of the Winds, where he encounters the four winds. Through Zephyr, the west wind, a Cupid-like figure, the king hears of the Isle of Bliss where the eternally young Felicia reigns. This place, to which he is eventually carried, is akin to the *locus amoenus* of classical tradition, a paradisiacal world of wish fulfillment that Atterbom has equipped with fountains, nymphs, the song of nightingales, and palms, a pleasant place for a frozen inhabitant of the North. Astolf spends three hundred years, which he experiences as only three months, in this seductive setting, enjoying his leisure, occupied only with pursuing his love games with the beautiful Felicia. This existence of uninterrupted pleasure, however, cannot satisfy him in the long run.

He returns to his native country, only to find that the ideas of the French Revolution and of liberalism have corrupted it. It is a satirical depiction of the society Atterbom feared would be born from the new, radical, liberal ideas. Astolf cannot tolerate it, and he tries to get back to his wonderful fairy island. He is overtaken, however, by an old man who is actually Time/Death.

Felicia's island, the domain of imagination and poetry, is also destroyed. With her sensuous love, Felicia has sullied the country of the imagination. Her mother, Nyx, the Queen of the Night, intervenes and brings her daughter back to the starry skies.

For a long time, Atterbom's play was regarded as unadulterated, unplayable closet drama. More recent research, however, has shown how well informed Atterbom was about the conditions of the contemporary theater and theatrical expression. There is a palpable kinship between his drama and Mozart's operas. Both *The Magic Flute* and *Don Giovanni* had been performed at the Royal Theater in Stockholm, *The Magic Flute* as early as 1812 and *Don Giovanni* in 1813. Moreover, during his long sojourn in Germany and Italy, Atterbom had many opportunities to see plays. In his stage directions, there are obvious reminiscences of the scenery conventions of the period, such as the rock cave. Zephyr has certain similarities to Cherubin in *The Marriage of Figaro*. It is possible that Atterbom was thinking of the opera format in the inserted songs, which were set to music at an early date. In 1945, the play became the basis for an opera by one of Sweden's leading composers, Hilding Rosenberg.

As is often the case in Atterbom, there are several levels in the play. In addition to the manifest plot, a symbolic-allegorical level touches not only on poetry but also on Swedish history. *Lycksalighetens ö* has also been interpreted as a play of initiation into the nature of love, in which Astolf is the novice and Felicia the initiator. Atterbom based his plot on a book of folktales that exhibit the main features of the fairy tale, but he added a profound aesthetic and philosophical superstructure to his original. In the play's large cast, there are several characters whose fates engage the reader. Among them is Astolf's betrothed, Svanvit, who is left to wither and die when the king abandons his country. Svanvit speaks a death poem, a farewell to life. It is simple on the surface, but Atterbom has mustered all the musicality and verbal suggestiveness he could effect at his best. In each stanza, partly by means of a suggestive technique of repetition, the emotional theme is taken further with a series of verbs in the same range of denotation and connotation: sleep, wither, swoon.

Although the play is rather uneven in style and in treatment of its subject matter, it contains scenes of great effectiveness. Atterbom shows us a sampling of different verse forms, among them blank verse, in dialogue passages. In between there are songs of the type "Stilla, o stilla" (Still, oh still). The play is too extensive to be staged in its entirety, but the same objections might be raised to similar plays in world literature, such as Goethe's *Faust* and Ibsen's *Peer Gynt*.

Atterbom was fervently engaged in the battle between the old school and the new. In this way he also entered into opposition with Tegnér, who felt a great affinity for men like Kellgren and Leopold. Tegnér reacted against what he called "carbuncle" poetry, that is, against the exotic, iridescent words Atterbom had such a weakness for. In a series of poems with the title *Recensionsblommor* (Review flowers), published in *Poetisk kalender* in 1821, Atterbom extends a conciliatory hand to Tegnér and others. Of the poems included in this suite, it is precisely the one dedicated to Tegnér that best illuminates Atterbom's changed attitude. Among other texts, Atterbom reviews Tegnér's "Epilog" and points to both what distinguishes and what unites the two poets. In the main, Atterbom can agree with Tegnér's demands, based on eighteenth-century values, for clarity and light, but he defends night and darkness, which found an important symbolic figure in Nyx in *Lycksalighetens ö.* Nyx is the goddess not only of night but also of dreams and death. For Atterbom, as well as for Novalis, night has a magical, charged content.

Atterbom became a professor of philosophy in 1827; a few years later, in 1835, he moved to a professorship in aesthetics and modern literature. In this capacity he published some studies in literature, first *Svenska siare och skalder* (6 vols.; 1841–55; Swedish prophets and poets). In these volumes, the idea raised as early as the first period of debate—that is, to write the history of Swedish literature—is carried out. There are portraits of all the great authors (e.g., Stiernhielm, Dalin, Bellman, and Lidner). Thus Atterbom did pioneering work in literature comparable to that of Geijer in the field of political history.

ERIK JOHAN STAGNELIUS: A PREMODERN POET

The author who was closest to Atterbom both in temperament and in world view was Erik Johan Stagnelius (1793–1823), in spite of the fact that, as far as is known, they had no personal contact worth mentioning. Along with Almqvist, Stagnelius is the most gifted of the Swedish romantics. He is modern in the sense that he expresses a bottomless despair at the harsh conditions of earthly life ("ett kvidande dårhus är världen" [the world is a wailing madhouse]) with perfect versification and in a singularly clear diction. His poems are often permeated by an obscure cosmology that has its roots in Neoplatonism and German theosophy, influenced by mystics such as Jakob Böhme (1575–1624) and by Böhme's interpreters among French and German romantics. The main thought is the idea of the Fall, that the soul once separated itself from the divine and is a prisoner in the sensual world. "In the harem of the World Sovereign / Anima is captive" is a typical formulation in one poem, "Fången" (The prisoner). But it is not necessary to know every detail of Stagnelius's cosmology in order to appreciate his poetry. In most of these texts, it is possible to discern the speaker's desperate conflict between overshadowing sensuality and awareness of the necessity for reaching some kind of freedom by renunciation.

Stagnelius published only a few works in book form during his life: the epic *Wladimir den store* (1817; Vladimir the Great); the poetry collection *Liljor i Saron* (3 vols.; 1821; Lilies in Sharon), which also contains the play *Martyrerna* (The martyrs) and the tragedy *Bacchanterna* (1822; The Bacchantes). His literary remains were reverently edited by the greatest critic of the period, Lorenzo Hammarsköld. The world of Stagnelius's literary texts, however, did not become available in its entirety until the twentieth century, when an authoritative edition by Fredrik Böök was published in 1911–18. Since that time, Stagnelius has increasingly come to be viewed as the central figure of Swedish romanticism.

Like several of the romantics, Stagnelius had a religious background. His father was bishop in Kalmar, in southeastern Sweden; Stagnelius first studied in Lund and later in Uppsala. After his studies, he ended up as a government clerk in the Office of Education and Ecclesiastical Affairs in Stockholm. He never established a regular bourgeois existence, however. He was sickly, abused alcohol and other drugs, and died when he was only thirty.

Stagnelius's first published work, *Wladimir den store*, is an epic hexameter poem in three songs, its subject matter taken from the Russian *Nestor Chronicle*. The main character, Wladimir, besieges the Christian city of Theodosia. In the first song, we meet him in the army camp, melancholy and brooding despite the splendor that surrounds him. His thoughts circle around "the sorry lot of human life . . . and the desolate riddle of night," that is death and dissolution. Wladimir is quite representative of the attitude toward life that characterizes Stagnelius's poetic world. In the night, he has a heavenly vision that admonishes him to stop his offensive against Christians. It does not stop him from carrying out the attack on Theodosia, however. A Byzantine princess with whom Wladimir falls in love is captured. He lets her go, but his fate is sealed, and he converts to Christianity so that he can marry her. The plot is of minor interest compared to the portrait of the main character, who has reached an existential nadir and so is ready for the conversion that occurs in the last song.

One passage in the poem foreshadows the Russian czar Alexander, the instigator of the Holy Alliance, and the mission he felt himself called to perform. A copy of Stagnelius's poem was given to the Russian minister in Stockholm. Unlike Tegnér, Stagnelius sympathized with the program of the Holy Alliance.

Stagnelius was very much under the influence of the neo-classical renaissance. He was familiar with Greek and Roman mythology and poetry and counted Horace, Ovid, and Propertius among his masters. Figures from classical mythology such as Orpheus, Endymion, Daphne, Venus, and Narcissus belong naturally in his poetry. To the classical poetic genres of elegy and ode he added sonnet and canzone. His most important and best-known play, *Bacchanterna*, has a classical subject.

"Endymion," one of Stagnelius's most read poems, is representative of this kind of topic. It tells how the moon goddess, Delia, comes down to earth and spends a night of love with a sleeping shepherd. The last stanza in the poem runs:

> When he wakens at last, what terrible emptiness
> His flaming soul will find around itself!
> Only in dreams will Olympus
> Descend to mortal men.

The poem contrasts night, with its divinely inspired dreams—creative night—to day, characterized by "terrible emptiness." The intervention of the invisible voice to plead with "the rose-wreathed bride on her bed of saffron," that is, dawn, to stop and let the shepherd remain in his heavenly dream, is typical of Stagnelius's attitude to night and dreams. A similar tribute to night is found in the love poem "Julia, veken i vår lampa" (Julia, the wick in our lamp), whose concluding stanza laments, "Soon with day I have got / Back my empty life." Poems such as "Natt-tankar" (Night thoughts) and "Till Natten" (To night) bear witness to the attraction this subject had for Stagnelius.

Even if the mythological-allegorical staging in "Till Natten"—with Cynthia carrying the moon as a lamp and sleep personified, with a poppy as its attribute—has its origin in classical poetry (Ovid), it is unmistakably Stagnelius's own voice greeting the night as "the wretch's only treasure." Night also has purely positive connotations in a frequently quoted line from another poem, "Vän! I förödelsens stund" (Friend! In the hour of devastation). Night is here ranked with creative chaos: "Night is the mother of day, Chaos the neighbor of God." The playwright Lars Norén used these sententious statements as titles for two of his plays in the 1980s. The poem is, as so often in Stagnelius, cleverly constructed according to the rhetorical figure that employs questions and answers (anthypophora). The poem begins by outlining a hypothetical crisis for the poetic "you," starting from the first line's "when your inside of darkness is covered," a phrase that generates concrete statements about the kind of crisis it is. Some questions follow: the first, "Say, who will save you then?" in its turn generates elucidative questions. At last there is the answer, which is introduced by the line "Only the holy Word that cried to the worlds, 'Let there be!'" (an allusion to the biblical story of creation).

Stagnelius's texts often bear witness to such a crisis for the speaker in the poem. In "Grymt, verklighetens hårda band" (Cruel, the hard constraint of reality), even the title of the poem announces a desperate situation for the speaker. "I'm groping in a wild, a night-filled desert," says one line. But—as one of the authorities on Swedish romantic poetry, Horace Engdahl, has pointed out—one has to make a distinction between the "I" who writes the poem, whose hand guides the pen, and the "I" of the poem. At the moment of writing, the crisis is always in the past. In "Grymt," the cure for the crisis is also given: "But the heaven-borne song consoles me."

In Stagnelius's texts, erotic love occupies a central position. Even when his topic is other existential spheres, Stagnelius's imagery is erotic. Several different phases can be discerned in his love poetry. In earlier texts, erotic love has strong, sensual coloration. Such is the case in the elegy "Allt sen människor först" (Ever since humans first), inspired by Propertius. The poem speaks of how "each softly swaying bosom arouses desire in my heart, / each dazzling glance turns my blood into flame." Many of his love poems are dedicated to a—quite certainly fictitious—female figure called Amanda. She becomes his muse, in a way similar to Petrarch's Laura or Dante's Beatrice. The numerous attempts that have been made to find a real-life model have been extremely speculative. One of his poems is simply entitled "Amanda"; it is an eloquent celebration of this enigmatic woman, along with an awareness that she is unattainable for the poem's speaker.

The rhetorical construction of this poem underlines its meaning. The first stanza, in a verse in which flowing iambs and anapests chase each other, tells concretely and symmetrically how both souls and rivers reach their goals. This makes an effective contrast to the vain yearning of the poem's speaker in the next stanza, who can never reach his goal, fulfilled love with the beloved. The attitude that recurs in several poems with or without Amanda, that is, the necessity of abstaining from earthly love in favor of a higher, nonsensual existence, is foreshadowed in this poem. This outlook is perhaps most clearly illustrated in a canzone rather typically entitled "Uppoffringen" (The sacrifice), which tells what is at stake in the first few lines:

> For you, like angels sweet,
>   I light for the last time
> My sacrificial fire, enclosed by heaven's wind.

Further on, the same poem tells how the sacrifice of earthly love "Frees the souls and purifies them."

A large part of Stagnelius's later poetry is characterized by departure from and farewell to life. This theme can be seen in "Flyttfåglarne" (The migratory birds), concerning a subject beloved by the romantics and also treated by Tegnér and Runeberg. In Stagnelius's version, the poem concludes with the prospect of another life beyond the grave, "Gilded by the fire of eternal morning."

For Stagnelius, however, death is not only the hope of eternal life. In "Till Förruttnelsen" (To putrefaction), death, signifying annihilation and dissolution of the body, is depicted with an empathy and concreteness reminiscent of Baudelaire's well-known "Le cadavre." Typically Stagnelius personifies putrefaction as a "bride" and dissolution as a wedding. That does not prevent him from describing the process with penetrating realism: "I maskar lös tanken och känslorna opp / I aska mitt brinnande hjärta." (My thoughts and my feelings dissolve into worms, / and my burning heart into ashes!).

Stagnelius seems to conclude that desire and renunciation are the lot of human life. He tries to fit this insight into a broader natural-philosophical or cosmogonic perspective, however. This cruel fate is characteristic not only of humans but of all of nature. In a magnificent poem of instruction, "Suckarnes Mystèr" (The mystery of sighs), this philosophy of life is proclaimed with great conciseness:

Two laws govern human life
Two forces turn everything that's born
Under the moon's precarious disk.
Listen, o man! The power to desire
Is the first. The necessity to renounce
Is the second.

The sigh, the inhalation and exhalation, becomes the overarching metaphor in the poem, and in it, all existence is described. The moon, the sea, the wind: in everything, the same effort of will, the same yearning, which must be renounced, is observed. The wave rolling toward the shore must turn back, the wind must die down. Each hopeful effort is followed by disappointment. It is all rendered in a throbbing, suggestive rhythm that points to one concrete example after another: "Do you see the sea? . . . Do you hear the wind?"

The neoplatonically inspired world picture that informs "Suckarnes Mystèr" recurs in several poems. Its most consistent rendering might be the remarkable, partly obscure "Se blomman! På smaragdegrunden" (See the flower! In its setting of emerald). This poem develops the idea of the soul, Anima, as a prisoner of matter, this time in a flower that is personified in a way reminiscent of Atterbom's suite of poems on this topic. The underlying philosophy has the same origin, but in Stagnelius, the temptations of sensuality are depicted with the concreteness of which only he is capable when he tells the fable of Anima's journey to the Demiurge, the World Sovereign, enthroned in his castle and surrounded by seductive splendor.

During his short life, in spite of the fact that it was made difficult by sickness and drug abuse, Stagnelius was tremendously productive in different genres. Some of his texts became available only much later, including a large number of plays and librettos (below). Beyond all literary theories and "isms," his position as a living poet has become more and more notable, celebrated by, among others, a late kindred soul such as Gunnar Ekelöf.

ERIK GUSTAF GEIJER AS POET AND HISTORIAN

Together with Atterbom, Erik Gustaf Geijer (1783–1847) was the most prominent ideologue of the romantic school. As a literary writer, however, he was rather limited in range. He came from a well-to-do foundry milieu in Värmland and, perhaps because of his origins, was more attuned to reality than, for example, Atterbom. Geijer studied in Uppsala and became professor of history there in 1817.

In his work, he exemplifies the many-faceted aspect of cultural reorientation signified by romanticism. As a result of this versatility, however, Geijer did not make any profoundly original contribution in the fields he attempted: poetry, philosophy, history, and music.

Geijer tried to advance his career in the traditional way and was awarded the Swedish Academy's grand prix. A study trip to England in 1809–10 was important, not least because he became aware of Shakespeare, who, with Goethe and Schiller, became a great inspiration throughout his life. One result of his English trip is his translation of *Macbeth* (1813).

Earlier, as a member of Götiska förbundet (the Old Norse League), Geijer had published some poems on Norse topics in the league's journal, *Iduna*, of which he himself was the editor. Some of them are of special interest because far into the twentieth century they were obligatory reading in Swedish secondary schools; in this way, they contributed to the consolidation of the old Norse renaissance in this century. That is particularly true of the twin poems "Vikingen" (The viking) and "Odalbonden" (The yeoman farmer).

"Vikingen" gives a picture of a temperament, a personality type—expansive, tragic-heroic—rather than a historically based portrait of the warlike seafarers. "Odalbonden" is of greater artistic interest. It expresses an appreciation of the free farmer that is highly typical of its period. Thorild had already written "The farmer is everyone's father still / Still in this day." This appreciation received theoretical justification in the political economy by so-called physiocratism with its emphasis on natural law. In these poems,

Geijer's strength as a poet is shown by his ability to formulate sententious maxims, often antithetically constructed, which have entered the Swedish language as familiar quotations. "Each pain has its own cry, / But health is silent" is one example of such formulation in "Odalbonden." Another is the following brief stanza:

The great lords with thunder and cries
Burn countries and villages down;
Silently the Farmer and his son build them up,
Sowing in blood-spattered earth.

His brief poems in the Goethe tradition, primarily from the 1830s, are of greater importance in Geijer's poetic production. The best known, one that is still alive, is "Tonerna" (The notes), which Geijer set to music himself but which nowadays is mostly performed to a completely different tune, that of Carl Leopold Sjögren (1861–1900). Geijer's poem runs:

Thoughts, whose struggles only night can see!
Notes, in you they beg for rest.
Heart that suffers from the din of day!
Notes, to you, to you it wishes to flee.

As so often in Geijer, the poetic text is built on antithetical juxtaposition of words rather than on elaborate imagery. Sometimes his short poems have elements of maxims of the type that can be read on wall hangings, as in "Höstsädet" (The autumn sowing) with its comparison between the farmer sowing his grain and the positive attitude to life of the poem's speaker: "He does what I do: buries his hope. / He believes as I do in Sun and Spring." The same trusting attitude is expressed in "Natthimmelen" (The night sky), some of whose features, however, may point to loneliness, isolation, and awareness of death: "The day is sinking, the sky turns to night. / Soon all I can see are the eternal stars."

As a historian, Geijer is a dominant precursor figure, for good and for ill. He exercised great influence, not least because as a lecturer he had great charisma. The period until the end of the 1810s is characterized by the historical philosophy of romanticism. For him, myth and fairy tales were important source materials. One does not find in Geijer's work much of the concern about source criticism that emanated from the somewhat younger German historian Leopold Ranke. Geijer's books *Svea rikes hävder* (2 vols.; 1825; The chronicles of the realm of Svea) and *Svenska folkets historia* (3 vols.; 1832–36; Eng. tr. *The History of the Swedes*, 1845) are nationalistic and conservative in spirit. In the 1830s, Geijer came into contact with the philosophy of Hegel and moved away from the conservative attitude he, like many other romantics, had adhered to earlier. His study of the French social theorist Alexis de Tocqueville's work *De la démocratie en Amérique* (1835; Democracy in America) impelled him in a democratic and liberal direction. The idea of the individual and of liberty had always been of central importance to Geijer, who was well read in philosophy. His frequently quoted statement that the history of Sweden is the history of its monarchs, partly characteristic of his view of history, provoked the young Strindberg, who made an attempt to write the history of the Swedish people from a more democratic standpoint. Geijer's last important work, *Människans historia* (The history of mankind) was published posthumously in 1856.

In 1838, Geijer started publishing a journal of his own, *Litteraturbladet* (The literature paper). To the dismay of many of his friends, he declared in the first issue that he had left the so-called historical school, that is, the movement in historical studies that emphasized tradition and organic political development. Instead, he adopted the position of the liberal contingent, as far as education, freedom of trade, and demands for constitutional reform were concerned. In the 1820s, Geijer represented the university in the estate Riksdag meeting at that time, and he was then a supporter of conservative ideas. In 1840, he rejoined the Riksdag as a liberal. Because Geijer had been one of the most prominent figures in the conservative camp, this political change of sides caused a sensation. If one studies his contributions to the topical debate of the 1830s and the collection of articles and aphorisms he published in 1837, entitled *Den blå boken* (The blue book), however, one realizes that he had gradually slid away from his conservative stance. Liberal ideas were gaining support abroad. Geijer also followed the debate about the drawbacks of industrialism, in part through the English journals he read regularly, and he had contacts with liberal Swedish industrialists. Part of the sensation of this so-called apostasy came from the fact that Geijer criticized the poetry of his former supporter, Atterbom, in an extensive review. Aesthetically as well, Geijer had distanced himself from romanticism and approached realism, as was evident in *Minnen* (1834; Reminiscences).

When Geijer broke with some of his conservative friends, he himself saw it as a step into the unknown. The liberals did not immediately receive him with open arms. The brief poem written in the shadow of his break with the conservatives, "På nyårsdagen 1838" (On New Year's Day 1838), has to be viewed against this background.

Alone in a fragile vessel the sailor
Ventures on the wide sea;
The starry sky flames above him,
Below, his grave roars horribly.
Forward!—That is the commandment of his fate;
And God dwells in the depths as well as in the heavens.

TEGNÉR: THE STANDARD BEARER OF CULTURAL IDEALISM

During the later part of the nineteenth century and for a large part of the twentieth, the figure of Esaias Tegnér, the man and his work, occupied a central position in Swedish cultural life. The modern breakthrough and cultural radicalism would gradually undermine his status. His weakened influence is also connected to the fact that the genres he cultivated, meditative poetry and verse narrative, had been supplanted by more vital genres. Nevertheless, his work is still so rich and permeated by a strong, unique personality that much in his textual world is alive by virtue of its own innate power.

Tegnér was born in a clergy home in Värmland in 1782. When he was nine years old, his father died, and he ended up in a foster home where, however, he was well cared for. His intellectual gifts were recognized, and he was sent to the University of Lund in 1799. Here he studied Latin, Hebrew, Greek, and philosophy. As was common for poor students at the time, he had to interrupt his studies to work as a tutor in wealthy families. In 1812 he became professor of Greek, but by then he was already well known as an author. During his years in Lund, he was the central figure in an academic clique, Härbärget (the Lodging), which was the counterpart of the Aurora League of the Uppsala authors. The closeness to Copenhagen and the Danish romantic movement was important for Tegnér. He declined an invitation to contribute to Atterbom's journal. In 1825, Tegnér was appointed bishop in Växjö in southern Sweden although he did not actually have any special interest in religious matters. He became bishop, not unlike other authors of the period, to have a somewhat secure income. Both Franzén and Wallin filled the same function; of course, this similarity may also be viewed as a sign of the religious renaissance implied by the romantic movement.

At the time, the road to literary recognition went by way of competition texts submitted to the Swedish Academy. In 1811, Tegnér received the grand prix for his patriotic poem "Svea," written in the shadow of the great catastrophe in Swedish history, the defeat against Russia in 1808–9 and the loss of Finland. One can read the poem as a grandiose sermon of rebuke to an enfeebled people—in alexandrines, to please the academy. An inserted iambic section, the so-called dithyramb passage, gives a vision of the last great battle, which almost acquires the character of apocalypse in an Old Norse key, from which a newborn, happier people will evolve. Tegnér had to tone down the most obvious allusions to Russia before he received permission to publish his poem.

In the first decades of the nineteenth century, strongly marked by the Napoleonic Wars and by the aftermath of the French Revolution, Tegnér was intensely engaged in foreign politics. Like Byron and Heine, he was fascinated by Napoleon's personality; in several poems, he takes a position for or against the emperor. That is partly true of a poem that is obligatory in every Swedish anthology of Tegnér's poetry: "Det eviga" (1810; The eternal). Napoleon is not mentioned by name in the final version of the poem, but he is still apostrophized as "The strong man" who uses his tool— the sword—to reshape the world. In opposition to this violent rampage, Tegnér places what might be called the golden triad of romantic cultural idealism: the right, the true, and the beautiful. These concepts are given the dignity of eternal, indestructible, universal lodestars by Tegnér. Thus his text becomes a battle poem, a spiritual resistance poem that concludes with a fervent appeal for the defense of these values: "So seize all that is true, dare all that is right, / and shape the beautiful with joy."

The poem is given life and completeness by Tegnér's expressive imagery, which, in the spirit of the eighteenth century, frequently uses personification: "But truth lives. Among axes and swords / she stands calm, with radiant forehead"; "Right gets arms, truth gets a voice." The imagery gives a kind of dynamism to the poem. "Hjelten" (1813; The hero), a monologue in which the speaker has Napoleonic features, defends the great person, who supposedly has been allotted a predestined task and "works blindly, as the spirit moves him." In this poem Tegnér expresses a dynamic view of history that was hardly in line with the antirevolutionary stand cherished by the romantics, that is, that old, fossilized social and political structures must be replaced by new ones: "What is decayed shall be toppled, / and the healthy new shall grow / out of destruction." We find another comment on the times in "Nyåret 1816" (The New Year 1816), which is a reaction to the Holy Alliance and to the policy of the Congress of Vienna. Like Byron, with whom he felt greater affinity, Tegnér regarded the reactionary politics embraced by Metternich and Castlereagh with great skepticism. Tegnér's main stylistic tool in "Nyåret 1816" is irony, otherwise primarily encountered in his letters. The next-to-last stanza runs:

Hello there! Religion is a Jesuit,
Human rights a Jacobin,
the world is free, and the raven white,
long live the Pope—and the Devil!

Tegnér as Speaker and Cultural Philosopher

On 4 November 1817, Tegnér gave an important and much-discussed speech in Lund on the occasion of the tricentennial of the Lutheran Reformation. After paying obligatory homage to Luther's contribution, Tegnér proceeds to a survey of the eighteenth century and the French Revolution. He renders discriminating judgment on the past century: its tolerance is praised, but its one-sided worship of reason is censured. Tegnér's real message, however, concerns the good and bad points of his own age. The romantic school, headquartered in Uppsala, is blamed—but not named—for its tendency toward obscurity and abstraction, and romantic poetry is characterized as a "ghost walking in the moonlight painting its blurry pictures." The liberation movements in Europe, which the representatives of the Holy Alliance wanted to stifle, do not frighten Tégner: "They only demand what the nature of the state itself demands, if it aspires to be an educational institution for humanity, and not a Negro plantation, with millions of slaves and a single Lord with his underbailiffs. They demand to make the laws they will have to obey themselves, to determine for themselves the burdens they will carry." Here Tegnér frames a manifesto for freedom and democracy. Later, when the Swedish liberals started to argue for their ideas of increased social justice more loudly and radically and appealed to him, Tegnér found this camp repulsive.

Many of Tegnér's texts are poems written for festive occasions or addressed to private people, dignitaries, or institutions. The most interesting is the "Epilog vid Magister-Promotionen i Lund 1820" (Epilogue at the conferring of masters' degrees in Lund, 1820). Like many of Tegnér's minor and major works, such as the Reformation speech, it was sold as an offprint and brought him a significant income. His cultural idealism is articulated with all the rhetorical brilliance he was capable of. He himself delivered this speech in verse form at the conclusion of the occasion; it thus made a special impression on the audience. Tegnér once explained that he "thought in images": his "Epilog" consists of a series of "pictures" or allegorical scenes.

The celebration took place in the cathedral, where a platform, called "Parnassus," had been erected. This setting gives Tegnér an opportunity to make connections to the Greek Parnassus and to the world of classical symbols and myths in general, to the "City of Apollo" by the Delphic oracle. He believes that these pagan deities have been ennobled by Christianity, but that does not prevent him from lingering in the classical world, for the laurel wreaths the young Masters of Arts have been awarded come from there. He retells the fable of Apollo's infatuation with Daphne, who flees from the god and is rescued by being turned into a laurel tree. Similarly, truth always flees the one who seeks it; it is impossible to reach the highest truth. This point is a part of Tegnér's lecture on the critical stance. "Don't believe every sailor's yarn you hear," that is, the students should not believe that they have found Truth, the Philosopher's Stone. Nevertheless, he dubs his young novices the champions of light against all the darkness and obscurity of the age.

The core of his proclamation may be summed up by the words "strength" and "clarity." The latter is chiseled into a concise maxim that thousands of Swedish students have taken along on the road of life in the form of a familiar quotation:

Hvad du ej klart kan säga, vet du ej;
med tanken ordet föds på mannens läppar;
det dunkelt sagda är det dunkelt tänkta.
[What you cannot say clearly, you do not know;
the word is born on human lips along with thought;
what is obscurely said is obscurely thought.]

Tegnér's philosophy of clarity has its origin in classicism, and it was particularly directed at the Uppsala romantics. In making a thought process concrete, he builds a metaphoric space, a crystal city in which "the light a thousandfold / shines back from its mirrored walls." For him, this image is a contrast to the biblical, dark Tower of Babel. It is this metaphor for clarity he holds up as a lodestar for his students as he sends them off to spread light and culture in those distant places where they will work. Tegnér gives the same mission to Alexander the Great in his poem "Alexander vid Hydaspes" (Alexander at Hydaspes) in which Alexander says, "I want to carry light and culture / From Hellas all around the world." Tegnér's cultural idealism has components of Hegelian philosophy of history: "The World Spirit works through human powers," it says, and it is up to the individual to contribute to the struggle for a better world.

Another of Tegnér's academic occasional speeches, given in 1829, paid homage to the Danish author Adam Oehlenschläger, who had been invited to Lund. This occasion acquired a particular historical importance because it became the starting point for so-called Scandinavianism. Tegnér formulated the motto of a new pan-Nordic feeling after all the wars: "The time of discord is past (and it should never have been / In the free and infinite / World of the spirit)."

Yet another speech in verse form is "Sång den 5 april 1836" (Song on 5 April 1836), intended to be read at the fiftieth anniversary of the Swedish Academy. This text is constructed as a summing up of Gustav III and his time, above all of the great authors and scientists who conferred brilliance on the period: Linné, Gyllenborg, Creutz, Bellman, Oxenstierna, Kellgren. These figures, and several others are each given a few lines of characterization: because of their effective formulation, they would long dominate the view taken of the Gustavians. Kellgren is apostrophized as a genius who "fought the battles, / the sparkling ones, for truth, for right and reason." Bellman is given "the trait of sadness on his forehead, / the trait of a Nordic singer, a rose-red sorrow," and over the whole of Gustav's reign, Tegnér throws that "luster . . . fantastic, foreign, wanton if you will," as a tribute to the king who, more than any other, had favored literature, theater, and other fine arts. Tegnér's encomium is an elegant essay with a touch of the esprit that distinguished Gustav's era.

Tegnér's Verse Narratives

The romantic verse narrative was a fashionable genre in this period. Goethe practiced it in *Hermann und Dorothea* (1798), and Byron developed it, in his particular diction, in a number of texts, such as *The Corsair* (1814) and *Lara* (1816). In Denmark, Oehlenschläger had used topics from Nordic myth and fairy tale in several texts, for example, *Helge* (1814). Tegnér felt great sympathy for these three authors. His hexameter narrative *Nattvardsbarnen* (1820; The child communicants) is a counterpart to Goethe's parsonage idyll. In this text, as well as in *Kronbruden* (1841; The crown bride), written in the same tone, Tegnér deals with contemporary subject matter, which is otherwise rather rare for him. In *Axel* (1822), he returns to the chaotic period of Karl XII's Russian war. The story is about a Swedish soldier who is sent as a courier to his native country by the king himself but is assaulted on the way back, is wounded, and is then cared for by a young girl with whom he falls in love. Fate does not permit their union, however. Disguised as a Russian soldier, she comes to Sweden to find her beloved. But she is wounded and dies in Axel's arms. The sentimental narrative was a great hit with the public and became one of Tegnér's most frequently read texts. It even gave occasion for parody. *Axel* has not endured well in the eyes of posterity, however.

Frithiofs saga (1825; Eng. tr. 1833), which Tegnér began in 1820, was a greater venture. The subject matter was taken from *Nordiska kämpadater* (1737; Norse warrior deeds), by Eric Julius Biörner (1696–1750), which introduced translations of Icelandic sagas, among them the one about Frithiof the Bold. *Frithiofs saga* consists of twenty-four songs, the classical epic division, in various meters: hexameter, ottava rima, blank verse, and imitation of *fornyrðislag* (an Old Norse verse form of eight-line alliterative stanzas). Tegnér relates twenty-four rather independent scenes or situations—several of dialogue-character—with the saga, which he uses rather freely as his point of departure.

Of course, Frithiof is not a realistic depiction of a viking. His character is rather contradictory. *Frithiofs saga* is primarily a love story. The young hero proposes to his foster sister, Ingeborg, but is rejected by her two brothers, Helge and Halvdan, as unworthy. In spite of his renown with arms, he is only the son of a farmer, and Ingeborg is the king's daughter. A more worthy suitor turns up, old King Ring. When he is also turned down and threatens war, Helge and Halvdan ask Frithiof for help. He is willing to give it, but as a reward he wants Ingeborg's hand. He is again turned down when it is revealed that he has been seeing Ingeborg in secret in the grove dedicated to Balder, where she has been placed by her brothers. As a punishment, Frithiof is sent on a risky tax-collecting expedition to the Orkneys. He succeeds in his task, but when he returns, he finds that Ingeborg's brothers have burned his farm, Framnäs, to the ground and married their sister to King Ring. Frithiof then seeks out King Helge, who is performing sacrificial rites in Balder's temple. Frithiof throws the purse with the taxes in Helge's face. In the ensuing commotion, he happens to jostle an image of the god, which falls into the flames; the whole temple burns down. Banned as a criminal, he goes into exile but cannot forget Ingeborg. He travels in disguise to King Ring's court, is eventually recognized by the king and becomes his friend. When King Ring dies, Frithiof is appointed guardian of the king's and Ingeborg's minor son by the Thing. Frithiof is reconciled with Halvdan, who now reigns by himself, and marries Ingeborg.

As is obvious from this summary, *Frithiofs saga* depicts a variety of moods. There are reminiscences of Homeric poetry, especially in the song in which Frithiof receives his paternal inheritance, meticulously described. There is the elegant, ironic-satirical "Frithiof spelar schack" (Frithiof plays chess); "Frithiof går i landsflykt" (Frithiof goes into exile), which is marked by a desolate Byronic mood; and "Rings drapa" (Ring's funeral elegy), colored by Norse mythology, which tells of the old king riding across the bridge to the realm of the dead, Valhalla, and being greeted as a peer by the Aesir.

Sometimes Frithiof gives the impression of a medieval knight, courteous and noble, as when he throws away his sword rather than succumb to the temptation of killing his sleeping rival, Ring. Ingeborg, passive and modest, is a bourgeois nineteenth-century girl who submits to being married to the man her guardians select. In general, Tegnér has attempted to modernize and humanize the old saga. That is most evident in the concluding song, "Försoningen" (The atonement). The temple of Balder, which burned down because of Frithiof, is rebuilt. Tegnér has the Balder priest speak of love and peace, with obvious allusions to Christianity, and presage the advent of this faith in the North.

For a long time, *Frithiofs saga* was something of a Swedish national epic. It mixes epic and lyric in a way that appealed to contemporary readers. The character descriptions work according to the principle of antithesis: the light-haired, sympathetic hero, Frithiof, is placed in opposition to the dark-haired, unsympathetic Helge, who is also associated with the dying belief in the Aesir. Twelve of the songs were set to music by Bernhard Henrik Crusell (1755–1838), contributing to the popularity of the work. Some of the songs, such as "Vikingabalk" (Viking code), were incorporated into the musical treasure trove of the schools and were sung far into this century. The songs were translated into both German and English. Longfellow, whose *Song of Hiawatha* (1855) is in part an attempt in the same genre, was familiar with Tegnér. He visited Sweden in the early 1830s and wrote an extensive essay on Tegnér for the *North American Review* (1837). Longfellow also translated *Nattvardsbarnen*.

Tegnér as Lyric Poet

Like most of the other romantics, Tegnér often spoke in his poems about the task of poetry; poetry and the creators of poetry are given an exalted, almost sacramental function. According to Tegnér, the poet must not occupy himself with vain brooding or fall into pessimism. In two relatively early poems, "Skidbladner" (1812) and "Sången" (1819; The song), he argues for poetics of this kind; the poems are partly addressed to the Uppsala romantics. In "Skidbladner," he speaks of the world of poetry as a golden ship with an eternal following wind, and in "Sången," he explains that "the poet has no sorrows / And the sky of song is ever clear." The task of the poet is not to sing of "griefs he himself has invented." Tegnér abandoned his view of poetry as a positive force for life in some of his later lyric poems. The greatest of these is "Mjeltsjukan" (Spleen). The date of this text is disputed, but strong arguments (e.g., in Tegnér's letters) have been advanced for 1825. The reason for the pessimism—*mjältsjuka* was an old word for melancholy—expressed in the text has also been debated. It seems quite obvious that when the poem was written, Tegnér had suffered from bad health for a long time. The text, however, speaks of a sudden reversal of outlook on life and zest:

Then a spleenish black elf appeared, and suddenly
the black one fastened his teeth on my heart:
and see, all at once everything turned empty and desolate,
and sun and stars suddenly turned dark.

The biographical interpreters who, along with the Danish critic Georg Brandes, want to see disappointed love at the root of Tegnér's melancholy can find arguments in the text to support the view that it is not the spleen but rather the heart, the stronghold and symbol of love, that is the seat of the disease: "O my consumed heart, bled dry!" and "My heart? There is no heart in my chest / only an urn containing the ashes of life."

Other critics have pointed out similarities to Byron and to the melancholy found in Shakespeare, for instance, in Hamlet's soliloquy on suicide. Tegnér's expressive imagery presents obvious comparisons to Shakespeare's, as in such lines as "The odor of death runs through human life / poisoning the air of spring and the splendor of summer," or when the poem's speaker exclaims, "Tell me, watchman, what is the time of night? / Will it never end?" or when he paints a night landscape with "weepy-eyed stars" and "the half-consumed moon," which makes one think of *Macbeth*. No matter which models and inspirations Tegnér may have had, the unique, personal note he strikes in "Mjeltsjukan" makes him one of the great writers of confessional poetry in Swedish literature.

"Den döde" (The dead man), dedicated to one of the women close to him in his later life, is another confessional poem. Tegnér gives his beloved a self-portrait in verse for her to have when he is dead; with its help, she will be able to tell what kind of person the poet was: "a changeable soul, who created his own torment / and finally burned out in his own flame."

The Letters as Documents of a Period and a Life

In an often quoted characterization of the young Tegnér, Erik Gustaf Geijer writes that all Tegnér said "gleamed." It is an attempt to explain his esprit. He spent his entire career in the provinces, outside Stockholm: first in Lund and then in the school and cathedral city of Växjö. He was an assiduous letter writer, however, and in this way he kept in touch with influential cultural figures in Sweden. In these letters, sandwiched between expositions on trivial official and promotion concerns, Tegnér's esprit blossoms: his ability to find striking images, his sarcasm, and his irony. In March 1817, he writes to one of his friends: "The serpent of time often sheds its skin; but I have never seen it more abominable than now, right now, as far back as history goes, even if he hissed nothing but hymns and his back were painted all over, like a gravestone, with Bible verses." In his method of enlarging an image into a concrete, striking construction, Tegnér's style points forward to modern poetry. Some of his metaphors evidently make their first appearance in his letters and are further developed in his poems and speeches. One of Tegnér's more intimate correspondents was the diplomat and writer Carl Gustaf von Brinkman (1764–1847), who developed letter writing and the cult of friendship into something of a lifestyle. When he wrote in a letter to Tegnér that he had been severely ill, Tegnér replies sympathetically in March 1826 but adds, "Of course I know that you will one day die like a man, as Socrates died, as all superior individuals must die, calmly and fearlessly."

Tegnér's last years were darkened by poor mental health; during one period, he was in a hospital in Schleswig. Geijer, who had borne such eloquent witness to the intellectual vitality of the young Tegnér, writes in some letters of his meeting with the mentally ill poet during a visit to Stockholm in 1840. Tegnér was then periodically calm and collected but later, as Geijer wrote to his wife, he fell "into fantasies, which are, among other things, that he is tremendously rich and will, only now, with his friends, be able to enjoy life." Tegnér died in 1846.

ROMANTIC PROSE WRITERS, 1800–1830

In Sweden, prose was hardly held in high esteem by the end of the eighteenth century and in the first decades of the nineteenth. Atterbom, who set the tone in aesthetic matters, did not write fictional prose, but in the group surrounding the Aurora League, there were two people in particular who would promote the novel and the short story. They were Vilhelm Fredrik Palmblad (1788–1852) and Clas Livijn (1781–1844). Palmblad translated short stories by such German romantics as Hoffmann, Tieck, and Fouqué which he published in *Poetisk kalender*. He also championed the novel as an art form in his essay "Dialog över romanen" (Dialogue on the novel), which was published in *Phosphoros* in 1812. He is at his best in relatively realistic texts like "Amala" (1817) and *Holmen i sjön Dall* (1819; The islet in Lake Dall). The first takes place in India, and the second mostly in Kashmir; thus, they are examples of the exoticism that characterized Swedish romanticism. In "Amala," a first-person narrator relates his experiences, in particular his unhappy love for the title character, a young dancer.

Palmblad's style is simple, clearly focused on the story itself. The text shows not a vague fairy-tale land but instead a war-torn, chaotic India, marked by English colonization. Palmblad had no first hand experience of India or, indeed, of any part of Asia, but that did not disturb authors of the romantic school. In any case, it is a contemporary tale, as is also true of *Holmen i sjön Dall*, but there is an *Arabian Nights* atmosphere in this novel with its inserted tales, its dreams, and its mysterious harem ladies. The narrator is the young Rustan, the son of the governor of Kashmir. In the beginning of the novel, he meets a beautiful woman on an island in Lake Dall, by whose shore he takes lonely walks. The lake with the strange island, where the heroine occupies herself with feeding dwarf deer, is described in terms reminiscent of the *locus amoenus* that fascinated other romantics as well: "This lake is strewn with a number of very beautiful islets, adorned with pavilions, mountains with vineyards, groves, and orchards." Rustan falls in love with the mysterious girl and wants to marry her, but because of perfidious intrigues on the part of the villain of the story, Jussuf, she disappears and the reunion takes place only in the final part of the narrative.

His contemporaries criticized Palmblad because he had depicted his main character and narrator, Rustan, more as a Westerner than as an Asian. If one views Palmblad's text as a paraphrase of *Arabian Nights*, which is reasonable, it may be possible to overlook such trifles. Because there is always a narrator who controls the perspective, even when he is listening to inserted tales, the composition remains firm though the plot meanders by surprising twists and turns. Among the relatively sparse and uneven attempts in the fictional genre offered by Swedish romanticism, Palmblad's texts have been too long neglected.

Clas Livijn's best-known work is the epistolary novel *Spader Dame* (Queen of Spades), which was published early in 1825, at about the same time as *Frithiofs saga*. It employs the devices common at this time for creating verisimilitude. A fictitious preface, signed "The Editor," states that the manuscript of the novel was found in a closet at the mental hospital Danviken and that it was written by an insane student. A fragmentary introductory section follows, signed with the initials of the main character, Z.S. This arrangement is reminiscent of the one employed by E.T.A. Hoffmann in his *Die Elixiere des Teufels* (The devil's elixir), published in 1812. The hero and letter writer of Livijn's novel is the student Schenander, who is about to start as a tutor in the family of a wealthy foundry owner and who falls in love with the owner's niece. It has already been decided that she shall marry the brutal officer Leyonbraak, however. As a result of a number of plots, the unfortunate student lands first in prison and eventually in a hospital for the insane.

One cannot overlook the fact that the story is partly a criticism of social conditions and class differences. Ultimately, Livijn's novel is about the opposition between the intellectual and a society distinguished by arbitrary justice and class prejudice. The points of contact with Goethe's Werther are evident. The interest in mental illness and its supposed kinship with genius also appears elsewhere in the romantic period. Livijn's text probably contains more allusions to contemporary conditions than a modern reader is able to find. Stylistically speaking, the text is uneven and bizarre, which may be intentional.

Fredric Cederborgh (1784–1835) existed outside the literary cliques. In addition to his work as a journalist and as a government official, he published several prose texts, among them the novels *Uno von Trasenberg*, (3 vols.; 1809–10) and *Ottar Trallings lefnads-målning* (4 vols.; 1810–18; Ottar Tralling's life depiction). Cederborgh writes in the tradition of the picaresque novel, and his protagonists move among different milieus in their odysseys through early-nineteenth-century Sweden, viewed through the spectacles of awakening liberalism. With his realistic style, Cederborgh accurately describes town and country, stagecoach inns and civil service departments. The stories are playfully artistic and rather loosely structured; high and low matters are mixed in a fashion that offended the arbiters of taste in this period. Cederborgh was severely criticized by the Uppsala romantics, and the Swedish Academy rejected a proposal to award him a prize. Literary institutions were not ready to accept the realistic novel as an artistic genre, but that was not the case of the growing crowd of literature-loving readers.

Ottar Trallings lefnads-målning, arguably Cederborgh's best novel, is, like Strindberg's much later *Röda rummet* (1879; Eng. tr. *The Red Room* 1967), a satirical reckoning with various institutions in a class society rife with corruption and class pride. On his odyssey, the protagonist makes the acquaintance of courts of law, prisons, and law offices. Ottar even spends a semester at the University of Lund, but since he does not know Latin and does not have the money to bribe his professors, he has no success there. Cederborgh's novel is what might nowadays be called "open." Verse, letters, and other documents are included, as well as frank comments on those phenomena the author disapproves of, such as Atterbom and his romantic school in Uppsala. The characterizations lean toward caricature: in this respect, Cederborgh reminds us of Gogol and Dickens. Contemporaries as well as posterity have compared him with the master of the picaresque novel, Le Sage, and his *Gil Blas.*

ALMQVIST: THE MAN OF MANY MASKS

Even more markedly than other romantics, Carl Jonas Love Almqvist (1793–1866), both in his personal destiny and in his texts, displays the conflict between the intellectual and society, with its values and prospects for making a livelihood. Early in his career, Almqvist comes across as a visionary, even a prophet, and a reformer of society. He came from a well-known family of government employees and received his academic degree in Uppsala before he took a position, in 1815, in the same central civil service department as Stagnelius, the Office of Education and Ecclesiastical Affairs. A visionary and a reformer of society, however, cannot in the long run content himself with being a minor government clerk. For a short period, 1824–25, Almqvist tried to establish himself as a latter-day Rousseau-type farmer; later he became the headmaster of a high school in Stockholm. He was ordained, in order to choose the same track as Tegnér, but he stumbled at the very start after he published his criticism of marriage in the novella *Det går an* (1839; Eng. tr. *Sara Videbeck*, 1919; *Why Not?* 1994). In the same year—like Geijer the previous year—he moved into the liberal camp and started contributing to the opposition paper *Aftonbladet* (Evening paper), which was despised by the establishment. Following accusations of an attempt to commit murder by poison, Almqvist was forced to leave Sweden in 1851. He then spent his life under various names and in various occupations in the United States. He returned to Europe in 1865, hoping to reestablish contact with his native country. He did not succeed, and in 1866 he died in Bremen, where he had used the name Professor Carl Westermann.

In 1817, Almqvist and some Stockholm friends founded the society Manna-Samfund (Society of Men), following the example of Atterbom's Uppsala circle. The society was based on Swedenborgian ideas, which also influenced Almqvist's first important work, *Murnis* (1819), embodying his—in many respects very personal—ideas about life after death. *Murnis* was not published until 1845, in a censored version; a complete edition did not appear until 1960. The reason is the supposedly pornographic elements in the passages in which Almqvist describes the lovers' meeting in an Edenic landscape with cypresses and silk grass. Eroticism and religiosity form a strange alloy in this poetic love scene, in which the sex organs are given suggestive, mysterious names. The zealous censors saw through this device, however. Another of Almqvist's important early texts, *Amorina* (1822), suffered a similar fate. *Amorina* belongs to a mixed genre of novel and play, prose and poetry. To a larger extent than the other Swedish romantics, Almqvist was prepared to listen to the appeal to break with the tyranny of genre. Unfortunately, the publication of *Amorina* was stopped by the intervention of an old relative, who feared that the book would hurt the career of its author. Instead, it was published in 1839, equipped with a long introduction of the same type as *Spader Dame* (above) but even more elaborate. The cast of characters consists of twin brothers, Rudman and Wilhelm Falkenburg, who are both in love with Henrika/Amorina, their half-sister and the stepdaughter of the vicar Libius. Johannes, a mentally ill murderer, is another figure at the center of the narrative. Almqvist is interested in the connection between criminality and madness, and Henrika, who assumes the part of Amorina, succumbs, like Ophelia, to madness; *Hamlet* was performed in Stockholm in 1819, and its importance for Almqvist's story should not be underestimated. Libius is a brutal and mean-spirited church functionary; Amorina, who represents natural, naive religiosity, provides the contrast.

Amorina is an uneven work in which scenes of shattering realism are mixed with lyrical passages, elements of vampirism, and other horror effects borrowed from German romanticism. The text may also be read as a Shakespeare-inspired chronicle play with a dash of the brilliant, demonic fantasy typical of all Almqvist's works. *Amorina* has also been interpreted as an attempt to put into practice the all-encompassing work of art, universal poetry. All genres are mixed here: dramatic, epic, and lyric. Perhaps that is what has tempted modern directors to venture the staging of this work. They are attracted by the dialectic between sublime and criminal, embodied by the saintly Amorina and the mentally ill murderer Johannes.

Törnrosens Bok

Almqvist's works are among the most singular and variegated creations in all Swedish literature. He organized the major part of his output within a fictional framework, publishing his texts under the title *Törnrosens bok* (The book of the briar rose), an original idea. In the late 1820s, he wrote his story *Jaktslottet* (publ. 1832; The hunting estate), which functions as a frame story for *Törnrosens bok*. The proprietor of the hunting lodge, Hugo Löwenstjerna, has gathered his relatives in his home to listen to stories, fairy tales "without connection among themselves, but making a single unity whose parts would be independent by themselves, yet lived in and through each other." The poetics is ingenious and equivocal, modeled on other frame narratives such as the one in *Arabian Nights*, which is mentioned in *Jaktslottet*. Perhaps Almqvist also received inspiration from Goethe's Boccaccio-influenced *Unterhaltungen deutscher Ausgewanderten* (1795; The recreations of the German emigrants) and from the new interest in the short story as an art form. Löwenstjerna represents an aesthetic concept with a certain didactic orientation. A different kind of poetics is represented by the mysterious guest, Richard Furumo, a literate farmer, strangely classless in outward appearance but the son of a former librarian at the estate. He makes a condition for his participation in the storytelling: he will always be allowed to follow his impulse and will not have to subject himself to structural principles such as chronology. This condition is in line with the poetics pronounced by the Don Juan character in one of Almqvist's plays, *Ramido Marinesco* (1834): "I paint this way, Donna Bianca, / for this is how it amuses me to paint."

Almqvist's "Songes," or dreams, a special kind of all-encompassing work of art, also belong to the hunting estate fictions. They were intended to be read, sung, and performed as living pictures. Almqvist himself composed the music, which is often artless and unsophisticated, like the text. His "Songes" have an obvious visual component that is made concrete with his singular naiveté. He himself describes his "Songes" as follows: "something that is different from plays but that closely approaches the idea of a tableau vivant in that it only includes a single situation. It is possible to give *sound* and *movement* to this situation, that is, to a certain extent." Most of the *songes* poems were written in the 1820s and became known through handwritten copies and performances in such places as Malla Silfverstolpe's salon; a collected edition was not published until 1849, two years before Almqvist's exile. The structural composition of these poems may be studied in one of the best known, "Marias häpnad" (Mary's astonishment):

The white lambs graze in the meadow;
The Jesus child walks alongside.
Astonished, Mary stops and cries,
"I see a halo around the child's hair!"

The *songes* poems are not always this brief, but there is usually an immanent "picture" that is brought to life by an element of dialogue. It is possible that, in this instance, Almqvist found his inspiration in some naive religious picture. The subject matter, however, is not always religious by any means. Sometimes his *songes* have features of folk songs about young love, as in "Hvarför kom du på ängen?" (Why did you come to the meadow?), which is still frequently sung today. The strain of social criticism, which became more marked in Almqvist with the passing years, is evident in the short, pithy, but cruel picture from Swedish history, "Häxan i Konung Carls tid" (The witch in the time of King Karl). In ten expressive lines, it tells of a poor old woman denounced as a witch. She is accused of having milked the minister's cow surreptitiously by putting sticks in a wall. The punishment was being burned at the stake. "The children were permitted to stand by the Mother's pyre" is the ironic comment in the last line.

Almqvist published two editions of his variegated collective work, *Törnrosens bok*, first the so-called duodecimo edition of 1833–51 in fourteen volumes and then an imperial octavo edition in three volumes, 1839–50.

Fairy Tale, Myth, and Vision

Fairy tale and myth underwent a renaissance through romanticism which was extremely fruitful for Almqvist. Sometimes he writes outright myths, as in the arch little creation story "Skönhetens tårar" (The tears of beauty). He often mixes different styles of narration and discovers that such hybrid genres can be used for satire and social criticism. That is the case in "Ormus och Ariman" (Ormazd and Ahriman), narrated by Richard Furumo in the circle at the hunting estate. The underlying myth is taken from the Persian *Zend-Avesta*, which had been translated into Swedish in a collection of texts based on religious history documents.

In "Ormus och Ariman," Almqvist's irony and satire are sometimes mischievous, as when, using reckless etymologies, he pretends to prove that the secretaries, that is, the civil servants, belong to a "caste of beggars scattered throughout Europe." Ormus, who in the beginning of the tale is identified as the principle of goodness, develops into a superbureaucrat with offices on the moon, whence he issues his edicts, including the priceless one about how the citizens should walk the streets. Ariman, the seemingly evil one, sabotages all this bureaucratically regulated existence. He is the romantic, even anarchistic, artist, a counterweight to Ormus's benighted attempts to rule and regulate everything, and he adds beauty to existence. He is described in the following manner: "A dark, tall figure, with fine but coal-black eyebrows, fiery eyes beneath his forehead, a kind of sadness lingering about his mouth. By preference, Ariman often walked alone. He did not build a house: he did not yearn for house or estate: he was no householder, regulator, or careful provider." "Ormus och Ariman" clearly shows the rift in Almqvist's romantic project, and one can see how it points to the more pronounced social criticism in the late 1830s. At the same time, Almqvist introduces his so-called rag aesthetics, summed up in the following lines from "Ormus och Ariman":

Why is the good man stupid—
Why is the clever one evil—
Why is everything in rags?

The tale concludes with this pessimistic grimace, which negates both ethics and aesthetics.

Like Atterbom and Tegnér, Almqvist discusses—partly in allegorical, fairy-tale form—the question of the essence, origin, and conditions of poetry, as in "Guldfågeln i paradis" (1822; The gold bird in paradise). The short, visionary "Skaldens natt" (1827; The poet's night) is more interesting. Here the first-person narrator is agonizing in doubts about his task as an artist; finally, in a vision, he receives a kind of calling or mission. It is significant for Almqvist's demonic view of art, however, that it has no moral loyalty. His fidelity is to the essence of art, but as the text says, "Its nature isn't to be straight, is it? — Art doesn't shoot in the same direction it aims." The view of life in "Skaldens natt" has similarities to Goethe's often-cited lines, "Ich hab' mein Sach' auf nichts gestellt" (I have based my course on nothing), a kind of zero declaration. Almqvist states, "Only remember to stand on nothing and to support yourself on nothing."

Because Almqvist was accused of attempted murder and left Sweden voluntarily, his work was neglected for a long time. His rehabilitation began with an influential essay by Ellen Key in 1894, in which Almqvist was introduced as Sweden's most modern author. Since then, his position as one of the country's most original writers has been reinforced, and the publication of all his works, which include poetry, plays, short stories, novels, essays, and articles on various topics, as well as letters and textbooks, is not yet finished. In his private life as well as in his works, Almqvist still appears enigmatic, elusive, and innovative. Further discussions of his works are found in the next chapter.

THE ROMANTIC PLAY

Plays, especially opera and popular comedy, enjoyed a time of glory during the reign of Gustav III, who had a special royal theater built. Gustav's death brought a period of decline, and in 1806, Gustav IV Adolf closed the opera house and stopped state subventions. After the end of absolute rule in 1810, the theater was reopened and periodically a special dramatic stage as well. The royal theater monopoly continued until 1842. That did not hinder the flourishing of the theater, however, and it was possible to see Mozart operas as well as Shakespeare and Schiller plays and, perhaps most of all, the new, popular melodrama. August von Kotzebue's plays in particular were extremely popular, as well as René Charles de Pixerécourt's melodramas, for example, *The Moors in Spain* and *The Count of Castelli*. As far as native authors are concerned, the plays of the extremely prolific Carl Magnus Envallsson (1756–1806) were frequently performed by touring theater groups in the provinces. His poetic comedy *Slåtterölet eller Kronofogdarne* (1787; The harvest feast, or The bailiffs) stayed in the repertoire a long time, not least because of its popular songs. The foundation for contemporary bourgeois plays had been laid in the last decades of the eighteenth century. George Lillo's crime drama *The London Merchant* was translated (from French) in 1767 and was staged very successfully, first in Göteborg and then in Stockholm. A Swedish adaptation of the play was also popular, but the arbiters of taste in the Swedish Academy, Leopold and Oxenstierna, were critical of the piece's departure from French theater aesthetics. The barriers had come down, however, and Pehr Enbom (1759–1810), one of Thorild's primary allies, published *Fabriksflickan* (The factory girl) in 1796, the first expression of conscious class awareness in Swedish dramatic literature. It is true that after the fashion of the time, the play has a sentimental dénouement in which the proletarian heroine turns out to be the daughter of a captain, but the play still conveys true pathos for "the poor factory wretches," as the author expresses it in his preface. Among other places, *Fabriksflickan* was performed in Göteborg in 1801.

In imitation of Shakespeare and Schiller, the historical drama was also cultivated, mostly by Bernhard von Beskow (1796–1868), who for a time managed Kungliga Teatern. His own history plays *Erik XIV* (1827–28) and *Torkel Knutsson* (1836) were important contributions to the genre.

The authors of this period, especially Atterbom, Stagnelius, and Almqvist, were geniunely interested in theater, which left a profound impression on their works. Atterbom's *Lycksalighetens ö* has been treated earlier. Stagnelius's most pronounced attempts to imitate the popular chivalric play were *Eröfringen af Ceuta* (1816; The conquest of Ceuta) and *Riddartornet* (1825; The knights' tower).

Stagnelius's effort in quite a different dramatic genre, *Thorsten Fiskare* (Thorsten the fisherman) is of greater literary value. The play was published only after Stagnelius's death, but it has been staged at Dramaten in Stockholm in recent years. Stagnelius here approaches the popular harlequinade, which was especially successful in pantomimes. The protagonist, Thorsten, is shipwrecked on an island and is brought to the court of the elf king, Germund. First, however, he is given a Harlequin costume by the king's maids. Stagnelius envisioned a fairy play with gnomes, elves, water sprites, and other nature deities, as well as songs and dances of the type common in pantomimes.

The closet drama *Martyrerna* (1821; The martyrs) deals with a Christian woman, Perpetua, who chooses a martyr's death rather than compromise her conviction. The play is set in Roman-occupied Carthage, and its subject matter is well adapted to the new watchword about Christian elements in literature which had recently been introduced, primarily by Chateaubriand in France.

The Stagnelius play that, because of its literary quality, has survived the best is *Bacchanterna* (1822; The Bacchantes), a rather difficult and contradictory text whose subject matter and form have been borrowed from classical Greek drama. The chorus has an important function in the play, as does the female leader of the chorus, who pronounces the accusation against Orpheus that clarifies the basic conflict, that is, that he speaks for only one way to conquer and pass beyond the threshold of death: asceticism and self-denial. The leader of the chorus speaks for love of life, the love of women, and "convivial pleasures."

Orpheus is killed by the furious Bacchantes but returns as a "shade" in the final scene of the play, delivering an epilogue that speaks of recon-ciliation between opposing life forces and condemns rite and sacrifice as externals. Only obedience to the one "who opens and shuts the copper door of Orcus" will wash away the contagion of the soul, it says, that is, the necessary insight will come through submission to the implacability of death. In this scene, the statement made by the tragic conflict is partly corrected. Orpheus offers to participate in the Dionysian sacrifice and contributes a ram, but the sacrifice is rejected by the Underworld. In this treatment of the Orpheus myth, Stagnelius has pushed the figure of Eurydice into the background and concentrated on Orpheus's conflict with the phallus-worshiping Bacchantes. The chorus is given great scope, as might be expected from a purely lyric poet like Stagnelius.

In Almqvist, it is possible to see how the theater component sometimes gets the upper hand of the epic in his two great novels, *Amorina* (1822) and *Drottningens juvelsmycke eller Azouras Lazuli Tintomara* (1834; Eng. tr. *The Queen's Diadem*, 1992). The different scenes in *Amorina* are called "pictures," and the connection with pantomime tableaux is palpable. There is often pantomime with dramatic musical accompaniment, something Almqvist would have experienced in the theater. Another popular form was the monodrama, a hybrid of music, recitation, and pantomime.

Almqvist's most stage-worthy plays are probably *Ramido Marinesco* (1834) and *Purpurgrefven* (The purple count). The former is a Don Juan play in verse in which the protagonist, Ramido, turns out to be the son of Don Juan. In a prefatory remark, Almqvist refers to Mozart's and Byron's treatments of the same material. His own version gives us a penitent Don Juan, one who tries to atone for the evil he has done by getting the women he has betrayed to hate him. But Almqvist carries the myth further by introducing Ramido, who regularly falls in love with young women who turn out to be his half-sisters. The idea is certainly bold. Ramido's tragic fate is completed when, on his return home, he falls in love with the picture of a woman Don Juan has painted. In his painting, Don Juan—like Almqvist himself in his writing—mixes poison in his paint. Thus the figure of Don Juan becomes still another representative of Almqvist's demonic view of art. The play has been performed in a radio version.

Purpurgrefven has also been performed successfully, both on the stage and on the air. It is a relatively realistic contemporary play without the chivalric romantic elements of *Ramido Marinesco*. The theatrical power and poetry of Almqvist's texts were demonstrated in 1951, when Dramaten offered an adaptation of *Amorina* directed by Alf Sjöberg, the premier director of the time. It proved a great success. That resulted in a staging of *Drottningens juvelsmycke*, first in an alternate theater in Stockholm, and later as a television play and as a full evening's performance on the national stage. The main character, Tintomara, has shown herself to be a rewarding theater figure; of course, she was borrowed from the world of the theater in the first place: she is supposedly a ballet dancer at the opera of Gustav III. Consequently, it is quite natural for one of Sweden's most prominent composers, Lars Johan Werle, to choose this figure as a central character in an opera entitled *Tintomara* (1973).

THE DISSOLUTION OF ROMANTICISM

A number of authors who may be considered romantic imitators were noted during their lifetimes but have been unable to hold their own in the eyes of posterity. Among them is Carl Wilhelm Böttiger (1807–78) who also, however, wrote lyric poems that still belong to the living treasure trove of songs, for example, "O, hur härligt majsol ler" (Oh, how wonderfully the May sun smiles), an obligatory spring song for male chorus. Another late romantic was Elias Malmström (1816–65), who succeeded Atterbom as professor in Uppsala and carried on Atterbom's research in literary history with *Grunddragen af den svenska vitterhetens historia* (1816–69; Outline of the history of Swedish literature). Carl August Hagberg (1810–64) has inscribed his name on the pages of Swedish cultural history in a special way. He translated Shakespeare's collected plays into Swedish (1840–51), and his interpretations influenced the view of Shakespeare for generations to come. When Shakespeare is quoted in Swedish, it is still in Hagberg's striking formulations. He was a professor at the University of Lund but also wrote historical novels in the tradition of Sir Walter Scott.

The romantic movement may, if one so chooses, be divided into several phases. Preromanticism started in the 1780s with Thorild and Lidner; a high romantic movement began with Atterbom's creation of a romantic school in 1809, and ebbed in the mid-1820s. Realistic elements then became more prominent, with Almqvist and Fredrika Bremer. Nevertheless, the romantic heritage manifested itself as an undercurrent through the rest of the nineteenth century, emerging in a forceful renaissance in the 1890s.

In its initial phase, Swedish romanticism received strong influences from Germany and England, but the basic ideas of the movement promoted a search for a national cultural identity. Among its most important and lasting contributions are the new interest in folklore, folk tales, and medieval ballads and the rediscovery of the Icelandic sagas. A striking democratic component helped weaken the aristocratic court culture. Before romanticism, poetic language in the modern sense did not exist in Sweden. Texts from the period of classicism were often characterized by shallow moralizing or didacticism, and authors were expected to confine themselves to the repertory of established genres as far as style, metrics, and imagery were concerned. Romanticism signified an expansion of the means of expression for poetic language. The period was also distinguished by more diverse literary activity. Several important critics appeared, and a forum was created, in the form of journals and publishing ventures, for literary debate and for influencing public opinion. Not until the Modern Breakthrough in the 1870s did a significant critical view of the premises of romanticism emerge.

Liberalism, Realism, and the Modern Breakthrough: 1830–1890

Birgitta Steene

5

THE AGE OF LIBERALISM (1830 – 1879)

In retrospect, the nineteenth century in Swedish literature emerges as the century of the middle class, whose social arrival in the 1700s had by then produced new groups of readers with somewhat different literary tastes than earlier generations of largely upper-class literates. Ideologically, the Swedish bourgeoisie felt closer to the Age of Enlightenment than to the religious, philosophical, and political concepts of the ensuing romantic era. Romanticism was viewed as conserving old values rather than responding to the new liberal ideas that, in the 1830s, began to spread north from England and the European continent.

European liberalism manifests itself in such political events as the French July Revolution of 1830 and the British Parliamentary Reform of 1832 and leads up to the February Revolution of 1848 and its impact on many parts of Europe, most notably in the national unification of such countries as Italy and Germany. The cultural ideas that emerge from these political changes emphasize a belief in reason and scientific progress; they speak up for the rights of the individual against social and religious authorities; and they express an attitude of optimism fed by the rapid technological transformation of European society.

Among the middle class, the family and family life held a central position; its most common pastime was reading aloud in the evening, as the head of the household gathered his wife and children around the fireplace. An important feature in the nineteenth-century middle-class family was the home library, which lent social prestige to the aspiring bourgeoisie. It is likely that this phenomenon, more than anything else, helped create a shift in literary taste. The didactic literature of a preceding age was replaced by books of entertainment that were often read quickly as the literary consumer tried to keep up with the latest best-selling fiction.

The family circle as a paradigmatic consumer group of literature can be related to an older, peculiarly Swedish cultural phenomenon instituted by the Lutheran state church—the so-called house examination, which, as early as the seventeenth century, laid the foundation for an unusually high literacy rate in Sweden. In the house examination, the head clergy within a given parish would conduct regular visitations and hearings in the homes of his parishioners to ensure an adequate reading knowledge or understanding of the Bible and other religious works deemed important in the Lutheran dogma.

By the 1830s, Luther's small catechism, the Swedish hymn book, and Johann A. Arndt's *postilla* (book of homilies) no longer constituted the only available material for the reading public. More secular books began to spread to all levels of the citizenry. From the middle of the century compulsory education increased this readership, as did an expanding university and administrative population. But the largest single group of literary consumers in the 1800s was constituted by women, despite the fact that they were still excluded from most institutions of higher learning.

Books continued to be associated with social advancement in Sweden throughout the century. When a new social group—the laboring class—began to gain a political voice toward the end of the 1800s, one of its basic aspirations was to get access to books (and education). One could claim that the period between 1830 and 1890 represents the real flowering of the Gutenberg Age in Swedish culture.

With expanding reading habits followed a redefinition of the writer's role. Before the establishment of the newspaper and other nineteenth-century outlets for literary works, the aspiring playwright, novelist, or poet was found in the traditional professions: Tegnér was a bishop, Geijer a university professor, and Almqvist a high school superintendent. By the middle of the 1800s, an author could live from his writing alone with an income comparable to that of a university professor. It is estimated, for instance, that August Strindberg earned about the same amount, in the 1880s, as a supreme court judge.

What were the tastes of the growing reading public in Sweden in the 1830s and on? Most popular were translations of European and American fiction. Subscription libraries, an early version of the Book-of-the-Month Club, were started, spreading the works (in inexpensive softcover editions) of such authors as Walter Scott, James Fenimore Cooper, Edward Bulwer-Lytton, and George Sand. It was through this form of publication outlet that the most successful native novelist of the time was discovered: Emilie Flygare-Carlén (1807–92). From the late 1830s and for many years to come, she produced a couple of novels a year and frequently challenged subscription publishers to outbid one another for exclusive rights to her works.

The growing reading public also had access to literature through the establishment of a commercial library system, often managed by local booksellers who lent books for a small fee. Another highly successful source of reading material was the family magazine, which gained in popularity in the 1850s and specialized in short fiction. Publications such as *Illustrerad tidning* (Illustrated paper) and *Svenska familjejournalen* (Swedish family journal) became lucrative outlets for contemporary Swedish writers who catered to the middle class. The prolific August Blanche (1811–68) produced, for instance, six brick-size novels in four years (1847–51) for three different magazine publications.

The age of the bourgeois *arrivé* delegated a new and important role to the newspaper. The 1830s signaled the breakthrough of the liberal press in Sweden. The first modern newspaper in the country, *Aftonbladet*, began publication in 1830. The editor, Lars Johan Hierta, combined his commitment to new political ideas with a shrewd business sense. Thus he came to personify not only the earliest form of mass media culture in Sweden but also the spirit of middle-class entrepreneurship.

Newspapers such as *Aftonbladet* and, later in the century, *Göteborgs Handels- och Sjöfartstidning* (The Göteborg commercial and maritime news) were important disseminators of contemporary liberal ideas and values associated with the rising bourgeoisie. They no doubt contributed to the change in Sweden's political structure that took place in 1866, when the old Riksdag composed of the four estates (the nobility, the clergy, the burghers, and the farmers) was replaced with a two-chamber parliament with representation based on age and income rather than social class or profession.

Newspapers were also significant in providing a forum for the *kåseri* (columnist section) and supplying space for the realistic sketch of everyday life and the literary genre painting. Several prominent writers contributed to *Aftonbladet* as columnists or literary authors: Carl Jonas Love Almqvist, Fredrika Bremer, Emilie Flygare-Carlén. By the 1850s, the newspaper had become an important competitor to the best-selling publisher and the commercial library with its introduction of the serialized novella and novel, which was to play as vital a role in the literary career of Viktor Rydberg as did the English newspaper for Charles Dickens.

It makes sense to use the year of the launching of *Aftonbladet* (1830) as a starting point for a discussion of the arrival of realism as a literary period in Sweden. Newspapers brought contemporary events and factual observations into the homes of the middle class. No doubt the reportage and the *kåseri* helped create a taste for a literature that dealt with realistic events in the present. The new press, political liberal thought, and literary realism emerged as interdependent phenomena in Swedish culture between 1830 and 1890. The gradual decline of the political and social power of the nobility and the clergy ran parallel to the rise of the new bourgeoisie, which based its influence and values on mercantile expansion and entrepreneurship rather than on inherited privileges and biblical rhetoric. It was the (upper) middle class that set the cultural tone, and authors representing nineteenth-century realism in Swedish literature frequently came from this social group or depicted its basic norms: a belief in progress, economic expansion, and social reform, and a desire to see authors explore "the lowly and little world" (Almqvist 1839).

As a literary mode, nineteenth-century realism was a reaction against the poetic aestheticism, exotic milieu painting, and imaginative historicism of the preceding Romantic Age. In his essay "Poesi i sak" (1839; Poetry of realism), Almqvist declares that "the final hour of the masquerade tolls," implying that literary artificiality is a thing of the past and that a new realistic form of fiction and poetry is in the offing.

Swedish nineteenth-century realism may have been aimed at the middle-class reader who sought entertainment in a depiction of contemporary issues and a local or domestic setting. But its scope broadened to include the life of the lower classes, especially in the countryside. A special prose genre, *folklivsskildring* (the popular or provincial sketch), brought a social pathos and a strong moral voice to Swedish literary realism and spawned other forms of prose fiction—what Almqvist calls "tendentious novels and didactic short stories." This streak of literary moralism could be seen as a national trait, an offshoot of the fusing of a strong Lutheran ideology with nineteenth-century revivalist and temperance movements, which gave rise to a new form of tendentious rhetoric.

Dates signaling new literary periods or trends are often arbitrary or at least nebulous. A single work or event seldom defines the beginning of a new literary era. At best it is a marker pointing in a given direction, and rarely does it imply a complete break with the past.

The Swedish nineteenth-century writer Carl Jonas Love Almqvist (1793–

1866) is living proof of the tenuous transition from one literary period to another. Almqvist has been called "a voyager from another planet," but the writer's self-characterization as a personality torn between the "poetic soul" of his mother and "the accountant soul" of his father is perhaps a more accurate portrait. It points to his mood swings, as a person and as a writer, between revivalist religion and mysticism on one hand and emotional detachment and realistic observation on the other. His composite "novel" *Amorina* is a case in point. Subtitled "Den förryckta frökens levnadslopp och sällsynta bedrifter" (The life cycle and strange deeds of a mad demoiselle), *Amorina* epitomizes much in Almqvist's enigmatic talent. On a personal level, it is an aggressive work, a critique of "the big madhouse," that is, the Office of Education and Ecclesiastical Affairs, where Almqvist worked between 1815 and 1823. Reminiscent of Kierkegaard's attacks on state clericalism and also of the Danish philosopher's intellectual passion, *Amorina* exposes a corrupt society governed by bigoted moralism and stupidity. One should keep in mind that the symbiosis of church and state in Sweden had, by Almqvist's time, turned ecclesiastical employees into a strong cadre of civil servants, who often seemed to govern by virtue of their established and petrified power rather than by faith and biblical practice. In the martyr Henrika/Amorina and the criminal outcast Johannes, Almqvist depicts two characters who are ostracized by such an unforgiving and intolerant church and society.

As a literary work, Almqvist referred to *Amorina* as his "poetic fugue," thus indicating its affinity to polyphonic musical composition. The term may adequately sum up the form and structure of the book, but it does not specify its main characteristic: its mood swings from sublime mysticism to grotesque humor, and its literary range from Gothic horror story and melodrama, involving murder and incest, to realistic and robust narrative, evoking the detailed scene-painting of a Bellman or a Strindberg. In *Amorina*, Almqvist exposes the power and excesses of his visionary personality, as well as his talent for storytelling and social critique. Both qualities are amply present in his major work, *Törnrosens bok* (The book of the briar rose). This multivolume prose work (first published in 1833–35, with later editions appearing in 1838–40, 1850, and 1851) contains both realistic everyday stories and imaginative excursions into distant times and places. Such bridging of romantic fantasy and realistic observation suited Almqvist's charged temperament, with its flights between idealistic *svärmeri* (ecstasy) and a desire to deal with the immediate and tangible world. But Almqvist's writing is also representative of a changing literary climate in Sweden. Between 1830 and 1880, prose fiction—the preferential genre of the middle class—emerged as a full-fledged competitor to drama and verse epic. Nevertheless, the literary ideals of the early 1800s lingered on into the epoch of realism and are noticeable in a certain flowery and emotionally excessive language. On the whole, such harkings back to an earlier literary style and mood are mostly found in poetry and especially in the historical novel, which next to the family novel and the realistic short story or novella was the dominant fiction in the period from 1830 to 1880.

HISTORICAL FICTION

In a volume of *Törnrosens bok* from 1834, we find Almqvist's most successful attempt at writing historical prose: the novel *Drottningens juvelsmycke eller Azouras Lazuli Tintomara* (1834; Eng. tr. *The Queen's Diadem*, 1992), subtitled "Berättelser om händelser näst före, under och efter konung Gustav III:s mord" (Tales about the events before, during, and after the murder of King Gustav III). The historical past, depicted in a light, vignette-like manner, is no more than a generation removed from Almqvist's own time, but the atmosphere has an aura of exotic distance and the setting relies on the legendary milieu of opera and masquerade that Gustav's reign had come to represent in the popular imagination. What gives Almqvist's novel its special quality is the way the author transcends the historical and documentary circumstances of the plot by inventing as his main character an enigmatically complex, androgynous ballet dancer, Azouras Lazuli Tintomara, who is unwittingly drawn into the conspiracy to murder the king. The beautiful Tintomara, an amoral creature of instinct who is oblivious to ethical codes, steals the queen's diadem. Led only by impulsive sentiments, she attracts both men and women but loves no one. She drives others to madness, suicide, and murder while keeping herself aloof from any human involvement.

Törnrosens bok opens with a frame story in which Almqvist introduces the reader to the hunting estate of Hugo Löwenstjerna, a jovial host and narrator of some of the ensuing stories. Almqvist's alter ego, however, seems to be the Byronic Richard Furumo, whose family name—literally, Pinemoor—also suggests an affinity with the dark Gothic landscape of Walter Scott's historical novels. It is Furumo who tells the story of Tintomara. Through his narrator, Almqvist can display his thorough knowledge of the Gustavian era; among other things he had studied the protocols from the masquerade ball assassination of Gustav III at the Stockholm Opera in March 1792. But Tintomara is a fictional character; Almqvist makes her the king's half-sister as well as a "specter" from a world of Neoplatonic myth. With an animal's sinuous grace and an aesthete's love of beauty, Tintomara becomes synonymous with art as pleasure, playfulness, and mystery. Richard Furumo seems to accept the Gustavian ballet dancer unconditionally as an emblem of romantic aestheticism and takes obvious delight in telling her story, thus echoing Almqvist's own, oft-quoted lines from *Ramido Marinesco*, another work in the same edition of *Törnrosens bok*: "I paint this way, Donna Bianca, / for this is how it amuses me to paint."

Richard Furumo is not only one of the narrators in *Törnrosens bok*; he is also, on occasion, a kind of stage manager who sets up and directs a series of tableaux vivants performed by the guests in Hugo Löwenstjerna's yellow salon and accompanied by Almqvist's "Songes" compositions. When juxtaposed to the story of the enigmatic and esoteric Tintomara, these lyrics, though appearing outside the actual plot of *Drottningens juvelsmycke*, seem nevertheless to reinforce the elusive and mysterious nature of Tintomara's persona and evoke, in Almqvist's own words, a vision of pure aesthetic bliss "on a heavenly morning . . . in an infinite faraway land of dream and beauty." The phantasmagoric quality of "Songes" balances Tintomara's unwitting cruel impact on her surroundings. Perhaps for the same reason, Ingmar Bergman was led to incorporate Almqvist's "Songes" as a framing device and intermittent "voice" in his 1994 staging of Shakespeare's *A Winter's Tale*, like Tintomara's story an often grotesque and puzzling tragicomedy.

Viktor Rydberg

Major historical prose works in Swedish literature between 1830 and 1880 often combine, as did Almqvist's story of Tintomara, a depiction of a past era with the author's personal ideology. In the 1850s, Viktor Rydberg (1828–95) published several novels in which he incorporated his own philosophy in the historical plot. A typical example is *Fribytaren på Östersjön* (1857; Eng. tr. *The Freebooter of the Baltic*, 1891), first serialized in *Göteborgs Handels- och Sjöfartstidning*. Set in the seventeenth century during a time of witch trials, sea piracy, and attempted revolutionary coups, the novel provides ample amounts of adventure and pathos, revenge and last-minute rescues, told in an episodic manner that seems dictated by its publication in the newspaper format.

Rydberg shared with Almqvist a temperament that oscillated between an involvement in the social issues of the day and an attraction to the exoticism and mystique of the Romantic Age. This ambivalence in emotion and intellect left its mark on his next historical novel, *Singoalla* (1857; Eng. tr. 1903), published in a Christmas calendar. Subtitled "En romantisk sagodikt" (A romantic fable) and set in the Middle Ages, the story depicts the love affair of a socially ill-matched couple, the Christian knight Erland Månesköld and the gypsy girl Singoalla. In later life Rydberg referred to this novel as his "favorite child," possibly because in it he most successfully fused his romantic penchant for a bygone age with episodes of striking realism, especially his account of a ravaging plague, for which he drew on his childhood experiences of a cholera epidemic that had killed his mother in 1834.

The philosophically most crucial of Rydberg's historical novels, *Den siste atenaren* (Eng. tr. *The Last Athenian*, 1869), was serialized in *Göteborgs Handels- och Sjöfartstidning* in 1859. The late classical period in Greece held both emotional and intellectual appeal for Rydberg: in keeping with the Hegelian dialecticism of his own time, he viewed the clash between Greek humanism and early Christian thought as a prelude to a synthesis of the best aspects of both philosophies. At the end of *Den siste atenaren*, the noble Krysantheus fights side by side against intolerance with the priest Theodoros, the latter a spokesman for Christian charity.

The same Hegelian synthesis of classical thought and Christian ethics forms the core of Rydberg's last novel, *Vapensmeden* (The armorer), from 1891. Set during the Swedish Reformation when sixteenth-century Roman Catholicism gave way to Luther's Protestantism, *Vapensmeden* projects as its main character the old fiddler Svante, who wanders through south-central Sweden with his young son, Gunnar. Father and son represent Rydberg's two ideals: the wise and caring humanist and the pure and innocent youth. Against this harmonious parent-child relationship, Rydberg contrasts the pious churchman Master Gudmund, who is a great lover of art and beauty, and his intolerant reformist son Lars, the personification of all the qualities Rydberg abhorred in a human being: fanaticism, power hunger, and smug egotism.

Zacharias Topelius
Both Almqvist and Rydberg were disciples of Walter Scott. In Swedish-speaking Finland they were joined by Zacharias Topelius (1818–98), like Rydberg a journalist and editor before being appointed a professor of history (at the University of Helsinki). Between 1853 and 1867, Topelius brought forth several volumes of *Fältskärns berättelser* (The tales of the military surgeon), first published in the newspaper *Helsingfors Tidningar*. Employing a narrative frame reminiscent of Almqvist's technique in *Törnrosens bok*, Topelius uses an old army surgeon from the reign of Gustav III as his storyteller, letting him narrate memories and legends from Finnish and

Swedish history. The tales cover the time span from the days of Gustav II Adolf and the Thirty Years' War in the early half of the seventeenth century to the successful coup of Gustav III in 1772. In other words, Topelius focuses his attention on the time in Sweden's history referred to as *Stormaktstiden* (Sweden's century as a great power); his foremost purpose, however, is not to glorify the past but rather to show the role played by Finland in Sweden's conquest of new territories in northern Europe. Like his older countryman Johan Ludvig Runeberg, Topelius felt committed to speak for Finland's identity as a nation, and like Runeberg, he did so by juxtaposing upper and lower segments of Finnish society and by combining social consciousness, realistic historical scene-painting, and narrative suspense. *Fältskärns berättelser* became a best seller all over Scandinavia, with new Swedish editions still issued in the 1980s. Topelius's other historical fiction has not reached the same degree of popularity.

Topelius wrote primarily within the genre of youth and children's literature. At the time of his death he had become known as "Uncle Zachris" to children all over Scandinavia. His model was Hans Christian Andersen. More moralistic than Andersen, Topelius appealed to the schoolteachers in the newly established public education system, and his historical tales, as well as *Sagor* (1847; Fairy tales) and *Läsning för barn* (1865–96; Eng. tr. *Stories for Children*, 1911), became standard anthologized fare in Swedish schools up to World War II.

Strindberg and Historical Fiction

Historical prose played an important role in Swedish fiction throughout the nineteenth century. Between the early novels of Viktor Rydberg in the 1850s and the historical short stories and novels by Verner von Heidenstam in the 1890s stands the contribution to the genre of August Strindberg (1849–1912). He was attracted to a new approach to the past voiced by French historians at the time, emphasizing the customs and living conditions of the people in lieu of the more traditional focus on military leaders and royalty. These ideas had met with a positive response in Denmark through Troels Troels-Lund's *Dagligt liv i Norden* (1879; Daily life in Scandinavia), but Swedish academicians remained skeptical.

Though Strindberg did not possess the scientific and methodical temperament of a Viktor Rydberg, he had become interested in doing cultural inventories of earlier Swedish epochs during his time as an assistant in the Royal Library in Stockholm. Some of this material resulted in his nonfictional works on Swedish history: *Svenska folket i helg och söcken* (1881–82;

The Swedish people on weekdays and Sundays) and *Gamla Stockholm* (1880–82; Old Stockholm).

Strindberg, however, used his historical material selectively to promote his own subjective ideas. He was frequently charged with anachronism and became an easy target for the historians of the day, who lived in a century that had a passion for the past "as it actually was," to quote a famous statement by the nineteenth-century German scholar Leopold von Ranke, that is, a view of the past as retrievable and objectively truthful evidence.

Strindberg's best-known prose works in the historical genre are several short story collections published beginning in 1882 under the title *Svenska öden och äfventyr* (Swedish destinies and adventures). By this time in his career Strindberg was drawn to naturalism, a literary program that emphasized the importance of heredity and environment in determining human destiny. This view left its mark on the first volumes of *Svenska öden och äfventyr*; additional stories published under the same title in the 1890s reflect his changing philosophical and literary allegiances at that time.

The 1882 edition of *Svenska öden och äfventyr* also reveals Strindberg's affinity for the thinking of the Swiss philosopher Jean-Jacques Rousseau, especially his ideas about the damaging impact of city life and cultural refinement on natural man. In the story "Odlad frukt" (Cultivated fruit), Strindberg uses a medieval Swedish setting to draw attention to thoughts expressed in Rousseau's educational book *Emile*, in which men of sophistication and culture are likened to sterile fruit. In "Pål och Per" (Paul and Peter), Strindberg associates overrefinement with middle-class city dwellers who survive only by parasiting on the natural growers of the soil, the farmers.

Strindberg's subjective voice breaks through loud and clear in his story "Utveckling" (Evolution), about the Renaissance monk Botvid, whose destiny anticipates the author's self-analysis of a divided and disharmonic soul in *Tjänstekvinnans son* (1887; Eng. tr. *The Son of a Servant*, 1966): "His soul was cut in two parts, always warring; he was the son of two epochs, and this gave him two ways of looking at things."

Overall, *Svenska öden och äfventyr* is a treasure trove for the student of Strindberg. Though the historical veneer may be thin, the author's lively style and imagination evoke bygone times and milieus. Ironically enough, as a schoolboy Strindberg had found his master in the historical genre, Walter Scott, exceedingly boring in his descriptions of setting and scenery. Now Strindberg himself brought to life the past history of the city of his birth and its natural surroundings. This landscape formed an emotional

"Proustian" core in his restless life, and he could always return to it for inspiration.

REALISTIC FICTION FROM ALMQVIST TO STRINDBERG, 1830 – 1870

Despite the popularity of historical fiction, the Swedish novelists and short story writers who emerged between 1830 and 1870 began to leave behind the exotic and distant lands of the romantic and neoromantic imagination. The focus shifted to middle-class men and women who occupy a more pedestrian and circumscribed space. Not surprisingly, women began to play an important role, both as writers and as characters, for the genre of realistic fiction catered to the domestic scene, that is, to a domain where women could offer special insights and new points of view.

One could claim—in a metaphorical if not always in a literal sense—that nineteenth-century realistic fiction discovers the bourgeois living room with its everyday atmosphere, its tone of propriety, its conversational mode. If travel is called for, it has a provincial, down-to-earth quality about it. Few people in the nineteenth-century realistic novel explore the wilderness by foot or on horseback or traverse the countryside in splendid carriages and charabancs. Rather, they travel, like Almqvist's Sara Videbeck in *Det går an* (1839; Eng. tr. *Sara Videbeck*, 1919; *Why Not?* 1994), by horse and buggy or by canal steamer and later by railroad. In such a realistic context, the literary plot revolves less around exciting incidents in dramatic landscapes and more around family disputes, arranged marriages, and everyday problems, often of an economic nature. We are in a world far removed from Rydberg's grandiose philosophical dichotomies and deeply classical learning. Instead, we are led into a way of life in which money has begun to replace wisdom as a normative guide and in which financial security and success, rather than land and title, are the criteria for social prestige.

At the same time, the characters we encounter in nineteenth-century realistic fiction before Strindberg's arrival on the scene largely inhabit a preurbanized society. Despite the impact of technological inventions such as the steam engine and the railroad, industrialism arrived later in Sweden than on the Continent or in England. The major demographic shift from the countryside into the cities is of much less cultural and economic importance in the period under discussion (1830–70) than are the emigration waves from the Swedish farmland to the United States, beginning in the 1830s and culminating in the 1870s, depleting the Swedish population by one-fourth. Not surprisingly, therefore, the realistic prose published in

Sweden before Strindberg's epoch-making novel *Röda rummet* (Eng. tr. *The Red Room*, 1967) in 1879 has a village or small-town quality about it. The poverty-stricken farmers who left the country for greener fields in North America attracted little literary attention. And in the absence of factory smokestacks, the working class plays only a minor fictional role.

The breakthrough of political liberalism in Sweden in the 1830s had a direct and profound impact on contemporary Swedish literature, which absorbed and promoted many of the new ideas. Such major writers as Erik Gustaf Geijer, Carl Jonas Love Almqvist, and Fredrika Bremer became sensitive to a growing demand for political reforms aimed at alleviating poverty, expanding educational opportunities, and creating a liberal climate for women and other powerless groups in Swedish society. Both Geijer and Almqvist underwent crucial intellectual "conversions" that not only put them in the vanguard of those advocating social reform but also changed radically their literary style and practice.

Geijer and Almqvist announced their new positions in official programmatic statements. In 1838, Geijer founded the journal *Litteraturbladet*; its first issue contained the account of his famous *avfall* ("apostasy") from the so-called historical school whose leader he had been at the University of Uppsala. Like other Swedish poets of the romantic period, Geijer had been a political conservative who supported the existing class structure as a divinely instituted system. Now, under the influence of liberal thinking, he adopted a new social philosophy. He spoke up for public education for all citizens. He advocated free trade and parliamentary reform. His guiding motto can be seen as the Swedish summary of political liberalism: "Obedience before existing law but an open right to demand a better one, and free discussion of the means to achieve it."

In the same year as Geijer's apostasy, Almqvist too broke with his romantic past and emerged, after a three-year silence, as a realistic writer of short fiction. Between 1838 and 1840, he published a series of novellas that established him as one of the founders of modern Swedish prose and as a keen social critic: "Kapellet" (1838; Eng. tr. *The Chapel*, 1919 and 1972), "Skällnora kvarn" (Skällnora Mill), "Målaren" (The painter), "Grimstahamns nybygge" (The Grimstahamn settlement), "Ladugårdsarrendet" (The farm lease), and above all the novel *Det går an*. In addition to his works of fiction, Almqvist published the sociophilosophical tract "Det europeiska missnöjets grunder" (1838; The causes of European discontent), in which he discusses the current social and political problems in Europe. His central point is the idea that man's "inner nature," created by God, must be the guiding principle in life. Almqvist distinguishes between two main groups of citizens: the common folk (*folket*) and the mob (*pöbeln*). The common folk are those people who live according to their inner divine nature, which includes compassion for others. The mob, on the other hand, lives according to egotistical desires. Its members' only ambition is to gain fame and titles for themselves. The mob is to be found most often among the so-called *förnäma*, that is, the snobs, whereas the common folk are found among the uneducated and less sophisticated minds.

Almqvist's long essay called "Den svenska fattigdomens betydelse" (1839; The importance of Swedish poverty) may be considered a companion piece to his discussion of the causes of European social misery. Inspired not only by the new intellectual climate that had produced the earlier essay but also by his personal idealistic experiments as a farmer in the province of Värmland, Almqvist now turned to an analysis of the Swedish national psyche. He finds two basic traits in the Swedish temperament: an ability to endure a frugal lifestyle and a capacity for staying young. He traces both characteristics back to the Swedish landscape and climate. These concepts form leitmotifs in the above-mentioned novellas, in which Almqvist creates situations that enable him to depict Swedish farmers and craftsmen who look on work as a playful occupation and not as a burden, who display a talent for acting quickly and opportunely, and who show an ability to rise above earthly tribulations.

Almqvist announced his new social and literary program in a series of articles titled *Poesi i sak* (1839; The poetry of realism) and in the preface to one of the volumes in *Törnrosens bok* named "Varför reser du?" (1839; Why do you travel?). Here he chose one of the oldest narrative devices in literature, the journey, as a metaphor for an exploration of contemporary Swedish life outside the capital. His didactic yet simple criterion rests on the assumption that all people and all facets of reality are worthy of literary treatment as long as the author pursues his task with genuine conviction.

Almqvist himself is the best example of the successful use of this new literary program. All his realistic novellas reveal his commitment to the subject matter and a personal knowledge of the depicted material. But only *Det går an* has a clear tendentious message. It was intended as a contribution to the current debate on the function and meaning of marriage and remains one of the most important feminist documents in Swedish literature. The reason for its modernity is not only its radical message but also its lively literary style.

The central character in *Det går an* (lit. "It is proper," "It can be done") is Sara Videbeck, the daughter of a glazier from the small town of Lidköping, who befriends a sergeant, Albert, during a journey by steamer and horse and buggy to Sara's home town. Despite his military profession, Sergeant Albert is clearly an atypical representative of the male sex. Baffled and somewhat at a loss, he listens to Sara's unorthodox ideas about "free marriage": Sara rejects both a religious and a civil ceremony; she advocates separate housekeeping for husband and wife; and she insists on a mutual promise to dissolve the liaison at the first sign of incompatibility. To be able to realize such a union, the woman must, like Sara herself, have a profession of her own.

Det går an caused a lively and at times bitter debate. The issues it raised continued to reverberate in Swedish literature during the rest of the century. Almqvist's novel can be seen as the literary starting point for what would be called, in the 1870s and 1880s, "the Great Scandinavian Morality Debate" (*den stora sedlighetsdebatten*) (below).

Fredrika Bremer and the Family Novel

As a literary practitioner Fredrika Bremer (1801–65) is akin to Almqvist. She shares with him an inclination toward sentimentality and melodrama, thus revealing her ties to an earlier romantic era. But she also blazes new trails and opens up new domains in the Swedish literary landscape. What Almqvist achieved in terms of *folklivsskildring*, realistic depiction of the common people in a rural setting, Bremer accomplishes within the realm of the realistic family novel with roots in English middle-class fiction. It is no coincidence that she names the main character in her first novel Beata Vardagslag (Betty Everyday Life) and assigns her the task of housekeeper, just as the title of the book *Familjen H**** (1830–31; Eng. tr. *The H——Family*, 1853) suggests Bremer's focus on the domestic scene and her view of the home as the center of life.

In the 1830s, Bremer befriended a young theologian and disciple of Kant, Per Böklin, who was to play a crucial role as her adviser and teacher. Yet she refused his proposal of marriage and opted to become the totally committed artist who lived her life through her work and used her growing literary reputation to sponsor social reform and promote political progress. In 1834, she published the novel *Presidentens döttrar* (Eng. tr. *The President's Daughters*, 1843) and, in the following year, *Nina* (Eng. tr. 1843). Both works are thinly camouflaged romans à clef that were rather negatively received. An indirectly contributing factor may have been the arrival of Balzac's novels in Sweden in 1833–34. Their starker realism and more merciless depiction of middle-class reality created new expectations among Bremer's readership. Almqvist advised her to broaden her subject matter beyond her own upper-class circles, but Bremer felt she was unable to transcend her own background with its rigid code of propriety.

At this critical time in her life, she came on a book by Erik Gustaf Geijer that was to have a decisive influence on her. In his memoirs, *Minnen* (1834; Reminiscences), a work in which Geijer utters the famous words "I thank God for the best of parents," Fredrika Bremer encountered a different, more genial family life than either Balzac's or her own, a more tolerant attitude between the generations and between different social groups. Her hope that a liberal and loving atmosphere could bridge generational and social gaps was heightened in the following year when she visited the Tomb estate in southern Norway, where she found a warm rapport between parents and children, masters and servants, clergy and congregation. Inspired, she began to work on another novel, *Grannarne* (Eng. tr. *The Neigbours*, 1972), which was published in 1837.

In *Grannarne*, Bremer follows the epistolary format that had been popular since the emergence of the novelistic genre in England with such works as Samuel Richardson's *Pamela* and *Clarissa*. It is a narrative approach that suited Bremer as it enabled her to combine her keen ability to observe everyday life in her own circles with an intimate and personal voice.

In Geijer's *Minnen*, Bremer heard an echo of her own belief that the roots of social growth were to be found "in the households, in the domestic traditions." In her next novel, *Hemmet* (1839; Eng. tr. *The Home, or Life in Sweden*, 1853), she develops her view of the family as a microcosm of society, "a contracted fatherland" as she calls it, which could have an ennobling influence on the individual as long as it provided an atmosphere of kindness and love. *Hemmet* depicts the Frank family, and again the novel borrows traits from Bremer's parental home. Her intention was to depict and advocate new options for women in Swedish society regardless of their class.

Published in the same year (1839) as Almqvist's *Det går an*, Bremer's novel invites comparison. Both authors insist on a woman's right to a profession of her own, but of the two, Bremer is by far the bolder visionary. Where Almqvist's main concern was the abolition of conventional marriage, Bremer advocates a totally new society in which women are to form "mouvemangspartiet" (the party of change). Bremer's alter ego, Petrea, insists that women take an active part in realizing a new industrial society in which all people will be well fed; only then will humankind be free to attain a true spiritual status and realize God's Kingdom on earth.

Like Geijer and Almqvist before her, Bremer published a literary program in which she singled out the Christian novel as the exemplary modern epic. Its tasks were to depict the single individual struggling for spiritual integrity but also to show life "in all its beauty, ugliness, greatness, small-ness, sweetness, bitterness; in one word, in all its truth."

Three years after publishing her literary program, Bremer attempted to put it into practice with her novel *Hertha, eller en själs historia* (1856; Eng. tr. *Hertha*, 1856). Subtitled "Teckning ur det verkliga lifvet" (Sketch from real life), Bremer's efforts at depicting her visionary realism backfired. Readers of the novel took its realistic purpose *ad notam*, and critics attacked it as immoral, claiming it would have a deplorable impact on family life. Despite Hertha's purity of body and spirit, Bremer's vestalian title figure was viewed as the embodiment of dangerous feminist tendencies. But years later, when the Fredrika Bremer Society was founded, its main publication was named after this novel.

Sophie von Knorring

During her visit to the Tomb estate in 1836, Fredrika Bremer listened to her hostess reading from a new Swedish novel, *Cousinerna* (The cousins). The anonymous author turned out to be another upper-class Swedish woman writer, Sophie von Knorring (1797–1848). She too was a practitioner of the family novel but lacked Bremer's visionary radicalism. Instead, she focused her attention on stories of unhappy marriages in which the women pine away while the author devotes much analysis to the psychology of illicit affairs. Von Knorring combines a basically conservative view of marriage with occasional insightful observations of women's responses to their circumscribed situations.

Sophie von Knorring ventured outside the realm of the landowning aristocracy, possibly also in response to Almqvist's clarion call in "Varför reser du?" that all human beings, regardless of social class, are interesting and worthy literary subjects. In 1843, she caused a minor sensation by publishing *Torparen och hans omgivningar* (Eng. tr. *The Peasant and His Landlord*, 1848), often referred to as Sweden's first peasant-class novel. The author's perspective is, however, entirely upper class, and her characterization reveals that she knew the peasants only through hearsay and gossip among the servants on her own estate. Today the novel is most interesting as a rebuttal of Almqvist's views on marriage in *Det går an*.

THE MELODRAMATIC TALE AND THE NOVEL OF INTRIGUE

In the middle of the 1840s, a new prose genre reached Sweden from the Continent: the sensationalist story of intrigue using stereotyped characters, schematic social conflicts, and melodramatic plots. The most successful originator of this type of prose fiction was the French author Eugène Sue, whose *Les Mystères de Paris* (Parisian mysteries) began to appear in Swedish translation in 1844. These and similar tales from the European metropolitan underworld were imitated in *Stockholms-mysterier* (1851) by Carl Fredrik Ridderstad (1807–86). From England came stories of intrigue of a somewhat different tradition: the Gothic horror story, often set in spooky rural surroundings, a narrative mode that survived in the melodramatic stories of Bulwer-Lytton, Frederick Marryat, and Dickens. The French melodrama, which tended to focus its intrigue on sex and violence, was soon to be criticized as immoral and threatening to bourgeois values. Though Eugène Sue's works were not totally devoid of social conscience, Swedish critics much preferred the English novel of intrigue, which seemed less sensational and more socially committed. Charles Dickens's works were deemed something of a model.

The melodramatic tale and the novel of intrigue offer easy solutions in an increasingly complex reality by steering the reader away from psychological intricacies of character to exciting physical action and emotionally tense conflicts that are often resolved by last-minute rescues or surprise reversals. Melodrama became associated with popular mass literature (and as such survives in today's soap operas), but melodramatic elements appear frequently in the works of writers of high literary ambition such as Almqvist, Rydberg, Bremer, Strindberg, and Selma Lagerlöf. All the novelistic genres discussed here—the historical novel, the family novel, the didactic novel, the novel of intrigue, and the social sketch—rely to some degree on the melodrama. But the works of Carl Anton Wetterbergh, Emilie Flygare-Carlén, and August Blanche seem particularly pertinent in this context.

Onkel Adam (C. A. Wetterbergh) and the Didactic Story

Though relatively unknown today, the pseudonym Onkel Adam was once referred to as the first Swedish author to have understood how to depict the poor. Carl Anton Wetterbergh (1804–89), who studied to become a medical doctor, had known poverty in his youth and frequently encountered its physiological effects in his patients. His professional life among the destitute set the tone for his tendentious literary activity; he aimed at writing for the masses, and he wished to advocate social reform. In *Genremålningar* (1842; Genre sketches) and *Penningar och arbete* (1847; Money and work), he called for better prison conditions, more even distribution of income, and greater religious tolerance. His stories and novels are full of sensationalist vignettes aimed at arousing the reader's sympathy for the underdogs in society. In addition to his fiction writing in book form, Wetterbergh frequently participated in the public debate by contributing serialized stories and articles to *Aftonbladet*.

Emilie Flygare-Carlén and the Novel of Intrigue

For a nation surrounded by water, Sweden has produced relatively little fiction focusing on life on the coast and in the skerries. To Strindberg, the Stockholm archipelago was important, but by and large Swedish prose writers have set their stories in the farmland countryside, the small town, or the big city. But with the novels of Emilie Flygare-Carlén (1807–92), the province of Bohuslän on the Swedish west coast gets its own storyteller. Her best works are those set in the milieu in which she grew up: *Rosen på Tistelön* (1842; Eng. tr. *The Rose of Tistelön: A Tale of the Swedish Coast*, 1844), *Enslingen på Johanniskäret* (1846; The hermit on the Johannis skerry), and *Ett köpmanshus i skärgården* (1859; A merchant home in the archipelago), though her weakness for stylistic incongruities, improbable catastrophes, and melodramatic incidents occasionally mars these novels. Behind her belabored sensationalism operates the idea of a conflict between atavistic nature and social constructs. Unbridled passion is often the catalyst for the catastrophe.

Flygare-Carlén has gone down in Swedish literary history as its most prolific writer of fiction. She had no formal schooling, but she had a shrewd business sense and turned her métier into a lucrative profession. Her greatest gift as a writer is her talent for epic storytelling involving a suspenseful intrigue. This remains an unmistakable feature in all her works, whether she tries to emulate French melodrama, as in *Ett rykte* (1850; A rumor), the English horror story, as in *En natt vid Bullarsjön* (1847; A night at Bullar Lake); or stories in the Swedish folk life genre, as in *Skuggspel* (1862; Shadow play).

August Blanche and the Story of Social Intrigue

One characteristic of melodramatic fiction is the passive and self-effacing role of women. Melodrama emphasizes physical action, daring rescue attempts, and catastrophic situations in which male strength is a prerequisite. Nowhere is this more obvious than in the novels of August Blanche (1811–68). Their world is a world of boys and men in which women play only a marginal role.

Like Flygare-Carlén, August Blanche tends to emphasize social rather than psychological motifs, often including a crime story of horrendous dimensions, as in *Banditen* (1848; Eng. tr. *The Bandit*, 1872). Blanche also tries to follow in Balzac's footsteps in *Den broderade plånboken* (1845; The embroidered wallet), whose main theme is the power of money. His most ambitious work is a thick novel, set in Paris during the 1848 revolution, titled *Sonen av söder och nord* (1851; The son of north and south), in which political conspiracies provide the backdrop for a love intrigue between the workingman Armand and a woman of the nobility. The unbelievable happy outcome of this love affair might be contrasted to Strindberg's handling of a similar liaison in his tragedy *Fröken Julie*.

Blanche's best-known work is a collection of short stories, *Hyrkuskens berättelser* (1863; The tales of the Coachman), in which the simple, domestic narrator doubles as a demonic lover. Blanche wrote these and other tales for *Illustrerad Tidning*, a literary magazine he began to edit in 1857. Here his forte as a writer of the realistic, often satirical vignette became obvious. Abandoning at last his weakness for intrigue and melodrama, he published four volumes of *Bilder ur verkligheten* (1863–65; Pictures from reality). In these episodic tales Blanche focuses on experiences from his own humble origin as an illegitimate child in Stockholm. He introduces students and schoolboys, craftsmen and tradespeople, artists and aspiring writers. Blanche sketches a milieu that Strindberg was to paint with consummate skill in his novel *Röda rummet*.

THE REALISTIC TRAVEL ACCOUNT AND THE MEMOIR

Our image of the nineteenth-century Swedish woman writer is probably conditioned more by the repressed life of Victoria Benedictsson than by the shrewd entrepreneurial success of Emilie Flygare-Carlén or the tenacious traveling of Fredrika Bremer in the New World, including the western frontier, the Deep South, and Cuba. All three of these writers came from a middle-class background. All of them were raised in small towns or in the countryside outside Stockholm. Though nineteenth-century middle-class values are usually associated with the emergence of liberal, social, and political ideas, the psychological climate that surrounded Benedictsson, Flygare-Carlén, and Bremer was definitely patriarchal, curbing the ambitions of women who did not follow the middle-class norm of prioritizing family, household tasks, and social representation.

Flygare-Carlén outwitted the male establishment in her successful business maneuverings, whereas Victoria Benedictsson succumbed to the pressures of male autocracy until she bowed out in a self-destructive act. Fredrika Bremer, on the other hand, left a more paradoxical legacy in the annals of nineteenth-century Swedish life and literature. Long looked on by (male) literary critics and biographers as the spinster aunt of Swedish belles lettres (Fredrik Böök, Karl Warburg), and presented in somewhat condescending terms, Bremer emerges in today's critical eyes (Birgitta Holm) as the foremost exponent of a truly international mind in her day and age and as an audacious spirit who set out to explore a world that no other Swedish writer of her time ventured into (with the exception of Almqvist, who escaped to the United States from Sweden, where he was suspected of poisoning a creditor). Bremer's travels to England, North America, and the Middle East are extraordinary accomplishments by a woman of the mid-nineteenth century. The literary results of these travels constitute her finest writing and mark the high point of Swedish travel literature of all times.

The travel book as a genre may correspond to a significant trait in the Swedish mentality, conditioned by the relative geographical isolation of the country and by a highly structured society, namely, *utbrytningsdrömmen*, the yearning to leave the home environment, the wish to fulfill oneself by breaking away from the restrictions imposed by an authoritarian society. Thus the Swedish travel book is often based on an urge to realize a vision rather than simply a romantic longing for the exotic.

The memoir, another well-established genre in Swedish literature, has perhaps a special appeal to a culture shaped by a religious dogma that does not provide for regular confession endorsed by the church, yet a culture that has remained guilt-oriented. The memoir or autobiography in Scandinavia has served the function, as Johny Kondrup has shown, of secularized confession.

The memoir book can also be seen as a precursor of the realistic novel. It is a genre in which the author aims at evoking an authentic picture of life as experienced at first hand. Early Swedish memoirs often focus on *hembygden* (the home province) and combine personal reminiscences with detailed accounts of local customs and traditions. A good example is Samuel Ödman's *Hågkomster från hembygden* (1830; Reminiscences from my home province), which gives a concrete picture of a Småland vicarage and of school life in the town of Växjö. The missionary preacher Petrus Laestadius fuses the travel book and the memoir in his *Journal* (1831–33), based on his experiences in the Lapland wilderness. Other noteworthy examples from the same time period are Geijer's *Minnen* and Nils Lovén's (Nicolovius) personal account, *Folklivet i Skytts härad* (1847; Folk life in Skytt County). Together with Almqvist's novellas, these memoirs, which were as much cultural documents as personal history, lay the foundation for the popularity of the provincial short story, which would culminate in the 1880s.

Both the travel book and the memoir date back to an age preceding the full breakthrough of realism in Swedish literature. The origin of the Swedish travel book is associated with the name of Jakob Wallenberg, whose seafaring experiences in 1769–75 resulted in *Min son på galejan* (My son on the galley). Carl Linné's detailed description of his travels around Sweden also helped establish the realistic contours of the travel genre, as did Per Kalm's accounts of his late-eighteenth-century voyages to America. His observations, coupled with an astute social analysis, might have served as a model for Fredrika Bremer's three-volume travel book from the New World, *Hemmen i nya världen* (1853; Eng. tr. *The Homes of the New World: Impressions of America*, 1854), written in the form of letters to her ailing sister back home during Bremer's visits to the United States in 1850–51 (also see Eng. tr. *America of the Fifties: Letters of Fredrika Bremer*, 1924).

In the prolific European accounts of North America that preceded Bremer's visit there, from Chateaubriand's idealized account of the noble savage in *Attala* and de Toqueville's incisive analysis of American democracy to Harriet Martineau's and Mrs. Trollope's travelogues, two basic views of the New World emerge: the visionary and the documentary. For some visitors, America remained a utopian possibility, an experimental new society, Hellas reborn; for others, the New World was an interesting economic and social experiment, full of hardships and populated by people who combined pragmatic ingenuity with considerable vulgarity. Bremer's accounts of life in North America draw on both these views. Long before her actual visit to the New World, she had read about the American continent in literature. In the early 1840s, de Tocqueville's work had fascinated her to such an extent that she had found it more intriguing than her own authorship. She began to see the New World not only as an expanding continent; it became her vision of a world of peace on earth. She was convinced that America had the answer both to the rights of women and to religious rejuvenation. In her novel from 1848, *Syskonliv* (Eng. tr. *Brothers and Sisters*, 1848), she depicted an idealistic project undertaken by a brother and sister, based on an experiment in a Massachusetts factory town in which the workers were said to experience "ennoblement, freedom, and happiness."

With her idealized view of North America, Bremer was bound to encounter some disappointments. Yet her visit became in many ways the fulfillment of a dream she had had since her youth to be able to experience a personal sense of freedom while absorbing vital new knowledge about reality. Her positive frame of mind never left her during her two years in the New World, and her account of her travels remains among the most balanced portrayals of life in America at the time.

Her curiosity and fearlessness took her into remote areas of the continent, from North Carolina's revivalist meetings to Wisconsin's wilderness. She studied social experiments such as modern open prisons and mental health programs in the Quaker town of Philadelphia, and she interviewed both slaves and slave owners in the Deep South. Her condemnation of slavery was unequivocal, and her analysis of it is one of the most incisive critiques of its practice in any literature. Though she was at times disappointed in her encounters with famous American thinkers, among them Ralph Waldo Emerson, she retained her faith in America. Comparing it to Old Europe, she saw it as a land with "a warmer heartbeat and a more energetic, youthfully strong lifestyle."

Swedish nineteenth-century novelists and short story writers before Strindberg appear more provincial than urban, in terms of both the setting they choose for their literary works and the perspective they assume as social observers. They fail, almost without exception, to depict their society in the broad scope of European writers such as Dickens, Balzac, and Thackeray, however frequently these realists are acknowledged as models. Though they never tire of reiterating their intention to promote realism in fiction, their portrayal of reality remains basically idyllic and firmly rooted in Christian idealistic thinking. They often express a strong social pathos and a solid faith in human goodness and social progress. Only rarely do they touch on the darkest streaks of the human psyche.

In many ways Bremer's statement in her novel *Familjen H**** can be taken as a motto for the early realistic novel and short fiction in Sweden before the Modern Breakthrough in the 1870s:

> The depiction of reality ought to resemble a clear brook which in its course reflects, in a pure and faithful way, the objects that are mirrored in its water, and through whose crystal surface one can perceive the bottom and all that rests upon it. All that the painter or author should permit his imagination to do in depicting the scene is to let it play the role of a sun ray, which without changing the unique features of an object, nevertheless gives to all colors a more lively sheen . . . and lightens up the brook's sandy bottom with purifying clarity.

POSTROMANTIC POETRY

The idealism that characterizes much of Swedish prose fiction between 1830 and 1880 leaves an even stronger mark on the poetic genre. In the previous literary period, the romantics had elevated poetry to a high artistic and philosophical status, which it retained—in spirit if not in quality—among the literary establishment, found primarily at the universities and in the Swedish Academy.

In the 1840s, poets such as C.W.A. Strandberg (Talis Qualis, 1818–77) from the university town of Lund and Gunnar Wennerberg (1817–1901) at Uppsala created the student song, a poetic subgenre built on the eighteenth-century troubadour tradition of Carl Michael Bellman but aiming at cementing a growing sense of fraternal mystique about life in academia. Rhetorical versification, set to music, became part of student marches and speech making. Wennerberg's collection, *Gluntarne* (1849), depicts a carefree and privileged student lifestyle marked by liquor, song, and academic pranks.

Talis Qualis began his career as a Hegelian disciple and advocate of republicanism but later in life chose to express his allegiance to King Oscar I by composing the Swedish Royal Hymn, "Ur svenska hjärtans djup" (1844; From the depths of Swedish hearts). Gunnar Wennerberg ended his professional life as minister of ecclesiastical affairs and a member of the conservative Swedish Academy. Both men lived in an era when royal support and recognition could be vital to an artistic or professional career. Both also represented the changing role of the universities in Sweden in the 1800s. No longer institutions to which the clergy sent their sons for higher education, the universities became the training ground for the offspring of the growing middle class, whose sons were to constitute the foundation of an ever-increasing *ämbetsmannaklass* (corps of civil servants), which by 1880 had attained considerable power in Swedish society. The growing cultural and political impact of the *ämbetsmannaklass* helps in turn explain the conservation of postromantic verse making in Swedish literature throughout much of the nineteenth century.

Apart from their own native romantic tradition with Esaias Tegnér as the leading figurehead, the Swedish postromantics valued such poets as Byron and Heine. In O. P. Sturzen-Becker (Orvar Odd, 1811–69), Heine's influence is easily detectable; his verse aims at intellectual and emotional simplicity rather than pathos. Other forms of postromantic verse making of some historical importance are folk and dialect poetry (Fredrik Dahlgren [1816–95]) and the *skillingtryck* (broadsheet), dating back to the sixteenth century but gaining new popularity after compulsory public schooling had increased the literacy rate among the lower classes.

But it is Tegnér's spirit that hovers over much postromantic Swedish poetry in terms of both imagery and rhetoric. At worst, as in the bombastic attempts that earned the future King Oscar II a second prize from the Swedish Academy in 1857, it is a poetry verging on parody. At best, it results in idyllic vignettes of bourgeois everyday life, in which the nationalistic rhetoric of the romantics has been toned down to suit the realistic tastes of a middle-class readership; this trend can be directly related to the arrival of Johan Ludvig Runeberg on the literary scene.

Johan Ludvig Runeberg

The first major challenge to Swedish postromantic poetry came not from a generation of Swedish poets but from Denmark (J. L. Heiberg and H. C. Ørsted) and later from Swedish-speaking Finland. In 1832, Johan Ludvig Runeberg (1804–77) published a series of critical articles in *Helsingfors Morgonblad* that were designed as an attack on the excessive chauvinism, "lion's roars," and precious "emerald" language of contemporary Swedish poetry. Runeberg did not hesitate to accuse Tegnér of producing "artistic bravura pieces," but his real target was Tegnér's many second-rate imitators. As an antidote to such epigonic poetry, Runeberg suggested a return to the Enlightenment poet Anna Maria Lenngren, whom he praised for being "natural" and for writing poetry using "the real and simple words of the heart."

Runeberg's critical action was in part prompted by experiences from his youth, when he spent time as a tutor in the interior farmland of Finland. There he discovered a lifestyle and a folk mentality whose authenticity was to provide him with poetic themes that would serve as a counterweight to the academic rhetoric of postromantic Swedish poetry. In the late 1820s, after moving to Helsinki as a writer and university teacher, Runeberg discovered, in a collection of Serbian folk songs that he translated from German, a lyrical style that seemed to express in a simple and authentic form the kind of folk culture he had met in the Finnish countryside. Later he would receive similar impulses from Finnish folk poetry, especially the *Kalevala*, a set of orally transmitted poems collected by his colleague Elias Lönnrot in the 1830s which would rapidly establish themselves as the national Finnish epic.

Despite his strong sense of rapport with the Finnish-speaking population and folk culture, Runeberg never became part of the so-called Fennomanian movement that advocated Finland's linguistic and cultural independence from Sweden. What mattered to Runeberg were the historical bonds between the two major ethnic groups in Finland. In view of his dual cultural allegiance, it seems fitting that Runeberg became the poet to write Finland's national anthem, "Vårt land" (1848; Our country).

When his critical articles appeared, Runeberg had already published his first collection of poetry, *Dikter* (1830; Poems), in which a cycle of poems called "Idyll och epigram" (Idylls and epigrams) is the most remarkable. It contains Runeberg's celebration of the Finnish farmer, "Bonden Pavo" (Pavo the farmer), who in his dogged perseverance epitomizes the spirit of the poet's country. It also includes his first depiction of the farmer/soldier fighting for his native soil, a motif Runeberg was to return to in his most famous work, *Fänrik Ståls sägner* (1848, 1860; Eng. tr. *The Tales of Ensign Stål*, 1938).

Idyll och epigram (1833; Eng. tr. *Lyrical Songs, Idylls, and Epigrams*, 1878), Runeberg's second collection of poetry, established him as a master of short lyrical poems focusing on love and heroism. In their simple yet rhythmically repetitious form, they attempt to reproduce the cadence of old oral folk songs.

Runeberg made his greatest literary contribution, however, in his epic poetry, which he began to publish in 1832 with the long narrative poem *Älgskyttarne* (The elk hunters). By combining a classical Homeric verse with an interest in historical motifs, derived from his reading of the novels of Walter Scott, Runeberg created a poetic tale full of realistic detail, bathos, love, and low-keyed heroism. He continued in the same genre with *Hanna* (1836), a love epic set in a provincial vicarage, and *Julkvällen* (1841; Eng. tr. *Christmas Eve, or the Angel Guest*, 1887), a wartime story in which the stoic mentality of a soldier's simple home is juxtaposed to the lack of heroism of a family on an upper-class estate. Late in the same year Runeberg attempted a more exotic theme in *Nadeschda* (Eng. tr. *Nadeschda: A Poem in Nine Cantos*, 1890), an expansive epic set in Russia, and in 1844 he published *Kung Fjalar* (Eng. tr. *King Fialar: A Poem in Five Songs*, 1912), a poetic narrative from the Viking Age, in part inspired by the *Songs of Ossian*, which had been translated into Swedish in 1842, and in part conceived as a contending piece to Tegnér's *Frithiofs saga*. But the public reception of Runeberg's non-national epics was rather critical, and the poet was asked in the press to return to his former Finnish motifs. He responded with the two volumes of *Fänrik Ståls sägner*.

No doubt Runeberg saw himself as Finland's national poet. That dictated his approach to his chosen subject matter, the war of 1809, when Sweden lost Finland to Russia. What he wanted to celebrate was the heroism of his people and the birth of a national spirit. His point of view was as idealistic as that of the postromantic Swedish poets he had attacked in the early 1830s. *Fänrik Ståls sägner* established Runeberg in both Swedish-speaking Finland and Sweden as a model patriot whose martial romanticism appealed strongly to the conservative establishment. As late as the 1890s, King Oscar II of Sweden would praise his protégé, the poet Carl Snoilsky, for writing in "the Runeberg spirit." Runeberg succeeded, in *Fänrik Ståls sägner*, in turning Sweden's loss of Finland in 1809 and its final demise as a great power into a glorious self-sacrificing act. Through unforgettable portraits of such fictionalized heroes as von Döbeln, Sven Duva, and Lotta Svärd, who emerge from both the officer corps and the foot soldiers' camp, Runeberg recreates a historic period by turning it into a fabled poetic reality.

Runeberg's poetry gained wide support in Sweden, all the way from the literary establishment, which approved of its patriotic spirit, to the so-called Namnlösa Sällskapet (Nameless Society), a group of signature poets who formed a literary circle in Uppsala in the 1860s. Led by a Norwegian lecturer, Lorenz Dietrichson, "the signatures" deplored the impact of Tegnér's abstract rhetoric on Swedish poetry and called for a new verse anchored in folk life and using the poetic works of Bjørnstjerne Bjørnson and Runeberg as its models. They published their literary attempts in a calendar called *Isblomman* (The ice flower). Although they aimed at revitalizing Swedish poetry, few of the signature poets lived up to their intentions. The only real talent among them seems to have been Carl Snoilsky.

Carl Snoilsky

The background of Carl Snoilsky (1841–1903) was ultraconservative. Both his parents stemmed from the Swedish nobility, and his life developed into an ambivalent challenge of his background. His first successful attempt to free himself from its impact came in 1864, when he traveled to Italy after finishing his academic studies at the University of Uppsala. Within a year he published a collection of poetry, *Italienska bilder* (1865; Italian pictures), in which he broke with the conventions of classical poetry, embraced a hedonistic lifestyle, and predicted Italy's political unification. Almost overnight he became the poet of the young and was admired by such critical and literary giants as Georg Brandes and Henrik Ibsen.

But Snoilsky's professional and private life was predetermined by his family; he was to pursue a diplomatic career and marry a suitable wife. Unhappy in both his work and his marriage, Snoilsky wrote little. A collection, *Sonetter* (Sonnets), from 1871 revealed his despair though in subdued form; he did not want to dwell on his own misery, a stance expressed in the poem "Noli me tangere"; instead, he portrayed political questions and imposed an elegant sonnet form to restrain his views and emotions, as in "Gammalt porslin" (Old porcelain). As a poet he was an official spokesman rather than a personal voice.

Eight more years went by before Snoilsky took his life in his hands; he resigned from his state department job and dissolved his marriage. In 1880, he remarried, left Sweden, and eventually settled for many years in Dresden, Saxony. His poetic creativity returned, and in 1881 he published *Nya dikter* (New poems), in which he staked out and demonstrated a new literary course of action. He turned his back on the aestheticism of his youth and focused on two clusters of motifs during the rest of the 1880s: social concern and nationalism. His poetic program was to write "in the simple form that thousands will understand," as he wrote in the poem "I porslinsfabriken" (In the porcelain factory). Again he became the voice of the antiestablishment; Strindberg and his contemporaries listened to him, but Snoilsky realized that his allegiance to the working class lacked emotional roots in his own life experience. When the king of Sweden, Oscar II, offered him support but urged him to abandon social themes and concentrate on poems with a patriotic foundation, Snoilsky followed the royal advice. The result was *Svenska bilder* (1894; Swedish pictures), a collection in which Snoilsky projected, in historical guise, his own disharmony, his longing to end his exile, and his sense of futility as a poet ("Kristina," "Aurora Königsmarck"). His attitude toward Swedish history ("Gustaf Vasa," "Kung Erik") was colored by his reading of the historian Anders Fryxell (1795–1881), whose anecdotal and populistic rendering of the past also inspired Strindberg in his cycles of historical dramas.

Snoilsky returned to Sweden in 1890 and, through royal intervention, was made head librarian of the Royal Library in Stockholm, a position he kept until his death. His frustrated and melancholy life and his formalistic poetic talent suggest a man born in the wrong age. He would have fit in better with the aesthetic and lyrical fin de siècle in Sweden. In the preceding more realistic and utilitarian decades, when he published his major works, he was bound to be a lonely and personally dissatisfied voice. Yet it should be remembered that for several generations of Swedish schoolchildren in the first half of the twentieth century, Snoilsky's *Svenska bilder* was as much of a modern classic reader as Selma Lagerlöf's *Nils Holgerssons underbara resa* (1906–7; Eng. tr. *The Wonderful Adventures of Nils*, 1907).

Viktor Rydberg

Toward the end of the 1860s, Viktor Rydberg became engaged in translating Goethe's *Faust*, completing the task in 1876. During this time he also rendered Edgar Allen Poe's virtuoso poem "The Raven" into Swedish. Rydberg belonged to a generation of writers for whom translation was considered excellent training for aspiring authors. Though well established as a novelist, Rydberg had yet to publish any poetry of significance. But his translations gave him good practice in versification, and Goethe's and Poe's works inspired him to use the poetic genre to express both philosophical and lyrical motifs. At the age of fifty-four, he issued his first collection of poetry, *Dikter* (1882; Poems). A second collection with the same title appeared in 1891. Despite their date of publication, both works belong to postromantic Swedish poetry rather than to the realism of the 1880s. In fact, Rydberg occasionally criticized his younger contemporaries for their devotion to photographic realism.

There are many parallels between Rydberg's fiction and his poetry. In his poems he often combines a classical rhetorical language to depict (melo)dramatic motifs from myth, as in "Prometheus och Ahasverus"; from folklore, as in "Tomten" (The goblin); or from his own childhood, as in "Träsnittet i psalmboken" (The wood cut in the hymnal). Though no pioneer and experimenter in terms of poetic form, Rydberg is nevertheless one of the foremost creators of philosophical poetry in Swedish literature and, in his idealistic verse, a worthy descendant of Tegnér. His themes frequently center on metaphysical quests, as in "Den flygande holländaren" (The Flying Dutchman), "Grubblaren" (The brooder), and "Vadan och varthän?" (Wherefrom and whereto?). Rydberg projects a vision of an enigmatic universe but finds solace in a belief in an idealistic and indestructible human spirit. His philosophical views reach their poetic apogee in the grandiose cantata he wrote for the four hundredth anniversary of the University of Uppsala in 1877. Sketching the spiritual history of humankind by using the Exodus myth in the Old Testament, Rydberg follows the children of Israel as they are guided by Moses toward the Promised Land, depicted as both a Platonic realm of ideas and an earthly utopia.

Rydberg's most remarkable poem in his second collection of poetry (1891) is "Den nya Grottesången" (The new grotte song). Choosing his dramatic motif from the Old Norse Poetic Edda, Rydberg transforms the mythic gold-making mill of Grotte into a metaphor for the plight of the contemporary laboring class. In the treadmill of capitalism, men, women, and children become victims of greed, profit making, and egotism. Though more radical in its vision than anything his younger contemporaries in Swedish literature produced, "Den nya Grottesången" did not become a political clarion call. August Strindberg had already shouldered the role of social iconoclast. Rydberg, now professor of history at the University of Stockholm and no longer a journalist in the liberal press, was viewed as part of the establishment. Still rooted in postromantic idealism, he seemed out of date despite the social indignation of "Den nya Grottesången."

August Strindberg

When Rydberg's *Dikter* appeared in 1891, the Swedish lyrical renaissance of the final decade of the century was still under way. But there had been signs of a radical liberation of traditional poetic language as early as 1883 when August Strindberg published his first volume of poetry, *Dikter på vers och prosa* (Poems in verse and prose). A year later Ola Hansson (1860–1925) made his debut with a collection of impressionistic poems, *Dikter* (1884; Poems), followed by *Notturno* (1885; Nocturne). The first volume in particular partakes of the literary zeitgeist of the 1880s in its use of compressed metaphors and newly formed compounds.

Ola Hansson's verse moves in the direction of rhythmic prose. In this respect Strindberg had been a forerunner by mixing poetry and prose with iconoclastic nonchalance. To write rhymed poetry required, to his mind, no special talent—as the poet Pedersen declares in Strindberg's early one-act play *I Rom* (1870; In Rome): "To put a rhyme at the end of a line / is a gift bestowed upon everyone."

In his *Dikter på vers och prosa*, Strindberg declared his thought to be more important than a verse foot or rhyme. The most startling and successful example of his "free verse" is the poem "Solrök" (Sun haze), in which the poet's subjective malaise anticipates fin-de-siècle symbolism and decadence. Ironically enough, Strindberg proves himself to be a skillful rhymer, so that many of his poems achieve their impact from his fusion of concise rhythm and rhyme, as in "Lokes smädelser" (The blasphemies of Loke) and "Esplanadsystemet" (The esplanade system).

Strindberg's *Dikter på vers och prosa* contained a poem titled "Sömngångarnätter, Första natten" (Sleepwalker nights, the first night), which was to form the first in a cycle of poetic nocturnal wanderings published in 1884 as *Sömngångarnätter på vakna dagar* (Eng. tr. *Sleepwalking Nights on Wide-Awake Days*, 1978). A fifth and final "Night" poem was added in 1889. In unrhymed couplets, a verse form Strindberg had used in the poetic version of *Mäster Olof*, he describes a philosophical journey, set against French scenery but revolving around the poet's imagined return to Sweden (he had left Sweden in September 1883).

Sömngångarnätter, conceived by Strindberg as a spiritual housecleaning ("therefore I clean my soul"), forms a bitter denunciation of contemporary ideologies and concludes with an apocalyptic vision, reminiscent of the thinking of the German philosophers Hartmann and Schopenhauer. Yet at the same time, Strindberg exhorts his reader to shun the mood of defeatism and to become *l'homme engagé*, working for the welfare of others. It was an attitude of social commitment that was in line with the period of the Modern Breakthrough. That Strindberg still aligned himself with the generation of the 1880s is corroborated by the fact that he dedicated his work to the two Norwegian realistic writers Jonas Lie and Bjørnstjerne Bjørnson, both of whom he had met in Paris. Bjørnson, however, detected Strindberg's emotional ambivalence in *Sömngångarnätter* and reviewed it without enthusiasm. But for posterity, the volume has come to represent, in the words of Henry Olson, "a monument over the two contending, basic tendencies in Strindberg's temperament—the need to doubt and the need to believe." This dualism in Strindberg's psyche can also be seen as emblematic of the tension between the politicized literature of the 1880s and the aestheticism advocated by the generation of writers making their debut in the 1890s. Strindberg was not to publish another volume of poetry until twenty years later. When he brought out *Ordalek och småkonst* (Word play and minor art) in 1905, he retained some of the earlier aversion to the "artificiality" and stylistic refinement of the poetic genre. In a letter to his German translator, Emil Schering, in 1902 he suggests that all art "should be a little careless, imperfect like a product of nature where not a crystal is without its flaw, not a plant without a defective leaf."

On the other hand, by the turn of the century Strindberg had been exposed to the poetic and symbolist drama of Maurice Maeterlinck. He had explored the vogue of fairy tales and nursery rhymes and had begun to incorporate poetic passages in his dramas. Several of the poems in *Ordalek*, notably "Holländarn" (The Dutchman) and "Trefaldighetsnatten" (Trinity night), had in fact been planned as verse dramas. The collection as a whole is uneven and improvised, but Strindberg's poetic skillfulness is revealed in "Stadsresan" (The city journey), a long poem in hexameter that he wrote after studying classical prosody. When his talent is coupled to a personal emotional chord as in "Chrysaëtos," he produces some of the finest imagistic works in Swedish modernist poetry.

THE MODERN BREAKTHROUGH

If *Aftonbladet*'s first publication in 1830 serves to signal the Age of Liberalism, August Strindberg's novel *Röda rummet* (The red room), issued in 1879, announces in Swedish literature the inter-Scandinavian period called the Modern Breakthrough. Usually associated with the 1880s and the writer's engagement in contemporary social issues, the period coincides in Sweden with Strindberg's realistic and naturalistic production and with the works of the so-called *åttitalister* (writers of the 1880s), specifically the literary group Det unga Sverige (Young Sweden), headed by Gustaf af Geijerstam (1858–1909). The Modern Breakthrough also announces the arrival on the literary scene of some outspoken women writers: Victoria Benedictsson (1850–88), Anne-Charlotte Leffler (1849–92), and Alfhild Agrell (1849–1923).

The Modern Breakthrough is a period of lively contacts among Scandinavian writers. In part it can be seen as a continuation of the pan-Scandinavian political movement of the 1860s and 1870s, which had engaged many students, writers, and intellectuals, among them Ibsen in Norway and Snoilsky in Sweden. The three countries included in the Modern Breakthrough, Denmark, Norway, and Sweden, had much in common socially and politically—including a precarious union between Norway and Sweden—and were undergoing similar changes in their internal structures and cultural outlook. They were patriarchal societies with a largely agrarian population ruled by a strong class of state and local administrators, including the officials of the Lutheran state church, whose power stemmed from the Age of Reformation in the sixteenth century. The writers of the Modern Breakthrough would frequently choose a state official or a clergyman to represent the conservative forces in Scandinavian society. In fact, the fight against the Lutheran state church became one of the major themes of the Modern Breakthrough, though its origin should be traced back to the Danish radical thinker, Søren Kierkegaard and his instigation of the so-called *Øjeblikket* feud in 1854. In a series of pamphlets Kierkegaard had attacked the Danish state church for its bureaucratic power structure and lukewarm commitment to Christian faith as an individual matter.

Despite new liberal constitutions in all three Scandinavian countries during the nineteenth century, there remained built-in conservative guarantees that prevented the lower classes—what Almqvist and later Strindberg were to refer to as *underklassen*—from gaining much political influence. Only 6 percent of the population in Sweden reached an income level, after the constitutional reform of 1866, that made it eligible to vote. An organized political consciousness-raising of this vast proletariat did not take place on a larger scale until the turn of the century, even though the first major strike in Sweden occurred in 1879, the same year Strindberg published *Röda rummet*. Recent historical research of the pan-Scandinavian movement suggests that its enrollment of the young intelligentsia may have deflected attention from local social problems and thus stalled the formation of a unified working class as a strong political front in Scandinavia until the end of the century.

Another reason for the relatively slow emergence of a political platform for the *underklass* is the delayed urbanization of the Scandinavian countries compared with England and the European continent. The industrialization of northern Europe was not completed until well into the twentieth century. Beginning in Denmark and Sweden, however, the second half of the 1800s brought new capitalistic impulses to Scandinavian society. A modern banking system was established and, in Sweden in particular, commerce was facilitated by the building of a network of railroads. But an economic depression set in during the 1880s and lasted until the turn of the century; it was coupled with a crisis in agricultural trade brought about by competition from American agriculture.

Nonetheless, the 1880s appear in retrospect more like a boom period. New businesses emerged and consolidated. In Sweden the steel and timber industries were growing. Communications were improved with wire services established within Europe and across the Atlantic. Under the impact of an expanding financial market, a flood of insurance firms and banking institutions began to build imposing city palaces. That was the start of the so-called *Gründer* Era, when power in society shifted to speculative investors and entrepreneurs. The urban landscape changed with the tearing down of old slums and the construction of new boulevards in an atmosphere of progress, as captured by Strindberg in his famous poem "Esplanadsystemet": "They tear down to get air and light / Isn't that reason enough?"

Strindberg's question becomes ironic in view of the many embezzlement scandals and bankruptcies that followed in the wake of the economic expansion. In *Röda rummet*, set in the author's contemporary Stockholm, economic swindles and questionable insurance affairs loom large. Soon other writers of the Modern Breakthrough would look on the *Gründer* mentality as the sign of a sick society, and economic subjects were to rank next to moral hypocrisy (supposedly endorsed by the church) and women's issues in importance among writers who saw as their central task "to set up problems for debate."

It was the Danish critic Georg Brandes (1842–1927) who with this famous slogan steered both Ibsen and Strindberg away from earlier historical and legendary subjects to the topical issues of the day. Brandes wished to bring a new cosmopolitan and European perspective into Scandinavian literary and political thinking. Though he did not coin the expression "the modern breakthrough" until 1883, Brandes had established himself as a controversial but leading literary critic (together with his brother Edvard) in Copenhagen in the 1870s. In 1871, he began a series of lectures titled *Hovedstrømninger i det 19de Aarhundredes Litteratur* (1872–90; Eng. tr. *Main Currents in Nineteenth-Century Literature*, 1903–5), and later in the same decade he went on a tour to Sweden. It is indicative of his influential though often controversial position in Swedish (and Scandinavian) literature that Brandes was attacked in sarcastic tones by Sweden's establishment poet Carl David af Wirsén but praised as a pathfinder for the writers of the eighties by Det unga Sverige's spokesman, Gustaf af Geijerstam.

The literature of the Modern Breakthrough aimed at creating both public and literary debate. It often touched on extremely sensitive issues in Oscarian Sweden, in an era whose moral and social attitudes had much in common with the Victorian Age in England. In its choice of contemporary realistic topics it also challenged the literary establishment found at the universities and in the Swedish Academy. The academy was dominated by its permanent secretary, Carl David af Wirsén, who saw it as his special task to preserve the moral and literary status quo. In the preface to his essay collection, *Kritiker* (1901; Criticisms), af Wirsén claims that for three decades he had devoted himself to examining "the philosophy, the spiritual conception that has formed the foundation of the works of the authors [of the Modern Breakthrough]. Such an undertaking has seemed to me simply necessary from a patriotic, religious, and ethical point of view in a time when often impure, unhealthy, and blasphemous thoughts have been smuggled into our society under the guise of belles lettres."

Af Wirsén spewed his venom on Ibsen (after the publication of *Gengangere* [1884; Ghosts]) and Bjørnson in Norway, and he was no doubt responsible for the fact that Strindberg never became a member of the Swedish Academy. He found support for his views in the philosophy of C. J. Boström, professor at the University of Uppsala, whose ideas had won wide acceptance among the student intelligentsia in the 1850s and 1860s. Emanating from Geijer's teaching during his last years as a professor of history, Boström's idealistic philosophy was built on the concept of God as the supreme personality and society as a hierarchy of lower personalities operating according to a preconceived pyramidical structure, reminiscent of the eighteenth-century concept of the great chain of being and serving to maintain the social status quo in Oscarian Sweden.

By contrast, Georg Brandes took his cue from several of the leading progressive minds of Europe. He paid personal visits to the social philosopher John Stuart Mill in England and the literary critic Hippolyte Taine in France. From the former, he adopted the concept of utilitarianism, a pragmatic philosophy stemming originally from Jeremy Bentham and aiming at creating a good life for as many people as possible regardless of social class or sex. Such ideas, though hardly revolutionary by today's thinking, seemed radical in nineteenth-century Scandinavia, for they departed from the established views of a society imbued with a Lutheran morality that preached a subservient role for women and promised the poor classes a spiritual reward in God's Kingdom rather than material improvements in their earthly life.

From the French critic Taine, Brandes developed his views on nineteenth-century determinism with its emphasis on the decisive impact of heredity and environment on an individual's destiny. Taine was also instrumental in forming Brandes's ideas on the importance of an author's personality in the genesis of a literary work. By transmitting his social and literary philosophy to the rest of Scandinavia, Brandes radicalized the intellectual climate there in the 1870s and 1880s. Strindberg's *Röda rummet* is the most striking example of this change in Sweden. It coincides in time with Ibsen's play *Et dukkehjem* (1879; A doll's house). Five years later, when Strindberg was brought to trial for blasphemy for publishing a collection of short stories, *Giftas* (1884; Eng. tr. *Getting Married*, 1972), his work appears in the midst of other Scandinavian literary "scandals": Bjørnstjerne Bjørnson's play *En hanske* (1883; A gauntlet), which attacks the moral double standard of the day; J. P. Jacobsen's novel *Niels Lyhne* (1880), which advocates a positivistic atheist point of view; Herman Bang's *Haabløse slægter* (1880; Hopeless generations), a work filled with spleen and erotic decadence that led to its public confiscation; and Hans Jæger's story of "free love," *Fra Kristiania-Bohêmen* (1885; From Christiania's bohemian life), which resulted in a trial in Norway and gave birth to an anarchistically colored radicalism that eventually proved too incendiary even for Brandes and some of his Scandinavian proselytes.

August Strindberg's expressive literary persona with its exuberant realistic power of observation and its hot-tempered rebellious spirit seems particularly well suited for the Modern Breakthrough period. Strindberg became its foremost artistic spokesman in Sweden. Yet at the same time he is perhaps too restless, self-centered, and idiosyncratic a mind to personify the period. He is part of it, but again and again, he also transcends it.

On the other hand, there is no doubt that Strindberg inaugurated the *modern* realistic era in Swedish literature and that in the early 1880s he saw himself and was seen as a central member, if not the leader, of the core group of avant-garde political and literary writers who called themselves Det unga Sverige. It was Strindberg who coined the name, in a letter referring to a radical coterie of students he met during his short stay at the University of Uppsala in the late 1860s. Only later did the name become associated with the Swedish Parnassus of the 1880s.

Apart from Strindberg, the 1880s in Swedish literature are dominated by the group of writers who called themselves Det unga Sverige (Strindberg disassociated himself from the group in 1884). Det unga Sverige was in many ways a remarkable constellation of literati who formed a coterie advocating *indignationslitteratur* (a literature of indignation). To a certain extent, the intellectual dynamics of the group transcend the individual literary contribution of its members. With Strindberg's 1879 novel *Röda rummet* serving as a beacon, and prompted by Georg Brandes's call for a socially conscious literature, Det unga Sverige, or *åttitalisterna* (the writers of the eighties), as the members were later named, signaled the arrival of modern literature and the impact of new scientific thinking in Sweden. They redefined the role of the literary writer as a bearer and unmasker of truth rather than an idealistic singer of beauty, and they engaged in a lively public debate, though mostly in smaller journals, since the major newspapers remained closed to them. They lived off their pens and often combined creative writing and critical activity. Their literary salons in Stockholm were public forums of a national rather than local character; some of the participants came from the southern province of Skåne: Ola Hansson, Axel Lundegård, Victoria Benedictsson. Yet as a group, Det unga Sverige never issued a literary manifesto. Its members were considered ideologically radical but fought more against traditional conventions than for political change. They seem to have viewed themselves primarily as forming a voice of opposition to the conservative elements in Oscarian Sweden.

Gustaf af Geijerstam

Det unga Sverige had no ideologue of its own of Georg Brandes's stature. Gustaf af Geijerstam (1858–1909), the group's central figure, was more important as an administrator and liaison person who maintained contacts with publishing houses, newspapers, and theater producers. Despite a promising start with tendentious works such as the short story collection *Gråkallt* (1882; Bleak and cold) and the educational novel *Erik Grane* (1885), which Melker Johnsson has termed the emblematic work of the Swedish 1880s, af Geijerstam became a victim of the decade's didactic trendiness and the main target of the subsequent generation's critique of the 1880s as bleak, pedestrian, and unpoetic.

The Women Writers of the 1880s

The 1880s combine intellectual liveliness and moral stuffiness. As the examples of Strindberg and Brandes show, it was possible for male members of the avant-garde to be politically radical but emancipatorily ambivalent. Thus, from within their own camp as modern writers, the women received mixed signals, which forced them constantly to reexamine their professional status and their gender role. In at least one instance, that of Victoria Benedictsson (pseudonym: Ernst Ahlgren) it served as the suicidal catalyst. In another case, that of Anne Charlotte Leffler, it resulted in an almost singular focus on what she called "kvinnlighet och erotik" (femininity or femaleness and eroticism). The fact that their professional commitment became incompatible with women's traditional domestic role was a contributing factor to both Leffler's and Alfhild Agrell's divorces. At the same time, however, all three of these women writers brought with them an intimate knowledge of the home scene, which they could use in their authorship in a decade that valued the realistic vignette. In that sense, they also carried on the legacy of the family novel from Fredrika Bremer's generation of women writers.

Anne Charlotte Leffler

The most celebrated of the Swedish women writers in the 1880s, Anne Charlotte Leffler (1849–92), had an outgoing temperament that made her a rallying figure in Det unga Sverige's literary salon. Making her debut under the pseudonym Carlot to protect her husband's reputation, she soon switched to using her maiden name as her pen name. Setting herself high standards—Ibsen of *Et dukkehjem* and Strindberg of *Röda rummet* served as her models—Leffler wrote both drama and prose but made her most lasting contribution in the short story genre. Between 1882 and 1890 she published several volumes of contemporary tales under the encompassing title *Ur livet* (5 vols; From life). Her intention was to unmask the hypocrisy of Oscarian Sweden, and her attitude may be summarized with the title of one of her stories from her second collection: "I strid med samhället" (1883; At war with society). Her weapon is a combination of indignation and satire. In "En stor man" (A great man), she ridicules the pomp and circumstance of the Swedish Academy while revealing that her celebrated protagonist is in reality a morphine addict and embezzler of family funds. In "En bal" (A ballroom dance), the formal scene gives the author an occasion to satirize the pretensions of the upper classes, including the host, a cabinet minister and social upstart who is pitifully sensitive to propriety and social convention.

By attacking the hypocrisy she observed around her, Leffler wanted to liberate the individual from the straitjacket of bigotry and social pretension. In her later writing this liberation came to focus more and more on women's right to express their eroticism, as in the novella "Aurore Bunge," about a socialite's erotic affair with a lighthouse keeper in the skerries, and the novel *En sommarsaga* (1886; A summer's tale), in which a sophisticated woman painter elopes with a viking of a teacher at a Norwegian folk high school.

Leffler's last work, the novel *Kvinnor och erotik 2* (1890; Women and eroticism 2), has a strong anchoring in her own personal experience. It depicts the love story of a Swedish woman, Alie, and an Italian nobleman and poet, Andrea Serra, and is the least didactic of her work. At the time of its publication, as she was getting ready to settle down in Italy in a new marriage, Anne Charlotte Leffler renounced officially the epithet *kvinnosakskvinna* (feminist).

Victoria Benedictsson (Ernst Ahlgren)

Whereas Leffler abandoned her pseudonym after her first publication, Victoria Benedictsson (1850–88) maintained her male writing persona throughout her brief career, even after its true identity had been revealed. It demonstrates clearly her desire to separate her domestic self as wife of an elderly postmaster in a small town in Skåne from her life as a writer and public figure. The final crisis in her life arises with great symbolic import when Ernst Ahlgren, the professional pseudonym, meets the critical guru of the 1880s, Georg Brandes, and Victoria Benedictsson falls in love with him—only to discover that her idol not only is lukewarm to her last novel, *Fru Marianne* (1887; Mrs. Marianne), but also views their liaison as no more than a fleeting affair. Crushed both as a writer and as a woman, Benedictsson/Ahlgren commits suicide. More than any writer of her generation, she embodies through her personal life a decade in Swedish literature that emphasized authenticity in lifestyle, an ambiguous equality between the sexes, and a rigorous ethical response to human actions.

Soon after her debut with the provincial stories *Från Skåne* (1884; From Skåne), Benedictsson established an intellectual friendship with Axel Lundegård (1861–1930), whose support was important to her in finishing her first novel, *Pengar* (1885; Money). In tracing the life of her main character, Selma, from girlhood and early marriage to emancipated independence,

Benedictsson contributed to the literature of indignation with its focus on marital incompatibility, monetary pressures, and the lack of opportunities for women for personal development. *Pengar* transcends, however, the theoretical tendentiousness of much of the literature of indignation in its psychological nuances, especially in its portrayal of Selma as a tomboy.

Benedictsson's second novel, *Fru Marianne*, is more epic in scope than the rather episodic *Pengar*. The key issue in the story, about a spoiled upper-class woman who marries a farmer, revolves around monogamous ethics, or what the author expressed in a letter to her friend Georg Nordensvan: "I really insist on the central idea—I mean that a man and a woman try to be faithful to each other throughout life." Mrs. Marianne's development from superficial socialite to diligent farmer's wife implies an adjustment to her husband's lifestyle and social position. That came as something of a shock to Benedictsson's writing colleagues, who were attuned to works criticizing the institution of marriage. In an official review, Brandes dismissed *Fru Marianne* as a sentimental *dameroman* (ladies' novel).

THE OBLIGATORY GENRE OF THE 1880S:
THE PROVINCIAL OR FOLK LIFE TALE

The realistic folk life tale introduced by Almqvist in the 1830s was very much in vogue throughout the 1880s. When Tor Hedberg (1862–1931), a member of Det unga Sverige, wrote a retrospective survey of the decade in 1891, he singled out the short story set in a provincial location as the "most mature" literary expression of his generation of writers. This interest in the provincial milieu was one of the few legacies of the *åttitalister* to be carried on by poets and prose writers of the 1890s: Heidenstam, Fröding, Karlfelt, Lagerlöf.

For Det unga Sverige, the provincial setting served both an idealistic and a realistic purpose: it represented a return to a simple and authentic life in Rousseau's spirit, away from the corrupting life of academia, high society, and urban bureaucracy; and it provided a subject matter in which the objective point of view advocated by the *åttitalister* could be tested. Partly influenced by Zola and the Goncours brothers in France, Swedish writers of the 1880s viewed people from the farming and labor segments of society as naturalistic models who revealed their essential human passions without the sophisticated duplicity of the educated classes. But people from the lower classes could also be singled out as victims of political injustice, on whom the writers could shower their social pathos. On the other hand, one can also detect in the literary portrayal of provincial folk—especially in Strindberg's and af Geijerstam's folk life themes—an occasional condescending attitude and a belief in the psychological inferiority of the rural mind.

Ever since the days of Peter Christen Asbjørnsen and Jørgen Moe in Norway, N.F.S. Grundtvig in Denmark, Gunnar Olof Hyltén-Cavallius in Sweden, and Elias Lönnrot in Finland, there had been a continuous interest in collecting and documenting the oral popular literature that survived in the provinces throughout Scandinavia. To this interest was added, in the 1860s and 1870s, a recording of provincial dialects. Dialect societies were formed at the universities. In 1873, Artur Hazelius founded Skandinavisketnografiska samfundet (the Scandinavian Ethnographic Association), a forerunner of the Nordic Museum and of Skansen, the open-air museum in Stockholm aimed at preserving folk life artifacts.

This scientific rather than personal approach to provincial lifestyle and traditions suited the writers of Det unga Sverige, for even when they had firsthand knowledge of the rural settings they depicted, they tended to view these milieus with naturalistic or scientific detachment. How closely related the new dialect and folkloristic sciences sometimes were to the folk life stories written by the *åttitalister* is demonstrated by the fact that Victoria Benedictsson spent time collecting dialect words in her province of Skåne and her colleague to the north, August Bondeson (1854–1903), worked as an ethnographer in his home province of Halland, while the foremost poet of the decade (next to Strindberg and Ola Hansson), Albert Ulrik Bååth (1853–1912), was a student of dialect in southern Sweden. Folklore and dialect studies provided an alibi for the realistic language of the Modern Breakthrough writers, who aimed at creating a literary style reflecting colloquial speech patterns.

Bondeson's exposure to ethnographic research resulted in several volumes of *Allmogeberättelser* (1884, 1888; Stories of the farming population) in which he includes a wide variety of portraits of crofters, well-to-do farmers, local politicians, railroad workers, and emigrants. His major work, *Skollärar John Chronschoughs memoarer* (1897–1904; Schoolteacher John Chronschoug's memoirs), uses similar documentary material in a more humorous vein.

Bååth's ethnographic experience in his youth shaped the rest of his life and might be compared with Johan Ludvig Runeberg's first and crucial encounter with the Finnish countryside in the 1840s. When Bååth as a young student met farmboys who voiced a curiosity to learn but had no academic ambitions, it seemed to him that "a new bright light" had opened up a wider perspective on life. He expressed this vision "full of air" in several collections of poetry: *Dikter* (1879; Poems), *Nya dikter* (1881; New poems), *Vid allfarväg* (1884; By the highway), and *På gröna stigar* (1889; On green paths).

Among the core group of Det unga Sverige, to which neither Bondeson nor Bååth belonged, the degree of firsthand exposure to the rural population varied. The interest of Gustaf af Geijerstam seems to have been more academic than personal. He researched his subject and used the documented material to expose not only the poverty but also the criminal psychology of his country models in *Fattigt folk* (1884, 1889; Poor people) and *Kronofogdens berättelser* (1890; The tales of the crown sheriff).

For Anne Charlotte Leffler, the folk life genre resulted in some of her finest literary achievements. In such tales as "Gusten får ett pastorat" (Gusten gets a parish) and "Moster Malvina" (Aunt Malvina), found in *Ur Livet*, Leffler's tendentious fervor is replaced by a drastic sense of humor.

Victoria Benedictsson's presentation of rural life and its people can take on a similar tone of levity, as in the story "Mor Malenas höna" (Mother Malena's hen), but on the whole she is more serious and intimate with her rural portraits than Leffler. Born on a Skåne farm, Benedictsson grew up in close proximity to her folk life subjects. In addition to her debut collection *Från Skåne*, with which she hoped to gain entry into Det unga Sverige, she used the same genre in *Folklif och småberättelser* (1887; Folk life and small tales).

Benedictsson's provincial countryman Ola Hansson also began his literary career writing short stories set in Skåne's rural milieu. His collection of *Slättbyhistorier* (Stories from Slättby), composed in 1881–83, was, however, rejected by the publishers and did not appear until 1927. Hansson's narrative style is indeed atypical of the 1880s in its impressionistic scene painting; to him it was more important to evoke images of the Skåne landscape than to expose folk life customs and people. In *Slättbyhistorier*, as in his other short stories and poetry, Hansson's affinity in terms of literary temperament is with the writers of the 1890s.

THE SWAN SONG OF THE EIGHTIES

Det unga Sverige was no homogeneous literary clique. As the decade wore on, there were many indications of the group's internal differences and of a shifting literary climate. Victoria Benedictsson's fragment of a novel titled *Modern* (The mother), which she worked on at the time of her death in 1888, turns out to be a critique of some of the basic attitudes of the eighties: their ideological fixation, superficial rationalism, and lack of genuine, subjectively experienced passion. Anne Charlotte Leffler's personal life story—her break from Sweden and marriage to an Italian duke—can be seen as a symbolic farewell to Det unga Sverige. Though Tor Hedberg continued to defend the literary program of the eighties and published a response to Heidenstam's attack on the decade's prosaic *skomakarrealism* (shoemaker realism) in 1889, the title of his rebuttal, *Glädje* (Joy), anticipates the more exuberant mood of the poets of the 1890s. Hedberg's later development as a lyrical poet drawn to symbolism confirms his gradual disenchantment with the ideology of the eighties. Gustaf af Geijerstam, the main proponent of *gråväderslitteraturen* (gray weather literature), also presented literary indications of a new development, though he himself never succeeded in fulfilling them. But one of his short stories published at the end of the 1880s, "Utan pengar" (Without money), suggests, as Gunnar Brandell has pointed out, an influence from the Norwegian Knut Hamsun's forthcoming first-person novel *Sult* (1890; Eng. tr. *Hunger*, 1899), fragments of which had been published in the Danish journal *Ny Jord* (Virgin soil) in 1888. *Sult* heralds, together with Selma Lagerlöf's *Gösta Berlings saga* (1891; Eng. tr. *The Story of Gösta Berling*, 1898), a new epoch in Scandinavian prose.

A more definite break with the literary perspective of Det unga Sverige was announced in 1887 with Ola Hansson's collection of short stories *Sensitiva amorosa* and in 1889 by Axel Lundegård's educational novel *Röde prinsen* (The red prince). Hansson's thin volume focusing on sensuous though virginal relationships between men and women caused a minor scandal. Together with his volume of poetry *Notturno* from 1885, *Sensitiva amorosa* expresses a modernistic sensibility pointing ahead to writers such as Vilhelm Ekelund and Pär Lagerkvist.

The contribution of Lundegård is more directly programmatic; he did not break new ground in terms of literary genre or focus. *Röde prinsen* is a conventional bildungsroman whose main character, Max von Rosenberg, might be contrasted to Strindberg's protagonist Arvid Falk in *Röda rummet* ten years earlier as the decade of the 1880s was approaching. Max is, as his family name suggests, an aristocrat; he shares none of Falk's affinity for social outcasts. He is a Nietzschean by temperament—Georg Brandes had introduced the German thinker a year earlier in a Copenhagen lecture— who expresses contempt for his newspaper boss as an *underklassräv* (lower-class fox) and for all those small and uneducated minds who cannot understand "the upper-class scent of the Red Prince's liberal mind." But *Röde prinsen* is above all a reckoning with Ibsen, whose rigorous moralism and serious debate drama had set much of the tone for the writers of the eighties:

"For much too long we have looked upon existence with the dark glasses of his writing temperament; now we long to approach light and dawn, long for May air and sunshine in life and literature. We shall sing hymns to the joy of life, burst into liberating laughter, dance in the light summer nights under the pine trees of our homeland, turn the sky blue and the world good in our poetry."

It was to be the task of the next generation of Swedish writers to realize Lundegård's vision of sensuality and joie de vivre. *Röde prinsen* was, as Lundegård himself stated, "the swan song of that movement in time to which, five years ago, I devoted my morning prayer."

STRINDBERG AND THE MODERN BREAKTHROUGH

Two reasons make Strindberg a natural rallying figure for the Modern Breakthrough generation in Sweden: his commitment to realism and his outspoken public voice. Gunnar Brandell has argued convincingly that Strindberg never deviated from his desire to depict the here and now; that he was never interested in exoticism; that when he wrote about utopias, they became *utopier i verkligheten* (utopias in reality); that when he later projected in writing his visions of Inferno, they were rooted in his observations of hell on earth. Defined in such a broad and expansive way, Strindberg's realism must include his subjective observations of his own life. Perhaps it is this subjective base, found also in such Modern Breakthrough writers as J. P. Jacobsen and Herman Bang in Denmark, that has led recent scholars of the period to redefine its scope and extend it to the symbolist 1890s.

THE MODERN BREAKTHROUGH AND PROSE FICTION

The dual role of Strindberg's literary persona as observer and participant is central to his first major work of fiction, the novel *Röda rummet* (1879; Eng. tr. *The Red Room*, 1967). Set in Stockholm in 1869–70, the plot revolves around a young journalist by the name of Arvid Falk and his initiation into modern Swedish society. In the beginning of the novel he is a naive young man, at times duped, at times shocked by the dissolute and corrupt world he encounters. In the end he appears ready to enter a bourgeois marriage, too disillusioned perhaps to challenge his society, though some readings of the text have suggested that Falk's personality harbors a subversive revolutionary.

Röda rummet has an episodic structure and a quick narrative pace that reveal its modernity: it is a product of the columnist's newspaper age and of the hectic rhythm of a growing urban environment. Its mood is rebellious; Strindberg freely admitted that he intended "to show a panorama of a society I do not love and that has never loved me." But he couches his personal indignation in a satirical tone and concludes that he has written his novel "without anger and effort." *Röda rummet* becomes a divertissement in which Strindberg allows himself to expose contemporary society but also plays with earlier literary prose forms, such as the picaresque story and the educational novel.

The satirical tone of *Röda rummet* cuts deeper in Strindberg's *Det nya riket* (1882; The new kingdom), a set of social commentaries that might be called Sweden's first mass media stories in the sense that they combine a tone of muckraking and slanted reportage with an acute sense of newsworthy material. Strindberg subtitled the work "Depictions from the era of coups and jubilee festivities" and proceeded to dissect Oscarian Sweden with plebeian glee. His motivation was twofold: as a social underdog he wanted to unmask the pompous players on the public scene, and as an angered author he sought revenge for the critique he had received for his cultural history *Svenska folket i helg och söcken* (1881–82; The Swedish people on weekdays and sundays).

Det nya riket became a succès de scandale. Strindberg used it as the reason for his leaving Sweden and going into voluntary exile in September 1883. But a more likely motivation was his desire to follow in the wake of other Scandinavian Breakthrough writers, many of whom—to the chagrin of Oscar II, who liked to see himself as an enlightened monarch and a man of letters—cultivated a contempt for Scandinavian provincialism by seeking out more cosmopolitan milieus. Brandes had lectured in Berlin; Ibsen had moved to Rome and Dresden; Jonas Lie and Bjørnstjerne Bjørnson were in Paris. Strindberg simply joined an ever-growing coterie of Scandinavian writers and artists who continued to flock to the European continent throughout the century. He traveled with his family and probably had no intention of remaining abroad very long. But another literary scandal intervened in his life, and in the end Strindberg did not return to live in Sweden until 1889, and then for a relatively short time.

The *Giftas* Trial

The overshadowing public debate associated with the Modern Breakthrough concerns sexual morality, the so-called *sedlighetsfejden*. The clarion call was Ibsen's play *A Doll's House* in 1879, whose main character, Nora Helmer, breaks up her marriage in order to reexamine her life. The "Nora woman," as Strindberg called her, became for him synonymous with the gender role debate that was underlying *sedlighetsfejden*.

When it came to feminist issues, Strindberg was genuinely and irascibly engaged in the debate as well as attracted to it for opportune reasons. When he published his collection of short stories, *Giftas* (Eng. tr. *Getting Married*, 1972), in 1884, he had in mind providing his new publisher Albert Bonnier with a "topical piece of publication," something up-to-date and sellable. But his own marriage to Siri von Essen was entering a turbulent phase; coupled with his sexual insecurity, it led him to assume an ambiguous position vis-à-vis "the woman question." In a famous preface with a faked interview, Strindberg presents an egalitarian vision of life between the sexes that appears amazingly radical for its day and age; it is, however, based on a fast-disappearing rural lifestyle, a back-to-nature pipedream inspired by Rousseau. How rooted this vision was in traditional gender roles rather than in new emancipation concepts becomes clear in many of the stories in *Giftas*, in particular perhaps "Ett dockhem" ("A Doll's House"), which was a direct response to Ibsen's drama.

Strindberg's authorial voice is strong throughout *Giftas*. Though he claims that his stories were based on sociological facts, they clearly reveal his personal point of view. His polemical attitude, however, is directed not at feminist issues as such but at Ibsen—"the Norwegian bluestocking"— and at Ibsen's failure to give a realistic picture of married life. In this way Strindberg could presumably win two battles: he could present his traditional view of marriage as the only functional and "natural" view, and he could outwit Ibsen as a modern realistic artist.

A year before Ibsen's play was staged in theaters throughout Scandinavia, George Drysdale's book *Elements of Social Science, or Physical, Sexual, and Natural Religion by a Graduate of Medicine* (1855) had appeared in Swedish translation. Drysdale, an English medical doctor, argued against sexual abstinence in both men and women, claiming that celibacy could lead to physical debility. Both Georg Brandes and Strindberg subscribed to Drysdale's views. In the first story in *Giftas*, "Dygdens lön" ("Reward of Virtue"), Strindberg depicts a young man, Theodor, who lives in celibacy for many years only to die shortly after getting married.

The story about poor Theodor threatened to become Strindberg's Swedish nemesis. Charged with "mockery and blasphemy," Strindberg had to return to Sweden to stand trial. It was not the sexual morality or the bold new ideas presented in the *Giftas* preface that was at issue, but rather young Theodor's first experience of the Holy Communion; Strindberg deprives Christ of his divine dimension and ridicules the sacrament as a political weapon used by the upper classes to control the dispossessed in society.

The case was dismissed, and Strindberg was acclaimed as the hero of the day by multitudes of people who assembled in front of the Grand

Hotel in Stockholm, where, with rhetorical graciousness, he addressed them as celebrators of the victory of free speech. But the triumph was short-lived, and in the long run the *Giftas* trial was going to appear to him in a negative light.

The woman question was a key issue to Det unga Sverige, and the appearance of *Giftas* caused a rift within the group, especially between some of the women writers and Strindberg, who suspected that the feminists' grand old lady, Sophie Adlersparre, had been instrumental in bringing about the *Giftas* trial. The role of central public figure among members of Det unga Sverige was taken over by Anne Charlotte Leffler, whose plays and works of fiction focused on emancipation issues. Leffler's home in Stockholm was for several years in the mid-1880s an open house and literary salon for young Swedish writers.

Strindberg and Autobiography

Strindberg, on the other hand, returned to the European continent. The *Giftas* trial served as a catalyst to bring out in the open a personal crisis that now worsened. His bitterness dictated the misogynist tone of a second volume of *Giftas* stories (1886). A year earlier he had published *Utopier i verkligheten* (1885; Utopias in reality), in which he still entertains a vision of the future as an idyllic, Rousseau-inspired, socialist state. Soon thereafter, however, he felt a need to "re-edit" his philosophical views. He declares himself no longer a deist but an atheist and gives up his socialist leanings; it now becomes crucial to him to reexamine his past. At age thirty-seven, he therefore sits down to write his autobiography. *Tjänstekvinnans son* (Eng. tr. *The Son of a Servant*, 1913) was published in three parts in 1886–87.

Tjänstekvinnans son is, like *Röda rummet*, a penetrating and dynamic exposé of Swedish life in the second half of the nineteenth century. Part autobiography, part cultural history, it inaugurates a strong tradition of literary self-portraits in Swedish belles lettres, from Hjalmar Söderberg to Jan Myrdal. Strindberg is anxious to point out that *Tjänstekvinnans son* is no confessional work in the spirit of St. Augustine or Rousseau, nor is it a memoir aimed at entertaining the reader with episodes from a public life. His ambition, expressed in the subtitle, is to examine "the evolutionary history of a soul" in a sociological, psychological, and historical light. His approach follows the precepts of "race, milieu, and moment in time" set down by Taine and promoted by Brandes.

According to Taine, a human psyche is disparate and chaotic. In his analysis of Johan, his alter ego in *Tjänstekvinnans son*, Strindberg agrees: "The self is not a thing to itself; it is a manifold of reflexes, a complex of drives and desires." But Taine also maintained that some major quality dominated in every psyche. Strindberg follows suit and concludes that "there were two fundamental traits in his soul complex . . . doubt and sensitivity to pressure!" His self-examination, together with his reading of the psychological research of the day, was to be instrumental to Strindberg in composing his dramatic works of the 1880s and in formulating his concept of the "characterless character" (i.e., a character who is complex rather than typecast), which he discusses in the famous preface to his play *Fröken Julie* (1888; Eng. tr. *Miss Julie*, in *Selected Plays*, 1986).

The title of his autobiography points at something central in Strindberg's psyche: his social insecurity and sexual ambivalence. It alludes to the story of the bondwoman Hagar in the Old Testament and her son Ishmael, fathered by the patriarch Abraham. Like Ishmael, the symbolic outcast, Strindberg viewed himself as a social pariah whose lower-class origin—his mother was a housekeeper before her marriage—predetermined him to feel strong sympathies with the lower classes. His relationship to his father was strained and bitter, and Steamboat Commissioner Strindberg was no role model to August. As a consequence, a complex psychological power play was to dictate much of Strindberg's personal life, in which social class, gender, and sexuality interact and in which his strong maternal identification feeds his social rebellion but also undermines his masculine self-image. In *Tjänstekvinnans son*, this ambivalence exposes us to a human being who is constantly railing against authority, secular as well as divine, until he rejects God and declares himself an atheist. In fictionalized form the same persona, filled with agonizing sexual self-doubt, emerges in a play like *Fadren* (1887; Eng. tr. *The Father*, in *Selected Plays*, 1986) and a prose work like *Le plaidoyer d'un fou*, originally written in French (1887; Eng. tr. *A Madman's Defense*, 1967). *Le plaidoyer d'un fou*, in particular, provides an instructive companion piece to *Tjänstekvinnans son*, in terms of both its duplicitous genre (fictionalized autobiography or first-person novel?) and its storytelling analogy to Strindberg's marriage to Siri von Essen, a period not covered in *Tjänstekvinnans son* until 1909, when a fourth part was added to the autobiography titled *Han och hon* (He and she).

Strindberg and the "Skerries Novel"
Implied in *Tjänstekvinnans son* are two central aspects of Strindberg's writing career: on one hand, his strong desire, from time to time, to abandon his literary métier (his "fictionalizing") and devote himself to sociocultural and scientific research; on the other hand, his obvious joy at using his verbal virtuosity to tell "fables," to structure reality in narrative

patterns. Throughout the 1880s these two ambitions continued to coexist in Strindberg's life. During his early years in exile he wrote not only *Giftas* but also—to his publisher's dismay—a two-volume cultural analysis of "the public discontent" titled *Likt och olikt* (1884; roughly, Varia). Later in the decade he produced a reportage from the French countryside, *Bland franska bönder* (1886; Among French peasants). But the following year he composed a novel about Swedish farmers in the Stockholm archipelago, *Hemsöborna* (1887; Eng. tr. *The Natives of Hemsö*, 1967). It appears that after each commitment to nonfictional writing, Strindberg returns to belles lettres with renewed creative exuberance. But it is also typical of his own ambivalence in the matter that he frequently upgrades his social and scientific works while occasionally dismissing the importance of his literary endeavors. Thus he referred to *Hemsöborna*, a classic in its genre in Swedish literature, as an "intermezzo scherzando" between more serious "battles."

Strindberg had intellectual curiosity but also intellectual pretensions. Studying his life is like having all the major ideas of his age pass in review, from Darwinism to Nietzscheanism, from socialism to occultism. Yet Strindberg's strength as a creator of literature does not lie at all in the ideational content of his works. Rather, it is to be found in his scene painting and in the dynamic emotional encounters of his characters. It is also lodged in the storytelling energy of his language. Nowhere is this more apparent than in his novel about the confident landlubber Carlson, who restores Madame Flod's farm on the island of Hemsö and marries the widow but succumbs to the elements and loses out to Mrs. Flod's son Gusten. It is an archetypal conflict between the entrepreneur and the settler, between the intruding outsider and the native who, like Gusten, lives in harmony with his surroundings. The spirit of Rousseau and Darwin are present, but not intrusively so.

In *Hemsöborna*, Strindberg returned to his "smultronställe" (favorite place), the island of Kymmendö, where he had spent a happy summer in his youth writing *Mäster Olof* and to which he would go back for his honeymoon with his first wife, Siri von Essen. The novel comes as close to a national prose epic as any Swedish work, for Strindberg not only recreates his memories with humor and great aplomb; he also captures a piece of social mythology in storytelling form—the mystique that recently urbanized Swedes still attached to a life close to soil and water. By assigning to the main character, Carlson, the role of enterprising newcomer on Madame Flod's island farm, Strindberg allows his reader the opportunity to explore Hemsö as both a visitor and a participant in the events there, a dual role that generations of city Swedes, vacationing in the archipelago, have experienced since Strindberg's days.

After *Hemsöborna*, Strindberg was commissioned by his publisher to return to the same setting for his next work of fiction. The result was a collection of stories, *Skärkarlslif* (1888; Life in the skerries). But now the spontaneity and lusty humor of *Hemsöborna* were gone, replaced by Strindberg's excursions into Nietzscheanism. Most interesting is the novella "Den romantiske klockaren på Rånö" (The romantic sexton on Rånö) for its use of dreams and visions, a foreshadowing of Strindberg's authorship in the 1890s. Like his subsequent novel *I havsbandet* (1890; Eng. tr. *By the Open Sea*, 1985), it signals a watershed in Strindberg's life, a psychological and religious crisis that develops his writing in a new and modernistic direction. This part of Strindberg's life and oeuvre is discussed below in a subsequent section.

THEATER AND DRAMA

The Nineteenth Century
The period between 1830 and 1880 meant an upsurge for the theater as an entertainment forum. The most popular genres were the melodrama, the popular comedy, and the historical drama. Though a royal monopoly, introduced by Gustav IV Adolf, controlled the national stages (the Opera and the Royal Dramatic Theater) and was not dissolved until 1881, private theaters were approved by the Riksdag in 1841, and the first one, Nya Teatern, opened in Stockholm in the following year.

The repertory did not differ very much between the royal stages and the private theaters. Operettas, native folk comedies, and French farces dominated, but Shakespeare's dramas also were performed; C. A. Hagberg's superb translations of Shakespeare, which were to attain the status of classics, appeared in 1847–51. *Hamlet* was produced for the first time in Swedish translation at the Royal Theater in 1853. The production inspired a number of Swedish playwrights, notably Edvard Bäckström (1841–86) and Johan Börjeson (1790–1866), to portray the royal house of Sweden on the stage. When Strindberg made his debut on the stage in the late 1860s and early 1870s, he too chose the historical genre and acknowledged his indebtedness to Shakespeare.

Shakespeare may also have been the inspiration for one of the most popular Swedish plays of the nineteenth century: F. A. Dahlgren's *Wermlänningarne* (1846; The people of Värmland). Dahlgren, who had translated *Romeo and Juliet* a few years earlier, moved the intrigue of two rivaling families in Verona to a farming community in central Sweden and provided a happy ending for his love couple, Anna and Erik.

The most popular Swedish playwright of the mid-nineteenth century was August Blanche. His best-known work for the stage is *Komedianterna eller Ett resande teatersällskap* (1848; The comedians, or A travelling theater company). A play in the vaudeville tradition, the title points to a phenomenon of growing popularity in the Swedish theater: the ambulatory stage companies that traversed the countryside, offering their repertoire at marketplaces, in so-called theater barns, or in newly constructed city theaters. Drama, which at the beginning of the century had tended to result in closet plays, meant to be read rather than staged, now catered to live audiences. Traveling by horse and carriage and later by railroad, the ambulatory theater companies provided a mixed entertainment fare, playing a popular role not unlike that of the cinema in the twentieth century.

The Modern Breakthrough, 1870–1890

August Blanche wrote several realistic dramas, among them *Läkaren* (1845; The doctor), which signal a trend toward contemporary subject matters, a development that was to culminate during the 1870s and 1880s. In this period of intense intellectual debate it is hardly surprising that drama, the most immediate and public of the literary genres, should attain a certain prominence. Many of the literary giants in Scandinavia at the time chose the stage as their forum: Henrik Ibsen, Bjørnstjerne Bjørnson, and August Strindberg. Some of the women writers of the Modern Breakthrough had a brief but timely success as playwrights. Anne Charlotte Leffler and Alfhild Agrell achieved more popular acclaim for their theater plays in the early 1880s than did Strindberg. Leffler's *Skådespelerskan* (1873; The actress) and *Sanna qvinnor* (1883; True women), as well as Alfhild Agrell's bourgeois drama *Räddad* (1883; Saved), were works of indignation, conceived in the Ibsen spirit; his influence is noticeable in the focus on conflicts emphasizing moral choice, in which men and women apply very different criteria to solve a problem. Leffler's and Agrell's male heads of household show no qualms about embezzling money or gambling away their wives' savings. Like Ibsen's plays from the late seventies and early eighties, Leffler's and Agrell's dramatic plots take place in a bourgeois domestic setting in which the outside world begins to make its presence felt. A few years later, when Leffler broadened this domestic perspective in *Hur man gör godt* (1885; How one does good) and in the double, or "parallel," drama *Kampen för lyckan* (1887; The struggle for happiness), coauthored with the Russian mathematician Sonja Kovalevskaja, she met less of an enthusiastic response.

August Strindberg and Modern Breakthrough Drama

Strindberg's international reputation rests on his dramatic production. In this genre he was an innovator and a pioneer. His naturalistic plays from the 1880s are still part of the world theater repertory, notably *Fadren, Fröken Julie, Fordringsägare* (1888; Eng. tr. *Creditors,* in *Selected Plays,* 1986), and *Den starkare* (1889; Eng. tr. *The Stronger,* in *Selected Plays,* 1986). His famous preface to *Fröken Julie* expresses his contempt for both the intellectual status of the contemporary theater and for the stereotypical aspects of the drama of his times. Strindberg proceeds to outline a new approach to drama and staging, which can be viewed as the manifesto of the modern realistic theater with its emphasis on greater concentration in dramatic structure, more psychologically complex characters, ensemble acting rather than star performance, and greater naturalness in diction and gesture.

Strindberg's temperament was dichotomous, that is, he was drawn to and inspired by conflict. The dramatic genre seems therefore his natural literary mode. He was also fascinated by the theater itself and maintained a lifelong contact with the stage. Two of his three wives, Siri von Essen and Harriet Bosse, were actresses. On three separate occasions he tried to found a stage of his own. His first two ventures were fiascos, including his Experimental Theater in Copenhagen in 1889, where *Fröken Julie* had its premiere.

Fittingly, Strindberg's debut as a man of letters was in the dramatic genre. After the one-act play *I Rom* and two historical plays, *Hermione* (1869) and *Den fredlöse* (1871; Eng. tr. *The Outlaw,* 1969), were produced at the Royal Dramatic Theater in Stockholm with modest success, Strindberg submitted *Mäster Olof.* It was a play conceived in the spirit of Shakespeare, with changing scenery, multiple plots, and numerous characters who were presented both publicly and privately—all in accordance with Brandes's prescription in his famous analysis of *Henry IV.* To this expansive format Strindberg added impulses from Schiller's historical dramas of ideas. His title figure, the young Lutheran reformer, is caught in a power play between the traditional church and the state but is also exposed to new revolutionary ideas aimed at overthrowing the present regime. The rebellious spirit represented by Gert, the Bookprinter, was partly inspired by the radical Paris Commune of 1871. This topicality no doubt helped sway the conservative Royal Dramatic Theater—the only available forum for a serious new drama in Sweden at the time—in its negative decision. But a more damaging reason was the fact that Strindberg gave Gert the last cue in the play, in the form of a strong denunciation of Mäster Olof, Luther's disciple in Sweden.

Such an unorthodox treatment of a revered historical personage, coupled with a dialogue written in contemporary realistic prose, made Strindberg a virtual persona non grata at the Royal Dramatic Theater. Despite several revisions throughout the 1870s, *Mäster Olof* was not staged until 1881. A version in rhymed poetry (*knittel*) was printed in 1878 but not performed until 1890. Perhaps as a gesture of postmortem atonement, the Royal Dramatic Theater celebrated its two hundredth anniversary in 1988 with a production of *Mäster Olof.*

Disillusioned, Strindberg did not return to the dramatic genre until the 1880s. A historical drama, *Herr Bengts hustru* (1882; Sir Bengt's wife), was performed with Siri von Essen in the lead. But the turning point did not come until his encounter with Zola's ideas about the naturalistic theater. There Strindberg found an advocacy of a conception of drama that was the very opposite of Shakespearean expansiveness, with a strict adherence to the classical unities of time, place, and action. Concentration of conflict and compactness of action were key principles. In addition, Zola emphasized the playwright's detached approach to his characters and subject matter, so that the dramatic presentation would achieve the quality of a scientific case study, which in turn should demonstrate a general psychological or philosophical truth.

Strindberg's first attempt at the new formula was *Fadren*. In retrospect, it seems clear that his conception of this play emanated as much from the older bourgeois drama as from Zola's dictum. He referred to his play as *ett sorgespel*, a Swedish variant of the German *Trauerspiel*, a common designation for a bourgeois drama with an unhappy end. He also raised an issue that has occupied playwrights and drama critics to this day: whether it is possible to write tragedy in bourgeois or democratic dress rather than in classical costume, and to present such a story within a modern scientific context rather than against a philosophical backdrop mirroring a divinely ordained vision of life. Strindberg's answer lay in his concept of the battle of the brains: the stronger and more powerful mind will outmaneuver a superior but sensitive psyche, and in this defeat of the nobler individual the playwright could depict a modern psychological drama of tragic proportions.

Fadren explores this thesis by pitting the Captain, a man of superior intellect and feeling, against his unscrupulous wife, Laura, whose machinations lead her to commit a bestial psychic murder by planting in her husband's mind a self-destructive doubt about the paternity of their child. Strindberg's model was not only his own family situation but a classical drama: the first part of the Aeschylus trilogy *The Oresteia*, in which

Clytemnestra emasculates and murders Agamemnon on his return from the Trojan War. With a reference to the Omphale-Hercules myth as well as to the poisoned robe that killed Agamemnon, Strindberg has Laura scheme to have the wet nurse put the captain in a straitjacket and render him helpless like a child. Both Aeschylus and Strindberg focus on women who feel their control at home threatened or undermined by their husbands.

Strindberg sent his play to Zola for approval but received only a hesitant response. Less than a year later, however, he mailed a confident note to his publisher, announcing himself as the Zola of the North. The occasion was *Fröken Julie*, a play about a young woman of the nobility who has a brief affair with her father's valet and coachman, Jean, and is destroyed by the event. Through this concentrated plot Strindberg realized his ambition to write a full-length naturalistic drama within the scope of a long one-act play, replacing conventional intermissions with a midsummer dance on stage and a mime performed by the cook, Kristin. Strindberg wished to create the verisimilitude of a real event taking place before the audience. The plot, too, he claimed, followed naturalistic guidelines, in that he had dramatized a case, "a motif from life itself as I heard it spoken of a number of years ago." This single motif proved, he argued, a law of nature—the survival of the fittest—all in accordance with Zola's naturalistic decrees. But the fate of an aristocratic lady and her father's plebeian albeit stylish valet no doubt evoked personal feelings in Strindberg, a commoner who had himself married a noblewoman out of love. The drama proved once more that his creative power sprang from ambiguities in his own psyche. He makes Jean a representative of the "new nerve and brain nobility" to whom Julie must succumb. To Strindberg, Julie's suicide is the result of an inevitable evolutionary process. In the preface to the play, he argues cynically that Julie's downfall is a relief, like clearing a park of its rotten trees in order to allow new growth to thrive. But in the play itself, his sympathies oscillate constantly between the two characters, and in an alternate early ending to the play he lets Julie dismiss Jean as a cowardly serf unable to hand her the suicidal razor.

Strindberg's preface was written after *Fröken Julie* was completed. It reveals his conscious attempt to disengage himself from his characters and transcend his private demon, so noticeable in the drama itself. His cool analysis of the title character as a creature of indeterminate sex is a case in point; it harks back to the ordeal of his *Giftas* trial more than to his empathetic portrayal of Miss Julie in the play: "Miss Julie is a modern character, not that the half-woman, the man-hater, has not existed always, but because now that she has been discovered she has stepped to the front. . . . The half-woman is a type who thrusts herself forward, selling herself nowadays for power, decorations, distinctions, diplomas, as formerly for money."

The discrepancy between Strindberg's depiction of Miss Julie in the play and his reference to her in the preface, where he is trying to abstract her, suggests an incompatibility between dramatic inspiration and theory. Even so, Strindberg persevered in his drive to author the epitome of a naturalistic drama. In *Fordringsägare*, he claimed to have carried "the new formula" to perfection. The outcome was a tight triangular melodrama set in an impersonal room at a Swedish spa. A cannibalistic theme, which Strindberg was to use repeatedly in his writing from then on, forms the core of the drama. Elsewhere he refers to it as the vampire motif; it forms a parallel to his concept of the battle of the brains. The three characters in *Fordringsägare*—a married couple (Tekla and Adolf) and their visitor (Gustaf), a former friend and Tekla's first husband—feed on and dissect one another in a drama that has both the stylization and black comedy tone of twentieth-century plays in the absurdist and theater-of-cruelty genres.

Strindberg had hoped to get both *Fröken Julie* and *Fordringsägare* produced at the Théatre Libre, an avant-garde stage started in 1887 by André Antoine in Paris. But neither Antoine nor any other stage wanted to touch the plays, prompting Strindberg to rekindle his old idea of starting a theater of his own. In late 1888, he opened the Scandinavian Experimental Theater in Copenhagen, for which he wrote three one-act plays modeled on Antoine's repertory in which amateurs performed short pieces called *quart d'heures*. Although the production collapsed after only two performances, two of the three plays, *Paria* (1889; Eng. tr. *Pariah*, 1913) and *Den starkare*, have appeared on numerous repertory bills since then. *Den starkare* was in due time to be singled out as a veritable tour de force in the modern theater. The brief one-act play unfolds as a power struggle between two women, Mrs. X and Mlle. Y, one of whom is silent. The psychological tug of war between the speaking woman, who reveals herself candidly, and the mute woman, who conceals herself behind her silence until unmasked, no doubt was of fundamental importance to Ingmar Bergman in his conception of the film *Persona*.

After the fiasco of the Scandinavian Experimental Theater, it was almost three years before Strindberg wrote again for the stage. He returned to Sweden, where he lived through the final phase of his divorce from Siri von Essen, culminating in a libel suit brought against him by his wife's friend Marie David. As this period in his private life was drawing to a close, it also seemed to him that the literary climate was due for a change. In an essay from 1889, titled "Om modernt drama och modern teater" (On modern drama and the modern theater), Strindberg criticized naturalism for having degenerated into "a working method elevated to an art form," and made a distinction between "grand naturalism . . . which enjoys the struggle of the powers of nature," and petty realism, which "includes everything, even the speck of dust on the camera lens."

Philosophically, Strindberg was soon to part company with Nietzsche, whose atheism and superman concept had helped shape the ideational context of many of his naturalistic plays. The religiosity of his childhood would show signs of returning, albeit in a different form, and his intellectual frame of reference was no longer going to be found in the tenets of the realistic and naturalistic 1880s.

STRINDBERG AND THE TRANSITION TO MODERNISM

Whatever may characterize literary genius, one of its trademarks is both to define and to transcend the time periods structured by literary historians. Like Almqvist before him, August Strindberg spanned two distinct eras in modern Swedish literature. As one of the figureheads of the Modern Breakthrough of the 1880s, Strindberg laid the groundwork for subsequent realistic treatments of Swedish society. As an experimenter with new literary forms and an explorer of the subconscious patterns of the human mind, Strindberg had also become, by the turn of the century, one of the crucial implementers of a new literary mode that was later to be given the name of modernism.

During the socially conscious 1880s, Strindberg had first and foremost a national and Scandinavian impact, though some of his naturalistic dramas were to become part of an international stage canon. As a representative of early modernist literature, he made contributions that would be much more seminal, reaching far beyond his geographical and linguistic origin. Strindberg's different roles as a realist in the 1880s and as an emerging modernist in the 1890s can be linked to his self-defined position as a writer, including his view of a prospective readership. In his Modern Breakthrough phase, Strindberg wrote for the most part with a Swedish or Scandinavian public in mind even when he lived abroad. Such work as *Röda rummet*, *Hemsöborna*, and *Fröken Julie* clearly address the society in which the author had grown up, its values and mores. Strindberg was, of course, sensitive to foreign impulses and wanted recognition abroad. Yet he defined his ambition at the time as either an attempt to undermine the petrified "ideals" of his native society by "grandiose spitting on all those things" or as a wish to become "the Zola of the North," that is, a naturalist within his own culture. Despite his long stay outside Sweden, his public debates and literary encounters occurred mostly within a Swedish (or Scandinavian) cultural context, as they did again during the final years of his life. But in the mid-1890s, his creative impulses became linked, in a very personal way, to various intellectual phenomena on the European continent. He now wrote some of his works in French—notably, *Inferno* (1897; Eng. tr. 1968) and, in part, *Legender* (1898; Eng. tr. *Legends*, 1912)—presumably for a Parisian readership. After his return to Stockholm in 1899, it is as though he has two different recipients in mind. On one hand, he writes a series of historical dramas based on figureheads and events in the Swedish past; through these dramas he tries to establish himself as Sweden's national writer. On the other hand, he maintains his foreign contacts through a prolific correspondence; he achieves a major success in Germany with his play *Dödsdansen* (1901; Eng. tr. *The Dance of Death*, 1976), in 1905, and two years later he founds his own Kammerspielhaus in Stockholm, Intima Teatern, modeled after the German director Max Reinhardt's playhouse in Berlin. For this stage he writes, in 1907–8, a series of chamber plays, which he doubted any established Swedish theater at the time would know how to produce.

These shifting channels of communication must not be construed to mean that Strindberg was merely a literary weathervane, always swaying with the taste and makeup of his public. He knew, for instance, that his *Drömspel* (1902; Eng. tr. *A Dreamplay*, 1973) and chamber plays broke new dramatic ground that might meet resistance among producers and spectators alike. But these dramas were linked to deeply personal events in his life in the 1890s, which forever changed his conception of reality. In order to convey his new vision to theater audiences, he had to cast his plays in a new dramatic form. In the final analysis, it is in this transformation of a self-experiential reality into literary and dramatic texts that Strindberg's restless and creative spirit reaches us.

The Inferno Crisis
In 1889, after seven years abroad, Strindberg had returned to live in Sweden. He had failed in his attempt to found an experimental Scandinavian theater in Copenhagen. He had separated from his first wife, and the divorce was to be finalized two years later. It was a period of economic and emotional hardship for Strindberg. Frustrated and almost destitute, he left Sweden again in 1892, this time to settle briefly among a coterie of Scandinavian and Continental bohemians and artists in Berlin. Here he met his second

wife, the young Austrian journalist Frida Uhl, but the marriage did not last long, and in 1894 Strindberg moved on to Paris, where he soon bid goodbye to Frida and their daughter Kerstin. The occasion also marks the beginning of a literary hiatus in his life. Though he had published in 1892–93 one full-length drama, *Himmelrikets nycklar* (Eng. tr. *Keys to Heaven*, 1965), and six one-act plays, among them *Leka med elden* (Eng. tr. *Playing with Fire*, 1969), *Moderskärlek* (Eng. tr. *Motherly Love*, 1987), and *Bandet* (Eng. tr. *The Bond*, 1969), once he had settled in Paris, Strindberg turned all his attention to an old ambition: to become a scientist. Influenced by alchemical and occult currents in French culture at the time, he sought to invent a formula for making gold. Like the alchemists, he disputed the existence of chemical elements and believed in the endless transmutation of matter. But it is doubtful that Strindberg shared the alchemists' view of gold as the ultimate manifestation of the spiritual in matter. He wanted above all to win recognition for himself as a bona fide chemist and to engage in a pursuit that he felt carried more social and masculine prestige than being a writer. It was always important for Strindberg to be viewed as a man of virility and as a man of the times.

Strindberg's neurasthenic and unstable psyche, his Parisian lifestyle (which included ample consumption of absinthe), and his poor physical and economic condition brought him closer and closer to a mental crisis. Beset by periods of insomnia and painful psoriasis, he spent some weeks in the St. Louis Hospital in Paris, temporarily calmed by the maternal care of a nun. But between 1895 and 1897 he was in a labile frame of mind and underwent a series of psychic upheavals. Haunted by paranoiac fears, he felt "electric currents" through his body and fantasized about enemies who stood in telepathic contact with "the powers," occult spirits sent to torment him.

There is a rationality to all madness, and Strindberg's case is no exception. Scholars are still debating the extent of his mental breakdown, and their findings range from declaring him "one of the great abnormals" (Vernon W. Grant) to giving him a clean bill of health with the exception of one week of acute paranoia (Johan Cullberg). Clinical diagnoses are, however, less relevant to the literary researcher than are the artist's own productive use of his mental upheavals. Strindberg found an operative explanation for his ordeals. Here his discovery of the eighteenth-century mystic Emanuel Swedenborg is crucial.

From the journals Strindberg kept at the time (1893–97), one can follow his development as a religious visionary and see how he appropriated Swedenborg to suit his own metaphysics. Life on earth was viewed either as a purgatory where human beings were chastened or as "an excrement hell" where the unredeemed pursued their existence, chained to bodily functions. Like Swedenborg, Strindberg invested reality with a spiritual potential, wiping out the borderline between a scientific and a mystical view of life. He adopted a monistic belief that all objects and phenomena, visible and invisible, actual and dreamlike, hung together and fused. Later, via the German philosopher Schopenhauer, his new codex incorporated Neoplatonic and Vedic thoughts, especially the conception of life on earth as an imperfect replica of a higher and purer reality. Strindberg could also couple the notion of earthly life as a fallen existence to the image of humankind as expelled from Paradise and forever partaking of an original sin, a view that had been a central part of his pietistic Lutheran upbringing.

His religious turning point, which Strindberg referred to as his "Inferno" and later described as "the big crisis at fifty; revolutions in my spiritual life, desert wanderings, devastation, Swedenborg's hells and heavens," transferred his own tribulations to a metaphysical plane. They were expiatory ordeals through which he made amends and atoned for his earlier life. At times, however, his agonies seemed to him out of proportion to his guilt-ridden experiences and actions, but he found a possible explanation in the *satisfactio vicaria* concept, that is, the thought that certain people were chosen by "the Eternal One" to endure vicarious suffering for the misdeeds of others. His literary world too became peopled with occasional Christlike atoners, such as Eleonora in the drama *Påsk* (1900; Eng. tr. *Easter*, 1976), the Student in the chamber play *Spöksonaten* (1907; Eng. tr. *The Ghost Sonata*, 1962), and Indra's daughter and the Lawyer in *Ett drömspel*. Such characters are surrounded by embodiments of the Swedenborg-inspired "corrective spirits," whose destiny on earth is to personify evil, intensify suffering, and conduce penance.

Spiritual conversions were legion among European fin-de-siècle artists, but Strindberg's Inferno period was no faddish whim of the moment. With hindsight we can see the crisis approaching. Toward the end of the 1880s, Georg Brandes had alerted Strindberg to Nietzsche's writings. As seems to be the case with most of the philosophical reading Strindberg did, he found in Nietzsche a confirmation of ideas that had already begun to take root in his own mind. Meeting with his fellow Swede and poet Verner von Heidenstam in Switzerland some time earlier, Strindberg had postulated a new ideal that rejected Christian ethics and democracy and advocated an elitist lifestyle to be pursued by modern man, now refined in body and spirit and intellectually triumphant over the plebeian rabble in society. This type of individual, related to Nietzsche's superman, was depicted by Strindberg in the novella *Tschandala* (1888) and in the short drama *Paria* (1890; Eng. tr. *Pariah*, 1987) but reached its most subtle and ambiguous treatment in the novel *I havsbandet* (1890; Eng. tr. *By the Open Sea*, 1984). Here, however, the main character, a fisheries inspector by the name of Axel Borg, succumbs to his intellectual inferiors in the skerries and self-destructs in a Christmas storm. Blaspheming Christ, "the idol of all criminals and rascals," Borg's deranged psyche seals his bankrupt destiny. "The individual is destroyed in his quest for absolute individualism," as Strindberg was later to summarize the theme of the novel. Another way to describe Borg's defeat is to point to the decadent aspect of his personality, his overrefinement and sensitivity, which make him an easy target for both the unscrupulous islanders and the uncontrollable forces of nature. *I havsbandet* suggests Strindberg's conception of his once beloved archipelago as a viable demonic force, over which Borg's scientific catalogs of flora and fauna have little ritualistic power. In the imagery of his native skerries, Strindberg projects, as it were, the dichotomy that was to form the symbiotic yet irreconcilable fusion of matter and spirit in his Inferno vision. In Borg's dying character this vision is implied in his final reverie: "Allmother, from whose bosom the first spark of life was lit, the inexhaustible fountain of fertility and love, the origin of life and the enemy of life."

Post-Inferno Production

Strindberg's entire life can be defined as a series of battles with real or imaginary opponents. Not surprisingly, his chosen form of expression was above all the dramatic genre. In the 1880s, the "enemy" was defined as establishment society, the humbug leaders of business and government, or as threatening feminists, the bluestocking phenomenon. In the 1890s, the struggle is internalized and becomes Strindberg's personal reenactment of Jacob's wrestling with God. This internalization can be found as early as Borg's character in *I havsbandet*. Like Borg's agonizing final words, Strindberg's religious conversion is no contemplative mystical experience but an ongoing argument between a human soul and "the powers" who dictate the unhappy conditions of life, exemplified in poetic form by Strindberg in the repetitive key line from *Ett drömspel*: "Det är synd om människorna" (Man is to be pitied). As this reiterated pronouncement suggests, Strindberg's religious rationale is related to a theodicy quandary in which the existence of evil is a more pressing reality than God's goodness and omnipotence.

This quest is deeply self-centered. Strindberg sees himself as particularly victimized by the evil of the world. On a moral level, one could interpret his conversion as a personal desertion of principle in which he attempts to evade his own responsibility in his many problematic relationships. He sets up various defensive arguments through which he can emerge as a victim rather than an instigator and perpetrator of conflict. The ultimate and morally "conclusive" act is to transfer the problem to a metaphysical level. Evil that causes suffering and guilt is God's punishment; earthly life is forever marked by an original Fall from grace; suffering is a process of liberation; existence on earth is a penal colony where human beings do penance. Only death can bring about a release. No human is to blame.

Strindberg attempts to present this new vision in such dramatic works as the trilogy *Till Damaskus* (1898, 1901; Eng. tr. *To Damascus*, 1975), *Påsk, Ett drömspel,* and several of his post-Inferno history plays. In fact, his midlife crisis colors most of his subsequent literary production up to his death in 1912. To begin with, he transposes his experiences in the prose works *Inferno* (1897), *Legender* (1898), and *Jakob brottas* (1899; Eng. tr. *Jacob Wrestles*, 1968). These works, though all based on the notes he kept during his distraught years, are somewhat different in tone and approach. We can see how Strindberg, in editing his journals, establishes an increasing distance to his psychic crisis and how he oscillates between different positions within the religious process. *Inferno* is by far the most striking of the accounts and unique as a confessional book in that it depicts the movement of a religiously oriented mind rather than the recapitulation of a convert. It contains no visions or promises of an afterlife but describes a preparation for a spiritual state that will be without physical encumbrances. *Inferno* maps a pilgrim's progress, a repudiation of man as a biological creature and an embracing of the ascetic life. As a motto for the book, one could use Strindberg's own words, "Born with a nostalgia for Heaven, I cried like a child over the dirt of existence."

Inferno conveys the image of a haunted man. Its sequel, *Legender,* projects a narrator who is compiling testimonials to verify the existence of an avenging God. In later editions, the work was expanded to include the fragment *Jakob brottas,* which is more defiant and inquisitive in tone. Above all, it uses a different authorial discourse, presented as a dialogue between the narrator and The Stranger, a divine messenger who, at the end, leaves the narrator to his own thoughts, a situation that is indicative of the aftermath of Strindberg's conversion. Instead of entering a time of peacefulness and quietude, Strindberg became embroiled in new conflicts and also experienced the most productive period of his life. For the next four years (1898–1903), he wrote an average of five dramas a year, publishing almost half his entire literary oeuvre between 1897 and

1909. During this time he also married again (1901) but three years later divorced his new wife, Norwegian-born actress Harriet Bosse. Both his wife and their daughter, Anne-Marie, presumably inspired some of his late work, such as *Svanevit* (1901; Eng. tr. *Swanwhite*, 1981) and *Sagor* (1902; Fairy tales).

Post-Inferno Drama: From Till Damascus to Stora landsvägen

Toward the end of *Jakob brottas*, the narrator likens himself to the biblical Saul, who on his way to Damascus was converted to the apostle Paul. Out of this analogy Strindberg shaped his *Till Damaskus* trilogy. Falling back on the dreamlike and unreal state of mind that he experienced during his psychologically intense stay in Paris, he attempted to create a dramatic form that would emulate the contours of our nocturnal psyche, the associative and seemingly illogical pattern of our dreams and nightmares. His post-Inferno plays coincide in time with Freud's first years of work in his Vienna clinic; Strindberg begins to explore the same subconscious arena that was to be the scene of Freud's *Traumdeutung* (Interpretation of dreams), a world that camouflages itself in our actions and reactions. But Strindberg casts his view in a religious post-Inferno mold. The facade does not tell the truth; it merely suggests a deeper pattern, which the divinely initiated can interpret. All events and happenings exist on two levels: the immediately naturalistic and the symbolic. The symbolic level serves as a road map, a sign of correspondences between the earthly and the divine.

Till Damascus is a conversion drama in which the main character, the Stranger, undergoes the various stages of religious change: resistance, defiance, repentance, acceptance. It is disguised as a station drama in which the Stranger's various stopovers are places of expiation. Part 1, an autonomous drama that is often discussed and performed by itself, opens and closes before the entrance of a church with a visit to an asylum as its peripatetic point. The various characters that appear to the Stranger can be viewed as doppelgänger who offer guidance or as corrective spirits who appear as warning examples, sometimes looming as guilt-ridden monsters before him. A woman referred to as the Lady accompanies the Stranger as a possible redeemer. But the dramatis personae lack autonomy and appear more like emanations of the Stranger's mind. The male-female conflict that formed the dynamic core of the naturalistic dramas has been replaced by a struggle between different contending sides within a single psyche, for whom life seems like a dream or chimera. The only time Strindberg returns to the furious contest between the sexes as the center of a drama is in the macabre two-volume play *Dödsdansen*. It is also the only post-Inferno work for the stage to retain fully the firm linear composition of the earlier naturalistic dramas.

The stylized form of drama that Strindberg begins to conceive in *Till Damascus* relies less on interpersonal character conflict than on explorations of a theme. Structurally, this dramatic method centers on a leitmotif that is varied, like a musical chord, throughout the play. Psychologically, the thought patterns follow the associative meanderings of our dreams and derive meaning from visual objects that serve both a functional and a symbolic role in the mise-en-scène. Epistemologically, knowledge is derived less from a dramatic struggle between human wills than from a demonstration of human guilt and suffering, as higher powers interfere in the lives of ordinary people. The play that above all others epitomizes this evolution in Strindberg's dramaturgy is the polyphonic drama *Ett drömspel*, in which his stage composition excels in parallel actions, contrasting effects, alternating dialogues, and group scenes, while his symbolist vision of life reaches its climax in the dramatized story depicting the descent to earth of the daughter of the Vedic god Indra.

The loosely constructed plot of *Ett drömspel* exposes Indra's Daughter to the plights of humankind. Part participant, part observer, she learns of the frustration of love, the misery of married life, the brevity of happiness, the social injustice on earth. In the end she returns to heaven, carrying with her the lament of the Poet, her Virgilian companion on earth, whom she meets in the elegiac Fingal's Cave, where the winds and the waves echo the sorrows of human beings. Indra's Daughter brings no salvation to the people she visits, only a possible explanation for their suffering as she retells the myth of Brahma's encounter with the earth spirit Maya. Finally, through an act of purification by fire, she ascends to the heavens, leaving behind all the people she has encountered.

In his famous preface to *Ett drömspel*, Strindberg summarizes the conception behind his new dramatic form. Dissolving the realistic spatial and temporal contours of his naturalistic stagecraft, he intends to project a drama in which "time and space do not exist" and in which the dramatic tale winds its way like a dream through a kaleidoscopic vision of life in which "characters double and split." The cohesive factor in the play is the "consciousness of the dreamer," variously interpreted as Strindberg, creator of the drama, as the transmutative Indra's Daughter, or as an invisible discursive voice in the play. Perhaps it is less important to identify the "dreaming consciousness" than to recognize its gradual movement from a psychological to a metaphysical level, thus expanding its experience beyond the realm of individual nightmare to a transcendental vision of life. For it is in this dramatized bridging of the physical world and a spiritual illusion of hope that Strindberg's dramatic language reaches its most poignant and beautiful levels, in terms of both spoken poetry and visual stagecraft. In that respect, Strindberg's literary and dramatic art alleviates the discordant theme of *Ett drömspel*.

At the end of his preface to *Ett drömspel*, Strindberg wrote: "As for the loose, disconnected form in the drama, it is only seemingly so. For on closer examination, the composition is found to be quite firm—a symphony, polyphonic, fugued here and there with the main motif returning, repeated and varied by the some and thirty voices in all tonal keys." On a smaller scale, like a change from an oratorio to a sonata form, Strindberg was going to pursue his musical concept of dramatic structure in the chamber plays he wrote in 1907–8. Referring to them as his opus 1 to 5, he wanted to design a series of dramas with few characters and a small scope, suitable to be performed at his Intiman Theater, a remodeled store seating only 161 persons.

One of Swedenborg's central concepts was that of vastation, which Strindberg interpreted as a form of unmasking and exposure of life behind the facade. The best known of his chamber plays—*Oväder* (1906; Eng. tr. *Storm Weather*, 1962), *Spöksonaten* (1907; Eng. tr. *The Ghost Sonata*, 1962), and *Pelikanen* (1908; Eng. tr. *The Pelican*, 1962)—use the functional and symbolic setting of a house to unravel social, moral, and spiritual secrets. In *Oväder*, the day of reckoning concerns the truth about a dissolved marriage. In *Pelikanen*, a mother's usurpation of her (dead) husband and children turns on her and destroys her. In *Spöksonaten*, the idealist Student enters a house of illicit kinships, fake costumes and pretensions, and alluring but poisonous flowers. This household belongs to the "Hummel family of vampires." The unmasking process, which parallels the Student's exploration of the house, is ultimately a form of spiritual awakening that leads closer to the moment of death. At the end of the play, Böcklin's painting "Die Toteninsel" (Island of the dead) is projected on the wall of the deathlike antechamber, "the hyacinth room."

The chamber plays demonstrate the pervasive power of evil in human life, destroying innocent and guilty alike. Though confined to the house and the family, the plays depict a total rejection of life that might be exemplified by the Son's bitter comment in *Pelikanen*: "My contempt for life, humanity, society, and myself is so boundless I wouldn't raise my little finger to go on living." Against such a pessimistic assessment of human existence, death comes as the liberator, as it did earlier for Indra's Daughter in *Ett drömspel*.

During his Inferno crisis Strindberg once wrote, "When I now throw a glance at my past, I often see myself in the guise of a hunter." It was in this role that he cast the main character in *Stora landsvägen* (1909; Eng. tr. *The Great Highway*, 1981), a play that has been called his literary testament. It represents a final codification of his lifelong experiential material, based on a process he describes in the prose fragment *Klostret* (1902; Eng. tr. *The Cloister*, 1969): "By ruminating his experiences in this way, he converted them imaginatively, and by this procedure, they became imprinted or fixed in his mind in such a way that he could have them at his disposal for future use as safely as assets put in a bank." *Stora landsvägen* is, like *Till Damaskus* and *Ett drömspel*, conceived as a *vandringsdrama* (road or quest drama). The journey of the Hunter is a via dolorosa between the seven stations of the Cross, but his role is not that of a Christ figure and he has none of the transcendental aura of Indra's Daughter in *Ett drömspel*. Rather, he is akin to the Stranger in *Till Damaskus*, possessing the same anguished frustration and punitive, bickering personality, but he has also absorbed some of the resigned spirit of the aging Strindberg.

Stora landsvägen was designed as a recitation text to be performed against a stylized backdrop. After the Inferno crisis, Strindberg had returned once more to Shakespeare, whom he now viewed as a supreme painter in words: "The spoken word is the main thing, and when Shakespeare's overly educated contemporaries could do without stage decor, we too can imagine to ourselves walls, barricades, and trees. . . . For all is make-believe on the stage."

The History Plays

On his return to Sweden a few months before turning fifty, Strindberg had quickly assessed the nation's renewed interest in its historical and rural past, which had left its mark on painting, literature, and the preservation of artifacts from the provinces. He now wrote *Kronbruden* (1902; Eng. tr. *The Crown Bride*, 1981), based on a Swedish folklore motif. But above all, he set about to write a series of historical dramas that were to cover some seven hundred years of Sweden's existence as a nation. He was encouraged in this undertaking by a successful production of *Mäster Olof* in Stockholm in 1897 and again in 1899. Once more he turned to Shakespeare and once more decided to depict the past "realistically," which in Strindberg's nomenclature meant adapting it to his own view of life. The discrepancy in character approach and mood between the history plays of his youth and his post-Inferno dramatizations of the Swedish past reflects Strindberg's changing life philosophy as formulated during the Inferno crisis. In some ways, his current belief that human life was controlled by supernatural agents made him susceptible to the past as myth and archetype and furnished him with a Shakespearean analogy. Strindberg's "powers" and corrective spirits operated through omens and portends, abundant in Elizabethan drama; they were enigmatic but ultimately harbingers of a divine and absolute will. One of his basic motivations in writing the history plays was to illustrate the ongoing retributive justice of a Supreme Will: "History is in its broad outlines Providence's own composition," he wrote in his collection of advisory essays, *Öppna brev till Intima teatern* (1909; Eng. tr. *Open Letters to the Intimate Theater*, 1966).

Strindberg's history plays are full of philosophical anachronisms and dramatic expediencies that require the telescoping of historical time and space. Through his renewed reading of Shakespeare, Strindberg found justification for such an approach; Shakespeare, after all, took plenty of liberties with Holinshed's history and the old chronicles. Talking about the genesis of his first post-Inferno history play, *Folkungasagan* (1899; Eng. tr. *The Saga of the Folkungs*, 1959), Strindberg wrote what might be termed his dramaturgical credo as a historical playwright: "I made it my task, after my teacher Shakespeare . . . to let the historical be the background and shorten historical time according to the demands of the theater in order to avoid the undramatic form of chronicles and narratives." Like his "teacher" Shakespeare, Strindberg used a vast perspective and panoramic setting for several of his history plays, painting a world of great contrasts in an attempt to make a whole age come to life on the stage. His fluid composition results in frequent scene changes, multiple character constellations, group scenes, and parallel plots. This dramaturgical design characterizes such plays as *Folkungasagan*, *Karl XII* (1901; Eng. tr. *Charles XII*, 1955), *Kristina* (1901; Eng. tr. *Queen Christina*, 1955), *Gustav III* (1902; Eng. tr. 1955), and *Gustav Adolf* (1900; Eng. tr. 1957). But even in the second of his eleven post-Inferno historical dramas, *Gustav Vasa* (1899; Eng. tr. 1959), Strindberg narrows the scope to focus more on the individual character of the title figure, an autocrat who is brought to Swedenborgian repentance. With its sequel, *Erik XIV* (1899; Eng. tr. 1959), he explores the persona of Sweden's madcap prince as a modern, fragmented character, genetically and psychologically doomed to certain crimes.

More and more, Strindberg approached the melancholy drama of Maurice Maeterlinck and adopted his own evolving "dreamplay" dramaturgy. In *Karl XII*, Strindberg designs a mood drama of a brooding monarch. Though the dramatic conflict stems from a tension between the warrior king and his impoverished people, there are few actual encounters between royal and popular wills. The play opens when the king returns to Sweden after defeat and imprisonment abroad. What is depicted is the last act of his short life; as Strindberg puts it through one of the characters in the play, "The king is a dead man whose body walks about like a ghost." Karl XII is a somnambulist character whose dreamlike consciousness echoes the conception behind *Ett drömspel* and *Spöksonaten.*

Strindberg began his cycle of historical dramas with a cohesive plan to demonstrate the providential workings of the past, using the contention for royal power as a dramatic locus. But the design became fragmented, and the result is a series of plays that have a great deal of variety in mood, conception of character, and dramaturgical design. Inspired by the anecdotal myth making about royal personages in popular history books of the times, Strindberg was intrigued by the theatrical and histrionic potential of some of the portrayed monarchs. He cast Queen Christina as an actress ruler and Gustav III, the opera and masquerade devotee, as a colorful dissembler. He was also motivated to write his final history dramas in the aftermath of a disappointing reception of his chamber plays. To prove, at least partly, that he could still produce entertaining and traditional drama, he composed *Siste riddaren* (1908; Eng. tr. *The Last of the Knights*, 1956), *Riksföreståndaren* (1908; Eng. tr. *The Regent*, 1956), and *Bjälbo-jarlen* (1909; Eng. tr. *Earl Birger of Bjälbo*, 1956), thus completing the chronology of his historical production from *Folkungasagan* to *Gustav Vasa*. But the variety that characterized the bulk of his history plays was gone and the genre had developed its own formula for Strindberg, as revealed in his comment about *Bjälbo-jarlen* in *Öppna brev till Intima teatern*: "When I wrote *The Earl of Bjälbo* I proceeded as usual. I read Starbäck's History. . . . To 'create atmosphere' and remove myself to a distant time, I did as I usually do in writing my historical dramas: I read Walter Scott. . . . As usual in my historical dramas I have placed Swedish history within the frame of world history." Strindberg remains, however, with Shakespeare and Schiller, one of the few playwrights in world drama who have pursued the historical genre combining a philosophical and moral vision with a feel for turning actual historical personages and political events into dramatic characters and plots. Some of Strindberg's twenty historical plays have been frequently staged and remain landmarks in the performance canon of the Swedish theater, notably *Gustav III*, *Gustav Vasa*, *Erik XIV*, and *Kristina*.

The Last Prose Works: From Götiska rummen *to* Svarta fanor
In a letter to Emil Schering, written in 1907 when Strindberg despaired about the Swedish reception of his dramatic production, he says: "The

secret of all my tales, short stories, fairy tales, is that they are dramas. When the theaters were closed to me for long periods of time, I got the idea of writing my dramas in epic form—for future use." The dramatic structure is evident in a number of the prose works Strindberg published during the last ten years of his life. In *Götiska rummen* (1904; The Gothic rooms), the composition is what Strindberg called "fugued," a term he had used in describing the dramatic form in *Ett drömspel*. The novel seems composed for many voices and an authorial chorus; descriptive commentaries on contemporary times alternate with long segments of dialogue. In another prose work from the same time, *Taklagsöl* (1906; Eng. tr. *The Roofing Feast*, 1989), the dramatic structure takes the form of a monologue by a dying man who becomes talkative under the influence of morphine. His rambling speech, filled with nightmarish visions, is reminiscent of such chamber plays as *Spöksonaten* and *Pelikanen* and anticipates an absurdist play such as Beckett's *Krapp's Last Tape*.

In writing his late prose works, Strindberg attempted to revive his role as social iconoclast. *Götiska rummen* was conceived as a companion piece to *Röda rummet*. The tone is as oppositional as in the work from 1879, but Strindberg's youthful spirit is replaced by a religious mood and an acerbic bitterness symptomatic of this time in his life. In connection with his third divorce in 1904, Strindberg's misanthropy reached new depths. He viewed human life as a grotesque penal colony peopled by criminal minds and vampires. In an entry note in his diary from 1904, he writes: "Life is so terribly ugly, we humans so abysmally evil, that if an author were to depict *all* he has seen and heard, no one would stand reading it. . . . Only semblance and illusion, lies, faithlessness, falsehood, auto-comedies. 'My dear friend' is my worst enemy. 'My beloved' ought to be written 'my hated one.'" It was in this mood that Strindberg composed *Svarta Fanor* (1907; Eng. tr. *Black Banners*, 1981), which was withheld from publication for three years. The book has the subtitle "Moral tales from the turn of the century." The first nine chapters deal with the infernal machinations of a group of hypocrites who illustrate the Swedenborgian thesis that hell is not a place but a state of mind, similar to the Sartrean definition of hell as "the others." A grotesque dinner at Professor Stenkål's becomes another Strindbergian ghost supper, revealing the bombast and false pretense of the household ("a gull was called a sea eagle, two bookshelves were called a library, a plaster bust of a grinnir.g Voltaire was called a work of art"). The main target of the book, Zachris, is depicted as a second-rate artist who feeds on the sufferings of his sick wife as food for publishable material, a vampire writer reminiscent of Chekhov's Trigorin in *The Seagull*.

Svarta fanor, a transparent diatribe against Strindberg's Swedish contemporaries, was viewed as an act of vengeance and proof of the author's deranged and barbaric mind, what his former friend Heidenstam called his "slave mentality." The scandal was similar to the one caused by Dante's placing, in *Divina commedia*, his enemies in the various circles of Hell. In *Svarta fanor*, well-known people in Strindberg's society were exposed as tormentors, inhabiting the infernal world created by the author. Though verging on libel at the time of its publication, the work is so grotesque in its caricature that it also takes on the stark quality of an evil fairy tale. Today the characters seem more like archetypes than real-life people. Nathan Söderblom, archbishop of Sweden and Strindberg's personal acquaintance, was surely right when he pointed out that "when the personal key has been lost with time, the demonic power of the fictional characters will remain, a power that no doubt stems from someone other than the smaller, nicer people who now recognize themselves."

Svarta fanor also incorporates Strindberg's religious viewpoints, lending the book a self-righteous tone. Strindberg claimed that he felt compelled to write it. But was it in order to castigate his contemporaries like some Old Testament prophet pronouncing his doom over a modern Babylon, or was it to purge himself of his venom so that he could once more master his own self? Certainly, his subsequent prose works, *Taklagsöl* and *Syndabocken* (1906; Eng. tr. *The Scapegoat*, 1967), two novellas of remarkable artistic control, seem conceived in a more balanced mood and are in that respect closer to *Ensam* (1903; Eng. tr. *Alone*, 1968), an autobiographical meditation that displays Strindberg's sense of transcendence of the personal: "I crawl out of my own skin and speak out of the mouth of children, women, and old men. . . . I live in all ages and I myself have ceased to be." *Syndabocken*, planned as an appendix to *Taklagsöl*, is a Hoffmann pastiche about a small-town lawyer, Libotz, who becomes a ridiculed pharmakos figure yet retains the composure of a man of integrity, while the townspeople represent faking and parasitical natures engaged in committing psychic murders under chameleonlike guises. They are the relatives of Hummel and the Cook in *Spöksonaten* and Zachris and his cohort in *Svarta fanor*. In his diary, published as *Blå boken* (1912; Eng. tr. *Zones of the Spirit: A Book of Thoughts*, 1913), Strindberg describes such people, who now proliferated in his mind, as mistletoe or sticky feeders and destroyers, personifications of evil: "There are sticky people, insufficient, empty people who cannot live on their own root but must sit on another's branch, like the mistletoe which is very sticky, so that one can make glue out of it. It is the sticky one who writes long letters about nothing, offers services to be able to put you in his debt, becomes enraged if you don't write eight pages to him about nothing."

The Finale: The Strindberg Feud and Exit

Svarta fanor constitutes one side of Strindberg's contentious nature, in which human beings are embodiments of evil within a moral and metaphysical universe defined through the Inferno vision. Another side of his belligerent temperament is represented by Strindberg the muckraker, who embroiled himself in public discussions on social, literary, and political issues. Among the last things he published before he died was a series of more than one hundred newspaper articles, his contribution to the so-called Strindberg Feud. Covering a time span of almost two years (1910–12), his publicist subjects ranged from an attack on the Swedish cult of King Karl XII, whom Strindberg had likened to "a barbarian, a rascal, the destroyer of the Swedish nation," to a critique of the legal system, military activism, and the contemporary theater. Young radicals adopted Strindberg as their spokesman, while the establishment turned its back on him once more. Although younger writers such as Erik Axel Karlfeldt and Selma Lagerlöf were admitted into the literary sanctum and eventually became members of the Swedish Academy and recipients of the Nobel Prize in literature (instituted in 1903), August Strindberg was never elected to the academy and his name was repeatedly bypassed by the Nobel Committee. In 1911, when the prestigious literary award went to the Belgian playwright Maurice Maeterlinck, radical and liberal forces in Sweden started a national campaign fund for an alternate Nobel Prize for Strindberg. He received it on his sixty-third birthday, a few months before his death in May 1912.

At the time of his death, it was still not uncommon for Strindberg's books to be "banned reading" in bourgeois families in Sweden. Yet tens of thousands of people, mostly students and socialists, marched in his funeral procession, an event under red banners that became as dignified as the funeral of any head of state. Strindberg's American biographer Vivian McGill provides a striking account of the occasion in her book *August Strindberg: The Bedeviled Viking*, which suggests the controversial legacy left by Sweden's greatest writer as social gadfly, venomous neurotic, and literary genius:

> The man in the hearse had been a scourge to them all. He had reviled them, betrayed their secrets, blasphemed their ideals. He had attacked the family, marriage, love, with ruthless concentrated fury. He had satirized schools, universities, art, science, business. No

person or institution had escaped his hatred and his evil tongue. Yet they paid homage to him, this enemy of society, marching thirty thousand strong to his grave, in a demonstration which has seldom been accorded to a private man. Like Hercules, his infamies were forgiven. By a sudden change of sentiment, the outcast had become a god. This procession which celebrated his apotheosis was no less than a national event.

Into the Twentieth Century: 1890–1950

Susan Brantly

6

Susan Brantly

THE AESTHETIC REVOLT OF THE 1890S

The literary 1890s has been given a host of epithets: neoromanticism, symbolism, decadence, fin de siècle, even the Golden Age of Swedish literature. However accurate any single term might be, the 1890s constituted a revolt against the naturalistic, socially engaged literature of the 1880s. The 1890s came to focus on the individual rather than the collective, on aesthetic and psychological issues rather than social problems, on fantasy rather than fact. The favored genres of the 1880s were prose and drama, the forms best suited for effacing the author and creating the illusion of photographic realism. In the 1890s, poetry flourished as a forum for subjective, symbolic expression. Rather than trying to capture a piece of external reality, the prose of the 1890s began attempting to evoke psychological states through the use of dreams, hallucinations, and ghosts. The aesthetic revolt of the 1890s contains many of the seeds that would grow into the modernism of the next century.

The initial proclamation of the program of the 1890s has traditionally been attributed to Verner von Heidenstam's essay "Renässans" (1889; Renaissance). In that essay, Heidenstam argues that the naturalism of the preceding decade served a valuable purpose in rejuvenating Swedish literature, but in his view, realism is boring and ugly. Instead, he calls for a return of beauty and imagination to literature. The importance ascribed to Heidenstam's essay is more a result of good timing than acute critical insight. The following year, Oscar Levertin and Heidenstam collaborated on "Pepitas bröllop" (1890; Pepita's wedding), an essay that continued the revolt against naturalism and established the 1890s alternative. The two authors posed the question, "Are not a poet's fantasies also a form of reality?" In 1892, Gustav Fröding contributed to the debate with his essay "Naturalism och romantik" (Naturalism and romanticism), in which he attributed Emile Zola's greatness to his use of symbolism and proceeded to demonstrate the incompatibility of great art and photographic realism. From his exile in Germany, Ola Hansson published throughout the early 1890s a series of articles that constituted a systematic rebuttal of the aesthetics of naturalism, chiefly inspired by his reading of Nietzsche. Strindberg, Hugo von Hofmannsthal (1874–1929), and Gerhart Hauptmann (1862–1946) partook of Hansson's essays with interest. This flood of essays indicates a level of critical self-consciousness among the authors of the 1890s which is without precedent. Literary criticism in general flourished during this decade, with Oscar Levertin its foremost practitioner.

One of the important spiritual fathers of the 1890s was Friedrich Nietzsche (1844–1900), especially as he was interpreted by Georg Brandes (1842–1927) and Ola Hansson. On one hand, Nietzsche's writings inspired an inclination toward elitism, aristocracy, and a cult of the exceptional individual above the masses. Such a stance must have seemed appealing in the wake of the democratic 1880s with its emphasis on the ordinary and everyday. On the other hand, Nietzsche's *Also Sprach Zarathustra* (1883; Thus spake Zarathustra) also provided an example of a new way of symbolic writing. In *Die Geburt der Tragödie* (1872; The birth of tragedy), Nietzsche describes the tension between the Apollonian and the Dionysian in ancient Greek art. The Apollonian element represents order, clarity, reason, and structure, whereas the Dionysian element represents chaos, oblivion, ecstasy, and destruction. Apollonian order keeps the Dionysian forces in check, and the dynamic interaction of the poles produces great art. A similar tension runs through much of the literature of the 1890s. The Dionysian lurks as a threat and a temptation, sometimes in the form of the fall of civilization, sometimes in the form of the subconscious. Adhering to a specific code of behavior or creating poetic order is a means of keeping Dionysian chaos at bay.

An international phenomenon that makes its presence felt in the literature of the 1890s is fin-de-siècle decadence, the roots of which are usually traced to French authors Charles Baudelaire (1821–67) and Joris-Karl Huysmans (1848–1907). The 1880s had an optimistic view of humankind and believed in progress. Darwin's theory of evolution seemed to describe a steady improvement of species with human beings at the pinnacle of evolution. To the decadents, the human species had peaked at an earlier point in time and had entered a phase of degeneration. Decadent literature brings with it a host of characteristic topoi: an obsession with abnormal psychological states, an interest in dead languages and cultures, a fascination with cruelty and destruction, an elitist horror of the mob, as well as a preference for exoticism, occultism, and "artificial paradises." The femme fatale and the dandy figured prominently in decadent literature. Heidenstam and especially Levertin were influenced by this trend, and traces may even be found in the work of Lagerlöf, Karlfeldt, and Fröding. Decadence reached its peak in Sweden in the next generation of writers at the turn of the century.

It is significant that Sigmund Freud (1856–1939) began publishing his work on psychoanalysis during the 1890s. He could not have had a direct influence on the authors of this period, since his reputation was not yet established and his writings came much later to Sweden. Nonetheless, Freud's interest in abnormal psychology and the irrational was entirely typical of the time. Many of the authors of the 1890s were on the track of the subconscious, and their symbolic use of dreams augurs Freud's *Traumdeutung* (Interpretation of dreams), published in 1900.

August Strindberg wrote some of his most significant dramas after 1890; however, Verner von Heidenstam, Selma Lagerlöf, Erik Axel Karlfeldt, and Gustav Fröding are the traditional pillars of the 1890s and, trailing behind them, Oscar Levertin. Several literary historians, Alrik Gustafson among them, have sought to isolate Heidenstam, Lagerlöf, Karlfeldt, and Fröding from the mainstream of European literature and treat them as a unique, vital outgrowth of the Swedish national spirit. Levertin is too obviously influenced by French decadence to be admitted into the group. These four authors have been characterized as robust, joyous, optimistic, and patriotic. Indeed, they share a fondness for regional folk culture. Lagerlöf and Fröding bring Värmland to life in their writing, and Karlfeldt immortalizes the folk culture of Dalarna in his poetry. Heidenstam becomes a monument of patriotism with his poetry collection *Ett folk* (1902; One people) and his historical novels. Certainly, with these authors a sense of humor returns to literature, which was more or less absent in the 1880s, if one does not count Strindberg's biting satire. Heidenstam proclaims in "Renässans" that "the age thirsts for joy." It is necessary, however, to qualify the description of these authors as joyful and optimistic. The joy in Heidenstam's writing has a note of forced bravado; for Fröding, humor is an act of self-defense against the absurdity he perceives in the world, and his humor often has dark undertones; Lagerlöf and Karlfeldt look with nostalgia on a disappearing way of life, threatened by industrialization and democratization. Their so-called romanticism bears the stamp of escapism. Sweden was changing rapidly. In 1889, the Social Democratic party was founded, with Hjalmar Branting (1860–1925) at the helm. The 1897 Industrial Exhibition in Stockholm pointed the way to the rapid technological development of the twentieth century.

Verner von Heidenstam

Appreciation for the literary achievement of Verner von Heidenstam (1859–1940) as a patriotic author has cast its pall over all his work, obscuring the fact that he was an important stylistic innovator in both poetry and prose. He was not a particularly learned man, but he traveled widely in the Near and Middle East and lived for a time in Rome, Paris, and Switzerland. He had the opportunity to steep himself in the ambience of the fin de siècle. His aesthetic instincts were quixotic, but they were right on the mark for the 1890s, and his early works were a sensation because of their exoticism, decadence, and freshness. Around the turn of the century, he began to cultivate his persona of national poet, which changed the tone of his writing. The "Strindberg Feud" of 1910 proved in the long run to hurt his status as poet laureate and entrenched him more deeply in political conservatism. He became a member of the Swedish Academy in 1912 and received the Nobel Prize in 1916, after which he fell silent as an author.

Heidenstam got the 1890s off to an early start in 1888 with his poetry collection *Vallfart och vandringsår* (Pilgrimage and wanderings). Many of the poems evoke the world of the *Arabian Nights*, its sensualism, beauty, and joy of life. The poet asserts that one should live life to the fullest while young, sparing no expense or effort, so as not to regret missed opportunities in old age. With contemporary decadence he shares a love of dead cultures. In *Vallfart och vandringsår*, the ancient Middle East is a vital, imaginative past world that is better than the poet's coldly materialistic contemporary world. Civilization has not progressed but is in a state of degeneration. A portion of the collection, "Ensamhetens tankar" (Thoughts of solitude), contains intimate, personal reflections quite new to Swedish literature and is the first step on the way to modernist lyric. The subjective musings of the individual are the central theme, not the general social problems of the 1880s. The poet's joy of life, presented with almost impudent insouciance, is tinged by an acute awareness of death. His celebration of life is a celebration on the brink of the modernist abyss. In "Kosmopoliten" (The cosmopolitan), Heidenstam writes of Sweden with mixed emotions and distances himself from the views of his countrymen in exile, who deplore the nation's lack of taste and elegance. In the process he formulates his own particular aesthetics, finding beauty in the ugly, and greatness in the humble poverty of his native land. The stance is reminiscent of Almqvist's in "Den svenska fattigdomens betydelse"; with Heidenstam, it is above all the affective pose of the born aristocrat.

After *Vallfart och vandringsår*, Heidenstam published the novel *Endymion* (1889). In the prologue, the prevailing "gray weather thoughts" of the age encounter some stray thoughts in a bookstore, and a discussion ensues as to how the novel should be composed. The device draws attention to the novel as a literary artifact: "You should not read my book out loud for your friend. It is in solitude I want to meet you." The story then proceeds in an ordinary third-person narrative—contemporary detractors described the book as a romantic Baedeker—but a quite innovative attempt had been made to incorporate the author as subject into the narrative. The theme of the novel is familiar: the materialistic barbarism of Western culture is pitted against the beauty and refinement of the Near East. The motif of barbarians destroying a superior culture hails from the fall of the Roman Empire and is a central theme of European decadence.

Heidenstam's next novel, *Hans Alienus* (1892), is something of a decadent bildungsroman. A mixture of prose and poetry, another means of escaping realistic narrative, the book is divided into three sections: "The Promise," "Hades," and "The Homecoming." With the exception of the poetic introduction, the first third of the book is narrated in a realistic prose style and the setting is contemporary Rome. Hans Alienus has a post in the Vatican Library and spends his time ensconced among the old tomes, savoring the beauty of the Roman Catholic Mass or enjoying the present moment. Catholicism holds a particular fascination for the 1890s, because of its sanction of beauty and the attraction of a monastic life spent in contemplation away from worldly cares. Offended by the materialism and science of the modern age, Alienus spends half his inheritance on a carnival procession that is to parody the modern spirit. The procession ends in chaos, not triumph.

The second section of the novel, "Hades," departs completely from the premises of realism. Hans Alienus enters the Underworld in order to visit the past. One of his hosts is the legendary ancient king Sardanapalus, who has created for himself an artificial paradise and who looks forward with sensuous pleasure to his spectacular self-immolation.

The social debates of the 1880s had produced the figure of the emancipated woman; the 1890s reacted with the paranoid counterimage of the femme fatale, the cruel and dangerous woman. "Hades" provides the Swedish 1890s with two splendid examples of this topos: Ahirab, pulling the wings from moths and throwing them still living in the fire, and a creature with the head of a beautiful woman and the body of a snake, who lures men to her and then sucks their brains out. The entire hallucinogenic journey through the Underworld is a voyage into the poet's imagination and a forerunner of expressionist prose. Two subchapters in "Hades," "The Lyre" and "The Chisel," could anachronistically be referred to as "metafiction," in that they self-consciously address the issues of artistic creation.

Hans Alienus's journey ends in defeat. In "The Homecoming," the protagonist returns to his brooding father in Sweden, from whom he had escaped as a young man to live instead with his sensuous Italian mother. The section is a mixture of realistic prose and visions that Alienus still carries with him from his visit to the Underworld. Father and son become reconciled and reach common ground through imagination and an interest in the past. After the death of his father, Alienus becomes a recluse and even loses the capability of communicating with ordinary people. He falls prey to his father's obsession with explaining life rather than living it, and like his father, he can find no explanations.

Heidenstam's second poetry collection, *Dikter* (1895; Poems), contains no remarkable innovations, and the intimate tone of "Ensamhetens tankar" is mostly absent. The poems quite often tell stories, most of which are set in Sweden. The exoticism of Heidenstam's earliest works has begun to pale, and from this point on, Swedish themes dominate his writing. A prevalent theme is the fear of aging and death. The immediacy of Heidenstam's cult of beauty is superseded by reflection.

With *Karolinerna* (1897–98; Eng. tr. *The Charles Men*, 1920), Heidenstam begins what has come to be considered his nationalistic production, though he has not yet made a drastic transition from his decadent aesthetics. Henceforth, his prose no longer deals with the present. When the book first appeared, the author was accused of having profaned the national hero Karl XII. In the wake of Strindberg's criticism, the novel was thought of as patriotic. This disparity of interpretation bears witness to the multiplicity of perspectives Heidenstam incorporated into the novel. The career of Karl XII is broken down into moments as they are experienced by the people whose lives he has affected. In prose, the technique of breaking up a course of events into scattered episodes seems quite modern. Karl XII is an inspiring military leader, but he may also be seen as a decadent hero on a grand scale. He is the last of a noble line; his reign coincides with the fall of the Swedish Empire, and the Russians are the barbarians from the east. Karl XII pursues and finds his tragic hero's death. The Swedish people display their own greatness as they rise to meet the challenge of such a perplexing ruler and pay with suffering and deprivation.

In Heidenstam's other historical novels, *Heliga Birgittas pilgrimsfärd* (1901; St. Birgitta's pilgrimage) and *Folkungaträdet* (1905–7; Eng. tr. *The Tree of the Folkungs*, 1925), historical themes continue to be interpreted through subjective individual experience. Heidenstam described St. Birgitta of the novel as a portrait of the author as an old woman. The worldly cult of beauty from Heidenstam's youth is defeated by the stern spiritualism of St. Birgitta. *Folkungaträdet* traces the emergence of Sweden as a nation from its mythic, chaotic past. There is a change in tone from the fall of the Swedish Empire in *Karolinerna* to the rise of the Swedish nation in *Folkungaträdet*, but the upward movement still carries a price of violence and treachery. *Svenskarna och deras hövdingar* (1908–10; Eng. tr. *The Swedes and Their Chieftains*, 1925) was Heidenstam's response to a request that he write Swedish history for schoolchildren. He found it difficult to reconcile his subjective experience of history with the generalizing pedagogic demands of a textbook.

Ett folk is a short poetry collection that represents the acme of Heidenstam's career as literary patriot. "Medborgarsång" (Citizen's song) became the anthem of the movement for voting rights: "It is a disgrace, a stain on Sweden's banner, / that the right to citizenship is called money." For a time, Heidenstam enjoyed some popularity in the labor movement, but workers felt betrayed when, too much the aristocrat, he did not take their side publicly during the general strike of 1909. In his final poetry collection, *Nya dikter* (1915; New poems), Heidenstam has returned to the more intimate tone of his earlier poetry, but the nationalistic pose is strikingly weak and testifies to the poet's waning powers.

Selma Lagerlöf

For many years, the literary reputation of Selma Lagerlöf (1858–1940) was affected by Oscar Levertin's condescending assessment of her as "just" a teller of fairy tales, whose literary strength rises from a well of folk belief and provincial mysticism. Levertin, himself steeped in stylized fin-de-siècle culture, presented Lagerlöf as a naive purveyor of folk traditions. Subsequent admirers have unearthed the symbolic richness and structural precision in her work. Lagerlöf herself compared writing to solving a mathematical problem. Her work is a combination of inspiration and calculation. She was awarded the Nobel Prize in 1909 and became the first female member of the Swedish Academy in 1914.

Selma Lagerlöf's literary debut, *Gösta Berlings saga* (1891; Eng. tr. *The Story of Gösta Berling*, 1898), owed little to the Heidenstam-Levertin essays, but it was greeted as the first work exemplifying their aesthetics. The joy Heidenstam thirsted for is evident in the description of the cavaliers' pact with the devil figure Sintram not to do anything sensible or useful for an entire year. There is no lack of imagination in the presentation of the figures around the Ekeby estate in Värmland. As pointed out by Vivi Edström, Lagerlöf gives her characters both a realistic and a mythic identity, much like the double exposure one finds in Carl Michael Bellman's poetry. Supernatural beings interact with the populace, but whether they have a real existence or are merely psychological representations is left open. With her colleagues of the 1890s Lagerlöf shares a nostalgia for the past. From the vantage point of a lackluster present, the narrator of *Gösta Berlings saga* looks back on the wildly romantic tales of a past age. The theme of the threatened estate, in this case Ekeby, recurs often in Lagerlöf's writing. It is inspired by her relationship to her own home estate, Mårbacka, but also serves as a symbol of the importance of history and tradition.

There is in Lagerlöf's writing an acute sense of divine providence and poetic justice, a notion implied by the title of her collection of stories *Osynliga länkar* (1894; Eng. tr. *Invisible Links*, 1899). This quality easily leads to the mistaken conclusion that the author was a religious writer. The presence of God, justice, and the immortality of the soul served aesthetic rather than religious ends in her writing. In *Gösta Berlings saga*, the philosophical cavalier, Uncle Eberhard, writes a learned book in which he irrefutably proves that God does not exist, death is at the end of everything, and love is a biological urge. When the young countess, Elisabet, hears of the contents of the book, she is distressed and claims that she could not live in such a world. Out of consideration for her, Uncle Eberhard locks his book in a chest, which is not to be opened until after the turn of the century. The narrator gives us every reason to believe that Uncle Eberhard's arguments are valid, but the choice is made to cling to the old beliefs for a while longer. In "Kejsarinnans kassakista" (The empress's treasure chest), from the collection *Drottningar i Kungahälla jämte andra berättelser* (1897; Eng. tr. *The Queens of Kungahälla and Other Tales*, 1917), the treasure chest is a symbol for divine providence. The Empress has left a treasure hidden among the people of West Flanders, which they are to use only in the case of extreme need. Although they never use it, the existence of the treasure as a last resort is a great solace to the people and improves the quality of their lives. In the people's imagination, the treasure is vast. In reality, it amounts to twenty gold thalers. The truth of the treasure or of God's existence is not of real importance: it is the belief that is a source of strength and beauty. Lagerlöf acknowledged the view of the 1880s that God is dead and man a biological mechanism, but she chose not to write about that world. Instead, in the neoromantic spirit of the 1890s, she sought unity and order in the beliefs of the past. In her own words, she found it useful to give her readers "rest, to let them believe in justice and the governance of God."

Lagerlöf's second novel, *Antikrists mirakler* (1897; Eng. tr. *The Miracles of Antichrist*, 1899), is set in Sicily and draws a comparison, common at the time, between socialism and Christianity. The novel was well received, probably because of the friendly face it gave to the threatening socialist movement, but the Swedish leader of this movement, Hjalmar Branting, criticized Lagerlöf for not understanding the difference between well-meant charity from above and a claim for social justice from below. Lagerlöf herself viewed *Antikrists mirakler* as an artistic failure. The Roman Catholic cultural tradition, however, continued to hold a special fascination for her, especially the legends of the saints, a genre she explored in *Kristuslegender* (1904; Eng. tr. *Christ Legends*, 1908).

En herrgårdssägen (1899; Eng. tr. *From a Swedish Homestead*, 1901) is a masterpiece of narrative and psychological observation. An interest in abnormal psychology was characteristic of the 1890s; the depiction of Gunnar Hede's voyage into madness and ultimate return to sanity through the agency of Ingrid, the woman who loves him, would make Sigmund Freud nod in recognition at several points. Lagerlöf's attempt to translate psychological turmoil into prose leads her down some modern paths. Psychological phenomena are given tangible form in a way that presages expressionism. Gunnar Hede regains his sanity by reliving his repressed past traumas through music, and he is called by Ingrid from the stranglehold of insanity in a way that would impress modern therapists.

Jerusalem 1–2 (1901–2; Eng. tr. *Jerusalem 1 and 2*, 1915–18) brought about an international breakthrough for Langerlöf. Uncharacteristically, she chose to write about a fairly recent event: the emigration of farmers from Dalarna to a religious colony in Jerusalem during the 1880s. The heroism of these individuals lies in their giving up home, tradition, and friends to follow their beliefs. It is the epic story of the proud and respected Ingmarssons; their roots are deep in the Dalarna soil and in ancient traditions, and they are faced with uncompromising moral choices. As part of the wave of nationalistic literature that arose around the turn of the century, *Jerusalem* is a monumental tribute to a vanishing peasant culture. The psychological insights it offers are timeless.

Herr Arnes penningar (1903; Eng. tr. *Herr Arne's Hoard*, 1923) offers a variation on the Faustian theme of the love of a good woman redeeming the reprobate male. It had been present in Lagerlöf's works since *Gösta Berlings saga*, but in *Herr Arnes penningar*, the love of Elsalill is not enough to redeem the sins of the cold-blooded murderer, Sir Archie. Elsalill does not consciously recognize Sir Archie as the murderer of Herr Arne's household, but the ghost of her murdered foster sister sees to it that this knowledge rises to consciousness. The ghost follows Sir Archie unseen, like a nemesis. In Lagerlöf's writing, nature often reflects an emotional climate. Thus in *Jerusalem*, the flooding of the Dala River forebodes the religious turmoil that will surge through the valley. In *Herr Arnes penningar*, the ice does not break up until the murder is solved and Elsalill's body is retrieved for burial.

The Swedish Board of Education asked Lagerlöf to write a book that could be used to teach Swedish children about their country. The result was *Nils Holgerssons underbara resa genom Sverige* (1906–7; Eng. tr. *The Wonderful Adventures of Nils*, 1907), probably her internationally best-known work. Lagerlöf had worked as a teacher and was able to find an imaginative approach to the subject; her effort proved far more success-ful than her colleague Heidenstam's attempt to write a Swedish history for schoolchildren. Nils, who has been miniaturized by an angry *tomte* (gnome), experiences the Swedish countryside with a flock of wild geese. Nobel laureate Czeslaw Milosz has characterized the double perspective of *Nils Holgerssons underbara resa*—both an overview from above and a study of detail near the ground—as a model of artistic creation in general.

Much of Lagerlöf's writing displays a tension between poles such as cultivation and wildness, nurturing women and irresponsible men, or even the Nietzschean Apollonian and Dionysian principles. Usually, good sense and order ultimately prevail; during the 1910s, however, the darker side of human nature looms larger, a reaction to the approach and outbreak of World War I. In *Körkarlen* (1912; Eng. tr. *Thy Soul Shall Bear Witness*, 1921), the drunkard David Holm has tortured his family to the brink of suicide, and in *Kejsarn av Portugallien* (1914; Eng. tr. *The Emperor of Portugallia*, 1917), the reader is drawn into the madness of the protagonist, Johannes. Each of these tales ends with reconciliation or consolation, but the desperate circumstances described seem at odds with Lagerlöf's well-ordered literary world. In six novellas from *Troll och människor 2*, (1921; Trolls and people 2), Lagerlöf writes of how the outbreak of World War I paralyzed her creativity. A pacifist message is found in her novel *Bannlyst* (1918; Eng. tr. *The Outcast*, 1920). In the first part of Lagerlöf's late trilogy about the Löwensköld family, *Löwensköldska ringen* (1925; Eng. tr. *The General's Ring*, 1928; *The Löwensköld Ring*, 1991), the ring, as pointed out by Vivi Edström, could be seen as a symbol of the nationalistic, belligerent spirit that causes war. A gift from Karl XII to one of his generals, the ring lies at the root of the distress and intrigue of several generations in the Löwensköld family. The trilogy of novels that begins with *Den Löwensköldska ringen* and ends with *Anna Svärd* (1928; Eng. tr. 1931) is the only major work by Lagerlöf that concludes with a question mark, rather than resolution; the reader is not told whether the male protagonist is redeemable or not.

Lagerlöf also wrote a series of autobiographical volumes under the collective title *Mårbacka* (3 vols.; 1922, 1930, 1932; Eng. tr. *The Diary of Selma Lagerlöf*, 1936). They are of interest not only as the memoirs of a remarkable woman but also as works of art by one of Sweden's greatest literary geniuses.

Erik Axel Karlfeldt

Erik Axel Karlfeldt (1864–1931) is perhaps the least controversial member of the 1890s Parnassus. It may have been a dubious honor that he was selected for membership in the Swedish Academy as early as 1904, when Carl David af Wirsén (1842–1912) was still at his post. Wirsén had adopted the role of national guardian of taste and morals in the 1880s and fought energetically against the naturalist school in general and August Strindberg in particular. He continued to object to the aestheticism of the 1890s. Karlfeldt's poetry, with its well-executed meters and nostalgic depictions of Dalarna and its peasant culture, did not offend the sensibilities of Sweden's most conservative critic. When Wirsén died in 1912, Karlfeldt took his place as permanent secretary of the Swedish Academy.

Karlfeldt did not make his poetic debut until 1895 with *Vildmarks och kärleksvisor* (Songs of love and wilderness). His poetic milieu is Dalarna. In "Fäderna" (The forefathers), he celebrates the traditional life of his rural home province. The peasants in Karlfeldt's poems are in harmony with nature and the seasons, robust people equally hard at work and at play. Other poems are devoted to beings of folklore and popular superstition lurking on the edge of the idyll of human culture and cultivation. Pan, a favorite figure of the 1890s, is a darkly erotic, Dionysian force and one of "the demons" that tempt and must be mastered. Karlfeldt's poetic world displays the tension between the Dionysian and the Apollonian as described by Nietzsche in *Die Geburt der Tragödie*, but the Apollonian generally prevails. In "Utbölingen" (The outsider), Karlfeldt approaches the symbolic technique of Selma Lagerlöf in his depiction of a black bird that whispers to the guilty the secrets of their hidden crimes. The black bird, Pan, the demons, and the witches are all avenues to the subconscious.

In his next collection of poems, *Fridolins visor och andra dikter* (1898; Fridolin's songs and other poems), Karlfeldt introduces the traveling minstrel Fridolin, who "speaks with peasants in peasant fashion / and with learned men in Latin." Comparisons have been made between Karlfeldt's Fridolin and Carl Michael Bellman's Fredman, but not to Karlfeldt's advantage. Karlfeldt's character gallery is much paler than Bellman's; Ollondal, Pillman, and Laxander lack distinctive features and leave no lasting impressions.

The collection *Fridolins lustgård och Dalmålningar på rim* (1901; Fridolin's garden of delights and peasant paintings in rhyme) is touched by the nationalistic mood around the turn of the century. Karlfeldt contributes to the trend with "Tuna Ting" (The tuna assembly), a poem about the men of Dalarna who came to the aid of Gustav Vasa when he seized the throne of Sweden. The theme points to Dalarna as midwife to the birth of the Swedish nation. Karlfeldt ends his collection with a poem about the apocalypse, a theme popular in the 1890s and also in modernism, whereas "Längtan heter min arvedel" (Longing is the name of my inheritance) is more in keeping with the private lyric poetry of the period. A comparison with the opening line of Pär Lagerkvist's poem "Ångest, ångest är min arvedel" (1916; Anguish, anguish is my inheritance) reveals an intensification of feeling emblematic of the shift from the 1890s to modernism. The 1890s displayed a melancholy longing for the past; modernism expresses anguish before the circumstances of the present.

The collection *Flora och Pomona* (1906; Flora and Pomona) is named after the goddesses of flowers and fruit. Botanical imagery and classical allusions abound, and the meter is markedly baroque. Karlfeldt's interest in baroque poetry is shared by the modernists, but Karlfeldt does not so much renew the forms as adopt them. The effect is conservative rather than revolutionary. *Flora och Pomona* is a more learned volume than its predecessors, and much of the imagery is inaccessible to the untutored reader. The demons of Karlfeldt's earlier poetry are present in "Häxorna" (The witches), but they bear the Latin names of the Middle Ages.

Flora och Bellona (1918; Flora and Bellona) is named for the goddesses of flowers and war. In these poems, Karlfeldt, the representative of poetic traditions with deep roots in Sweden's past, attempts to come to grips with the turmoil of World War I and the Russian Revolution, but the battle is not entirely successful. "I Marsvind" (In the wind of March [or Mars]) reassembles the cast of Fridolin's poems for a discussion of current events. Fridolin gazes out the window and glibly remarks: "What do we care about the Czar? / Look at the starling, look at the starling!" In keeping with the duality of the collection's title, political upheavals in another part of the world are here contrasted with enduring nature; the flippant apoliticism of the lines, however, caused Victor Svanberg to warn of a "Karlfeldt danger" in 1928. "Till Bellona" (To Bellona) marshals a procession of wars through the ages to its culmination in the technological warfare of the present time. The poet struggles with the urge to flee to his pastoral world of Dalarna but also realizes that its time is forever past, and Fridolin's song is "tömd och dömd och glömd" (exhausted and condemned and forgotten).

Dalarna makes a comeback in Karlfeldt's final collection, *Hösthorn* (1927; Autumn horn). The poet prefers not to dwell in the modern world, though he expresses pity for the generation that grew up knowing war and that now must confront the rapid advances of society. He offers advice to youth that seems valid today: "Put aside your headphone in a quiet hour / and listen to your inner instrument." "Sub luna" is one of Karlfeldt's most enduring poems; the opening line in Latin of each stanza is darkly suggestive as it celebrates a different aspect of the poet's life and the universal themes of love, song, drink, and death. After Karlfeldt's death in 1931, two final volumes of his poems and speeches were published: *Tankar och tal* (1932; Thoughts and speeches) and *Karlfeldts ungdomsdiktning* (1934; Karlfeldt's early poetry).

Gustaf Fröding

Gustaf Fröding (1860–1911) did not share in the official honors bestowed on his fellow writers. Heidenstam, Lagerlöf, and Karlfeldt each received formal recognition in the form of memberships in the Swedish Academy and Nobel Prizes. In 1892, when Fröding was awarded a stipend by the Swedish Academy, he donated it to the movement for general voting rights. Whereas Heidenstam, Lagerlöf, and Karlfeldt each could play the traditional part of poet as public oracle, Fröding fell into the more modern role of poet as outsider. Throughout the decade, he struggled with mental illness, and his poetry was written during and in between stays in sanatoriums. In 1898, he suffered a serious breakdown, which put an end to his public life as a poet. The poetry of Fröding's final years was published posthumously and proved to be a stunning source of poetic innovation. His poetry contains a legacy of romanticism and traces of the fin de siècle; more enduring, however, is the view of Fröding as "a modernist before modernism."

The title poem of Fröding's first poetry collection, *Gitarr och draghar-monika* (1891; Eng. tr. *Guitar and Concertina*, 1925), advises the reader to listen for two strains in his poetry. The guitar accompanies the dark, bitter, and melancholy strain, and the concertina evokes the cheerful, funny, and burlesque strain. Fröding's great popularity is largely due to the poems in the latter category with amusing and irreverent depictions of folk life; in "Våran prost" (Our dean), the parish dean warns of fire and brimstone from the pulpit and invites the church council members to a lavish table and schnapps afterward. Another example is "Jan Ersa och Per Persa" (Jan Ersa and Per Persa), in which two farmers pursue a bitter rivalry even into the grave. There is a note of compassion and implied social criticism in "Elin i Hagen" (Elin in the meadow) and "Lars i Kuja" (Lars from Kuja). Elin drowns her illegitimate child, and Lars lives a life of unceasing toil without hope of change or improvement.

The darker "guitar" strains are found in the second part of Fröding's early collection. The description of inner states is here reinforced by concrete imagery. The technique, which presages expressionism, is found in "En ghasel" (A ghasel). Here the poet looks at life through a barred window, and in the final stanza we learn that the bars are internal: "and not until I myself am broken, will the bars be broken." Fröding makes use of a Persian meter, the ghasel, which entails frequent repetition of a word, in this case *gallret* (the bars). In "Hydra," the poet relates a fevered dream in which he is a weak Hercules fighting against the Hydra, a symbolic representation of the poet's struggle with anguish. Similarly, in "Mefisto," the title figure represents a self-critical aspect of the poet himself. Fröding's use of dreams could be seen as typical of the 1890s, but his evocations of inner struggles in symbolic form are quite advanced.

In *Nya dikter* (1894; New poems), Fröding shows proof of a social conscience more typical of the 1880s. A poem such as "Den gamla goda tiden" (The good old days) could be read as an ironic commentary on the period's nostalgia for the peasant life of the past. Poverty is not ennobling. "The good old days" sanctioned the exploitation of the working class. In "Tronskifte" (Accession to the throne), Fröding notes that humankind has entered a new age. The slow and deliberate king Chronos is dead, and his heir, the Modern Age, is in a great hurry and is leaving many of the old guard behind in the dust. Although Fröding writes of the past, he does not avoid the present to the same extent as Heidenstam, Lagerlöf, and Karlfeldt. He addresses the cult of the Nietzschean superman in a pastiche of *Also Sprach Zarathustra*. Zarathustra informs his disciples that he has told them to love themselves and cultivate their own interests, but he has never told them to trample others on their way to the heights. Fröding warns against the dangers of egoism in the 1890s cult of the individual.

The title poem of *Stänk och flikar* (1896; Sprinklings and tatters) describes an essentially modernist view of a fragmented reality. The poet cannot describe a totality, only "sprinklings and shreds." The same thought lies behind the series of poems about the Holy Grail, the first of which appears in this collection. The grail represents the lost unity of reality, for which the poet longs. In this collection, Fröding continues to experiment with nontraditional techniques, as in "Drömmar i Hades" (Dreams in Hades).

One of Fröding's most beloved poems is "Ett gammalt bergtroll" (An old mountain troll). The poem resembles "En fattig munk från Skara" (A poor monk from Skara) and "Skalden Wennerblom" (The poet Wennerblom) from the earlier collections, in that it describes an unloved yet lovable outsider. The monk has committed every deadly sin and Wennerblom is an alcoholic, but both are treated with sympathy. The lonely mountain troll can establish a relationship with people only by eating them. The themes of eroticism and the moral double standard of the age run through many of the poems in this collection. In "En morgondröm" (A morning dream), the graphic depiction of intercourse and orgasm was considered shocking and the poet was brought to trial for immorality. Although the court cleared him of the charge, Fröding did not recover from the experience; it undoubtedly contributed to his mental collapse.

In *Nytt och gammalt* (1897; New and old), Fröding displays his flair for the absurd, another quality he shares with modernism. *Nya dikter* (1894; New poems) contains a poem about the Wandering Jew, who after viewing centuries of human life can only smile at the strangeness of everything. Fröding's sense of humor is in large part responsible for his great popularity, but his sense of the absurd is a reaction to a chaotic and frightening world view. In *Gralstänk* (1898; Sprinklings from the grail), Fröding develops the theme of a fragmented reality. The collection also contains lengthy meditations on good and evil and the possibility that these terms have no absolute value. The poet reacts in part to Nietzsche's *Jenseits von Gut und Böse* (1886; Beyond good and evil) and in part to his own complex feelings of guilt. In "Maskin i olag" (Machine out of order), he takes the 1880s scientific view of man as a machine literally and with his usual humor describes a machine that falls apart because desire is not properly balanced in terms of the will. *Gralstänk* was the last poetry collection published before Fröding's own breakdown.

Poems not included in Fröding's major poetry collections were published in *Efterskörd* (1910; Late harvest), *Reconvalescentia* (1913), and *Återkomsten* (1964; The return). These poems display a will to explore the limits of poetry in a way that anticipates many of the movements within modernist poetry in the twentieth century. In his youth, Fröding experimented with an artificial language and wrote poems that were melodious nonsense. A similar concentration on sound and rhythm rather than meaning was later to be found in the poetry of the futurists and the dadaists. Fröding's sensitivity to the auditory qualities of language makes some of his poems (such as "Säv, säv, susa" [Rush, rush, whisper]) approach onomatopoeia. In "Gråbergs sång" (Granite's song), a *carmen figuratum*, or what was later called a *calligramme* after Apollinaire, the text assumes the form of a cliff. Drawing pictures with poetry was a practice of baroque poets which resurfaced in the so-called concrete poetry of the twentieth century. Further modernist experimentations are found in poems such as "Den skapande nyskapade" (The creative newly created), in which Fröding ignores the rules of syntax. In the role poem "Ett gammalt bergtroll," he gives voice to a consciousness beneath the human. He takes this even further in "Snigelns visa" (The snail's song), "Myra med barr" (Ant with needle), and "Vargsång" (Wolf song), in which he writes from the perspective of a snail, an ant, and a wolf, respectively.

Oscar Levertin

The literary production of Oscar Levertin (1862–1906) has been overshadowed by the works of Heidenstam, Lagerlöf, Karlfeldt, and Fröding. Nonetheless, Levertin played an important role in shaping the aesthetics of the 1890s, and his work constitutes the most direct link connecting the 1880s, the 1890s, and the new generation of authors at the turn of the century. His strong sympathy for French culture made him more susceptible to the literary trends on the Continent. At the same time, he deeply admired Verner von Heidenstam's literary vitality, even though he himself was more inclined toward passive aestheticism. A denizen of the urban landscape, he thrived among classic works of art and ancient books. The provincial folk elements in the literature of the 1890s Parnassus were foreign to his personal tastes. In 1897, Levertin became the literary editor for *Svenska Dagbladet* and in this post was one of Sweden's most influential literary critics. From 1899 he held a professorship at the humanistic faculty of Stockholms högskola (Stockholm College).

The chronology of his debut places Levertin among the writers of the 1880s. He was an enthusiastic member of Det unga Sverige (Young Sweden) and produced two collections of realistic, socially engaged novellas: *Småmynt* (1883; Small change) and *Konflikter* (1885; Conflicts). Levertin had great respect for Georg Brandes and nourished hopes of becoming his Swedish counterpart. During a stay in a Swiss sanatorium for tuberculosis patients, he was sought out by Heidenstam. This meeting decisively changed Levertin's aesthetic views; together the two composed "Pepitas bröllop." In that essay, Levertin distances himself from his earlier writing, which he felt possessed too great a reverence for reality. He accuses himself of having collected real details as a hat-check boy collects tips.

The immediate literary response to the meeting between the two writers was Levertin's first poetry collection, *Legender och visor* (1891; Legends and songs). The shift in genre from prose to poetry was significant; Levertin is indeed best remembered for his poetry. Many of the poems from this first collection contain settings from the Middle Ages and myth. An overriding theme in Levertin's poetry is the juxtaposition of Eros and Thanatos, love and death. "Florez och Blanzeflor" is one of many such poems. Levertin's poetry lacks the joy and humor present in the work of his 1890s colleagues; instead, melancholy and pessimism prevail. *Nya dikter* (1894; New poems) makes an attempt to endorse frivolity in "De visa och de fåvitska jungfrurna" (The wise and the foolish maidens), in which the poet praises the wastefulness of the foolish maidens over the miserliness of the wise, but this effort seems merely to be a nod to his friend Heidenstam. *Dikter* (1901; Poems) contains one of Levertin's most famous poems, "Folket i Nifelhem" (The people of Nifelhem), a dark sketch of the Swedish national character. "Alienor," from the same collection, treats the topos of the *femme fragile*, or delicate, ailing woman. In the general context of fin-de-siècle aesthetics, the love for the *femme fragile* often represents the aesthete's love for his decaying culture. This decadent fascination with death and dissolution is also evident in "Dykaren" (The diver), in which the title figure is caught in a dead and sunken world at the bottom of the sea. In *Sista dikter* (1907; Last poems), published posthumously, the poet speaks in apocalyptic terms of "the world's death song."

Levertin did not stop writing prose after his meeting with Heidenstam. Under Heidenstam's influence; he put the finishing touches on a generally overlooked novel, *Livets fiender* (1891; Life's enemies). The short novel is a showcase of decadent motifs. The protagonist, Otto Imhoff, belongs to an old, noble family. He suffers from hypersensitivity, nervousness, and a feverish imagination. He is an aesthete who lists the contents of his library, savors paintings, and is fond of Wagner. *Livets fiender* is a city novel in which the reader follows the protagonist on his rounds of Stockholm and shares in his impressions. Imhoff's hypersensitivity develops into an abnormal persecution mania. The novel recalls Joris-Karl Huysmans's *A rebours* (1884; Against the grain) as well as Ola Hansson's depictions of nervous impressions in *Sensitiva amorosa* (1887) and *Parias* (1890). An unusual feature of the novel is an allegorical chapter, perhaps in emulation of Heidenstam's prioritizing of the imaginative over the real. Two female figures, Caritas and Scepsis, encounter each other across the centuries from Golgotha to the present.

Levertin's passionate interest in the rococo and the reign of Gustav III resulted in several fine essays and monographs on the subject, but his *Rococo-noveller* (1899; Rococo stories) have fared less well among critics. A cosmopolitan, Levertin felt more at home in the cultured past than in the romantic folkloristic past of Lagerlöf and Karlfeldt. His short novel *Magistrarne i Österås* (1900; The scholars in Österås) also has a historical theme and constitutes Levertin's attempt to join the nationalistic wave. *Kung Salomo och Morolf* (1905; King Solomon and Morolf) is the last poetry collection published during Levertin's lifetime and is generally considered his best poetic effort. The King is cultured, reflective, hesitant, and melancholy. His brother Morolf is wild, spontaneous, and joyful. Critics have identified the figure of Morolf as Heidenstam, Karlfeldt, and/or Fröding. It seems safe to say that *King Salomo och Morolf* represents Levertin's reflections on his own role in the 1890s as compared with that of his more popular colleagues. The King feels that his melancholy tunes will be forgotten whereas Morolf's songs will endure.

TURN-OF-THE-CENTURY PESSIMISM AND
PARALYSIS OF THE WILL

It has become traditional to classify a small group of authors under the rubric *sekelskiftet* (turn of the century) and to distinguish them from the authors of "the Golden Age of Swedish literature." A chronological distinction is to an extent arbitrary. Hjalmar Söderberg (1869–1941), the quintessential author of *sekelskiftet*, made his literary debut in 1895, the same year as Erik Axel Karlfeldt. Other members of this group, however, belonged to a much younger generation of authors. The authors of *sekelskiftet* picked up the strains of fin-de-siècle decadence that were in evidence throughout the 1890s and turned them into the fashion of the day. Oscar Levertin was their literary idol. A young Bo Bergman (1869–1967) and Hjalmar Söderberg read Levertin's "Florez och Blanzeflor" in an Uppsala café and felt that Swedish literature had obtained a new voice. Skåne poets, such as Vilhelm Ekelund (1880–1949) and Anders Österling (1884–1981), were particularly influenced by Ola Hansson's poetry. Whereas Heidenstam, Lagerlöf, Karlfeldt, and Fröding were perceived as particularly Swedish phenomena, the authors of the turn of the century were deeply influenced by a long list of foreign models: Baudelaire, Verlaine, Rimbaud,

Maeterlinck, Huysmans, Wilde, Swinburne, Stefan George, Hofmannsthal, Rilke, d'Annunzio, Bang, Jacobsen, and Obstfelder.

One of the dominant features of the literature of *sekelskiftet* is the belief in biological determinism. The scientific wave of the latter half of the nineteenth century did away with God and made humankind a product of genetics, upbringing, and environment. At first, this world view was received positively, and scientists felt confident that they could eventually explain every mystery of the natural world and provide a natural order to replace the divine order. The authors of *sekelskiftet* analyzed the implications of this world view for the individual and posed the question, If everyone is a product of genetics, upbringing, and environment, then what role can free will play? The answer arrived at was "none"; not surprisingly, the most telling poetic image from the era is the marionette. In the title poem of Bo Bergman's *Marionetterna* (1903; The marionettes), man lives his life, but everything "is but a pull of the strings." Man's behavior is determined by factors beyond his control. The notion of biological determinism results in a paralysis of the will, apathy, and existential weariness. Bergman writes of his poetic generation in "Vårfrost" (Spring frost): "We were born old, and our kind / had gray hair in the cradle." The attitude is a far cry from that of the writers of the Golden Age, who reacted to the 1880s world view with flights of fancy and a call for joy.

The authors of *sekelskiftet* also differ from their 1890s predecessors in their choice of milieu, with a marked preference for a contemporary urban environment rather than provincial settings of the past. Both Bergman's novellas and Söderberg's novels are set in Stockholm. In his poem "Stadsbarn" (Children of the city), Bergman follows the lead of the "city poets" Baudelaire and Verlaine. The typical denizen of the urban landscape is the flaneur, who observes life but rarely participates. Anders Österling writes in "Sen vandring" (Late wandering): "it is my lot / in solitude, like a distant illusion / to observe life with its noise and light." If drawn into a course of events, the flaneur tends to view his own actions with ironic distance; a dandy, he may divide his attention equally between details of dress and existential questions. Aestheticism, style, and beauty are valued commodities.

Because man is viewed as ruled by his biological urges, eroticism takes a central place as the most compelling. Sven Lidman (1882–1960) and Bertil Malmberg (1889–1958) shocked the public with a hedonistic cult of sensual pleasure in their first poetry collections. Söderberg's characters are often guided, consciously or unconsciously, by erotic attraction. Freud's theories can be applied quite fruitfully to his literary contemporaries, although they had no direct knowledge of his work.

Eros and Thanatos, love and death—the two absolute experiences of the biological organism—are often juxtaposed in the writing of the turn of the century, as they were in Levertin's work. Sven Lidman is particularly fascinated by the idea of the beautiful death, popular in Continental decadence as well as in Heidenstam's early writing. In *Primavera* (1905), Lidman calls for "the courage to perish in the flame of fate, / to obey the voice of destruction in the blood." Suicide is viewed as an alternative to the meaninglessness of life. Pessimism is the overriding mood of *sekelskiftet*, and its poetry is rife with apocalyptic visions and hallucinogenic imagery. Hjalmar Söderberg's essentially realistic prose is spiced with symbolic dream sequences. Stylistically, these features presage modernism.

Such a depressing view of life proved to be difficult to maintain in the long run, and for several of the authors, the literary mode of the turn of the century was a passing phase. Anders Österling would later disavow the decadent works of his youth and count his actual literary debut as *Årets visor* (1907; The year's songs), a pleasant cycle of poems dedicated to the changing seasons. Both Bergman and Österling began writing poems about the quiet dignity of ordinary objects. Bergman did not lose his fin-de-siècle aestheticism but abandoned the pessimism. Sven Lidman made the radical change from a decadent to a bourgeois realist with a concomitant shift from poetry to prose. The connection of pessimism with modernism is significant. The world view of the turn of the century lies at the root of modernist angst.

Hjalmar Söderberg

Hjalmar Söderberg (1869–1941) is the most eloquent spokesman of *sekelskiftet*. The relatively few works that he published scandalized contemporary Sweden. For the last half of his life, Söderberg chose to live in Copenhagen and died there during the German occupation. His writings were deeply imbued with the concerns of his day, but they have by no means become obsolete. The existential quandaries of his characters still resonate in the hearts of modern readers. Söderberg's clear and concise prose style has become classic.

During the 1890s, Hjalmar Söderberg worked as a journalist and wrote stories for various newspapers and journals. The first of his five story collections, *Historietter* (Short stories), appeared in 1898. These stories display an astonishing range of stylistic variety. The collection begins and ends with allegories. In "Tuschritningen" (The ink sketch), the implied moral is that there is no meaning in life, just as there is no hidden image in the ink sketch. The howl of the masterless dog in "En herrelös hund"

(A masterless dog) evokes humankind's anguish at being left in a world without God. "Sotarfrun" (The chimneysweep's wife) and "Sann historia" (True story) are fairy tales with a cynical twist. "Drömmen om evigheten" (The dream of eternity), "Skuggan" (The shadow), "Duggregnet" (Drizzle), and "Mardröm" (Nightmare) are symbolic stories that make use of unreal, nightmarish situations. The tales are the direct ancestors of Pär Lagerkvist's *Onda sagor* (1924; Evil tales) and subsequent modernist prose. Some of the prose pieces in *Historietter* contain social satire, and others describe the fates of pathetic individuals trampled by life. This mosaic of stories expresses a pessimistic view in which a cold, hard look at life reveals only futility and failure; the beautiful and the good are merely illusions. Every word in a Söderberg story is important; the author's admiration for Baudelaire is evident in the prose poem character of some of the short stories. Söderberg's other short story collections include *Främlingarna* (1903; The strangers), *Det mörknar över vägen* (1907; The road darkens), *Den talangfulla draken* (1913; The talented dragon), and *Resan till Rom* (1929; The journey to Rome).

Söderberg's actual literary debut occurred in 1895 with *Förvillelser* (Delinquencies), a novel about a young man ensnared in a web of biological determinism; the actions of the protagonist, Tomas Weber, are propelled by his biological urges rather than guided by careful consideration. Weber remains unaware of the forces shaping his existence, and the results are catastrophic as he drifts into disastrous liaisons with a young boutique attendant and a woman of his own class. The protagonist of Söderberg's next novel, *Martin Bircks ungdom* (1901; Eng. tr. *Martin Birck's Youth*, 1930), is much more reflective than Tomas Weber. In many ways, Martin is *too* much so. His introspective nature paralyzes his ability to act. He is torn between his dreams of love and life and the paltry reality available to him. He has dreams of being a poet, but he comes to the realization that poetry may capture truths but never the Truth. Financial necessity forces him to become a civil servant and to resign himself to his routine job and the "pitiful happiness" of a clandestine relationship with his mistress.

Doktor Glas (1905; Eng. tr. *Doctor Glas*, 1970) is the most sophisticated of Söderberg's novels. The diary format allows the reader to follow the protagonist's reasoning and experience of events with greater understanding of Glas's motivations than Glas himself. The doctor believes his motives to be objective, but his "objectivity" is compromised by his attraction to Helga Gregorius and his revulsion for her husband, Pastor Gregorius. Seizing his professional advantage, Glas proceeds to murder the pastor. Contemporary readers assumed somewhat naively that the novel was a defense of ethical murder, reflecting the author's opinions. But Glas's act achieves nothing, and the message is one of futility. Söderberg does not offer a solution to Glas's moral dilemma; instead, he uses the doctor's situation to expose the fragile moral ground on which society rests.

Söderberg's last novel, *Den allvarsamma leken* (1912; The serious game), takes up the familiar themes of determinism and eroticism by following the complicated relationship between Lydia Stille and Arvid Stjärnblom over the course of several years. Lydia searches for love and finds more or less satisfying sexual relationships. Both Arvid and Lydia are driven by inclinations and instincts they cannot fully explain. With a technique Söderberg may have borrowed from the Danish writer Herman Bang (1857–1912), the novel presents characters from earlier novels. These intertextual references suggest that each individual novel is merely a part of the highly complex web of life. The cynical Markel, the romantic Martin Birck, and the ironic Henrik Rissler function as a Greek chorus, each providing commentary from his particular point of view.

Hjalmar Söderberg is one of the few Swedish authors to write plays of any merit in Strindberg's immediate wake. His best-known play, *Gertrud* (1906), is based on the same material as *Den allvarsamma leken*, but viewed from the perspective of the female protagonist rather than the male. The men in Gertrud's life cannot fulfill her dream of love. In her marriage, Gertrud must compete with her husband's interest in politics. Similarly, in her earlier relationship with an author, Gertrud's rival was his writing. For her latest love interest, a young musician, Gertrud is merely a conquest. Söderberg makes use of scenic elements and music to underscore the erotic motivations of the play, features that point to an influence from Strindberg. *Aftonstjärnan* (1912; The evening star) is a one-act play set in a café, a setting reminiscent of Strindberg's one-act play *Den starkare*. The viewers' attention is drawn from one conversation to another, as though they were eavesdropping. One table is commenting on uncanny dreams; a doctor is reading a three-hundred-page dissertation on the will; an engineer is given a small loan by the waitress; and an old man exerts his will by humiliating her with the power of money. *Ödestimman* (1922; The hour of fate) has, quite uncharacteristically, a fictional setting. Inspired by the events leading to World War I, Söderberg seeks to expose in this play the dangers of nationalistic myths as chauvinist and humanist interests collide.

Martin Birck called for an author who did not sing but spoke clearly. Söderberg himself began to question whether or not fiction was a suitable means of conveying ideas, since it can be easily misunderstood or dismissed. In *Hjärtats oro* (1909; The heart's unrest), the author speaks directly to the reader about his opinions on current ideas and events. This move away from fiction is not unrelated to the general shift in literature from symbolism to realism at this time; Söderberg's pessimistic world view remains constant, however. His concern is truth, but his tactic for approaching truth is to reveal untruths, a rather early "deconstructive" approach. In *Jahves eld* (1918; Jehovah's fire), *Jesus Barabbas* (1928), and *Den förvandlade Messias* (1932; The transformed messiah), Söderberg goes about puncturing the myths of Western religion. Moses and Jesus are presented as clever political leaders who used religious myths for their own worldly purposes.

Vilhelm Ekelund

Vilhelm Ekelund (1880–1949) is one of Sweden's most original poets; as a result, he was largely misunderstood by publishers and the general public. "That my poetry you deeply despise / is the only thing that has cheered me," wrote Ekelund in *Dithyramber i Aftonglans* (1906; Dithyrambs in evening glow). Both Strindberg and Hansson took up free verse as a temporary poetic experiment. Ekelund was the first Swedish poet to adopt free verse as a consistent form of expression; it cast aside regular meter and end rhyme yet was tightly disciplined and paid close attention to alliteration, assonance, and rhythm. Only a small selection of connoisseurs appreciated the subtleties of Ekelund's verse. He became something of a poet's poet and as such had a great impact on the modernists. He lived in exile in Germany and Denmark from 1908 to 1921.

Ekelund published his first poetry collection, *Vårbris* (1900; Spring breeze), at the age of twenty. His poetic development over the following six years was striking. In his first collection, he follows in the footsteps of the Skåne poets Ola Hansson and A. U. Bååth (1853–1912) and poetically explores the countryside of southern Sweden. Free verse has not yet entered his poetry, and some poems, such as "Skördefest" (Harvest feast), are reminiscent of Karlfeldt's depictions of folk life, while others show a French symbolist influence and include prose poems in the fashion of Baudelaire. Another stimulus is Arthur Schopenhauer (1788–1860), who praised pure contemplation and the experience of beauty. According to Schopenhauer's aesthetics, the poet's soul should be a clear mirror of eternal ideas. This aesthetic stance becomes even more apparent in Ekelund's second collection, *Syner* (1901; Visions), in which the poet begins to use free verse. The first poem, "Till Skönheten" (To beauty), registers the harmony and beauty of a landscape from a vantage point above the earth. Beauty is, in a sense, holy and brings about a transcendence of the earthly. Ekelund attempts to make his poetic soul receptive to the moods and beauty of various natural settings. At other times, it is the landscape that reflects the poet's soul, as in "Vägen" (The road), in which a lonely walk down a foggy road becomes a symbol of the poet's isolation and disorientation.

Vilhelm Ekelund's poetic development follows a path from provincial poetry to metapoetry. The metapoetic element is strongest in *Melodier i skymningen* (1902; Melodies in twilight). The line "Sonett, in i ditt tempel vill jag stiga" (Sonnet, I wish to enter your temple) sums up Ekelund's approach toward poetry at the time, an attitude of reclusive cultivation of art for its own sake. Poetry is a holy temple—or ivory tower, in which the poet may escape the world. In *Elegier* (1903; Elegies), the temple of poetry is invaded by Eros, viewed as a barbarian. The conflict between pure aesthetic contemplation and erotic yearning makes the poet long for a sanctuary beyond this world, as in the Baudelairean "Hemlängtan ur världen" (Homesickness out of the world). The tone changes in Ekelund's two collections from 1906, *Havets stjärna* (The sea's star) and *Dithyramber i Aftonglans*, in which Eros is no longer a threat to poetic activity but sublimated into poetry.

This change of attitude was brought about by Ekelund's exposure to Nietzsche. In *Antikt ideal* (1909; The ideal of classical antiquity), Ekelund describes the cult of beauty in modern poetry and his own earlier production as decadent and cowardly. Instead, he endorses the aesthetic stance of ancient Greece as presented by Nietzsche. The Greeks affirmed both good and evil in life, and Greek drama "appeals first of all to the will, the courageous instinct; not to the sense of beauty." Under the influence of Nietzsche, Ekelund began writing discursive prose and aphorisms. His conversion to prose has certain aspects in common with the general shift in literature to realistic prose in the 1910s. Like the *tiotalisterna* (the writers of the 1910s), Ekelund reaffirms the existence of the will and finds poetry ethically inferior to prose, but unlike the *tiotalisterna*, he places private, existential problems above collective, political issues. His prose production and his stoic attitude toward the grim aspects of life were to impress the Swedish modernist poets of the 1940s. In *Nordiskt och klassiskt* (1914; Nordic and classical), Ekelund writes: "You deceive yourself, you suffer a loss, if you are afraid of that which is empty, false, and bottomless. There you realize your human destiny and win salvation from pettiness." Ekelund helped deromanticize poetry. Instead of conveying the higher insights and powers of an oracle, poetry in Ekelund's hands becomes a vehicle of existential experience. After a life-threatening illness, Ekelund altered his heroic posture, and the graceful, restrained poetic gesture returned.

In 1907, John Landquist (1881–1974), Anders Österling, and Sigfrid Siwertz (1881–1970) traveled to Paris together, where they heard the lectures of the French philosopher Henri Bergson (1859–1941). Bergson argued against the principles of biological determinism, which held that human behavior is purely mechanical. He maintained that free will exists, although free acts are the exception. Mechanical behavior can become habitual, and a free act results from a fully conscious decision. Siwertz wrote of his encounter with Bergson, "I suddenly had the cheeky courage to believe in my own free will." Instead of passive reflection, Österling proposed action in *Hälsningar* (1907; Greetings): "Build yourself a world / if the world does not suit you!" The following year, Landquist published *Viljan* (1908; The will), in which he affirmed free will, humankind's creative capabilities, and the ethical responsibility that attends free will.

Landquist's views had a profound effect on the *tiotalister*. Landquist was an old friend of Siwertz and Sven Lidman. Another member of the group, Elin Wägner (1882–1942), was married to Landquist from 1910 to 1922. Landquist's *Viljan* is no doubt the book being read by the Doctor in Hjalmar Söderberg's play *Aftonstjärnan*. Söderberg was not moved by Landquist's arguments and continued to believe in biological determinism. The younger generation of writers, however, experienced the resurrection of the will as a great release. It brought about a shift from apocalyptic pessimism to optimism and from symbolic poetry to prose realism. Elin Wägner, Gustaf Hellström (1882–1949), and Ludvig Nordström (1882–1942) drew on their journalistic experiences and treated contemporary political and social issues. The *tiotalister* were concerned with the world at large rather than the private musings of the individual.

Traditionally, the writer's profession in Sweden had been accessible primarily to the monied classes, which could afford higher education. This tradition was beginning to change, and the first two decades of the new century saw the emergence of a new type of author, the *proletärförfattare* (proletarian writer) or *arbetarförfattare* (working-class writer), the former term implying a greater degree of political activism than the latter. The establishment of folk high schools and lending libraries enabled members of the working class to obtain the skills necessary to become writers. They had difficulty breaking into the accepted literary establishment, but their work could reach the public through newspapers and publishing companies run by the labor movement. Martin Koch (1882–1940), Gustav Hedenvind-Eriksson (1880–1967), Maria Sandel (1870–1927), Ragnar

Jändel (1895–1939), and Dan Andersson (1888–1920) wrote about conditions and experiences new to literature.

Swedish society was in a state of transition. *Folkrörelser* (populist movements) organized at the end of the nineteenth century had become influential social factors. There were generally three types of movements—religious, temperance, and labor—and it became common to perceive oneself as part of a group. A fierce battle was fought over the right to vote. Before 1909, the only people entitled to vote were men of property; thus both women and the working class were disenfranchised. Demonstrations and a strike were held in 1902, but it was not until 1909 that the law was changed to enable all men to vote. In 1905, the union with Norway was dissolved after a long period of nationalistic controversy. The conservative King Oscar II died in 1907, and with him much of the veneration for the old form of government by a privileged class. In 1909, workers called a general strike that failed. The strikers felt bitter that the older generation of authors had not openly supported them, and the "Strindberg Feud" followed, during which Strindberg once again became the champion of the working class.

The rapid changes in society demanded the attention of literature. The *tiotalister* and the *proletärförfattare* provided that attention. At first, the mood was optimistic. Humanity was capable of creating a better world fueled by commerce and technological advances. Ethical choices could be made for the benefit of all classes. This initial mood of optimism received a serious shock in the form of World War I. The scope of the conflict rocked the proletarian dream of international worker solidarity. The wartime uses of technology shook the *tiotalister*'s faith in industrialization. Voices in the women's movement argued that men were responsible for the vast destruction. In 1919, women were granted the right to vote.

Middle-Class Realists
The *tiotalister* might be compared with the Modern Breakthrough writers of the 1880s because of their taste for realism and interest in social issues. Whereas the earlier writers elicited aggressive attacks from the society they sought to depict, the *tiotalister* spoke in tune with their times. The *borgerliga realister* (middle-class realists), as this group is also called, offended few by criticizing egoistic capitalism while warmly supporting industrialization. Elin Wägner's advocacy of feminist causes surely met with mixed reactions, but they were mild compared with the outrage that had been directed at Ibsen's *Et dukkehjem* (A doll's house). In the 1880s, authors sought to reveal pieces of objective reality, with the result that the narrative voice

receded and the realistic subject matter commanded the attention. There was a belief that science would eventually provide a complete picture of existence, although some great mysteries still remained. The *tiotalister*, on the other hand, were driven by an urge to explain everything and to account for all causes and effects. Frequently, an omniscient Godlike narrator confidently guides the reader through events, such as in Ludvig Nordström's *Planeten Markattan* (1937; The shrewish planet): "So listen now and look, Serious and Future Swedes, and you will see and hear, how it has been and probably never shall be again." The omniscient narrator views circumstances and events with distant irony and, not infrequently, humor. In all fairness, it should be noted that Elin Wägner possesses a somewhat broader narrative register than her colleagues and generally allows her readers to draw their own conclusions. The authors of the 1880s dealt almost exclusively with the present; in contrast, the *tiotalister* often provide a historic dimension to explain contemporary conditions. One such example is Gustaf Hellström's *Snörmakare Lekholm får en idé* (1927; Eng. tr. *Lace Maker Lekholm Has an Idea*, 1930), in which Hellström follows the Lekholm family through three generations.

Unlike the writers of the 1880s, some of the *tiotalister* showed a distinct inclination toward religion. Sven Lidman became a preacher for the Pentecostal movement. Elin Wägner held a private belief akin to that of the Quakers. In her *Den namnlösa* (1922; The nameless one), the first-person narrator, Rakel, tries to follow her convictions about the will of God, even though they do not always coincide with the orthodox views of her brother, the minister. Ludvig Nordström writes in "Evighetsbössan" (The eternity rifle), from *Idyller från kungariket Öbacka* (1916; Idylls from the kingdom of Öbacka), about the path he took to an "unfashionable" belief in God to provide life with meaning. Individual will is important, and man strives to exert his will in concert with the will of God. Nordström developed a fairly idiosyncratic utopian vision of the universe, which he gave the name "Totalism." Under divine guidance, humankind is progressing toward a goal in which all countries are combined into one world state, the binding principle of which is world commerce; thus people attain moral perfection and war becomes impossible. Nordström sought to spread the gospel of Totalism in the four volumes of his novel *Petter Svensks historia* (1923–27; The history of Peter Swede).

Even the *tiotalister* who were not particularly religious, Hellström and Siwertz, tended to view life on earth as an ordered totality. Instead of God, it was genetics or a course of predestined evolution that provided the teleological order. This tendency of the *tiotalister* is in sharp contrast to the modernist view of reality as fragmented and chaotic. The *tiotalister* typically focus on a microcosm that reflects the totality. Nordström sets a large part of his short stories and novels in Öbacka, the town "that I know best and that certainly suffices to show all sides of the nation, yes, of all mankind" (*Planeten Markattan*). Against this background, he systematically examines the different levels of society in the short story collections *Fiskare* (1907; Fishermen), *Borgare* (1909; Burghers), and *Herrar* (1910; Gentlemen). Hjalmar Bergman uses the town of Wadköping in much the same way, but the world he paints is quite different from Nordström's. In *Snörmakare Lekholm*, Hellström makes a single family his microcosm. One member of the family remarks, "It is rather strange that it didn't take more than two generations, his sons and grandsons, to crystallize practically all the types one usually calls genuinely Swedish." It is noteworthy that only the family's sons are of consequence.

Even if humankind's fate is in the hands of higher powers, divine or evolutionary, free will is still an important factor. Individuals must participate in society's evolution. Sigrid Siwertz confronts fin-de-siècle apathy in his novel *En flanör* (1914; A flaneur): "The world is not built by coincidences, but by decisions." Of the *tiotalister*, Elin Wägner is the author most actively engaged in trying to affect the policies of society. *Norrtullsligan* (1908; The Norrtull League) brings to literature the hitherto unexplored circumstances of unmarried female office workers, and *Pennskaftet* (1910; The penholder) energetically pleads the cause of women's right to vote. Wägner also considered peace and disarmament important issues for feminists. Ludvig Nordström's journalistic volume *Lort-Sverige* (1938; Filth-Sweden) caused a sensation by exposing unsanitary living conditions in the Swedish countryside.

The male *tiotalister* shared a fascination with economics. In Nordström's Totalist utopia, economically successful people are good people. Technological advancement and industrialization have a positive value. In a more cynical mood, Nordström exposes the flaws of "Credit-Sweden" in *Planeten Markattan*. The overextension of credit and incidents of bankruptcy are common disasters in the novels of the *tiotalister*. Gustaf Hellström's Lekholm family suffers from bankruptcy, and it takes two generations for them to recover and begin to realize the dream of social mobility that was the original idea of Lekholm the Lace Maker. In his masterpiece, *Selambs* (1920; Eng. tr. *Downstream*, 1922), Siwertz provides a chilling study of the egoism of a family of rapacious capitalists. In general, Siwertz views industrialization positively; city expansion and the investment of capital are good and useful enterprises. Capitalism goes wrong when ethics fail to prevent a fall into a Darwinian state of nature where only the fittest survive. Tord Selamb, a man who has read too much Nietzsche and Darwin, degenerates into a ruthless animal on his windswept island in the skerries. Although less obvious about their animalistic greed, his siblings are just as heartless in their pursuit of money. The Selamb dynasty collapses under the weight of its avarice; it is a source of comfort that the only heir to the Selamb fortune is the ethical Georg Hermansson.

The "mass egoism" Siwertz fears is socialism. One of the potential heirs of the Selamb fortune is Peter Selamb's unsavory illegitimate son, who was raised in a slum. As Siwertz presents him, the child of the working class is clearly an unsuitable steward of society. Peter's son will meet his end as a drunk. In general, the *tiotalister* looked on the working class with suspicion, if not fear. Sven Lidman maintained his affinity for the aristocracy from his youthful decadent phase and wrote a five-part series about the aristocratic family Silfverstååhl. In his novel *Köpmän och krigare* (1911; Merchants and warriors), he sees the aristocrats taking over the powerful role of the capitalists and maintaining their superior position in society. Lidman became disenchanted with capitalism and the general direction in which society was moving. In *Huset med de gamla fröknarna* (1918; The house with the old ladies), he writes bitterly, "Modern society no longer consists of nobility, clergy, burghers, and farmers, but has changed its form of representation and gone over to a democratic two-chamber system: the rich and the poor." Lidman's sympathy is hardly with the proletariat; it is rather with the impoverished aristocracy. The old gentlewomen of his novel must quietly and heroically defend themselves from the crass and barbaric advances of a capitalist society.

The *tiotalister*'s faith in industrialization and humankind's ability to create a better world was seriously shaken by World War I. Industry produced war machines for the purpose of destruction, not progress. Civilization had not progressed far enough to prevent humanity from reverting to the behavior of the Darwinian jungle. Siwertz at first approved of the war as a heroic and nationalistic enterprise, but the realities of the conflict changed his romantic notions, and his mistrust of human nature and capitalism is vented in *Selambs*. Eventually, his optimism reasserted itself in his later popular fiction. Nordström retained his optimistic Totalist vision, although he came to acknowledge the presence of losers in the economic system.

Elin Wägner considered war a male preoccupation, and in *Släkten Jerneploogs framgång* (1916; The success of the Family Jerneploog), she urges women to band together in protest against the war. In *Dialogen fortsätter*

(1932; The dialogue continues), Wägner argues that admitting women into political life is an important step toward abolishing war. In *Åsa-Hanna*, generally viewed as her best novel, the war causes Wägner to meditate over the difficulties of remaining a good person in a world filled with evil. There is in Wägner's authorship an increased interest in individual psychological and moral struggles, as in *Den namnlösa*; here the troubled individuals living in the parsonage form yet another microcosm with general validity.

Gustaf Hellström also treats a private moral struggle in *Carl Heribert Malmros* (1931). Malmros is a policeman who plays peacemaker in a small-town labor conflict. He incurs the enmity of both sides and is condemned to social isolation, which results in his suicide. Even in *Snörmakare Lekholm*, Hellström showed signs of a growing skepticism toward the progress of modern society. Staffan Lekholm, the most promising member of the next generation of Lekholms, is killed at the end of the novel in a motorcycle accident, a victim of modern technology. In *Storm över Tjurö* (1935; Storm over Tjurö), Hellström's skepticism has turned into pessimism. A little island in the skerries is ruined by the arrival of summer guests and the economic competition they introduce among the natives. The island becomes a microcosm of Europe on the verge of the Second World War.

Hjalmar Bergman (1883–1931) has much in common with the *tiotalister* and is typically included in it, but his dark world view and narrative innovations set him apart. He is dealt with separately in the context of the onset of modernism in Sweden.

The First Generation of Working-Class Writers

Although the so-called *arbetarförfattare* are usually treated together, they do not make up a particularly homogeneous group. The individual members displayed considerable differences in literary styles and political outlook. Their common working-class backgrounds provided them with a different view of society from that of the *tiotalister*. As members of the working class, they were better acquainted with the toll that industrialism had taken in terms of monotonous labor and worker exploitation. Although they tended to share a belief in the human will and humankind's creative potential, the working-class writers understood that the will can be too easily squelched by abysmal material circumstances. Their writing often bears witness to a stylistic freshness in comparison with the standard realism of the *tiotalister*. It is more concerned with expressing the hitherto unexpressed than with traditional literary procedure.

The working class had received literary treatment before, but not from the inside. Maria Sandel could write from her own experience of the strain of tedious labor and the vulnerability of proletarian women in a male-dominated society in *Droppar i folkhavet* (1924; Drops in the sea of humanity) and *Mannen som reste sig* (1927; The man who stood up). Women were relegated to the periphery of the workers' movement, and Sandel called for the inclusion of women in worker solidarity. She could also give expression to the frustrations of the failed general strike of 1909 in *Virveln* (1913; The whirlpool). Gustav Hedenvind-Eriksson drew from his own experience as a lumberjack, a navvy, and a jack-of-all-trades in northern Sweden in *Ur en fallen skog* (1910; From a felled forest) and *Vid Eli vågor* (1914; By the waves of Eli). Technically, Martin Koch had his roots in the lower middle class, but he rebelled and worked for a time as a house painter. He demonstrates a passionate identification with the working class throughout his writing. *Arbetare. En historia om hat* (1912; Workers: A story of hate) was written in the aftermath of the disappointing general strike. At the beginning of the novel, the narrator observes the parade of the "faceless masses" on their way to work. Gradually, this amorphous group is endowed with faces, names, and destinies.

Working-class writers occasionally found it necessary to invent new forms of expression to depict a sphere of existence that had no literary precedents. In some cases, the result is drastic realism; in others, expressive symbolism. The writing of Koch and Hedenvind-Eriksson comes very close to a modernist approach. In *Arbetare*, Koch makes use of shocking metaphors to describe the figures on the street. For example, he writes of a run-down alcoholic couple: "They resemble two filthy sex organs that thoroughly understand one another." Such a metaphor would be unthinkable in the writing of the *tiotalister*. Koch uses another evocative metaphor to describe some of the workers: "There are men who resemble machines and are nothing but machines—huge, enormous, with hard muscles connected to thick limbs. When they laugh, there is a noise like steam being released, teeth gleam as though greased with fat and oil between an occasional black rotten hole in the maul." It is a short step from Koch's drastic metaphors to expressionism.

Koch's major novel, *Guds vackra värld. En historia om rätt och orätt* (1916: God's beautiful world: A story of right and wrong), follows the unsavory career of the thief Frasse Karlsson-Gyllenhjelm, which ends with his suicide. World War I robbed Koch of his faith in ultimate human goodness, yet he felt that evil should be confronted without blinking. Working-class writers showed great respect for the power of language: the person who expresses himself well can achieve what he wants; those who lack the words stay where they are. Frasse becomes imprisoned in his thief's jargon: "With this dismal language, through whose thick muck no beam of spiritual light can force its way into his consciousness and no glimmer can work its way out—with this he lives." The ninth section of the novel, "At the bottom of the sea," shows strong traces of expressionism. Here the author seeks to enter the subjective realities of the men in prison. One man has killed his wife over a few hundred hard-earned crowns and feels he was right to do so. Koch reveals the black farce of the justice system, which imposes the same set of rules and punishment on widely varying individuals and circumstances. Frasse's opposite is Sven Lilje, a student of philosophy who believes in "God's beautiful world," where man is recognized and respected for his human value and not used as a tool and instrument. Sven's idealism and faith in humankind is shaken when his fiancée is raped and murdered. The novel ends with the moral that one must persist in working for the good, despite the evil in the world.

Hedenvind-Eriksson also experienced World War I as a great shock, but his optimism and faith in human goodness remained intact. After the war, he abandoned straightforward realism and adopted a symbolic, coded, allegorical form of writing. In his first novel after the war, *Tiden och—en natt* (1918; Time and—a night), a snowstorm could be seen as symbolizing the onslaught of World War I. Hedenvind-Eriksson departs from ostensible realism in *En dröm i seklets natt* (1919; A dream in the century's night), whose middle section is a ghostly, dreamlike vision with abrupt scene changes. After the Second World War, he dropped political allegories and turned to the timeless sphere of saga and myth in such books as *Jämtländska sagor* (1941; Jämtland tales) and *Sagofolket som kom bort* (1946; The saga people who vanished). The author found the medium of realism inadequate for expressing universal truths. His unfailing sense of optimism sets him apart from the mainstream of modernism with which he shared some technical concerns.

The working-class writers divided their attention between existential questions and social and political issues. The givens of society are highly questionable. How does one find one's way and make moral choices under adverse material circumstances? Ragnar Jändel approached this and other questions in his poetry and in autobiographical novels such as *Vägledare* (1921; Guide), *Det stilla året* (1923; The quiet year), and *Jag och vi* (1928; I and we). *Barndomstid* (Childhood) was published in 1936, when the younger generation of working-class writers was making the autobiographical genre popular. *Den trånga porten* (1924; The narrow gate) traces the development of a disadvantaged boy into an author. Sten Erling experiences as a youth the power of words and becomes politically active. After working for a political newspaper for a time, he comes to a realization: "He understood that there was something in human beings that had nothing to do with society and social conditions. . . . He saw that man was first and last alone, alone with his mystery, with life, with death or—if one wanted or was able to say it—with God." This realization results in the decision to focus on his own authorship rather than on political writing. His comrades feel he has betrayed them and their cause.

Dan Andersson is the poet of proletarian lamentations. Much of the working-class poetry at the time resembled battle hymns meant to incite workers to fight for the revolution and to urge solidarity. Andersson is more interested in the existential weariness of individuals whose daily life is a struggle. He lends the dignity of the poetic genre to the working class: "There are no words for the song / about those who have lived hidden" ("Strid och vår" [1913; Strife and spring]). Andersson's poems often contain a mixture of the shocking and the sublime, as in "Sista natten i Paindalen" (The last night in Paindal), from *Kolvaktarens visor* (1915; Eng. tr. *The Charcoal-Burner's Ballad and Other Poems*, 1943). Berg, a charcoal burner, lies on his deathbed reviewing his life; he feels remorse for having beaten his wife and cries with stirring pathos: "Am I an animal or a man, soot or earth?" "Spelmannen" (The fiddler), in *Svarta ballader* (1917; Black ballads), is worlds apart from Karlfeldt's cheerful Fridolin: "I play in order to forget that I exist." Andersson's poetry is characterized by melancholy and at times a latent death wish. As fate would have it, the poet met with a premature accidental death in a hotel in Stockholm. His beautiful and rhythmic poetry has been set to music and has won lasting popularity, in the best sense of the word.

TRADITION VERSUS INNOVATION: THE CRADLE OF SWEDISH MODERNISM

"Modernism" is a difficult term to define because of the great variety of its manifestations. The concept can be approached from three different angles. To begin with, modernism represents a new way of thinking about the world. Modern life brought such rapid and fundamental changes that traditional views of humanity, God, government, and art proved inadequate. From a different viewpoint, modernism in literature may be characterized by a system of formal innovations and tendencies. From yet a third angle, "modernism" may be used to designate a literary period, the parameters of which are widely debated; they vary greatly depending on whether or not an international or a national perspective is applied. A work of art that falls in the intersection of all three of these approaches might be labeled "modernist" without reservation.

In the wake of Charles Darwin, science replaced God as a purveyor of meaning and order in the world. In the modernist world view, however, science is suspect. Rapid developments in technology result in the dehumanization of large portions of society and the increased aggressiveness that culminates in the First World War. Science becomes a tool of the powerful, not a guarantor of order. With the loss of divine order and meaning, the world is perceived as inherently absurd, chaotic, and meaningless. An overview of creation is no longer possible, only fragmented perceptions. All human order is seen as an imposition on the chaotic disorder of life. The modernist abyss recurs as a symbol of the dizzying threat of meaninglessness that haunts human existence.

The artistic act is central to modernism, since it represents a creation of order, or an attempt to perceive the world. Modernist art possesses a high degree of self-consciousness: art is not reality. Terms such as "metapoetry," "metafiction," and "metatheater" refer to poems about poems, novels that examine their own fictional genesis and process, and dramas that break with theatrical illusion. Traditional literary forms are deemed insufficient for the new age. Special value is placed on formal experimentation and innovation. Realism is no longer considered viable. The artist does not report a world; he or she creates it. The relation between language and the external world is problematic; as a result, issues of communication and subject/object relationships are highly complex. The artist is no longer a member of a community but an outsider, subject to alienation and angst.

The formal innovations of modernism brought about an unparalleled renewal of literature. Each genre adapted to the new world view in its own way. Poetry became the favored genre of modernists, although the role of the poet had changed drastically. Ingemar Algulin has identified an "Orphic retreat" in modernist poetry: the poet is no longer a divine oracle who sings of the harmony and unity of creation. Nor does he celebrate the culture to which he belongs. Modernist poetry eliminates the long epic poem and adopts a non-narrative, compressed format. The poem is no longer a public utterance but an intimate act of communication or, in T. S. Eliot's definition, "the voice of the poet talking to himself, or to nobody." The concentrated format of modernist poetry is an arena for exploring the subject/object relationship, for testing the limits of language, and for finding a new poetic idiom.

Modernist poetry abandons many of the structuring methods of traditional poetry: rhyme, meter, division into stanzas. Within the general mode of free verse, modernist poets may experiment with alogical, musical, or compressive structures. Musical structure does not imply that a poem should be sung. On the contrary, poetry has shifted from vocal lyric to instrumental, replacing the rhythmic and melodious tones of traditional poetry with repetition, counterpoint, and other analogous features of musical composition. Again according to Algulin, compression is a central technique of modernist poetry. It may take the form of syntactic compression, which is the use of words or phrases laden with specific associations for the reader; allusive compression, which entails references to traditional literature and the cultural complexes they represent; and visual compression, which may include different kinds of typographical experimentation. Finally, modernist poetry makes use of associative imagery that goes beyond the traditional functions of ornamentation or characterization. An image is often meaningful in itself, expressing thoughts or feelings beyond the reach of verbal explication.

The novel was perceived by many to be the heir of the epic, the genre that depicts a broad panorama of life and provides a coherent account of events, all from a settled, ethical viewpoint. The modernist world view called the very possibility of the epic into question and brought about a crisis in the novel. A preoccupation with the problems of representing reality in narrative produced novels self-consciously aware of the complexities of their own form and the fictionalization process. Modernist experiments often depart from a logical, sequential, chronological, plot-centered structure. Modernist prose, in its concern with the representation of inward states of mind, resorts to stream-of-consciousness narration, surrealist imagery, or the problematic first-person narration, to name only a few possible approaches; the new psychoanalytic theories play an obvious role in these explorations of consciousness. The relationship between the narrator and the reader is no longer self-evident. The narrator may not be a reliable guide to events, and thus the reader must participate in deciphering or creating the meaning of the text.

Modernist drama seeks to move away from the illusion of the missing fourth wall of naturalist drama. The stage may become an arena for the interaction of symbolic or dreamlike figures. The nonverbal potential of the theater experience is fully used: silence, stage design, costume, mime, and music. Communication is problematic; dialogue may be superseded by monologues. The audience no longer sits securely in the darkness of the auditorium but may be addressed or otherwise drawn into the performance experience. The real is contrasted with the illusory, as in Brechtian drama, in which actors step out of their roles in order to break the theater illusion.

Modernist drama need not depict a course of action designed to conform to Aristotelian structure but may instead explore moods, present fragments, or remain static. A crisis in social values makes the possibility of tragedy or comedy problematic. Instead, modernist drama may experiment with the absurd, tragicomedy, black comedy, or some other variation.

Literary scholars have spilled a good deal of ink trying to establish the dates of a modernist literary period. "Premodernist" traits can be located in the literature of romanticism, as well as earlier works stretching as far back as Plato's *Symposium*. "Postmodernism" is still in the process of defining itself but has not done so in a manner that enables us to identify a "death year" for modernism. Attempts have been made to trace international modernism in the twentieth century to around 1910, the following two decades marking a peak with the appearance of various -isms: futurism, surrealism, dadaism, vorticism, concretism, and so forth. The picture is rather different from a Swedish perspective. Scholars generally agree in identifying the 1940s as the modernist decade in Swedish literature, despite earlier isolated manifestations around the time of World War I.

Why did modernism take so long to establish itself in Sweden? The reasons are many and complex, but one may point to two significant factors: the vitality of traditional literary forms in Sweden, and Sweden's policy of neutrality during the two world wars. During the 1910s, three of the pillars of the Swedish Golden Age were still literarily active: Heidenstam, Lagerlöf, and Karlfeldt. The writers of the 1890s generation began their literary careers as rebels of the imagination, but by the 1910s, they had become members of the literary establishment and living national monuments. Karlfeldt became permanent secretary of the Swedish Academy in 1912 and, as such, an important arbiter of public taste. The most influential literary critic at the time, Fredrik Böök (1883–1961), was a conservative partisan of the 1890s generation. He supported the middle-class realists and the idyllic poets but reacted with hostility or incomprehension to signs of modernism.

For most of the Western world, World War I (1914–18) was the cataclysm that galvanized modernist movements and confirmed the modernist view of the world. Sweden's policy of neutrality served as a buffer against this central experience of Western culture, whereas her neighbor to the east, Finland, endured the trauma of the Russian Revolution (1917) and the Finnish Civil War (1918). This cultural upheaval opened the gates for a strong school of Finland-Swedish modernist poets. Because of its isolation, Sweden was better able to adhere to its literary tradition, and the cultural impact of the world war was delayed.

Pär Lagerkvist perceived the import of the war immediately (just as he would be among the first to warn of the threat of another war in the 1930s): "What a wave of brutality has broken over us, devastating, transforming!" (*Modern teater*, 1918). Birger Sjöberg described the impact of World War I as follows: "Then came a time, that tramped on the ground, / and traditions got split and broken" (*Kriser och kransar*, 1926). The majority of Swedish authors, however, may have experienced the war as Hjalmar Bergman's Jac Tracbac, "who knew about as much about the World War as a blind and deaf man knows about a volcanic eruption— a general, incomprehensible shaking and trembling" (*Clownen Jac*, 1930). The wave of World War I that washed away the edifices of tradition in other countries, clearing the way for modernist experimentation, did not reach Sweden. The foundations of tradition were undermined, but the structures still stood. Therefore, the Swedish pioneers of modernism were engaged in a more intensive struggle with tradition than their European counterparts. The last bastions of tradition crumbled after the onslaught of the Second World War.

Hjalmar Bergman

Hjalmar Bergman (1883–1931) has long been placed by critics among the middle-class realists of the 1910s, and with some reason. Like Nordström, he frequently returned to a small-town milieu, Wadköping, to chart the foibles of Swedish society in general. Like Hellström and Siwertz, he wrote family chronicles that reflect a larger social context. Bergman's father was a bank director, and the author could trace the flow of money in society as well as any *tiotalist*. Contemporary critics of Bergman complained of a lack of realism in his novels, however. His vision of reality did not coincide with prevailing taste. The *tiotalister* were generally optimists; Bergman was a pessimist whose stories usually end on a dissonant note. While his colleagues rediscovered the will, he believed in determinism. The *tiotalister* employed omniscient narrators who could explain cause and effect to the reader; Bergman's narrators are sometimes unreliable and leave important things unsaid, and the reader is faced with the unaccustomed task of helping decipher the text. Bergman is best loved as a humorist, but his humor has a quality different from that of his colleagues. From a superior vantage point, the *tiotalist* narrator pokes gentle fun at the inhabitants of the world. Bergman's narrator is not superior but a part of an essentially cruel and absurd world in which tragedy hides behind a mask of comedy.

Without subscribing to modernism in any programmatic fashion, Bergman incorporated in himself many of its conflicts and concerns. His perception of the world was essentially modernist and clashed violently with the traditional bourgeois values with which he was raised. For him, the modernist struggle with the weight of tradition was personal and a matter of life and death. Like most modernists, Bergman possessed a keen interest in formal issues; his narrative experiments were unprecedented in Sweden and remarkable even from an international perspective.

Bergman's youthful works—*Maria, Jesu moder* (1905; Mary, Mother of Jesus), *Solivro* (1906), *Blå blommor* (1907; Blue flowers), *Junker Erik* (1908; Squire Erik), and *Savonarola* (1909)—give little evidence of formal experimentation, but in *Hans nåds testamente* (1910; Eng. tr. *The Baron's Will*, 1968), Bergman begins to find his own style. On the realistic level, the novel is an amusingly told tale of complicated family relationships. The eccentric Baron Bernhusen de Sars wants to play matchmaker between his illegitimate daughter, Blenda, and his housekeeper's son, Jacob, and to leave them all his money, thereby irritating his detestable sister, Julia, whose sons expect to inherit the Baron's fortune. On the mythical level, the Baron attempts to play God in his own little Garden of Eden and seeks to write a happy scenario for his Adam and Eve. The snake, in the form of his sister, arrives on the scene, teaches Blenda and Jacob shame and succeeds in shattering the idyll. Blenda likes only stories with happy endings and refuses to marry Jacob because she does not think that their marriage will make a good story. Happy endings do not exist in Bergman's world; in his next novel, *Vi Bookar, Krokar och Rothar* (1912; We Books, Kroks, and Roths), we meet Blenda again as the discontented wife of Per Hyltenius, Julia's son. *Hans nåds testamente* can be read as comic realism. Its modernist flavor lies in the shattering of the harmonious romantic fiction by the absurdity of life and the self-reflective discussion of happy endings.

Vi Bookar, Krokar och Rothar is Bergman's counterpart to the great financial chronicles of his contemporaries, but his interpretation of the finance circles was not received favorably. In this story of greed and exploitation, everyone, on all levels of society, is selfish and looks after his own interests, including the alleged moralists. The problems of the workers' slums are not solved through careful management and planning. Money becomes available because Blenda Hyltenius cynically purchases Abraham Krok as her lover. The fates of many people are decided by an erotic whim.

Bergman's formal experiments became more daring during the years of World War I. At about this time, his father died without leaving an inheritance, and Bergman was forced to try to live by his pen. In *Loewenhistorier* (1913; Loewen stories), he traces the decline of a failed artist, Leonard Loewen. The portrait of an artist is a favorite genre of self-reflective modernists, such as Franz Kafka (1883–1924), who wrote "Der Hungerkünstler"

(1922; The hunger artist), and James Joyce (1882–1941), who wrote *A Portrait of the Artist as a Young Man* (1916). Bergman's treatment of the theme of the artist culminates in his last novel, *Clownen Jac*. The cryptic first-person narrative of *Loewenhistorier* adds to the "modern" impact. In *Komedier i Bergslagen* (3 vols.; 1914–16; Comedies in Bergslagen), Bergman continues his formal experimentations. *Två släkter* (1914; Two families) possesses an expressionistic quality, and *Dansen på Frötjärn* (1915; The dance at Frötjärn) is a Lagerlöf pastiche. *Knutsmässo Marknad* (1916; St. Knut's Fair) is considered one of his narrative masterpieces. The author here plays with the concepts of comedy and tragedy. A performance of Voltaire's tragedy *Zaïre* constitutes an ironic parallel to events in the story. The bizarre quirks of actors and audience make the tragedy quite funny. That is a summation of Bergman's own literary technique in a nutshell. In *Mor i Sutre* (1917; Mother of Sutre), he experiments with unreliable narration. Narrative statements that the reader is accustomed to accepting as objectively true turn out to have a subjective cast.

Independently of Pär Lagerkvist and the German expressionists, Bergman wrote during 1916–17 a group of dramas with distinctly expressionist qualities. Less abstract than Lagerkvist's dramas, Bergman's plays present characters who are highly symbolic but still shown in their social context. Some vestiges of traditional dramatic form remain. Bergman gives a group of three dramas the collective title "Marionette Plays" (2 vols.; 1918–19), borrowing the favorite symbol of the fin-de-siècle determinists. The forces that determine the fate of Bergman's characters are not predictable, scientifically established instincts, however, but irrational, cruel, and uncontrollable powers. The "Marionette Plays" are *Dödens arlekin* (1917; Death's harlequin), *En skugga* (1917; A shadow), and *Herr Sleeman kommer* (1917; Eng. tr. *Mr. Sleeman Is Coming*, 1944). Three additional plays were written about the same time but not published until 1923: *Spelhuset* (The gaming house), *Vävaren i Bagdad* (The weaver of Baghdad), and *Porten* (The gate). Bergman was very much in the mainstream of modern drama; his plays met with only qualified acceptance by the public and the theater establishment.

The most modernistic of Bergman's novels, *En döds memorarer* (1918; A dead man's memoirs), has a highly sophisticated narrative and a complex symbolic network. A childhood reminiscence with mythic undertones dissolves into a surreal perception of adulthood. Here Bergman pursues the antimimetic direction of modernist prose. In one scene, the narrator meets himself dressed as a sailor from a toy ship he had in his childhood; in another scene, his father's watch loses its hands but continues to run.

Such experimentations with time, stemming from the Bergsonian distinction between mechanical time measured by clocks and subjective time as experienced by the individual, is characteristic of modernist prose.

In retrospect, Bergman's modernistic experimentation emerges as an artistic triumph. At the time, his works were commercial disasters, a serious problem for a man forced to make a living from his pen. Concealing once again his dark philosophy behind the mask of comedy, he experienced his first popular success with *Markurells i Wadköping* (1919; Eng. tr. *God's Orchid*, 1924). The novel is a comic masterpiece of enduring popularity. The account of Harald Hilding Markurell's megalomania and his blatant attempts to secure through bribery the successful outcome of his beloved son's matriculation exam is high comedy. The hilarity of the novel masks what is essentially a double tragedy: the ruin of Markurell's adversary and Markurell's own painful realization that it is not he but his adversary who is the biological father of his adored son.

Herr von Hancken (1920; Mr. von Hancken) is a jovial, historical pastiche set in 1806, in which Bergman parodies the tone of Frederik Cederborgh's picaresque novels. As in *Markurells in Wadköping*, it is ultimately the story of the protagonist's painful self-realization and reconciliation. The same could be said of the masterly *Farmor och Vår Herre* (1921; Eng. tr. *Thy Rod and Thy Staff*, 1937). The third-person narration, the customary tool of the omniscient narrator, is deceptive, and the picture that emerges of Grandmother, the Borck matriarch, has been filtered through her memory and consciousness. Grandmother perceives herself as a competent administrator of her family's affairs, but the chorus of complaints by relatives at the end of the novel makes it evident that she has been a tyrannical egoist. She falls from power at the hands of her greedy and unsympathetic relatives. Chastised, she gains the ability to listen and accepts the affection of her grandson Nathan, the only family member who was not dependent on her.

A similar theme is present in *Chefen Fru Ingeborg* (1924; Eng. tr. *The Head of the Firm*, 1936), in which the protagonist's insights prove fatal. The narrator collaborates in the attempts of Ingeborg to repress the knowledge that she is passionately in love with her future son-in-law, a moral nihilist. As in other works, Bergman invokes the mechanisms of Greek tragedy in this story of a modern Phaedra; however, tragic fate is determined not by anthropomorphic gods but by random, uncontrollable forces. Ingeborg sees her repressed passion in the symbolic guise of a beggar and a forest fire. Unable to reconcile her illicit love with her bourgeois values and sensibilities, she commits suicide.

The style of Bergman's plays changed radically after the failure of his expressionist experiments. He succeeded in the theater with fairly simple comedies, such as *Swedenhielms* (1925; Eng. tr. 1968), *Patrasket* (1928; Riffraff), and dramatizations of *Hans nåds testamente, Markurells i Wadköping*, and *Farmor och Vår Herre*. In the 1910s and 1920s, the Swedish film industry was experiencing a golden age and produced such famous artists as directors Victor Sjöström (1879–1960) and Mauritz Stiller (1883–1928) and actress Greta Garbo (1906–90). Bergman was intrigued by the artistic potential of the cinema. He felt that in film one could "let the story flow as it wants and float just as capriciously, surprisingly, illogically as life itself." He wrote numerous scenarios for silent films, although his initial artistic ambitions were thwarted by the director, who had final say. Bergman's involvement in the film industry resulted in a brief sojourn in Hollywood in 1923. In the late 1920s, as his health declined because of the abuse of alcohol and drugs, he produced some uneven novels that seemed to court public success: *Flickan i frack* (1925; The girl in tails and tie), *Jonas och Helen* (1926; Jonas and Helen), *Kerrmans i Paradiset* (1927; Kerrmans in Paradise), and *Lotten Brenners ferier* (1928; Lotten Brenner's holidays).

Bergman's last novel, *Clownen Jac* (1930; Eng. tr. *Jac the Clown*, 1995), can be read as a lengthy epitaph of his literary career. The artist is a clown who uses his own fear to earn money and make the public laugh. The novel is a bitter commentary on modern society in which public appeal and commercial value are the criteria by which art is judged. Jac the Clown, whom we met as Nathan in *Farmor och Vår Herre*, lives in a huge mansion in southern California, for Bergman the center of the superficial art market. In one performance, Jac tries to confront his audience directly, revealing the tricks of his trade and the sadism inherent in humor. The audience becomes hostile, and Jac realizes that it is a mistake to be honest with one's audience. He replaces his confessional monologue with a simple, slapstick sketch with an uplifting moral. The public loves it. This episode parallels the public failure of Bergman's own experimental period and the subsequent success of his facile comedies. Resigned, Bergman endorses bourgeois values over the crazed life of the artist, as illustrated by the fate of the sisters Caroline and Sanna. Caroline, the daughter of solid bourgeois parents, is a picture of health and good nature, whereas Jac's illegitimate daughter, Sanna, is transported to California and becomes a grotesque caricature of her father the artist. Thus Bergman ends his career with a highly pessimistic view of the future of art.

Pär Lagerkvist

Pär Lagerkvist (1891–1974) is considered one of the pioneers of Swedish modernism. In 1913, the young author traveled to Paris, where he encountered the latest movements in modern art, particularly cubism. The resulting essay, *Ordkonst och bildkonst* (1913; Verbal art and pictorial art), is a landmark of modernist aesthetics in which Lagerkvist argues against realism and the limits it imposes on the poet's imagination. The artist should be allowed to create worlds no one has ever seen. Personal, confessional, and psychological considerations should be replaced by aesthetic concerns and universal issues. The modern artist might profitably derive inspiration from primitive art and such models as the Bible, Icelandic sagas, eddic poetry, and Oriental art.

Lagerkvist made his literary debut with *Människor* (1912; People), an emotional tale about a tormented individual and his love/hate relationship to his family. In *Två sagor om livet* (1913; Two tales about life) and *Motiv* (1914; Motifs), Lagerkvist makes uneven attempts to put his own aesthetic theories into practice. *Järn och människor* (1915; Eng. tr. *Iron and Men*, 1988) is a collection of short stories about World War I. The author omits specific details that identify where the stories take place. The effect is a commentary on the mechanisms of war in general. The bloody, inhuman nature of war is a product of technological advancement and the invention of new and terrifying war machines. Vulnerable human flesh is effectively contrasted with hard and destructive iron.

Lagerkvist's artistic breakthrough came with his poetry collection *Ångest* (1916; Anguish). From the fragments of tradition the poet builds a monument to modernist angst. The stark, hostile landscape of the title poem is an expressionistic materialization of the inner anguish of the poet. The view of the world that informs the rest of the collection is modernistic in its darkness, sense of isolation, and antimimetic imagery. At the same time, Lagerkvist keeps a tight hold on the building blocks of tradition. In *Ångest* and subsequent collections, he makes use of rhythmic, rhymed, hymnlike meters. In many cases the modernistic sensibility of a poem contrasts with the ordered rhythm of the form. "Nu löser solen sitt blonda hår" (Now the sun loosens her blond hair), from *Kaos* (1919; Chaos), borrows the traditional form and imagery of hymns only to undermine the comforting message. The beauty of spring and the early morning hour is not a sign of God's grace but rather an accident of astronomy and physics. Although Lagerkvist may at times use language and imagery hitherto unknown in poetry (such as "stinking refuse heap!"), he generally obeys the rules of syntax.

Lagerkvist's contribution to theater is as original as his contribution to poetry. In the essay *Modern teater* (1918; Eng. tr. *Modern Theatre*, 1961), the author argues for a dramatic form to represent the new age, which is chaotic, violent, and fantastic. The practice of peering through the transparent fourth wall of naturalistic drama cannot do justice to the times. In pretending to create a secure illusion of reality, naturalistic drama fails to use the full potential of the theater. Stage scenery should not merely create a mood or a realistic illusion; it should spring from the imagination of the artist as a meaningful component of the work of art. Lagerkvist dismisses the plays of Ibsen and holds up Strindberg's late dramas as a source of inspiration. He is aware of the early expressionist theater in Germany, but he criticizes Max Reinhardt for lacking a consistent aesthetic program.

In his own first plays, Lagerkvist gives expression to a vision marked by the confusion, brutality, and darkness in the wake of the First World War. *Sista människan* (1917; Eng. tr. *The Last Man*, 1988) shows an eerie, unrealistic stage landscape; it suggests a frozen, desolate earth following some major catastrophe that has left everything in ruins. Among the ruins, barely human creatures scrape out an existence in hostile competition. The main character, Gama, is blind, and his physical affliction is also a symbol of the limitations of his spirit. He longs for contact, but his love is tainted by egoism and turns to hate. The hostility of the human condition proves fatal to the boy Ilja, a symbol of innocence, who dies when he witnesses his mother being murdered by his father. The play is a bleak and pessimistic comment on human life after the war. *Den svåra stunden* (1918; Eng. tr. *The Difficult Hour*, 1961) consists of three one-act plays dealing with the theme of death. The influence of Strindberg's *Ett drömspel* is felt in the suspension of time and space and in certain absurd touches.

The mood of *Himlens hemlighet* (1919; Eng. tr. *The Secret of Heaven*, 1966) is similar to that of *Sista människan*. The setting is a barren planet whose curved surface is populated by deformed and crazed individuals. Many of the inhabitants are seeking something: the meaning of life, a staircase to heaven, a certain coin with a hole in it, a string that will make all of life harmonious. The search is futile. The characters inhabit a modernist world where wholeness, order, and communion have been replaced by fragmentation, chaos, and isolation. The play contains symbolic figures that will reappear in subsequent Lagerkvist works: the Executioner, the Old Man Sawing Wood, and the Dwarf. Innocence, in the form of The Young Man, enters the stage but is distressed by the hostility of the inhabitants and their meaningless existence. He establishes a communion of sorts with a young woman, but when he realizes that she is mad and that their contact is an illusion, he jumps off the globe in despair, a sacrifice to the modernist abyss.

At the beginning of the 1920s, after his initial reaction of pessimism and hopelessness following the war, Lagerkvist attempts to reconcile himself with life. In *Det eviga leendet* (1920; Eng. tr. *The Eternal Smile*, 1934), he translates his antimimetic approach into prose. He returns to the same imagined afterlife he described in the last part of *Den svåra stunden*. The dead sit around in an infinite sea of darkness, alone or in small groups, and spend eternity going over their experiences in life. One among them rises and suggests that they band together to seek out God and demand of him an explanation of life's confusion and anguish. When the legions of the dead find God, he turns out to be an old man sawing wood. He humbly explains that he has not meant anything in particular with life. He simply wanted people not to have to be satisfied with nothing. A note of consolation is struck in connection with the children that God claims to have created when he was feeling happy. The innocence of the child at play brings out the eternal smile and an acceptance of the manifold richness of life. *Den lyckliges väg* (1921; The way of the happy man) continues along the path of reconciliation with poems honoring human love and expressing an affirmation of life:

> O world, how do you remain
> so dear to me,
> when you refuse
> the things I desire.

In the play *Den osynlige* (1923; The invisible one), symbolic figures enact a perpetual cycle of the human spirit: from repression toward an era of light to apocalypse. Despite an apocalyptic ending, the Invisible One identifies himself as the spirit of humankind and in his last line exits "toward light, toward light."

Onda sagor (1924; Evil tales) is a collection of short prose pieces, most of which could be labeled prose poems. The tales are concise and display a technical virtuosity of narrative presentation. "Kärleken och döden" (Love and death) is a narrative gem only a paragraph long. A first-person narrator relates the episode of his own death at the hands of a burly cherub with a crossbow. The situation is illogical and absurd but evokes the despair and pain of unrequited love. "Hissen som gick ner i helvetet" (The elevator that went down into hell) is another bizarre tale of a tawdry modern hell in which psychological torture has replaced the old-fashioned physical punishment of hellfire and brimstone. In "Far och jag" (Father and I), a mysterious train serves as a symbol for the existential anguish that separates a young boy from the secure, religious world of his father. In this tale, Lagerkvist returns to his childhood Småland. The same environment with the small-town railroad station at the center is the setting for his autobiographical novel *Gäst hos verkligheten* (1925; Eng. tr. *Guest of Reality*, 1936). The novel describes the child Anders's perceptions of life and those around him and his frantic fear of death; it follows the process of his gradual alienation from the secure religiosity of his home to the threshold of adulthood.

Hjärtats sånger (1926; Songs of the heart) manifests a growing ambivalence toward the redeeming powers of love. Tones of isolation and suffering are struck in the poems in the first half of the collection. The second half consists of poems in praise of love, "our only home." In the play *Han som fick leva om sitt liv* (1928; Eng. tr. *The Man Who Lived His Life Over*, 1971), Daniel, a shoemaker, is given a chance to do things over when his first attempt at life results in the murder of his wife, Anna, in a moment of panicked, existential claustrophobia. The second time around, Daniel is able to make it through this difficult moment with the help of Anna's love. Having successfully suppressed his own violent emotions, however, Daniel has neglected to take the despondency of his son seriously and to prevent his suicide. Although the author still makes use of an illogical "dreamplay" dramaturgy, the situation depicted in this play is not as abstract or stripped of realistic detail as those in his earlier dramas.

Earlier than most writers of his generation, Lagerkvist was disturbed by the events in Hitler's Germany that led to the Second World War. The First World War had inspired in the young author feelings of anguish, futility, and hopelessness. The mature Lagerkvist took up the cause of humanistic ideals and their defense in the face of Nazi barbarism. His campaign against Nazi ideology pervades his literary production throughout the 1930s and part of the 1940s. In the play *Konungen* (1932; Eng. tr. *The King*, 1966), the monarch of the title has been too consumed by his own spiritual doubts to try to change the traditional barbaric practices of his kingdom. When a revolution sweeps through the kingdom, the dying king admonishes a follower to believe in ideals and not to fall prey to doubt as he did. Similarly, Lagerkvist rallies to the support of ideals threatened by a political situation. *Bödeln* (Eng. tr. *The Hangman*, 1936) appeared as a novel in 1933 and as a play in 1934. The executioner of the title is the agent used by humanity to give vent to its violence and aggression. The first part of the work takes place in the Middle Ages. The hangman is sitting in a tavern, and his presence gives rise to fear and anecdotes of violence and fantastic superstitions surrounding his person. In the second part, which takes place in a jazz café in Nazi Germany, the hangman is still sitting at his table, but this time he is the object of admiration and adoration, a reminder that the barbarism and brutality of the prevailing order exceeded that of the Middle Ages. Years before the excesses of the Nazi regime were known to the public, Lagerkvist points to the consequences of such a violent ideology: café guests chat about castrating political opponents, one guest is killed because of a moment of wavering solidarity, and the members of the black jazz band are beaten and killed because they dare to eat in the same room as the white guests. Lagerkvist continued his fight for humanism with the prose works *Kämpande ande* (1930; Fighting spirit), *Den knutna näven* (1934; Eng. tr. *The Clenched Fist*, 1988), *I den tiden* (1935; In that time), and *Den befriade människan* (1939; Man liberated); with the poetry collections *Vid lägereld* (1932; By the campfire), *Genius* (1937), *Sång och strid* (1940; Song and battle), and *Hemmet och stjärnan* (1942; The home and the star); and with the dramas *Mannen utan själ* (1936; Eng. tr. *The Man without a Soul*, 1944) and *Seger i mörker* (1939; Victory in the dark).

The scope of Lagerkvist's vision and dramatic power is demonstrated in such plays as the realistic/lyrical *Midsommardröm i fattighuset* (1941; Eng. tr. *Midsummer Dream in the Workhouse*, 1953) as well as *De vises sten* (1947; Eng. tr. *The Philosopher's Stone*, 1966), a Faustian drama with post-Hiroshima echoes, and the oratorio-like *Låt människan leva* (1949; Eng. tr. *Let Man Live*, 1951).

Lagerkvist's literary production after the Second World War to the end of his life is dominated by the novels that secured his international fame. In these works, the author who referred to himself as a "religious atheist" returns to the timeless questions of good and evil, of faith and doubt. Lagerkvist's final poetry collection, *Aftonland* (1953; Eng. tr. *Evening Land*, 1975), can be read as a poetic summation of his religious probings in his late novels. Each of these novels has a historical, biblical, or mythical setting.

Dvärgen (1944; Eng. tr. *The Dwarf*, 1945), which could be seen as an epilogue to Lagerkvist's wartime writings and an attempt to assess humankind's relationship to evil, is set in Renaissance Italy, a time of the cultural strides of Leonardo da Vinci and the deadly politics of Machiavelli and the Borgia family. The narrator of the novel is the Dwarf, an agent of evil whose warped perception of people and events in the court of the Prince provides a chilling perspective. The Dwarf is most comfortable in times of war, and his master, the Prince, makes use of his talent for treachery in triumphing over his enemies and the nobler, "humanistic" side of his own nature. When the conflicts are over, the Dwarf, although he has been acting on the Prince's orders, becomes a scapegoat and is chained in the dungeon, but he is confident that the Prince cannot do without his services and that he will be called on again. The duality inherent in the Renaissance as well as in the individual human being is illustrated by the contrast between the Dwarf and the Prince, who is a humanist in the pursuits of art, science, and philosophy.

Barabbas (1950; Eng. tr. 1951) tells the story of the criminal who was released in Christ's stead. Barabbas is a rough and brutal denizen of the darkness who is momentarily dazzled by the light that surrounds Christ when he first sees him. Barabbas witnesses the crucifixion and becomes obsessed with the figure of Christ. Doctrines such as "Love thy neighbor" are foreign to Barabbas, however, and he is perplexed by the calm, spiritual happiness of some early followers of Christ. Beset by doubts, he cannot overcome his fear of death. At the end of the novel he finds himself in Rome and becomes involved in spreading a fire that he has heard was set by the Christians. He is imprisoned and condemned to be crucified. In the figure of Barabbas, the man who felt himself both drawn to Christ and repelled by him, who both wants to believe and demands rational "proof," Lagerkvist offers a spiritual self-portrait; at the same time, Barabbas could be seen to represent the existential dilemma of modern man.

Barabbas's encounter with Christ was a source of constant doubt and unease. *Sibyllan* (1956; Eng. tr. *The Sibyl*, 1958) also tells of the dubious nature of a meeting with God: "God will never abandon the person in whom he has taken up his abode, even if he only remains as a curse." Ahasuerus, the Wandering Jew, was cursed with eternal life after his one meeting with Christ. In order to gain insight into his own fate, Ahasuerus seeks out an old priestess of the Oracle at Delphi, who was driven from her service in the temple when it was discovered that she was pregnant. The sibyl, once greatly loved by the god she served, now lives a hard existence on the fringes of civilization with her idiot son. Both Ahasuerus and the sibyl have cause to wonder about the cruelty of the divine. The mysterious ending of the novel calls into question even more acutely the nature of God.

Ahasuerus reappears in the novel *Ahasverus död* (1960; Eng. tr. *The Death of Ahasuerus*, 1962), which, together with the novels *Pilgrim på havet* (1962; Eng. tr. *Pilgrim at Sea*, 1964) and *Det heliga landet* (1964; Eng. tr. *The Holy Land*, 1966), describes a spiritual pilgrimage. Ahasuerus meets Tobias, a criminal who has decided to make a pilgrimage to the Holy Land because of a dead old woman with the stigmata whom he found in the forest. Tobias's obsession with his pilgrimage makes Ahasuerus understand that there must be something holy, a sacred spring beyond our reach that God's cruel capriciousness prevents us from attaining. When Ahasuerus perceives Christ as another victim of this cruel God, he can free himself from his curse and is finally able to die. In the second novel, Tobias has bought passage with a group of pirates, among them Giovanni, to the Holy Land. Both Tobias and Giovanni are criminals and murderers, yet at the same time, good men. The same paradoxical duality or synthesis of good and evil is found in the figures of the Hangman, the Prince, Barabbas, and Ahasuerus. In *Det heliga landet*, Giovanni and Tobias are stranded in a strange region. They take up their abode in an abandoned temple. With the help of mysterious female figures, each is able to make peace with the divine. Throughout Lagerkvist's writing, women are shown to have direct contact with the wellsprings of love and the divine.

Lagerkvist's final novel, *Mariamne* (1967; Eng. tr. *Herod and Mariamne*, 1968), further explores the human paradox. Herod is a cruel and tyrannical warrior king whose only redeeming quality is his love for the good Mariamne. But it is a possessive love, and driven by jealousy and suspicion, the king has Mariamne killed. Herod is a man of the desert, Lagerkvist's symbol for spiritual desolation. He builds himself a huge temple as a bulwark against his fear of death and oblivion. But death ultimately comes to Herod after an evil life: "He was an image of mankind, who fills the earth, but whose numbers one day will be wiped from it, and as far as anyone can understand, will leave no memory behind."

Finland-Swedish Modernists

The first poetry collection of Edith Södergran (1892–1923), *Dikter* (1916; Poems), appeared the same year as Lagerkvist's ground-breaking collection *Ångest*. Whereas Lagerkvist did not find many followers in Sweden, Södergran's modernist precedent was followed by other strong Finland-Swedish poetic voices: Elmer Diktonius (1896–1961), Gunnar Björling (1887–1960), and Rabbe Enckell (1903–74), to name only the best known. The peak years of Finland-Swedish modernism extend from Södergran's debut in 1916 until shortly after 1930. In the initial years, Hagar Olsson (1893–1978), critic, novelist, and playwright, helped form a united front of modernism and met the outrage of established critics with considered aesthetic arguments. Toward the end of the peak years, the modernists produced their own journal, *Quosego* (1928–29), in which modernist aesthetics was further explicated by Rabbe Enckell. After 1930, the individuals that formed this group of modernists went on to develop in their own particular directions.

The life of Edith Södergran was brief and tragic. She endured poverty, the brutality of the Finnish Civil War, and her own slow death from tuberculosis. Much of her poetry entails a search for strength in the face of adversity and a preparation for death; feminists, Nietzscheans, and Christians can all find affirmation in the different moods of her poetic production. *Dikter* constitutes a poetic revolution. "Vierge moderne" makes successful use of the catalog technique of Walt Whitman (1819–92). "Stjärnorna" (The stars) provides an example of Södergran's concrete imagery:

> Listen, a star fell with a clang!
> Do not walk out in the grass with bare feet
> my garden is full of splinters.

The star, the traditional symbol of the ideal, shatters and becomes dangerous. At the same time, the garden is not a piece of external reality but a part of an inner landscape. Södergran is numbered among the foremost poetic expressionists.

Septemberlyran (1918; September lyre) had a controversial introduction in which Södergran declares, "I possess the power of the word and the image only with complete freedom, that is to say, at the cost of rhythm." In other words, traditional meter restricts the poet's choice of words. *Septemberlyran* parallels Vilhelm Ekelund's affirmation of free verse and acceptance of a Nietzschean heroic stance before life. "Triumf att finnas till" (Triumph of existing) gives expression to this heroic attitude toward life. Södergran often takes an ecstatic tone; she is the poet in possession of the lyre of the gods: "I am Orpheus. I can sing as I wish" ("Orpheus"). The ecstatic, almost shamanistic tone continues in *Rosenaltaret* (1919; Rose altar). In "Till fots fick jag gå genom solsystemen" (On foot I crossed the solar systems), she provides another expressionistic image of a soul as large as the universe:

> Somewhere in space hangs my heart,
> sparks fly from it, shaking the air,
> to other limitless hearts.

Framtidens skugga (1920; Shadow of the future) is more subdued and conscious of the immanence of death. Södergran died at age twenty-nine, and *Landet som icke är* (1925; The land that is not), which was published posthumously, indicates that she had turned to a religious view of death. The title poem of the collection expresses the poet's longing for a world beyond this one.

"If the purpose of art were to anesthetize, to make us forget life, then a hammer blow to the head would be the simplest and best kind of art," writes Elmer Diktonius in his debut book, *Min dikt* (1921; My poetry). Modernism and political engagement are not necessarily mutually exclusive. For the young Diktonius, political revolution and revolt against literary tradition were complementary pursuits. His signature poem "Jaguaren" (The jaguar), from *Hårda sånger* (1922; Hard songs), describes the poet's role: "To bite is necessary as long as bites give life / to rend is holy as long as rottenness stinks." The poet tears down the old to make way for the new. "Maskinsång" (Machine song), from *Stark men mörk* (1930; Strong but dark), uses a highly modern structure—a suggestive mechanical rhythm on the verge of onomatopoeia combined with verbal counterpoint—to express a critique of the dehumanization of the worker in the machine age. "Röd-Eemili" (Red Eemili), from the same collection, is a modernist ballad. The traditional form of the ballad is exploded and the grim tale of Eemili, member of the Red Guard, is told in cryptic flashes and fragments. Diktonius, an accomplished musician, used musical structuring devices such as syncopation and counterpoint in the composition of his poems. Perhaps the most obvious example of musical influences in his poetry is "Symfoni i ord" (Symphony in words), from *Gräs och granit* (1936; Grass and granite). Diktonius also proved to be an innovator in modernist prose with *Janne Kubik* (1932). The narration is characterized by elliptic phrasing, jumbled chronology, and shifting perspectives, and the novel concludes with a metafictive commentary on the composition of the work.

Södergran felt restricted as a poet by the demands of meter and rhyme. Gunnar Björling's protest against poetic limitations goes even further. Language itself is limiting. The rules of syntax and grammar impose obligations on the poet. There are not always words available to express the manifold possibilities of life. A poem from *Solgrönt* (1933; Sun green) reads as follows:

> You
> that day and the evening
> you
> the sun-illuminated
> your air-clear
> head.

There are no verbs in the poem, only gaps for the reader to fill in. Björling's poetry can be compared to an experimental laboratory in which language is broken down into its fundamental elements. The poet attempts to dispel the hierarchy of language in which nouns, verbs, and adjectives, because of their great number and variety, command the most attention. He is interested in the "cement" of language: conjunctions, pronouns, prepositions, modal verbs, and so on. Syntactic and visual compression are among Björling's most common tools.

One single poem is my book
one single poem are all my books
a poem is my life

says the poet in *Ord och att ej annat* (1945; Words and that nothing else). Life is unlimited, incomplete. When life is completed, it is dead; when a sentence is completed, it is a dead system. In Björling's work of the 1920s, the influence of dadaism is noticeable. In general, however, his production displays an impressive philosophical and aesthetic consistency from his debut in 1922 to his twentieth poetry collection in 1955.

In his articles in *Quosego*, Rabbe Enckell established himself as a modernist theoretician. In his view, modernist poetry should capture fleeting, momentary experiences through sketches, improvisation, associative flight, incoherence, or interruption. He often uses the behavior of insects and small animals to evoke his point. In a metapoetic poem about his own production in *Vårens cistern* (1931; The spring's cistern), Enckell refers to his poems as "matchstick poems" that flare up and illuminate the poet's face. To begin with, Enckell's poems are self-reflective, expressive of the poet's mental life. Through the influence of Diktonius, Enckell developed a greater interest in external reality. His use of words and imagery is concise and precise. An often-cited poem from *Landskapet med den dubbla skuggan* (1933; Landscape with the double shadow) provides an example of how Enckell with a few strokes of the pen translates a sound into words:

A bird knits fine melodies
in white air.
It shimmers brightly
and a blue thread
hangs mute in the air.

After a personal crisis in the 1930s, Enckell adopted what has been called a "classicist" view of modernist poetry; combined with this attitude was an interest in myth as a source of eternally human qualities. Eventually, Enckell came to advocate "pure poetry," that is, poetry that does not serve extra-aesthetic purposes, whether religious, political, or social.

Birger Sjöberg

When Anders Österling repudiated the decadent poetry of his youth, he called instead for a poetry of nature and everyday life, intimate, with an appreciation for detail, life affirming, and with attention focused on things in the intimate sphere. The collection Österling published toward the end of the war, *Idyllernas bok* (1917; Book of idylls), was quite popular, maybe as a welcome relief from news of the war. A number of poets followed Österling's lead and gained the collective title of *intimister* (intimate poets); among them were Sten Selander (1891–1957), Gunnar Mascoll Silferstolpe (1893–1942), and Karl Asplund (1890–1978). These poets affirmed tradition and bourgeois values and wrote of home, family, and the countryside in melodious verse. In general, their poetry was the antithesis of modernism.

In this poetic climate, Birger Sjöberg (1885–1929) made his debut with *Fridas bok* (1922; Frida's book). The subtitle of the collection reads, "Small-town songs about Frida and nature, about death and the Universe." Much of the irony in the collection relies on the juxtaposition of the limited, small-town perspective with the problems and concerns of the big, outside world. The irony is inherent in the nickname of the small town: Little Paris. Little Paris is a charming Swedish idyll, paternalistically administered by the Alderman, where amateur choral groups sing patriotic songs at their meetings. The fictive bard of Little Paris is a self-educated shop assistant who has come into contact with the world's great ideas and scientific discoveries via the encyclopedia. His muse is Frida, a representative of middle-class, Swedish values.

The shop assistant sees it as his task to enlighten Frida and to share with her the wisdom he has gleaned from his sources. Thus, some of his poems deal with the rather unusual poetic topics of Martian canals and moving pictures. One attempt to educate Frida is narrated in the poem "Samtal om Universum" (Conversation about the universe). The shop assistant lectures Frida about astronomy and implies that there is no God and that nature is capricious and arbitrary. He brushes against one of the central tenents of modernism, but the point dissolves into a personal misunderstanding between the poet and his beloved Frida, who is unable or unwilling to understand the implications of what she has been told. The lighthearted moments of *Fridas bok* far outweigh the serious moments. The poems were all set to original music by the poet and performed by him with great success. Sjöberg proved to be a disciple of Carl Michael Bellman, to whom he pays homage in the poems "Fjäriln på Haga" (The butterfly of Haga) and "I Gustav Tredjes år" (In the years of Gustav III). In *Fridas bok*, Sjöberg works within the parameters of Swedish lyric tradition and adds his own original touches. Like his *intimist* contemporaries, he paints an idyll and pays homage to traditional Swedish values, but the homage is undercut by double-edged irony.

Sjöberg's prose work, *Kvartetten som sprängdes* (1924; The quartet that exploded), is a lengthy, small-town epic written in an ironic and highly entertaining style. A cast of idiosyncratic characters weave their way through a dizzying parade of events. Beneath the humor, however, there is a perplexing undercurrent of bitterness and disillusionment. The main character, Cello, is a failed artist. He had dreams of becoming a great cellist and then a great poet, but financial necessity made him a journalist for a small-town newspaper. Cello's cozy marriage strikes one as yet another sad compromise of his artistic dreams. The interests of art are not compatible with love or money. The quartet explodes because of imprudent stock speculations and the bankruptcies of the early 1920s. The small-town idyll is shaken, but not devastated. Those who are struck by the financial blow must simply collect their energies for an economic comeback.

Sjöberg's dedication to the Swedish idyll was always equivocal, but this ambivalence was masked in irony. When critical voices railed against the escapism of the idyllic trend in Swedish poetry, Sjöberg felt personally singled out and underwent one of the most surprising lyric transformations in Swedish literary history. *Kriser och kransar* (1926; Crises and wreaths) is considered by many the most important poetry collection of the decade and a milestone in Swedish modernism. The first poems of the collection are reflections on the role of the poet. "Ej för lagrar löpa!" (Don't run after laurels!) is the title of one of the poems and the gist of Sjöberg's newfound resolve. The poet should not be concerned with popularity but should write for himself and his art. Instead of public acclaim, the poet finds his strength in the serious embrace of solitude. A series of poems, beginning with "Av raka linjen" (Of the straight line), tells the story of a respected businessman who is exposed as a criminal. The "story" is told in collage fashion; the reader pieces together the tale from episodes and images. The cryptic compression of Sjöberg's poem is modernistic. A similarly fragmented tale is told in "Konferensman" (Conference man), in which a clergyman participating in a religious conference has a nervous breakdown. His urgent question is, "What does the Lord mean?" The ordered world of the clergyman is broken down into modernist chaos. The poems of *Kriser och kransar* are not shorn of their social context. Sjöberg attacks the pillars of bourgeois culture: the poet, the businessman, the clergyman, and the teacher. In his attack on tradition, he does not abandon meter and rhyme but uses other modernist techniques such as alogical structure, compression, and associative imagery. He also experiments with language, using nonsense words, elliptic syntax, and abrupt shifts from formal language to everyday speech. It is above all Sjöberg's

innovative use of imagery that has been emulated by subsequent generations of poets.

When Sjöberg died in 1929, he left behind more than three thousand
unpublished poems. *Fridas andra bok* (1929; Frida's second book) was
published shortly after his death. The tone of this collection is not sub-
stantially different from that of the first. It includes the popular "Längtan
till Italien" (Longing for Italy) inspired by "a colorful southern landscape
on a tin of lemon drops." In "Naturlig förklaring" (Natural explanation),
however, the shopkeeper directly attacks Frida's illusions, without the usual
consideration of her feelings. The poems of *Fridas tredje bok* (1956; Frida's
third book) reveal a crumbling idyll.

"Svar på beställning" (Filling an order), in *Minnen från jorden* (1940;
Memories from Earth), is a metapoetic critique of idyllic poetry and the
commerciality of art:

> There came an order for chaffinch songs
> and some other flowery wares
> . . . In the rosewood were worms
> wiggling, black, and nimble.

The finished product is rejected by the customer because of the worms.
The title poem of *Syntaxupproret* (1956; The syntax rebellion) provides a
vision of the breakdown of language at the edge of the modernist abyss,
paradoxically expressed in rhythmic, rhymed stanzas, whereas most of the
poems in the collection tend to torture syntax more blatantly. The poet
engages in virtually untranslatable word games, such as the suggestive
juxtaposition of "amor" (amour, love) and "amortering" (amortization).
Sjöberg's contemporary audience had little appreciation for his modernist
innovations and preferred instead his Frida poetry. Not until modernism
made its breakthrough in Sweden in the 1940s did Sjöberg's inventiveness
receive full recognition.

Karin Boye

Karin Boye (1900–1941) is best known for her powerful, moving poetry,
much of which is traditional in form but modern in impact. Boye is more
of a formal innovator in her prose. She possessed a thorough knowledge of
psychoanalytic theory and underwent analysis herself. She became the poet
of dualities in the modern psyche: duty vs. desire, male vs. female, superego
vs. id, illusion vs. reality, surface vs. depth, and tradition vs. innovation.

Boye made her poetic debut with *Moln* (1922; Clouds). The collection
is dominated by rhythmic, rhymed verse, although an occasional free-verse

poem is inserted. Her debut poetry consists of elevated personal lyric, contemplative and concerned with existential problems. What is there to turn to "When our gods fall / and we stand alone among splinters," she asks with a nod to Vilhelm Ekelund's poem "Till skönheten" (To beauty). *Gömda land* (1924; Hidden lands) continues in much the same vein as her first collection. The long poem "Asar och alfer" (Aesir and elves) gives expression to one of Boye's many dualities: the Aesir rule over external phenomena and tradition; the elves rule over all that is nameless and wild. "Sköldmön" (Shield maiden) became Boye's signature poem. A shield maiden fights alongside a male warrior and falls, unnoticed by her male partner. The poem may be read as a symbolic depiction of the lot of woman in a male world; from an expressionistic perspective, it treats conflicting female and male elements in the poet's personality. The theme of the shield maiden reappears in *Härdarna* (1927; The hearths):

Armed, erect, and enclosed in armor
I went forth—
but of fear was my coat of mail made
and of shame.

The armor of the shield maiden consists of psychological defense mechanisms, but the poet claims, "I want to meet the forces of life weaponless."

In 1927, Boye became a contributor to *Clarté*, a journal with leftist political sympathies and radical aesthetic interests. Her essays demonstrate her revolt against her upper-middle-class background. In the 1930s, she turned to prose. In her first novel, *Astarte* (1931), a glance at the ocean serves as a model of our perception of daily phenomena: all we see at a glance is the surface of the water. Beneath the surface lurk unknown depths, bizarre creatures, and predators. In *Astarte*, Boye turns her glance to the myths of modern society and the depths they conceal. The gods have been demoted. The goddess Astarte is now a mannequin in a department store window, worshiped by the followers of fashion. A tweed suit with a cape broadcasts a message of practicality and romanticism. Behind this superficial image lie millennia of sacrificial lambs, ships that transport the wool, and the dockworker whose labor has contributed to the suit. The striking narrative of *Astarte* is broken up into segments that illuminate the various characters in the novel and lay bare the illusions created by movies and women's magazines.

Boye's next novel, *Merit vaknar* (1933; Merit awakens), is a psychological exposé of sex roles and marriage. *Kris* (1934; Crisis) is a radical renewal of the autobiographical novel, in a decade dominated by autobiographical novels. It tells the story of Malin Forst, age twenty, whose crisis is brought about by the disparity between her own observations about life and what she has been taught in her girls' school. Tradition and religion dictate a view of life at odds with what Malin feels and perceives. Boye uses a collage technique in her narrative. Some segments relate, in a fairly straightforward manner, Malin's deeds and thoughts, but there are also documents and dialogues addressing her crises. Thus Malin is discussed by a Medical Man, a Theologian, a Humanist, a Cactus Grower, a Nice Person, and other figures. Malin 1 argues with Malin 2, and the White and Black forces of life play a symbolic chess game over her. In modernist fashion, there is not a single objective account of Malin's struggle; the perspective is splintered.

Boye returned to poetry in *För trädets skull* (1935; For the tree's sake). Traditional meters have yielded to free verse, and the imagery is more radical, as in "Min hud är full av fjärilar" (My skin is full of butterflies). The themes of personal pain and longing are more tangible: "I am sick from poison. I am sick from a thirst, / for which nature did not provide any drink." Perhaps the best-known poem of this volume evokes the pain of transition and renewal: "Of course it hurts when buds are bursting. / Why else would spring hesitate?"

För lite (1936; Too little) is a novel written in straightforward, controlled prose. It is a portrait of an artist and explores the familiar theme of the incompatibility of art and family life. Boye's last novel, *Kallocain* (1940; Eng. tr. 1966), is a dystopia along the lines of Aldous Huxley's *Brave New World* (1932) and a reaction to the totalitarian developments in Nazi Germany and Stalinist Russia. It describes a future in which totalitarian states fight over the control of the world. In this world, "the State is everything; the individual is nothing." Boye depicts a militaristic society in which the population's only loyalty is to the State. Leo Kall, an ambitious and loyal citizen, invents a truth serum that is given the name *kallocain*. Kall is slow to realize the import of his invention. The last realm of privacy, the mind, is invaded by the State, and thoughts are subject to criminal prosecution. The novel is both a powerful political statement and a subtle study of the psychology of the individual and the possibility of human trust under totalitarianism.

Karin Boye took her own life in 1941. *De sju dödsynderna* (1941; The seven deadly sins) was published posthumously. The title poem is only a fragment, part of a meditation on sin from a psychoanalytic perspective. "De mörka änglarna" (The dark angels) expresses a hope of reconciliation for the questioning outsider.

Tradition under Siege

During the 1920s and 1930s, the literary tradition found some highly capable defenders. During World War II, in particular, many authors felt an urgent need to uphold the values of the humanistic tradition in the face of the cultural barbarism and anti-intellectualism of totalitarian states. Traditional literary choices were no longer self-evident, however. Modernist impulses from abroad and tentative experimentations inside Sweden suggested an alternative.

The relationship of Hjalmar Gullberg (1898–1961) to modernism was problematic. Educated in Lund in the 1920s, he absorbed the high-spirited atmosphere of irony and skepticism that was the hallmark of this university town. Erudite and a virtuoso of rhyme and meter, he schooled his own poetic talents by reworking masterpieces by Goethe, Racine, Heine, Baudelaire, and others into Swedish. Typical of his playful irony is his poetic suite about Adjunct Örstedt in *Ensamstående bildad herre* (1935; Eng. tr. *Gentleman, Single, Refined,* 1979). Örstedt socializes with abstract concepts in a rather concrete fashion. In one poem, he follows *das Ewig-Weibliche* (the eternal feminine) upstairs, and in another, Kant sends him *das Ding an Sich* (the thing-in-itself) through the mail. Gullberg has a particular fondness for short, narrative poems with a twist, such as "Sjön" (The lake) in *Att övervinna världen* (1937; To overcome the world).

In Gullberg's poetry, the Western cultural tradition is often represented by the gods, especially those of Greek mythology. "Vid Kap Sunion" (At Cape Sunion), from *Kärlek i tjugonde seklet* (1933; Love in the twentieth century), is an invocation of the cultural values and beauty of antiquity, whose ruins are outlined against our contemporary sky. In "Himmelsk familjebok" (Heavenly lexicon), the poet notes that the gods have fled. There is no place for them in modern society. In the aftermath of World War II and the breakthrough of modernism in Sweden, Gullberg fell silent as a poet for almost a decade. *Dödsmask och lustgård* (1952; Death mask and garden of delights) is dominated by free verse and demonstrates that he was quite capable of expressing himself in the modernist idiom. He does so with regret, however. The poet is compared to the dismembered Orpheus in "Sjungande huvud" (Singing head). The divine, harmonic music of Orpheus has abandoned the poet and poetry. All that is left are fragments. *Terziner i okonstens tid* (1958; Terza rima in the age of un-art) is a collection of poems written in the sophisticated meter of Dante in defiance of an age Gullberg deems devoid of art. In the poem "Landskapet är ett själstillstånd" (The landscape is a state of the soul), he protests against the solipsism of expressionism, which denies external reality an integrity of its own. Gullberg's last collection, *Ögon, läppar* (1959; Eyes, lips), is a solemn preparation for death, written during his final illness. His poetic idiom is here whittled down to a stark and moving simplicity.

At the beginning of his career, Johannes Edfelt (1904–) was often compared to Gullberg because of his formal strictness. His view of the world, however, lacks Gullberg's playful irony and has much in common with modernism: we are situated in chaos, in a sea of isolation, with recourse only to temporary escape. Edfelt takes issue with the modernist dictum that chaotic times require a chaotic poetic form; his resistance entails imposing poetic order on chaos and seeking values in the disorder. One source of relief from our isolation is love. In his later poetry, Edfelt seeks a possible source of order in the Jungian collective unconscious. In *Bråddjupt eko* (1947; Precipitous echo), he writes that the poet's task is to experiment, to capture in words clues that lead "to the nucleus of the self, situated under the external world's confusing rubbish." Most of Edfelt's poetry is written in stringent rhymed meter; he also writes prose poems, however, a traditional form that allows the free expression the modernists sought to achieve with free verse.

Both Edfelt and Gullberg are representatives of an erudite, elevated poetic tradition. Nils Ferlin (1898–1961) is a bohemian and more closely aligned with the traditions of folk poetry in the manner of Dan Andersson and certain of Gustaf Fröding's poetic moods. Ferlin's poetry has none of the inaccessibility and cryptic compression of modernist poetry; it is clear and often written in straightforward rhymed couplets. Many of his poems have been set to music. The poet's apparent simplicity has brought him wide popularity but has also hurt his literary reputation. Ferlin's perspective is that of the social outsider. His language is closer to slang and everyday speech than elevated poetic diction. With dark humor, he treats the themes of a rootless existence and acceptance of a meaningless life. "Stjärnorna kvittar det lika" (It makes no difference to the stars), from *En döddansares visor* (1930; Songs from a dancer of death), underscores that humanity is no longer the center of an animated universe: "The stars don't care if someone is born or dies." The title poem of *Barfotabarn* (1933; Barefoot child), "Du har tappat ditt ord" (You have lost your word), compares humankind's existential situation to a barefoot child who has lost his shopping list. The child no longer has words or direction and is chased away by the shopkeeper. In the title poem of *Med många kulörta lyktor* (1944; Eng. tr. *With Plenty of Colored Lanterns*, 1986), the poet tells how the colored lanterns of his youth all went out one by one.

Ferlin felt himself to be outside both the literary establishment and modernism, which grew to dominance in Sweden during his poetic career. He adopted an ironic adversary posture toward both. In the poem "Gammal poet" (Old poet), from *Goggles* (1938), the old poet who writes songs about nature is called old-fashioned by a modern voice. The days of traditional poetry are numbered. "När skönheten kom till byn" (When beauty came to town), from the same collection, tells the story of how Beauty is chased out of town by Wisdom. Although Ferlin never abandoned rhymed verse, he did write some free verse in later collections. In one such poem, "Frälsning" (Salvation), from *Kejsarens papegoja* (1951; The emperor's parrot), he launches a sharp attack on housebroken modernism in the form of Nobel laureate T. S. Eliot at a cocktail party, who claims that we must all be crucified in a more difficult manner than Christ.

Evert Taube (1890–1976) belongs to Sweden's strong tradition of troubadours and is one of its best-known and loved representatives. Taube always nursed ambitions of being considered a "serious artist," but his career as a performer long stood in the way of this goal. He gently defended the dignity of the troubadour by paying homage to Bellman and translating medieval Provençal troubadour verse in the 1950s. Taube began performing shortly after World War I, and his first song collection, *Sju sjömansvisor och Byssan Lull* (1919; Eng. tr. *Sea Ballads and Other Songs,* 1968), introduced his alter ego, Fritiof Anderson. Fritiof is a sailor who has had adventures and romantic entanglements in various parts of the globe. When Taube grew too old to imitate young Fritiof, he invented Rönnerdahl, a mature family man. The geographical setting of Taube's poems shifts from Bohuslän to Argentina, from Roslagen to Cuba and Italy. Common features are romantic dialogues, idyllic natural settings, dance, and an occasional shipwreck. Taube's poetry gained its renown in performance, and his songs, highly original and profoundly Swedish, lose an essential dimension without his music. Defying the accepted artistic criteria of the age in which he lived, they did not win serious recognition until the 1950s; today few people would question his inclusion in the Swedish literary canon.

Agnes von Krusenstjerna (1894–1940), the great-great-granddaughter of Erik Gustaf Geijer, was raised in the lap of tradition. She started her career as a novelist in the 1910s with some fairly thin romantic tales. Her marriage to the literary critic David Sprengel (1880–1941) resulted in a major change in her prose. Sprengel encouraged her to follow the model of the Modern Breakthrough and write realistic social criticism. Her devastatingly critical eye was turned on the faults and hypocrisies of her own upper-class world. Her suite of novels about Tony—*Tony växer upp* (1922; Tony grows up), *Tonys läroår* (1924; Tony's apprenticeship), and *Tonys sista läroår* (1924; Tony's last year of apprenticeship)—are first-person accounts based on autobiographical material. The suite constitutes a female anti-bildungsroman; instead of the traditional path of education and integration into society, Tony's road leads to disillusionment and mental breakdown. The first-person narrator relates events in the past tense with a degree of analytical distance, but during her stay in a mental hospital, her anxiety attacks are suddenly described in an immediate present tense.

In the 1930s, Krusenstjerna produced a suite of seven novels with the collective title *Fröknarna von Pahlen* (1930–35; The Misses von Pahlen). Publication of the series was interrupted by public outrage because of the author's explicit treatment of sexuality. Arguably, the furor may in part have been due to the fact that a woman was adopting the belief in the redeeming nature of the sexual drive released from moral conventions; the belief owed much to Freudian theory and was a key concept in the program of the primitivist movement in the Swedish 1930s. The interruption of the series resulted in the so-called Krusenstjerna debate, in which Karin Boye and Eyvind Johnson among others rose to the author's defense. Krusenstjerna's last suite of novels, *Fattigadel* (1935–38; Impoverished nobility), remains uncompleted because of the author's death in 1940. The series is a roman à clef in which the author unmercifully turns on her family. Krusenstjerna was not a formal innovator, but her novels provided a frontal attack on the moral weight of tradition.

Both Frans G. Bengtsson (1894–1954) and Fritiof Nilsson Piraten (1895–1972) were, like Hjalmar Gullberg, products of the student life in the Lund of the 1920s. Bengtsson, erudite poet, novelist, and essayist, in many ways picked up the baton of the 1890s. His poetry is characterized by formal elegance. He is best known for his two prose epics, however: *Karl XII* (1935–36) and *Röde Orm* (1941–45; Eng. tr. *The Long Ships*, 1954). *Karl XII* has been referred to as both a biography and a novel. In his choice of topic and admiration for the hero, Bengtsson followed in the footsteps of Verner von Heidenstam. The work is a tragic, romantic account of a major figure from Sweden's national past. The tone of *Röde Orm*, on the other hand, leans more toward comedy and lusty burlesque in the depiction of the Viking Age. The Icelandic saga style is replicated to great effect, and the telling of the picaresque adventures reveals considerable familiarity with both Old Norse and Old English sources. As an essayist, Bengtsson has few equals in Swedish literature. Some of his best-known collections are *Silversköldarna* (1931; The silver shields), *De långhåriga merovingerna* (1933; The long-haired Merovingians), and *Sällskap för en eremit* (1938;

Company for a hermit). *A Walk to an Ant Hill, and Other Essays* (1951) is a collection of selected essays in English translation.

Fritiof Nilsson Piraten's most famous book is his first, *Bombi Bitt och jag* (1932; Eng. tr. *Bombi Bitt: The Story of a Swedish Huckleberry Finn*, 1933). The novel is a tale of youthful adventure and initiation into adulthood. Piraten's work, characterized by a zest for storytelling, enjoys enduring popularity. His oeuvre contains such literary gems as *Bokhandlaren som slutade bada* (1937; The book dealer who stopped bathing) and the title story of *Småländsk tragedi* (1936; Småland tragedy). Piraten's literary world, however, is not merely idyllic; it can also be cruel, bizarre, and absurd.

LITERATURE DEMOCRATIZED:
WORKING-CLASS WRITERS OF THE 1930S
(*by Rochelle Wright*)

For more than fifty years, social scientists have examined and analyzed Sweden as an illustration of both the benefits and the flaws of the modern social welfare state. It is sometimes easy, therefore, to forget that urbanization and industrialization came late to northern Europe. As recently as the turn of this century, Sweden was primarily an agrarian nation, and a poor one. Society was highly stratified. Though compulsory schooling had largely eradicated illiteracy, a higher education was usually outside the reach of sons (let alone daughters) of impoverished parents, and without this training, middle-class professions were closed to them. Historically, living by the pen—presupposing, as it generally does, not only an education but also leisure time and some measure of underlying financial security—had been the province of the middle and upper classes. Authors from working-class backgrounds were rare; those few who found publishers for their works usually went unacknowledged either by critics or by a wider audience.

Before this century, to the degree that the common people were portrayed in literature at all, they were thus seen through the prism of the middle- and upper-class imagination. This perspective may often have been sympathetic, but it was also condescending and prone to stereotype of the sort exemplified by the title of Marie Sophie Schwartz's *Mannen av börd, kvinnan av folket* (1858; The man of noble birth, the woman of the people). Even a master like Strindberg, however much he may have chosen to regard himself as the son of a servant, viewed the peasant population from outside and above. *Hemsöborna* is indubitably a comic masterpiece with a folksy tone, displaying considerable familiarity with the flora and fauna of the Stockholm archipelago and the customs of the human inhabitants, but its author was a summer visitor, not a year-round member of the rural population.

The dominance, in the literary profile of the 1930s and well beyond, of writers who not only came from humble backgrounds but chose to write about their class of origin is unprecedented in Sweden and a unique phenomenon in world literature. Still, the rise of the working-class or "proletarian" writer did not occur in a vacuum. The first two decades of the twentieth century were a period of profound and lasting social change. As already noted, populist organizations and causes, in particular the folk high school and temperance movements, did much to raise the level of literacy among the rural poor by providing access to libraries and encouraging the reading of belles lettres. Literary figures such as Jack London, Maxim Gorky, and Martin Andersen Nexø, as well as the relatively few Swedish writers who had portrayed the common people from the vantage point of personal experience—in particular, Martin Koch and Gustaf Hedenvind-Eriksson—often became sources of inspiration and role models for the *trettiotalister* (thirties generation).

The ascent of the proletarian writer is also correlated with the rise to dominance of the Social Democratic party, which stressed an international orientation as well as individual and collective self-improvement through education. The struggle to gain political representation for disenfranchised groups went hand in hand with the party's encouragement of members to write; its various publishing organs actively supported fiction and poetry by untried authors even when it was not directly polemic. The gradual establishment of the welfare state thus made possible an environment in which workers, and working-class writers, could find their voice.

The writers most directly associated with this flowering of literature by and about, and to some degree for, the working class—Vilhelm Moberg (1898–1973), Ivar Lo-Johansson (1901–90), Jan Fridegård (1897–1968), and Moa Martinson (1890–1964)—had many experiences and characteristics in common. All of them grew up in poverty, even deprivation, as the children of farm workers, crofters, small farmers, or manual laborers. None had more than a few years of formal schooling or came from backgrounds that valued reading for its own sake, and as a result they were largely self-taught, their periods of literary apprenticeship long. Though they were involved, to varying degrees, in national and international political debate and became committed socialists (albeit with individualist or rebellious leanings), they all retained, in many of their best works of fiction, a strong provincial anchoring. Perhaps most important, their respective literary productions all encompass a prominent autobiographical component.

Vilhelm Moberg

Vilhelm Moberg was the first to achieve critical and popular success, with his novel *Raskens* (1927; The Rask family), set on a soldier's croft in Småland, the author's home province, during the previous century. Drawing on both oral tradition—Moberg's father, grandfather, and great-grandfather had all been soldiers under the former military system, according to which each village provided maintenance for its own defenders—and his personal familiarity with rural customs that had remained unchanged for centuries, Moberg recreates a vanishing way of life. The chronicle is thus an important document of social history as well as a psychologically convincing work of fiction. *Raskens*, like many later works, is enriched by Moberg's judicious use of Småland dialect, not only in dialogue but also occasionally in the third-person narrative voice.

The conflict between the security provided by the innate conservatism of a tradition-bound rural society and the attraction of modernization and technological progress is the theme of Moberg's next two novels, *Långt från landsvägen* (1929; Far from the highway) and *De knutna händerna* (1930; The clenched fists). The protagonist, Adolf of Ulvaskog, can neither see any possible benefits in change nor accept its inevitability, and with age he becomes increasingly entrenched and inflexible. The central symbol of the work, the clenched fists of the second novel's title, suggests his tragedy of fate: as his grip hardens, what he desires slips through his fingers; when he tries to clutch his children to him, he succeeds only in driving them away. A related theme, the opposing demands of individualism and social integration, is the focus of the powerful love story *Mans kvinna* (1933; Man's woman).

As a child, Moberg had been deeply scarred by the narrow-mindedness of his home environment, its lack of understanding of, even hostility toward, literature and the life of the imagination, and its bleakly fundamentalist religious orientation. He nevertheless came to appreciate the positive aspects of rural culture: its continuity, its harmony with the natural world, its folk wisdom and pithy sayings. As an adult he identified with and admired this social structure while simultaneously feeling compelled to reject and escape it. This irreconcilable dilemma, explored from different perspectives, is the theme of several major works of autobiographical fiction. In *Sänkt sedebetyg* (1935; Eng. tr. *Memory of Youth*, 1937), the authorial alter ego, Knut Toring, looks back at his childhood and youth in Småland in an effort to understand why he cut himself off from his roots and moved to the city; in subsequent volumes of the series, *Sömnlös* (1937; Eng. tr. *Sleepless Nights*, 1940), and *Giv oss jorden!* (1939; Eng. tr. *The Earth Is Ours*,

1940), discontent and alienation lead him to try to return home, with only qualified success. This act is a fictional projection, for once having moved to Stockholm, Moberg never resettled in Småland.

In the later autobiographical novel *Soldat med brutet gevär* (1944; partial Eng. tr. *When I Was a Child*, 1956), the protagonist, Valter Sträng, resolves the same conflict by choosing to write about the society of which he no longer is a part: his fiction will focus on the "little people," as Moberg's own did. A bildungsroman in accordance with the classic German model, *Soldat med brutet gevär* is less personal than the autobiographical trilogy of the 1930s; the narrative voice not infrequently regards the young authorial alter ego with humor and irony as he searches for an objective truth about himself and the world around him and gradually evolves a personal philosophy and mission in life. Like *Raskens*, this novel is also an important work of social history. Because Valter Sträng is a representative individual, more typical of his time and social class than his creator, his thoughts and experiences provide a broad panorama of various political and social currents—socialism, pacifism, temperance, the folk high school movement—among the rural poor during the first decades of the twentieth century.

Moberg was a rebel and iconoclast, an outspoken atheist and republican long after the Social Democrats ceased calling for a separation of church and state and the abolition of the monarchy. During the war years, he maintained a very active profile, courageously protesting the Nazi regime in the sole Swedish newspaper to defy government-imposed limitations on freedom of the press, Torgny Segerstedt's *Göteborgs Handels- och Sjöfartstidning* (The Göteborg commercial and maritime news). The historical novel *Rid i natt!* (1941; Eng. tr. *Ride This Night!* 1943), set in seventeenth-century Småland, addresses issues of political oppression and armed defiance that are thinly disguised descriptions of the contemporary political situation in countries occupied by Germany. Both the author's own stage version of the work and the 1942 film directed by Gustaf Molander were highly acclaimed. During the 1950s, Moberg devoted much effort to uncovering and calling attention to political and legal corruption in Sweden, which he satirizes as "Idyllia" in the scathing novel *Det gamla riket* (1953; The ancient kingdom).

Moberg's attraction to the subject of emigration to America was a natural one. Småland, where farms were small and the soil poor, had experienced a mighty exodus over many decades. In the preceding generation of Moberg's family, his parents were each alone among their siblings in remaining in Sweden; an important motif in *Soldat med brutet gevär* is the effect of emigration on those who were left behind. When the author decided to embark on a major literary project devoted to this recent folk migration, he first turned to family and local lore and to letters sent home by Swedes in the United States. Eventually, his research took him across the Atlantic as well, primarily to Swedish settlements in the upper Midwest and to California, where he briefly settled. The series swelled from a projected three volumes to four: *Utvandrarna* (1949; Eng. tr. *The Emigrants*, 1951), *Invandrarna* (1952; Eng. tr. *Unto a Good Land*, 1954), *Nybyggarna* (1956; Eng. tr. *The Settlers*, 1978), and *Sista brevet till Sverige* (1959; Eng. tr. *Last Letter Home*, 1978).

The emigrant tetralogy focuses on the true pioneers, those who left Sweden in 1850, before the years of mass emigration, and settled in the upper Midwest when it was still largely uninhabited wilderness. Moberg deliberately creates representative fictional characters to illustrate various historical reasons for emigration and attitudes toward and reactions to America. Until the group of Swedes reaches Minnesota (about halfway through *Invandrarna*), the emphasis is collective, with approximately equal attention given to the small farmer Karl Oskar Nilsson; his wife, Kristina; his brother, Robert; Kristina's uncle, the lay preacher Danjel Andreasson; his follower, the former parish whore, Ulrika of Västergöhl, and his hired hand, Arvid; and a neighbor, Jonas Petter. This approach never becomes schematic because Moberg's extensive use of interior monologue allows the reader to share the thoughts and feelings of each individual.

Karl Oskar hopes that in America, where soil is fertile and free from stones, hard work and self-reliance will be rewarded and a brighter future will await his children. In large measure his expectations are met. Because later volumes of the tetralogy concentrate increasingly on daily life on his farm, the main story line follows the stalwart, earthbound pioneer and settler as he gradually achieves prosperity and participates in the building of a new community based on principles of democracy and self-determination. Even Karl Oskar, however, underestimates both the physical hardships the settlers must endure and the psychological difficulties of adjustment. Only those with few or unsatisfactory personal ties in the old country and nothing to lose in the new are unequivocally satisfied with their decision: Ulrika attains respectability and marries an American Baptist pastor, while Jonas Petter, fleeing a miserable marriage in Sweden, eventually finds peace of mind and solace in the arms of Svenska Anna. For would-be prophet Danjel, the outcome is less clear-cut: though free to follow his conscience and worship as he pleases in the New World, he is humbled by adversity and plays no prominent role in local religious life.

Kristina, unlike her husband, leaves Sweden with considerable reluctance, painfully aware that ties with loved ones and the homeland are forever severed, and is never truly transplanted in American soil. Another contrasting temperament and fate is embodied by Robert, the imaginative, romantic dreamer and idealist who seeks freedom and gold but, broken by his encounter with harsh reality on the California trail, finds only disillusionment and death. Karl Oskar's accomplishments notwithstanding, a tone of nostalgia and melancholy thus comes to the fore as the series progresses. In old age, Karl Oskar himself returns in his thoughts to the land he left behind, as he sits with a map of his home parish tracing the paths he and Kristina walked in their youth. Moberg knew that for the first generation of settlers, no matter how many acres were cleared and put to the plow, the emotional cost of emigration was high. His gripping epic tale has found more readers in Sweden than any work except the Bible and has so convinced them of its authenticity that tourists in Minnesota's Chisago County still search for Kristina's grave. Jan Troell's films based on the tetralogy, *Utvandrarna* (1971; *The Emigrants*) and *Nybyggarna* (1972; *The New Land*), won critical praise and a large international audience.

The novel *Din stund på jorden* (1963; Eng. tr. *A Time on Earth*, 1965), which Moberg also dramatized, concerns a Swedish American of the author's own generation. Albert Carlson has never truly adapted to his new homeland but discovers after a return visit to Sweden that neither can he be repatriated, for the land of his birth has changed beyond recognition. Without roots, without meaningful human attachments, he experiences a profound existential alienation from which only death can release him. In part a deeply personal confession, *Din stund på jorden* also affords Moberg the opportunity to criticize the superficiality and materialism of contemporary American life and to speculate about the threat of nuclear holocaust. His progressive disillusionment with the United States is also revealed in the afterword to the second edition (1968) of the essay collection *Den okända släkten* (1950; Eng. tr. *The Unknown Swedes*, 1988), in which he contrasts the vision of freedom and opportunity that had attracted earlier generations of immigrants with the contemporary reality of the Vietnam War.

The preindustrial, conservative, tradition-bound society of rural Småland into which Moberg had been born had vanished by the postwar years. His fiction looks back on it with increasing nostalgia but at the same time retains an awareness of the hardships and injustice people endured in times past and incorporates a passionate plea for liberty and social justice. *Förrädarland* (1968; Land of traitors), set in the seventeenth century, focuses on the plight of the common people along the border between Småland and Skåne, which then separated Sweden from Denmark. Moberg's final work, which remained incomplete at his death, abandoned the fictional guise altogether. The two published volumes of his extremely personal, idiosyncratic narrative history of Sweden, appropriately titled *Min svenska historia* (1970–71; Eng. tr. *A History of the Swedish People*, 1972–74), discuss important events of the past from the point of view of their impact on the common people.

Though his literary reputation rests primarily on his fiction, Moberg also wrote more than thirty plays. The dramatic works that have best endured in the repertory are folk comedies such as *Kassabrist* (1925; Shortage of funds) and *Marknadsafton* (1929; Market day eve). Simple in structure and often predictable in outcome, these early plays nevertheless feature vivid characterizations and amusing dialogue. In addition to stage versions of his novels, Moberg's serious dramas include *Vår ofödde son* (1945; Our unborn son), which debates moral issues related to abortion, and *Domaren* (1957; The judge), based on an actual judicial scandal. *Domaren* was filmed in 1960 by Alf Sjöberg.

Ivar Lo-Johansson

Ivar Lo-Johansson grew up in Sörmland, the province just south of Stockholm. Whereas Moberg's forebears were small farmers and soldiers, Lo-Johansson's parents and many relatives in previous generations had been *statare*, or estate workers, a category of nonlandowning agricultural laborers attached to large baronial estates who were paid primarily in kind rather than in cash. Lacking mobility or the possibility of social and economic advancement, they lived in a closed, virtually feudal society that had remained largely unchanged for centuries and were the most impoverished and oppressed group among the rural proletariat.

The microcosm of such an estate becomes the setting and subject of Lo-Johansson's *Godnatt, jord* (1933; lit. "Goodnight, soil"; Eng. tr. *Breaking Free*, 1990), the first major work among the many autobiographical novels produced by self-educated writers of his generation. Lo-Johansson's stated goal was to write a collective novel about an entire social class as part of a larger literary program aimed at both documenting the estate-worker system and bringing about its abolishment, but the narrative is also a moving, intimate psychological portrait of the author as a child. This apparent internal contradiction is nevertheless fused into an artistic whole. It is, in fact, the alternation of perspectives between the realistic, objective portrayal of the circumscribed world of the estate on the one hand and the lyrical, empathetic expression of the dreams, aspirations, and frustrations of the young Mikael Bister on the other that lends the novel its rhythm and balance. *Godnatt, jord* may justifiably be regarded as a watershed in Swedish fiction.

Lo-Johansson's first published works, in the 1920s, were four travelogues, the result of his intention to record the lives of ordinary laborers in each country he visited. After *Måna är död* (1932; Måna is dead), a personal novel that explores the conflicting demands of love and the desire for renown, he devoted more than a decade to the plight of the estate workers. *Godnatt, jord* was followed by more than a hundred short stories in three volumes (*Statarna* [2 vols.; 1936–37; The estate workers] and *Jordproletärerna* [1941; Proletarians of the soil]) that trace the history of the estate-worker system from its inception in the eighteenth century to the present through selected vignettes from everyday life. Two novels with contemporary settings, *Kungsgatan* (1935; King's Street) and *Traktorn* (1943; The tractor), concern, respectively, the fate of impoverished young people who flee the countryside for the city and the difficult process of agricultural modernization.

Bara en mor (1939; Eng. tr. *Only a Mother*, 1991), the most important work of this period after *Godnatt, jord*, resembles the earlier novel in that the setting is an estate during the first decades of this century. In *Bara en mor*, however, despite an ongoing analysis and implicit indictment of a social network that makes small allowances for individuality or divergence from the norm, it is the penetrating psychological study of the title character, an estate-worker wife and mother named Rya-Rya, that dominates. Because of one minor youthful error in judgment—she bathes naked in the lake on a hot summer day—Rya-Rya's life is thrown off course. She becomes a social outcast whose considerable energy and talent are channeled into proving herself to be better than her reputation—to no avail, for the collective oppressive forces of a system she cannot escape ultimately wear her down. Alf Sjöberg's 1949 film of the novel admirably captures Lo-Johansson's characters and milieu.

Because so much of his early fiction concerns agricultural laborers, Lo-Johansson is often regarded as the founder and chief practitioner of *statarskolan* (the estate-worker school) in Swedish literature; the system was eliminated in 1945, in no small part because of his efforts. By the 1950s, the abject poverty, both economic and spiritual, and the oppressive, hierarchical structure of rural society that characterized the environment of his childhood had largely been eliminated by the developing welfare state, and the southern suburbs of Stockholm were encroaching on the forests and fields of Sörmland. Unlike Moberg, however, Lo-Johansson reveals little ambivalence or sense of loss when he examines the past once again by turning to his personal experiences for subject matter. The first novel of the eight-volume autobiographical series published between 1951 and

1960, *Analfabeten* (The illiterate), gives a moving portrait of the author's father and his love of the land he tills, but the common theme of the first four volumes is the protagonist's determination to break away, to foil the expectations of those around him, to assert his independence and find his own path. In this regard he resembles Mikael Bister in *Godnatt, jord*, but in the later series, despite the use of a first-person narrator, the presentation of the authorial alter ego is less subjective and more analytical. When Lo-Johansson describes his life as a country peddler (*Gårdfarihandlaren* [1953; Eng. tr. *Peddling My Wares*, 1995]) and manual laborer or fledgling reporter in the capital city (*Stockholmaren* [1954; The Stockholmer]; *Journalisten* [1956; The journalist]), the point of view is often distanced and ironic, though events related deviate very little from biographical fact. The fictional component of the narrative thus derives primarily from the author's interpretation of and attitude toward his former self rather than from a manipulation of external events. In later volumes of the series, as the time frame of the story approaches the time of writing, the authorial alter ego and the narrative voice begin to merge.

Lo-Johansson also published four volumes of memoirs, *Pubertet* (1975; Puberty), *Asfalt* (1979; Asphalt), *Tröskeln* (1982; The threshold), and *Frihet* (1985; Freedom), which differ from previous autobiographical works both in their subject matter—there is surprisingly little overlap among the various narratives—and their interpretation. The memoirs largely ignore the emotional life of the author, concentrating instead on formative events and environments to which he was exposed, and thus in some respects are more a chronicle of the times than a personal history. Lo-Johansson has described the progression from *Godnatt, jord* to the memoirs as a gradual stripping away of the fictional artifice, but he also points out that each retrospective reinterpretation presents events in the light of the author's current circumstances and attitudes. Different accounts may therefore express "truths" that are contradictory but not mutually exclusive.

Though his extensive production, encompassing more than fifty volumes, is dominated by long novels of epic scope, Lo-Johansson considered the most challenging literary genre to be the short story. After a hiatus of more than twenty-five years, he once again turned to this form between 1968 and 1972, publishing seven volumes of "Passion stories," each of which centers on a deadly sin. These tales of greed, lust, and prevarication demonstrate a stylistic mastery unsurpassed even by the vigorous prose of his earlier works. This personal artistic renewal led to a renaissance of Swedish interest in shorter fiction.

Lo-Johansson's concern for minority groups that lack adequate political representation extended well beyond his social class of origin. Thus, for instance, he lived among and wrote about gypsies and campaigned for improved conditions for the elderly. The novel *Geniet* (1947; The genius) and subsequent essays formulate a plea for greater understanding of the problems of adolescence and for openness in sexual matters. An active participant in Sweden's cultural debate for nearly sixty years, Lo-Johansson wrote extensively about questions of literary history and theory and energetically promoted the works of younger authors from working-class backgrounds who carried on the tradition of his generation. His own best works—*Godnatt, jord, Bara en mor, Analfabeten, Gårdfarihandlaren*—rank among the great achievements in the genre of realistic fiction.

Jan Fridegård

Jan Fridegård's main contribution to the body of autobiographical fiction published in the 1930s was the Lars Hård trilogy: *Jag, Lars Hård* (1935; Eng. tr. *I, Lars Hård*, 1985), *Tack för himlastegen* (1936; Eng. tr. *Jacob's Ladder*, 1987), and *Barmhärtighet* (1936; Eng. tr. *Mercy*, 1987). These novels differ from those of his contemporaries, however, in that the author's alter ego is not a child growing to adulthood but a man in his twenties, chronically unemployed, who has returned to live with his parents while trying to determine what to do with his life. Lars Hård is arrogant, cynical, lazy, and insolent—characteristics that led contemporary critics to reject the books about him as morally repugnant—but he is also insecure, sensitive, and easily hurt. As the first-person narrator looks back on events described, he pokes fun at the posturing and egocentrism of his former self. A similar double vision may be found, for instance, in Moberg's *Soldat med brutet gevär* and Lo-Johansson's autobiographical narratives of the early 1950s, but the Lars Hård books stand alone in that regard among fictional autobiographies of the 1930s. Fridegård's novels also diverge from those of his contemporaries in their lack of overtly stated social perspective. Though one can analyze the protagonist's situation and temperament in terms of the class struggle, neither Lars Hård nor the author offers this interpretation. The protagonist remains an individualist and angry rebel who in no manner identifies with his proletarian roots, and his experiences are presented neither as typical nor as the product of repressive social and economic conditions. In contrast, Hampe Faustman's film *Lars Hård* (1948) views the title character as formed by his environment.

Fridegård's trilogy set in Viking times—*Trägudars land* (1940; Eng. tr. *Land of Wooden Gods*, 1989), *Gryningsfolket* (1944; Eng. tr. *People of the Dawn*, 1990), and *Offerrök* (1949; Eng. tr. *Sacrificial Smoke*, 1990)—reveals a more obvious social orientation. An amateur archaeologist, Fridegård cultivated a lifelong interest in history and prehistory. The trilogy incorporates a vast amount of factually accurate, and largely unromanticized, information about that era drawn from many sources, foremost among them Rimbert's *Life of St. Ansgar*, into an exciting narrative. On the historical level, it describes the clash of paganism and Christianity, and on the individual level, the thrall Holme's struggle for independence and social justice. Holme may be regarded as the literal ancestor of the impoverished agricultural laborers among whom Fridegård grew up—his parents, like Lo-Johansson's, had been estate workers—who figure in much of the rest of his fiction.

During the 1940s and 1950s, Fridegård published two volumes that continue the chronicle of his fictional alter ego Lars Hård (*Här är min hand* [1942; Here is my hand] and *Lars Hård går vidare* [1951; Lars Hård moves on]) and three semiautobiographical novels set in the environment of his childhood in rural Uppland (the province just north of Stockholm): *Lyktgubbarna* (1955; Will-o'-the-wisps), *Flyttfåglarna* (1956; Birds of passage), and *Arvtagarna* (1957; The inheritors). He once again turned to the historical novel in the five-volume "soldier" series—*Svensk soldat* (1959; Swedish soldier), *Soldathustrun* (1960; Soldier's wife), *Mot öster—soldat!* (1961; Eastward, soldier!), *Soldatens kärlek* (1962; The soldier's love), and *Hemkomsten* (1963; Homecoming)—which takes place in the late eighteenth and early nineteenth centuries, when Sweden was more or less continuously at war. The strength of these works lies in their gripping, detailed descriptions of sea battles in the various Baltic campaigns and in revelations of the hardships experienced by ordinary soldiers and sailors, rather than in psychological realism. Fridegård's fascination with occult phenomena, an outgrowth of his interest in folklore, is reflected in several novels, for instance, *Torntuppen* (1941; The weather cock), *Porten kallas trång* (1952; The narrow gate), and *Sommarorgel* (1954; Summer organ). In the 1960s, he published four volumes of memoirs (*På oxens horn* [1964; On the horns of the ox], *Lättingen* [1965; Lazybones], *Det kortaste strået* [1966; Short end of the stick], and *Tre stigar* [1967; Three paths]) that are personal and impressionistic rather than, like Lo-Johansson's, informative and analytical.

Moa Martinson

The literary 1930s were a male-dominated generation, for if it was difficult for working-class men to find the time and financial independence to devote themselves to writing, it was doubly so for working-class women.

Moa Martinson (Helga Maria Swartz) was born out of wedlock and grew up in the slums of the industrial town Norrköping and among estate workers in the surrounding countryside. She married at nineteen, bore five children, buried two of them, and endured her husband's bouts of depression and eventual suicide while struggling in isolation to educate herself and publish articles in the socialist press. Her second marriage, in 1929 to Harry Martinson, was a union that, it has been observed, gave birth to two writers. Her first novel, *Kvinnor och äppelträd* (1933; Eng. tr. *Women and Apple Trees*, 1985), was published when she was forty-three years old.

Moa Martinson's subject matter is the experience of working-class women. Virtually everything she wrote either is autobiographical or derives from female oral tradition. She is among the first in Swedish literature to give detailed accounts of physical labor performed by women, both in the home and in employment outside it, and she is also the first to describe the sensations of a woman giving birth. In contrast to the male proletarian writers of her generation, who tend to focus on camaraderie among men while describing young women in terms of potential erotic conquests and old ones as gossiping busybodies, Martinson creates a literary world in which strength, reliability, and concern for others are female characteristics, while men are often absent, shadowy figures. She recognizes, furthermore, that the political agenda of the ruling Social Democratic party may be at odds with the right of women to full equality of opportunity. Several works of fiction confront this issue without ultimately resolving it.

In the autobiographical series *Mor gifter sig* (1936; Eng. tr. *My Mother Gets Married*, 1988), *Kyrkbröllop* (1938; Church wedding), and *Kungens rosor* (1939; The king's roses), the protagonist closely resembles her creator, as her name—Mia—suggests. Mia is a strong female role model, independent-minded and feisty, a fighter who survives a childhood of abject poverty, physical abuse, and neglect with her curiosity, exuberance, powers of observation, and sense of self-worth intact. Eventually, her developing political awareness helps her understand her own experiences in light of larger social and economic forces. She is disturbed that leaders of the workers' party do not pay enough attention to women's concerns but nevertheless comes to believe it essential that women support socialism because it ultimately will benefit all members of the proletariat.

An autobiographical tetralogy published in the 1940s and 1950s (*Den osynlige älskaren* [1943; The invisible lover], *Du är den enda* [1952; You are the only one], *Klockor vid sidenvägen* [1957; Bells along the silk road], and *Hemligheten* [1959; The secret]), based on the early years of Martinson's first marriage, offers a less sanguine view. Trapped in a relationship with a violent, uncommunicative husband and with two small children to care for, the author's alter ego, Betty, finds that the gradual awakening of her interest in philosophical and social issues and a rudimentary political coming-of-age do nothing to help her escape. Whereas Mia is a self-aware heroine striving for specific political and social goals, Betty, a more typical representative of her gender and class, is a victim of circumstances she does not fully comprehend.

Another important series of novels, the "Östergötland Epic," made up of *Vägen under stjärnorna* (1940; The path beneath the stars), *Brandliljor* (1941; Flame lilies), and *Livets fest* (1949; The feast of life), gives a historical panorama of Moa Martinson's home province by tracing the lives of the occupants of a single farm through several generations. Other works continue to draw directly on her own life, such as *Armén vid horisonten* (1942; The army at the horizon), *Bakom svenskvallen* (1944; Behind Swedish fortifications), and *Kärlek mellan krigen* (1947; Love between the wars). In her later years, Martinson was also a popular lecturer and newspaper columnist. As a writer, one of her greatest strengths is precisely the personal, idiosyncratic voice in which she addresses her audience. By using interior monologue and syntactic patterns that approximate the fragmented or run-on quality of actual speech—narrative techniques that sometimes resemble stream of consciousness—she draws the reader into her fictional world. Recent feminist literary critics have accorded her the attention she deserves.

The Urban Scene

At the turn of the century, less than half of Sweden's population lived in metropolitan areas, so it is not entirely historical coincidence that most of the working-class writers of this generation grew up in the countryside and that provincial settings dominate in their works. An exception among them is the prolific if uneven Rudolf Värnlund (1900–1945), whose autobiographical novel *Hedningarna som icke hava lagen* (1936; Heathens outside the law) is set on the proletarian South Side of Stockholm. His fiction is often weighted down by extensive ideological debate, to the detriment of structure and pace, but Värnlund was also among the first in Sweden to discover D. H. Lawrence, whose influence is apparent in *Det druckna kvarteret* (1929; City block of drunks). In the last decade of his life, Värnlund turned increasingly to drama, in which regard he also stands alone among his contemporaries.

Though Lo-Johansson, Moberg, and Moa Martinson promoted collective goals through their respective productions, it was Josef Kjellgren

(1907–48), best known as one of the Five Young Men associated with the advent of modernism, who became the foremost practitioner of the collective novel with *Människor kring en bro* (1935; People around a bridge). Like Värnlund, Kjellgren turned to an urban environment in his depiction of the long, complex process of constructing Stockholm's Västerbron (West Bridge). Fictional chapters about the lives of various workers, both on the job and in the private sphere, alternate with segments providing documentary and statistical information. The lengthy descriptions of specific work tasks reveal Kjellgren's firsthand experience with manual labor. His faith in and enthusiasm for technological progress epitomizes the functionalist doctrine of the 1930s, and his emphasis on pride and camaraderie among workers is at the same time compatible with the goals of the Social Democratic movement, whose reforms characterized the decade.

If urban working-class settings are relatively rare in Swedish fiction before World War II, the industrial novel has found even fewer practitioners, no doubt because industrialization is such a relatively recent phenomenon. Folke Fridell (1904–85) had been a laborer in a textile mill for nearly thirty years before publishing *Tack för mig—grottekvarn* (1945; I've had my fill, people-mill). Like most of his subsequent novels, it is set in a small-town factory environment and draws on his own experiences to address matters ranging from the tedium of performing repetitive tasks to the need for a democratic restructuring of the workplace. In *Död mans hand* (1946; Dead man's hand), Fridell's mouthpiece, David Bohm, asserts that better conditions and higher pay are not enough—workers also need to find meaning in the jobs they perform. *Syndfull skapelse* (1949; Sinful creation) concerns a factory worker who suddenly takes a week off to reflect on his situation, to the consternation of everyone he knows. Though Fridell's early fiction in particular often functions as an exposé of dangerous and unsanitary conditions, its most significant contribution has been to stimulate philosophical debate about the role of the industrial worker in contemporary society. Several later works are openly autobiographical, like so many other narratives by writers of humble origin.

The working-class writers who came to the fore during the 1930s represent both a continuation and an expansion of the realistic, socially aware vein of Swedish literature that has its origins in the Modern Breakthrough. Like their predecessors from that period, they believed that literature has a didactic purpose: it should communicate ideas and information to a broad readership in order to promote discussion and effect social change. Accordingly, most of their works have a strong historical, political, and sociological bent and are written in clear, easily accessible prose. The differences in focus and orientation among them notwithstanding—many of which may be traced to their respective childhood experiences—their choices of subject matter and theme reveal striking similarities. The authors all place ordinary people—struggling crofters and small farmers, downtrodden estate workers, impoverished manual laborers—at the center of their imaginative worlds and champion principles of individual liberty, egalitarianism, and social justice. Despite their personal commitment to progressive socialism, much of their fiction may nevertheless be characterized as conservative, with respect to both subject matter and style. It looks back in time (either to the writers' formative years or to previous centuries) and preserves for posterity a vanishing rural culture. Though the authors often display indignation rather than nostalgia, a desire to reform rather than to perpetuate, the collective effect of their works is to give shape and voice to the rural proletariat at precisely the historical moment when it was forever disappearing. Their literary orientation is likewise traditional, hearkening back to the straightforward, chronological structure and omniscient third-person narrator or apparently guileless first-person storyteller of the nineteenth-century novel. Whereas other Swedish writers from working-class backgrounds born around the turn of the century, such as Eyvind Johnson, Harry Martinson, and Artur Lundkvist, were influenced by the modernism of contemporary international literary movements, with few exceptions these experimental trends are conspicuously absent from the works of the writers under discussion.

The writers of the 1930s played a significant role in setting Swedish literature on a fruitful course. Many important novelists of the postwar period—Per Anders Fogelström, Sara Lidman, Sven Delblanc, Kerstin Ekman—were to build on their work.

TURNING THE TIDE FOR MODERNISM

In 1930, after years of a booming economy, the Stockholm Exhibition brought into focus Sweden's dreams for an industrial future. Ludvig Nordström's Totalist utopia seemed an attainable goal. The Swedish illusion was soon shattered by the financial crash that occurred in the wake of the fall and suicide of Sweden's chief industrialist, Ivar Kreuger, and the growing threat of war. Even though Sweden managed to maintain a strained neutrality during the Second World War, it was impossible to ignore the effects of the conflict on Finland, Norway, and Denmark.

The 1930s proved to be a turning point for modernism in Sweden. Previously, there had been isolated proponents such as Hjalmar Bergman, Birger Sjöberg, and Pär Lagerkvist, whereas modernism had established itself much more easily in Finland, in part because of the efforts of Hagar Olsson, who orchestrated a group defense of the movement. In the 1930s, Swedish authors rallied to the cause of modernism, presenting a collective front despite many individual differences in the group. The anthology *5 unga* (1929; Five young men), on whose cover the contributors were listed with eye-catching typography as erik asklund, josef kjellgren, artur lundkvist, harry martinson, and gustav sandgren, was a gauntlet thrown down to academically schooled literary critics on their own territory. The new aesthetics was defended vigorously and competently in such journals as *Clarté, Bonniers Litterära Magasin, Spektrum,* and *Karavan.* It is a convenience of literary history to separate this new generation of modernists from such working-class writers as Ivar Lo-Johansson, Vilhelm Moberg, and Moa Martinson, but in actuality, all these authors had close contact with one another. Generally speaking, the modernists placed greater emphasis on revolutionizing the literary forms, whereas the working-class realists staked new territorial claims with regard to subject matter. Both groups were actively involved in questioning the assumptions of traditional bourgeois society.

Modernism is a highly international phenomenon, and its proponents expanded Sweden's cultural horizons dramatically. From Paris, Eyvind Johnson wrote articles on Joyce, Proust, and Gide. Karin Boye translated T. S. Eliot's *The Waste Land* with Erik Mesterton (1903–). Gunnar Ekelöf introduced the French surrealists. Artur Lundkvist closely watched the developments abroad and wrote essays on Carl Sandburg, William Faulkner, and a host of others. The majority of the modernists were seasoned travelers whose foreign experience taught them that cultural values are not absolute. Martinson, the world nomad, and Ekelöf, the eternal outsider, drew on examples from foreign cultures to debunk cultural myths of the Western world.

The writings of Sigmund Freud and Carl Jung had made inroads in Sweden by the 1930s. Early in the decade, the reading of Freud and D. H. Lawrence inspired a wave of "primitivism" or "vitalism," the glorification of the redeeming power of the sex drive, released from the straitjacket of moral convention. Jung's writings on archetypes and the collective unconscious strongly affected the symbolic expression of the modernists. In the afterglow of the Stockholm Exhibition, poets such as Lundkvist sang the praises of the new industrial world, similar to the futurists' worship of wet asphalt and dynamic machines. Soon, however, the affirmation of technological advances was transformed into a sense of betrayal, as the war machine rolled into motion.

Eyvind Johnson

After a materially and emotionally impoverished childhood in one of Sweden's northernmost provinces, Eyvind Johnson (1900–1976) left home at the age of fourteen to make his way in the world as a manual laborer. Eventually, he became politically involved with the Young Socialist movement and moved to Stockholm. Unemployed and with ambitions to be a writer, he left for Berlin and then Paris in 1921. On the Continent he acquainted himself with several of the central figures of modernism: Freud, Proust, Gide, and Joyce; in turn, he himself became an inspiration for the new generation of modernist writers, such as Lundkvist and Martinson, when they made their literary debuts in the late 1920s. A towering figure in Swedish literature, Johnson was elected to the Swedish Academy in 1957 and shared the Nobel Prize with Harry Martinson in 1974.

Johnson's earliest works, *De fyra främlingarna* (1924; The four strangers), *Timan och rättfärdigheten* (1925; Timan and justice), and *Stad i mörker* (1927; Town in darkness), share the themes of struggles with class loyalty, generational conflicts, small-town environments, and indecisive heroes. Rather than telling a tale in a continuous sequential narrative, Johnson shows a preference for breaking a narrative into segments, as in *Timan och rättfärdigheten*, a story about the son of a factory owner who rebels against his father and sides with the workers. In *Stad i mörker*, Johnson pursues two intertwining stories. *Stad i ljus* (1928; City in light) is the tale of an author starving in Paris during the course of a day, a subject that bears a strong resemblance to Knut Hamsun's *Sult* (1890; Hunger). The tracking of the protagonist around Paris is interrupted, however, by an account of his background and by narrative segments approaching prose poems. Early on, Johnson experimented with several narrative modes, a technique he perfected in his later works.

Minnas (1928; Remembering) has a much darker tone than that of his previous novels and takes a bleak look at the tyranny of memory and the unpredictable forces that shape lives. Memory is an important theme in Johnson's authorship. In his preoccupation with time, Johnson aligns himself with the greatest writers of the twentieth century. One can point to an influence from Marcel Proust's *A la recherche du temps perdu* (1913–27; Eng. tr. *Remembrance of Things Past*) or to the works of Thomas Mann. In *Minnas*, however, impulses from Freud and Hjalmar Bergman are even more apparent. The memories of the characters are not savored, as they are in Proust; they are repressed and denied. These repressed memories eventually cause ruin, despair, and mental collapse.

Kommentar till ett stjärnfall (1929; Commentary to a falling star) presents a bustling and complex cross-section of life in Stockholm during the 1920s. One narrative line in the novel follows the fate of a self-made, respected businessman, his deep-seated fears and insecurities about his economic position, and his ultimate breakdown. It is narrated with a Joycean stream-of-consciousness technique, the first such occurrence in Swedish literature, since Strindberg's *Taklagsöl* was, strictly speaking, not an inner monologue.

Avsked till Hamlet (1930; Farewell to Hamlet) represents a turning point in Johnson's authorship. His early works are filled with indecisive Hamlet figures; there are two sides to Hamlet, however. On the one hand, he is indecisive, but on the other hand, he is a person of high moral demands and a strong urge to build a better world. In *Avsked till Hamlet*, Mårten Torpare, who describes himself as a Hamlet interpreter, leaves ambivalence behind and affirms his social engagement. This development parallels the shift in Johnson's writing at this time. Mårten Torpare appears in five novels from the 1930s, as a spokesperson for the author and an ironic foil for the narrative perspective. *Bobinack* (1932) recommends a primitivist return to nature as a protest against the spirit of capitalism. Mårten Torpare here functions as a commentator and critic of bourgeois culture. The many narrative threads of *Bobinack* all spiral out from an initial car accident in which most of the central figures are involved. *Regn i gryningen* (1933; Rain at dawn) further examines the primitivist alternative to bourgeois culture.

Johnson made a unique contribution to the legion of proletarian auto-biographies that flourished during the 1930s with his novels about Olof: *Nu var det 1914* (1934; Eng. tr. *1914*, 1970), *Här har du ditt liv* (1935; Here you have your life), *Se dig inte om!* (1936; Don't look back), and *Slutspel i ungdomen* (1937; Finale in youth). The novels follow the experiences and personal development of Olof during the five years after he leaves home at age fourteen. The reader has access to Olof's thoughts, which sometimes are related with great immediacy and sometimes with critical distance. One feature that makes Johnson's novels different from the other autobiographies of the day is the "fairy tales" that break the otherwise realistic frame of reference. These "detours around reality," as Johnson called them—later literary scholarship might choose the term "magic realism"—complement important thoughts or themes from the rest of the novel. The narrative of the last volume, *Slutspel i ungdomen*, is more experimental than those of the previous three, and the "fairy tale" of this final volume brings modernist self-reflection and musical composition techniques to the genre of proletarian autobiography.

The Second World War brought about a sharpening of Johnson's political awareness and a strong commitment to Western democratic ideals. The novels Johnson produced before and during the war fall within the category of the so-called *beredskapslitteratur* (literature of militant preparedness), in that each contains a strong warning against Nazism, not least the threat from Swedish Nazi sympathizers. *Nattövning* (1938; Night maneuvers) deals with a group of Swedish Nazis. Johnson had always been a pacifist, but his alter ego in this novel, Mårten Torpare, advocates the use of force in furthering the cause of peace. In *Soldatens återkomst* (1940; The soldier's return), Mårten Torpare comments, "One should prevent others from killing. If necessary, one should prevent them by force." Johnson's most ambitious project during the war was the Krilon trilogy: *Grupp Krilon* (1941; The Krilon group), *Krilons resa* (1942; Krilon's journey), and *Krilon själv* (1943; Krilon himself). The trilogy is an intricate allegory for the Second World War. Krilon, a Stockholm real estate agent, is the representative of Western democratic values and a Churchill figure. His adversaries are the nefarious businessmen Staph and Jekau, whose names point to Germany and the Soviet Union, respectively. The novels, in part a running commentary on contemporary events, employ a number of shifting narrative modes. Johnson pursues his allegory with a mixture of realism, dream sequences, propaganda, and satire.

After the war, Eyvind Johnson's interest in personal memory expanded to an interest in cultural memory, that is, history. Motivated by a need to deal with the atrocities of the recent past and to discover a means of living with those memories, Johnson views both memory and history as living parts of the present. His attempts to evoke the simultaneity of past and present generate highly sophisticated narratives. *Strändernas svall* (1946; Eng. tr. *Return to Ithaca*, 1952) is a realistic retelling of Odysseus's journey from his captivity on Calypso's island back to Ithaca, where he must deal with Penelope's suitors, who are beleaguering his island. Johnson subtitles the book "A Novel about the Present." Odysseus is a warrior who must come to grips with the violent acts he committed during the Trojan War and return to his political and administrative duties, the first of which is killing Penelope's suitors. His situation parallels that of Europe after the war. Johnson thematicizes the modernist concern with representing reality. Odysseus's realistic adventures contrast with the literary form the protagonist gives them in his tales and yet again, the author seems to suggest, with the form in which they will be recast by Homer.

Drömmar om rosor och eld (1949; Eng. tr. *Dreams of Roses and Fire*, 1984) takes place in Cardinal Richelieu's seventeenth-century France. Urbain

Grainier—the name thinly disguises that of the historical priest Urbain Grandier—is tortured and burned for witchcraft because he opposed the cardinal. Contemporary parallels to these historical events could be found in the Stalinist trials of the 1930s and the Czechoslovakian trials of the 1940s. Truth and justice are brutally perverted for political ends. The novel dispenses with a logical, sequential narrative structure. There are several narrative filters between the reader and the events, and the course of events is presented in fragments with an erratic chronology. The narrative is highly self-reflective. *Lägg undan solen* (1951; Put away the sun) provides a double exposure of refugees hiding in a mountain hut and rebelling Roman slaves in a similar situation two thousand years earlier. Johnson shows the same concern with multiple time layers when he again takes up his personal past in *Romantisk berättelse* (1953; Romantic tale) and *Tidens gång* (1955; The passage of time), which deal with his experiences in Berlin and Paris in the 1920s.

Molnen över Metapontion (1957; The clouds over Metapontion) integrates three levels of time in its narrative. There is the tale of Themesto-genes from Xenophon's *Anabasis*, whose fate parallels that of the Jewish archaeologist Jean-Pierre Lévy and the Swede Klemens Decorbie. The two meet in a concentration camp during the Second World War. A third level entails Decorbie's visit in 1950 to the places out of *Anabasis* that had been described by Lévy. History, he claims, is not a futile repetition: "Every event is a completely new event. That is why life still exists. And that is why we can all hope."

Hans nådes tid (1960; Eng. tr. *The Days of His Grace*, 1968) is a more conventional historical novel set during the reign of Charlemagne. It describes a crushed revolt in Lombardy; to contemporary readers the parallels with the Hungarian uprising of 1956 were obvious. Again, the novel operates on several levels and offers different narrative perspectives. It tells the story of the protagonist Johannes's continued protests against the emperor, which land him in prison. The rebellious youth swears to kill Charlemagne. Ironically, fate instead transforms Johannes into the emperor's private secretary.

Livsdagen lång (1964; Life's long day) is a fantastic tale of lovers, Donatus and Astralda, who meet only every few hundred years over a span of a millennium in an eternally recurring pattern. The basic sameness of human experience is emphasized by the fact that the characters carry memories from earlier incarnations across the centuries. *Favel ensam* (1968; Favel alone) tells of a group of Nazi victims in modern England who try to deal with their experiences. The novel ends with an affirmation of a need for utopias. Johnson's last work, *Några steg mot tystnaden* (1973; A few steps toward silence), is "a novel about captives." The captives are prisoners of the past. The narrative features multiple time levels (ranging from 1973 back to 1477), a shattered chronology, fragments, and several narrative filters. This last novel is in many ways a summation of Johnson's lifelong concerns: his opposition to oppression, his commitment to humanistic ideals, and his explorations of the past as personal solace and a means of understanding the present.

Artur Lundkvist

Artur Lundkvist (1906–91) was the son of a poor farmer in northern Skåne. Despite an uncomprehending environment, he knew from a very early age that he wanted to become an author. He sent off his first hand-printed manuscript at the age of twelve, but his actual debut had to wait until he was twenty-two. The most prolific author of his generation, Lundkvist published more than eighty books and wrote copious articles in newspapers and journals, in which he comes through as an indefatigable "cultural laborer," an internationalist, and a champion of modernism. Perhaps more than any other single writer, he explosively expanded Sweden's cultural horizons through his travel depictions and his essays on and translations of modern authors from other countries. In 1968, he was elected into the Swedish Academy.

Lundkvist's early poetry is marked by his burning urge to introduce modernism into Sweden. This impulse made him the driving force behind *5 unga*. Inspired by Elmer Diktonius, Carl Sandburg, Walt Whitman, and D. H. Lawrence, Lundkvist's first poetry collections, *Glöd* (1928; Ember), *Naket liv* (1929; Naked life), and *Svart stad* (1930; Black city), are characterized by free verse, a positive view of progress and technology ("The screaming of the factory whistle should be for us a cry of joy"), and an affirmation of life's primal urges, which Lundkvist prefers to call "vitalism" rather than "primitivism." The poetic short prose in *Jordisk prosa* (1930; Earthly prose) is the first sign of what was to evolve into a battle with "the tyranny of genre." *Vit man* (1932; White man) contains signs that Lundkvist's infatuation with the machine age has diminished. The smoke of factories is described as "industrialism's veil of mourning."

In 1932, Lundkvist made his first trip abroad to Africa, which he wrote about in *Negerkust* (1933; Negro coast). In *Självporträtt av en drömmare med öppna ögon* (1966; Self-portrait of a dreamer with open eyes), Lundkvist writes, "All journeys are, for the most part, illusions that get shattered." His meeting with colonial Africa shattered his dreams of the primitivist paradise he thought he would find. At the same time, an unfortunate love affair called into question the mythic image of woman that Lundkvist had developed in his vitalist poems. The conflict of dream and reality is at the center of the novel *Floderna flyter mot havet* (1931; The rivers flow to the sea), the novellas in *Himmelsfärd* (1935; Ascension to heaven), and the poetry of *Nattens broar* (1936; The night's bridges). For Lundkvist, the urge to bridge the gap between dream and reality, the individual and the collective, and inner and outer became an important source of creativity.

In the mid-1930s, Lundkvist developed an interest in surrealism, which he wrote about in the influential essay collection *Ikarus' flykt* (1939; The flight of Icarus). For Lundkvist, the inward turn to the subconscious entailed a search for Jungian archetypes and a sense of unity in the collective unconscious. His voyage into the surreal interiors of his soul coincides with increasing aggression in world politics. *Sirensång* (1937; Siren song) contains a surrealist version of Dante's walk through a dark wood, in which, among other surrealistic moments, "A bird / hurtled with outspread wings to the ground / and burst into flames." *Eldtema* (1939; Fire theme) continues in a surrealistic vein and attempts to dissolve the border between the individual and the world.

Once Modernism became an accepted movement in the 1940s, Lundkvist turned on it with a critical eye. "I am with the revolutionaries, as long as they have not achieved their goal," he wrote of himself in 1962. He took issue with modernist poetry that had become too intellectual, too harmonious, or too pessimistic. One alternative was "panic poetry," which he described in an essay of the same name from 1947. Panic poetry is convulsive, surprising, fragmentary, and suggestive. Another suggestion was the "impure poetry" of Pablo Neruda, a poetry that incorporates naturalistic detail, such as earth and blood, into poetic images.

During the 1950s, Lundkvist entered his most political phase. His journeys to Africa, India, the Soviet Union, and China raised his social and political consciousness, and he, in turn, sought to convey his observations to Sweden. In the paranoid mood of the cold war, Lundkvist's friendly reports of the Soviet Union and China were highly controversial. He was a strong advocate of "the third viewpoint," that is, a view of the world situation independent of the political aims of the superpowers. *Malinga* (1952) is a description of a journey to an absurd fictional country that bears a strong resemblance to Sweden. Lundkvist also invents the "apholyricism," a mixture of aphorism and lyric, one example being, "He promised to love her all his life. And she soon died of boredom." *Spegel och en natt*

(1953; Mirror and a night) is another fictive travel piece. From this point on, prose dominates Lundkvist's writing. *Darunga* (1954) is a novel about a successful revolution in a Latin American country which prefigures, in an uncanny fashion, Castro's revolution in Cuba. On a less political note, Lundkvist's poetry collection *Liv som gräs* (1954; Life as grass) contains animal portraits and an affirmation of the vegetative forces of life in the symbol of grass.

In the 1960s, when Sweden's literary scene became highly politicized, Lundkvist stopped writing political literature and turned instead to private reflections and an interest in genre. His experiments in genre are prose equivalents to modernist experimentation in free verse. Just as meter and rhyme should not dictate the poet's choice of words, genre should not dictate the author's form of expression. Lundkvist's experiments with poetic prose and proselike poems grew bolder toward the 1970s.

During the late 1950s and the 1960s, Lundkvist wrote a host of collections of short, poetic prose pieces of a dreamlike quality, which he sometimes arranged in suites: *Berget och svalorna* (1957; The mountain and the swallows), *Det talande trädet* (1960; Eng. tr. *The Talking Tree*, 1982), *Orians upplevelser* (1960; Orian's experiences), *Berättelser för vilsekomna* (1961; Tales for the lost), *Sällskap för natten* (1965; Company for the night), *Sida vid sida* (1962; Side by side). *Ur en befolkad ensamhet* (1958; From a populated solitude) is a "novel surrounding an ego." *Agadir* (1961; Eng. tr. 1980), generally considered one of Lundkvist's finest poetic works, is an epic poem based on his eyewitness experience of a devastating earthquake in Morocco.

Lundkvist reflected on his role as a poet in his 1966 autobiography, *Självporträtt*, and in the collections *Ögonblick och vågor* (1962; Moments and waves) and *Texter i snön* (1965; Texts in the snow). "I am soft as a stone and hard as a jellyfish," from *Ögonblick och vågor*, is an important personal manifesto, written in the "catalog" style of Södergran's "Vierge moderne." Among other things, the poet claims: "A poem must be incoherent or else it dies of perfection," "I do not know my destination, therefore I wander with joy," and "Reality does not care about being, only becoming." Life is moving, changing, dynamic—and art must follow its example.

In the late 1960s, Lundkvist developed an interest in history. His historical novels, written with a mixture of imagination and fact, tend to portray a meeting of cultures and the reevaluation that such a collision entails: the cultural clash between Danish and Swedish in Skåne of the 1600s, the confrontation of East and West during the Crusades of the eleventh century, viking travels to Baghdad, European emigration to Trinidad of the 1600s, the meeting of Jewish and Babylonian cultures, or the conquest of the known world by Genghis Khan and Alexander the Great.

In the 1970s, Lundkvist's genre mixtures contain more than just prose and poetry: lyric and epic, factual essay and fable, biography and fiction, music and prose, pictorial art and prose are only a few of his permutations. In the majority of these works, there can be no talk of a plot in any ordinary sense of the term. *Långt borta, mycket nära* (1970; Far away, very close) is described as a collage, a "prose mosaic," whereas *Antipodien* (1971) is a hybrid of essay and fable, at some points describing a voyage to Australia, and at others, strange and fantastic places. *Lustgårdens demoni* (1973; Paradise's demonism), *Fantasins slott och vardagens stenar* (1974; Imagination's castles and everyday stones), and *Livsälskare, svartmålare* (1974; Lovers of life, painters of darkness) blend essays, poems, biography, descriptions of pictorial art, and prose. *Världens härlighet* (1975; The glory of the world) is a mixture of poems and prose poems that includes the splendid "Elegi för Pablo Neruda" (Elegy for Pablo Neruda). In *Flykten och överlevandet* (1977; Flight and survival), referred to as "an epic between poetry and prose," we find an amusing modern version of the Song of Songs. Lundkvist attempts to create a "prose symphony" in a series of three suites of prose poems: *Sett i det strömmande vattnet* (1978; Seen in the flowing water), *Skrivet mot kvällen* (1980; Written toward evening), and *Sinnebilder* (1982; Emblems). *Färdas i drömmen och föreställningen* (1984; Eng. tr. *Journeys in Dream and Imagination*, 1991) is an account of visions the author had while lying in a coma for two months after a heart attack. True to form, Lundkvist, the intrepid traveler, journeyed through unknown territory and returned to write about it.

Harry Martinson

After a difficult childhood as a ward of his home parish and a vagabond, Harry Martinson (1904–78) went to sea and became a coal stoker. In 1927, he returned to Sweden in order to become a poet. His subsequent marriage in 1929 to fellow author Moa Martinson became the stuff of literary legend. In 1974, he shared the Nobel Prize in literature with Eyvind Johnson. His literary career is a lengthy critique of civilization as seen through the eyes of the "world nomad."

Martinson's first poetry collection, *Spökskepp* (1929; Ghost ship), is replete with nautical themes. The concrete details drawn from his own experiences at sea lend the poems the authority of reality. At the same time, the brief glimpses of life at sea possess a symbolic depth that implies a greater existential context. For example, in "Osaliga" (Unblessed), eerie voices of drowned sailors cry out in the fog, "Where are we? Where do we come from?" These are also questions of individuals lost in existence. The poetic method in the first collection is not expressionist—the poetic images are not mere projections of the poet's soul—instead, Martinson explores the symbolic potential of images taken from reality. The *5 unga* anthology, which also appeared in 1929, meant a great deal to his early poetic career in terms of critical attention and support from his fellow poets.

The title of *Nomad* (1931) brings up an important theme in Martinson's writing. The nomad is not bound by cultural prejudice and has an outsider's perspective on the phenomena of life. Many of the poems in *Nomad* are nature miniatures inspired by the example of Rabbe Enckell. But whereas Enckell's "matchstick poems" were meant to illuminate the poet's face, Martinson's miniatures illuminate a piece of reality. Within the infinitely small, Martinson finds associations to the infinitely vast.

Resor utan mål (1932; Journeys without destination) and *Kap Farväl!* (1933; Eng. tr. *Cape Farewell*, 1934) are prose depictions of world travels, which combine realism with the symbolic pregnancy of poetry. Martinson further embellishes on his ideal figure of the "world nomad." The existential position of the nomad is enviable: refusing to be caught by the stagnation of civilization, he can maintain his spiritual independence. Anticipating later ecological concerns, Martinson also elaborates the view of "geosophy," the thoughtful stewardship of the earth, which would make better use of technology to improve people's lives.

A strong reverence for nature runs through all of Martinson's writing. World political events in the mid-1930s precipitated a crisis in his authorship and caused him to question the example of nature in *Natur* (1934; Nature). The imagery of *Natur* is not as accessible as before, and the collection shows influences from surrealism. In "Fabel om djungeln" (Fable about the jungle), the brutal "law of the jungle" lies at the root of an apocalyptic vision: "Many fear / —blue with historic shivers— / the fall of the entire jungle." The cruel element of nature is part of the impulse that propels humankind into war. The associative brilliance of Martinson's linguistic imagination is legendary. In "Noshörningen" (The rhinoceros), the armored rhinoceros kills out of "pansarskräck," a term that combines the word for armor (*pansar*) with that of panic fear (*panisk skräck*). The juxtaposition of war and animal fear is achieved in the poet's typical compounding of words. Nature has two sides, one that is violent and one that is beautiful, dignified, and calm. Even though the fear inspired by the violence of nature dominates the collection, the calmer side of nature is also addressed, as in "Solen och pojken i byn" (The sun and the boy in the village).

Like so many other working-class writers, Martinson turned to auto-biography. *Nässlorna blomma* (1935; Eng. tr. *Flowering Nettle*, 1936) and *Vägen ut* (1936; The way out) examine the shaping of Martin Tomasson from his birth until he puts out to sea as a teenager. The reader gains access to Martin's self-absorbed speculations about the world while the narrator retains a critical and unsentimental distance from Martin's weaknesses. Martin's youthful musings—Do the angels wash their own robes in Heaven or do they send their laundry down to Hell?—turn the values of the adult world inside out. As usual, Martinson's prose is characterized by poetic depths, verbal virtuosity, and surprising and playful associations.

Svärmare och harkrank (1937; Hawk-moth and crane-fly), *Midsommardalen* (1938; Midsummer valley), and *Det enkla och det svåra* (1939; The simple and the difficult) are Martinson's contribution to *beredskapslitteraturen* during the Second World War. Martinson returns to nature in his search for lessons in humanism. His affinity with the tradition of Linné has been noted by many critics and acknowledged by the author himself. He does not see the need for humankind to follow the "law of the jungle." Humankind is not imprisoned by its instincts but, by force of reason, can choose a course of action. Martinson has moved beyond simple primitivism toward a humanist view of life that emphasizes the power of sense and rationality.

Verklighet till döds (1940; Reality to death) and *Den förlorade jaguaren* (1941; The lost jaguar) are also reactions to the war and especially a condemnation of the abuses of technology. In *Verklighet till döds*, Martinson writes of his experiences as a volunteer in the Finnish Winter War. He also points to another war within Western culture: that between the poet and the engineer. Exactness, quantification, and technology are robbing humankind of its humanity, the purview of the poet. In *Den förlorade jaguaren*, Martinson attacks the American films of the 1930s as a medium of cruelty and as anesthesia of the imagination.

After a hiatus of eleven years, Martinson returned to poetry in *Passad* (1945; Trade wind). The poem "Passader" (Trade winds) moves through human history and evokes the world's loss of unity with the symbol of Gondwanaland, the ancient continent in which all continents were joined. The trade winds, much like the mind of the poet, pass over the globe from coast to coast and from culture to culture, providing a type of unity and an eternal airing of the world and the spirit. Technology has shrunk the world, removed its mysteries, so that the expedition to the unknown must aim toward "internal nomadic coasts." Martinson adopts the position of the wise humanist who, like the Taoist Li Kan in "Li Kan talar under trädet" (Li

Kan speaks beneath the tree), approaches understanding through intuition and contemplation.

Martinson further expands on his humanistic philosophies in *Vägen till Klockrike* (1948; Eng. tr. *The Road*, 1955). The philosophical cigar maker, Bolle, becomes a vagabond who, from his outsider's position, observes and reflects on the behavior of those who have a fixed address in life. Bolle is sensitive to the limits and smokescreens of language: "Silence can fit everything in, but language can only take one thing at a time." Only nature possesses truth; man always deals in plausibility. Man has dreams, so that he can get around "his own bones and chains." From his fellow humans, Bolle merely desires tolerance and basic decency. The final section of the novel breaks with the realistic premises of the rest of the work: after Bolle dies, he has a long talk with Charon and is then reincarnated in the Brazilian jungle.

With *Aniara* (1956; Eng. tr. 1991), Martinson presents a space age epic set in a dystopian future. Twenty-nine of the poems had already appeared in the 1953 collection *Cicada*, preparing readers for the mixture of lyricism and science fiction that characterizes *Aniara*. The story of the spaceship Aniara is told in 103 "songs" of varying meter. The epic is rife with allusive compression: the names of characters and the meters of the poems resonate with literary and cultural associations. Martinson creates a language suggestive of a world dominated by technology. The Goldonder Aniara is evacuating its passengers from the radioactively contaminated earth. Thrown off course by an asteroid, Aniara is hurtled into deep space with no chance of return. The passengers' only link with the earth is through the Mima, a sophisticated supercomputer with almost human properties. When news reaches the ship that the earth has blown itself to pieces, the Mima ceases to function and the ship's contact with history, roots, and culture is broken. Aniara's journey without a destination becomes a metaphor for humankind's cosmic situation. The mimarobe, the caretaker of the Mima, bears the role of the poet who creates illusions to distract the passengers from the meaninglessness of their journey or tries to sort the splinters of the Mima. *Aniara* is Martinson's most pessimistic vision of the human condition in the atomic age. It is also one of the twentieth century's most impressive literary accomplishments.

Gräsen i Thule (1958; The grasses in Thule) contains short poems in the form of contemplations on nature and life, fragments of real or imagined mythology, and glimpses of foreign cultures. *Vagnen* (1960; The wagon) begins with meditations on the functions of poetry and the limits of language. Martinson expresses his hatred of heedless technology in the section devoted to the modern juggernaut of death, the automobile. In "Skändad död" (Dishonored death), he captures the dehumanization of the Second World War:

The death one gave millions
was an animal death.
Where Charon's boat waited before,
lay a cattle barge.

As a contrast to the vastness of space in *Aniara*, Martinson again creates nature miniatures in the short prose pieces of *Utsikt från en grästuva* (1963; View from a tussock). *Dikter om ljus och mörker* (1971; Poems about light and darkness) contains a varied assortment of meditative poems. In *Tuvor* (1973; Tussocks), the poet returns to nature for its calm and wisdom. In the highly politized cultural climate in Sweden, the last decade of Martinson's life was embittered by insensitive criticism and even ridicule of his work and a questioning of his and Eyvind Johnson's worthiness to share the Nobel Prize. The result was that Sweden's best-loved poet published little during this time, although he continued writing. The works published after Martinson's death are *Längs ekots stigar* (1978; Along the paths of the echo), *Doriderna* (1980; The Dorids), *Aniara-Bollesagor* (1983; Aniara-Bolle tales), and *Ur de tusen dikternas bok* (1986; From the book of a thousand poems).

Gunnar Ekelöf

Unlike Lundkvist and Martinson, Gunnar Ekelöf (1907–68) did not come from a working-class background; however, his troubled childhood with a mentally ill father and an insensitive mother served to free him from a sense of obligation to established tradition. Reidar Ekner has stated that Ekelöf's break with poetic tradition was more complete than that of Södergran, Diktonius, Lagerkvist, or Sjöberg, and Ekelöf's example made it virtually impossible for later generations of poets to write in a traditional manner. At the same time, Ekelöf's poetry displays a cultural erudition and a sense of history unequaled in the twentieth century.

Ekelöf became acquainted with the art and literature of modernism during a stay in Paris in 1929–30. Readers could tell at a glance that *sent på jorden* (1932; Eng. tr. *Late Arrival on Earth*, 1967) was something new because of the poet's use of visual compression. The poems contain no capital letters, and "apoteos" (apotheosis) is written in the form of an arrow, which points downward to a symbol for eternity. In "sonatform denaturerad prosa" (sonnet form denatured prose), Ekelöf breaks down both sonnet structure and syntax. In some poems, the poetic self, a central human consciousness, is strangely absent. Objects are paired with verbs that lend them animation: "the flowers sleep in the window and the lamp stares light." In "osynlig närvaro" (invisible presence), the human presence is obliquely implied: "a yawn dragged itself across the floor / and drowned in the sink." Ekelöf referred to *sent på jorden* as a suicide book. The mood is sometimes despairing, and the self is in jeopardy.

Dedikation (1934; Dedication) is supplied with an epigraph from Rimbaud: "I say: one must be a seer, one must make oneself a seer." In this collection and in the two following, *Sorgen och stjärnan* (1936; The sorrow and the star) and *Köp den blindes sång* (1938; Buy the blind man's song), Ekelöf adopts a poetic role inspired by the symbolists and the romantics. The poet becomes a medium of higher insight. He abandons the typographical oddities of his first collection, and although he primarily writes in free verse, one occasionally stumbles across rhymed stanzas in these collections. Ekelöf's chief source of romantic inspiration is Stagnelius; these two poets share a longing for the reintegration of the self into the cosmos. Both modernists and romantics are concerned with the relation of the self to the world. Ekelöf strikes a note of modernist anxiety at the isolation of the self in "Ökenstämningar" (Desert moods), from *Sorgen och stjärnan*:

Endless void
that separates soul from soul!
In the ego's world
my soul withers.

Ekelöf is also influenced by the surrealists, who maintain that the poet should rely on impulses from his subconscious in order to penetrate beyond the surface appearances of reality. The surrealist position can be detected in the poems that deal in dreams and unusual imagery. The title poem of *Dedikation* is something of a modernist credo, professing love for the body and soul, ironic envy of the thing-in-itself, and "hatred of the crushing general ignorance, of the state and laws, the family and the church, lies and fear." In other words, Ekelöf expresses the modernist rebellion against the institutions of tradition; he does not celebrate the society to which he belongs.

In *Färjesång* (1941; Ferry song), Ekelöf abandons the subjective self-absorption of the romantic poetic role and moves toward an illusionless scrutiny of humankind's role in the world. The poet is not the inspired prophet of higher powers but a witness involved in human life; the poem becomes not an aesthetic forum but a means of exploring existential conditions. The self is perceived as a vacuum filled with social conventions:

In reality you are no one.
The legal system, human worth, free will
are all pictures painted with fear in reality's empty room.

Nonetheless, the poet believes in the person who stands alone, who tries to come to grips with the external factors that shape him, who does not blindly follow the dictates of the collective. The poet is a modernist outsider. Ekelöf distances himself from dualities such as good/bad or true/false and points to a synthesis: "Life is neither day or night / but dawn and dusk."

Ekelöf's individualism and encouragement of asocial behavior should be viewed against the background of the Second World War, in which the pressures of the collective caused its members to commit atrocities. The poet's asociality, his debunking of cultural myths, serves a social function. Ekelöf's rebellion against ideologies and fixed standpoints is even clearer in *Non serviam* (1945), the very title of which asserts the poet's independence. Ekelöf affirms an essential meaninglessness in life, but with little trace of existential acrophobia on the brink of the modernist abyss. "Samothrake" (Samothrace) is a poem about humankind's voyage through history, symbolized by the ship of the dead. Nike, the goddess of victory, is the elusive figurehead of the ship, and the rowers will never get any closer to her no matter how long they row. Final victory and meaningfulness are unattainable, but striving toward them propels humanity through history. "Röster under jorden" (Voices from underground), from *Om hösten* (1951; In the autumn), is one of Ekelöf's most famous poems, in which cryptic symbolism and musical construction describe a descent and ascent through different historical ages.

Strountes (1955; Nonsense) initiates another phase in Ekelöf's authorship. Ekelöf himself described the three collections *Strountes, Opus incertum* (1959), and *En natti Otočac* (1961; A night in Otočac), as antiaesthetic and antipoetic. He further debunks the notion of the poet as a higher individual and poetic imagery as elevated and extraordinary. Esaias Tegnér and his poem "Mjeltsjukan" (1825? Spleen) are the objects of spirited parody in "Epilog" (Epilogue); in other poems, the nonsensical, the absurd, the paradoxical, and the bizarre are used to great effect. *Opus incertum* begins with "Poetik" (Poetics), in which the poet states:

This is the search for a meaningless
in the meaningful
and vice versa

. . . .
What I have written
is written between the lines.

Language is unreliable; the search for meaning always leads elsewhere.
En Mölna-Elegi (1960; Eng. tr. *A Mölna Elegy*, 1971) is a masterpiece of
allusive compression. For example, the brief comment of the Old Actor—"I
was just contemplating a promemoria / about the punctuality of ladies . . .
—Victoria!"—invokes all the associations and implications of the corridor
scene in Strindberg's *Ett drömspel*. *En Mölna-Elegi* is rife with such literary
and cultural references. The structure is musical in terms of the chorus of
voices in which each strikes its own note and in terms of the simultaneous
pursuit of two different themes in two different languages, Latin or Greek
on one page and Swedish on the opposite page.

Ekelöf's last great poetic project was a trilogy made up of *Diwan över
fursten av Emgión* (1965; Diwan about the Prince of Emgión), *Sagan om
Fatumeh* (1966; The tale of Fatumeh), and *Vägvisare till underjorden* (1967;
Eng. tr. *Guide to the Underworld*, 1980). The poet wrote this trilogy in
large part in Turkey during a burst of inspiration brought on by the sight
of a Byzantine Madonna that had been worn down by kisses. Ekelöf was
interested in the East throughout his poetic career and used it as a foil
against which the arbitrary nature of Western values could be tested. He
returns to the prophetic tones of his earlier collections, and his cultural
eclecticism is apparent. *Diwan över fursten av Emgión* tells a story, but the
tale is fragmented. The chronology is broken and the pieces shuffled. The
Prince of Emgión has been captured by his enemies on his way home from
war and is blinded and tortured. In the grip of his great suffering, the Prince
invokes a vision of the Virgin, whose identity is more that of a universal than
a Christian female deity. Throughout Ekelöf's poetry, a female figure—the
Princess, Nike, the Virgin—represents a sense of unattainable fulfillment or
victory. *Sagan om Fatumeh* is a mystical love story that also has the flavor of
an erotic dance with death. Fatumeh is a prostitute loved by a prince, but at
the same time, she is his shadow and his destiny. In contrast to the Virgin,
Fatumeh is obtainable. Ekelöf conceived of the trilogy architecturally: the
poems about the Prince of Emgión and about Fatumeh form two pillars;
Vägvisare till underjorden is an arch between them in what remains an
unfinished structure.

Ekelöf's prose includes the essay collections *Promenader* (1941; Prome-
nades), *Utflykter* (1947; Excursions), *Blandade kort* (1957; Shuffled cards),
and the posthumous *Lägga patience* (1957; Playing solitaire). These works
show Ekelöf's impressive scope of knowledge and his eclectic amateurism—

in the best sense of the word—and some of the pieces are a source of illumination for his poetry. *Partitur* (1969), an uncompleted poetry collection, was also published after the poet's death.

THE MODERNIST BREAKTHROUGH

The Second World War left a deep mark on the generation of authors who spent their youth watching international aggressions assume proportions that defied comprehension. In the 1940s, an explosive outburst of modernist writing inaugurated what is considered the modernist breakthrough in Swedish literature; it was during this decade that modernist aesthetics took over the literary institution and set the tone of Swedish literature. The new writers published their aesthetic views in newspapers and high-quality journals: *Prisma* (1948–50), *40-tal* (1944–47), *Utsikt* (1948–50), and *Poesi* (1948–50). Perhaps most symptomatic of the changed attitude toward modernism was the new progressive bent of one of Sweden's major newspapers, *Dagens Nyheter* (The daily news).

In Sweden the postwar years were a period of rapid economic growth, increasingly progressive social measures, and a higher standard of living for all. This positive atmosphere of growth contrasted sharply with the darkly pessimistic and chaotic mood of the literature of the 1940s. Revelations from Nazi concentration camps and the explosion of the atom bombs in Japan caused most to feel that they were living in a doomed world where humanistic values had lost all meaning. One of the striking features of the generation was a mistrust of ideologies and claims of truth. The Second World War had demonstrated the frightening results of submitting oneself to an ideology. Under the influence of the writings of Sartre and Camus, authors focused on existential questions: How is one to live in a chaotic world with no truth or values? How does one make the right choice? The questions were of timeless and universal actuality, and literature avoided personal or historically specific solutions.

In general, the literature of the 1940s has been described as exclusive, intellectual, cynical, incomprehensible, pessimistic, and often indecent. A theme of petrification recurs, suggesting that any imposition of form on the chaotic flow of life causes a type of death and evoking a sense of spiritual paralysis in the frozen climate created by the war. Poets depict a complex, fragmented world in complex, fragmented images. Free verse is the only viable medium of expression. Rubble is all that is left of the cosmos, whose praises were sung by traditional poets. Prose writers reject the naturalist premise that reality can be captured in prose. Inspired by Faulkner and

Kafka, they conduct formal experiments that break all illusions of reality. Drama plays a lesser role. Strindberg is still the undisputed master of modern drama in Sweden. A few members of this generation also practice a new and unexplored genre: radio plays, a premonition of the future media age.

The Poetry of the 1940s

The debut made by Erik Lindegren (1910–68) in the 1930s with *Posthum ungdom* (1935; Posthumous youth) was unremarkable. If anything, it recalled the poetry of the fin de siècle. The career of Lindegren as a poet was inhibited by the war and timid publishers. In 1942, he published privately his astonishing collection *mannen utan väg* (Eng. tr. *The Man without a Way*, 1969). Considered perhaps the most important poetry collection of the decade, it was reissued by Bonniers in 1945. In an unpublished introduction to *mannen utan väg*, Lindegren wrote that "poetry's special task now is to experience and express the abysses of the age, its dizzying precipices with as much physically insistent tangibility as possible."

Lindegren sought to evoke the precipices of human experience by contrasting a disciplined form with chaotic, disturbing imagery. Each of the forty "exploded sonnets" consists of seven two-line strophes. The couplets have no capital letters or punctuation other than parentheses, so the flow of the language is unhampered. Lindegren thought of the imagery in the poem as musical, its appeal being to the feelings rather than logic. It is difficult to grasp a meaning from the startling array of disparate elements and clashing concepts in this poetry, but a sense of desolation and anguish conveys itself nonetheless. Not surprisingly, Lindegren became the primary target of the charge of incomprehensibility leveled by Sten Selander (1891–1957), a charge already met within the poems themselves: "false simplicity cannot speak the truth"; a complex world requires complex poetry. The lyric "I" of the poem is not personal; this core of the self is splintered, ambivalent, difficult to identify.

The title of Lindegren's next collection of poetry, *Sviter* (1947; Suites), has musical connotations. More accessible than his "incomprehensible" sonnets, many of the poems are indeed structured musically. "Arioso," one of the most frequently cited love poems in Swedish literature, is mystically erotic and vibrant with controlled ecstasy. Intensity of feeling, beauty of imagery, and a striving for transcendence reveal Lindegren as a modern romantic in the poems of *Sviter*. "Vid Shelleys hav" (By Shelley's sea) carries on a dialogue with the dead poet in stanzas alternating between a first- and a second-person speaker. In "Hamlets himmelsfärd" (Hamlet's ascension), Hamlet ascends to heaven, full of knowledge but with his mouth sewed shut. Other poems, such as "Kosmisk moder" (Cosmic mother), offer poetic commentaries on the surrealistic paintings of the Halmstad artist group.

Lindegren's final collection is *Vinteroffer* (1954; Winter sacrifice), whose very title invokes the theme of frozenness and petrification. The most famous poem is "Ikaros" (Icarus), in which Icarus does not crash into the sea but instead continues upward until he transcends reality: "Reality crushed / without Reality born!" The theme of ascension, a movement away from reality, is common in Lindegren's poetry, but the speaker in "Poet" is bound to the earth: "life is all-too-close / (like solidified lead)." In "Murar" (Walls), the poet's tool is petrification, and with plaster he erects walls "which I eat, smash and erect anew."

Karl Vennberg (1910–95) also had an unremarkable poetry collection behind him when he published *Halmfackla* (Straw torch) in 1944. Vennberg was one of the primary program formulators of the 1940s. His initial poems avoid cryptic imagery and engage in a direct criticism of the age. The poet tells us directly in "Om det fanns telefon" (If there had been a telephone) that the mauled body whose revival is hopeless is the corpse of Western culture. One of Vennberg's major themes is the distrust of beliefs and of those who think they possess the truth and want to force their truth on others. The poet shares this distrust with most of his generation. In "Den verklige tekännaren" (The real tea connoisseur), Vennberg is darkly ironic toward those who choose a belief as they would a brand of tea.

In *Tideräkning* (1945; Reckoning of time), Vennberg finds, in "Att leva" (To live), the words to express his generation's pessimism about Sartre's views on existential choice: the individual is faced with a choice "between the indifferent and the impossible." In "Tidsreplik" (Timely response), he attacks the traditional poets who create their beautiful lines while armies mass. The symbolism of *Fiskefärd* (1949; Fishing trip) is less direct than in previous collections. Vennberg still criticizes those who claim to possess the truth, but there is also a note of resistance against total despair: "Deep in the darkness / you must protect your life" ("Du måste värna ditt liv" [You must protect your life]). Against the background of the cold war, his poetry in the 1950s moves between pessimism and resignation. After a period of silence in the 1960s, Vennberg returned to poetry in 1971. The poems, marked by a new simplicity, express intensity, fatigue, and even bitterness.

Ragnar Thoursie (1919–) writes with a fractured, staccato syntax. *Emaljögat* (1945; The glass eye) shows his tendency to think in images: Stagnelius is placed in a tree, where the romantic poet can play with the air. Beneath him are the murky depths of reality, populated by bearded cod-females who want to be scratched. "Skolavslutningen" (Graduation) portrays in flashing images how the school officials ("Twelve men of wood, with beards, staffs, crosses, keys / swords and books") transform the students into wooden replicas of themselves. Thoursie explores the individual's position in life; whereas *Emaljögat* is somewhat despairing, *Nya sidor och dagsljus* (1952; New sides and daylight) offers a more affirmative approach to existence with the assertion that it takes courage both to be oneself and to function in society.

Sven Alfons (1918–) gives expression to a sense of nostalgia for the world that was lost in the chaos of the war in his collection with the telling title *Backspegel mot gryningen* (1949; Dawn in the rear-view mirror). Humankind is left to "sift the remains of that which has lost its worth." In "Vid en grå förtröstans spegel" (By a mirror of gray confidence), the poet describes "the last bard," who has lost his function in a degraded world and who ends his life blind and "transformed to stone"—yet another variation on the theme of petrification.

The poetry of Elsa Grave (1918–) is characterized by grotesque, shifting styles that frequently evoke a nightmarish sensation. In one well-known poem, "Svinborstnatt" (Pig bristle night), from *Bortförklaring* (1948; Subterfuge), the poet addresses the relativity of values by adopting the perspective of a sow who dreams of "streams of blue milk / where a speck of cream still conceals / the black corpse of a fly." Grave expressed a preference for the "impure poetry" advocated by Artur Lundkvist in the 1940s. She is notable for bringing specifically female experiences, such as motherhood and abortion, into the purview of modernist poetry.

The collections published by Werner Aspenström (1918–) during the 1940s are typical of the decade. "Skriket" (The scream), from *Skriket och tystnaden* (1946; The scream and the silence), emblemizes the cry of anguish of an entire generation. In *Snölegend* (1949; Snow legend), whose title reflects the theme of snow and frozenness so characteristic of the 1940s, Aspenström's cryptic imagery is reminiscent of Lindegren's poetry.

In the 1950s, Aspenström adopts a humorous tone to confront the views of his generation. In "Mätarlarven" (The inchworm), from *Litania* (1952; Litany), the perspective is that of an inchworm who finds that "eternity is much too large today" and decides to remain on his cherry leaf. Aspenström's poetry becomes less abstract and contains more reality than the typical poems of the 1940s. *Dikter under träden* (1956; Poems under the trees) offers a variation on the popular modernist Icarus theme; rather than long for wings, the poet wishes to sing the praises of the sole of the foot and the art of staying on earth and having weight ("Ikaros och gossen Gråsten" [Icarus and the lad Graystone]). In "Dialog" (Dialogue), the poet cautions his modernist colleagues: "Do not imagine that you revolutionize worlds / by revolutionizing words or styles." In "Du och jag och världen" (Eng. tr. "You and I and the World," 1980), from *Trappan* (1964; The staircase), Aspenström takes a down-to-earth approach to the classic modernist quandary over the self's relationship to the other and to the world:

Here we go now.
The one with the white galoshes
is you
The one with the black galoshes is I.
And the rain that falls over us both is the rain.

Other poets who were part of the modernist breakthrough include Axel Liffner (1919–), Ann Margret Dahlquist-Ljungberg (1915–), Folke Dahlberg (1912–66), Bernt Eriksson (1921–), and Arne Nyman (1918–).

Prose in the 1940s
The originality of the narrative art of Tage Aurell (1895–1976) was not appreciated until the 1940s, although he had published three solid works in the 1930s: *Tybergs gård* (1932; Tyberg's tenement), *Till och från Högåsen* (1934; To and from Högåsen), and *Martina* (1937). Aurell's novel *Skilling-tryck* (1943; Dime novel) and the short stories in *Smärre berättelser* (1946; Eng. tr. *Rose of Jericho and Other Stories*, 1968) and *Nya berättelser* (1949; New tales) were well received in the literary climate of the 1940s. Aurell's tales are usually set in the countryside or in a small town. Despite the provincial settings, the action is not historically determined, and thus the existential circumstances depicted have a timeless quality. Aurell tends to write about simple, even weak, people who are not successfully integrated into society. His prose is highly concentrated, and his novels, although only about a hundred pages long, often produce the effect of lengthy epics. The author pares away unnecessary images, metaphors, or adjectives; events, usually related in the present tense, are left unexplained, and it remains for the reader to fill in the gaps between the significant moments in the tales and to discover the hidden implications of the dialogue. The result is an almost cryptic but highly suggestive style.

Walter Ljungqvist (1900–1974) also made his debut in the 1930s with early Ernest Hemingway imitations, the most successful of which was *Ombyte av tåg* (1933; Changing trains). Ljungqvist's contribution to the experimental prose of the 1940s was *Azalea* (1948), a novel of symbolic and allegorical depths, in which the characters confront the author of the novel and discuss how it should progress in a manner reminiscent of Luigi Pirandello's play *Sei personaggi in cerca d'autore* (1921; Six characters in search of an author).

Sivar Arnér (1909–) is less experimental than the other prosaists of the 1940s, but moral analyses in his works are typical of the often confused moral stance of postwar Sweden. Arnér's novels in the 1940s deal with the consequences for the individual involved in conflict. The title novella of *Skon som krigaren bar* (1943; The shoe that the warrior wore) tells of a shoemaker who freezes to death rather than make boots for a baron who is planning to wage war. The shoemaker preserves his integrity, but his gesture will not change the course of events. In *Plånbok borttappad* (1943; Lost wallet), a hot-dog vendor, with moral right on his side, engages in subterfuge in order to mete out justice to a rich customer who has abused a weaker customer. His efforts result in ruin and suicide for the "innocent" parties. In *Knekt och klerk* (1945; Soldier and clerk), a monk loses his moral superiority when he becomes involved in conflict. Arnér's message is generally pacifistic, at the same time pointing to the futility of all action. In subsequent works, the author explores questions of identity, particularly in the context of marital relations.

The highly cerebral novels of Willy Kyrklund (1921–) are stylistically bold with a preference for absurdity, myth, and shifting narrative perspectives. His lean volumes present challenging "thought models" and describe humankind's existential plight in a meaningless world and the relativity of language. Kyrklund's characters often struggle with biological determinism and contingency. His first novel, *Tvåsam* (1949; Twosome), could be seen as a dialogue between Sartre and Kafka. In the novel *Mästaren Ma* (1952; Master Ma), the Master's wisdom is ironically contrasted with his wife's earthy comments and the know-it-all remarks of his disciple. The Eastern influence on Kyrklund's writing is also evident in his collections of novellas: *Ångvälten* (1948; The steamroller), *Hermelinens död* (1954; The ermine's death), and *Den överdrivne älskaren* (1957; The exaggerated lover). In *Polyfem förvandlad* (1964; Polyphemus transformed), the author makes use of the modernist collage form; the equally modernist suspicion of language plays a key role in *Den rätta känslan* (1974; The right feeling) and *8 variationer* (1982; 8 variations).

Gösta Oswald (1926–50) died in a drowning accident at age twenty-four, but the work he left behind indicates that he might have become one of the great experimental writers of Swedish modernism. *En privatmans vedermödor* (1949; A private individual's hardships) is both intellectual and exclusive in its allusive compression. The novel addresses the crisis of the individual in a world controlled by collective interests. The poems in *den andaktsfulle visslaren* (1946; the reverent whistler) are musically constructed. Oswald's posthumously published works *Rondo* (1950) and *Christinalegender* (1963; Christina legends) bear witness to a desire to revolutionize traditional epic form.

A cross-section of authors of the 1940s became known as members of the "hard-boiled" school. These writers were mainly responsible for the epithet "indecent" that came to be applied to the entire generation. The laconic style of Hemingway served as a model for these authors, whose occasional descriptions of raw violence shocked the public. The significant works in this line included Thorsten Jonsson's (1910–50) *Som det brukar vara* (1939; As it usually is) and *Fly till vatten och morgon* (1942; Flee to water and morning), Peter Nisser's (1919–) *Blod och snö* (1941; Blood and snow), Olov Jonason's (1919–) *Parabellum* (1943), and Mårten Edlund's (1913–87) *Tag vad du vill ha* (1944; Take what you want).

Stig Dagerman

Stig Dagerman (1923–54) became the "boy wonder" of the 1940s generation when he made his debut at the age of twenty-two as the master of a sophisticated, suggestive, symbolic prose style. He grew up in a troubled working-class environment and, like Eyvind Johnson, became involved with the anarcho-syndicalists, who advocated a socialist state without a bureaucratic superstructure. In a sense, it could be seen as the individualist's socialism. Like Kafka, with whom he has been compared, Dagerman departs from realism and creates the haunting sense that humankind is in the hands of blind, absurd, uncontrollable forces. Like Faulkner, he employs indirect narrative techniques and depicts violent and destructive subconscious impulses. Dagerman was highly productive for the five years following his debut; after another five-year period during which his creativity was paralyzed, he took his own life.

Ormen (1945; Eng. tr. *The Snake*, 1995) explores the central forces of angst and guilt, symbolized in expressionistic fashion by the snake of the title. The novel is structured not as a continuous epic but rather as a collection of short stories. Much of the action takes place in military barracks, and the novel captures the specific character of those gray and anguished war years, intensified to the level of nightmare. The snake that the protagonist has caught and keeps in his knapsack releases primitive fears; a young woman commits the desperate act of pushing her mother from a train, and in the soldiers' barracks the presence of the snake keeps the soldiers awake; to ward off their terror, they tell stories, which turn into powerful illustrations of human beings' existential circumstances.

Dagerman abandons realism entirely in *De dömdas ö* (1946; Island of the condemned) with a depiction of an expressionist landscape. A group of people is shipwrecked on an island without food and water, facing certain death. The island is inhabited only by ominous blind birds and aggressive lizards. Under these extreme conditions, the civilized shell surrounding the characters cracks and their primitive selves come to the fore.

Nattens lekar (1947; Eng. tr. *Games of Night*, 1959) is a collection of short stories that demonstrates Dagerman's technical virtuosity. Some tales are fairly realistic, and the narrative point of view is that of a child or an adolescent. "Var är min islandströja?" (Where is my Iceland sweater?) is an exercise in stream-of-consciousness technique. Other tales reveal depths of allegorical symbolism. The same year also saw publication of *Tysk höst* (1947; German autumn), which is a report from the rubble of postwar Germany.

In *Bränt barn* (1948; Eng. tr. *A Burnt Child*, 1950), Dagerman turns to psychological realism. The narrative point of view is generally that of Bengt, a youth in a working-class neighborhood of Stockholm. His emotional world is chaotic. After his mother's death, his father lives openly with his mistress, who later becomes Bengt's stepmother. The boy's anger with his father's behavior temporarily blinds him to the fact that he is sexually attracted to his stepmother. The conflict drives him to attempt suicide.

The events in *Bröllopsbesvär* (1949; Wedding difficulties) take place during a twenty-four-hour period. A farmer's daughter is going to marry a coarse and boastful butcher, who is not the father of the child she is carrying. The unexpected appearance of the child's father is one of many surprises in this story of grotesque, tragicomic, and burlesque dimensions. A carnival atmosphere prevails in which all norms are revoked and anything can happen, yet beneath the apparent humor of the novel lurk dark and disturbing depths.

A collection of Dagerman's short stories entitled *Vårt behov av tröst* (1955; Our need of consolation) was published posthumously. It contains the often anthologized "Att döda ett barn" (1955; To kill a child). As a playwright, Dagerman was not as stylistically innovative as in his prose. His plays include *Den dödsdömde* (1947; Eng. tr. *The Condemned*, 1951), *Skuggan av Mart* (1947; The shadow of Mart), *Ingen går fri* (1949; No one goes free), *Streber* (1949; Social climber), *Den yttersta dagen* (1952; Doomsday), and the radio play *En spelmans mössa* (1955; A fiddler's cap).

Lars Ahlin

Lars Ahlin (1915–) is an unusual member of the 1940s generation in that his art is inspired by a religious vision. Ahlin's view of the world is influenced by Luther's statement that man is both sacred and sinful. Since everyone is sacred, every human being has equal value, regardless of social hierarchy or moral pretensions. And since everyone is sinful, one needs to care about the material circumstances that affect human behavior. Ahlin's novels often focus on those who have been pushed out of society and their possibilities for regaining a sense of community. With the authors of his generation Ahlin shares an interest in existential issues and a distrust of those who claim to possess the truth and sit in judgment over others.

Like the modernists, Ahlin opposed a naturalistic illusion of reality in the novel, but at the same time, he took issue with the common modernist view that art should be an end in itself; a novel is an act of communication that gains its meaning only in interaction with the reader. Author as well as reader should identify with the characters, for whom the author acts as an intercessor. Humor plays an important part as a reconciling force in Ahlin's fiction. Like Dostoevski, Ahlin attempts to integrate low and equivocal characters into serious moral discourse.

Ahlin had already formulated all his aesthetic views when he made his debut with the novel *Tåbb med manifestet* (1943; Tåbb with the manifesto), based on his own experiences of unemployment during the 1930s. Tåbb is a firm believer in the *Communist Manifesto*, but according to that document, he has lost his value, since he does not have a job. He is ultimately led to reevaluate his faith in the manifesto; everything and everyone has value, and an ideology that generates a value hierarchy is inherently false. Tåbb rejects the manifesto and becomes a reformist social democrat to work for the improvement of everyone's material circumstances. Although Tåbb takes himself very seriously, the reader is given a more humorous view of him.

Inga ögon väntar mig (1944; No eyes await me) is a collection of short stories that contains the popular "Kommer hem och är snäll" (Coming home and being nice). The novella takes up the separate sets of expectations of a married couple. Their seemingly irreconcilable differences of opinion are—temporarily—bridged when they sacrifice their selfish demands and recognize their need of forgiveness and then find solace in the act of physical love. Ahlin often plays male and female expectations against each other. Earthly love is a unifier that brings a sense of true community. Ahlin's other collections of short stories include *Fångnas glädje* (1947; Joy of the imprisoned) and *Huset har ingen filial* (1949; The house has no annex).

Min död är min (1945; My death is my own) has a broad gallery of characters, many of whom feel themselves to be failures because they have accepted society's hierarchical view of success. There is much that is grotesque in the novel, and the unmasking of the characters is at times painful. *Om* (1946; If) is one of Ahlin's most interesting novels in terms of formal experimentation. The reader is constantly reminded that a novel is a linguistic construction; the illusion of reality is broken in a manner reminiscent of Brecht's *Verfremdungseffekt* (alienation effect) in theater. Ahlin's narrator encourages the reader's identification with the novel: "Bengt who is you who is I who is anyone." *Jungfrun i det gröna* (1947; The maiden in nature [bot. *Nigella damascena*]) shows that the idea of an autonomous individual is a myth; everyone is dependent on other people and material circumstances. In *Egen spis* (1948; A hearth of one's own), Ahlin adopts a lighter, satiric tone.

Fromma mord (1952; Pious murders) tells of Aron, who returns to his hometown of Sundsvall to reconcile himself with his past. In this he fails, and the primary obstacle to reconciliation and happiness of others is the idea of "piety." As Ahlin develops the concept, piety is the means by which people selfishly strive to obtain salvation for themselves. It is possible to be pious in terms of religion, but the word can also be applied to political ideology or economic power. A pious murder entails turning other people into agents of one's own salvation; in the process, they cease being human beings with independent worth and integrity.

Kanelbiten (1953; Eng. tr. *Cinnamoncandy*, 1990) is a young girl's coming-of-age story. *Stora glömskan* (1954; The great forgetfulness) introduces thirteen-year-old Zacharias, a boy who studies life intensely and possesses a sensitive understanding of other people. *Kvinna, kvinna* (1955; Woman, woman) begins a series of novels about marriage in which male and female longing are contrasted. *Gilla gång* (1958; Normal course) is a lighthearted treatment of an aging couple's affection.

Ahlin's most remarkable marital tale is *Natt i marknadstältet* (1957; Night in the fairground tent). The action does not progress in a straight line. The main story centers on a married couple and, in essence, takes place in the course of one day, but it is interrupted by numerous flashbacks, intertwined destinies, and commentaries. One of the characters involved in the marital drama is Zacharias, whom we met in *Stora glömskan*. Wife and husband have different views on life and love. For her, love is a gift; for him, love must be earned. Her approach to life is humorous; his is deadly serious. He is a victim of the hierarchical thinking Ahlin sees as the root of all evil. The wife loves her husband, but he does not feel worthy of her love.

Because of his desperate need to prove his worth, which according to Ahlin he already possesses, he resorts to criminal means and intends to trample others in his climb upward. His wife, out of love, kills her husband, in order to prevent him from "murdering" other people to attain his own ends.

Ahlin's novel *Bark och löv* (1961; Bark and leaves) is about the artist and his artistic medium. "The artist is a lover" engaged in an interaction with his reader. After *Bark och löv*, Ahlin fell silent as an author for more than twenty years. In 1982, he returned with *Hannibal Segraren* (Hannibal the victor), a historical novel that he coauthored with his wife, Gunnel Ahlin. The novel is an independent sequel to Gunnel Ahlin's novel *Hannibal sonen* (1974; Hannibal the son). Treating a historical theme was highly unusual for Ahlin, whose previous works dealt exclusively with a contemporary world. The author's creative powers had been revived. His next novel, *Sjätte munnen* (1985; The sixth mouth), moves in familiar territory and is set in Ahlin's native Sundsvall. The theme of a son's love for his reprobate father is familiar from *Om*. Ahlin's narrative art in *Sjätte munnen* has grown somewhat simpler, and the same can be said of *Vaktpojkens eld* (1986; The watchman's fire), a collection of novellas that deals with everyday reality. Ahlin's longest novel, *Din livsfrukt* (1987; The fruit of your life), deals once again with the inherent equality of all people in the figure of a socialist millionaire. During his career, Ahlin also wrote two seldom-discussed plays, *Lekpaus* (1948; Play break) and *Eld av eld* (1949; Fire of fire).

Lars Gyllensten

Of the 1940s generation, Lars Gyllensten (1921–) proved the most vigorous opponent of the tyranny of ideology and those who believe they are in possession of the truth. As a scientist—he was professor of histology at the Karolinska Institute for close to twenty years—Gyllensten learned that the tools and procedures we use to explore reality determine our results; therefore, no objective knowledge is possible. The existential strategy he proposes is *trolöshet*, a term implying both "faithlessness" and "lack of belief." The *trolös* individual is protean, constantly trying new attitudes and abandoning them when they reveal their limitations. This open approach to life is a safeguard against prejudice and intolerance. Kierkegaard's pseudonymous narrative strategy suggested to Gyllensten a compromise between unavoidable subjectivity and impossible but desirable objectivity. In his fiction, he adopts numerous narrative and existential attitudes, or roles, and plays them against one another. His prose production forms an organic whole in which formulations, names, motifs, images, and themes recur from book to book, where they are varied and developed. With a term borrowed from the American pragmatist Charles S. Peirce, the method is "an infinite inquiry."

Gyllensten's first published literary work, *Camera obscura* (1946), was a poetry collection issued under the pseudonym Jan Wictor. The poems were a deliberate spoof of the obscurity of the poetry of the 1940s, concocted late one night by Gyllensten and a friend from medical school, Torgny Greitz (1921–). Several critics treated the collection with serious respect, and when the hoax was revealed, it fueled the debate about "incomprehensible" poetry.

Gyllensten's serious debut came with *Moderna myter* (1949; Modern myths), which sets off a dialectical chain that runs from work to work. *Moderna myter* proclaims the bankruptcy of naiveté, that is, the blind belief in ideologies or -isms; instead, one must learn to live without such props and illusions. The narrative stance is ironic. *Det blå skeppet* (1950; The blue ship) is the antithesis of *Moderna myter* in which an ironic intelligence analyzes the possibilities of naiveté. In *Det blå skeppet*, young Abraham listens to and relates the disillusioned tales of the ship's crew and chooses "att satsa på undret," to stake all on the miraculous as an immanent counterpart to Kierkegaard's "leap of faith."

Barnabok (1952; Child's book) is a continuing step in a dialectic with no synthesis in sight. The first-person narrator has an "infantile" attitude toward life and people. This attitude is tested in his choice between two women who, in a sense, represent the two poles of the previous works. Together the works form a "dialectic trilogy" demonstrating how naiveté can lead to disappointment and destruction. *Carnivora* (1953) consists of sixty-six short prose pieces written with furious satirical verve and illustrating the Nazi mentality.

Barnabok dealt with an infantile consciousness with no self-control. *Senilia* (1956) explores attitudes associated with old age: the need to exercise complete control over existence and to order phenomena in familiar categories in an effort to prevent pain or surprises.

Senatorn (1958; The senator) and *Sokrates död* (1960; The death of Socrates) each deal, in a way, with men possessed by ideology. In the first novel, Antonin Bhör is an official in a communist state. Like the protagonist in *Senilia*, he is striving for structure and order in his existence. Political ideology has provided that order for him, but his faith in the state he serves begins to falter and he is seized with a desire to transcend his own being. His doubts cause a serious existential crisis. During a trip for rest and relaxation, Bhör has an affair with a woman who is in similar existential despair. Unlike Bhör, she does not want a protective shell to form around her, and her nymphomania is a symbol of her longing to transcend her own boundaries. Both protagonists seek something larger than themselves, something that transcends their reality.

In *Socrates död*, Xantippa complains to her husband, "You can only destroy, pick things apart that are alive only as long as they are whole." The main criticism, however, is directed at Socrates' willingness to drink the cup of poison in order to secure immortality for himself and his ideals. Contrasted with this attitude is "the little life," the life of the women in the service of life itself. The parallels in the novel between Socrates and Christ conceal a criticism of Christianity and other belief systems. In a sense, both Socrates and Christ could be seen as "desperadoes," a term the author explains in the book *Desperados* (1962): "I am firmly convinced that only evil comes from all-too-firm convictions"; however, he goes on to mock his own assertion, claiming that he may have overstated. The desperadoes are people with firm convictions, people whose compulsion to assert their convictions leads to destruction.

In journals, newspapers, and volumes of collected essays, Gyllensten offers a continual commentary on his own work. *Nihilistiskt credo* (1964; Nihilistic credo), whose title is a typical oxymoron, is the volume of essays in which he advocates the principle of *trolöshet*. The attitude is not synonymous with indifference, as shown by the stream of articles and commentaries on contemporary events in which Gyllensten enters into polemics and takes stands in a demonstration of existentialist engagement. Typical of his authorship is this alternation and mutual elucidation of fiction and factual prose. In the latter category is the volume of essays *Ur min offentliga sektor* (1971; From my public sector). *Lapptäcken—Livstecken* (1976; Patchwork quilts—Signs of life)—the semiological joke of the title is untranslatable—shows Gyllensten as a brilliant essayist whose erudition spans the worlds of science, philosophy, and religion.

Kains memoarer (1963; Eng. tr. *The Testament of Cain*, 1967) was originally intended to be a part of the novel *Juvenilia* (1965). The editing of an unusual papyrus proves to be problematic. The documents are not all in good condition, and from this fragmented, unreliable evidence the editor pieces together information about the Cainite sect, whose beliefs turn traditional religious faith upside down. The Cainites, recognizing the evil of the world, worship Satan and Cain, who have both set themselves up against God. The Cainites' way of life appears both enlightened and humane. Cain is the original iconoclast and destroyer of accepted beliefs; his act of smashing the petrified masks of the gods is viewed as an ultimately beneficial measure. In his writing, Gyllensten himself assumes the mythic role of Cain the iconoclast.

By its title, *Juvenilia* alludes to both *Barnabok* and *Senilia*. *Juvenilia* explores an attitude to life different from childish naiveté or aged petrification. The presentation of Cain in *Kains memoarer* lies at the root of the protagonists' search for a way of living. Iconoclasm is tested as a means of transcending the patterns and conceptions that threaten to encase the self. The fragmented composition of the novel as well as the fragmented identities of the characters reflect the thesis of the novel. Whereas the characters of *Juvenilia* are open to the reality of suffering, the lotus eaters in *Lotus i Hades* (1966; Lotus in Hades) lead an existence free from pain, love, restrictions, suffering, and fear, but this existence is synonymous with being dead.

Diarium spirituale (1968) represents a turning point in Gyllensten's authorship. Up to this point, Gyllensten has played the role of Cain the iconoclast, debunking cultural myths, picking apart ideologies, and exposing the limits of fixed attitudes. In *Diarium spirituale*, he points to the epilogue of Cain's story. After the murder of his brother, Cain lived for a time as a beast, but then he became a builder of societies. Gyllensten sets out to imitate Cain, and invoking the examples of the great system builders in Swedish literature—Swedenborg, Linné, and Strindberg—and of mythic figures such as Orpheus, he wills his way toward creativity and a constructive relationship to the world.

This new attitude is tested in *Palatset i parken* (1970; The palace in the park), which follows the mythic pattern of Orpheus's descent into Hades. A middle-aged man returns to a boardinghouse where he stayed while in school, a place haunted by memories like the shadows in Hades. The novel is fragmentary, and layers of memory merge into one another in a fashion reminiscent of Strindberg's *Ett drömspel*. Ultimately, the novel attempts to establish a constructive relationship between the individual and the world. The same striving underlies *Mänskan, djuren, all naturen* (1971; People, animals, all of nature), which blends fictional sketches with essayistic reflections and scientific and philosophical quotations. Gyllensten here develops his epistemological interpretation of elective affinities: we are capable of comprehending only that which we have already partially understood; we identify as truth that which is related to ourselves.

The structure of *Grottan i öknen* (1973; The cave in the desert) resembles a shattered Chinese box. There are three levels to the story, and splinters of each level can be found in the other. The first level is church father Athanasius's biography of the hermit Antonius. The second level is a kaleidoscopic view of Athanasius's life with anachronistic fragments of contemporary life. On the third level, a man returns to a boardinghouse where he lived while in school (a variation on the theme in *Palatset i parken*) and writes the biography of a modern hermit, whose withdrawal from society entailed doing what good he could in a home for the incurably ill. The progression is here from total isolation in the desert to a more "engaged" form of isolation.

I skuggan av Don Juan (1975; In the shadow of Don Juan) is about the legendary swordsman and seducer of women, a figure who also held great fascination for Kierkegaard. Don Juan is driven by a compulsion to assert himself and his will, a compulsion that leads to his downfall. The name of Don Juan's servant, Juanito (Little Juan), points to the fact that he is a distorted version of his master. Juanito has little will or courage, but this lack brings him a better fate than the swaggering master in whose shadow he lives. Gyllensten returns to the topic in *Skuggans återkomst eller Don Juan går igen* (1985; The return of the shadow, or Don Juan haunts). In this novel, an aged and penitent Don Juan longs for a way to endure life.

In *Baklängesminnen* (1978; Backward memories), the usual progression of a memoir, from youth to maturity, is turned backward. The novel takes up the question of the "right way of reading" sought by the biblical interpreters of the Middle Ages. It is a search not only for the right way of reading books but for a way of reading the Book of Life. The same theme is present in *Huvudskallebok* (1981; Skull book) and *Rätt och slätt* (1983; Pure and simple).

Sju vise mästare om kärlek (1986; Seven wise masters on love) has a contemporary, realistic frame in which the narrator tells of a brief, passionate encounter in Seville. This episode gives rise to a string of Buddhist legends dealing with love. The Eastern notions of reincarnation and karma alter the usual Western perspective on injustices in life. Suffering in one life is compensated for in another. Before perfection can be attained, countless forms of existence must be experienced.

In his collection of essays and aphorisms *Just så eller kanske det* (1989; Just so or maybe so), Gyllensten suggests that we ought to praise the world we live in—in order to make it worthy of praise. The thought is developed in the novel *Det himmelska gästabudet* (1991; The heavenly banquet). A handful of people are gathered in Heaven, and in the manner of the *Decameron* or *Canterbury Tales* with echoes of Plato's *Symposium*, each has a story to tell. From this vantage point, the same as Pär Lagerkvist's in *Det eviga leendet*, the guests attempt to find a meaning to life on earth in the face of sufferings and indignities and the certainty of death. Through the stories, Gyllensten offers some possible attitudes to life. *Det himmelska gästabudet* ends in humble praise and wonder before the immensity of creation.

In *Anteckningar från en vindskupa* (1993; Notes from an attic), the protagonist is a postmodernist counterpart of Dostoevsky's Underground Man, an uncommitted observer of life and suffering. By his own admission, he is the prototypical Western man, spiritually poor and "amoral in an innocent shamelessness," who lives in a society of heedless consumerism. The novel offers a chilling view of yet another existential position as part of Gyllensten's unique dialectical authorship.

The six decades between 1890 and 1950 saw more technological advances and social changes than ever before in Sweden's history. Correspondingly, there was more formal innovation in literature than ever before as authors sought to keep up with the rapid pace of social change. During these years, a belief in humankind's ability to shape its destiny was affirmed by some literary voices (the *tiotalister* and social realists among the working-class authors, for example), only to be seriously questioned by modernist views as waves of global warfare swept through Europe. Each new development in history has caused a reevaluation of humankind's place in the universe, and literature continues to be an important agent of humankind's reappraisal of itself.

Literature after 1950

Rochelle Wright

7

In Sweden, as in much of the rest of the world, the years immediately following the Second World War and most of the 1950s were characterized by political and economic regrouping. When the shortages of the war years gradually gave way to expansion, prosperity, and growth, there was a corresponding rise in the overall standard of living. Democratic social reform was the hallmark of the period, as Per Albin Hansson's vision of a *folkhem* (people's home) providing cradle-to-grave security for all individuals was translated into progressive legislation. The educational system was democratized by extending obligatory schooling to nine years, and taxation policy was revised to help level economic inequalities. Though a cold war was developing between the American and the Soviet spheres of influence, Sweden's foreign policy continued to stress nonalignment, an active neutrality referred to as *tredje ståndpunkten* (the third standpoint). In general, however, there was reduced emphasis on international affairs and increased attention to national concerns and the purely private sphere.

The *fyrtiotalister* (1940s generation) is the last group for whom the traditional decade division so beloved of Swedish literary historians is a meaningful one. Their common philosophical or existential stance—pessimism and angst—was a natural response, even in neutral Sweden, to the horror and devastation of the war and its aftermath. In contrast, the 1950s reveal little unanimity in the literary scene; pluralism is, in fact, the single most striking feature of the period. In the absence of a clearly delineated collective profile among new writers, some of the most important literary works of the decade were produced by established authors, among both the social realists and the poetic modernists. For example, the epic tradition came to renewed prominence with Vilhelm Moberg's emigrant tetralogy and Ivar Lo-Johansson's eight-volume series of autobiographical narratives; prose fiction also continued to encompass the philosophical, moral, and religious concerns of Lars Ahlin and the experimentation, skepticism, and dialectic approach of Lars Gyllensten. Gunnar Ekelöf, rather than any younger colleague, was the dominant lyric voice of the decade. Other major poetic contributions by older writers include Pär Lagerkvist's *Aftonland* (Evening land), published in 1953, and Harry Martinson's *Aniara,* which appeared in 1957.

NEW PROSE WRITERS AFTER THE WAR

The most direct inheritor of the epic narrative tradition of Vilhelm Moberg and Ivar Lo-Johansson is Per Anders Fogelström (1917–), a social realist cut in the 1930s mold. Unlike most of the writers of that earlier generation, however, Fogelström grew up in an urban environment, the working-class South Side of Stockholm, and it is the lives of members of the urban, industrial proletariat, past and present, and the growth and development of the city itself that is the subject matter of his fiction. His first important novel, *Sommaren med Monika* (1951; The summer with Monika), is actually the third in a series of works chronicling disaffected young people in the postwar period; the success of Ingmar Bergman's film of the same name (scripted by Fogelström) gave added momentum to the careers of both men. During the 1950s, Fogelström also published, among other works, the autobiographical *I kvinnoland* (1954; In women's country), but it was the five-volume *Stad* (City) series of the 1960s—*Mina drömmars stad* (1960; City of my dreams), *Barn av sin stad* (1962; Children of their city), *Minns du den stad* (1964; Do you remember the city?), *I en förvandlad stad* (1966; In a city transformed), and *Stad i världen* (1968; City in the world)—that established both his popularity with readers and his reputation with critics.

The time frame of the series is more than a hundred years, beginning in 1860 when an impoverished boy named Henning Nilsson arrives in the country's capital hoping to improve his lot. By focusing on Henning, his wife, and their descendants, and on several generations of another family, that of Henning's friend Ture Lindgren, called Tummen, Fogelström traces the city's growth from a relatively isolated, largely preindustrial town to a modern metropolis. Though the fictional characters are portrayed with sensitivity and psychological insight and their struggle to overcome hardship and carve out bearable lives for themselves is described in moving detail, it is the city that becomes the true protagonist of the narrative. An avid collector of Stockholm lore, Fogelström imparts a vast amount of historical information—on city planning, construction, and architecture but also about the lives of the inhabitants: tasks performed by manual laborers in occupations that no longer exist, patterns of socializing, and everyday domestic details. This material, albeit intrinsically fascinating, occasionally threatens to overwhelm the fictional superstructure.

His next novel, *Café Utposten* (1970; Café outpost), draws on a specific historical incident of 1908, the bombing by three Swedish anarchists of the *Amalthea,* a ship bringing English strikebreakers to their shores. The theme, however, is a universal one: the conflict between revolutionaries who accept and even promote violence in service of a just cause, and proponents of peaceful reform. The four-volume *Kamrater* (Comrades) series—*Upptäckarna* (1972; The explorers), *Revoltörerna* (1973; The rebels), *Erövrarna* (1975; The conquerors), and *Besittarna* (1977; The possessors)—concerns Fogelström's own generation, which came of age between the world wars and whose youth coincided with the rise of social democracy and the welfare state. The first volume, set in 1927 in the author's childhood environs, a working-class Stockholm neighborhood, introduces three eleven-year-old boys and their families. The narrative stresses the boys' optimism, enthusiasm, and spirit of discovery in the face of economic want. In succeeding volumes, each set approximately ten years apart, both the evolution of their respective careers and the vicissitudes of their personal lives are intended to illustrate the process by which individuals from unpretentious, even impoverished backgrounds could become affluent members of the middle class—though social mobility alone is no guarantee of happiness.

Another Folgelström series, *Vävarnas barn* (1981; Children of the weavers), *Krigens barn* (1985; Children of the wars), and *Vita bergens barn* (1987; Children of White Mountains District), turns to an earlier period in the history of Stockholm, the eighteenth and early nineteenth centuries. In the first volume, the author implicitly provides a realistic correlative to the prevailing positive image of cultural and literary flowering during the reign of Gustav III, when the vast majority of the population endured conditions that were unspeakably miserable. The time frame of the second book is more or less the same as that of Jan Fridegård's *Soldat* (soldier) series, but Fogelström emphasizes the effect of the ongoing wars on the urban proletariat rather than on those who fought or the rural population. The final volume, which brings the action up to the mid-nineteenth century, connects this series with Fogelström's own earlier *Stad* books both chronologically and by reintroducing several characters from *Mina drömmars stad*. Fogelström's achievement is thus to have portrayed the development of Stockholm from the perspective of the working class through three centuries and more than a dozen novels. His interest in history takes a more personal turn in *Komikern: Roman om en teaterfamilj* (1989; The comedian: Novel of a theatrical family), which is based on the life of his grandfather, the actor Fredrik Deland. In the novel *Mödrar och söner* (1991; Mothers and sons), Fogelström returns to typical themes and motifs: changes in the Stockholm district of Kungsholmen in the decades around 1900 provide a backdrop for the fictional narrative. *Hem, till sist* (1993; Home, at last), a memoir, concentrates on the author's family background and childhood but also describes the inception of the *Stad* series.

Though Birgitta Trotzig (1929–) also sets much of her fiction in past centuries, localizes it to a particular area of Sweden (the province of Skåne, specifically in or near Kristianstad), and focuses on society's outsiders, it is difficult to imagine a writer whose philosophical orientation is more unlike Fogelström's. To Fogelström, poverty and deprivation are the product of specific political, economic, and social circumstances that can be identified, described, combated, and ultimately overcome. Trotzig is by no means indifferent to political and social issues: while living in Paris for many years, she experienced the repercussions of the Algerian conflict firsthand and began speaking out against the evils of war and colonialism long before public consciousness was raised about U.S. involvement in Vietnam. The orientation of her fiction, however, is toward the metaphysical. In the world view of her short stories and novels, suffering and injustice are not merely external conditions but manifestations or reflections of an impoverished inner world that is unique to each individual, difficult to grasp, and virtually impossible to vanquish.

A convert to Roman Catholicism, Birgitta Trotzig offers variations on related moral themes and wrestles with the theodicy problem: why does suffering exist, and how can an omnipotent God allow it to continue? Why do human beings, despite good intentions, so often fail in their efforts to love one another? These issues are formulated in her first important novel, *De utsatta* (1957; The exposed), which takes place in Skåne at the end of the seventeenth century, when the province repeatedly had changed hands between Sweden and Denmark. The main character, a minister named Isak Graa, is caught in this political struggle, removed from his calling, and forced to become a beggar. Humiliated and cast out from society through no fault of his own, he becomes a sort of provincial Job figure suffering at the hands of an incomprehensible fate or indifferent God. *En berättelse från kusten* (1961; A story from the coast) explores similar timeless issues in a different historical setting, the late Middle Ages.

Sveket (1966; The betrayal) reveals certain plot parallels to Vilhelm Moberg's *De knutna händerna*. In both novels, a man confuses love for his daughter with his own need to dominate and control, and this failure of empathy leads to the daughter's death. In *Sveket*, however, the betrayal is far more complex, for Tobit's all-consuming love has its roots in guilt at having failed the girl's mother, and his inability to love selflessly ultimately stems from his parents' rejection of him.

The parent-child relationship is also central to several other novels by Trotzig. In *Sjukdomen* (1972; The illness), parental insufficiency once again has dire consequences for the next generation. Albin Ström's flaw is not lovelessness—he is supportive and caring toward his son Elje—but his lack of a language to express what he feels and consequent failure to teach the boy to communicate. Without words to establish contact with others, Elje cannot formulate his own identity and remains amorphous, contourless, anonymous. His illness, schizophrenia, is the ultimate breakdown in communication: a total separation from reality that leads to a confused act of violence against another.

Dykungens dotter (1985; The marsh king's daughter) evinces many thematic parallels with earlier novels: the effect of actions and choices on subsequent generations, the difficulty of true communication, the inefficacy of love in sparing others from harm. Set in the present century, the story follows an unnamed girl, later simply called "Mojan" (Skåne dialect for Mom), and her descendants. As a result of a sexual encounter with a sailor, the untamed, uncivilized "marsh king" of the title, the girl bears an out-of-wedlock child. She tries to make a life for herself and her daughter in town, but the combined pressures of hard labor, social ostracism, and the periodic but unpredictable return of her lover render her ineffective at protecting the girl, who goes her own way and in turn bears a child. After the daughter's death, Mojan focuses her love and attention on her grandson but again is powerless to stave off his downfall. Whether heredity or environment plays the greater role in the progressive downward spiral of the action remains an unanswered question.

Birgitta Trotzig's narratives have sometimes been called legends or sagas because of their timeless and universal qualities. Trotzig often blurs distinctions between genres by incorporating poetic or essayistic passages in her prose; she has published volumes of short stories, essays, and prose poems as well as the novels for which she is best known. Though her prose is dense and the subject matter often painful, there are also passages of great lyricism and visionary power, frequently with biblical overtones, that serve to mitigate her descriptions of seemingly unredeemed human suffering. A remarkably consistent and self-contained writer, Birgitta Trotzig was elected a member of the Swedish Academy in 1993.

Whereas Trotzig stands apart, Pär Rådström (1925–63) is considered by many the quintessential voice of the 1950s, a writer who treats ennui, spleen, and the search for meaning in the specific context of that decade. In his trilogy about Greg Bengtsson, *Tiden väntar inte* (1952; Time doesn't wait), *Greg Bengtsson och kärleken* (1953; Greg Bengtsson and love), and *Ärans portar* (1954; The gates of glory), Rådström creates an antihero who flounders through life, out of touch with his own needs and desires and unable to establish emotional bonds with others. The first novel takes place in a provincial backwater where social life centers on Saturday evenings in the City Hotel dining room. The young protagonist, nominally employed as a fledgling journalist, spends much time and emotional energy writing the "history" of an imaginary country he calls Baravia; by creating a land of make-believe where he alone is sovereign, he flees the impotence and tedium of his everyday life. His ostrichlike behavior reflects the self-involvement of an alienated generation.

The remaining novels of the trilogy are mostly set in Stockholm, where Greg Bengtsson now works writing advertising copy. Marriage, entered into unreflectively, only increases his disaffection, since he and his wife rarely communicate successfully, and he retreats farther and farther into alcoholism and another imagined universe, a projected but unwritten novel about life at sea. In *Ärans portar*, the colorless Greg becomes a less important figure than his next-door neighbor, an ambitious if somewhat vacuous photographer improbably named Astolf Felixsson. Through Astolf's circle of acquaintances, Rådström provides a portrait of a group of *strebers* who buy the "right" things and cultivate the proper attitudes while utterly lacking any true ideology or even taste; they are blissfully unaware that this veneer of culture only partially masks their superficiality.

Various characters in Rådström's works have traits in common with their creator. Role playing, masks, and alter egos all figure directly in the innovative autobiographical novel *Sommargästerna* (1960; The summer guests), in which the narrator Pär Rådström becomes acquainted with his fictional counterpart Paul Renberg and then pursues him when he mysteriously disappears. The narrative also comments on and explains how it came to be written, but the author avoids more speculative and philosophical aspects of the metanovel, proclaiming that he has merely chosen an unusual technique to tell his story. *Översten* (1961; The colonel) continues to explore themes related to personality formation and the search for authenticity in a world increasingly dominated by icons of popular culture; here the protagonist tries—and fails—to find coherence through a cult of Gustav IV Adolf.

Several of the best stories in the collection *Ro utan åror* (1961; Rowing without oars) focus on children, such as the little boy in "På tillväxt" (Catching up), who has been held back from beginning school. The world of childhood and adult reality are often disconnected in Rådström's fictional universe. This lack of continuity suggests an underlying reason for the dislocation and rootlessness of many of his adult characters, a theme that is overtly explored in the novel *Mordet* (1962; The murder). Here the protagonist murders the child within him, mistakenly believing that this act will eliminate his self-pity and force him to face reality, but because he has never integrated his internal child with his adult personality, he is unable truly to move on.

Pär Rådström's unmistakable style is a peculiar mixture of breezy conversational jargon, stream of consciousness, and literary quotations and allusions; the early novels also parody old-fashioned journalese through the self-conscious use of plural verbs and inverted word order. The 1980s saw a resurgence of interest in Rådström, in part perhaps because of a more general nostalgia for the 1950s. His works deserve consideration not just as typical documents of the time, however, for their satiric tone often disguises a more serious theme. The underlying melancholy and weariness that paralyze so many of Rådström's characters are not attributable to the decade in which they live but rather reflect their inability to come to grips with fundamental existential issues that everyone must confront.

The term *nyprovinsialism* (new provincialism) was coined in the 1950s to refer collectively to the regional anchoring of several important prose writers of the postwar period. In fact, the term is misleading. Though the dominance of Stockholm in Swedish literary and cultural life and in the publishing industry was long-established, works of literature had not evinced such a narrow, exclusive focus in previous decades. Certain writers of earlier generations are inextricably associated with their home provinces: the Värmland of Selma Lagerlöf and Gustaf Fröding, and the Småland of Vilhelm Moberg. Norrland, the sparsely populated northern half of the country that is largely covered by forests, is the setting of several earlier Swedish classics: Martin Koch's *Timmerdalen* (1913) and Eyvind Johnson's four-volume autobiographical novel *Romanen om Olof* (1936–39). These works and many of Moberg's novels had helped establish a tradition of social awareness in regional literature by concentrating on society's least fortunate members.

Chronologically, Stina Aronson (1892–1956) bridges the gap between such older writers as Koch and Johnson and those whose careers began after the war; though her debut came as early as 1921, her most important works were published in the late 1940s and early 1950s. Her novels and short stories reveal a profound awareness of the difficult lives of the impoverished inhabitants of Norrland as well as a deep appreciation of the expansive, barren beauty of the landscape. The novels of Björn-Erik Höijer (1907–) are also set in the north of Sweden; the autobiographical narratives about his alter ego Martin, in particular *Martin går i gräset* (1950; Martin walks in the grass), call to mind Eyvind Johnson's masterpiece. Sven Rosendahl (1913–), himself from a prosperous Stockholm suburb, locates his fictional universe both in Norrland and in the equally isolated and remote *finnskogar* (forests originally settled by Finnish immigrants) of Värmland. The best-known among his many novels is *Gud fader och tattaren* (1951; God and the gypsy), a penetrating study of a social outcast and his attempt to overcome prejudice against his origins.

The literary career of Sara Lidman (1923–) has undergone several transformations. In the 1960s and 1970s, she turned away from fiction entirely to concentrate on political issues and documentary reporting. During the 1950s, however, she published four novels set in the interior of Norrland that established her as one of the most original new voices of the decade.

Sara Lidman's Norrland, in and near the fictional village of Ecksträsk (based on Missenträsk, where she grew up), is a sparsely populated, inhospitable landscape where impoverished farmers struggle to survive. Rarely do they even visit a town in their own province; the rest of Sweden is so remote that it seems like a foreign country. Because of this isolation, moral dilemmas and interpersonal conflicts must be resolved without intervention from the outside, through the interplay of individual conscience and collective village mentality. These, in turn, are largely determined by the dictates of evangelical Christianity; virtually all Lidman's characters are steeped in biblical language and lore, even those who choose to ignore the Bible's teachings.

Tjärdalen (1953; Valley of the charcoal burners), her first novel, focuses on both individual and collective guilt. The farmer Nisj discovers that his charcoal burner, which would have provided him with desperately needed cash, has been destroyed by the village ne'er-do-well, called Räven (the Fox). Räven is literally trapped by his own act, however, since the burner collapses on top of him, breaking his leg. The angry villagers carry him home but leave him unattended, and by the time a doctor is called, gangrene has set in and his life cannot be saved. Though Petrus, the village elder, had not known of these events in time to intervene, he feels a sense of personal responsibility and is distressed by the others' lack of charity; they become less than fully human, he believes, if they cannot tolerate an aberrant person in their midst. But when a well-to-do farmer takes advantage of Nisj's desperate situation by buying his charcoal for a pittance, Petrus does not intervene, since he himself owes the purchaser money. In his own eyes, he is now just as guilty as the villagers.

Hjortronlandet (1955; Cloudberry land) centers on a group of impoverished crofters in the hinterlands whose economic situation is even more precarious than that of the Ecksträsk villagers. These crofters have settled on free government land, available as a result of a policy aimed at populating and cultivating Norrland's interior, but the government inspectors have little understanding of the actual conditions the pioneers face. The focus of the novel is not, however, misguided social policy but the way human potential is crippled in this setting: the gifted Märit, encouraged by the schoolteacher to continue her studies, instead stays home, becomes pregnant, and eventually dies of tuberculosis.

Though both *Tjärdalen* and *Hjortronlandet* are collective novels that illustrate the complex and interconnected personal, social, and economic structure of rural society, their primary emphasis is on individual psychology, not least with respect to the women who respond to and comment on, but rarely influence, the action. Sara Lidman's next two novels, *Regnspiran* (1958; The rain bird) and *Bära mistel* (1960; Bearing mistletoe), share a female protagonist, the strong-willed and independent-minded but unhappy and misguided Linda Ståhl; the collective is represented primarily in terms of attitudes Linda tries to combat and rebel against. The rain bird of the first novel's title is a bird of ill omen, associated with Linda. Unloved as a child, as a young woman she becomes vengeful, betraying in turn several people who trust her, yet she is not deliberately and consciously malicious. In the second novel, Linda falls blindly in love with an itinerant musician and abandons a life of economic security to accompany him on his travels. The object of her passion, however, is homosexual, and during the course of enduring indifference and mistreatment from him, she gradually achieves insight into the nature of selfless love.

In Sara Lidman's novels, words and grammatical forms indigenous to Norrland appear not only in dialogue or interior monologue but also in strictly narrative sequences. Colloquial, fragmentary, and stream-of-consciousness passages and the formalized cadences and rhythms of the Bible merge into a unique and powerfully suggestive stylistic voice.

Sven Fagerberg (1918–), who was influenced by and has written about the international modernist movement, reveals an interest in myth and Eastern philosophy in his dense, complex first novel, *Höknatt* (1957; Hawk night). *Svärdfäktarna* (1963; The fencers), in which Zen plays a prominent role, adds an element of social satire. Having held a high position in a multinational corporation, Fagerberg is familiar with the world of business and finance and skewers it in several works, notably *Kostymbalen* (1961; The costume ball) and *Det vitmålade hjärtat* (1966; The heart painted white), which uses conventional devices of the detective story to unravel the corrupt machinations underlying a successful financial empire in a country he calls Yamanien. In Johan Bergenstråhle's film version from the following year, *Made in Sweden*, the anticapitalist aspect of the novel is oversimplified to make it correspond to a more orthodox Marxist view. Fagerberg's criticism of bureaucratic structures and high technology continues in *Revolt inifrån* (1969; Revolt from within).

By incorporating essayistic digressions and self-contained myths or fairy tales into the fictional superstructure, Fagerberg often crosses genre boundaries and creates narratives that can be read on several levels. His *oeuvre* encompasses an apparent contradiction: he celebrates the power of intuition and mythical or symbolic interpretations of reality, at the same time honing an intellectual, analytical approach to problem solving.

NEW POETS IN THE 1950S

Though it is difficult to isolate common characteristics among prose writers who came to prominence in the 1950s, in many instances their respective connections with various predecessors are apparent: Fogelström, and in a less direct manner, Lidman, build on the epic tradition and social consciousness of the working-class writers of the 1930s, whereas Trotzig may be regarded as an inheritor of the pessimistic, existential orientation of the 1940s. For poets, the situation was more complex. Poetic modernism came late to Sweden, but new poets in the first decade or so after the war did not experience the liberating impact of its breakthrough. They were nevertheless forced to come to grips with modernism and choose whether to build on the movement or to question it.

Some poets turned to the past, away from free verse forms to rhyme and meter, and to the traditional subject matter of poetry: personal issues of an aesthetic, philosophical, and metaphysical nature. Albeit vaguely defined, this stance was sometimes called neoromantic. It incorporated a strain of religious mysticism as well as the cultivation of anonymity through the assumption of different roles and identities and a playful self-consciousness expressed in irony, parody, and pastiche. New Criticism, the nascent critical school, sanctioned this shift to internal rather than external concerns through its emphasis on the primary nature of the text itself, rather than the context surrounding it. Many of the newest poets were themselves academically trained in the study of literature, and criticism, not the political and social debate in which the 1940s generation had been involved, was the focus of their interest. In some cases, the extreme youth of those making their debuts and their consequent lack of experience—several became published writers while still enrolled in secondary school—may have militated against involvement in the nonliterary concerns of the day.

Among new poets in the 1950s there were no immediately apparent leading figures as there had been in the previous decade. Instead, there were various competing literary coteries, often clustered around a short-lived journal. The first of these was called—somewhat ominously, given the lack of unanimity that was to characterize the decade—*50-tal* (The fifties). In another sense, the name was prophetic, however, for during its brief life span, from 1950 to 1952, the journal served as a venue for virtually all the important new poets of the time. The collective profile of this generation, as described by Bo Setterlind (1923–91) in the 1951 article "De nya romantikerna" (The new romantics), was an emphasis on individualism, aesthetic concerns, and religion, and a refusal to moralize or take a stand on topical issues.

The group calling itself Metamorfos, which included Lennart Nilsén-Somre (1923–), Paul Andersson (1930–76), Petter Bergman (1934–86), Urban Torhamn (1930–), Ingvar Orre (1932–), Svante Foerster (1931–80), and Lasse Söderberg (1931–), also proclaimed neoromanticism as a literary ideal, only to quarrel about the meaning of the term. Despite a high public profile, they offered no coherent literary program. With respect to image, at least, the group followed the lead of American beat poets; rather than establish a journal, they preferred to distribute stenciled copies of their poems and read them aloud at jazz clubs. Much of their work nevertheless hearkens to the past; it is characterized by imagery derived from, among others, Swedish romantic poets Atterbom and Stagnelius. In particular, the figure of Paul Andersson and his poem "Elegi över en förlorad sommar" (1953; Elegy on a lost summer) served to epitomize the role of the poet as outsider and romantic rebel. An anthology of the Metamorfos poets, *Sex unga lyriker* (1954; Six young poets), put out by Folket i Bild's (FIB:s) lyrikklubb, sold ten thousand copies.

In keeping with the proclaimed "new provincialism" of the decade, various groups outside Stockholm also attained prominence, notably Ingemar

Gustafson (1928–), Majken Johansson (1930–93), and Göran Printz-Påhlson (1931–) in Lund, who drew on the modernist tradition and on the existential orientation of the preceding decade reviving forgotten verse forms such as the villanella. Gustafson and Johansson each turned from an ironic, skeptical stance to religion, the former by converting to Roman Catholicism (whereupon he changed his name to Leckius) and the latter by joining the Salvation Army. Their respective religious conversions influenced both the subject matter and style of their work, as formal experimentation gives way to traditional Christian imagery. Printz-Påhlson's poetry displays vast learning and carries on an implicit intertextual discourse—in fact, Printz-Påhlson was the first to introduce the concept of intertextuality to Sweden. His study of poetic modernism, *Solen i Spegeln* (1958; The sun in the mirror), was the most important critical work of the decade. An anthology of his poems, *Säg minns du skeppet Refanut?* (Say, do you remember the ship *Refanut?*), appeared in 1984.

Several of the poets making their debuts in the years around 1950 who, in retrospect, stand out as the most important voices of the postwar period were not affiliated with any particular movement or group, though their work incorporates certain salient characteristics of the literary climate of the time. Lars Forssell (1928–) epitomizes the scope and breadth of poetic concerns during the 1950s. In an essay from 1949, he argues that there is no inherent contradiction between being committed to serious literature and simultaneously working in the vein of light entertainment. In keeping with this belief, he published popular verse and song lyrics as well as erudite and esoteric poems; flexible and versatile, Forssell deliberately cultivates variety and eclecticism, even within a single collection.

Forssell earned a bachelor's degree at Harvard University, and an Anglo-Saxon orientation is apparent in his reflective poetry, in particular with regard to the works of T. S. Eliot and Ezra Pound (he introduced the latter to a Swedish readership). He is reluctant to reveal his own identity or point of view; instead, he displays his learning by playing with masks and assuming the roles of various historical and fictional characters. A favorite persona is that of the fool or jester, a protean figure who shifts character and whose utterances may be interpreted on several levels. His second collection, *Narren* (1952; The jester), explores the ambiguities implicit in the role: the clown is simultaneously truth-sayer, performer, analyst, and mirror. An essay on Charlie Chaplin from the following year stresses the same qualities. In *Telegram* (1957), Forssell's motifs and voices range from the sublime to the whimsical, from Odysseus and Penelope to Winnie-the-Pooh. Later collections include a series of poems about Nijinski (*Röster*

[1964; Voices]) and political poems and songs in *Jack uppskäraren* (1966; Jack the Ripper). A central motif is fear—of death, of aging, of humdrum routine—counterbalanced by the positive motif of the security of love.

In contrast to the relative obscurity of some of his serious poetry, Forssell's light verse and popular song lyrics, in particular those in *Snurra min jord och andra visor* (1958; Spin, my earth and other songs), have been widely performed and recorded. Inspired by French cabaret tradition, Forssell has also translated and recast French songs into Swedish. Many texts convey a political message. *Visor svarta och röda* (1972; Songs black and red) contrasts the theme of love with its opposite force, violence and oppression. Forssell has sometimes worked directly with performers.

In the late 1960s and early 1970s, Forssell's serious poetry, too, becomes more straightforward and immediate, in part because of an increased political bent. *Oktoberdikter* (1971; October poems), for instance, concerns the Russian Revolution, and Lenin, the speaker in one series of poems, grapples with the familiar question of whether noble ends ever can jústify repressive means. In the collection *Försök* (1972; Attempt), Forssell's external stimulus is more immediately topical: the U.S. bombing of Hanoi. Subsequently, Forssell turns toward more personal subject matter. He also explores the possibilities of traditional verse forms by publishing a collection of sonnets (*Sånger* [1986; Songs]).

Forssell is also a distinguished dramatist. The short one-act play *Narren som tillhörde sina bjällror* (1953; The jester who belonged to his bells) uses wordplay, rhythmic incantation, and rhyme to create an absurdist quality; the theme, as in poetry centering on the jester motif, concerns questions of mask and identity. In *Mary Lou* (1962), the title character, broadcasting for the Nazis during the Second World War, encourages American soldiers to desert by pretending to be seductive. The contrast between her radio persona and her "ordinary" self is another manifestation of role playing, but the play also explores issues of loyalty to political systems and moral principles as well as to oneself.

Söndagspromenaden (1963; Eng. tr. *Sunday Promenade,* 1968) illustrates how a dreamer and play-actor manages to draw others into his magic circle. A confrontation with brutal reality has apparently tragic results, but the play concludes with a reassertion of the power of the dream. *Galenpannan* (1964; The madcap) continues to investigate the ambiguity of definitions of madness and sanity, of illusion and reality. The title character is the deposed Swedish King Gustaf IV Adolf, who after his removal from the throne lived abroad under the name "Överste [Colonel] Gustafsson." His "madness" is shown to be remarkably astute and internally consistent, at

least with respect to an understanding of political events. The companion piece *Christina Alexandra* (1968) focuses on another much-maligned
Swedish monarch, Queen Christina, both before and after her abdication
and self-imposed exile. Though in his afterword Forssell refers to the
work as a dream play that permits anachronisms and the rearrangement of
chronology, he nevertheless attempts to provide a psychologically consistent interpretation of Christina's personality and motivation: she is a deeply
unhappy individual, wounded, contradictory, and incapable of wholeness.
Forssell also offers a social perspective and context: voices of the people
provide a sort of ongoing chorus, pointing out that Christina is utterly
unaware of the poverty and suffering that prevail outside the monarch's
sheltered circle. Despite the reference to dream-play technique, Forssell
does not draw directly on Strindberg's expressionistic theater or his play
Kristina.

Several plays of the 1960s and 1970s have political themes. *Sverige,
Sverige eller Borgerlighetens fars* (1967; Sweden, Sweden, or The farce of the
bourgeoisie) uses slapstick and disjointed dialogue to satirize those who are
concerned with image rather than substance. *Borgaren och Marx* (1970; The
bourgeois and Marx) recasts Molière's *Le Bourgeois gentilhomme* as a send-
up of the pursuit of radical chic and politically "correct" jargon, simultaneously making the point that Molière's message—that social climbers always
blow as the wind blows—is timeless. *Haren och Vråken* (1977; The hare and
the vulture) is a skillful pastiche of the world of Carl Michael Bellman as
seen from a modern, class-conscious perspective. Fredman, Ulla Winblad,
and Bellman himself are characters, and the play effectively incorporates
several well-known Bellman songs. Ulla, who is annoyed at Bellman for
writing such scandalous things about her, has broken with her previous
life and purchased an inn called Haren och Vråken located in Haga Park.
Her main goal in life is to protect her fifteen-year-old daughter, Anna-
Britta, from the misery she herself has experienced, especially with respect
to men. This idyll is shattered when Captain Rytterstjärna kidnaps the girl
and rapes her, in retaliation for which Ulla's friends condemn and hang
him. General Piper, previously a friend and admirer of Ulla, now displays
solidarity with his fellow aristocrat by ordering his men to surround the inn
and set it on fire with everyone except Bellman inside. The name of the inn
thus becomes a metaphor for the victims and oppressors in society, and the
triumph of the status quo within the play reflects events on a larger stage,
for the action is set on 19 August 1772, the day of Gustav III's bloodless
coup. Art, in the person of Bellman, supports the status quo and gains from
its support while hunting real-life models from the lower classes. *Haren*

och Vråken is a powerful work that conveys a social and political message without preaching.

Forssell's fascination with the outsider or rebel comes to the fore in several plays based on actual persons, notably *Show* (1971), whose central figure closely resembles Lenny Bruce, and *Lasse i Gatan eller Pirater* (1982; Street-Lasse, or Pirates), which draws on the career of the notorious pirate who, after coming to the assistance of Karl XII, was ennobled under the name Lars Gatenhjelm. *Pirater* includes musical numbers and is composed in a variety of poetic forms ranging from free verse to rhymed couplets, thus displaying the author's linguistic virtuosity. In contrast, dialogue in the partly autobiographical *Bergsprängaren och hans dotter Eivor* (The dynamite blaster and his daughter Eivor) from 1989 is unadorned and realistic. Set in Stockholm of the 1930s and subtitled "A naturalistic tragedy," it reveals a world where class differences are insurmountable and good intentions can do little to alleviate suffering. Forssell, a multifaceted writer and a master of several genres, was elected to the Swedish Academy in 1971.

Östen Sjöstrand (1925–), essayist, translator, and editor as well as poet, reveals a markedly international orientation in a period otherwise noted for turning inward. His interests, like Forssell's, are eclectic. Attracted to Christian mysticism, he became a convert to Roman Catholicism in the early 1950s. While religious themes and motifs continue to be prominent in his poetry, his orientation expands to become more mythic. A strong interest in the natural sciences, dating back to his school days, and a commitment to environmental issues long before they had coalesced into a movement coexist with his religious concerns. In an important essay, Sjöstrand testifies to his powerful affinity with music, which is expressed in the rhythms, sounds, and structures of his poetry; a long-standing collaboration with the Swedish composer Sven-Erik Bäck (1919–94) resulted in the opera *Gästabudet* (1951; The banquet) and an oratorio, among other works. Sjöstrand also translated into Swedish the libretti of others, notably W. A. Auden's text to Stravinsky's *The Rake's Progress*.

Sjöstrand's poems may be described as free meditations in a conversational tone, though their subject matter is often complex and visionary. Drawing on medieval light mysticism and on the Platonic tradition in poetry, particularly the works of the Swedish romantic poet Stagnelius, Sjöstrand perceives the spark in each individual soul as capable of lighting the way to religious ecstasy and ultimately to God. Like music, dreaming is a source of energy and power, a way of coming into contact with one's innermost self. In *I vattumannens tecken* (1967; In the sign of Aquarius),

Sjöstrand views the contemporary nihilistic, technological, materialistic age as leading to an apocalypse that in turn will usher in a second coming. A later collection, *Strömöverföring* (1977; Transfer of current), concentrates on the human sphere and in particular on the love motif. Several of the poems in *Strax ovanför vattenlinjen* (1984; Just above the waterline) refer to Baudelaire; the section "Återkomster" (Returns), about revisiting familiar places, features imagery associated with the sea.

The subject matter of Sjöstrand's poems is sometimes language itself and its potential for communicating inner experience. In his work, the tension between thesis and antithesis leads not necessarily to the resolution of synthesis but rather to new approaches to eternal existential problems. The process of investigation is itself an end. Sjöstrand's work, sometimes regarded as dense and esoteric but acclaimed by critics, earned the author election to the Swedish Academy in 1975. *The Hidden Music*, a volume of his poetry in English translation, was published in 1975, and a selection of poetry and prose, *Toward the Solitary Star*, appeared in 1988.

Tomas Tranströmer (1931–) holds a unique position among his Swedish contemporaries as a poet of international acclaim. Thus, virtually his entire production has been translated into English by skilled translators, including Robin Fulton, Leif Sjöberg, and such noted American poets as May Swenson and Robert Bly; Tranströmer has in turn translated Bly into Swedish. Two volumes, *Selected Poems, 1954–1986* (1987) and *Collected Poems* (1987), translated by Bly and Fulton, respectively, gather material that had appeared in various other collections and scattered poetry journals and offer the English-language reader the unusual opportunity of comparing different renditions of the same poems.

A partial explanation for Tranströmer's renown across linguistic and cultural boundaries may be that the most important features of his style, the combination of straightforward syntax with startling metaphor, survive translation relatively unscathed. Precise, concrete, yet bold and daring, Tranströmer's metaphors are used to capture a specific instant or sudden insight, freezing it in time and in the reader's imagination. They are often surrealistic in the technical sense of the term: they encapsulate the metamorphosis of experience by freeing the mind from habitual ways of ordering reality, with the result that the physical universe, the everyday world, may suddenly seem unreal. Tranströmer's imagery juxtaposes in startling ways the world of nature with signs of present-day technological civilization, so that dead mechanisms become animated and a lost mystery is restored. Because his imagination combines factual precision with visionary insight, his poems transform the abstract into the concrete and particular.

In contrast to much poetry of the 1950s, Tranströmer's work bridges the gap between object and word.

A gifted amateur pianist, Tranströmer has described music as providing serenity and a retreat from the turbulence of the modern world. Though rhythm is important in his poetry, his imagination is nevertheless primarily visual rather than aural, a quality that no doubt facilitates the work of the translator. Another contributing factor to the attention he has attracted outside his homeland is the universality of his subject matter; many of his most remarkable poems are about the natural world or spiritual immanence. Particularly in his early work, he strives to find an impersonal, anonymous voice in which the poet's individuality is absent.

Unlike many of the poets of his generation, Tranströmer did not receive his academic training in literature. A practicing psychologist, he has not been associated with any particular literary circle or trend, and he only occasionally participated in topical literary and cultural debate. The fact that he pursued his own interests regardless of the prevailing political climate drew fire from more doctrinaire poets, especially during the 1960s and 1970s, when he was accused of being elitist and escapist. His work is not ideological, but in a broader sense it is often concerned with human history, with the world surrounding the contemporary individual, from which there is no escape. Tranströmer does not, however, focus on specific events but rather sees human endeavor from a more universal perspective, in the context of the natural world.

Tranströmer attracted immediate attention in 1954 with his debut collection, *17 dikter* (17 poems). Here and in subsequent collections, *Hemligheter på vägen* (1958; Secrets along the way); *Den halvfärdiga himlen* (1962; The half-finished heaven), the poet functions as an observer, a witness, and objectifies his own role by referring to himself in the third person. This characteristic stance remains relatively unchanged until *Östersjöar* (1974; Baltics), which consists of a single long poem. It focuses on a locale for which he feels a particular affinity, an island in the Stockholm archipelago. By Tranströmer's own account, this poem represents a renewal; in it, the poet speaks in his own voice, in a conversational tone.

Tranströmer's production may be self-contained, but it is not static. In his later collections, the gradual movement of the poetic voice from the role of apparently objective, dispassionate observer toward a greater personal involvement leads to a correspondingly darker vision and an increased awareness of insecurity and pain. In particular, *Sanningsbarriären* (1978; Eng. tr. *Truth Barriers*, 1980) represents a shift in Tranströmer's orientation. Though the earlier volumes *Klanger och spår* (1966; Sounds and tracks) and *Mörkerseende* (1970; Night vision) included material from his work life, the long poem "Galleriet" ("The Gallery") in *Sanningsbarriären* abandons entirely the mask of anonymity. Here, the poetic "I," spending the night in a motel along the highway, is kept awake by visions of faces of his patients, demanding to be noticed, acknowledged, remembered. These fragmentary, surrealistic images induce a sense of helplessness and an awareness of both the difficulty and the necessity of truly "seeing" others. Though Tranströmer sometimes chooses to work with older verse forms, prose poems are prominent in *Det vilda torget* (1983; The wild market square) and *För levande och döda* (1989; For the living and the dead).

Tranströmer's brevity and concentration, his spare, terse, even ascetic style, provides a marked contrast both with the sometimes flamboyant, overladen neoromanticism of certain other poets who made their debuts during the 1950s and with the political and confessional poetry that dominated the 1960s and 1970s. His total production is quite small—it can be gathered in a single volume—but its impact on poetry, in both a Swedish and an international context, has been powerful.

CONCRETE POETRY AND "NEW SIMPLICITY"

Poetry is generally considered the dominant genre of the 1950s. The sheer number of new poets who were published in the early years of the decade and their preeminent role in literary debate have contributed to this perception. Another factor was the establishment, in 1954, of FIB:s lyrikklubb, dedicated to publishing inexpensive volumes of high-quality poetry in large editions. Stig Carlson, a poet in his own right and the editor of the series from its inception until his death in 1971, probably did more than any other single figure, before or since, to disseminate poetry to a relatively wide audience.

In spite of the self-reflexive quality often associated with poetry of the period, and a fondness on the part of many poets for extravagant, elaborate metaphor, it is important to note that a more realistic, socially involved poetic tradition also continued through the 1950s, represented, for example, by Stig Sjödin and Birger Norman. In fact, the very issue of *50-tal* in which Setterlind's article on neoromanticism appeared also included an essay by Walter Dickson on an apparently opposing ideal, "Den nya realismen" (The new realism). (Dickson, himself a novelist, not a poet, wrote *Storbasens saga* [1950; The foreman's story], which draws on family oral tradition to chronicle the building of Sweden's railroads, and *Carmania* [1952] and its sequels, which provide a socialist perspective on urban emigration to America.) The apparent prominence of poetry appears in a different light when one considers publication statistics. With the exception of books put out by FIB:s lyrikklubb, volumes of poetry virtually never appeared in editions exceeding fifteen hundred. Then as now, the majority of the reading public preferred prose to poetry and realism to formal experimentation; by far the most popular works of the decade were Vilhelm Moberg's emigrant novels.

The lack of unanimity that characterized the 1950s became, if anything, more pronounced as the decade drew to a close. On the one hand, there was a brief flowering of literary experimentation as certain poets focused almost exclusively on the aural and visual aspects of poetry rather than its semantic content. The journal *Odyssé*, under the aegis of Öyvind Fahlström (1928–76), had proclaimed the virtues of concrete poetry as early as 1953 but met with little response. By the early 1960s, however, Fahlström's ideas began to catch on with avant-garde poets, in particular Bengt Emil Johnson (1936–), Åke Hodell (1919–), Lars Norén (1944–), and Jarl Hammarberg-Åkesson (1940–). Their works, in which sound combinations and progressions and the typographical arrangement and appearance of letters and words on the printed page elicit direct sensory response rather than reflection or analysis, push the definition of poetry to its furthest limits.

Simultaneously, however, a reaction arose against poetry that seemed not only irrelevant but self-indulgent because it was inaccessible to most readers and appeared to address an audience composed only of other poets. A renewed emphasis on the communicative function of poetry came to the fore. Göran Palm (1931–) is the writer most closely associated with the demystification of poetry that gradually occurred in the early 1960s and a style that came to be called "nyenkelhet" (new simplicity). Palm had established a public profile during the 1950s as a critic and as editor of the journal *Upptakt* (1955–58), but his first collection of poetry, *Hundens besök* (The dog's visit), appeared in 1961. In "Megafonen i poesiparken" (The megaphone in the poetry park), he calls into question the entire modernist tradition by satirizing the use of metaphor for its own sake and poetic obscurity in general. Palm also rebels against empty metaphysics. His intimate, conversational style is an attempt to establish direct contact with the reader, a tendency that is further developed in "Själens furir" (The soul's sergeant), the long, central poem in his second collection, *Världen ser dig* (1964; The world sees you). The poet engages the reader in a dialogue and includes his audience in a collective "we."

The works of Sonja Åkesson (1926–77) may also be regarded as part of the movement against perceived obscurity. The tone of her first two collections, *Situationer* (1957; Situations) and *Glasveranda* (1959; Glass veranda), is startlingly informal. Unlike many of her contemporaries, Åkesson had little formal education and had not pursued an academic degree. Her training ground as a poet was a study group organized by the education wing of the Social Democractic party. For subject matter, she turned to what she knew best: everyday life, in particular that of an ordinary housewife. She was not, however, unschooled in literature; in "Självbiografi" (Autobiography), from the collection *Husfrid* (1962; Domestic peace), she describes her own situation in part through quotations from, responses to, and ironic comparisons with Lawrence Ferlinghetti's poem of the same title. Sonja Åkesson's poetic voice is down-to-earth and distinctly female; by deflating various romantic myths about relations between the sexes, Åkesson provides a contrast and counterbalance to the elevated discourse of certain male contemporaries. She is the first Swedish poet to equate racism with sexism, in "Äktenskapsfrågan" (The marriage question), in which the repeated line "Vara vit mans slav" (Be white man's slave) refers to a married woman rather than a black. In many respects, Åkesson is a precursor of the feminist new wave that is an important aspect of literature of the 1970s.

Sandro Key-Åberg (1922–91) also found the language of everyday conversation suitable for poetic expression. In *Bildade människor* (1964; Educated/Created/Pictured people), he creates a form he dubs "prator" (chatterings). As the untranslatable play on words of the collection's title indicates, the poems are pictographs that enclose a text on the page within the physical contours of the speaker, often to humorous or satiric effect. The manner in which language may be misused to distort or disguise meaning is one of Key-Åberg's recurring themes. His infallible ear for dialogue is shown in particular in his "scenprator" (stage chatterings), collected in *O* (1965; Eng. tr. *O and an Empty Room*, 1970). These provide no stage directions and no information on the speakers, but merely identify different voices, and thus are ideally suited to public readings or radio performance. A typical pattern is one of recurrent misinterpretation and misunderstanding, as the speakers, whether unwittingly or willfully, talk past each other. *Härliga tid som randas* (1968; Great times dawning), about atomic warfare, and *Två slår den tredje* (1981; Two against one), about warfare within the family, are more conventional plays. A common theme in many of his works is the manner in which language can be used as a weapon. Key-Åberg puts an ironic twist on discussion about poetry's communicative function by using linguistically simple structures to illustrate the breakdown of communication. The handbook

Poetisk lek (1961; Poetic play) encourages everyone to give poetry writing a try.

Even in his earliest collections, such as *Skrämdas lekar* (1950; Scared folks' games) and *Vattenträd* (1951; Water tree), Key-Åberg reveals a social conscience and concern for the oppressed and downtrodden. Toward the end of the 1950s, this stance became more prevalent among other writers as well, and a gradual shift occurred from esoteric aesthetic concerns toward a political awakening. The production of Folke Isaksson (1927–) illustrates this progression. His debut, *Vinterresa* (1951; Winter journey), and other early collections follow in the footsteps of Rilke. *Det gröna året* (1954; The green year) established his reputation as a nature poet. The conflict between elegiac idyll and the consciousness of social problems becomes apparent in *Blått och svart* (1957; Blue and black). He also continues to write portrait poems, however, such as "Almqvist i landsflykt" (Almqvist in exile) in *Teckenspråk* (1959; Sign language). The step to political awareness is complete in *Terra magica* (1963), whose dominant motifs are the concentration camp Theresienstadt and the Algerian war of independence.

Setterlind, whose public persona was that of the quintessential romantic, was also among the first to herald the move toward a more socially conscious stance. As early as 1954, in *Poeten och samhället* (The poet and society), he warns against literature in the service of oppressive political regimes, and in *Pandoras ask* (1957; Pandora's box) he examines the materialism of American society with a critical eye. Nevertheless, if a common thread can be found in his extensive poetic production of nearly forty collections, it is an emphasis on religious motifs; several of his hymns found their way into the Swedish hymnal. Setterlind also published travelogues, many works of prose fiction—most notable among them two autobiographical novels about his childhood, *Pojken som trodde på Djävulen* (1962; The boy who believed in the devil) and *Mor Augustins diamanter* (1968; Mother Augustin's diamonds)—and a memoir, *Från dörr till dörr* (1985; From door to door).

EXPERIMENTAL PROSE AND "DISENCHANTMENT"

During the brief flowering of concrete poetry in the early 1960s, several novelists experimented with new approaches and techniques. Torsten Ekbom (1938–), in his *Ord och Bild* essay "Romanen som verklighetsforskning" (1962; The novel as research into reality), a polemic against the traditional emphasis in narrative fiction on individual psychology, provides the theoretical underpinning for his own work. His first novel, *Negationer* (1963; Negations), employs some techniques of the French "New Novel" in that it lacks a conventional plot and instead describes the world in terms of what can be observed through the senses. This cinematic approach is disjointed and fragmented rather than fluid, as the first-person narrator gropes toward some tentative and incomplete understanding. In *Spelöppning* (1964; Opening in the game), the text is open in an even more obvious manner because it requires the reader to play an active role in interpretation. *Signalspelet* (1965; Signal game) uses a collage technique; apparently random pieces of text are assembled in such a manner that they suggest the contours of a story.

Björn Håkanson (1937–) also employs collage structure in *Generalsekreteraren* (1965; The secretary-general). Here 125 sections or fragments are arranged and juxtaposed so that they describe a progression. Håkanson refers to the work as a bildungsroman, though there is no single identifiable individual with whom the development is associated. Ambiguities and apparent inconsistencies also militate against a single interpretation of the textual material. In his poetry from the early 1960s, Håkanson is associated with the "new simplicity" movement; like many of his contemporaries, after the middle of the decade he turns away from the private sphere to concentrate on political and social issues.

A collage technique is also used by Erik Beckman (1935–95) in his novel *Hertigens kartonger* (1965; The duke's cartons). Here the different voices belong to soldiers in Churchill's cortege, and the tension in the text derives from the implied contrast between order (military discipline) and chaos (the random voices themselves). Beckman's texts, whether prose, poetry, or drama, often revel in theatrical flair and absurdist flights of fancy and sabotage the reader's expectations. The author employs seemingly irreconcilable elements borrowed from "new simplicity" and concrete poetry within the same text.

A common thread in these prose experiments is distrust in the fictional artifice, which in turn derives from an epistemological stance: the belief that no complete and accurate perception of the world around us, of reality, is possible. Skepticism toward all systems of belief and consistent or coherent world views is a hallmark of the early 1960s, when the so-called *trolösheten* (disenchantment with all belief systems) debate flourished. Proponents of *trolösheten* included older writers such as Lars Gyllensten and Karl Vennberg as well as Håkanson and his contemporaries. By proclaiming relativism, the lack of an ideological position, to be a positive goal and calling into question the assumption of a collective set of cultural values, they opened the way for an appreciation of non-Western cultures and a newfound awareness of the Third World. Because of the widening of horizons this discovery implied as well as in response to the U.S. involvement in the Vietnam War, the political climate by the mid-1960s became more polarized. *Trolösheten,* now interpreted pejoratively to mean "normlessness," thus bore the seeds of its own demise.

LITERATURE TURNS POLITICAL

As many writers rejected "bourgeois individualism" or even stopped producing belles lettres entirely, the tradition-bound poetry so typical of the 1950s was considered irrelevant. It was nevertheless a single poem, "Om kriget i Vietnam" (1965; On the war in Vietnam), by Göran Sonnevi (1939–), that served to crystallize the political awareness of the 1960s. Sonnevi shows how television images bring the horrors of the war into Swedish living rooms. His poem touched off an intense debate on the role of literature in consciousness raising and in bringing about political change. Aesthetic values were no longer perceived to be of supreme importance, and moral and ethical issues were seen not as abstractions but rather as concrete social and political dilemmas present in the here-and-now. This ideological orientation, though not unilateral, characterizes most literature of the period, regardless of genre.

Even before the war in Indochina became a focal point of international concern, interest in the Third World had a direct impact on Swedish literature because it led to a renewal of the genre of travel literature, whose long and illustrious tradition dated back at least to eighteenth-century botanist Carl von Linné's accounts of his journeys to various Swedish provinces. A more immediate influence on writers of the 1960s were Artur Lundkvist's books from the late 1950s on Greece and Iran; Lundkvist did not focus on the exotic aspects of foreign cultures but rather attempted to understand them on their own terms. Jan Myrdal (1927–) and Sven Lindqvist (1932–) traveled farther afield. Myrdal's *Resa i Afghanistan* (1960; Journey in Afghanistan) revels in the author's openness to new experiences and impressions but also offers penetrating cultural and political analysis. Myrdal attracted international attention with the first of several books about China, *Rapport från kinesisk by* (1963; Eng. tr. *Report from a Chinese Village,* 1966), which draws heavily on interviews with inhabitants in an isolated spot in the north of the country. A follow-up volume, *Kinesisk by 20 år senare* (Eng. tr. *Return to a Chinese Village,* 1984), appeared in 1983. Several of Myrdal's books on China discuss and interpret the communist revolution and its aftermath, though *Sidenvägen* (1977; Eng. tr. *The Silk Road*, 1979), set in China's remote and nearly inaccessible interior, is a more conventional travelogue. Myrdal also writes about prerevolutionary Cambodia (*Ansikte av sten* [1968; Eng. tr. *Angkor*, 1970]), Albania (*Albansk utmaning* [1970; Eng. tr. *Albania Defiant*, 1976]), and India (*Indien väntar* [1980; Eng. tr. *India Waits*, 1984). His travel books are illustrated with the drawings and photographs of Gun Kessle.

A committed socialist, Myrdal views non-Western cultures ideologically; he recognizes the dangers of Eurocentrism and its attendant tunnel vision. His gripping and powerful autobiographical volume, *Samtida bekännelser av en europeisk intellektuell* (1964; revised Eng. tr. *Confessions of a Disloyal European*, 1969), is both an analysis of the author's progressive discovery of his own and his culture's limitations—a self-induced exercise in consciousness raising—and a cry for commitment, rational analysis, and political action.

Myrdal's high profile as a public figure engaged in political debate, particularly during the 1960s and 1970s, sometimes eclipsed his role as a writer. As early as the 1950s, however, he had published four novels casting himself as a sharp critic of bourgeois mentality. His play *Myglaren* (1966; Pulling strings) satirizes bureaucrats' jockeying for position through behind-the-scenes contacts. *Karriär* (1975; Career) uses a fictional construction to explore various political constellations. Turning once again to autobiographical subject matter, Myrdal published the memoirs of his childhood in three volumes: *Barndom* (1982; Eng. tr. *Childhood*, 1991), *En annan värld* (1984; Another world), and *Tolv på det trettonde* (1989; Twelve going on thirteen). His portrayal of his famous parents, the social scientists Gunnar and Alva Myrdal, may be ruthless, but he is equally brutal and frank about his own earlier self, and the reader sees a connection between the parents' rational, no-nonsense attitude toward childrearing and the rational, systematic approach to problem solving evinced by the adult Jan Myrdal. More important, Myrdal has an uncanny ability not merely to reconstruct childhood scenes but to capture specific images and sensations as experienced from the perspective of the child. The memoirs thus convey the impression of a life relived rather than recreated.

Lindqvist, too, lived and traveled in China. His experiences there and elsewhere in Asia are summarized in *Kina inifrån* (1963; Eng. tr. *China in Crisis*, 1965) and *Asiatisk erfarenhet* (1964; Experience of Asia). More than two years of exploration of various countries in South America resulted in *Slagskuggan* (1969; Eng. tr. *The Shadow: Latin America Faces the Seventies*, 1972) and *Jord och makt i Sydamerika* (1973–74; Land and power in South

America). *Elefantens fot* (1985; The elephant's foot) reports on journeys in Afghanistan and Pakistan. Like Myrdal, Lindqvist is a politically committed writer, but particularly in his earlier works, he strives for stylistic elegance as well as political analysis.

The essay is the genre of choice for Lindqvist. Sometimes he is polemic, as in *Reklamen är livsfarlig* (1957; Advertisements are life-threatening), sometimes reflective, as in *Myten om Wu Tao-Tzu* (1967; The myth of Wu Tao-Tzu), which debates the philosophical and moral issue of the retreat into aestheticism versus social and political action. The artist cannot merely vanish into his work of art, alluring though this dream may be, Lindqvist proclaims. Instead, he must turn outward, go into the world in hopes of changing it, while still recognizing that democracy and freedom, at least as defined in the Western tradition, may not always be attainable goals. The focus of Lindqvist's concern is thus the connection between the personal and the political. In *Gräv där du står* (1978; Dig where you're standing), he links questions of individual identity with the search for historical accuracy and urges people to conduct their own investigations into the past.

Lindqvist probes his own private history in *En älskares dagbok* (1981; Diary of a lover) and *En gift mans dagbok* (1982; Diary of a married man), which use diaries and letters to look back on and scrutinize earlier phases of his relationship with his wife and their circle of friends. In *Bänkpress* (1988; Bench press), the focus is on loss and the attempt to overcome pain and the fear of emptiness through physical exertion.

The works of Gunnar Helander (1915–) drew early attention to the apartheid system in South Africa. A missionary and school administrator in that country from 1938 to 1956, Helander wrote as many as seven novels dealing with racial conflicts. Among the best known are *Endast för vita* (1951; For whites only), *Svart symfoni* (1952; Eng. tr. *Black Rhapsody,* 1956), *Storstadsneger* (1955; Eng. tr. *Big City Zulu,* 1957), and *På vår tids språk* (1960; In the language of our time).

Per Wästberg (1933–) made his debut while still in his teens with *Pojke med såpbubblor* (1949; Boy with soap bubbles). Throughout the 1950s, his fictional universe is circumscribed but idyllic, limited but comfortable. Wästberg is among those whose world view was radically altered as a result of the encounter with the Third World, in particular with the institutionalized racism of Rhodesia and South Africa. *Förbjudet område* (Forbidden area) and *På svarta listan* (Blacklisted), both from 1960, register the shock of this newfound awareness. A supporter of prodemocracy movements throughout Africa, Wästberg focuses on political issues in *Afrika—ett uppdrag* (1976; Africa—An assignment). He also published several anthologies of African literature and a volume of critical essays, *Afrikas moderna litteratur* (1969; Africa's modern literature).

Wästberg's later fiction often incorporates an African motif. The setting of the trilogy *Vattenslottet* (1968; The water castle); *Luftburen* (1969; Eng. tr. *The Air Cage,* 1972)—filmed by Bengt Forslund in 1973—and *Jordmånen* (1972; Eng. tr. *Love's Gravity,* 1977) shifts from Stockholm and environs to Botswana and back, and the experience of Africa has a significant impact on two of the characters. The private sphere is nevertheless central to these novels, which may also be regarded as reflecting a proclaimed personal ideal of the 1960s, that of the guilt-free, open love relationship. Incest and infidelity are treated matter-of-factly rather than judgmentally, with sensitivity and insight rather than sensationalism. Africa plays a more important role in *Eldens skugga* (1986; The shadow of the fire) and *Bergets källa* (1987; The mountain spring), in which a successful Swedish diplomat sets out for Cameroon to retrace the footsteps of a deceased relative. He uncovers many secrets of the colonialist venture, builds a friendship with an African cousin, and begins to penetrate the mysteries of present-day Africa, only to be taken hostage by an obscure terrorist group. In the subsequent volumes, *Ljusets hjärta* (1991; Heart of light)—the title refers, of course, to Joseph Conrad's *Heart of Darkness*—and *Vindens låga* (1993; The flame of the wind), he has returned to Stockholm and is engaged in discovering his own emotional landscape through a love relationship with the evocatively named Ellen Mörk ("Dark").

Two novels of Sara Lidman from the early 1960s, *Jag och min son* (1961; Me and my son) and *Med fem diamanter* (1964; With five diamonds), are set in Africa. The first work employs a white protagonist, an egotistical, self-pitying Swede of questionable ethics who is oblivious to the brutal apartheid system within which he operates, to illustrate the bankruptcy of a policy of neutrality. The main character of *Med fem diamanter* is an African who struggles unsuccessfully to maintain his personal integrity and self-esteem in a climate of repression and discrimination.

For more than a decade, Sara Lidman wrote no fiction, choosing instead to concentrate on reporting and direct political action. In the mid-1960s, she traveled to North Vietnam; *Samtal i Hanoi* (1966; Conversations in Hanoi) reveals her conviction that the North Vietnamese cause is a just struggle against colonialism and imperialism. Throughout the war in Indochina she, together with Jan Myrdal, was one of the most prominent Swedish spokespersons against U.S. involvement in the conflict. Lidman also demonstrates her commitment to social justice in the interview book *Gruva* (1968; Mine), which describes conditions among mine workers in northern Sweden and was instrumental in bringing about a strike there the following year.

Radical social criticism of indigenous Swedish conditions is also a characteristic stance in the novels of Lars Görling (1931–66) and Bosse Gustafson (1924–84). Görling's *491* (1962; Eng. tr. 1966) concerns a group of juvenile delinquents and an experimental open living situation that is designed to rehabilitate them. The narrator, Nisse, one of the boys, resists being rescued. He reveals corruption in high places, calls into question the motives of the experiment's sponsors, and rejects the very notion of forgiveness, which is seen as yet another act of oppression. Vilgot Sjöman's 1964 film captures the brutality and violence of the world Görling portrays.

Each of Gustafson's best-known novels critically examines a particular facet of contemporary Swedish society. *Press* (1968) attacks the irresponsible practices of sensationalist journalism; *Förrädarna* (1970; The traitors) reveals judicial sleight-of-hand during a spy trial; *Systemet* (1971; The system) criticizes alcohol policy (the title alludes both to the colloquial term for government-run liquor stores and to "the system" in general). Though Gustafson is clearly a product of the political awareness of the 1960s, the problems he addresses and the hypocrisy he castigates remain topical. Another theme that he has turned to repeatedly is loss, bitterness, and loneliness in love relationships, in such works as *Kungsleden* (1964; King's trail) and *Nyckel* (1974; Key).

The traditional definition of the author's role was expanded during the 1960s. The pattern of the writer and observer who becomes a participant and agitator was a common one. Göran Palm's *En orättvis betraktelse* (1966; An unjust reflection) takes up the question of Western versus non-Western perspective on culture, democracy, and social welfare. Seen from the viewpoint of the Third World, Western affluence and progress are based on exploitation and oppression, a point Palm continues to hammer home in *Indoktrineringen i Sverige* (1968; Indoctrination in Sweden). *Vad kan man göra?* (1969; What can be done?) urges readers to combat the status quo, first by educating themselves and then through involvement. The impact of the book can be gauged by the fact that ninety thousand copies were sold—an unusually high figure for a serious work of nonfiction.

Palm combines a documentary, journalistic approach with his own demand for participation and action in two books about the firm L. M. Ericsson, for which he collected information by working anonymously on the factory floor. *Ett år på LM* (1972; A year at LM) and *Bokslut från LM* (1974; Final report from LM) call for a radical reorganization of the work situation, but Palm never loses sight of the workers' individuality in his discussion of collective goals.

In different ways, Myrdal, Lindqvist, Wästberg, Lidman, Görling, Gustafson, and Palm all challenge themselves and their fellow writers to view themselves, their calling, and their heritage in a new light. In part because of their efforts, during the 1960s the very definition of literature itself changes. It now encompasses not only the essay and the travelogue but also what earlier had been classified as political journalism. These genres may be referred to as "documentary," but the word does not imply objectivity; rather, the writer openly avows a point of view and offers an interpretation. The function of the text is to enlighten and educate, to engage readers in a dialogue and instill in them the same desire for reform that inspires the writer. The reader is no longer merely a passive receiver but a coparticipant.

The genre of "rapport" (report) books, many of which included the word itself in the title, is especially prominent in the late 1960s. The subject matter is drawn from a wide variety of circumstances and geographic locations. Of particular note, in addition to works already mentioned, are *Rapport från medelsvensk stad* (1969; Report from an average Swedish town), a book on Västerås by Sture Källberg (1928–); and *Rapport om kvinnor* (1969; Report about women), a series of in-depth interviews by Karin Mannheimer (1934–), which became a central document in the women's movement. Some authors of "rapport" books describe their own situations. Maja Ekelöf (1918–89) worked for many years in a strenuous, low-paying job as a cleaning woman, simultaneously trying to find time to rear her children and satisfy her irrepressible curiosity about the world around her through systematic reading. *Rapport från en skurhink* (1970; Report from a scrub pail) traces her efforts to overcome obstacles of birth and class by educating herself. Her evolving political awareness becomes a moving testimony to the desire for self-improvement. Perhaps inevitably, the conservative columnist Erik Zetterström ("Kar de Mumma") parodied not only Ekelöf's book but the entire genre in *Rapport från en ishink* (1970; Report from an ice bucket).

During the 1960s, the definition of literature also expands to include genres previously felt to be beneath consideration in any serious context, literature intended primarily to entertain: science fiction, the detective story, "popular" literature in general. The ten police procedurals that Maj Sjöwall (1935–) and Pär Wahlöö (1926–75) published between 1965 and 1975 mark a high point in an increasingly sophisticated genre and found a wide international audience. They skillfully incorporate political discussion and social criticism within the detective novel framework while painting vivid portraits of Sergeant Martin Beck and his co-workers. In the influential volume *Demokratins kultursyn* (1962; Democracy's view of culture), Bengt Nerman (1922–) calls into question the notion of absolute values in literary matters and states that the concepts of "high" and "low" literature are relative.

THE DEMOCRATIC THEATER

The demand for radical democracy in literary matters had the most powerful impact on theater and drama. In Sweden, the opening of international barriers and the end of censorship after the Second World War led to a focus on imported drama. Indeed, Strindberg and Ibsen aside, there was little native theater tradition to fall back on. Though Pär Lagerkvist and Hjalmar Bergman had both written significant works for the stage, they were seldom performed. In the 1940s and 1950s, no major new Swedish playwrights had emerged; Ingmar Bergman's dramatic exercises and Stig Dagerman's plays were overshadowed by their films and novels, respectively, and Lars Forssell's most important stage works lay in the future.

What Sweden did have was a tradition of strong directors whose personal interpretation determined every aspect of a theatrical production. The 1930s Strindberg productions of Olof Molander (1892–1966), which combined psychological acuity with visionary power, were considered definitive for decades. Alf Sjöberg (1903–80), whose stagings of Shakespeare had been high points of the 1940s, made greatly admired productions of Almqvist's *Amorina* and *Drottningens juvelsmycke* in the 1950s. Beginning in the mid-1940s, Ingmar Bergman established himself as a theater director of note, though internationally he became far better known for his films. By the mid-1960s, Molander had reached the end of his career, but Sjöberg (himself an acclaimed film maker as well) was still a powerful force, and Bergman was head of Dramaten, the Royal Dramatic Theater in Stockholm, from 1963 to 1966.

The gradual dying out of independent touring companies was compensated by the founding, in 1933, of Riksteatern (the National Theater), which was intended to bring high-quality theater even to remote areas of the country. Despite this effort, theatrical life was heavily concentrated geographically. The financial difficulties experienced by private theaters also led, in the postwar years, to the almost complete dominance of institutional theaters, in particular Dramaten. In the 1950s, state-subsidized, permanent companies outside the capital city existed only in Göteborg, Malmö, and Helsingborg.

In an earlier generation, Per Lindberg (1890–1944) had hoped that the new genre of radio drama would reach a wide audience across class barriers. Though there was a steady stream of Swedish-language radio (and later, television) productions, beginning in the 1930s, and many established authors were challenged to write for the new media, their works never had the impact Lindberg envisioned—in part, perhaps, because of the increasing dominance of imported popular culture. Alf Sjöberg had also striven to expand the theater audience—he saw theater as a popular art form intended for all people—but his theoretical orientation and interest in experimental technique militated against success in that regard.

Theatrical reform in the 1960s is a reaction against centralization and against directors perceived to be authoritarian and antidemocratic, yet it arose within the institutional theaters themselves, particularly at Göteborgs stadsteater (the Göteborg Municipal Theater), where the director, Lennart Hjulström, and a group of young actors and writers, including Kent Andersson (1933–) and Bengt Bratt (1937–), formed a working collective to create and perform their own material. Social relevance and immediacy were among their goals. Inspired by the style of cabaret and review performance, which flourished throughout the 1950s and 1960s, they emphasized improvisation and an intimate relationship with the audience.

The first collaboration, in 1967, was *Flotten* (The raft), a satire of the social welfare state. The raft is a microcosm for Sweden, ostensibly floating off toward bliss. But life aboard is no idyll, and conflicts come to a head when a shipwrecked foreigner is rescued and joins the passengers. The title of *Hemmet* (1968; The home) refers to the old folks' home where the action is set, but it is also an ironic allusion to the "people's home" of Social Democratic policy, which supposedly guarantees comfort and security for all but actually has shunted old people aside. *Sandlådan* (1970; The sandbox)—written by a single member of the team, Kent Andersson—reveals how social indoctrination begins in childhood. *Tillståndet* (1971; The condition), which takes place in a mental institution, criticizes the care the patients receive and shows the detrimental effect on everyone of passivity and lack of social involvement. Though all these plays have an obvious and biting social message and are intended to be thought-provoking, they are not tendentious because the message is conveyed in part through humor. With them the Göteborg group succeeded in attracting an audience that was younger and less well off than the middle-aged, upper-middle-class patrons who comprised the traditional theatergoing public, but in some quarters their efforts were considered controversial.

Various "free" theater groups outside the purview of the large institutional theaters also began to arise during the late 1960s and 1970s, not all of them in the capital city. Among the more ambitious may be accounted Oktober, with a permanent stage in Södertälje from the 1970s, and Skånska teatern (the Skåne Theater), in Landskrona, led by Peter Oskarson (1951–), who moved his base of operations to Folkteatern (the People's Theater) in Gävle in the 1980s. With *Pjäsen om Norrbotten* (1970; The play about Norrbotten), Norrbottensteatern (the Norrbotten Theater), in Luleå, directed attention to issues relevant to northern Sweden, in particular the lack of work opportunities that forced many to move south. In Stockholm, Fria Proteatern (the Free Pro theater) and Narren (the Jester) were among the pioneers and attracted audiences with a mixed repertory ranging from works of Italian playwright Dario Fo to collaborative efforts within the companies.

Among established non-Swedish dramatists, Bertolt Brecht (who had lived briefly in Stockholm in the 1930s) was congenial to directors and actors in the 1960s and 1970s because of his conviction that theater could and should be an instrument of social reform. Ralf Långbacka (1932–), based in Göteborg, had encountered the Brecht tradition in Berlin during the 1950s and staged his works throughout the 1960s. The documentary theater of another German, Peter Weiss (1916–82)—a resident of Sweden since 1939, though he continued to write primarily in his native language—was especially influential during the 1960s. *Die Ermittlung* (1965; Eng. tr. *The Investigation*, 1967), based on transcripts from the Auschwitz trials, is not political theater that incites to action but an examination of a particular moment in history and its moral implications. Peter Weiss, who had published prose in Swedish and had established himself as an experimental film maker and visual artist during the 1950s, played a prominent role in public debate against the Vietnam War. His belief in moral responsibility also comes to the foreground in the novel trilogy with the collective title *Aesthetik des Widerstands* (1975–82; the aesthetics of resistance), which draws on his own experiences before, during, and after the Second World War and explores the intersection of art and politics.

THE DOCUMENTARY NOVEL

In the politicized climate of the 1960s, when nonfiction reporting was elevated to the status of literature, distrust in the fictional artifice, in fabulation, in purely imaginative speculation was a common attitude, one that may be discerned in several of the most important prose fiction writers of the period. Per Olof Sundman (1922–92) was early associated with "new provincialism" because much of his fiction is set in Jämtland (northwestern Sweden, near the Norwegian border), where he lived for many years. The geographic setting nevertheless serves primarily as a backdrop allowing him to explore fundamental issues of epistemology and narratology. Sundman believes that since it is ultimately impossible for anyone to understand completely another's emotions or motivations, it is inappropriate for the writer of fiction to pretend to such knowledge. Consequently, like a behaviorist psychologist, he describes external reality without attempting to interpret it; it is up to the reader to impose a framework of meaning on these observations. Thus Sundman is a documentary realist in the strictest application of the term; like practitioners of the French New Novel (with whom he is contemporaneous) and prose experimentalists such as Torsten Ekbom, he confines himself to recording information that may be gleaned through the senses. His literary antecedents, however, reach farther back, to the laconic, compressed style of the Icelandic sagas.

Sundman's first collection, *Jägarna* (1957; The hunters), introduces several of his most important themes. In four stories, a physical hunt for someone who is missing serves as a metaphor for the search for understanding of other human beings. In "Anakoreten" (The anchorite), a car salesman leaves big-city life behind and isolates himself under primitive conditions in a remote, rural area. His reasons for doing so are never explained and difficult to deduce, which is precisely Sundman's point; the preface to the story includes the passage, "You cannot see with his eyes, cannot hear with his ears, nor can you feel with the tips of his fingers."

Undersökningen (1958; The investigation) explores the issue of our imperfect understanding of others in a social context. A provincial official is supposed to establish whether a big-city engineer living temporarily in the area to supervise the building of a power plant may be breaking a temperance ordinance. The official conducts a series of interviews with the man's relatives and co-workers with the intention of remaining dispassionate, but the evidence he uncovers is contradictory and misleading. There is thus no objective "truth" accessible to him. Like the reader of a fictional narrative, he must nevertheless try to make a judgment and reach his own conclusions. Sundman's painstakingly detailed descriptions of the Jämtland environment create an illusion of a concrete reality that stands in sharp contrast to the shadowy contours of the impenetrable individual psyche. The same premises underlie his next work, *Skytten* (1960; The marksman), which returns to the hunting metaphor: an apparent accident during a moose hunt leads to a search for an elusive individual and an equally elusive attempt to piece together what actually happened.

Sundman's documentary novel *Expeditionen* (1962; Eng. tr. *The Expedition*, 1967) is set not in northern Sweden but in Africa, and draws on H. M. Stanley's account of his journey into the interior of the Congo. Though it is possible to read the narrative as a parable for European exploitation of the Third World, Sundman is equally interested in questions of perspective and point of view. The story alternates between two narrators, one a rigid military officer and the other an Asian who is familiar with both European and native mentalities. Their versions differ yet overlap; each offers a perspective on events that casts a revealing light on typically European attitudes and questions the purpose of the expedition.

The novel *Två dagar, två nätter* (1965; Eng. tr. *Two Days, Two Nights*, 1969) grew out of a short story in Sundman's first published collection, *Jägarna*, his subsequent use of this story for a filmscript, and his active collaboration with the director (Yngve Gamlin) in making the film, *Jakten* (1965; The hunt). The original story about two men who are members of a posse and succeed in tracking down and capturing a young criminal in the wilderness is rich in possibilities. There is the inherent suspense and drama of the capture and wounding of the armed desperado and the logistics of returning him to civilization. The novel adds a new dimension to the story by focusing on the interaction of the two capturers, a policeman and a schoolteacher. As in all his works, Sundman avoids psychological interpretation. His strict behaviorism and passion for exact detail allow for discussions of the nature of violence and the use of force but also for memorable portraits of the protagonists with hints of complex relationships. *Två dagar, två nätter*, in Sundman's own words "a chamber play set in the wilderness," is one of his most disciplined works and arguably his finest artistic achievement.

Like Sir John, the Stanley figure in *Expeditionen*, the title character of *Ingeniör Andrées luftfärd* (1967; lit. "Engineer Andrée's air voyage"; Eng. tr. *The Flight of the Eagle*, 1970) is a monomaniacal leader obsessed with the quest for glory, prestige, and national honor. Once again, Sundman constructs his novel from documentation of actual events, in this case the ill-fated attempt in 1897 of three Swedes to reach the North Pole by balloon; remains of the expedition, including diaries, notes, and undeveloped film, were found in 1930. The novel purports to be the diary of Knut Fraenkel, the only member of the group who in actuality did not record his thoughts.

The lack of scientific justification for the enterprise and the likelihood that it would fail was clear to impartial observers from its inception. Sundman's narrative focuses on how the judgment of participants and sponsors was clouded by a blind faith in science and technology and a preoccupation with self-aggrandizement and chauvinistic posturing. From the moment of takeoff, when the steering capacity of the balloon is lost, the expedition is doomed, and after landing only sixty hours later on the ice, the three passengers proceed inexorably toward their death. As Fraenkel, who initially had admired Andrée as a visionary hero, gradually becomes disillusioned and aware of the absurdity of the quest, the emphasis shifts to an exploration of the relationships between the men. Sundman's interpretation of individuals and events is in keeping with the facts of the expedition insofar as they are known (as is demonstrated in his companion volume of annotated documentation, *Ingen fruktan, intet hopp* [1968; No fear, no hope]), yet his account *is* a fictional reconstruction, since many questions of motivation and psychology cannot be answered by the documents. *Ingeniör Andrées luftfärd* is a powerful indictment of nationalistic fervor and tunnel vision as well as a gripping tale of three human beings' struggle against the elements and among themselves. Jan Troell's 1982 film of the same title was an international success.

Berättelsen om Såm (1977; The story of Såm) is a modern-day retelling and reinterpretation of one of the best-known prose texts of Old Icelandic literature, *Hrafnkel's Saga*. Like the source text, Sundman's version investigates questions of morality and power in a social framework. His interest in issues pertaining to the rights of the individual versus the rights of society led him to become involved in politics, both on a local level and, after 1968, as a member of parliament for a decade. Sundman was elected to the Swedish Academy in 1975.

In addition to Sundman, two important practitioners of the documentary technique are P. O. Enquist (1935–) and Per Gunnar Evander (1933–). Enquist's first major work, *Magnetisörens femte vinter* (1964; Eng. tr. *The Magnetist's Fifth Winter,* 1989), is based in part on the life of the German hypnotist and healer Anton Mesmer. The documents that form part of the narrative, however, are fabricated. By creating a smokescreen of factual source material, Enquist lulls the reader into a sense of false security and confidence in the reliability of the account in the same way the novel's protagonist, Friedrich Meisner, plays with his clientele's expectations to distort their ability to distinguish between illusion and reality. Just as he is both a charlatan and, apparently, a miracle worker, this account of his activities is a fiction that may approach the truth. *Hess* (1966), which centers on the career of Nazi official Rudolf Hess, takes this pseudodocumentary technique one step further by presenting a hodgepodge of notes and material, some of it "real" and some fictional, without any attempt to organize and interpret it. Enquist thus questions the validity of trying to pin down a verifiable "truth" about any individual or sequence of events.

It is precisely the difficulty faced by the investigator/narrator who must sift through contradictory evidence to reach an understanding of a complex historical situation that becomes the focus of Enquist's best-known work, *Legionärerna* (1968; Eng. tr. *The Legionnaires*, 1973). In the closing days of the Second World War, 167 soldiers from the Baltic states, most of who had been conscripted into the German army, fled to Sweden. After six months of vacillation, the Swedish government decided to send them back to their respective homelands, in opposition to the wishes of the men themselves, who feared for their lives under Soviet rule. The forced repatriation was a topic of heated debate, and public opinion as to the morality of the Swedish decision was sharply divided. Enquist's account of these events incorporates extensive research into the political aspects of the episode and also makes an effort to gauge its long-range effects, by ascertaining, for instance, the fates of the various men after their return. Throughout the narrative he carries on a continuous inquiry into his own preconceived notions, prejudices, and inclinations, and analyzes how these factors inevitably affect his perception of events. Though he is able to uncover a vast amount of information, the investigation is ultimately unsatisfactory because it is impossible for him, or for anyone, to be a purely objective observer. Enquist collaborated on the script of Johan Bergenstråhle's film *Baltutlämningen* (1970; The extradition of the Balts), based on his novel.

Sekonden (1971; The second) draws on an actual incident in Swedish sports history—the discovery that a champion hammerthrower had set his records using an underweight hammer—to explore the role of organized sports in contemporary society as well as the evolution of Swedish social democracy. The fictional narrator, the son of the disgraced athlete, turns to his father's earlier life and family history in an attempt to come to grips with why the man cheated. He discovers that the deception came about through a misguided sense of solidarity in the form of internalized pressure not to fail his compatriots. Originally an extension of class and national loyalty, athletics has gradually become an end in itself. Enquist takes up related questions in a nonfictional format in the essay collection *Katedralen i München* (1972; The cathedral in Munich), which uses the Olympic Games as a springboard for open-ended commentary.

Individual alienation and disillusionment with society are the focus of the stories in *Berättelser från de inställda upprorens tid* (1974; Stories from the age of canceled rebellions), most of which are set in California, where Enquist briefly lived and taught. The sense of futility that pervades the stories stems both from the perception that the United States has betrayed the principles on which it was founded and from a more general awareness that the various social revolutions of the late 1960s have become derailed.

In the historical novel *Musikanternas uttåg* (1978; Eng. tr. *The March of the Musicians*, 1985), events take place in Enquist's native northern Sweden during the period leading up to and immediately following the 1909 general strike. The political radicalism of the more industrialized south, embodied in the socialist agitator Johan Elmblad, meets with little response among this pious, conservative population, yet steadily deteriorating wages and conditions eventually lead to a wildcat strike among sawmill workers. On opposite sides of the struggle are young Nicanor Markström, a disciple of Elmblad, and his uncle Aron, a spy for the company. The conflict has dire consequences for them both: Nicanor is badly injured in a fight, and Aron commits suicide after his treachery is revealed. The title of the book alludes to the Grimm brothers' fairy tale "The Town Musicians of Bremen." Like the old animals in the story, the characters in Enquist's novel pull up stakes and leave when they no longer can find any purpose in their present life: they emigrate to Brazil.

The style of Enquist's later novels has little in common with the documentary technique that characterized his early prose works. *Nedstörtad ängel* (1985; Eng. tr. *Downfall,* 1990), set in the present, is short but intense and lyrical. Subtitled "A Novel about Love," its interwoven narrative strands focus not on eros but on agape. The experimental form incorporates parallel plots as well as hallucinations, dreams, and songs. *Kapten Nemos bibliotek* (1992; Eng. tr. *Captain Nemo's Library,* 1992) is set in Norrland in the 1940s, in Enquist's childhood milieu, but it is anything but a realistic autobiographical account. The narrator, switched at birth with another baby, is restored to his biological parents at age six. The effect on his identity and sense of security is catastrophic, and a major theme of the novel is his attempt to reconstruct the past and his sense of self through narration. Dreams, hallucinations, and projections all play a role in this process. The Captain Nemo of the title is the Jules Verne character, who comes to represent ultimate authority—a Godlike figure who is posited as the repository of all answers. Enquist has composed a complex, multifaceted tribute to the power of the imagination to shape our perceptions of reality and make it endurable.

In the mid-1970s, Enquist suddenly shifted the focus of his authorship from prose fiction to drama. The interplay of art and reality, persona and inner self is a common theme in three plays grouped under the rubric *Triptyk*. *Tribadernas natt* (1975; Eng. tr. *Night of the Tribades*, 1977) features a situation and characters loosely based on an actual event: Strindberg's attempt, in 1889 in Copenhagen, to raise some money through a performance of his one-act play *Den starkare*, starring his soon-to-be exwife Siri von Essen. In the Enquist drama, the couple engages in vicious sparring that simultaneously abounds in black humor. Strindberg reveals the unpleasant personal traits already known to anyone familiar with his biography—he is a jealous bully, constantly compelled to try to dominate—and Siri shows herself to be a worthy opponent as she plays on his insecurities and punctures his bombast. Enquist's intriguing implication is that an unconscious motivation for the writing of *Den starkare* may be found in Strindberg's unresolved feelings for Marie David, Siri's purported lover. Especially to an audience familiar with the real-life, behind-the-scenes drama, *Tribadernas natt* is very effective theater. The play was translated into several languages and achieved success abroad as well. Enquist also provided the script for a 1984 television biography, *Strindberg: ett liv* (Strindberg: A life).

Till Fedra (1980; To Phaedra), based on Racine's *Phèdre* rather than Euripides' *Hippolytus*, treats the classical motif in stylized, elevated language. *Från regnormarnas liv* (1981; From the lives of the rain snakes) is again set in Copenhagen, though earlier in the nineteenth century. Its three main characters are among the most prominent literati of the day: Johan Ludvig Heiberg and his wife, Johanne Luise Heiberg, and H. C. (Hans Christian) Andersen. Andersen, refusing to believe that his fairy tales—which reshaped the entire prose tradition in Scandinavia and are internationally famous today—will have any lasting literary value, hopes to find fame and glory by writing for the stage and has turned to the Heibergs for help. Johanne Luise has learned to play the role of grande dame, but it is not a part she was born to. She recognizes that, different though they may be, she and Andersen are kindred spirits: both come from lower-class backgrounds and do their utmost to hide or gloss over their origins. Their authentic voices are often repressed or denied, though ghosts from the past (one of them physically present on the stage) continue to haunt them. Questions of identity and integrity are also central to the one-act *I lodjurets timma* (1988; Eng. tr. *Hour of the Lynx*, 1990), in which a young murderer, a psychologist, and a pastor grapple with existential issues. Enquist published a memoir, *I min morfars hus* (In my grandfather's house), in 1988.

At first examination, several of Per Gunnar Evander's early novels seem typical of the 1960s and early 1970s in that they are constructed as reports based on documentary material. Evander has cited Per Olof Sundman as the contemporary he most admires, and he undoubtedly is indebted to his older colleague with respect to narrative technique. The parallel is nevertheless misleading. Though both writers provide descriptions of observable, apparently verifiable phenomena and behavior, in Evander's work the appearance of factual validity is false, for the documents referred to within the fictional construction do not actually exist. In this regard his narratives more closely resemble certain works of Per Olov Enquist, notably *Magnetisörens femte vinter* and *Hess,* in which the distinction between "fact" and "fiction" is blurred.

The diary of Hadar Forsberg and the papers surrounding an investigation of his disappearance provide the apparent documentary basis for *Uppkomlingarna* (1969; The upstarts), Evander's breakthrough novel. Forsberg records that his house was invaded and occupied by a band of ragamuffin boys claiming to be his sons; their ill-treatment of him is presumed to have led to his death. The wildly fantastic and absurd contents of the narrative are in sharp contrast to its dry, reportorial style. The reader may interpret the account as an allegory of Third World revenge for the ills of colonialism and imperialist oppression or may regard the boys as simply a manifestation of Forsberg's psychic disturbance.

Sista dagen i Valle Hedmans liv (1971; The last day of Valle Hedman's life) is a similar "investigation" into events surrounding an accident that causes the death of a roof layer. An illuminating comparison may also be made with Sundman's *Undersökningen,* in which the investigator's inconclusive results suggest to the reader that no insight into another's motivation and psychology is possible. In Evander's narrative, the painstakingly collected and pedantically formulated information at first seems to become an end in itself; only when the reader acts as a co-investigator by trying to piece together an interpretation does it become meaningful. Though Valle Hedman's feelings remain inaccessible, the material lends itself to an analysis of the pressures of working against the clock and more generally to the effect of increasing mechanization and industrialization on the skilled craftsman or small businessman.

The text of *Tegelmästare Lundin och stora världen* (1970; Foreman Lundin of the brickworks and the wide world) purports to consist of descriptions of and commentary on sixty-one photographs. Once again, the story they tell must, as it were, be read between the lines, and it concerns both the fate of one individual and a shift in the economic structuring of society.

From the early 1970s, Evander largely abandons formal experimentation with different narrative strategies and instead concentrates on exploring, in more conventionally straightforward accounts, psychological dilemmas in their social context. He does not share Sundman's fascination with the extraordinary individual in unusual circumstances. With few exceptions, Evander's characters seem to be unremarkable people who manage to get by from day to day, yet they suffer from a variety of psychic ailments, the most common of which are lack of self-insight, alienation, and a dearth of meaningful attachments to others that has its source in a failure of parental love. Their isolation, which is often physical as well as emotional and spiritual, may be viewed as a particularly Swedish dilemma. Though the welfare state can guarantee cradle-to-grave economic security for all, emotional security and happiness are determined by intangible factors that cannot be controlled by social planners.

The first novel that reveals this shift in technique and emphasis, and the first work by Evander to reach a wide audience, is *Det sista äventyret* (1973; The last adventure), which was filmed in 1974. Jimmy, the young protagonist, has been dominated and controlled by his mother and fiancée. Afraid to express his resentment through open rebellion at home, he instead deflects his repressed anger and engages in disruptive behavior while doing military service; a series of macabre but comic incidents eventually results in his expulsion from the army. Subsequently, while employed as a substitute teacher, he becomes obsessively involved with one of his pupils. Since he is unable to confront the true source of his internal conflict, he eventually suffers a complete breakdown. In an unconventional residential group-therapy program, he gradually gains self-insight, and his ability to function begins to return.

The protagonist of *Måndagarna med Fanny* (1973; Mondays with Fanny), Robert, is almost completely out of touch with his feelings and uses alcohol as an escape from tension. His marriage functions on a surface level, based on routine, but lacks warmth and depth. During Robert's weekly visits to the hospital to visit his dying father, an abusive and vindictive tyrant, the source of his emotional repression in the parent-child relationship becomes clear. The visits also lead to his involvement with a young nurse, Fanny, however, with whom he gradually learns to be open and spontaneous.

In *Härlig är jorden* (1975; Glorious is the earth), a young teacher is distraught and overwhelmed by a sense of abandonment after the end of a love affair. He resists the attempts of friends and colleagues to reach out to him, and the resulting social isolation intensifies his sense of paralysis until he is perilously close to total collapse. In order to be healed, he must break free from his self-involvement and allow the past to recede, a process that has just begun when the narrative ends.

Lungsnäckan (The snail) and *Fallet Lillemor Holm* (The case of Lillemor Holm), which appeared half a year apart in 1977, are a logical outgrowth of Evander's interest in the dysfunctional individual and therapeutic methods and techniques; these narratives investigate a relationship between patient and psychologist from both perspectives. *Lungsnäckan* is supposedly the autobiographical novel written by Lillemor Holm shortly before her suicide; the second work is the therapist's account of their dealings with each other. For years, Evander maintained that Lillemor Holm was the actual author of the text attributed to her and that the casebook novel was based on fact. Both works, however, are fictional, and the double perspective offered by the "novel" versus the "documentary account" serves once more to point out the slippery nature of objective reality, let alone psychological truth.

Evander examines biblical subject matter from an unconventional point of view in *Judas Iskariots knutna händer* (1978; The clenched fists of Judas Iscariot). In subsequent novels in a contemporary Swedish setting, psychological distress is often described both realistically and symbolically. The main character in *Ängslans boningar* (1980; Dwelling places of fear) compulsively digs a tunnel in an attempt to flee existential anguish. *Orubbat bo* (1983; Undivided estate) reveals a father's written testament to his daughter—a sort of journal or diary—after his suicide. In *Mörkrets leende* (1987; Smile of darkness), the protagonist's feelings of guilt at having failed others cause him to revisit an important place in his past, both physically and in his dreams. Evander's characters are often isolated and cut off from intimate human contact, yet the author implies that only through relationships with others can life attain meaning.

The late 1960s were a watershed in Swedish literature. The cultural climate of the period, with its political and social involvement and lack of concern for aesthetic and metaphysical issues, had a profound effect. The belief that literature should be anchored in and correlate to conditions in what was somewhat narrowly perceived as "the real world" was associated with the dominance of prose genres, despite the historical importance of lyric poetry in Sweden. This phenomenon led, in turn, to the revitalization in the 1970s of the novel as traditional realistic narrative. Several distinct yet related and sometimes overlapping directions may be isolated. The documentary trend of the 1960s broadened to include a renewed interest in the epic historical novel as well as realistic narratives set in the present, many of which revealed skepticism about social and political developments. A younger generation of writers from working-class backgrounds contributed both to the genre of historical fiction and to the analysis and critique of present-day society, and numerous women writers with a feminist orientation set about redressing the historical imbalance between the genders by drawing attention to it in their works.

THE HISTORICAL NOVEL

The historical novel that sets out to explore a fairly recent past comes to prominence around 1970. Its antecedents are found in the historical and social orientation of working-class writers of the 1930s generation, several of whom were still publishing decades later. Like their predecessors, the latter-day practitioners of the genre of historical fiction—Sven Delblanc, Kerstin Ekman, Göran Tunström, Lars Ardelius, Hans Granlid, Gunnar Sandgren, Sara Lidman—often compose multivolume series that trace the lives of one or more protagonists and their descendants through many years. The works are frequently set in the author's home region and may draw in part on his or her own experiences and family history as well as on archival research.

The renewed interest in historical topics also derives from the political consciousness that arose during the mid-1960s and the awareness that one must understand the past in order to analyze the present and prepare for the future. Distrust of the fictional construct had led, in the 1960s, to reportorial books, to documentary novels, or to the abandonment of fiction entirely. Now fiction again is regarded as a legitimate means of exploring and revealing the historical past. In some of the novels, however, the pretense of narrative omniscience or objectivity is abandoned, since it is acknowledged that the writing of any narrative necessitates selection, arrangement, and interpretation. Documentary techniques are used self-consciously and self-reflectively; the narrator may draw the reader's attention to the very process of storytelling and to the fact that this account—indeed, any account—is only one possible version or interpretation of events. Multiple narrative perspectives employed within the same text may serve the same function. This emphasis on the role of the author as fictional creator rather than objective reporter allows for a more open, nonlinear structure and style than was the case with the social realists of the 1930s.

Sven Delblanc (1931–92), one of the greatest masters of Swedish prose since Strindberg, displays wide range within his oeuvre. In addition to the historical novels for which he is best known, he published reflective, philosophical fiction, a picaresque burlesque, memoirs, plays, and several insightful collections of essays on Swedish literature (he earned a doctorate in that field from Uppsala University; one of his principal scholarly achievements was to coedit with Lars Lönnroth the multivolume literary history *Den svenska litteraturen* [1987–90; Swedish literature]). A deep pessimism, tempered by the refusal to give up hope, characterizes his philosophical novels. *Eremitkräftan* (1962; The hermit crab), his debut, is a political allegory set in an imagined dystopia where contrasting social structures coexist. The protagonist Axel flees the totalitarian environment of the Prison and takes up residence in the White City, where apparent freedom and permissiveness are mere window dressing disguising a more insidious form of mind control. Disillusioned, he returns of his own accord to the Prison yet continues to dream of a third possibility: a society in which personal liberty might coexist with cooperation and responsibility for the general welfare.

In keeping with the cultural climate of the 1960s, several other Delblanc novels of that decade have similar political implications. *Prästkappan* (1963; The cassock), set in late-eighteenth-century Prussia, turns the classical myth of Hercules upside down: the central figure, Hermann, instead of overcoming a series of obstacles, undergoes one defeat after another. His picaresque adventures are comic and grotesque, but *Prästkappan* is also a pessimistic novel of ideas in which idealism and the desire for freedom are vanquished by the forces of tyranny and oppression. In *Homunculus* (1965; Eng. tr. 1969), a similar theme is projected into a future world that closely resembles our present one: an inventor who aspires to make the perfect human being in his laboratory becomes a pawn in a global power struggle. Cornered by forces beyond his control, he grows desperate and can no longer create. *Nattresa* (1967; Night journey) incorporates fantasy elements as well as topical social criticism to reveal how an artist learns to reject the allure of radical individualism and become a committed socialist. Despite a message that, on the surface, seems formulaic, Delblanc's narrative is a deeply felt personal testimony, and the author drops the fictional artifice to explore the same complex of ideas in *Åsnebrygga* (1969; Asses' bridge). Based on the diary he kept while a visiting professor at the University of California, Berkeley, in 1968–69, this "bridge back to the novel" reveals, not for the last time, that his temperamental tendency toward defeatism and paralysis stems from formative childhood experiences. Delblanc resolves, however, to overcome the allure of "the dark land" within himself by choosing to live *as if* meaningful action were possible. In response to others' demands that authors engage in political debate and that literature be topical and relevant, he defends his own artistic creation and the writing of fiction in general by asserting that the artist may take a stand through his characters and within the fictional universe.

The fictional universe that he subsequently creates, in four historical novels that won him a wide reading public and were made into a popular television series, is centered on Hedeby, based on the small town in Sörmland where he grew up. The time frame of the tetralogy—*Åminne* (1970; River memory), *Stenfågel* (1973; Stone bird), *Vinteride* (1974; Winter lair), and *Stadsporten* (1975; The town gate)—is approximately a decade, from 1937 until after the Second World War. Taken together, these collective novels provide a kind of social history of a Swedish microcosm and illustrate how the sometimes imperfectly realized goals of social democracy gradually supersede the stratified culture and deeply conservative values of rural and small-town life. The traditions of a collective that addresses common concerns of the village are exemplified in *Åminne* by the annual ritual, performed by everyone in the community, of clearing the river of underbrush. Delblanc's apparent nostalgia for this now-vanished way of life does not, however, impede his pure delight in fabulation, which frequently gives the novels a rollicking, fast-paced, comic aspect.

Delblanc's narrative technique is complex. Events are related largely from the perspective of the author's fictional alter ego, the adult Axel Weber, but also through the eyes of Axel as a child and through the thoughts of other characters. Perhaps most tellingly, the narrative voice frequently interrupts itself to remind the reader that omniscience is impossible: memory is imperfect, and our knowledge of others limited. This distancing effect keeps the reader continually aware of the fact that the narrative, like any fictional reconstruction, is only part of the actual story. At the same time, by encouraging the reader to see characters and situations from several points of view, Delblanc makes his public a part of the interpretive process and deepens our response.

One motif that appears throughout the tetralogy is the distinction between public persona and private self, best illustrated by Axel Weber himself. When reality, in the person of his violent, unpredictable father, threatens to overwhelm him, he withdraws into his own inner world where he is untouchable and safe. In order to function outwardly, however, he must learn to break out of this paralysis. The conflicting impulses of objectification and immobility as opposed to the potential for flight, for living freely, are metaphorically captured in the title of the second novel, *Stenfågel*.

In the Hedeby series, the autobiographical aspect of the narrative nevertheless plays a relatively subordinate role. Delblanc turned more directly to his own family history in several subsequent works. *Kära farmor* (1979; Dear grandmother) is partly based on his father's family, though the author is more interested in the psychology of contrasting character types than in historical accuracy. The tetralogy *Samuels bok* (1981; Samuel's book), *Samuels döttrar* (1982; Samuel's daughters), *Kanaans land* (1984; The land of Canaan), and *Maria ensam* (1985; Maria alone) concerns his maternal grandfather, here called Samuel Eriksson, and his descendants. A theme of tragic inexorability connects all four volumes, as the devastating combination of a hereditary strain of mental illness and a hostile environment leads to the unhappiness, defeat, or death of various family members. At the same time, the narratives are a testimony to the struggle to find meaning and dignity within these constraints.

Samuel, a minister forced by necessity to eke out a living teaching school, dies poor and insane, leaving a legacy of spiritual defeat but also of respect for the intellectual and imaginative life and of love, kindness, and consideration for others. His daughter Maria trains as a teacher and attains autonomy and financial security, only to sacrifice them when she marries. In keeping with the family tradition of female servitude, she follows her husband when he emigrates to Canada, where a combination of pressures—economic hardship, lack of communication in her marriage, constant homesickness for Sweden, the death of a newborn daughter—causes her gradually to lose her religious faith and the comfort it provides. This alienation is ultimately spiritual rather than geographic, as Maria painfully discovers after returning to Sweden in the final volume of the series. Worn down and broken, she eventually commits suicide. A note of hope is nevertheless provided by the fate of her youngest child, Delblanc's alter ego, again called Axel Weber. As a boy he showed signs of having inherited the mental instability of his grandfather and two of Maria's siblings, but given a chance for an education, he displays intellectual brilliance and begins to make friends. Samuel's legacy can ultimately be positive and life-affirming.

In both the Hedeby series and the tetralogy about Samuel and his family, Axel Weber's father, Fredrik, is presented as an abusive tyrant whose sudden outbursts of rage are a source of terror to his wife and children, though little information is given about the cause of his behavior. In the harrowing memoir *Livets ax* (1991; Gleanings from life), Delblanc directly addresses and confronts the impact his father had on his early development. His goal, however, is not revenge but understanding, both of his father and of himself. Delblanc's anguished grappling with existential questions makes this personal testimonial deeply moving. A second volume, *Agnar* (1993; Chaff), which focuses on his teenage years, was published posthumously.

Delblanc periodically returned, usually in a historical setting, to the theme of the relationship of the artist or philosopher to society and its rulers. *Kastrater* (1975; Eng. tr. *The Castrati,* 1979), which includes Sweden's King Gustav III among the characters, concerns patronage and exploitation. The drama *Den arme Richard* (1978; Poor Richard) uses Richard Strauss to epitomize the artist who serves whoever happens to be in power while claiming to serve only music. Yet after the lights go up, the audience hears Strauss's "last reply and defense," the finale of *Der Rosenkavalier.* The beauty of the work itself endures. Delblanc addresses the same issues at a greater historical remove in the novel *Ifigenia* (1990; Iphigenia), a bitter but savagely funny reinterpretation of one of the most famous events of classical antiquity. Here the artist is forced to accommodate the demands of those in power, to compromise himself, but the artistic creation again takes on a validity of its own.

Delblanc's affinity for historical allegory is also apparent in the ironically titled novel *Speranza* (1980; Eng. tr. 1983), which demonstrates the powerlessness of idealism and innocence in a world where might makes right. The play *Senecas död* (1982; The death of Seneca), about the philosopher who tries to enter the political arena to no avail, also draws a parallel to contemporary events. In *Jerusalems natt* (1983; Jerusalem's night), "might" is embodied by the military and political power of Rome in the first century A.D., and the far-reaching philosophical debate includes the intriguing notion that an important feminine component of Jesus' teachings has been lost or eradicated because the authors of the Gospels were male.

Both in the various novels in which members of his own family play important roles and in his philosophical fiction, Delblanc uses a historical setting to explore timeless existential questions. The Hedeby tetralogy concentrates on the intersection of social "progress" and self-realization. In the Samuel series, the focus turns inward to center on rootlessness and loss of faith and the struggle to find meaning without the anchor faith may offer. The various plays and novels set in the more remote past—or in a nonspecific future time—explore a wide range of questions having to do with freedom, constraint, responsibility, and creativity. Delblanc's literary production is noteworthy for both its intellectual depth and its stylistic brilliance.

Kerstin Ekman (1933–) began her literary career in the early 1960s by publishing detective novels. The genre was too confining, however, and she signaled her decision to leave it behind in *Pukehornet* (1967; Devil's horn), which takes its title from the slum district of Uppsala where the action is set. The plot begins conventionally enough, with a death and subsequent coverup. An abrupt shift in point of view, however, reveals that this account is a fictional reconstruction, an imagined scenario. The mystery is never solved. *Pukehornet* is a complex narrative that investigates how people piece together their own realities in an ongoing search for meaning and coherence.

Menedarna (1970; The foresworn) concerns a historical figure, the Swedish-American labor agitator and songwriter known in the United States as Joe Hill. Unlike many works published during the late 1960s and early 1970s, *Menedarna* does not strive for historical accuracy or documentary realism. Rather, Ekman demonstrates how stories and songs about Joe Hill distort his character, motivation, and politics by turning him into a mythical martyr figure, a symbol. Just as *Pukehornet* confounded the constraints of the detective genre, *Menedarna* deliberately sabotages the notion that there is an objective, verifiable truth about individuals or events.

Mörker och blåbärsris (1972; Darkness and blueberry brush) takes place in northern Sweden in an isolated area largely untouched by the benefits of the welfare state. The central action revolves around the confused, and ultimately anguished, reaction of the widow Helga to a brief, spontaneous three-way sexual encounter involving her lover and stepdaughter, and her gradual recovery from emotional collapse. In its detailed description of the harsh yet beautiful landscape as well as its psychological insight, *Mörker och blåbärsris* bears a resemblance to the Norrland novels of Sara Lidman.

Kerstin Ekman is best known for her tetralogy of historical novels set in Sörmland: *Häxringarna* (1972; Magic circles), *Springkällan* (1976; The spring), *Änglahuset* (1979; Angel house), and *En stad av ljus* (1982; A city of light). The first three novels, which incorporate considerable research as well as family oral tradition, show the growth and development of the town of Katrineholm from around 1870, primarily as observed and experienced by working-class women and children through several generations. This focus on women's lives is intended to provide an alternative history that contrasts with and partially compensates for the predominantly male viewpoint that traditionally prevailed among writers of both history and fiction, even those whose subject matter was the impoverished and dispossessed. Ekman's goal is to bring into the foreground those who would otherwise be forgotten.

Häxringarna centers on Sara Sabina Lans, the gritty, determined wife of a poor soldier; her daughter Edla, who dies in childbirth at age fourteen; and Edla's daughter Tora. Tora, too, bears an out-of-wedlock child and then is left a widow with two small children to support. Like her grandmother, who found no task too filthy or distasteful to take on if survival depended on it, Tora displays courage and tenacity when struggling to make the best of a difficult situation: she borrows money from her former employer and begins baking bread to sell in the town square. The title refers to the impenetrable forces that govern human fate, here associated specifically with biological destiny. Both Sara Sabina and Tora demonstrate that it is possible to maintain dignity in the face of adversity.

In *Springkällan,* the narrative focus expands to include Tora's friend Frida, also a widow with children. Through detailed descriptions of physical labor performed by various female characters, Ekman shows the gradual improvement in their circumstances and implicitly in the overall Swedish standard of living—but also the physical and emotional cost. The underground spring of the novel's title represents renewal and hope as well as the hidden currents connecting human beings to one another and the unseen patterns underlying all life.

Änglahuset reveals a gradual shift from external to internal concerns. Unlike women in previous generations, Tora's daughter-in-law Jenny and Frida's daughter Ingrid no longer have to toil merely to survive. Instead, they must attempt to find purpose and meaning in a society where their roles no longer are predetermined. The search for inner coherence and the role of the narrative process itself in that effort becomes the central focus of the final volume of the series, *En stad av ljus,* in which Jenny's stepdaughter, Ann-Marie, is the first-person narrator. With its emphasis on the subjective nature of truth, the limitations of our individual perceptions, and the importance of selectivity, interpretation, and arrangement in the versions of reality we convey to others and to ourselves, *En stad av ljus* hearkens back to *Pukehornet* and *Menedarna.* Storytelling is Ann-Marie's method of imposing order on the world around her and of shaping her own identity. By producing a coherent account from memory fragments, visual images, or scraps of fact, the narrator actually creates her personal history, or at least one possible version of it. On a broader scale, this is precisely what Kerstin Ekman has done in the entire tetralogy.

In *Rövarna i Skuleskogen* (1988; The robbers of Skule Forest), the importance of the narrative process is examined in an even larger context: the course of human history. The novel's protagonist, Skord, is a troll who lives among human beings for five hundred years, a participant in their affairs but simultaneously, by definition, always an outsider. Skord first learns about the world around him by listening to others' stories; later he attempts without success to find a more universal truth through systems of metaphor or analogy. Ultimately, it is only by regaining access to the intuitive, "troll" side of his nature, represented by his connection to the forest and its creatures, that Skord can construct a meaningful narrative of his own life. At the same time, *Rövarna i Skuleskogen* demonstrates that history itself is a series of interlocking stories, a collective narrative of our shared past.

Hunden (1986; The dog) is a short, lyric novel about a puppy who gets lost, survives in the wild, and gradually is tamed again. The natural world is described from the animal's point of view but without anthropomorphism or sentimentality. The documentary realism of *Häxringarna* and *Springkällan* is conspicuously absent in *Knivkastarens kvinna* (1990; The knife-thrower's woman), a long prose poem composed of associations alluding to an abortion and to violence directed at women.

Händelser vid vatten (1993; lit. "Events by the water"; Eng. tr. *Blackwater*, 1995) recapitulates many aspects of Ekman's earlier production: it incorporates some characteristics of the detective story, it gives a sharply etched picture of particular times and places, and it describes the landscape of northern Sweden with insight and sensitivity. The complex, interlocking plot, with numerous unexpected developments and revelations, offers plenty of suspense, but the primary strength of the novel is its psychological acuity. *Händelser vid vatten* received the Nordic Council award for the year's best work of Scandinavian fiction as well as a prize as the best Swedish detective story.

Kerstin Ekman was elected to the Swedish Academy in 1978, only the third woman to be so honored. In celebration of the academy's two hundredth anniversary in 1986, she published *Mine Herrar . . .* (Dear sirs . . .), a learned discussion of the inaugural addresses made by academy members, which traditionally summarize the careers of their immediate predecessors. In 1989, however, Kerstin Ekman and Lars Gyllensten withdrew from the academy, believing it should have taken a firmer stand in protest of the death threats against Salman Rushdie. Though sometimes categorized as a documentary realist, Ekman displays a broad range that also encompasses a pronounced element of lyricism and subjectivity.

Göran Tunström (1937–) made his debut as early as 1958 but came to prominence in the 1970s with three novels set in Sunne in his home province of Värmland: *De heliga geograferna* (1973; The holy geographers), *Guddöttrarna* (1975; The goddaughters), and *Prästungen* (1976; The parson's kid). The first two novels are associative, nonlinear narratives that move back and forth in space and time; the central characters, the minister Hans-Christian Wermelin and his wife, Paula, are loosely based on Tunström's parents. *De heliga geograferna* concerns the search on the part of the narrator, their son Jakob, for his deceased father, and the attempt to make him come alive again, to recreate him through narrative; in *Guddöttrarna*, Jakob is both a child within the story and a more conventional adult narrator looking back on events. Both novels explore aspects of a common theme: that different individuals have fundamentally divergent ways of viewing and perceiving the world. Paula experiences psychotic breaks; members of the Geographical Society promote an idealistic vision not only of expanding their horizons but of bringing the Second World War to a close; the women who, in *Guddöttrarna,* band together to grow and sell carrots, share practical, collective goals. Tunström demonstrates that words sometimes function to separate people from each other, because, by attempting to define and capture experience, they can limit awareness. But it is possible to bridge the gap: Hans-Christian learns to be open to his wife's experience and share her sense of oneness with the cosmos.

Prästungen is a more openly autobiographical and down-to-earth depiction, characterized by humor and delight in fabulation, of Tunström's childhood and youth. An abrupt change is apparent in *Ökenbrevet* (1978; The desert letter), a first-person account of the experiences of Jesus before the ministry described in the Gospels. Jesus is presented as a product of his time and place, sensitive to political issues and their moral implications. He is capable of mystic revelation but is not necessarily the son of God.

The structure of *Juloratoriet* (1983; Eng. tr. *The Christmas Oratorio,* 1995) resembles that of a musical composition, with themes, counterthemes, and leitmotifs. The rehearsal and performance of Bach's great choral work become emblems of hope and joy, a way of transcending grief. Once again, the setting is Sunne, but the town is less a provincial backwater or a microcosm of Swedish society than a stage for existential suffering and ultimately for affirmation and love.

The plot of *Tjuven* (1986; The thief) involves an elaborate plan through which the protagonist, Johan, believes he can rescue himself from poverty and degradation, and his cousin Hedvig from confinement in a mental hospital, by stealing and selling one of Sweden's great national treasures, the Codex Argenteus (Silver Bible)—the only surviving text in Gothic. After years of academic study, Johan eventually tracks down, in an Italian monastery, a lost Gothic manuscript that predates the Silver Bible. This text, given in blank verse, tells a tragic story of the author's doomed attempt to preserve his language and culture against the barbarian onslaught. The plan Johan has made, too, is doomed to failure, for by the time he has won enough accolades to gain him access to the coveted volume, it is too late to help Hedvig. *Tjuven* is a reflection on guilt and betrayal, on the potential human cost of great artistic or scholarly endeavor; it is formulated as an appeal to posterity in the person of Johan's infant son.

Despite the autobiographical and provincial roots of many of his novels, Tunström is hardly a typical epic realist. In fact, his grappling with issues that at heart are moral or spiritual and his vision of mystic wholeness attainable through intuition and empathy suggest that he is the inheritor of a long romantic tradition. Tunström's production contains drama and poetry as well as fiction. His play *Chang Eng* (1987), for instance—about the Siamese twins who were exploited by P. T. Barnum—centers on questions of autonomy and connection that are relevant to all human beings.

Lars Ardelius (1926–) is another established writer who turned to the historical novel in the 1970s after an eclectic literary career. His works of the 1960s are characterized by formal experimentation. *Plagiat* (1968; Plagiarism), for instance, purports to be an autobiographical story of childhood. Since much of the text is a patchwork of unidentified quotations from other literary autobiographies, however, the reader has no easy way of identifying which portions are "authentic" and original and which are not. *Plagiat* is thus both a send-up of the collage technique and a sardonic commentary on the genre of autobiographical fiction.

An obvious social orientation is apparent in Ardelius's novels of the early 1970s. *Gösta Berglunds saga* (1970; The saga of Gösta Berglund)—the title is an ironic allusion to Selma Lagerlöf's Gösta Berling—is a satirical portrait of an exploitative industrial leader, who is contrasted with two of his employees. The narrative demonstrates that despite social reform and the reorganization of business practices, distinctions of socioeconomic class remain over a period of nearly fifty years. *Kronprinsarna* (1972; The crown princes) reaches the same conclusion. Here the impact of environment on individual psychology is depicted through the vastly different life experiences of identical twins reared separately from middle childhood on. One twin, with the advantages of wealth and educational opportunities, becomes a prosperous architect; the other, brought up in poverty, becomes a manual laborer and develops a drinking problem. As adults they have nothing in common. In *Smorgasbordet* (1974; The smorgasbord)—the absence of diacritical marks in the title is deliberate—Ardelius's satire is directed at Swedes who live abroad: their complacency, their refusal to confront their own roles as oppressors, and their stereotypical nostalgia for the homeland.

The historical trilogy *Och kungen var kung* (1976; And the king was king), *Tid och otid* (1978; Good times and bad), *Provryttare* (1981; Traveling salesman) is an ambitious attempt to trace fundamental changes in

Swedish society from the loss of Finland in 1809 to the eve of the Second World War. The first novel shows, through the loosely intersecting fates of many characters in several generations of various families, the rise of the bourgeoisie to a dominant role in society. An important motif is that the participants themselves have little or no understanding of the historical process of which they are a part. The narrative technique— Ardelius presents a jumble of episodes and situations that apparently have little connection to one another—reflects the confusion and uncertainty experienced by the characters and forces the reader to impose a retroactive interpretation, a process that recapitulates the effort of historians to find patterns and trends.

Tid och otid is primarily concerned with the working class and its awakening to political consciousness and power through the socialist movement. *Provryttare* alternates two representative settings and sets of characters to demonstrate, once again, that the chasm between workers and more privileged groups remains even after the rise to power of the Social Democrats. Ardelius's view of both human psychology and the course of history is deterministic: individuals who are oppressed will either go under or find others whom they can dominate, and in any society a dominant group will establish itself. Yet his novels are not schematic. His characters are portrayed with great acuity and insight, every nuance of their thoughts and observations registered in a clear, flexible style.

In the prose debut of Hans Granlid (1926–), *Nertrappning* (1969; Winding down), the neurotic antihero Halvar Halvdan Hand looks back on and analyzes, with phenomenal verbal inventiveness, both his disastrous personal life and his misguided political fanaticism. Neither the relentless subjectivity of the narrative nor its rejection of ideological excess was in accord with the spirit of the time. Granlid, like Delblanc an academic, had already established himself as a specialist on the historical novel with the study *Då som nu* (1964; Then as now). His own subsequent historical novels—*Rackarsång* (1974; Horse butcher's song), *Flickan Kraft* (1975; The Kraft girl), *Själasörjaren* (1978; The shepherd of souls), and *Enkelt ursprung* (1979; Humble origins)—resemble those of many of his contemporaries in that they have a provincial setting (Västmanland) and focus on outcast and downtrodden members of society in previous generations; the protagonists of the first two novels are a horse butcher and a prostitute, respectively.

Granlid makes no pretense to documentary realism, however, but continuously breaks into the narrative with subjective commentary and questions about life's meaning and purpose. In *Flickan Kraft*, the text is not a straight prose narrative at all; it incorporates various other genres, including poetry and dramatic dialogue, learned discourses on abstruse topics, and typographical innovations in a sort of collage that is reminiscent both of the experimental works of the early 1960s and the romantic novels of C.J.L. Almqvist.

The next two novels are stylistically somewhat more conventional but continue to center on the same existential issues: *Själasörjaren* explores the question of how someone who is both intelligent and religious could be taken in by fascist ideology during the 1930s; *Enkelt ursprung,* the most straightforward narrative in the series, is autobiographical in origin and portrays Granlid's parents. In the memoir *Upptrappning—övningar i livskonst 1926–1969* (1988; Winding up—Exercises in the art of living, 1926–1969), Granlid examines himself and his times.

With respect to style, Gunnar E. Sandgren (1929–) is a more direct descendant of the epic realists of earlier generations. His first two novels, *Förklaringsberget* (1960; Mount of transfiguration) and *Löftesdalen* (1961; Valley of promise), depict a revivalist movement in Småland during the early years of the century; the formal experimentation that characterizes Granlid is conspicuously absent. Throughout the 1960s, Sandgren continued to go his own way, ignoring prevailing trends and ideologies. In his historical novels, he frequently turns to remote or obscure eras. *Fursten* (1962; The sovereign) concerns Russian prisoners of war in Sweden in the eighteenth century and features extensive debate on metaphysical issues. *Floden hem* (1967; The river home) and *Järnsparven* (1973; The passerine) are about the Ostrogoths in sixth-century Italy. In *Prinsen* (1979; The prince), he recreates the figure of Hamlet, basing his account on Saxo Grammaticus rather than Shakespeare. Sandgren's view of history has points in common with that of Ardelius: human beings are seen as trapped in a course of events they cannot control.

After many years of involvement in international political issues, in the late 1970s Sara Lidman once again began writing fiction set in the interior of Norrland, in the parish of Lillvattnet. Her five-volume series, *Din tjänare hör* (1977; Thy servant heareth), *Vredens barn* (1979; Children of wrath), *Nabots sten* (1981; Eng. tr. *Naboth's Stone,* 1989), *Den underbare mannen* (1983; The wonderful man), and *Jernkronan* (1985; The iron crown), covers approximately the last quarter of the nineteenth century; the exterior action centers on the attempt to bring the railroad to this remote, isolated part of the country. Though the central character and primary mover in the railroad venture is Didrik Mårtensson, the story is anything but linear. Many separate, individual narrative strands involving other residents, some reaching considerably further back in time, are also woven into the chronicle.

The main plot line traces Didrik's gradual rise to a position of relative strength and control and his subsequent fall from grace. An idealist, Didrik has a vision of how his home district will benefit from being connected to king and capital city. He becomes the protégé of powerful men, including the local sheriff and an important businessman, who help him establish himself as a shopkeeper as part of their own efforts to exploit the natural resources of the interior, and gains political leadership himself on a smaller scale. But when the railroad does arrive, it causes social upheaval, discontent, and increased poverty rather than prosperity. Eventually, Didrik, who has borrowed heavily to cover his generosity in extending credit to others, suffers bankruptcy and imprisonment. Though his intention was to help his friends and neighbors, his efforts have instead resulted in the virtual disintegration of the community, and he himself has been the unwitting pawn of forces he does not fully understand.

Sara Lidman employs a kind of heightened realism in her recreation of a bygone and—even to Swedes—foreign world. Her attention to linguistic detail is especially striking. Even more than in earlier works, she employs dialect words and phonetic spellings not only in direct discourse, where they serve to exemplify differences in social class, education, and place of residence, but also in descriptive passages. Phrases and cadences of the Old Testament permeate the characters' speech and thoughts, and biblical allusions widen the scope of the story. Interior monologue often approaches a stream-of-consciousness technique. The use of dialect in particular creates difficulties for the uninitiated reader, a problem Lidman recognizes and addresses by providing translations and commentary. Yet these ethnographic aspects of the narrative are not its primary focus. Instead, the entire series can be read as a cautionary tale in keeping with a particular kind of morality, the pietistic Christian world view most of the characters share. Various motifs and images introduced early in the series recur and evolve in succeeding volumes, linking the disparate events of the story. Sara Lidman's greatest achievement may well be to have given modern readers, the products of an urban, secularized culture, intimate access and insight into a society, a way of life, and a mode of thinking that is far removed from their everyday lives.

Though Torgny Lindgren (1938–) made his debut in 1965, the weight of his literary career falls after 1982, when *Ormens väg på hälleberget* (1982; Eng. tr. *Way of a Serpent*, 1990) was published to unanimous critical praise. *Ormens väg*, a dark tale of injustice and oppression, takes place in a remote village in northern Sweden in the second half of the nineteenth century. When the parents of a young girl, Tea, cannot pay the rent in cash, she is compelled to grant sexual favors to the local shopkeeper and landlord. After Tea ages, the shopkeeper's son demands payment from her daughter instead, despite the fact that she is his own half-sister; finally, the narrator, Tea's son, takes his revenge.

Like Sara Lidman, Lindgren weaves Bible quotations and paraphrases as well as Norrland dialect into his narratives, which possess both a colloquial and a stylized, timeless flavor. The author turns directly to the Bible for subject matter in *Bat Seba* (1984; Eng. tr. *Bathsheba,* 1989), which expands on and elaborates the story of King David. As divine ruler David has no qualms about using his power, and his reign is portrayed as brutal and violent; he is humanized only by his love for Bathsheba, who has no qualms using *her* power over him. *Merabs skönhet* (1983; Eng. tr. *Merab's Beauty and Other Stories,* 1990) and *Legender* (1986; Legends) are collections of short stories that range widely through time and space. Here Lindgren consciously borrows from an oral narrative style with its delight in storytelling for its own sake.

Historical time and place do not play a central role in *Ljuset* (1987; The light), though it is set in northern Sweden during the Middle Ages. The story concerns the complete collapse of values and moral conventions in a small village decimated by the plague. In part, the narrative is wildly fantastic with elements of grotesque humor. *Ljuset* is an odd blend of tall tale and morality play. Lindgren turns to pre-Christian myth in *Kärleksguden Frö* (1988; Frej, the god of love), which purports to be a conventional biography of the best-known Norse fertility god. The irreverent and comic interpretation of the gods and goddesses and their erotic adventures nevertheless leads to a serious reflection on the limitations of power in a world governed by inexorable fate.

The trajectory of Lindgren's career, like that of Kerstin Ekman, moves beyond the constraints of documentary realism to embrace imaginative, fantastical fictional constructs as an equally valid way of interpreting timeless aspects of the human condition.

SOCIAL CRITICISM AND BUREAUCRATIC SATIRE

During the 1960s and 1970s, literature with a social and political orientation dealt not only with war and oppression in the international arena or the historical effort to eliminate traditional barriers of wealth and class within Swedish society. There was also a growing perception that, despite the implementation of policies of reform, fundamental flaws had developed in Sweden's postwar social democracy. Criticism of the status quo focused on the expansion of an impersonal bureaucracy that had lost touch with those it ostensibly served. The process of urbanization, industrialization and technological advancement, and structural change in society was also seen as having led not to equal opportunity for all but to loss and alienation; with it went the absence of a sense of connection to tradition and cultural heritage and the disappearance of such fundamental human values as care and concern for others. Writers who explored these issues from various perspectives include P. C. Jersild, Göran Hägg, Björn Runeborg, Stig Claesson, and Lars Gustafsson.

The novels of P. C. Jersild (1935–) reveal a vivid imagination as well as a sharp satiric edge. In both *Till varmare länder* (1961; To warmer lands) and *Prins Valiant och Konsum* (1966; Prince Valiant and the co-op), everyday Swedish reality is contrasted with a fantasy realm; the "warmer lands" of the first novel's title, it gradually becomes clear, are not an underdeveloped country but Hell. *Ledig lördag* (1963; Saturday off) begins as a humorous depiction of a company party but evolves into a nightmare of being trapped for a week in a continuously moving subway train. In *Calvinols resa genom världen* (1964; Calvinol's journey through the world), perhaps the most inventive of the early novels, the title character is a picaresque traveler who moves through geography and time and whose experiences yield startlingly untraditional interpretations of historical events.

Grisjakten (1968; The pig hunt)—filmed by Jonas Cornell in 1970—purports to be the diary of a loyal civil servant who has been assigned the task of eliminating all the pigs on the Baltic island of Gotland. Narrative tension is provided by the contrast between the absurdity of the effort and the objective, analytical detailing of how the slaughter is to be effected. The functionary is never told why the pigs should be eradicated, but he does not question the decision—his job is merely to follow orders. To the reader, the parallel to the mentality that made possible the Holocaust is obvious. In *Vi ses i Song My* (1970; See you at Mai Lai), the narrator is again a bureaucrat doing his duty, which involves manipulating both people and language to preserve the appearance of democratic decision making; ironically, he himself is being manipulated by a higher administration to serve its own ends.

Stumpen (1973; The stump), *Barnens ö* (1976; Eng. tr. *Children's Island*, 1986), and *Babels hus* (1978; Eng. tr. *House of Babel*, 1987) are firmly anchored in contemporary Swedish reality. All concern, in one way or another, those who are outside the mainstream of society. The protagonist of *Stumpen* is an alcoholic. Reine Larsson in *Barnens ö* is a boy of nearly eleven who is emotionally, and to some degree physically, abandoned by his mother. Rather than letting her send him off to camp, Reine decides to go AWOL and spend the summer alone trying to come to grips with the big existential questions he fears will no longer interest him once puberty arrives. Reine dreads adolescence because it leads inevitably to adulthood, and the adult world he observes is often cruel and absurd. By portraying the Stockholm of the mid-1970s through the eyes of an intelligent, imaginative child, Jersild finds a perspective that is simultaneously naive, funny, and wise. *Barnens ö* was filmed in 1980 by Kaj Pollack.

Babels hus, set in a large Stockholm hospital, draws on Jersild's own professional experience as a medical doctor. The hospital with its staff and patients serves as a microcosm for Swedish society. It is well organized, rational, and generally efficient but also highly stratified and hierarchical. High-status subgroups, in particular doctors, promote and perpetuate themselves. Their clients, the patients, receive excellent medical care but are treated impersonally and become isolated and lonely, as is illustrated by the fate of Primus Svensson, an old man who suffers a heart attack and eventually dies. The reference to the Tower of Babel reflects Jersild's perception that different subgroups speak different languages and thus often fail to communicate with one another.

Some of Jersild's novels use a future setting to criticize tendencies in contemporary society. *Djurdoktorn* (1973; Eng. tr. *The Animal Doctor,* 1975) sketches a bleak picture of a world in which natural resources are depleted and the state has become an enormous bureaucracy regulating virtually every aspect of citizens' lives. The protagonist, a middle-aged woman veterinarian named Evy Beck, is progressively marginalized after she protests the treatment of experimental animals at the Alfred Nobel Institute for Medical Research, which like the hospital in *Babels hus* functions as a microcosm. The rats that viciously turn on one another when an uncontrolled population explosion in a closed environment causes overcrowding—a purposeless experiment Evy unsuccessfully tries to halt— serve as a metaphor for the situation of human beings on planet Earth.

En levande själ (1980; Eng. tr. *A Living Soul,* 1988) depicts an even more insidious future dystopia where science and technology are used to manipulate and experiment on people. The first-person narrator, the "living soul" of the novel's title, is Ypsilon, a disembodied human brain in a laboratory aquarium. Though his personal memories have been removed by electric shock treatments and he is utterly helpless, subject to the whims of his experimenters and the commercial interests that control them, he retains a full range of human emotion and is capable of experiencing love as well as despair over his situation. The narrative ends abruptly when Ypsilon, no longer considered useful, is simply eliminated. *En levande själ* contains passages of striking lyricism and beauty. Despite the bleak premise, it is a moving testimony to the human spirit.

The events in *Efter floden* (1982; Eng. tr. *After the Flood,* 1986) take place in the aftermath of a nuclear catastrophe that has left most of the world uninhabitable. Now, thirty years later, virtually all traces of culture and civilization have been eradicated. Surviving human beings, among them the narrator, Edvin, are brutalized and cruel, interested only in self-preservation. Once again Jersild speculates on what qualities are essentially human, and once again his vision of the future is deeply pessimistic. The novel ends when a virus wipes out the few people who remain.

Den femtionde frälsaren (1984; The fiftieth savior), set in eighteenth-century Venice, is a religious allegory that posits a son born to Jesus and Mary Magdalene, whose descendants through the centuries are bearers of faith. *Geniernas återkomst* (1987; Return of the geniuses) covers an even greater chronological span, from prehistory to the future, and gives an imaginative and speculative view of human history. In the final chapter, geniuses of the past have been brought to life again through modern biotechnology and genetic tinkering. *Holgerssons* (1991) provides a wildly fanciful continuation of Selma Lagerlöf's famous children's story, *Nils Holgerssons underbara resa genom Sverige* (1906), in which the fictional character confronts his creator. *En lysande marknad* (1992; A wide-open market), in contrast, harks back to the bureaucratic satires of the 1960s and 1970s. Set in the not-too-distant future, it explores the ramifications of our present-day information society, with data banks and the poten-tial for electronic espionage, in a marketplace governed by unregulated competition. Jersild posits that an enterprising person could successfully operate alongside the criminal justice system, serving as judge, jury, and executioner.

In the nonfiction book of essays *Humpty-Dumptys fall* (1990; Humpty Dumpty's fall), Jersild discusses many of the issues dealt with in his fiction: the relationship between ethics and technology, and the fundamentally different world views formulated or conveyed through science, art, and religion. *Fem hjärtan i en tändsticksask* (1989; Five hearts in a matchbox), a memoir, describes the author's childhood in a lower-middle-class Stock-holm suburb and his path toward both medicine and literature.

Jersild's ability to incorporate highly specialized technical and scientific knowledge in a context of fantasy and imaginative speculation, combined with his biting social criticism, gives him a distinct profile. One of the most widely read authors among his contemporaries, he bridges the gap between "serious" and "popular" literature.

Like Jersild, Göran Hägg (1947–) is a satirist whose works sometimes extrapolate from present circumstances into the future. Hägg takes as his particular subject the analysis of a society that has become compartmentalized through the growth of bureaucratic hierarchies that have lost sight of their supposed purpose—if indeed they ever had one. His major theme is the depersonalization that occurs when an individual becomes a cog in the bureaucratic machinery and the insidious implications for society when its members become automatons. Within this overall pattern, he concentrates specifically, like Jersild in *Babels hus,* on the role of language. Hägg exposes fashionable buzzwords as being divorced from any semantic content, and illustrates how the growth of technical jargon and "officialese" causes individuals and the work-related subgroups to which they belong to become more and more isolated from one another.

Lejontecknet (1977; The sign of Leo) is set at a fictitious government agency with no designated function whatsoever other than paper pushing, where the director's primary tool for career advancement is his mastery of administrative jargon. The novel begins as a satire of bureaucratic inefficiency but expands to encompass a broader exploration of the influential and sometimes pernicious and manipulatory role of linguistic smokescreens in contemporary society. The traditional language of literature and of humanistic endeavor is irrelevant or dying out, as illustrated by others' attitudes toward the aspiring poet Agneta. Her later experiences are chronicled in the sequel, *Agneta hos kannibalerna* (1986; Agneta with the cannibals), a scathing view of the publishing world and the cultural elite.

Det automatiska paradiset (1979; The automatic paradise) focuses on education and the accompanying terminology. Though pedagogical theory in methodology courses is couched in impenetrable abstractions that are of little practical use, the protagonist, Christer Björkström, discovers, after finding a job at a government-sponsored adult education organization, that he actually enjoys teaching. Unfortunately, however, an administrator with a military background establishes a hierarchical bureaucratic structure that totally isolates the individuals who make decisions from the classroom teachers. Goals are formulated no longer as educational objectives but in terms of efficiency. It becomes clear that the real purpose of the school, high-sounding phrases notwithstanding, is to depress artificially the unemployment statistics.

Hägg pillories another level of the educational establishment in *Doktor*

Elgcrantz eller Faust i Boteå (1983; Doctor Elgcrantz, or Faust in Boteå), set in a university literature department. Much of the satire and humor derives from the title character's mastery of and ironic commentary on the jargon of literary criticism, which reflects current theoretical trends but has little correlation with the text ostensibly being discussed. Mårten Elgcrantz eventually elects to join the private sector, where he believes his language skills can be put to use without necessitating the sacrifice of his integrity. The futuristic vision of the novel's last chapter challenges this assumption. A middle-aged Mårten is now the head of a government agency where culture, defined as entertainment, is entirely in the service of the industrial and political power structure. Having figuratively speaking sold his soul, Mårten is now consigned to Hell.

Hägg's novels reveal the manner in which the officially sanctioned style of discourse, whether administrative mumbo-jumbo, the bromides of pop psychology, the impenetrable abstractions of pedagogy, or overly theoretical academic jargon, distorts or disguises meaning. Words are used to hide laziness, indifference, self-aggrandizement, and lack of content; their true function is to provide window dressing. The ability to manipulate them is essential to success, but because real communication is no longer a goal, this skill is associated with an attitude of cynicism and value-neutrality. A fundamental irony in the eyes of the author is that Sweden's outward movement toward democracy, leveling, and equalization of opportunity has not led to these objectives but rather has resulted in the creation of a new class structure based on mastery of new types of jargon.

A prolific writer since the early 1960s, Björn Runeborg (1937–) combines an interest in individual psychology with broad social concerns. In early works, his fictional characters are generally ordinary people living in small towns or the suburbs, struggling to get by. They are lonely and isolated, searching for happiness and a sense of purpose, but lack control over the circumstances that dictate their lives. In *Lönen* (1969, The salary), for instance, a low-paid worker cannot make ends meet and sinks deeper and deeper in debt, which in turn causes him to withdraw from contact with others; the potential for violence lurks just below the surface.

Runeborg emphasizes that social and political issues affect people in their private lives, often in ways they themselves do not understand. Attempting to take action against the negative effects of capitalism and industrial "progress" is not, however, necessarily an exercise in futility. The protagonist of *Stenhugg* (1970; Stone cut), discovering that he will be replaced by a computer at his factory job, moves to northern Sweden to try to start up an abandoned quarry. The locals think he is a profiteer, beat him up, and send him packing—yet before he leaves, they decide they would like to hear more about his plan. Similarly, in *Riddaren från Mjölby* (1978; The knight of Mjölby), the owner of a small firm fights back when he is bought out by a multinational company. That effort ends in failure, but a note of hope is nevertheless introduced through a collective enterprise to provide day-care facilities for the community. This initiative may not be able to combat the increasing dominance of enormous multinational corporations, but it may serve the social good in a smaller context.

A common motif in many of Runeborg's novels is the unanswered question of how to go about creating a just society, one that preserves and defends individual rights and makes possible personal happiness and a sense of security. Several works center on potential leader figures—a politician in *Valkamp* (1973; Election battle) and *En folkets man* (1975; A man of the people), a businessman in *Ur en företagsledares liv* (1974; From the life of an industrialist). But they also have difficulty setting a course of action or controlling the outcome of events because too many factors lie outside their sphere of knowledge or expertise. Runeborg's novels, as well as his plays written for the stage, television, and radio, are generally realistic, anchored in the everyday experiences of his characters.

The subject matter of Stig Claesson—Slas—(1928–) is those whom the welfare state has forgotten. In *Västgötalagret* (1965; Västgöta warehouse) and *Döden heter Konrad* (1967; Death's name is Konrad), the setting is Stockholm's working-class South Side, where Claesson grew up. *Bönder* (1963; Farmers), however, concerns the precarious situation of small farmers, and the trilogy *Vem älskar Yngve Frej* (1968; Eng. tr. *Ancient Monuments*, 1980), *På palmblad och rosor* (1975; On palm leaves and roses), and *Henrietta ska du också glömma* (1978; You should forget Henrietta, too) takes up various aspects of the retreat from the countryside to the city and the isolation of those who are left behind. In *Vem älskar Yngve Frej,* the main characters are four old people who refer to themselves ironically as ancient monuments, relics from the past, and a young Stockholm photographer and his girlfriend who meet them while on vacation. The Stockholmer wants to help them find stimulation and companionship by attracting tourists to their home, but in the end they prefer to be left alone. Their lifestyle may be the product of a bygone era, but it is the only one they know and are comfortable with.

In *På palmblad och rosor,* a solitary old woman in a cottage, bedridden and lame, becomes an emblem of what has been lost or left behind in the name of social progress. In the traditional agrarian culture of the past, a support network of neighbors and kin would have cared for her; today she is alone. *Henrietta ska du också glömma* is a love story that illustrates, through its protagonists, that city and countryside are separate worlds.

Many of Claesson's novels focus on individuals whose existence is seemingly aimless, who suffer from rootlessness and lack of meaningful contact with others. *En vandring i solen* (1977; A wandering in the sun) is an understated exploration of existential anguish. *Ni har inget liv att försäkra* (1979; You have no life to insure) concerns, in a broader sense, the perception that the postwar generation has been misled and deceived. In *Utsikt från ett staffli* (1983; View from an easel), Claesson (himself a painter and illustrator) presents a self-deprecating satire of the role of the artist in contemporary society. *Kärlek rostar inte* (1988; Love doesn't rust), in contrast, portrays an artist who discovers, through a bizarre case of unrequited love, that he can help make experience meaningful to others.

The melancholy, pessimistic undercurrent of Claesson's novels is tempered by his style, in which repetition and short, abrupt formulations often contribute to a laconic, humorous effect. His novels have found a wide audience, and many of them (*Vem älskar Yngve Frej, På palmblad och rosor, Henrietta ska du också glömma, En vandring i solen*) have been filmed.

Lars Gustafsson (1936–) established himself as a writer of both prose and poetry early in his career and proceeded to become one of the most widely translated Swedish authors of his generation, particularly in Germany. In Sweden, he was the influential editor of BLM (*Bonniers litterära magasin*) from 1962 to 1972, during which time the journal carried on a wide-ranging debate on cultural and political as well as strictly literary matters and became a forum for the dominant leftist currents of the time. Gustafsson continued to maintain a high public profile in his homeland, even after the early 1980s when he moved to the United States and a teaching position at the University of Texas at Austin (*Tennisspelarna* [1977; Eng. tr. *The Tennis Players*, 1983] describes a year spent there as a visiting professor).

Gustafsson's most important prose works are five thematically interlocking novels collectively titled *Sprickorna i muren* (The cracks in the wall): *Herr Gustafsson själv* (1971; Mr. Gustafsson himself), *Yllet* (1973; Wool), *Familjefesten* (1975; The family gathering), *Sigismund* (1976; Eng. tr. 1985), and *En biodlares död* (1978; Eng. tr. *Death of a Beekeeper*, 1981). Though each tells a separate story, they all feature protagonists named Lars whose birthday and childhood experiences are those of the author. Like many other novels published during the 1970s, the earlier volumes in particular comment on circumstances in contemporary Sweden: the expansion of impersonal institutions and bureaucracies and of official hypocrisy that attempts to disguise the loss of personal freedom and diminishing of democratic ideals. Gustafsson's view of Swedish society is pessimistic, yet a refrain that occurs in all five novels is, "We'll start over. We won't give up." This sentiment expresses both the attitude of the various fictional protagonists and the response of Gustafsson himself to the conditions he describes.

In the first novel, perhaps the most directly autobiographical, an author and editor looks back on the literary trends of the 1960s and takes stock of his own situation. He begins to distrust his own mastery of words as he sees that they have been used to shore up a corrupt moral system and have become a substitute for life. In search of a positive, life-affirming value, he wonders whether love is possible in the present age.

The protagonist of *Yllet* is a mathematics teacher in a provincial backwater who discovers he has a genius in his class. No one else is interested in helping the boy reach his potential; his parents merely want him to stay out of trouble, and the school principal worries that a gifted pupil is a threat to the democratic principles of the educational system. More important, the boy finds both his talent and life in general to be meaningless, a realization that leads to his senseless death. The teacher, whose own capabilities have never been fully explored, experiences a moment of solidarity and fellowship participating in a political demonstration, but he, too, dies in an accident shortly thereafter. The novel is a reflection on human potential that remains unfulfilled, in part because society has no mechanism for reaching out to those who do not fit the mold.

Familjefesten more directly concerns the public sector and the insidious, hidden mechanisms of power: the main character publicly exposes government involvement in an environmental disaster but is ultimately powerless to stop it. The novel is less a political satire than a paranoid thriller. The several narrative strands of *Sigismund*—including a science-fiction fantasy—form a complex investigation of identity and layers of reality. There are fewer direct correlations to perceived conditions in Sweden; the wildly fantastic depiction of Hell nevertheless evinces certain correspondences. *En biodlares död*, a first-person account of the confrontation of one individual with existential issues as he awaits death, completes the movement away from political and social concerns, though external circumstances are mentioned in passing. Paradoxically, the pessimism of earlier volumes is largely absent, for the protagonist achieves wholeness through the experience of pain.

Gustafsson holds a doctorate in philosophy from Uppsala University, and a speculative, metaphysical orientation is apparent in many of his novels, particularly those published during the late 1950s and 1960s. He also alludes to and borrows from the conventions of various fictional genres: the subtitles of *Vägvila* (1957; Resting place), *Poeten Brumbergs sista dagar och död* (1959; The last days and death of Brumberg the poet), *Bröderna* (1960; The brothers), and *Följeslagarna* (1962; The companions) identify them as a mystery play, a romantic tale, an allegorical narrative, and an adventure story, respectively. *Den egentliga berättelsen om herr Arenander* (1966; The real story of Mr. Arenander) reveals a shift from philosophical debate and the attempt to systematize reality to the more immediate social orientation of *Sprickorna i muren*.

In the 1980s, Gustafsson continued to experiment, through complex narrative structures, with questions of identity: in *Sorgemusik för frimurare* (1983; Eng. tr. *Funeral Music for Freemasons*, 1987) and, most notably, the tour de force *Bernard Foys tredje rockad* (1986; Eng. tr. *Bernard Foy's Third Castling*, 1988), which features, in the first of three interlocking stories, a complicated espionage adventure involving decapitated bodies, Nazi war criminals, the superpowers, cruise missiles, and the fate of the Western world. A veritable gold mine for scholars in search of intertextual references, the novel has a boxes-within-boxes construction: in each of the three sections, the protagonist is named Bernard Foy, but the first two are apparently projections emanating from the mind of the third. By its reference to the chess move, the title of the novel suggests its oblique and nonlinear progression. Gustafsson uses narrative sleight of hand to demonstrate that reality is multivalanced and appearances are deceiving. *En kakelsättares eftermiddag* (1991; Eng. tr. *A Tiler's Afternoon*, 1993), about an old workman who sets to a task only to discover that he has gone to the wrong address, reveals thematic parallels to *En biodlares död* in its focus on isolation and emptiness.

Among Gustafsson's short stories are *Berättelser om lyckliga människor* (1981; Eng. tr. *Stories of Happy People*, 1982) and the science-fiction narratives in *Det sällsamma djuret från norr* (1989; The strange animal from the north). His short fiction through the mid-1980s is published in *Samlade berättelser* (1987; Collected stories). The range of literary and philosophical allusions in his texts makes Gustafsson a remarkably self-conscious as well as challenging writer. His social criticism, like Jersild's, is frequently a strategy to facilitate discussion of fundamental existential issues.

WORKING-CLASS LITERATURE REVISITED

In connection with the renaissance of prose fiction during the 1970s, there emerged a new group of writers from working-class backgrounds whose subject matter is their own class of origin. Virtually without exception they share the political and social perspective of the self-taught writers who made their debuts around 1930; they aim both at documenting living and working conditions among the ordinary people and at criticizing circumstances in hopes of bringing about change. Like their predecessors, these working-class writers made important contributions to historical fiction through their depictions of the unlanded rural poor of previous generations, the growth of industrialization, the evolution of labor unions, and the emergence of the Social Democratic party, but they also describe the current situations of factory workers, sailors, truck drivers, and pensioners. Again like their literary role models, they tend to cultivate a straightforward, realistic narrative style.

Several of them, in fact, were very nearly contemporaries of the 1930s generation. Gunnar Adolfsson (1906–83) had been a laborer, a journalist, and a communist member of parliament before turning to literature. His tetralogy *Träskoland* (1964; Land of wooden clogs), *Fattigmans tröja* (1965; Poor man's coat), *Stolpar med röda ringar* (1966; Poles with red rings), and *Nattens spelmän* (1969; Night's fiddlers) has many points in common with Vilhelm Moberg's novels, in particular *Soldat med brutet gevär*. Set in the glass district of Småland during the first decades of the century, the tetralogy traces the effect of industrialization and rapid social and political change on the impoverished rural population. The parallel to Moberg is less evident in Adolfsson's emigrant novel *Född i våra dalar* (1970; Born in our valleys), which features not stalwart pioneers who settle the American Midwest but migrant laborers forced by the famine of 1869 to search for work on the large estates of Pomerania. *Mäster Påvels hytta* (1974; Master Påvel's glassworks), another historical novel, describes the arrival of the first glassblowers to Småland in the early seventeenth century. Adolfsson also followed an established pattern among working-class writers by publishing a series of memoirs: *Vägar vida* (1971; Wide ways), *Människobukett* (1981; Human bouquet), *Virvelvind* (1982; Whirlwind), *Timglasets sand* (1983; Sand in the hourglass). Rather than focusing on childhood, they are primarily concerned with the author's involvement in politics and the labor movement.

Karl Rune Nordkvist (1920–), another epic realist in the tradition of the 1930s generation, grew up in Norrland and, like Adolfsson, received little formal education and worked at a variety of jobs. Most of his fiction concerns middle-aged men from working-class environments who perceive themselves as losers. In *Nattvägen* (1970; Night way), the protagonist commits suicide when he is ostracized because of his political convictions, and the main character's death in *En dag i oktober* (1972; A day in October) may have similar causes. *Hösten lång* (1977; All through the autumn) incorporates a detailed criticism of developments in the contemporary welfare state, in which the Social Democrats' promises of economic security and social equality have not been fulfilled. In the autobiographical series *Solens barn* (1982; Child of the sun), *Slaktarens hus* (1985; The butcher's house), *Septembers ljus* (1987; September light), Nordkvist depicts his childhood environment in a small railroad town. Nordkvist's understated style and sympathetic yet unsentimental perspective on people and events lend the account authenticity and authority.

The tetralogy of Bunny Ragnerstam (1944–) about the growth of the workers' movement in the southern Swedish town of Kristianstad during the 1880s—*Innan dagen gryr* (1974; Before day dawns), *Uppbrottets timme* (1975; Hour of departure), *Vredens dag* (1977; Day of wrath), and *Skall jorden bliva vår* (1978; Shall the earth be ours)—has many similarities with other historical series published in the 1970s, but it reveals a more specifically political focus and a strict adherence to documentary form (actual documents are interfoliated in the narrative). Through a representative selection of characters, the novels portray a wide variety of attitudes and responses among the working class and those who oppose its reform efforts.

In the two novels collectively called *En svensk tragedi* (A Swedish tragedy)—*Uppkomlingen* (1980; The upstart) and *Ett prima liv* (1983; A top-notch life)—Ragnerstam narrows his focus to a single protagonist, Bertil Larsson, and shifts the locale to a small mining town in central Sweden, beginning in the 1920s. Larsson, a soccer star in his youth, never achieves the breakthrough he had envisioned but uses sports as a way of escaping his working-class origins. His subsequent descent into alcoholism and his son's career in advertising both illustrate how, in Ragnerstam's view, lack of connection with one's roots has negative consequences, both personally and for the solidarity that is essential to social reform. In his emphasis on documenting the social history of an entire class, whether through collective novels or by portraying one representative individual, Ragnerstam has much in common with Ivar Lo-Johansson and his literary program of the 1930s.

Some working-class writers concentrate on depicting work environments. Erik Johansson (1914–) did not make his literary debut, *Fabriksmänniskan* (1976; Factory person), until after his own retirement from a factory job. In that novel and the sequel, *Bakom fabriksmurarna* (1978; Behind factory walls), he explores the question of why culture (in the traditional sense of appreciation for the fine arts) has not flourished in the welfare state. His protagonist, Tok-Alfred (Crazy Alfred), is the odd man out, a nonconformist who, like Folke Fridell's fictional protagonists, pursues his own idealistic goals despite collective opposition. In *Alfred och Isabella* (1989; Alfred and Isabella), Johansson contrasts the situation of young people faced with few job prospects, exorbitant rents, and large debts to repay with that of pensioners, who have fewer material cares but suffer from lack of love and companionship.

The novels of Ove Allansson (1932–), himself a sailor for many years, mostly concern life at sea. *Ombordarna* (1971; Those on board) documents the social hierarchy and working and living conditions aboard a trawler, with particular emphasis on the relentless monotony. A similar factual basis is found in *Här seglar Manfred Nilsson* (1975; Here sails Manfred Nilsson). *Sjömän* (1984; Sailors) is a nonfiction history of the occupation from the turn of the century to the present. Novels not set at sea also have a social or political thrust. In *Zeppelinaren* (1976; The zeppelin), based on an actual incident in the 1930s, a guerrilla group disguised as members of a symphony orchestra rent a zeppelin and attempt to overthrow the Nicaraguan dictator Somoza. Life in the United States and U.S. cultural imperialism abroad are criticized in *New York blues* (1981) and *Gud är amerikan* (1987; God is an American), respectively. Though his fiction is generally realistic, Allansson also incorporates an oral tradition of tall tales and burlesque humor as, for instance, in *Containerbröderna* (1979; The container brothers), in which an old sailor sets up housekeeping in a container and has himself shipped around the world.

Reidar Jönsson (1944–), in *Hemmahamn* (1973; Home port), a collective novel about life aboard a cargo ship, also stresses the human cost of isolation and terrible working conditions. In other works, Jönsson focuses on work-related issues on land. When the middle-aged textile worker Erik Hansson in *En borgares död* (1971; Death of a burgher) loses his job, he reacts with anger and depression, refusing to participate in the system's attempt to shift him to a worse position. He begins to recover his sense of self-worth through a gradual political awakening, as he sees how his fate is part of an economic and political system. *En borgares död*, like Johansson's factory novels and the works of Folke Fridell, argues that laborers' work must be perceived as meaningful. Another aspect of the search for meaning and fulfillment in life is shown in *Emilia, Emilia* (1972), a documentary novel about a widow who finds that material well-being and security do little to alleviate her isolation. *Levande livet* (1976; Living life) draws a parallel between an athlete selling his skills and workers selling their labor. In both cases there may be hidden risks to health, and the payoff is uncertain.

In Jönsson's autobiographical novel *Mitt liv som hund* (1983; Eng. tr. *My Life as a Dog*, 1990), set in the late 1950s, the father is mostly absent, the mother dies of tuberculosis, and the boy Ingemar Johansson moves among foster homes. Lasse Hallström's 1988 film, *Mitt liv som hund,* became an international success by bringing out the charm of the boy while downplaying the story's pessimistic undertones. Jönsson's sequel, *En hund begraven* (1988; Eng. tr. *My Father, His Son,* 1991), allows the reader to follow Ingemar into adulthood.

Jan Fogelbäck (1943–) also writes from personal experience. The protagonists of *Goliat* (1976; Goliath), *Bussbolaget* (1977; The bus company), and *Körjournal* (1979; Driving log) are all drivers, for an oil company, the municipal transportation organization, and a trucking firm, respectively. Fogelbäck describes work tasks in great detail. He emphasizes the role unions play in eliminating unsafe, stressful conditions and demonstrates the effect of work-related tension on people's personal lives.

LITERARY FEMINISM

One of the most significant outgrowths of the politicized climate of the late 1960s, in Sweden as well as internationally, was the reemergence of feminism, which had an immediate impact on Swedish literature. Though female writers from earlier generations had attained prominence within the predominantly male literary establishment, with few exceptions they had been forced to do so on the establishment's terms rather than their own. A new awareness of the suppressed, disguised, or hidden female literary heritage and tradition came about as critics reexamined the works of, for instance, Victoria Benedictsson, Selma Lagerlöf, Agnes von Krusenstjerna, and Moa Martinson in light of feminist theory. The articles and essays in *Kvinnornas litteraturhistoria* (1981; Women's literary history) provided an alternative view of prominent women writers, resurrected others who had been forgotten, and raised questions about why women's voices had often not been heard.

Beginning in the 1970s, many female writers consciously and deliberately provide a counterbalance in their fictional worlds to the domain traditionally associated with men: war, politics, and great historical events. Like Kerstin Ekman in her Katrineholm series, they focus on the domestic sphere and the private lives of female characters. Many of the women writers who came to prominence during the 1970s also explicitly promote a feminist agenda and seek to document various aspects of the struggle for respect and equality in relations between the sexes.

Märta Tikkanen (1935–), from the Swedish-speaking minority in Finland, reached an international audience with the novel *Män kan inte våldtas* (1975; Eng. tr. *Manrape,* 1978) and the long, autobiographical prose poem with the ironic title *Århundradets kärlekssaga* (1978; Eng. tr. *Love Story of the Century,* 1984), which exposes, with raw intensity, the emotional roller-coaster ride of marriage to an alcoholic. A stage version of this work has been widely performed both inside and outside Scandinavia. *Rödluvan* (1986; Little Red Riding Hood) expands on the fairy tale in an associative, psychoanalytical narrative that explores women's internal landscapes.

In her novel *För Lydia* (1973; For Lydia), Gun-Britt Sundström (1945–) retells one of the most famous love stories in Swedish literature, Hjalmar Söderberg's *Den allvarsamma leken* (1912; The serious game)—but from the woman's point of view and transposed to a contemporary setting. *Maken* (1976; The husband) depicts the marriage of an academic couple in which both partners are struggling to preserve autonomy and integrity.

In *Dotter till en dotter* (1977; A daughter's daughter), by Inger Alfvén (1940–), the protagonist, a successful social worker, gradually realizes that she has fallen into a traditional female trap of dependence and subservience in her marriage, despite her husband's lip service to equality. By examining the lives of her sister, niece, mother, and grandmother and comparing them with her own, she discovers patterns of inherited or acquired behavior. Eventually, she is able to reject the roles of domestic drudge and patiently waiting, all-forgiving wife and struggle toward increased assertiveness and self-reliance.

Inger Alfvén's other novels also focus on female discontent and the search for meaningful lives and satisfying love relationships. In *Städpatrullen* (1976; The cleaning patrol), three women try to find independence through mutual support and employment outside the home. *s/y Glädjen* (1979; The good ship joy) concerns a woman on an extended sailing trip with her husband, undertaken to help her cope with grief over the death of a child. Her effort to discover, or imaginatively and empathetically recreate, events leading up to the tragic deaths of the boat's previous owners indirectly assists her own emotional recovery. The historical novel *Arvedalen* (1981; Heritage valley) evinces parallels with Kerstin Ekman's Katrineholm tetralogy and with Enel Melberg's novel *Modershjärtat* (1977; A mother's heart), in that it traces the lives of women through several generations of the same family, concentrating on their efforts to escape socially or biologically prescribed roles and find a sense of purpose and meaning on their own terms. Complicated love relationships involving three or more people are the focus of *Ur kackerlackors levnad* (1984; From the lives of cockroaches), in which the entanglements illustrate that one person's dream of freedom may oppress or even destroy another's autonomy, and *Lyckansgalosch* (1986; Lucky dog), which depicts a classic triangle situation involving a long-married couple and a younger woman. In *Judiths teater* (1990; Judith's theater), the narrative perspective alternates between two women, a mother and daughter who have successively been involved with the same man, an egocentric poet.

Some works by women writers during the 1970s are overtly autobiographical or confessional. The trilogy of Ann-Charlotte Alverfors (1947–) about Gudrun—*Sparvöga* (1975; Sparrow-eye), *Hjärteblod* (1976; Heart's blood), and *Snabelros* (1977; Trunk rose)—chronicles a young girl's coming of age in what today would be called a dysfunctional family, her teenage rebellion, and the unplanned pregnancy that puts an end to it. *Linneas resor* (1979; Linnea's journeys) has a wider scope, as the title character travels around Sweden in search of love and herself, eventually awakening to the awareness that her conception of love is a romantic myth. Iconoclastic revolt characterizes the various authorial alter egos in the novels of Kerstin Thorvall (1925–). In *Det mest förbjudna* (1976; The most forbidden), the protagonist, Anna, tries to liberate herself from the influence of a repressive, puritanical mother by engaging in a series of sexual affairs. The confinement of marriage and children is rejected in *Oskuldens död* (1977; The death of innocence); *Ensam dam reser ensam* (1979; Single lady travels solo) embraces the frank pursuit of sexual pleasure but suggests that ultimately it can do little to relieve existential angst. The contributions of Anna Westberg (1946–) to the autobiographical genre are *Paradisets döttrar* (1978; Daughters of paradise) and *Gyllene röda äpplen* (1979; Golden red apples). In later works, her scope widens. *Valters hus* (1980; Walter's house) illustrates the contrasting temperaments of a husband and wife but without polemical emphasis, since each is portrayed with insight and empathy. The protagonist of *Sandros resa* (1986; Sandro's journey) is an androgynous Italian boy who becomes a love object for both men and women from many countries.

In a literary climate that was receptive to women's issues and concerns, several somewhat older women writers also came to prominence or drew renewed attention during the 1970s. Gerda Antti (1929–) cultivates a spare, straightforward, colloquial prose style in her short stories and novels which creates a sense of shared intimacy between reader and fictional characters. Most of her narratives—the stories in *Inte värre än vanligt* (1977; No worse than usual), the novels *Ett ögonblick i sänder* (1980; One moment at a time), *Jag reder mig nog* (1983; I guess I'll get by), and *Det är mycket med det jordiska* (1987; [freely] Life isn't easy)—focus on middle-aged women who to others are ordinary and unremarkable but whose inner lives are rich and reflective.

While still in her early twenties, Sun Axelsson (1935–) was considered a promising poet, but she subsequently lived abroad for many years and published relatively little. Her autobiographical trilogy *Drömmen om ett liv* (1978; Eng. tr. *A Dreamed Life*, 1983), *Honungsvargar* (1984; Honey wolves), *Nattens årstid* (1989; Night's season) describes her childhood and youth in Göteborg, provides a fascinating retrospective on the literary scene in Stockholm during the 1950s, and traces her involvement with and eventual rejection of a noted Chilean poet. Axelsson avoids self-indulgence by providing a double perspective on events: the naiveté of the author's younger self is contrasted with the feminist interpretation and analysis of the narrative voice.

Ulla Isaksson (1916–) began publishing in the 1940s; her subsequent extensive production included the novels *Kvinnohuset* (1952; House of women), about individual personalities and approaches to life within a female collective; *Dit du icke vill* (1956; Whither thou does not want), set in the seventeenth century and centering on a woman accused of witchcraft; and *Klockan* (1966; The bell), in which the fate of an eight-hundred-year-old church bell becomes a metaphor for Sweden's secularization. She also provided two filmscripts for Ingmar Bergman: *Nära livet* (1958; Brink of life) and *Jungfrukällan* (1959; The virgin spring). Over the years, many of her works dealt with female psychology and life experiences. *Paradistorg* (1973; Paradise square)—filmed by Gunnel Lindblom in 1976—nevertheless antagonized feminist critics and brought about a lengthy debate in the press with its implication that maternal instinct and responsibility are the exclusive purview of women. In *De två saliga* (1982; The blessed pair), however, she presents a marriage in which the husband recognizes his culpability in his wife's oppression. *Födelsedagen* (1988; The birthday) examines tangled, mixed emotions in mother-daughter relationships. Several decades older than most women writers associated with the feminist new wave, Ulla Isaksson in part shares their concerns, but her works also reveal connections to those of an earlier generation of feminist authors, to Ellen Key and Elin Wägner, who emphasize the personal and societal importance of motherhood.

Heidi von Born (1936–) made her debut as early as 1956 with a volume of poetry and also wrote short stories and plays, but beginning in the early 1970s, her main venue became the novel. Through her depiction of people who are outcasts or on the fringes of society, who are weak and vulnerable, physically or psychologically handicapped, she functions indirectly as a social critic. In her narratives, individuals—portrayed with psychological insight and empathy, often through interior monologue— are always the primary focus of attention. In *Dagar som de faller* (1972; As the days come), the protagonist is a single mother of two, living in a relationship of mutual dependence with an alcoholic. *Den tredje handen* (1974; The third hand) centers on a retarded girl who has been abandoned by her divorced parents; only in an institution does she find the warmth and attention she needs. In *Simulantens liv* (1977; Life of a malingerer), an old hypochondriac grasps at security through ritualized acts and tries to overcome his fear of death.

In the 1980s, Heidi von Born published a tetralogy about a brother and sister growing up in the 1950s: *Hungerbarnen* (1981; Children of hunger), *Kungariket Atlas* (1984; The kingdom of Atlas), *Den vita öknen* (1986; The white desert), and *Tiden är en tjuv* (1989; Time is a thief). The development and growth of the city of Stockholm in the last several decades provides a backdrop to the story, but the central theme is the devastating effect in later life of childhood neglect—not just material deprivation but lack of security and love. Other acclaimed novels are *Hummerkriget* (1983; The lobster war) and *Månens vita blod* (1988; The white blood of the moon).

Margareta Ekström (1930–) began writing in 1960, well before the feminist new wave of the 1970s. A major practitioner of the short story, she often focuses on female characters and their love relationships. Her narratives are rarely political or polemical. She is particularly sensitive and insightful in her portrayal of old people, for instance in several of the stories in *Dödens barnmorskor* (1976; Eng. tr. *Death's Midwives*, 1985). Selected stories from this collection and five others are included in *Den femte årstiden* (1983; The fifth season). A representative selection of her short fiction in English translation is found in *The Day I Began My Studies in Philosophy and Other Stories* (1989).

In addition to poetry and children's books, Ekström has also published several novels. *Flickorna* (1963; The girls) concerns the mutual dependence of two emotionally starved and lonely sisters. In contrast, *När de red omkring* (1969; When they rode about) is a picaresque novel in which two lovers experience wildly fantastic adventures. *Kvinnan som reste med Montaigne* (1981; The woman who traveled with Montaigne) intersperses fiction with the author's diary. Particularly in her short fiction, Ekström attains a stylistic clarity and concentration reminiscent of Söderberg.

In the late nineteenth and early twentieth centuries, more than 1.2 million Swedes left their native land for other countries, primarily the United States. Most of them departed for economic reasons; others sought religious or political freedom. The vast majority never returned permanently to Sweden.

In the second half of the twentieth century, the situation is reversed. Sweden, now prosperous, has become home to about a million immigrants from many different countries searching for jobs and economic security or fleeing terror and oppression. Once again, most immigrants stay.

This influx of people who are not ethnic Swedes has had a profound effect on Swedish society, though less on Swedish literature per se, since many immigrant writers express themselves in their own tongues. An important exception is Theodor Kallifatides (1938–), who emigrated to Sweden from Greece in the early 1960s. An aspiring writer in his homeland, he determined that his literary language would henceforth be Swedish and systematically set about mastering it. He has described the transition from one language to another as the longest journey anyone can undertake, a journey that inevitably ends in a sort of limbo. That he nevertheless quickly made Swedish his own is indicated by the fact that he took a Swedish university degree five years after his arrival and served as editor of the journal *BLM* from 1972 to 1976.

Most of Kallifatides' fiction, however, is set in Greece. His trilogy *Bönder och herrar* (1973; Eng. tr. *Peasants and Masters,* 1977 and 1990), *Plogen och svärdet* (1975; The plow and the sword), and *Den grymma freden* (1977; The cruel peace) shows the effect of the Second World War and the ensuing civil war on the small Greek village of Jalos and its inhabitants. The trilogy resembles other epic historical series published in Sweden during the 1970s in that it takes place in the author's home district, though the district in question is not Sörmland, Värmland, or Norrland but the Peloponnesus.

Utlänningar (1970; Foreigners), Kallifatides's first novel, draws on his own experience to depict the situation of Greek immigrants to Sweden—the cultural and linguistic barriers to their acceptance by the Swedish mainstream but also their support of one another. *Utlänningar* was filmed by Johan Bergenstråhle in 1972 under the title *Jag heter Stelios* (My name is Stelios). Several other novels concern confrontations with memories and with the past. In *En fallen ängel* (1981; A fallen angel), an old friend who has suffered torture and imprisonment under the Greek junta suddenly appears in the narrator's Stockholm apartment. A father's struggle against the Nazi occupation of Greece and postwar neofascism comes alive for his son through an account found after the older man's death in *Brännvin och rosor* (1983; Akvavit and roses). *En lång dag i Aten* (1989; A long day in Athens) recalls the author's father. Less tied to the Greek environment is *Kärleken* (1978; Love), which explores a love triangle in contemporary Sweden.

The largest groups of immigrants arrived, like Kallifatides, after 1960, but before, during, and immediately after the Second World War, some refugees from Nazi Germany or survivors of the Holocaust settled in Sweden. For writers or future writers among them, the subsequent choice of literary language was largely dependent on their age. The German-language poet Nelly Sachs (1891–1971) never shifted to Swedish; Peter Weiss (1916–82) wrote in both German and Swedish; his younger brother Alexander (1926–) only in Swedish. Zenia Larsson (1922–) also belongs entirely to Swedish literature. A Polish Jew, she has described her harrowing experiences in the Lodz ghetto and in concentration camps in the trilogy *Skuggorna vid träbron* (1960; Shadows by the wooden bridge), *Lång är gryningen* (1961; Long is the dawn), and *Livet till mötes* (1962; Heading for life). The novels of Rita Tornborg (1926–), also of Polish-Jewish extraction, are set in Sweden and written in Swedish, but many of her characters are Jewish immigrants, outsiders to contemporary Swedish society, for instance in *Hansson och Goldman* (1974; Hansson and Goldman) and *Salomos namnsdag* (1979; Solomon's nameday). *Friedmans hus* (1976; Friedman's house) portrays Jewish immigrants to Sweden in the mid-nineteenth century through the memoirs of an old man looking back on his experiences and examining his motives. *Systrarna* (1982; The sisters), a family chronicle in an entirely Swedish milieu, explores complicated relationships both in the present time of the story and in the past of a remembered childhood. Tornborg's narratives may also include mystical or magical elements, as in *Rosalie* (1991), whose title character—on the surface just an ordinary young wife and mother—experiences a series of adventures in which past and present, Sweden and Poland, intertwine.

Several authors with deeper roots in Swedish soil also give literary expression to experiences of fruitful or problematic confrontations of Swedish and Jewish cultures. The celebrated actor Erland Josephson (1923–) deals with Jewish themes in plays, such as *Dr Meyers sista dagar* (1964; Dr. Meyer's last days). His novel *En berättelse om herr Silberstein* (1957; Eng. tr. *A story about Mr. Silberstein*, 1995) exposes hidden racism and anti-Semitism in Swedish society. The autobiographical reflections in *Rollen* (1989; The role), *Sanningslekar* (1990; Truth games), *Föreställningar* (1991; Performances), and

Självporträtt (1993; Self-portrait[s]) primarily offer inside views on the theater and on acting, but here, too, the author addresses the question of Jewish identity.

THE VINDICATION OF POETRY

In general, the period from the mid-1960s through the early 1970s was not a high water mark for the lyric genre. Leftist ideology, with unprecedented media support, was inimical to the personal and existential topics that constitute much of the traditional subject matter of poetry, and proved inimical to poetry in general unless it illuminated some aspect of topical political issues.

Modernism resurfaces in the 1970s, only to be attacked or undermined on several fronts: by the notion of postmodernism, which—declaring modernism itself to be dead, or at least a dead end—features an eclectic, sometimes tongue-in-cheek borrowing from various earlier traditions, and by the easy accessibility of popular culture and music. The line between literature and entertainment, already challenged in the 1950s by such authors as Lars Forssell and ignored in the 1960s by songwriter Cornelis Vreeswijk (1937–87), becomes even more blurred in the 1970s and 1980s, when poets such as Jacques Werup (1945–) perform their own texts to rock music, and rock star Ulf Lundell (1949–) publishes several popular novels and composes a song, "Öppna landskap" (Open landscapes), enthusiastically proposed by some as a new national anthem.

In some critical quarters, this perceived crisis of poetry in an era of mass media domination led to a declaration, in the early 1970s, that poetry itself was dead (a statement that calls to mind similar ones, issued periodically, about the novel). Pronouncements to that effect proved somewhat premature. In the aftermath of the concrete poetry and "new simplicity" movements of the early 1960s, it became clear that both had expanded the boundaries of the poetic idiom. By establishing the outer limits for poetic discourse, they also opened the way for a return, in subsequent decades, to more traditional approaches. The ideological bent of the late 1960s, an apparent constraint, in fact led to politically and socially aware poetry with a wider focus, especially with regard to environmental and feminist concerns.

In his early collections, published during the 1960s—*Hyllningarna* (1963; Homages), *Essäer om Bror Barsk och andra dikter* (1964; Essays on Bror Barsk and other poems), and *Gubbdrunkning* (1965; Old man's drowning)—Bengt Emil Johnson (1936–) showed himself to be among the most gifted of the concrete poets. As a musician, he proved especially sensitive to the aural qualities of language. While the purely typographical eccentricities of the concrete style diminished, he continued to be an innovator and experimenter, creating startling new compounds, fragments, and juxtapositions.

Skuggsång (1973; Shadow song) (the reference is to the less full-throated way birds sing in the fall) establishes Johnson as a sensitive nature poet. In four collections devoted to seasons of the year, *Rötmånad* (1976; Dog days), *Efter vanligheten* (1978; As usual), *Vinterminne* (1981; Winter memory), and *Upprört* (1982; Agitated), he tries to capture fleeting moments in time, the traces of an external reality that cannot be grasped, only approximated through language. Here and in *Hemort* (1984; Home place), he also explores his own position and role within the natural world, the boundaries between self and other. Johnson's playful quality comes to the fore in *Tal till folket* (1975; Speeches to the people), which parodies public rhetoric. In later collections—*Utsatt* (1985; Exposed), *För resten. Improviserade dikter o. dyl.* (1987; By the way. Improvised poems, etc.)— the poems are linguistically more straightforward and accessible than previously, though composed in a variety of forms.

The early efforts of Lars Norén (1944–) are also associated with the concrete poetry movement. Norén made his debut at nineteen with *Syrener, snö* (1963; Lilacs, snow). The surrealistic qualities of this first collection become even more pronounced in subsequent volumes, which push the boundaries of modernism to their furthest limits and reflect a perception of the world as fundamentally chaotic, schizophrenic, and hallucinatory. Norén bombards the reader with words that are stripped of an obvious context. His poems are fragmentary and apparently unstructured, associative rather than linear; meaning is broken down rather than accumulated. Two central motifs that nevertheless emerge are an angst-laden sexuality and a preoccupation with death. *Encyklopedi* (1966; Encyclopedia) and *Stupor* (1968; Stupor) are constructed as enormous catalogs of references, both to violence and brutality in the international political arena (Vietnam, the Holocaust, suffering in the Third World) and to the music, drugs, and lifestyle of the 1960s counterculture, that form a sort of visionary collage.

Though virtually all his poetry is intensely personal, Norén sometimes assumes another persona or tries to penetrate another's state of mind. *Viltspeglar* (1972; Game reflectors) includes a series of first-person poems composed as letters ostensibly written home by a soldier during the Thirty Years' War. A section of *Kung Mej och andra dikter* (1973; King Me and other poems) focuses on the painter Carl Fredrik Hill (1849–1911), who became mentally ill. Two subsequent collections—*Dagliga och nattliga dikter* (1974; Daily and nightly poems) and *Dagbok augusti–oktober 1975* (1976; Diary August–October 1975)—employ a diary style and appear to serve a therapeutic purpose, as Norén examines his own separation anxiety and the Oedipal constellation that is the ultimate motivating force behind much of his writing.

This reductionism and compression continue in *Order* (1978; Order), *Murlod* (1979; Plummet), *Den ofullbordade stjärnan* (1979; The incomplete star), and *Hjärta i hjärta* (1980; Heart in heart), in which Norén's technique often centers on the repetition of certain key nouns. The frame of reference in these later poems is internal and self-contained; they are often obscure and difficult to interpret yet strangely beautiful. Norén is acutely aware of modernist tradition and has been particularly influenced by Paul Celan. Since around 1980, most of Norén's prolific output has been drama rather than poetry.

Lars Gustafsson's attraction to bizarre adventures and his sense of play are reminiscent of a 1950s sensibility, but his straightforward language and syntax reflect the concern for poetry's communicative function that dominated in the early 1960s, when he made his poetic debut. In his poetry, philosophical speculation is often demystified; abstract dilemmas are presented in concrete images. The poet's persona is frequently that of an observer and commentator who displays intellectual curiosity and great learning. He is both a rationalist in his search for explanations and answers and a romantic in his realization that some matters remain impenetrable.

These characteristics are all apparent in his early collections: *Ballongfararna* (1962; The balloonists), *En förmiddag i Sverige* (1963; One morning in Sweden), *En resa till jordens medelpunkt och andra dikter* (1966; A journey to the center of the earth and other poems), and *Bröderna Wright uppsöker Kitty Hawk och andra dikter* (1968; The Wright brothers visit Kitty Hawk and other poems). The overtly political orientation so typical of the literature of the 1960s is largely absent, though in the fourth collection, the Wright brothers' dream of flight is contrasted with subsequent technological developments that led to violence and terror. A more representative direction for Gustafsson is found in the title poem of the third volume, in which the reference to Jules Verne is inverted as the journey becomes a metaphor for the search for a center within each human being. *Kärleksförklaring till en sefardisk dam* (1970; Declaration of love to a Sephardic lady), with its rich, associative montage structure, contains most of the themes and motifs of *Sprickorna i muren* in compressed form. The portrait sketches in *Varma rum och kalla* (1972; partial Eng. tr. *Warm Rooms and Cold,* 1975) are less complex and allusive. In the 1970s, Gustafsson turned increasingly from free verse to fixed forms, as in *Sonetter* (1977; Sonnets). His most openly philosophical collection is *Artesiska brunnar cartesianska drömmar* (1980; Artesian wells, Cartesian dreams).

Gustafsson's collected poetry through 1980, *Ur bild i bild* (1982; From image into image), includes introductory commentary by the author. Other collections are *Världens tystnad före Bach* (1982; partial Eng. tr. *The Stillness of the World before Bach and Other Poems,* 1988) and *Fyra poeter* (1988; Four poets), in which he assumes four fictive identities to explore different poetic approaches. Functioning as a more conventional literary critic in *Strandhugg i svensk poesi* (1977; Eng. tr. *Forays into Swedish Poetry,* 1978), he offers insightful personal interpretations of fifteen representative poems by others.

With his first two collections, *Etnografika* (1960; Ethnographica) and *Skiljaktigheter* (1963; Differentiations), Reidar Ekner (1929–) established himself as one of the poets associated with the "new simplicity" of the early 1960s. His searing account of his young daughter's death from cancer in *Efter flera tusen rad* (1974; After several thousand rads), written both as therapy for himself and in hopes of helping others face terminal illness, is extraordinarily moving in its testimony. Subsequent collections—*Varje meddelande om att motståndet skall uppges är falskt* (1974; Every report that resistance will cease is false), *Den svenske toalettsabotören* (1975; The Swedish toilet saboteur), *Halvvägs mot mörkret* (1979; Halfway toward darkness), *Mellan polerna* (1982; Between the poles)—reveal an increasing political awareness, particularly with regard to the need to conserve irreplaceable natural resources. Similarly, in *Under trädkronorna* (1987; Under the tree crowns), he serves as a spokesman for ecological causes. Ekner, who holds a doctorate in literature and is a specialist in the poetry of Gunnar Ekelöf, is also a translator and critic.

Attention was riveted on Göran Sonnevi (1939–) in 1965 with the publication of his powerful poem "Om kriget i Vietnam" and the ensuing public debate. Through the remainder of the 1960s and beyond, he functioned more than anyone else as the officially sanctioned poet of the New Left. In the collections *Ingrepp-modeller* (1965; Interventions-models), *och nu* (1967; and now), and *Det måste gå* (1970; It has to be possible), his subject matter is the world around him and his point of view is anti-imperialist and anticapitalist. Gradually, however, his utopian faith gives way to an awareness that many revolutions have failed and that socialism requires an existential stance. Ideology can lead to liberation but also to violence and more oppression.

A key concept in Sonnevi's poetry is the notion of structures, the various external and internal patterns that govern or limit people's lives. With Noam Chomsky, Sonnevi sees language itself as one such structure. His interest in words as bearers of meaning comes to the fore in *Det oavslutade språket* (1972; The unfinished language) and subsequent collections. Beginning with *Det omöjliga* (1975; The impossible), Sonnevi's range widens both technically and thematically. This lengthy cycle of poems contains short, apparently fragmentary texts arranged in an order that cumulatively lends them meaning. What is impossible, according to Sonnevi, is to liberate ourselves from structures imposed on us. Love can do little to counteract the violence in the world, but at the same time, it represents the only possible escape from it. Similarly, we must try to break free by finding new ways of expressing ourselves, by learning a new language.

Språk; Verktyg; Eld (1979; Language; tools; fire), *Dikter utan ordning* (1983; Unordered poems), and *Oavslutade dikter* (1987; Unfinished poems) demonstrate an increasing sophistication and complexity. Once again, individual fragmentary poems are positioned in a sequence that illuminates them. These collections reveal a visionary, mystical aspect as Sonnevi explores the relationship between the individual and the cosmos; simultaneously, he displays an intellectual, cerebral approach in his use of philosophical and mathematical models. In contrast, all the poems in *Små klanger, en röst* (1981; Small resonances, one voice) contain fourteen lines. Though they are not conventional sonnets, each text attains remarkable concentration and intensity because of the fixed form.

The rhythmic, musical qualities of Sonnevi's poetry become more pronounced in later years with texts that seem intended for oral delivery. He is familiar with and builds on an international modernist tradition as well as the poetry of Swedish predecessors, notably Gunnar Ekelöf.

In his early collections, *Det nödvändiga är inte klart* (1969; The necessary isn't obvious) and *Namn och grus* (1973; Names and gravel), Tobias Berggren (1940–) resembles Sonnevi in his criticism of existing political and social structures, but like Sonnevi, he gradually moves beyond a rigid Marxist interpretation and analysis. He also shares Sonnevi's interest in linguistic theory and stresses the manner in which language itself shapes our perception of the world. In contrast to Sonnevi's short, fragmented texts, Berggren's tend to be longer, more internally coherent narratives.

By his own account, Berggren writes three kinds of poems: "process" poems that are learned and intellectual; ecstatic, intense, visionary lyrics; and short "Asian" verses that may seem simple, even banal, but that approach fundamental truths. Drawing on his knowledge of history and myth, he is able to interweave a mythological subtext with a depiction of present-day actions and events in a "process poem" like "Europa, en exil" (Europe, an Exile), in *Bergsmusik* (1978; Mountain music). It is at once a journey through contemporary Europe and an exploration of the mythic structures that underlie everyday experience. Journeys, both into the world and through the labyrinth of language, are the unifying motif of *Resor i din tystnad* (1976; Travels in your silence). *Threnos* (1981) explores the paradox of tangible, visible surface and impenetrable essence. Here and elsewhere, the image in a mirror, with its interplay of light and darkness, is a central metaphor for the poet's perception.

The natural world is, for Berggren, a metaphoric system. His nature poetry, often set on the Baltic island of Gotland, features seashores and detailed descriptions of plant life and includes short "Asian" poems about the seasons of the year. Music, always important to Berggren, becomes a central structural device in *24 romantiska etyder* (1987; 24 romantic études), composed in analogy to Chopin's preludes. These poems are compressed, intense encapsulations of mood.

In his eclectic and openly acknowledged borrowings from other poets (Dante, Blake, Eliot, Ekelöf), Berggren demonstrates a frame of reference that might loosely be termed postmodern. He fuses a romantic conscious-ness with a social conscience, metaphysics with politics. At the same time, he is himself a modernist, both in his self-conscious awareness of the poem as created object, as artifactapolinaire, and in his perception of the world as ultimately unknowable.

Kjell Espmark (1930–), a member of the Swedish Academy since 1981 and professor of literature at the University of Stockholm whose specialty is poetic modernism, is himself a poet. Though his debut was in the late 1950s, he is best known for the trilogy with the collective rubric *Sent i Sverige* (Late in Sweden): *Det offentliga samtalet* (1968; Public discourse), *Samtal under jorden* (1972; Discourse underground), and *Det obevekliga paradiset* (1975; The relentless paradise). Poems in these vol-umes are vignettes from contemporary Sweden, the objective descriptions of an impersonal observer. Collectively, they give a pessimistic view of a social democracy in which power corrupts and a revolution has gone astray. Three subsequent collections—*Försök till liv* (1979; Attempts at life), *Tecken till Europa* (1982; Signals to Europe), and *Den hemliga måltiden* (1984; The secret meal)—expand on this awareness by encompassing other countries and the course of history. Human beings are seen as victims of circumstances and conditions they cannot control. Swedish politics and society, seen from various perspectives, is again the primary focus in the novel series *Glömskan* (1987; Forgetfulness); *Missförståndet* (1989; Misunderstanding); *Föraktet* (1991; Contempt); *Lojaliteten* (1993; Loyalty); and *Hatet* (1995; Hatred).

In the late 1970s and in the 1980s, a number of poets at least temporarily abandoned free verse, which had dominated Swedish poetry ever since the modernist breakthrough, and began employing conventional verse forms. Some, like Lars Gustafsson and Lars Forssell, turned to international tradition and composed sonnets. Blank verse is generally considered primarily an Anglo-Saxon form, since it lends itself well to the natural cadences of the English language. Swedish does not fall with the same ease into iambs, but in *Sverige, en vintersaga* (1984, 1989; Sweden, a winter tale), Göran Palm—in the early 1960s the foremost proponent of "new simplicity"—produces a two-volume epos in blank verse. His model, as the title indicates, is Heine's *Deutschland, ein Wintermärchen*. Palm's political and social perspective is much the same as in his earlier works: his portrait of Sweden, past and present, is critical and bitingly satiric. He attacks injustice, inequality, and lack of freedom wherever he observes it. He castigates the authorities and an unwieldy bureaucracy and chastises Swedes in general for their complacency and self-centeredness. In the second volume, he is particularly concerned about the ecological problems that threaten not only Sweden but the entire planet. Throughout, Palm's language is fluid and expressive. *Sverige, en vintersaga* is a remarkable achievement.

Like Sonja Åkesson, about whom she published an important essay in *Kvinnornas litteraturhistoria*, Kristina Lugn (1948–) writes mostly about the private or domestic sphere. Again like Åkesson, Lugn uses straightforward and direct language. Whereas Åkesson tends to be descriptive and ironic when she examines herself and her own situation, however, Kristina Lugn—like many writers whose roots are in the women's movement—is usually confessional, even shockingly so. Her most common poetic persona is nevertheless no feminist but a frustrated, rejected woman in search of love who is bitter and angry, unsatisfied sexually, and disgusted by her own body. This persona appears to be in desperate need of consciousness raising; her isolation and alienation lead to depression and despair, which she fends off with pills. Matrimony is no solution to her plight, as the titles of several collections suggest: *Till min man, om han kunde läsa* (1976; To my husband, if he could read), *Döda honom!* (1978; Kill him!), and *Om ni hör ett skott* (1979; If you hear a shot); the last-named consists of a single long poem, strange, grotesque, and darkly humorous, about a miserable marriage. Similarly, the depiction of childhood in *Percy Wennerfors* (1982) is anything but idyllic; the imaginary companion of the title is not a wish-fulfillment playmate but a sinister figure who undermines the child's self-confidence. Lugn's sixth collection, *Bekantskap önskas med äldre bildad herre* (1983; Seeking acquaintance of cultured elderly gentleman), was a great success both with critics and with the public, and in 1984, all her previously published poems were reissued in the volume *Lugn, bara Lugn* (the untranslatable pun of the title may be rendered either "Lugn, only Lugn" or "Just simmer down"). The collection *Hundstunden* (1989; Dog time) breaks no new thematic ground but contains many striking images. Without being a "popularizer" in the negative sense of the term, Kristina Lugn proves that poetry can speak to a large audience outside a small literary coterie if it strikes a responsive chord.

The multifaceted Elisabet Hermodsson (1927–)—poet, artist, essayist, songwriter, and novelist—grew into feminism during the politicized 1960s, when both socialism and Christianity provided underpinnings to her search for social justice. Her feminism may also be seen as an attempt to overcome the limitations imposed by a single philosophical stance or point of view. *Disa Nilsons visor* (1974; The ballads of Disa Nilson), which she also recorded, is a tribute to Birger Sjöberg's *Fridas visor* and simultaneously a corrective. Sjöberg's "lilla Paris" (little Paris) (in actuality Vänersborg) and the love object Frida are described only through the eyes of her admirer. Hermodsson transposes the setting to Gotland and provides a female perspective, that of Disa Nilson, who in many ways is Frida's opposite: spontaneous, open, receptive to new experiences, in harmony with the natural world. The poems in *Gör dig synlig* (1980; Make yourself visible) revolve around a related motif: how women have tended to see themselves through the male gaze rather than defining themselves. The anthology *Kvinnors dikt om kärlek* (1978; Women's poetry about love), edited by Hermodsson, addresses the question, albeit indirectly, whether there is a specifically female viewpoint on or experience of love. Hermodsson is not programmatic, however. The songs of *Vad gör vi med sommaren, kamrater?* (1973; What do we do with the summer, friends?) and *Vakna med en sommarsjäl* (1979; Awaken with a summer soul), for instance, have more to do with nature and the search for psychic wholeness than with political issues, and the poems in *Stenar skärvor skikt av jord* (1985; Stones, shards, layers of soil) focus entirely on the natural world and ecological concerns.

Just as Elisabet Hermodsson alludes to Sjöberg, another troubadour, Cornelis Vreeswijk (1937–87), an immigrant from Holland, is inspired by Bellman, that most Swedish of all songwriters. In a series of song collections from the 1960s—*Ballader och oförskämdheter* (1964; Ballads and effronteries), *Ballader och grimascher* (1965; Ballads and grimaces), *Visor och oförskämdheter* (1965; Songs and effronteries), and so on—Vreeswijk creates a gallery of characters who, like Bellman's, provide a cross-section of bohemian and working-class Stockholm. Bellman's humor and irony, his sympathy for those who are defenseless and downtrodden, his melancholy, and his profound awareness of mortality may all be found in Vreeswijk's songs. Like Bellman, Vreeswijk borrows eclectically from various musical traditions and styles; some of his songs are translations, reworkings, or pastiches of American texts and tunes, recast in his own idiom—full of contemporary loanwords as well as borrowings from poets of previous centuries—and performed in Stockholm dialect. Vreeswijk also recorded an album of Bellman songs in a raucous, melancholy blues mode that brings out their emotional force. Especially during the 1970s, his texts incorporate a sharper, more direct social criticism than is found in his predecessor. In his last work, *Till Fatumeh* (1987; To Fatumeh), his style is concentrated and his message bleak as he confronts his impending death. Vreeswijk's production demonstrates that it is possible to be derivative to the highest degree and yet utterly original.

American idiom may have influenced Gunnar Harding (1940–) through the beat poets; he translated their works, as well as those of French surrealists and Russian modernists, into Swedish. In his role as editor and critic he is an important disseminator of foreign poetry. His own poetry is anchored in a specific time and place and may focus on a particular individual, as in *Blommor till James Dean* (1969; Flowers for James Dean), *Guillaume Apollinaires fantastiska liv* (1971; Eng. tr. *The Fabulous Life of Guillaume Apollinaire,* 1970, 1982), and *Starnberger See* (1977; Lake Starnberg), in which Ludwig II of Bavaria is the central figure. Portrait poems are also found among the English-language selections in *They Killed Sitting Bull and Other Poems* (1973). Visual rather than aural qualities dominate in his work, though he borrows an associative and improvisational technique from jazz. In spite of his attraction to the avant-garde, Harding's poetry is not "difficult" or inaccessible. Other collections—*Tillbaka till dig* (1980; Back to you), *Gasljus* (1983; Gaslight), *Stjärndykare* (1987; Star divers)— tend toward the introspective and personal.

The poetry of Katarina Frostensson (1953–) often evinces a fragmentary quality. There is seldom a narrative line, and metaphors are sparse. Instead, the poems revolve around repetitions and associations, with an emphasis on qualities of rhythm and sound. They attempt to register sensory input from the external world rather than describe or analyze, so an exact meaning or significance is difficult to pin down. Precisely for this reason, in her early collections—*Imellan* (1978; Between), *Rena land* (1980; Pure land),

Den andra (1982; The other), and *I det gula* (1985; In the yellow)—
Frostensson is implicitly critical of bureaucratic language that attempts to
codify meaning and of the social system that produces it. *Stränderna* (1989;
Seashores) makes explicit that her fundamental distrust of language derives
not from its lack of semantic content but from the inflexibility of words
and their failure to convey the mutability of the world. *Monodramer* (1990;
Monodramas) consists of four lyrical dramatic monologues, all with the
same initial reference point; one of them, *Nilen* (The Nile), was performed
at Dramaten in 1989. This shift to drama appears to have opened up and
freed a new vein in her authorship, for many of the poems in *Joner* (1991;
Ions) echo medieval ballads, folk songs, and hymns. Katarina Frostensson
has also translated French literature, both poetry and prose, into Swedish.
In 1991, she was elected to the Swedish Academy, the youngest member
chosen in more than seventy years.

DRAMA AFTER 1970

The revitalization of theatrical tradition in the late 1960s and 1970s led
most immediately to political theater as promoted by the collaborative
efforts of collectives within various companies, but it also gave rise to the
socially oriented plays of such established authors as Lars Forssell, the philosophical dramas of Sven Delblanc, and the psychological and existential
plays of P. O. Enquist. Agneta Pleijel (1940–), like Kent Andersson and
Bengt Bratt, was associated with Lennart Hjulström in Göteborg. The
first play she coauthored, *Ordning härskar i Berlin* (1970; Order reigns
in Berlin), is documentary theater, based on the historical record of the
failed 1918–19 revolution in Germany, and very Brechtian in its distancing
effects and interpolated songs. In subsequent works, Pleijel focused on
female characters. *Kollontaj* (1979) concerns a political dilemma and its
repercussions in the private sphere. Alexandra Kollontai, a Soviet diplomat
under Stalin, held heretical views, but in her public role she continued
to defend Soviet policy. The play offers a plausible explanation for her
behavior—her belief that the Soviet Union was the last bulwark against
fascism—but at the same time calls into question her moral stance. A
historical perspective is provided by Mayakovsky and the futurist poets.
At first they see the revolution as removing all barriers to artistic freedom
of expression, but during the course of the action they themselves are
eliminated one by one. *Berget på månens baksida* (1984; The mountain on
the dark side of the moon) also illuminates a remarkable woman of the
past, the Russian mathematician Sonja Kovaleski (Kovaleskaia), who in the

1880s became Sweden's first female professor. Here the conflict is between her professional aspirations and her love for a man who neither understands nor supports them. *Sommarkvällar på jorden* (1986; Summer evenings on earth), subsequently filmed by Gunnel Lindblom, has a Chekhovian quality, as a mother and three adult daughters with their families gather at the summer home and confront their existential dilemmas. The issues here are entirely personal and center on dreams of love and fulfillment and the conflicts that arise when two dreams are mutually exclusive.

Before he wrote for an adult audience, Staffan Göthe (1944–) was the author of half a dozen children's plays, and a playful quality is found in much of his work. Göthe reveals connections to absurdist tradition with its emphasis on black humor and the irrational. In *Den gråtande polisen* (1979; The weeping policeman), for instance, the angels literally sing, and in *En uppstoppad hund* (1986; A stuffed dog), various dogs that have been preserved by a taxidermist comment on the action. The theatrical Cervieng family of this play appears in several others by Göthe, notably *La Strada del Amore* (1985). In *En uppstoppad hund,* they are contrasted with the Ljungs, "typical" Swedes who avoid conflict and emotional involvement.

Conflict and powerful emotions are precisely what characterize the plays of Lars Norén, virtually all of which revolve around traumatic, Oedipal parent-child relationships. *Orestes* (1980) explores the Greek myth as a family drama. The implication is that everyone reenacts archetypical love-hate relationships and no one can escape this fate. *Modet att döda* (1980; The courage to kill) follows this thought to its logical conclusion: the play ends with a son killing his father because that is the only way he can free himself from the relationship. *Natten är dagens mor* (1982; Night is mother to the day) and *Kaos är granne med Gud* (1982; Chaos is the neighbor of God)—both titles refer to a poem by Stagnelius—feature the same family constellation, two sons and their middle-aged parents. The characters alternate between declarations of undying love and displays of relentless hate with little transition and no explanation; what appears to be random violence, presumably stemming from deep-seated psychological problems that have been repressed for years, unexpectedly breaks out from time to time. This family grouping is largely unchanged in *Stillheten* (1986; The stillness); *Höst och vinter* (1989; Autumn and winter) varies the pattern slightly by substituting daughters for sons. In *Underjordens leende* (1982; Subterranean smile), adults slip into bizarre, infantile behavior when under stress. *Hebriana* (1989) and *Endagsvarelser* (1990; One-day creatures) focus on a lost generation that now is approaching middle age without having resolved childhood conflicts.

Like Strindberg, with whom he has often been compared, Norén writes dialogue that seems jagged because of its many lacunae; much of the meaning lies between the lines. The influence of O'Neill is also obvious in Norén's work, and his masterpiece to date, *Och ge oss skuggorna* (1991; And grant us the shadows), acknowledges the debt. *Och ge oss skuggorna* is O'Neill's *Long Day's Journey into Night* set a generation later. The characters are Eugene O'Neill, Carlotta (his third wife), and his two sons from a previous marriage; the occasion is O'Neill's sixty-first birthday. Not only does the action in Norén's play recapitulate much that happens in O'Neill's, there are also deliberate verbal echoes of *Long Day's Journey*. Yet for all its borrowings, *Och ge oss skuggorna* does not seem derivative; it creates its own unique atmosphere of confrontation and claustrophobia. With this work, Norén established himself as a playwright on a par with his eminent predecessors.

HUMORISTS AND ENTERTAINERS

The Swedish troubadour tradition that can be traced from Bellman through Evert Taube and Nils Ferlin to Elisabet Hermodsson and Cornelis Vreeswijk also encompasses a tradition of musical parody. In the 1920s and 1930s, entertainers and songwriters Karl Gerhard (1891–1964) and Ernst Rolf (1891–1932) performed in musical reviews that, borrowing from cabaret performance style, lampooned the status quo in satiric couplets. Whereas elegance and charm were Rolf's strong suits, Gerhard incorporated a more sophisticated political and social thrust, especially before and during the Second World War, when the barbs of his antifascist texts challenged restrictions placed on freedom of speech. During the 1940s and 1950s, Ulf Peder Olrog (1919–72), himself a folk-song specialist, parodied the entire song tradition with *Rosenbloms visor* (1945–55; Rosenblom's songs). Povel Ramel (1922–) was responsible for introducing the so-called crazy style of the 1950s, which featured wildly surrealistic and subversive nonsense games with words and an equally eclectic parody of musical styles. Although primarily known as a musician and performer, Ramel also produced texts that appeared in published collections, such as *Min galna hage* (1957; My crazy playpen) and *Lingonben* (1978; Lingonberry bones).

The literary parody is the particular venue of Tage Danielsson (1928–85). In *Tage Danielssons Bok* (1963; Tage Danielsson's book), he offers, with the motivation that in the current media age people soon will not recognize printed material, a brief sample of every genre he can think of. *Grallimatik* (1966)—the untranslatable title scrambles the word for "grammar book"—deals with semantics and provides an analysis of the physiology of nonsensical utterance, and *Tage Danielssons Postilla* (1965; Tage Danielsson's book of homilies) pokes holes in the pontificating platitudes of self-styled guardians of morality. In *Samlade dikter 1967–67* (1967; Collected poems, 1967–67), Danielsson shows a mastery of poetic forms, a talent for pastiche, and a healthy skepticism toward poets who take themselves too seriously. *Sagor för barn över 18 år* (1964; Fairy tales for children over 18) and *Tage Danielssons mytologi: Ny svensk gudalära* (1978; Tage Danielsson's mythology: New tales of Swedish gods) are amusing and satirical commentaries on contemporary life. Danielsson's social criticism has a more serious aim in his libretto to Lars Johan Werle's opera *Animalen* (1980; The animal), with its message promoting disarmament and peace.

Hans Alfredsson (1931–) also began as a humorist, for instance with the parody *Rosa rummet* (1967; The pink room), an up-to-date version of Strindberg's satirical novel *Röda rummet,* but the scope of his literary production widened to encompass other styles and genres as well. *Den befjädrade ormen* (1979; The plumed serpent), set in viking times, concerns a confrontation between European and Native American culture. *En ond man* (1980; An evil man) is ostensibly a detective story, but the factory owner referred to in the title becomes an emblem of what is wrong with contemporary Sweden. *Tiden är ingenting* (1981; Time is nothing), a family chronicle covering a century and a half, resembles many other historical novels of the 1970s and 1980s in that it examines social changes brought about by technological advancement.

Until Danielsson's death, the team of Alfredsson and Danielsson was best known for its performances. Their comic routines in various musical reviews derive from the student tradition of the *spex,* a series of loosely strung together numbers that parody a particular style and historical period. Alfredsson and Danielsson also collaborated on a number of films, some of them based on their own literary texts. In the best of them—*Äppelkriget* (1971; The apple war), which has an ecological theme, and *Picassos äventyr* (1978; The adventures of Picasso), a commentary on the commercialization of art—a serious social message is conveyed through humor and gentle irony. The contribution of "Hasseåtage" (their joint signature) to Swedish cultural life is considerable, albeit difficult to categorize.

THE POSTMODERN MUSE

An awareness of literary tradition and the free-spirited borrowing from many different sources and styles are characteristic of postmodern sensibility. During the late 1970s and the 1980s, the historical novel and the autobiographical narrative, genres with a long and distinguished history, find new practitioners; other prose writers draw eclectically from crime fiction and the ghost story or construct narratives that turn inward to focus on psychological or existential dilemmas. Individual authors may shift their emphasis from one genre to another or move freely back and forth among them. Generalizations about common patterns and trends, or even about single authorships, become difficult or impossible.

To cite one example, Agneta Pleijel, an established dramatist known especially for her political theater, turned to poetry with the collections *Änglar, dvärgar* (1981; Angels, dwarfs) and *Ögon ur en dröm* (1984; Eng. tr. *Eyes from a Dream*, 1991) and subsequently published three acclaimed novels. *Vindspejare* (1987; Wind watcher), firmly anchored in the established tradition of the multigenerational family chronicle, is based in part on the experiences of the author's grandfather, who shelved his artistic dreams and emigrated to Java. It offers a condensed colonial history and simultaneously, as a metanovel in which the author comments on the creative process, explores new thematic territory. *Hundstjärnan* (1989; Eng. tr. *The Dog Star*, 1992), told from the point of view of a young girl, concerns parental betrayal and abandonment and thus represents yet another new direction. *Fungi* (1993), a historical novel with a documentary basis, incorporates elements of an exotic adventure story with extensive philosophical debate.

Similarly, Lars Andersson (1954–) borrows from many disparate currents in contemporary prose fiction without losing his own distinctive voice. Two of his novels incorporate plot features of the murder mystery: the psychological thriller *Brandlyra* (1974; Lyre of fire) and *Snöljus* (1979; Snow light), in which a deadly virus may be on the loose. The perception in *Snöljus* of a society that has lost track of human priorities, where individual rights and safety are subordinate to the schemes of some insidious hidden power and ecological disaster is just around the corner, has much in common with the jaundiced or apocalyptic view of Sweden in many other contemporaneous novels. *Snöljus* and *Vi lever våra spel* (1976; We live our games), however, also revolve around existential questions, particularly about the ways in which human beings are trapped: by language, by the roles they play for one another, by the way their culture forces them to define themselves—all central issues in contemporary linguistics, psychology, and philosophy as well as literature. In a similar vein, *Löv till läkedom* (1986; Leaves for healing) is less a conventional novel than an extended philosophical dialogue. Two historical novels are fundamentally different in their approaches. *Bikungskupan* (1982; Bee king's hive), about a nineteenth-century student who moves from discipline to discipline in search of himself, has a documentary basis. *Pestkungens legend* (1988; The plague king's legend), though set in the Middle Ages and featuring King Magnus Eriksson among the characters, alludes to saga and myth. Andersson also displays great virtuosity with regard to narrative structure. *Snöljus*, for instance, is a montage with many shifting points of view.

The reinterpretation of myth is a main focus of the works of Marianne Fredriksson (1927–). Her first two novels, *Evas bok* (1980; The book of Eve) and *Kains bok* (1981; The book of Cain), are extrapolations of the story told in the book of Genesis; the third, *Noreas saga* (1983; Norea's saga), draws on apocryphal accounts of a daughter born to Adam and Eve. In Fredriksson's version, the departure from Eden was actually a flight from a sort of collective unconscious, timeless and amoral, to a world of individuality, governed by conscience and moral choice. Both *Noreas saga* and two novels with a contemporary setting, *Simon och ekarna* (1985; Simon and the oaks) and *När Gud skrattade* (1993; When God laughed), suggest that people have a capacity for mystical, visionary experience that often is lost or repressed. *Den som vandrar om natten* (1988; He who wanders in the night) is a philosophical parable that takes place at the time of Jesus; *Gåtan* (1989; The riddle) incorporates a mystery motif with a story of incest and confused identities in a modern setting. In *Syndafloden* (1990; The flood), Fredriksson again turns to Old Testament subject matter. Here the story of Noah and his family becomes a parable for contemporary humanity's sinfully negligent treatment of God-given resources.

Vibeke Olsson (1958–) also turns to the distant past with a series of six novels in which ancient Rome is seen through the eyes of a female Christian slave and her descendants: *Hedningarnas förgård* (1982; The forecourt of the heathens), *Kvarnen och korset* (1984; The mill and the cross), *Sabina* (1985), *Sabina och Alexander* (1986; Sabina and Alexander), *Krigarens sköld* (1988; The warrior's shield), and *En plats att vila på* (1989; A place to rest). Similarly, *Kastellet* (1992; The fortress) is set in Germania, on the periphery of the Roman empire. Like Marianne Fredriksson, Vibeke Olsson uses faraway settings to explore fundamental issues in interpersonal relations and timeless existential questions.

Other writers reveal an orientation toward social criticism with a clear anchoring in the present, particularly during the 1970s. This stance characterizes two early novels by the prolific Jacques Werup (1945–) —*Streber* (1972; Careerist) and *Swiss made* (1975)—as well as the poetry collection *Tiden i Malmö på jorden* (1974; Eng. tr. *The Time in Malmö on the Earth*, 1989). *Casanovas senare resor* (1979; Casanova's later journeys) displays his talent for caricature and parody. *Shimonoffs längtan* (1983; Shimonoff's longing) is a fictional biography that explores the respective attractions of adventure and security. In *Pornografens död* (1988; Death of the pornographer), the vivid descriptions of erotic exploits are part of a deathbed coming-to-terms with existential questions, which is also a theme in the poetry collection *Den skräddarsydda sorgen* (1982; Tailor-made grief). Nature plays an important role in Werup's poetry, particularly in the collections *Fläckar av liv* (1977; Spots of life) and *48 dikter från Österlen* (1980; 48 poems from Österlen), but other common motifs are the search for freedom and the need to keep asking questions. *Stjärnan i periferin* (1987; The peripheral star) celebrates passion and romantic love. Werup's frequent sojourns in Paris and the French provinces are reflected in a number of travel articles, some of which are collected in *Den elektroniska synden* (1989; The electronic sin) and *42 minuter från Paris* (1992; 42 minutes from Paris). With the collection of poetry *Septemberljus* (1990; September light) he returns to Österlen in Skåne, its landscape, people, and changing seasons.

In the first three narratives of Klas Östergren (1955–), *Attila* (1975), *Ismael* (1977; Ishmael), and *Fantomerna* (1978; The phantoms), the protagonists are young men of his own generation searching for an identity, security, and satisfying love relationships. *Gentlemen* (1980; Gentlemen) is less autobiographical and more sophisticated, both technically and thematically. Two brothers, Henry and Leo, illustrate diametrically opposed ways of coping with life: Henry systematically represses all negative feelings and ritualizes everyday events to lend them meaning, whereas Leo, a poet, lies on his bed and broods or goes on alcoholic binges. Through two interlocking detective stories in which the brothers are involved, the narrative expands to incorporate an implicit condemnation of Sweden's murky role in international business and politics. The historical novel *Fattiga riddare och stora svenskar* (1983; Poor knights and great Swedes) also includes a complicated intrigue involving gangsters and the powers-that-be and gives a vivid picture of Stockholm in the 1930s. In two subsequent works, Östergren's emphasis shifts from the social or historical panorama to inner concerns. In *Plåster* (1986; Band-aid), two middle-aged hospital patients who have suffered heart attacks discuss their situations; *Ankare* (1988; Anchor) centers on a single individual, a smuggler who is struggling with his conscience, his memories, and his alcoholism. *Handelsmän och partisaner* (1991; Businessmen and partisans) concerns isolation and alienation in both an interpersonal and social context.

A similar movement from the external to the internal underlies the work of Eva Runefelt (1953–). Though she made her debut with a novel, *I svackan* (1975; In the hollow), based on her own experience caring for patients in a hospital, she is best known as a poet. Most of her texts, collected in *En kommande tid av livet* (1975; A future time of life), *Åldriga och barnsliga trakter* (1978; Aged and childlike places), *Augusti* (1983; August), and *Längs ett oavslutat ögonblick* (1986; Along an unfinished moment), refer to small, transitory incidents or experiences that are conveyed with extraordinary attention to sensory detail. Runefelt becomes progressively more involved in an existential quest for connections and correspondences that will eliminate the boundaries of the individual ego.

Much of the writing of Ernst Brunner (1950–) has autobiographical roots, an orientation that has been common in Swedish prose at least since Strindberg. He frequently approaches the same subject matter first in a poetry collection and then in a novel. Like Eva Runefelt, he found working in a hospital a formative experience; his first collection, *Jag ändrar ställning klockan tre* (1979; I change positions at three o'clock), is set in a ward for chronic patients, which is also the work environment of the protagonist in *Känneru brorsan?* (1980; D'ya know my brother?). *I det stora hela* (1982; On the whole) and *Dans på rovor* (1983; A bed of turnips) both center on his perceptions as an exchange student in Leningrad and are highly critical of the rigid Soviet political system and its bureaucracy. Similarly, both *Separator* (1986) and *Svarta villan* (1987; The black villa) are set in Tullinge, where Brunner, the son of Austrian immigrants, grew up. Here the community of workers from various European countries employed by Alfa-Laval, which manufactures milk-processing machinery, serves as a microcosm of Sweden's evolving multicultural society as viewed from the child's perspective. The novel *Kocksgatan* (1991; Cook Street) is a rollicking slice of life from the 1970s on Stockholm's South Side, the author's home as an adult. Brunner has also explored the life and works of the Finland-Swedish poet Edith Södergran from several perspectives. Thus all the poems in *I det stora hela* take place in the instant of her death. A doctoral dissertation on Södergran's expressionism, *Till fots genom solsystemen* (1988; On foot through the solar systems), was followed by a novel, *Edith* (1992), about her life. Whether drawing on his own experiences or imaginatively reconstructing those of others, Brunner is an epic realist with a remarkable feel for evocative detail.

Stig Larsson (1955–), in contrast, registers a reality that exists only within the fictional universe itself, where chronology and logical sequence are absent or confused. He cultivates a minimalist style in his novels, which often seem to lack a plot entirely. Since Larsson refuses to analyze or offer psychological motivations, his fictional protagonists all seem strangely flat and contourless. This pattern remains constant in *Autisterna* (1979; The autistic ones), *Nyår* (1984; New year), *Introduktion* (1986; Introduction), and *Komedin 1* (1989; Comedy 1). In his poetry collections—*Minuterna före bilden* (1982; The minutes before the image), *Samtidigt, på olika platser* (1982; Simultaneously, in different places), *Deras ordning* (1987; Their order), and *Händ!* (1988; Happen!)—he also strips away semantic content and simply records what appear to be random comments or observations, devoid of the imagery and metaphor usually associated with poetic language. Larsson's theme, the meaninglessness of contemporary existence, is expressed through his form. In addition to poetry and prose fiction, Larsson has written for the stage and television. His play *VD* (Head of the firm), about a boss who pays an unexpected visit to an employee and his girlfriend in order to sabotage and manipulate them, was performed at Dramaten in 1987 and on television the following year; *Straffångens återkomst* (Return of the convict), which premiered in 1991, is reminiscent of Norén's family dramas in its emphasis on role playing and psychological trauma.

Jonas Gardell (1963–), novelist, dramatist, and stand-up comedian, describes a basically cruel world peopled by lonely, alienated, or seemingly trivial characters. His debut novel, *Passionsspelet* (1985; Passion play), centers on the love story of two boys, Hampus and Johan. Faith in the redeeming power of love, whether homosexual or heterosexual, is questioned, yet never entirely abandoned, in the subsequent novels *Odjurets tid* (1986; Time of the monster), *Präriehundarna* (1987; The prairie dogs), and *Vill gå hem* (1988; Want to go home). Gardell's narrative stance oscillates from ruthless observation to tender compassion to an often unsettlingly sudden comic vision. The play *Isbjörnarna* (1990; Polar bears) gives a devastating portrait of Ilse, an egoistic and power-hungry mother in her early seventies whose two daughters are vainly vying for the affection she reserves for her absent son. Gardell's interest in female psychology is also apparent in *Fru Björks öden och äventyr* (1990; Mrs. Björk's adventures and experiences). In the novel *En komikers uppväxt* (1992; The adolescence of a comedian), young Juha tries to protect his exposed position in the pecking order and win acceptance and friends by playing the clown, hiding his vulnerability behind the mask of a comedian.

With *Dikter kring Sandro della Quercias liv* (1979; Poems on Sandro della Quercia's life), Niklas Rådström (1953–) purports to have written a lyric biography of an artist of the Italian Renaissance whose irrepressible curiosity about the world around him also typifies his age. The poems interfoliated in the text, however, are not Sandro della Quercia's but Rådström's own; the documents, like the figure, are fictitious. Just as della Quercia's inquisitiveness is symptomatic of Rådström himself, this role playing and hiding behind masks is a characteristic pose. The poems in *Skuggan* (1982; The shadow), for instance, are composed in rhyme and meter and reveal a tone of romantic longing and introspection that is reminiscent of the 1950s. Rådström continues to experiment in *Landskap* (1983; Landscapes), which contains short stories ranging from fables and legends to ghost stories and realistic narratives. A second lyrical biography, *Den helige Antonius frestelser* (1986; The temptations of St. Anthony), features a historical figure, but the interpretation of his character is unconventional, for St. Anthony is tempted not by the devil but by the rich possibilities of life itself. *Berättat om natten* (1988; Told at night) offers more conventional ghost stories; the novel *Månen vet inte* (1989; The moon doesn't know) celebrates Rådström's grandmother, who first made him aware of his imaginative resources. In yet another change of focus, the poems in *Pappskalle* (1990; Numbskull) display Rådström's playfulness with words, his wit and offbeat humor. The historical novel *Vänd ditt timglas* (1991; Turn your hourglass) is both a mystery and an adventure tale, set in the Stockholm of Bellman and told from the perspective of a boy who witnesses the murder of Gustav III. Rådström is also the author of several children's books.

By referring to and borrowing from a wide variety of traditions and styles, Niklas Rådström demonstrates a self-consciousness often identified with the postmodern spirit. In this regard, just as Pär Rådström has been considered the quintessential author of the 1950s, his son Niklas may be regarded as a representative voice of the 1980s and beyond.

Women Writers

Cheri Register

8

In April 1979, a special Nordic literary prize was awarded to the Finland-Swedish novelist and poet Märta Tikkanen. It was a grass-roots alternative to the prestigious Nordic Council prize, created to protest the fact that the council had never chosen a woman to receive its annual honor. Money to finance the award was solicited from female writers and literary scholars throughout Scandinavia in a word-of-mouth campaign. Märta Tikkanen was not the only deserving writer, but she was an appropriate symbolic choice. In her poetry collection *Århundradets kärlekssaga* (1978; Eng. tr. *The Love Story of the Century,* 1984), a first-person narrator reveals how her husband's alcoholism affects her life. The book had caused a stir among readers, who took it as an exposé. Henrik Tikkanen was, after all, a prominent writer whose own work played on the image of the creative artist drowning his angst in alcohol. Märta Tikkanen's poems offer *en annan synpunkt,* another viewpoint, challenging this particular masculine mystique with the grim reality experienced by the wife and the children of the alcoholic:

Such an honest account
of alcoholism
say the wise men in the book review sections
Strange, that none of them
feel there's something missing—
like the smells, for example

In awarding Märta Tikkanen their prize, those who funded it were urging that the literary establishment pay belated attention to human creativity's "other viewpoint" by reexamining and reevaluating literature written by women over several centuries. This strategy grew out of a series of pan-Scandinavian seminars on women and writing at which female poets, novelists, playwrights, and journalists made contact with literary historians studying the works of earlier writers who had been neglected, underestimated, or even ridiculed in the authoritative histories of Scandinavian literature. The writers talked about obstacles they encountered in getting their works published and reviewed, which corroborated the scholars' thesis that women's writing had been limited by discrimination in the literary "marketplace." The scholars talked about the works they had discovered and offered new readings of familiar works, information that the writers eagerly received as precedent for their own literary aspirations.

This special attention to women's literature, as the creative expression of women's experiences and perspectives on life, can be traced directly to the new women's movement that emerged in Europe and North America in the late 1960s. In the United States, the feminist revival generated a new interdisciplinary field, women's studies. Swedish academic institutions, with their rigid bureaucratic structure, have been more resistant to such influences, but research and teaching pursued on the margins of academe are gradually finding their way into the center and revising the literary canon. Evidence of change can be seen in the appearance of new editions of works long out of print, which are now regarded as classics—for example, Fredrika Bremer's *Hertha* (1856), Victoria Benedictsson's *Pengar* (1885; Money) and her diary, *Stora Boken* (The big book), and Elin Wägner's *Pennskaftet* (1910; The penholder).

Much of the credit for persistence in this endeavor goes to Karin Westman Berg, of the University of Uppsala, who in the mid-1960s initiated a weekly seminar on women's literature that served for many years as a forum for scholars doing research on individual female writers. She also directed the first government-funded research project on women's literature, which got under way in 1979. After her retirement from the university in 1981, the national Ministry of Education named her an honorary professor and established an academic position in women's literature in her name. This action, too, was in response to a petition by writers and literary scholars. By the mid-1980s, doctoral candidates were producing dissertations on women's literature at all the Swedish universities. Outside academe, collaborative efforts such as the series *Kvinnornas litteraturhistoria* (The women's history of literature, begun in 1981) invited a wider reading public to reexamine women's literature.

Rediscovering lost or neglected writers and fitting them into the canon has been the first task of the recent scholarship. This volume, as a whole, reflects the progress that has been made to this point. Yet to interpret and evaluate women's works in an enlightening and judicious way, scholars need to view them in a context different from the one that has been the backdrop for a predominantly male literary history. This context—the changing social conditions that shaped women's lives—does not always correspond to the distinct periods into which Swedish literary history is usually divided. In some cases, a female writer may have derived more inspiration from seemingly obscure female predecessors than from her male contemporaries, or she may have been open to an entirely different set of foreign influences than those generally credited with altering the course of Swedish literature.

This chapter is intended as a complement to the history recounted in the preceding chapters. It traces a female literary tradition that exists within the history of Swedish literature. It is necessarily sketchy, and many of the writers included here are treated more extensively elsewhere in the book, as they should be. The comments made here are precisely those that require "another viewpoint." The emphasis is on features of their work that illuminate the cultural context of women's writing or show continuity and interdependence among female writers.

The standard artistic representation of Sweden's first known female author, St. Birgitta (1302–73), described by Stephen Mitchell in chapter 1 as "hard at work, listening to voices from heaven, pen in hand," can function as an icon for the female writer, listening hard for inspiration that is not mediated by external masculine authority. As the leading religious figure of pre-Reformation Sweden, Birgitta has received scholarly attention from several different perspectives. Feminist scholars approach her Revelations both as documents in women's cultural history and as literary works that contain particularly female themes and imagery. Because she took religious orders after raising eight children and overseeing a large household, her life encompasses both halves of what is usually seen as an either/or choice for medieval women of wealthy families: marriage or the convent. Her spiritual writings are infused with the imagery of domestic life. God is likened to a washerwoman rinsing souls or to the still in which beer is brewed. Christ, speaking to Birgitta in a vision, urges her to regard her soul as a "sweet and pleasant" cheese that fills her body, the form in which it takes shape. Earlier scholars have found these similes absurdly prosaic, but they offer a rare view into daily life on a fourteenth-century Swedish estate. At the same time, they offset the patriarchal imagery of God that has dominated both Catholic and Lutheran tradition, and they make it possible to posit a female spirituality.

Recent feminist interest in Birgitta hearkens back to the work of Emilia

Fogelklou (1878–1972), the first Swedish woman to receive a doctorate in theology, who wrote her dissertation on Birgitta in 1919. In a later work, *Bortom Birgitta* (1941; Beyond Birgitta), Fogelklou shows a resemblance between Birgitta's spiritual vision and pre-Christian folk beliefs and rituals that were preserved by women well into the Christian era. She characterizes Birgitta as a successor to the "seeresses" who performed a shamanistic function in pagan Scandinavia. Fogelklou finds evidence of pre-Christian beliefs especially in Birgitta's reverence for Mary as the mother of Jesus. Mary's motherhood is very graphic and physical. In one vision, Birgitta feels Jesus quickening in her own womb as Mary tells about the Annunciation, and in another, she witnesses the birth itself. Mary loosens her hair, a folk practice thought to ease the child's passage through the birth canal, and then gives birth on her knees on bare ground. Birgitta ends her account of the vision by asking rhetorically why, if it was a woman who first touched the Lord's body, women should be considered unclean after childbirth. Nevertheless, other visions, particularly those involving female adversaries, show that she shared Roman Catholicism's contempt for women as sexual beings. By excluding women from the priesthood and equating female sexuality with original sin, Christianity had deprived women of authentic religious practice. Birgitta found a place of influence within the church for herself and for a spirituality derived from her life experience.

The next person in this history is as enigmatic as Birgitta and as anomalous: a woman entrusted with political power. Queen Christina (1626–89), by her own account a masculine soul in a female body, has long baffled historians, who could not reconcile her aspirations with her sex. She becomes far less problematic when seen in conjunction with her contemporary and social acquaintance Agneta Horn (1629–72), whose memoirs, *Beskrifningh öfwer min wandringestidh* (1657; Description of my wandering time), offer critical insight into an experience not uncommon to women of the Swedish nobility: the prospect of an unwanted marriage. In both their lives and their autobiographical writings, Christina and Agneta Horn struggled with the legally crippling and morally deadening impact of marriage, which would subordinate them to the will of their husbands. Both women exalted love as the proper foundation for a lifelong partnership, as did the French précieuses of the same period. In her intellectual history, *Kvinnosyn i Sverige* (1973; Views on women in Sweden), Ruth Nilsson documents a raging public debate about the institution of marriage and the relative place of men and women in it. Between 1628 and 1669, there were eighteen Latin treatises on marriage written by Swedish theologians and jurists defending the conservative view that the wife's subordination was ordained by nature.

Christina's and Agneta Horn's private writings, as well as Christina's highly public actions, must be understood in light of this debate, which was the Swedish variant of the Continental *Querelles des femmes*.

These three women do not, however, constitute the beginning of a conscious and deliberate female literary tradition. Their writings were not available to the women of their time or even those of the generations immediately following. Agneta Horn's autobiography might still be unknown were it not for the special interest in women's history shown by Ellen Fries (1855–1900), the first woman to complete doctoral studies at a Swedish university. She found the manuscript on a shelf at the Uppsala University library in 1885 and began publishing excerpts from it in *Dagny*, a women's rights magazine.

An actual, continuing tradition begins in the late seventeenth century with the poetry of Sophia Elisabeth Brenner (1659–1730). Brenner was one of many women of the upper class who engaged in the art of poetry, but she did so with a rare consciousness of herself as a writer by profession. She was unique in having a classical education, which, in her own words, "depended only on happenstance and not at all on intention." She simply took the initiative to follow her brothers' Latin lessons. She also benefited from having a father with liberal views on women's education and a husband who encouraged her literary aspirations. The Brenners socialized with the leading male writers of the day, who were well aware of her work.

Brenner's poems were reproduced and distributed at the time of writing and then collected into two volumes entitled *Poetiska dikter* (Poetic writings), in 1713 and 1732. The collection contains 152 poems, written in Swedish, German, French, Italian, Dutch, and Latin. Brenner was well read in those languages and thereby familiar with Continental writings on natural law and the equality of the sexes. The occasional poem was her primary genre, and she used her wedding poems to promote harmony and equality between husband and wife as life partners. Her range of themes is as encompassing as her own life. She wrote poems in honor of political events, in which she took a lively interest. Yet she also wrote about the hardships of domestic life, a topic she knew well, having borne fifteen living infants, only six of whom survived into adulthood. A poem written to celebrate the publication of a handbook on pregnancy and childbirth, *Den Svenska Jordegumman* (1697; The Swedish midwife), contains a line that could well be her motto: "It is a noble thing to know how yourself." Brenner's reputation, if not her poetry, was known outside Sweden—even as far away as Mexico, where Sor Juana Ines de la Cruz dedicated to Brenner a poem in which she asserted women's right to take up the pen.

Brenner and her successor, Hedvig Charlotta Nordenflycht (1718–63), suffered a common fate in literary history. Because they continued to write throughout their lives, they have been portrayed in caricature as middle-aged poetesses, as though that were an absurdity. Brenner has been called *hedersgumman,* "that good old woman," and given little credit for her part in the emergence of a native literature. A caption under Nordenflycht's portrait in a multivolume Swedish literary history that served as the major reference work until 1988 reads, "The antique lyre is ill-suited to the Sunday-dressed matron's bourgeois corpulence." Current female writers have commented that the continuation of this stereotype has made it difficult for them to claim the authority implied in authorship. Literary historian Martin Lamm's equivocal summation in 1918 of Nordenflycht as poet is quite typical: "With her obvious faults, her author's vanity, her female obstinacy, her lack of logical consistency, her inability to judge the world objectively, she is nevertheless one of our literature's most imposing figures." The grounds for belittling Nordenflycht's work are precisely its strongest and most distinctive features. One is her subjective lyricism, a personal candor seen in some of Sophia Brenner's poems about the difficulties of childbirth and the loss of children. Nordenflycht was the first Swedish writer whose authorial voice was purposefully subjective. The title of her first poetry collection, *Den sörgande turturdufwan,* (1743; The sorrowing turtledove), combined with the unrequited passion for a younger man expressed in her last poems, stamped her as "lovesick" even during her lifetime, despite her influential position in Stockholm's literary circles. "Den sörgande turturdufwan" refers specifically to the death of her chosen husband less than two years into a marriage long delayed because her brother, her legal guardian, refused to permit it. It presages a theme that runs throughout Swedish women's literature, the desire for a mate who is worthy of an intelligent woman and respects her natural equality.

Another aspect of Nordenflycht's work that has subjected her to ridicule is her feminism, which was heartfelt and vociferously expressed throughout her career. As "the Shepherdess of the North," Nordenflycht was a leading proponent of the philosophy of Jean-Jacques Rousseau. When Rousseau published a letter questioning women's intellectual and artistic capacity, Nordenflycht was moved to write a long poem, "Fruentimrets Försvar Emot J. J. Rousseau" (1761; The woman's defense against J. J. Rousseau), in which she catalogued women's achievements through time and attributed women's social inferiority to three causes: reigning prejudicial assumptions about women, restrictive upbringing, and limitations placed on women's activity. These were the conditions of her own life as well. As a widow whose brother had inherited the family wealth, she depended for her living on the commissions she earned for occasional poems and flattering homages to wealthy patrons and, finally, on an author's pension from the Swedish parliament.

Poet Anna Maria Lenngren (1754–1817) has fared better in literary history, in part as a contrast to Nordenflycht. Where Nordenflycht created a public persona for herself as author, Lenngren retreated into anonymity after her marriage in 1780, though she certainly continued to write and publish. Where Nordenflycht was openly feminist, Lenngren's attitudes and behavior in regard to the feminist issues of her time are sometimes puzzling. Her male contemporaries characterized her as a virtuous and unpretentious housewife, inclined by nature to domesticity. Lenngren herself wrote of her fondness for her sewing table, yet there is evidence that the sewing table is where she kept her writing materials.

The poem of greatest interest to scholars of women's literature is "Några ord till min kära Dotter, i fall jag hade någon" (1789; Some words to my dear daughter, if I had one), which advises a young woman to avoid manly pursuits, such as writing, that will distract her from her proper obligations and expose her to ridicule. Generations of Swedish teachers taught this poem as Lenngren's credo, in which she forswears the literary ambitions of her youth. Generations of female students have suspected that the poem is a bitterly ironic statement about the social risks faced by a woman who wants to write. The truth is not easy to establish. Ruth Nilsson warns against reading the poem as a personal statement of any kind. Lenngren was, above all, a skilled practitioner of poetic form. She was fond of exercising those skills to the limits of the genre, of taking existing formulas and reconstituting them. Parts of this poem seem to be dictated by the advice-giving genre, parts seem ironic, and parts seem sincere. The question that presents itself is: if Lenngren was so highly regarded as a satirist, why should we not read this poem as satire? It seems to satirize the conventions of the day as well as the women who oppose those conventions without regard for their reputations. Regardless of its intention, it tells the reader that eighteenth-century Sweden was not an entirely fruitful climate for women writers.

The romantic period of the early nineteenth century was no more hospitable to creative women. Those with the desire to write turned mainly to the private genres—letters and diaries. There has been recent interest in *Årstadagboken* (The Årsta diary), a private record of life on a Swedish estate, kept by Märta Helena Reenstierna between 1793 and 1839 but not published until 1946 to 1953. The memoirs of Malla Montgomery-

Silfverstolpe (1782–1861) are most appreciated for their insider's view of the literary elite that gathered at her salon in Uppsala. As Bertil Nolin notes in chapter 4, there were a few women in this circle, but none attained reputations like those of their male contemporaries. Indeed, the genres and themes of Swedish romanticism were virtually inaccessible to women. A century and a half after Sophia Brenner's accidental Latin lessons, women remained uneducated in classical literature, knew local folklore but not Old Norse myths and heroic legends, and had little opportunity to learn about poetic meter as such. The idealized masculinity and elitism of the literary brotherhoods with their heroic code names was alien to women. It would not be easy to conceive of oneself as subject in a genre that reserved a symbolic function for Woman. Reigning public opinion can be summed up in a statement by Per Daniel Amadeus Atterbom: "Sometimes nature itself makes exceptions and puts positive, masculine genius in a female body. From this anomaly come educated women, artists, and heroines, of whom three or four have justifiably won the world's admiration. Their lot, however, is not to be desired. They must surrender all claim to feminine happiness."

These early decades were undoubtedly a time of creative ferment for women, however. Increased literacy and leisure time among women of the *borgerskap,* the bourgeoisie or middle class, enlarged the female reading audience, and sentimental and Gothic fiction imported from England and the Continent aroused interest in a literature that at least used settings where women were present. In 1828, an anonymously published Danish book, *Hverdags-Historier* (Everyday stories), opened with this manifesto-like pronouncement: "All my stories are true everyday stories. They bear the imprint of the earth from which they spring. They are fruits of life, not of learning and profound study. Domestic and social life, individual relationships and intrigues are the sphere from which they are taken, and I admit frankly that I assign these daily, domestic circumstances a great importance. That is, for all humans, the most intimate, the source from which their happiness and unhappiness spring." The author was Thomasine Gyllembourg (1773–1856), member of the Heiberg family, well known in the Danish theater.

That year, 1828, also marked the appearance of one of the most path-breaking works in Swedish literary history: Fredrika Bremer's *Teckningar utur hvardagslifvet* (Sketches from daily life), which continued in three volumes, the last published in 1831. Literary scholar Birgitta Holm, in her critical series *Romanens mödrar* (Mothers of the novel, begun 1981), has done a subtle textual reading of *Familien H****, the second two volumes of the Sketches, using an interpretive method devised by American feminist scholars Sandra M. Gilbert and Susan Gubar in their book *Madwoman in the Attic* (1979). Holm credits Bremer (1801–65) with transforming the novel from entertainment to art, replacing romanticism with realism, and altering the perspective of literature from the aristocratic outlook of the eighteenth century to the bourgeois liberalism of the nineteenth. Holm is intrigued by Bremer's use of a marginal figure as narrator: the servant, Beata Hvardagslag, who is an ever-present observer but not really part of the family. She does not stand in the wings, unseen, but intervenes in the action and then withdraws again as etiquette demands. She is at once nearly omniscient and limited in what she can say, an ambiguous position suggestive of the place assumed by the female writer. Indeed, Beata tells her readers that she wrote poetry in her youth and "did not burn the gravy," an explicit refutation of the advice in Lenngren's "Några ord . . ."

In Bremer's career, we see the evolution of a woman's authorship from sheer delight in the rush of creativity—in the feeling expressed in a letter to a friend that "an alien power within me wrote" and the words "danced out of my head or my heart"—to a world-changing sense of literary vocation. Bremer sought to counter "the poisonous sorcery" in sentimental novels that distorted young women's view of reality and replace it with female characters "who through power and will conquer all external opposition and bring their talents to bear, so that they obtain independence and bliss for themselves and benefit others (or society)."

There were enough new, appreciative readings of Bremer's work in the 1970s and 1980s to constitute a Fredrika Bremer revival. In books, journal articles, and papers delivered at special Fredrika Bremer symposia, scholars and critics have examined Bremer's impact on the legal changes benefiting women in midcentury, especially the emancipation of unmarried women, her relationship to other writers, her religious beliefs, her contacts with women's rights advocates in the United States, and the reception of her novels in other countries. Bremer was truly an international figure in her time, admired by the likes of Hawthorne and Longfellow and emulated by other female writers. When British publishers balked at doing translations of her early works, Mary Howitt and her husband William proceeded at their own expense, translating the books from German until Mary had mastered Swedish. By 1845, Bremer was sending Mary Howitt her manuscripts, so the novels appeared in English almost simultaneously with their Swedish publication. Louisa May Alcott's *Little Women,* published thirty years after Bremer's *Hemmet,* contains an allusion to Petrea's red nose that is left unexplained, as though it had become a common idiom among novel readers.

Bremer was not the only female novelist to gain prominence in Sweden at midcentury or the only one whose works were popular abroad. Marie Sophie Schwartz (1819–84) was the best-selling author. Sophie von Knorring (1797–1848) and Emilie Flygare-Carlén (1807–92) were, as Birgitta Steene points out in Chapter 5, more given to generic formulas and to a conservative vision of women. Because of that, they have received far less attention in the recent scholarship on women's literature. A stereotypical and sentimentalized literature intended for women was also well represented in the periodical literature that came into fashion in the 1840s.

By 1859, the kind of literary program that Bremer advocated had its own forum in *Tidskrift för hemmet* (Magazine for the home), founded by Sophie Leijonhufvud Adlersparre (1823–95), known by her abbreviated signature, Esselde (S L——d). In preparation for the World's Exposition in Vienna in 1873, Esselde wrote an essay, "Qvinnan inom svenska litteraturen" (The woman in Swedish literature), the preface for an attempted but incomplete bibliography of women's writings from 1300 on. A second generation of editors, Sigrid Leijonhufvud and Sigrid Brithelli, completed the bibliography in 1893 in time for the Chicago World's Fair. It was the first effort undertaken in Sweden to trace the achievements of female writers and offer them as evidence that women's literature was worthy of support and encouragement. Esselde was also instrumental in the founding in 1884 of the women's rights organization Fredrika Bremerförbundet, which adopted *Tidskrift för hemmet,* renamed *Dagny,* as its official organ. (It is still published under the name *Hertha,* the title of a Bremer novel.) Esselde deserves a place in Swedish literary history as mentor, supporter, and original publisher of many female writers, from now obscure ones to Selma Lagerlöf.

By the 1880s, however, a new generation of writers saw Esselde as a formidable taskmistress whose ideological preferences must sometimes be resisted in the name of authorial independence. She phrased her appeals for women's emancipation in terms of a distinctive feminine character that could raise the moral tone of Swedish society. The younger generation felt confined by this notion of femininity, attributed it to oppressive material conditions, and appealed instead for greater individual freedom. This was the view expressed in *Framåt* (Forward), the publication of Göteborg's Women's Association, a short-lived (1886–89) but influential rival to *Dagny.*

The period known as the Modern Breakthrough was certainly a break-through for women's literature as well. No fewer than 137 Swedish women debuted as writers in the 1880s, twice as many as in each of the preceding four decades. There were many reasons for this increase: greater access to education; a gender imbalance in the population that required many women to remain single and thus be self-supporting; the legal emancipa-tion of single women, which allowed them greater economic independence and choice of marriage partners; the beginnings of urbanization, which broke old social patterns and opened gender roles and sexual mores to renegotiation; an active women's movement that encouraged women to enter new fields; and finally, a new orientation in literature that brought issues of social oppression and individual freedom to the center—the very issues that women struggled with in their private lives. Fredrika Bremer had introduced these themes three decades earlier, but it was the prominence of male-authored works about freedom-seeking women, such as Ibsen's *Et dukkehjem* (1879; A doll's house), as well as Georg Brandes's championing of a socially engaged "tendenslitteratur," that gave them validity.

The popular acceptance of *kvinnofrågan*, the woman question, as an appropriate theme for literature did not make authorship trouble-free for women, however, as the Danish scholar Pil Dahlerup has illustrated in a reexamination of the Modern Breakthrough from the women's point of view. Male writers could urge resistance to the dominant institutions of government, church, press, and so on and then return to the solace of their marriages or the mutual support of bohemian café life. Women, however, had to resist directly, before they could even write, by challenging the institution whose oppression they felt most keenly—marriage. This could be a lonely endeavor. Furthermore, the answers that men of the stature of Brandes and Ibsen and Strindberg gave to the woman question became the authoritative ones. There was room for female characters who were heroically true to their internal sense of justice and for others who were neurotic and sexually stunted. But there was not ready empathy for female characters who felt ambivalent about the obligations imposed on them and the options open to them.

Ambivalence can be called the hallmark of the literature written by women in the 1880s. Ingeborg Nordin Hennel (1984) has made an analysis of grammatical and stylistic features, use of conversation, and metaphors in eight short story collections from the decade, four by men and four by women. She concludes that the women's texts show a juxtaposition of polar opposites: extreme caution and discretion side by side with exaggeration and hyperbole. Their metaphors also swing from pole to pole. She calls this an "ambivalence-generated breaking of norms" of prose style and asserts, moreover, that "the female writers lack an authoritative narrative voice— an 'I'—using instead a form of camouflage in order to approach what for them was a delicate issue, the role of writer." Ambivalence about the role of the writer, and its compatibility with the experience of the woman, is seen most vividly in the life and works of Victoria Benedictsson (1850–88), known by the pseudonym and alter ego Ernst Ahlgren. The Danish critic Jette Lundbo Levy poses the problem this way in her book *Dobbelblikket* (1980; The double view):

> There is in her a contradiction that the tragic and heroic doesn't immediately resolve. Namely this: she could write diary entries and letters that include exact and precise descriptions of those experiences of insecurity, pain, and great hopes that she experienced in her departure from and resistance to a narrow and useless female role— but why then could only bits of these experiences, in disguised and distorted form, find expression in the novels and short stories she wrote? Why can she see so clearly? And why can't she find forms of expression that are adequate for this clear vision?

A partial answer lies in the fact that the prescriptions for a politically correct literature of protest excluded much of women's authentic experience, provoking female writers to conform to these prescriptions, to challenge them at their peril, or to sneak their personal truths in "in disguised and distorted form." Benedictsson succeeded with *Pengar* because she took on the institution of marriage and portrayed a woman in rebellion against it. Selma is, however, distinctly more ambivalent about her actions than Ibsen's Nora is. *Fru Marianne* (1887), on the other hand, was read as a retreat from radicalism rather than a protest against the sham equality and hypocritical sexual tolerance of the intellectual and artistic elite. Under the tutelage of a natural and robust husband, Marianne becomes a natural and robust woman, with her sexuality and her equality affirmed.

The differences in how men and women actually experienced the issues of the day became especially evident during "the morality debate," a public argument about the double sexual standard which raged throughout Scandinavia in 1886 and after. The debate was perceived as an either/or matter: the radicals—Brandes, Strindberg, et al.—advocated complete sexual freedom, whereas the conservatives—including a leading faction of the women's movement—advocated a single standard of chastity for women and men alike. Women who ordinarily aligned themselves with the radicals on aesthetic and political questions were expected to take the radical position on sexuality as well, both in their writing and in their personal behavior. That was not an easy matter for women who had come of age with no education about sexuality, who had agreed to marriages with older suitors because of parental pressure or economic need, who had no access to birth control, and who feared both the "fallen woman" stigma applied to prostitutes and infection with venereal disease, which was rampant among middle- and upper-class men. These were the internalized sources of women's ambivalence, but there were external checks as well. The quick demise of *Framåt* in 1889 is a good illustration. The publication of "Pyrrhussegrar" (Pyrrhic victories), a short story by Stella Cleve—a pseudonym for Mathilda Malling (1864–1942)—that deals frankly with a woman's erotic feelings, caused such a scandal that Göteborg's Women's Association was obliged to dissociate itself from the magazine, advertisers boycotted it, and the editor lost not only her editorship but also her regular job at a school for girls. Both their male contemporaries and many later historians of the Modern Breakthrough failed to understand that to women living in this social environment, sex was not just a biological drive, a natural right, or an unmitigated source of pleasure: frequently, it was a commodity of exchange, as the title of *Pengar* indicates.

As the decade wore on, a new interest in human psychology began to replace naturalism's focus on material causation. Among its effects was a tendency to equate the ambivalence about sex portrayed in women's literature with *sexualskräck*, sexual fear, or frigidity. Even infertility was regarded as a sexual failing. In the preface to *Giftas I*, Strindberg writes: "An infertile or childless woman is greatly to be pitied, but she is, nevertheless, an aberration from nature, therefore she cannot see the relationship between man and woman correctly and her word ought not to have any significance. That is why one ought not to give the word of Sweden's four currently writing female authors any importance in this question, because all four live in childless marriages."

In this process of psychologizing, the biographies of the women who wrote the novels, short stories, or plays became conflated with the content and characters in their works. Furthermore, the popular perception of these writers/characters became the inspiration for male authors' own studies of the feminine personality. Both Ibsen's Hedda Gabler and Strindberg's Fröken Julie, for example, are said to be in part modeled on Victoria Benedictsson. In a critical biography of dramatist Alfhild Agrell (1849–1923), Ingeborg Nordin Hennel (1981) makes the claim that how a woman of the Modern Breakthrough fares in literary history depends on how well her life conforms to the female types prevalent in the most highly regarded literature of the time. Victoria Benedictsson, like the Norwegian-Danish Amalie Skram, lives on as a tragic figure whose confusion about sex, love, and her own womanhood led her to suicide. Anne Charlotte Leffler (1849–92) wound up as the passionate Duchess of Cajanello, acting out her erotic freedom in marriage to a younger man and then dying at age forty-three after the birth of her first child. Alfhild Agrell, on the other hand, kept on writing into old age, with neither heroism nor tragedy to recommend her. In restoring Agrell to the canon of Modern Breakthrough writers, Nordin Hennel is careful to say that she is not claiming for her any superior aesthetic quality. The most interesting question about the women of this period is not whether they wrote as well as Strindberg, for example, but how they managed to negotiate the tension between expanded opportunity to write and the literary establishment's restrictive and often contradictory expectations about what they ought to be writing. Victoria Benedictsson's personal motto, *Arbete och sanning*, work and truth, was nearly impossible to live by.

Swedish literary history describes an abrupt shift in literary fashion from the 1880s to the 1890s. Alfhild Agrell, Mathilda Malling, and Amanda Kerfstedt (1835–1920) were the only women of any prominence to survive that shift and alter their writing styles and genres to satisfy new reader expectations. Malling turned to historical fiction. A novel set during the French Revolution was published anonymously in 1894, perhaps to avoid the stigma of association with "Pyrrhussegrar." Agrell even changed her author's persona, publishing some very popular *kåserier* and provincial tales under the name Lovisa Petterkvist, not just a pseudonym but a lighthearted and scatterbrained narrator who stands in sharp contrast to the characters in Agrell's tendentious plays.

Among the most prolific women writers of the 1890s are a remarkable number of authors of children's literature. The works of Ottilia Adelborg, Elsa Beskow, Helena Nyblom, Anna Maria Roos, and the hymnist Lina Sandell are classics of Swedish children's literature. For those who also illustrated their books, the choice of audience was in part determined by the exclusivity of the arts establishment. Following on the popularity of Jenny Nyström's illustrations and her creation of the first genuinely Swedish picturebook, *Barnkammarens bok* (1882; Nursery book), writing and illustrating for children offered women more likely access to critical acclaim and an income than practicing the "high arts."

The undisputed greatest Swedish writer of the turn of the century was a woman: Selma Lagerlöf, (1858–1940). Despite—or perhaps because of—her genius, critics and historians have had some trouble with Lagerlöf's gender.

Down to the present day, there has been disagreement and confusion about how to categorize her: was she a *naiv sagotant,* naive teller of fairy tales, as Oscar Levertin characterized her, who spun out tales that hung in the atmosphere of the rural provinces, waiting to be saved from extinction? Or was she an intelligent, educated woman who skillfully wove together strands of folklore, history, and Continental literature? The first summation quickly degenerated into a female stereotype. The second is an attempt at revision, which places her intellectual gifts on a par with those of the leading men in Swedish literature. More recent scholarship has further revised Lagerlöf's portrayal by tracing feminist political tendencies in her work. A major aim of these revisions is to save her from the fate of the anomaly and root her in a social context that gives her work particular historical significance. Selma Lagerlöf, however, was, and remains, an anomaly: an uncommonly gifted writer with a depth of vision into the human psyche that probes beneath time and place and human events. On her admission to the Swedish Academy in 1914, an editorial in the women's magazine *Idun* compared her with earlier female writers and concluded: "What her [female] predecessors had, whether of vision and emotion, of pathos and merriment, in some tendency or other toward a Swedish character, is drawn together in Selma Lagerlöf in a grand and rich composition, poetry's splendid rose of color and scent. Pondering, mysticism, religious feeling, ecstasy for nature, joie de vivre, extravagance of life—all that which forms the rushing stream in the soul of the Swedish people and makes it so variable and difficult for the interpreter—is present in Selma Lagerlöf's writing, which is simultaneously visionary and naive."

Anomalous as she is, Lagerlöf belongs firmly in this specialized women's literary history because both her working life and her imagination put women at the center. In the short story "Mamsell Fredrika," she pays her debt to Fredrika Bremer as a literary predecessor and advocate for single women. Single and self-supporting throughout her life, Lagerlöf surrounded herself with female friends and colleagues. Though she was an aesthetician rather than an activist, she associated with women working on behalf of women's rights and turned initially to Esselde to seek publication for her stories. Her novels and stories take place in a moral universe in which women are the arbiters of what is good and true in human life. Women engage in existential questions that go beyond the matters of behavioral propriety and individual freedom that concerned Bremer and her contemporaries and the women of the Modern Breakthrough. Young women—often poor, orphaned, or, like Lagerlöf herself, physically disabled—bear weighty moral burdens and function as saviours in mythlike fashion. The surface naiveté of her narrative style can keep readers from seeing how creatively Lagerlöf uses the perspective of these seemingly vulnerable women to achieve a fresh, critical, and even transformative vision into the human condition.

In 1911, Selma Lagerlöf was the featured celebrity speaker at an international congress of women's suffrage organizations held in Stockholm. Her speech, entitled "Hem och stat" (Home and state), made a grand impression, and it has been cited since to claim Lagerlöf as a feminist. In it, she made the case that the mores and values that reigned in the home, particularly the preindustrial household managed by women, ought to be the model for governing the state. To some in the audience it was a provocative statement, though it was, for the most part, a reiteration of ideas widely accepted among Swedish women. Often called "the Ellen Key line," elements of it found their way into the official program of the liberal women's organizations and onto the pages of *Morgonbris* (Morning breeze), the Social Democratic women's publication.

Ellen Key (1849–1926)—regarded, like Lagerlöf, as a woman of genius—had, during the 1870s and 1880s, written reviews of women's literature in *Tidskrift för hemmet,* taught classes at the Stockholm Workers' Institute that were attended mainly by women, and founded a discussion group called Tolfterna, the Twelfths, to bring together women of different social classes. In 1896, she changed the direction of Swedish feminism with an essay entitled "Missbrukad kvinnokraft" (Misused womanpower). In highly charged language she accused the leading women's organizations of persuading women to "line up like zeroes behind a male cipher" in order to be taken seriously. The women's movement had failed women, she said, by emulating male behavior and values rather than calling for a new social order built on women's *egenart,* or distinctive character, especially the emancipation of women as *könsvarelser,* sex-beings. Above all, true emancipation required that motherhood be treated as women's "highest cultural task," a core human experience around which all social life should be organized. Given as Key was to hyperbole and misstatement, her essay was easily dismissed as reactionary by those it offended. As she continued to elaborate her thesis, however, it appeared more visionary, and eventually it became so familiar that even a revered figure like Selma Lagerlöf could espouse it at an international gathering.

Overall, the Ellen Key line had less impact on women's rights organizations and their political activity than on the literature of the following decades, where it left obvious traces. Key herself exerted influence not only as a reviewer but also as friend and adviser to two generations of writers. In a letter dated March 1887, Key described her recent activity: "Once I went and saw Ernst Ahlgren's new play, *On the Telephone,* such a lovely piece, one evening I was at Alfhild Agrell's and heard her new drama, and one time at Anne Charlotte's [Leffler] to hear hers; I am a sort of *hjälpmadam,* hired woman, to the authoresses." In a voluminous correspondence with Marika Stiernstedt (1875–1954), Elin Wägner (1882–1949), Anna Lenah Elgström (1884–1968), and many other writers of the new century, Key offered encouragement, advice, criticism, praise, and even practical help. When Key learned that Swedish-American novelist Hilma Angered-Strandberg (1855–1927) was sick and penniless, she appealed to her circle of writers for help. Reminding Elgström that her husband had given her an expensive ring for Christmas, she asked her to ask him to spare some money for Angered-Strandberg and added, "Then write personally to her, as a young author-sister to an elder" Elgström, like Key's other correspondents, was already offering support to younger, debuting authors. She provided editorial help, money, and hand-me-down clothes to a Fru Gustavsson, who appealed to her by letter in 1915:

> "A Pregnant Woman's Hunger" has been lying for a long time at *The Social Democrat*'s editorial office. They don't read such things there, of course, and if they read it, they don't understand it. Now I ask you to read it and, if it doesn't require far too many changes, to send it with a few words to *The Social Democrat.* I beg you to do it. Maybe the beginning could be omitted with no loss, but the description of the pregnant woman's hunger is so true. I would throw it in the trash if it weren't so. Please excuse me for asking you to read it. But where do you turn in such a case? I want to thank you for all that you have written. I have lived my life among ruffians and prostitutes, I am young, but so tired. When I read your works I am happy nevertheless.

Six years later, Gustavsson published her first novel, *Anna Holberg,* under the name Maj Hirdman (1888–1976), one of the few women generally included in coverage of the proletarian writers.

A sampling of novels and short stories written by the women who debuted in the first two decades of the twentieth century would reveal a set of themes and images compatible with Ellen Key's vision of women as *samhällsmödrar,* social mothers. We see young women at work in the city, looking ahead to a new social order, whether it be Cecilia, Elin Wägner's middle-class *pennskaft* (penholder, i.e., journalist), or the factory workers and unwed mothers of the short stories of Maria Sandel (1870–1927). We see a reverence for the preindustrial household and for elderly women who preserve aspects of that dying culture. Elin Wägner, for example, adopted the *nyckelknippa,* the ring of keys that was the rural housewife's mark of authority, as her personal logo. We see attempted relationships between men who are emptied of virtue by fin-de-siècle decadence and women who long for a chance to show moral courage. We see selfless young women fending off a hostile, excessively masculine world, either the threat of rape and battering or, in fantasy and historical fiction, images of battling warriors surrounding a castle inhabited by peace-loving women. The association between women and peace became especially vivid with the approach of the world war. Pacifism and the movement for women's suffrage were rallying points that brought women writers into frequent contact and cooperation. Ellen Key's correspondents did, to a large degree, constitute a literary and political sisterhood.

Elin Wägner was a member of the Swedish delegation to the 1915 Women's Peace Congress in The Hague, which was intended to unite women of all countries in active opposition to the war. She returned home disillusioned with the congress's failure to overcome nationalist sentiment and predicted that "the lesson that the opponents of feminism will draw from the World War will be that they need not reckon with any unified, independent female will for the foreseeable future." Critic Sarah Death maintains that Wägner's fiction took a turn at this point, demonstrating that "her belief in the need for women's solidarity is accompanied by a deep-rooted pessimism about their capability of achieving it." This pessimism is also apparent in Ellen Key's postwar writings and might be posited as a theme in women's literature of the postwar period. The trend away from political engagement does not mean conciliation with the status quo, however. Instead, women's literature of the next two decades becomes still more concerned with exploring what it is that sets women apart from the world of men and its images of them. A poem by the Finland-Swedish poet Edith Södergran (1892–1923) is emblematic of this postwar disillusionment:

> We women, we are so close to the brown earth.
> We ask the cuckoo what he expects of spring,
> we embrace the rugged fir tree,
> we look in the sunset for signs and counsel.
> Once I loved a man, he believed in nothing . . .
> He came on a cold day with empty eyes,
> he left on a heavy day with lost memories on his brow.
> If my child does not live, it is his . . .

The belief that women are closer to the natural life force and thus irreconcilably different from men, the masters of the industrial age, was a common theme in women's literature between the world wars. From the perspective of modern-day women's studies scholars who see gender as primarily a social construct, this belief appears antifeminist. Yet it was accompanied by seemingly greater authorial self-assertion than was seen in previous generations. In her second volume of poetry, Södergran answered critics who had ridiculed her disregard for rhyme and meter: "My self-confidence comes from the fact that I have discovered my dimensions. It does not behoove me to make myself smaller than I am." Novelist Agnes von Krusenstjerna (1894–1940), who gained prominence in the 1920s with a series of female apprenticeship novels, the Tony books, told a journalist in 1933: "There already burned within me then a desire to write really bold books—such as would amaze and alarm the world and make my family turn from me. I wanted to *épater les bourgeois* [provoke the burghers]. No, maybe I wanted rather to reveal the truth to people—the truth about women." Krusenstjerna certainly did amaze and alarm the world. Her seven-volume novel series, *Fröknarna von Pahlen* (The Misses von Pahlen), aroused a new morality debate, "the Pahlen controversy," in 1934. Conservative Swedish nationalists charged Krusenstjerna with weakening the public morality by attacking the family and promoting sexual freedom. Well into the 1950s, Swedish public libraries required special permission for teenage girls to check out Krusenstjerna's books.

The truth about women was, in the literature of the 1920s, 1930s, and 1940s, often erotically charged, since female sexuality was virtually new subject matter in need of authentic portrayal. The truth was to be found by probing into the psyche, through complex portraits of novel characters, or through revealing poetic imagery. Stina Aronson (1892–1956), Karin Boye (1900–1941), and Maria Wine (1912–) are prime examples of this approach. Of course, psychoanalysis and eroticism were also prominent tendencies in literature written by men in these years, particularly that called "primitivism," in which the primal woman, erotic and ever receptive, is the standard symbol of nature unspoiled by industrial culture. Female writers, however, see primal woman from "another viewpoint," as subject rather than object, which often allows them to mock men's use of her. For example, Artur Lundkvist's poem "Kvinnan" (Woman), from the collection *Vit man* (1932; White man), presents a photographic double exposure, with a woman superimposed on the landscape:

We experience you as land
and shore and sea, as cosmos.

Your thighs are covered with golden grass,
in your limbs run red springs.
Your maternal breasts are mountains
Filled with flowing gold.
You are as simple as a handful of dust
You are the mystery.

In contrast, Agnes von Krusenstjerna's *Av samma blod* (1935; Of the same blood) contains a scene in which some artistic men from the city get lost in the country late at night while searching for their runaway wives. Suddenly, the Great Mother rises up out of the landscape and scares them out of their wits. As a response to numerous literary bathing scenes in which nubile Venus-like women frolic unashamed in the water, Moa Martinson's *Kvinnor och äppelträd* (1933; Eng. tr. *Women and Apple Trees*, 1983) opens with two middle-aged women in the bathhouse. That two married women should take up the habit of bathing weekly is nearly scandalous:

Soon Fredrika stands there in all her fifty-year-old white plumpness. Mother Sofi's daughter is like a reed beside the big woman, and Mother Sofi, little and thin, would look like a pitiful plucked hen if it weren't for her sparkling eyes and curly, light hair. Her mouth is sunken, and the wrinkles beginning to show in her energetic, firm little face. Her breasts hang like two small, loose sacks from having nursed so many eager little mouths. The touchingly thin body, which was like a girl's, was more graceful than any of her daughters' when she wore a dress. It resembled a curious living rune stone when her clothes came off. Her stomach was one single scar, knot against knot, scar against scar, with big, broad, shimmering streaks here and there. "Terribly ruptured blood vessels, you have," the neighbor used to say at Sofi's childbirths. Mother Sofi often stared at her stomach during the bath nights. Like a skinny woman Buddha she sat there, gazing down on the scarred knots, her mouth tightening, and sometimes tears fell, dropping on her poor belly, and sometimes she said bitterly, "Such a miserable scrap heap." Fredrika would never say anything then, just busied herself making coffee and hummed a tune.

Though vastly different in their social origins, Krusenstjerna and Martinson (1890–1964) show an affinity that has led several recent scholars to view them in tandem. Both portray strong-minded women in settings that are exclusively female, or virtually so. The male characters in their works tend to be either threatening or ineffectual. It is relationships among women—mothers and daughters, friends, employers and servants—that move the plot along and carry moral or philosophical content. Both authors deal frankly with sexuality, pregnancy, and childbirth and with the costs borne by women whose sexual behavior breaks social norms. They show how the erotic, receptive woman so prevalent as a literary symbol becomes an object of contempt in everyday life. Because of her rural working-class origins, Martinson is sometimes simply appended to the list of proletarian writers as a popular novelist and the wife of Harry Martinson. Her literary debut at the age of forty-three was encouraged, however, by publication in the feminist magazine *Tidevarvet,* edited by Elin Wägner, and she had attended the "citizenship school" at Fogelstad operated by *Tidevarvet*'s founders, the Frisinnade kvinnor (Free-Minded Women).

Although the women's movement as such went into a relative period of decline after the achievement of suffrage in 1921, discussions of how women might manage civic duty, the combination of career and motherhood, more egalitarian marriages, and the like continued in popular novels such as Dagmar Edqvist's *Kamrathustru* (1932; Comrade wife) and Eva Berg's *Ny kvinna* (1936; New woman). Many prolific female writers found a wide readership but little critical acclaim, their works being regarded as light entertainment, or *underhållningslitteratur.* They include Irja Browallius, Gertrud Lilja, Alice Lyttkens, the Finland-Swedish Sally Salminen, Berit Spong, Gunhild Tegen, and Viveka Starfelt. While female experience continued to be a core subject of entertainment literature in the 1950s, a woman who sought serious attention from the literary establishment was better advised to address her attention to "universal" philosophical or moral themes. Ulla Isaksson (1916–) recalls making a decision to forgo exclusively female subject matter and to rely on male protagonists in order to safeguard her literary career. Sara Lidman (1923–) created a memorable and complex female protagonist, Linda Ståhl, in *Regnspiran* (1958; The rain bird) and *Bära mistel* (1960; Bearing mistletoe), but she won more notice for her politically-engaged novels and documentaries.

Like the United States and Western Europe, Sweden experienced an eruption in political and artistic values in the 1960s and 1970s. Journalist Eva Moberg's essay "Kvinnans villkorliga frigivning" (1962; The conditional emancipation of women) opened the "sex role debate," a fervent public discussion of what was natural to men and women and what was due to discrimination and childhood socialization patterns. By the end of the decade, both liberal and socialist women were organizing in pursuit of equality and justice. Gender patterns were among many systems of belief being called into question. Literature itself was being subject to redefinition, with a movement away from formal and aesthetic concerns toward engagement with contemporary social problems. Documentary reportage vied with fiction and poetry for literary ascendancy. The "report book" became a popular genre, one accessible to nearly anyone with a message to convey. Cleaning woman Maja Ekelöf, for example, called attention to the conditions of life and work of women at the bottom of the employment scale with the publication of her journal, *Rapport från en skurhink* (Report from a scrub pail) in 1970. Many women, young, old, some from the margins of society, debuted as authors in this period with works that featured women's issues as central themes. The female writer who best represents the experimentation with form and content that marked the 1960s is poet Sonja Åkesson (1926–77), known as a *folkhemsrealist*, one who painted unsparing portraits of daily life in the Swedish welfare state. Her narrative poem "Självbiografi" (Autobiography), a pastiche of Lawrence Ferlinghetti's poem of the same name, begins

> I live a quiet life
> at Drottinggatan 83 A in the daytime.
> Wipe kids' noses and wax floors
> and copper pots
> and cook rutabagas and sausage.

It wanders on through Swedish manners, childhood memories, adolescent sexuality, the daily news, the mundane and the horrifying, and then poses the question, "Where do I find an instrument / for all my shut-in air?" Åkesson provided the instrument—the frank and often ironic voice—for the young, working single mother, the psychiatric patient, and the elderly woman dying alone of cancer.

The explicit attention paid in the 1970s to women's experience as a literary theme helped generate a deliberately feminist or at least woman-centered literature. Three genres from that decade are especially worthy of mention: the confessional autobiography, the novel of social history, and experimental literature that introduces new female imagery. There are many examples of the confessional genre, but one of exceptional quality is the three-volume series by Sun Axelsson (1935–), *Drömmen om ett liv* (1978; Eng. tr. *A Dreamed Life,* 1983), *Honungsvargar* (1984; Honey wolves), and *Nattens årstid* (1989; Night's season). In these works, Axelsson portrays a young writer's vain search for love and comradeship with male writers in the 1950s. The outstanding author of social history in fictional form is Kerstin Ekman (1933–), the third woman admitted to the Swedish Academy (along with Selma Lagerlöf and Elin Wägner), who was later joined by Gunnel Vallquist (1918–), Katarina Frostenson (1953–), and Birgitta Trotzig (1929–)—four women among fourteen male writers. Ekman debuted as a writer of mystery novels in 1959 but made a dramatic shift in the mid-1970s to epic novels set in rural Sweden that are meticulous in their detail about the daily lives of women of varying social origins and fates. This "dailiness," the intricacy of plots, and the nature of the moral dilemmas the characters encounter are reminiscent of the novels of Elin Wägner and Moa Martinson. Ekman herself has cited Alfhild Agrell, Maria Sandel, and Maj Hirdman as inspirations. Elisabet Hermodsson (1927–), poet, essayist, visual artist, novelist, and composer and performer of ballads, is the bold experimenter. Hermodsson's work is concerned primarily with spiritual and aesthetic questions: whether there is a female poetic language or whether women have a particular affinity with nature and the creative process that runs counter to the dominance of rationalism and technological efficiency in Swedish society. As a young poet, she was befriended by Emilia Fogelklou, and her world view, sometimes called "ecofeminism," has much in common with the outlook promoted by Elin Wägner and her colleagues in *Tidevarvet*. Hermodsson's writing tends to be innovative in form and very serious in intent, but her most popular work is also the most accessible and humorous. Composed as an homage to Birger Sjöberg and his contribution to the Swedish ballad tradition, *Disa Nilssons visor* (1974; The ballads of Disa Nilson) portrays a modern sister to Sjöberg's Frida whose mission is a corrective one: "No matter how charming Frida may otherwise be—sensitive and kind, etc.—she is nevertheless lacking those features that could make her meaningful for the female future that humanity is in such great need of. Now I don't want to claim that Disa Nilson completely upsets our traditional role pattern, in any case not so much so that Disa's beloved is some kind of silly masculine goose. No, Disa is not mainly interested in revenge—even though that would be tempting for her—her motives are more positive." The important thing about Disa's contribution here is that she appears in the world of the ballad as *subject* and not as object.

It is too soon to predict which works of the 1980s and 1990s will come to stand as exemplars of their time. It is safe to say, however, that the number of women writers and the gifts they bring to the task are widening the perspective of Swedish literature so that "the other viewpoint" will be no longer "other" but essential to the whole.

Literature for Children and Young People

Maria Nikolajeva

9

BEFORE THE TWENTIETH CENTURY

The very first book in Swedish addressed to young readers, *Een sköön och härligh jungfrw speghel* (A young maiden's beautiful and wonderful mirror), was published in Stockholm in 1591. It was a translation from German; foreign books in translation—German and later English—dominated children's reading in Sweden until the end of the nineteenth century. Among original Swedish books for children, several important landmarks can be mentioned, such as the 1624 *Insignis adolescentia* and *Insignis puertia* tales of Petrus Johannis Rudbeckius (1578–1629) and the 1684 *Barnabibel* (Children's Bible) of Haquin Spegel (1645–1714), as well as Carl Gustaf Tessin's and Olof von Dalin's educational epistles and fables. Some of the original books from the past century are still read today, among them *Lille Viggs äfventyr på julafton* (1871; Little Vigg's adventures on Christmas Eve) by Viktor Rydberg. A decisive role for the emergence of original children's literature was played by the Finland-Swede Zacharias Topelius, whose *Läsning för barn* (1865–96; Eng. tr. *Stories for Children,* 1911) was a collection of fairy tales, poems, and plays for the young. It was all the more important since the first collection of Swedish folktales adapted for children did not appear until 1899. Of course, the tales of Hans Christian Andersen enjoyed great popularity all over Scandinavia.

The second half of the nineteenth century saw the emergence of a number of children's magazines with contributions by new authors and illustrators who were to play a leading role in the evolution of children's literature. From this period dates the famous *Barnbiblioteket Saga* (Children's library Saga), a series of children's books that had an unprecedented spread, thanks to low prices and efficient methods of distribution. The series included translated classics as well as newly written children's literature in Swedish.

At the turn of the century there was an ongoing lively debate in Sweden on child education; books such as Ellen Key's famous *Barnets århundrade* (1900; Eng. tr. *The Century of the Child*, 1909) drew the attention of educators and writers to the special needs of children as reading public. This was the heyday of authored fairy tales, often of dubious quality, but with some brilliant exceptions, such as the works of Helena Nyblom (1843–1926) and Anna Wahlenberg (1858–1923); in the genres of poetry and nursery songs, Alice Tegnér (1864–1943) deserves special mention; the picturebook in the tradition of British authors Walter Crane and Kate Greenaway also became popular. Two names may be evoked here: Jenny Nyström (1854–1946), whose *Barnkammarens bok* (1882; Nursery book) is considered the first truly Swedish picturebook, and Ottilia Adelborg (1855–1936), the author of the charming *Prinsarnes blomsteralfabet* (1894; The princes' alphabet of flowers) and *Pelle Snygg och barnen i Snaskeby* (1896; Peter Neat and the children of Candy Village), a variation on the eternal didactic theme of cleanliness. The most prominent author and illustrator, still widely read today, was Elsa Beskow (1874–1953). Idyllic yet realistic images of a small town in the series about the three aunties in *Tant Grön, tant Brun och tant Gredelin* (1918; Eng. tr. *Aunt Green, Aunt Brown, and Aunt Lavender,* 1928) alternate in her works with breathtaking adventures in enchanted forests, as in *Puttes äventyr i blåbärsskogen* (1901; Eng. tr. *Peter's Adventures in Blueberry Land,* 1975), or imaginative stories about gnomes, as in *Tomtebobarnen* (1910; Eng. tr. *Children of the Forest,* 1970). Realism and magic are intertwined in these stories in which text and picture are inseparable. The stories may seem somewhat didactic to modern readers, but their charm and humor are still strong.

Another author who is still enjoyed today is Ivar Arosenius (1878–1909); his *Kattresan* (1909; The cat journey) is a simple and amusing story in verse, in which each episode is accompanied by a plain little picture—a forerunner of the modern comic strip.

THE MORAL JOURNEY: TWO MAJOR CLASSICS

The years 1906 and 1907 mark a turning point in Swedish children's literature with the appearance of two crucial books: *Barnen ifrån Frostmofjället* (1907; Eng. tr. *The Children of the Moor,* 1927), by Laura Fitinghoff (1848–1908), and *Nils Holgerssons underbara resa genom Sverige* (1906–7; most recent Eng. tr. *The Wonderful Adventures of Nils,* 1991), by Selma Lagerlöf, one of the best-known and most translated Swedish books of all times. These books have some features in common.

Nils Holgersson, a work commissioned by the Swedish Board of Education, was originally intended as a book on Swedish geography for schoolchildren. Not content with simply describing one Swedish province after another, Selma Lagerlöf found a unifying element in the story of Nils, a teenage problem boy reduced to Tom Thumb dimensions who travels with a flock of wild geese the entire length of Sweden and back. This ingenious plot device enabled Lagerlöf to give the story at least three additional dimensions: an adventure story, as Nils and his companions dodge the pursuit of Smirre, a troublemaking fox; a child's point of view provided by Nils's midget perspective; and a panoramic survey of Sweden from above, literally a bird's-eye view. In addition, Åsa, the little gooseherd, and her brother Mats are introduced as a complement, duplicating Nils's journey on foot.

The views of the future and of progress in *Nils Holgersson* are basically positive. At the same time, Lagerlöf shows astonishing ecological awareness of the threat to humankind's truce with nature when she puts words of warning into the mouth of the old and wise lead goose, Akka, who plays the role of mentor and guide for Nils.

In *Barnen ifrån Frostmofjället,* too, everything is seen and experienced through the eyes of the children. Laura Fitinghoff wished to create a fundamentally new type of children's book, one that would be relevant for all classes of children. Therefore, she attempted to picture a society with which both rich and poor children could identify. Her book does indeed present a vast picture of Sweden, but unlike *Nils Holgersson,* it is not the author's contemporary Sweden but the lost country of her own childhood, the period of the great famine of the 1860s. The main theme of both books, the journey, constitutes an essential pattern in children's literature; the narrative structure of home—departure—adventure—homecoming is in turn a variation on the archetypal pattern of the folktale or quest tale. The Frostmo children and Nils Holgersson as well as Åsa and Mats are forced to leave home; exposed to the dangers of the world and of adult life, they feel alienated and unwanted. Nils's situation is reminiscent of Mowgli's in *The Jungle Book;* it comes as no surprise that Kipling served as a model for Lagerlöf.

The driving force behind the journey is a quest, not as in the traditional adventure story, a search for excitement and treasure, but for a safe home. The Frostmo children find home and security in the end; Åsa is reunited with her father, though Mats dies on the way. Nils not only returns home but also gains spiritual maturity, and the book assumes the dimensions of a modern psychological novel. This is probably the reason it is still enjoyed today.

Barnen ifrån Frostmofjället and *Nils Holgersson* are typical products of their time and of the neoromantic movement of the 1890s, as well as of the pedagogical endeavors for the young that enlisted the talents of some of the best authors: besides Selma Lagerlöf, Verner von Heidenstam in the field of history and Sven Hedin in world geography. In addition, Anna Maria Roos (1862–1938) wrote a series of primers, *Sörgården* (1912; Southern farm), read by generations of Swedish schoolchildren.

IDYLL AND ADVENTURE:
BOOKS FOR GIRLS AND BOOKS FOR BOYS

The period from 1907 up to 1945 contributed little to the genre of childen's literature, and the efforts could be best described as conventional and mediocre. *Bland tomtar och troll* (Among gnomes and trolls) was an annual classic appearing from 1907. It owed its popularity more to the great artistry of the illustrator, John Bauer (1882–1918), than to the quality of the tales. Many books for girls described happy and comfortable children in cozy homes, often during summer holidays, or typical Cinderella stories in which a poor, nice, and hardworking girl gets her prince; books for boys were filled with pranks and thrilling adventures. Today they are mostly forgotten, with the possible exception of two or three: *Ullabella* (1922), by Marika Stiernstedt (1875–1954), which portrays a girl's growing up from the age of three to her happy engagement, or *Helga Wilhelmina* (1933), by Jeanna Oterdahl (1879–1965), a story of a poor girl's road to higher education and independence.

Another exception in the main trend of prewar children's literature is *Pelle Svanslös* (1939; Pelle No-Tail) and its sequels by Gösta Knutsson (1908–73). In these humorous adventure stories, cats who act very much like humans are the protagonists. But although the characters were supposed to have real-life counterparts in the academic world of Uppsala, the general idyllic tone of the 1930s prevails in most of these stories.

In one respect, the period was important for the development of children's literature: foreign classics were translated into Swedish and served as models for Swedish authors. Among them were such familiar titles as *Anne of Green Gables* (Sw. tr. 1909), *The Secret Garden* (Sw. tr. 1912), *Pollyanna* (Sw. tr. 1914), *Peter Pan* (Sw. tr. 1921), *Just William* (Sw. tr. 1923), *Winnie-the-Pooh* (Sw. tr. 1930), *The Wind in the Willows* (Sw. tr.

1932), *Mary Poppins* (Sw. tr. 1935), and *The Wizard of Oz* (Sw. tr. 1940). In the process, children's literature was established as a separate kind of literature, and the strict differentiation between boys' and girls' books became more pronounced (the distinction clearly marked by bindings with green or red spines).

The year 1945 is usually viewed as a watershed in children's literature in Sweden with a strong showing of new talent: Astrid Lindgren (1907–), Tove Jansson (1914–), Lennart Hellsing (1919–), and Marta Sandwall-Bergström (1913–). The last-named's *Kulla-Gulla* (Eng. tr. *Anna All Alone*, 1978) is interesting as a children's book written in the tradition of adult *statar* literature (literature about estate workers), portraying a poor, abused child.

The simultaneous appearance on the literary scene of a great number of new writers of children's books was hardly a coincidence. The publishing climate was favorable throughout the 1940s. Sweden, spared during the Second World War, had been able to give immediate attention to the needs of the young. In the aftermath of the war experience, earlier idyllic tales and traditional stories of adventure were reappraised in a more critical light, and children's literature was enriched with regard to subject matter, style, form, and expressed values.

ASTRID LINDGREN: THE PIONEER

Of all the newcomers in 1945, Astrid Lindgren has made the greatest contribution to children's literature in Sweden and the world. Writing in every conceivable genre and style, she has consistently broken traditional rules and norms.

Astrid Lindgren's first book was an epistolary girls' story, *Britt-Mari lättar sitt hjärta* (1944; Britt-Marie opens her heart). Even in this first book, Lindgren transcends the conventions of the genre in her use of ironic distance and parody. If Astrid Lindgren had not written anything else, she would probably still be remembered for this innovative contribution to the popular genre.

Pippi Långstrump (1945; Eng. tr. *Pippi Longstocking*, 1950) is the most revolutionary children's book in Sweden. When Astrid Lindgren unequivocally took the child's part against the adult world, it upset all earlier pedagogical notions. Moreover, the book's antiauthoritarian stance is well matched by humor, nonsense, slapstick, and verbal acrobatics unheard of before. The emancipatory impact of *Pippi* on Swedish children's literature is enormous.

It is Lindgren's particular genius to go to the core of each genre and promptly turn it on its head. In *Pippi Långstrump* and two sequels, *Pippi Långstrump går ombord* (1946; Eng. tr. *Pippi Goes on Board*, 1957) and *Pippi Långstrump i Söderhavet* (1948; Eng. tr. *Pippi in the South Seas*, 1959), and later in *Barnen på Bråkmakargatan* (1958; Eng. tr. *The Children on Troublemaker Street*, 1964) and *Madicken* (1960; Eng. tr. *Mischievous Meg*, 1962), Lindgren makes fun of the conventional adventure story for boys by making the traditional rascal a girl. As early as the *Pippi* books we notice the genre convergence that will later be such a characteristic feature of children's literature: elements from pirate stories, robinsonades, the search for treasure, and classroom humor—all in intertextual relation to previous works for both children and adults; this is undoubtedly one reason why *Pippi* is appreciated by readers of all ages.

In her detective stories, *Mästerdetektiven Blomkvist* (1946; Eng. tr. *Bill Bergson, Master Detective*, 1952) and sequels, Astrid Lindgren never deviates from the child's perspective; she takes the child's part in the sentimental vagabond story *Rasmus på luffen* (1956; Eng. tr. *Rasmus and the Vagabond*, 1968); and in *Lillebror och Karlsson på taket* (1955; Eng. tr. *Karlsson-on-the-Roof*, 1971) and *Karlsson flyger igen* (1962; Eng. tr. *Karlsson Flies Again*, 1977), she offers an unexpected solution to children's loneliness in the figure of Karlsson, a fat and selfish little man with a propeller on his back. A deep trust in her young readers makes Lindgren confident that they will be able to see through the conceited and self-centered Karlsson, who is basically a comic figure. At the same time, to be able to fly is the secret dream of almost every child, and like the airborne Nils Holgersson, Karlsson is a brilliant realization of such a longing.

Probably the most important of Astrid Lindgren's early books is *Mio, min Mio* (1954; Eng. tr. *Mio, My Son*, 1956), Sweden's foremost contribution to the fantasy tradition. At first sight, the story is a typical example of the genre: an ordinary boy is transported to a distant country outside space and time; here he is sent off on a quest to meet and defeat an evil enemy. But unlike most fantasy tales, in this story the ties with the real world are never lost. All the characters in the magic world of Faraway Land have their counterparts in reality; Jum-Jum (Eng. Pompoo) corresponds to Mio's friend Benka (Benny), and My Father the King, to Benka's father; even the wonderful horse Miramis has a pedestrian counterpart back in the real world.

Astrid Lindgren rejects the traditional happy homecoming and never brings Mio back to his real world as most authors of fantasy would do; she lets him remain in Faraway Land. Mio does not seek adventure for its own sake; his quest is prompted by his deep unhappiness in the real world. But the magic journey is not an impotent escape into daydreams; it is a psychodrama that enables the protagonist to cope with his inner problems. Young readers will not necessarily realize that, for the denouement is camouflaged by the fairy-tale code with its durative time. We are not sure whether the adventure has actually taken place or is a figment of the boy's imagination, and whether, at the close of the book, he is in fact still sitting on a park bench in Stockholm. Almost twenty years after *Mio, min Mio,* Lindgren was to deal with a similar theme in *Bröderna Lejonhjärta* (1973; Eng. tr. *The Brothers Lionheart,* 1975), in which the psychodrama is deepened by the presence of death.

Emil i Lönneberga (1963; Eng. tr. *Emil and His Piggy Beast,* 1973) is another intertextual response to boys' books, more specifically stories about the mischievous boy. *Emil i Lönneberga* has some traits in common with this genre; it is episodic in character and full of humor and farcical incidents as it pokes gentle fun at the grown-up world. But unlike the static protagonists of the conventional stories, Emil undergoes changes and develops; from being a rascal he becomes the hero of the community and will in due time, the author assures us with a stroke of true comic genius, end up on the Municipal Board. This transformation of a prankster into a hero follows a typical folktale pattern. The *Emil* books indeed have features in common with folktales. For the setting, Lindgren draws on her own childhood in the southern province of Småland; in this rural locale she places various comical characters, such as a simple-minded maid, a fine lady, a stingy father, a good-natured farmhand. The tone is that of an oral narrative; the author repeatedly turns directly to the reader with questions and commentaries as if she were an oral storyteller.

Astrid Lindgren holds a unique position in children's literature. It is difficult to single out followers in the younger generation of authors. Her greatest contribution is to have created an extremely favorable climate for the art form and to have opened up avenues for new genres and styles. In the process she raised the status of children's literature.

IN THE MOOMINVALLEY

Like Astrid Lindgren, the Finland-Swedish author Tove Jansson defies narrow classification. Unlike Lindgren, she creates books that seem to be quite homogeneous and form parts of one series, from the less-known *Småtrollen och den stora översvämningen* (1945; Little trolls and the great flood) to *Sent i november* (1970; Eng. tr. *Moominvalley in November,* 1971).

It may be tempting to regard Moominvalley as a typical fantasy in the manner of Tolkien and the Moomins as a Finnish variation on the hobbits. The differences, however, are obvious. The Moomin series is by no means a heroic saga in its employment of irony, parody, and naivism; the Moomin books offer a child's viewpoint as a camouflage for adult reflection. Unlike the hobbits, the Moomins are projections of ordinary humans, and the books can be read as family stories about troublesome children and grown-ups representing the full range of human characteristics: a protective mother, a self-assured father, a mad scientist, a hypochondriac, and so on. It is evident that the author addresses a double audience: children will discover adventure in *Kometjakten* (1946; Eng. tr. *Comet in Moominland*, 1968) and *Farlig midsommar* (1954; Eng. tr. *Moominsummer Madness*, 1961) or magic in *Trollkarlens hatt* (1948; Eng. tr. *Finn Family Moomintroll*, 1958), while older readers and adults will be able to appreciate the parodical autobiography in *Moominpappans bravader* (1950; Eng. tr. *Exploits of Moominpappa*, 1966).

Literary scholars have also pointed to a development in the Moomin series from simple fairy tales to a sophisticated, symbolically charged discourse. *Pappan och havet* (1965; Eng. tr. *Moominpappa at Sea*, 1967) in particular is rich in symbols and archetypes and invites various psychoanalytical interpretations. The title story in *Det osynliga barnet* (1962; lit. "The invisible child"; Eng. tr. *Tales from Moominvalley*, 1964) could, for instance, be read as a case study of suppressed identity.

Another Finland-Swedish author, Irmelin Sandman Lilius (1936–), has a great deal in common with Tove Jansson; both create an imaginary world that, on closer scrutiny, turns out to be a miniature replica of their own reality with deep roots in the landscape of southern Finland. But the romantic stories by Sandman Lilius lack the irony found in Jansson's books; they are more like traditional local legends and family sagas.

THE 1960S AND 1970S: SOCIAL COMMITMENT

The title of Astrid Lindgren's *Bullerby* series (1947–52; Eng. tr. *Happy Times at Noisy Village*, 1963) has in Swedish become a symbol of idyllic harmony and a happy cloudless childhood. These books stand in striking contrast to the children's literature of the 1960s with its numerous lonely, abandoned, and insecure protagonists. Authors in this period seem to compete to write about problematic relationships and conditions: divorces, unmarried mothers, alcoholic fathers, sibling rivalry, school problems— all of a sudden, children's literature is invaded by an avalanche of social problems emphasizing the dark sides of reality. In this world of lonely, unhappy children who have cruel comrades, indifferent parents, and uncomprehending teachers, there is no room for the idyllic or for sentimental solutions of conflicts. Feelings of fear and despair prevail. Many of the earlier taboos in children's literature are now openly discussed in deliberate defiance of the previous attitude that wanted to shield young readers from the problematic aspects of society. This new development was, of course, a direct result of the extensive debates on children's rights, child abuse, and so on. During the 1970s, a few unique laws were passed in Sweden giving childhood a more secure status. Children's book author Gunnel Linde (1924–) was in the vanguard of this movement.

Often a particular problem is reflected in the title of a book; thus, for example, the child's longing for a real father is indicated in such titles as *Pappa Pellerins dotter* (1963; Eng. tr. *Pappa Pellerin's Daughter,* 1966) and *Nattpappan* (1968; Eng. tr. *The Night Daddy,* 1971), by Maria Gripe (1923–), or *I stället för en pappa* (1971; Eng. tr. *And Leffe Was instead of a Dad,* 1973), by Kerstin Thorvall (1925–). Almost everything in a child's life is presented as a problem: getting a new sibling, starting school, moving into a big city.

At the same time, more serious questions are dealt with, such as the child's response to death. In contemporary Sweden, where most old people die in hospitals and the majority of children never see a dead person, death becomes something unreal and frightening. With increasing frequency, death and a child's contemplation of death becomes a secondary motif, sometimes even the central theme, in children's books.

The majority of Swedish children's books of the period show deep psychological insight. The new themes and subject matters forced the authors to experiment with new forms, new poetics, and new stylistic devices, among them the abundant use of present tense in order to make the reader experience a character's situation with greater immediacy.

Clearly, the traditional narrative with an omniscient narrator was no longer adequate to enter the child's mind and conceptual world as demanded by the new subjects. Thus in *Elvis Karlsson* (1972; Eng. tr. *Elvis and His Secret,* 1976) and its sequels, Maria Gripe interprets the boy's thoughts and feelings; the effect is all the greater for her use of advanced literary language. Everything in the books is described not only through Elvis's eyes but through his sensitive mind. The result is a more sophisticated realism than in the books from the 1940s and 1950s. The titles of *Hemligt i huvet på Samuel Elias* (1974; Secret in the mind of Samuel Elias), by Rose Lagercrantz (1947–), or *Jättehemligt* (1971; Top secret), by Barbro

Lindgren (1937–), reflect the same effort to enter the child's most secret thoughts. In the latter book and its two sequels, the diary form is used and the style and way of thinking of a young person are brilliantly rendered.

The search for identity is a common denominator in most of these books. The protagonists are extraordinary, alienated children who have difficulty establishing contact with the world around them. The series about Hugo and Josefin (1961–66; Eng. tr. *Hugo*, 1970; *Hugo and Josephine*, 1969; *Josephine*, 1970) by Maria Gripe demonstrates how children adapt to their surroundings: the girl Karin by conforming; Hugo by refusing to conform, whereas Josefin, who is only slightly different, does not fit in.

The characters' names become important as symbols of identity. Although Josefin's real name in Gripe's novels is Anna Grå, she does not feel mature enough to use it. To her, there is a direct and concrete connection between name and identity; she writes her "real" name in the bottom of a shoebox and hides the box in a closet to wait for the day when she will be grown up enough to use it. The children in *Den vita stenen* (1964; Eng. tr. *The White Stone*, 1966), by Gunnel Linde, invent new names for themselves; their new identities help them cope with their problems. In Maria Gripe's series about Elvis, the boy's mother pinned great expectations onto her son. But little Elvis Karlsson has a strong personality, strong enough to live with another person's name; he knows that "I am myself, Elvis is Elvis, but Elvis Karlsson is not Elvis Presley." When Presley dies, the boy's mother wants to change his name, but by this time Elvis has outgrown the problem; the name is part of his own identity.

Friendship is also a key to identity. The protagonist often finds help and support from another child. Very often—indeed, more often than in real life, as shown by special studies—it is a child of the opposite sex. Such cross-gender friendships are usually described as first love, romantic and innocent, but with a wide range of attending adult passions such as rivalry, jealousy, and despair. Again, the central theme of these books is often reflected in the titles, as in Maria Gripe's *Hugo och Josefin; Martins Maria* (1970; Eng. tr. *Maria and Martin*, 1975), by Hans-Eric Hellberg (1927–); *Moa och Pelle* (1981; Moa and Pelle), by Kerstin Johansson i Backe (1919–); or *Malin och pojken med mössan* (1975; Malin and the boy in a cap), by Birgitta Bergman (1938–).

Friendship provides help and support and offers a possibility to create and retain one's identity. The relationships are rarely equal, however; one of the children is described as the stronger: Annarosa in *Elvis*, Hampus in *Den vita stenen;* Hugo in the series about Hugo and Josefin. The stronger partner helps the other child overcome his or her loneliness. As Maria Gripe puts it in *Elvis:* "I have myself and I have you. You have yourself and you have me. Together we are four."

A friend of the opposite sex often plays the part of a missing or inadequate parent. Adults, notably parents, are presented as absent or selfish and destructive. Elvis's mother has become a symbol of a negative parent; she is stupid, ruthless, and tyrannical, but she is also unhappy and uncomfortable with herself. In the long run, it is her young son who must help and support her. The *Elvis* series is as much the story of a mother as of a young boy. In most books, the grown-ups are dimly visible in the background and seem to have only minor parts in the protagonists' inner lives. When an adult plays an important role in a child's life, it is usually an outsider or, at best, a grandparent, as in *Morfars Maria* (1969; Eng. tr. *Grandpa's Maria*, 1974), by Hans-Eric Hellberg. Schoolteachers are on the whole obtuse, deaf to the child's needs, or totally absent despite the fact that some books have school settings or deal with problems connected with school.

Few of the books offer tangible solutions to the problems. They often deal with isolated periods in a child's life and lack plot development; the endings are simple or nonconclusive: Christmas arrives, the school year ends, the child moves to the countryside, gets a puppy, or has a birthday. Although such a composition may convey a sense of "real life" or, indeed, present an honest picture without easy solutions, the questions raised remain unanswered, and critics and readers may be justified in viewing the literature of the period as unduly pessimistic. In many cases, the social "message" is too obvious and little attention is paid to literary quality.

Such preponderance of subject matter over literary form is particularly noticeable in the so-called immigrant literature, that is, juvenile books dealing with the situation of immigrant children in Sweden. This concrete social issue, however, is dealt with rather superficially and with some preconceived notions. Even the best immigrant stories from the 1970s, such as *Jag heter Gojko* (1972; My name is Gojko), by Runa Olofsson (1937–), or *Tack—håll käften* (1972; Thank you—shut up), by Gun Jacobson (1930–), expose prejudices toward immigrants rather than offer insights into their genuine situation. The books depict the immigrant children's difficulties with language and adjustment to the culture and the ways of the new country, the hostility of the Swedish surroundings, but they fail to touch the essence of the immigrant experience. The immigrant child becomes a cliché, characterized by recurrent features: loneliness, depression, feelings of inferiority, and loss of identity, whereas such advantages as belonging to two cultures, for example, are never stressed.

The politicized 1960s and 1970s produced works in which the "message"—usually a Marxist one—was preached with great zeal, providing few or no opportunities for young readers to reflect for themselves. At best, this literature opened up new and challenging subject areas for literary treatment.

BOOKS FOR TEENAGERS

The emergence of "teenage culture" in the 1950s and early 1960s gives rise to a new type of literature, the teenage novel. Teenage culture is discovered by adults, who both encourage and exploit it as a potentially profitable market for clothes, records, magazines, and books. There is a rich harvest of books aimed at teenagers. J. D. Salinger's *The Catcher in the Rye* (1951) is sometimes pointed out as a model; it was translated into Swedish in 1953. But the very first Swedish teenage novel had appeared in 1949: *Den svarta fläcken* (The black spot), by Harry Kullman (1919–82). It deals with juvenile delinquency and treats the problem with unprecedented openness and sympathy for the young. The style, however, is still very conservative, and there is no attempt to capture a contemporary idiom of slang and colloquialisms.

The teenage novel makes its definitive appearance in Sweden in the 1960s, accompanied, typically, by such epithets as "socially critical," "problem-oriented," and "problem-realistic." The characteristic motifs of the 1960s and 1970s are loneliness, exposure in the world of adults, the teenager's conflicts with others and the self, and a sense of lost direction, as exemplified in such titles as *Vart ska du gå?—Ut* (1969; Where are you going?—Out) and the sequel, *Vart ska du gå?—Vet inte* (1975; Where are you going?—Don't know), by Kerstin Thorvall. The novels tell about crossing borders and breaking norms and introduce topics that had earlier been strictly taboo: sex, violence, alcohol and drug addiction. Authority is automatically challenged, whether in the form of parents, teachers, society, or the world at large. Swedish publishers promptly exploited the new trend and offered books in attractive covers and with striking titles that did not correspond to the contents.

The term *brukslitteratur* was coined to describe books that introduce burning issues for teenagers in school, such as teenage sex and unwanted pregnancy, as in *Tre veckor över tiden* (1973; lit. "Three weeks overdue"; Eng. tr. *Mia Alone*, 1975), by Gunnel Beckman (1910–90), as well as teenage parenthood, as in *Peters baby* (1971; Peter's baby), by Gun Jacobson. *Tre veckor över tiden* discusses the dilemma of a young girl who must choose between education and a career or children and family. The author provides an easy way out: it was all false alarm, and Mia is spared the choice this time. Nevertheless, the long waiting in uncertainty has allowed her to reflect on her life and situation.

"Gender stereotypes" is another key term in teenage fiction. A recurrent theme is the girl locked up in her home, a prisoner in a "doll house." A typical novel by Maud Reuterswärd (1920–80) bears the title *Flickan och dockskåpet* (1979; lit. "The girl and the dollhouse"; Eng. tr. *A Way from Home*, 1990). One of the few attempts to portray a strong and self-confident girl is *Stridshästen* (1977; Eng. tr. *The Battle Horse*, 1981), by Harry Kullman, a story set in the 1930s and focusing, like all Kullman's novels, on class struggle.

Gunnel Beckman's *Tillträde till festen* (1969; Eng. tr. *Nineteen Is Too Young to Die*, 1971; also translated as *Admission to the Feast*) is the story of a girl who learns that she has leukemia. It is presented in the form of letters written to a friend, in imitation of a confused and unaffected personal style. The technique allows for some distance to events and a possibility for self-reflection. Some social problems are also touched on: the parents' divorce, the father's alcoholism, and stereotypical sex roles. But the narrative structure, the condensed time frame, and the fresh and direct language provide a deep insight into the character's situation and make this work stand out above most teenage novels of the period.

A number of books concern the subject of teenage suicide—in thought or in action. Written from the teenagers' viewpoint, these books take without reservation the young people's side against the adult world. Other books deal with identity crises, whether expressed as fear of losing one's identity or as hope of finding it. Most of the books are well-meaning in their attempts to offer consolation or a way out of the crisis. Quite a few characters, however, fail to find their identity. The solution often lies in compromise and pain or, in extreme cases, in death or suicide.

POETRY FOR CHILDREN

The tradition of nursery rhyme in Sweden dates back to Jenny Nyström's *Barnkammarens bok* (1882; Nursery book) and to *Svenska barnvisor och barnrim* (1886; Swedish nursery songs and rhymes), by Johan Nordlander (1853–1934), and later other volumes such as *För barn och barnbarn* (1925; For children and grandchildren), by Hugo Hamilton (1849–1928).

The foremost proponent of poetry for children, however, is Lennart Hellsing (1919–). His children's verse has its roots in folklore (he has translated samples from the English *Mother Goose*) and appeals to imagination and feeling rather than to reason. Hellsing is a true master of nonsense, beginning with his first collections, *Katten blåser i silverhorn* (1945; The cat blows a silver bugle) and *Nyfiken i en strut* (1945; [freely] Curious, are you?).

In accordance with the tenets of the nursery rhyme, Hellsing constructs his universe as *mundus inversus,* the upside-down world, where "all squares are round, and all circles have four corners"; where Mr. Cucumber (Sw. *herr Gurka*) dances the waltz and the mazurka; where small children bite the king's ears or read books sitting on the king's nose. Such Hellsing creations as Krakel Spektakel, Kusin Vitamin, and Opsis Kalopsis have become part of the national gallery of literary figures.

Hellsing's poems are classical in their strict observance of rhyme and meter. A linguistic virtuoso, Hellsing uses language as his real subject matter. The play on words is his favorite device, as in *Krakel Spektakel* (1959), in which he rhymes verbs of motion with place names; in *Sjörövarbok* (1965; Eng. tr. *The Pirate Book,* 1972), the comic effects are largely based on the endless rhymings with the many names of the captains:

Pirate King
    does the fling.
Pirate Lamotte
    does the gavotte.
Pirate Schmaltz
    dances a waltz.
Pirate Marston
    dances the Charleston.

At the same time, the poems are extraordinarily visual, each verse or stanza forming a complete little picture. Hellsing's poetry has attracted some brilliant illustrators to children's literature. The verses are dynamic, abounding in verbs and stimulating movement, active games, dance, and singing. Most of Hellsing's poems have been set to music and are today widely sung in Sweden. In a sense, Hellsing has realized the notion of a children's *Allkunstwerk.*

Whereas the sensitive poetry of Britt G. Hallqvist (1914–) follows the Hellsing tradition rather closely, the modernistic poetry in free verse of Ingrid Sjöstrand (1922–) or Siv Widerberg (1931–) offers a more rational approach with short sketches from a child's everyday life, as in Widerberg's

I collected postage stamps.
Daddy gave me half a kilo.
I did not collect postage stamps anymore.

On balance, Hellsing, despite his formal traditionalism, appears to stand closer to mainstream modernistic poetry as expressed in the absurdism of the 1940s or the concretism of the 1950s.

ORDINARY CHILDREN AND WILD BABIES: MODERN PICTUREBOOKS

The impulses for the emergence and development of modern picturebooks came to Sweden from Denmark and marked a break with the picturesque and romantic style of the Elsa Beskow tradition. Instead, simple, everyday themes and down-to-earth stories are introduced, as in Inger (1930–) and Lasse (1924–) Sandberg's stories about Lena, Niklas, or little Anna in the 1960s. The titles reveal the contents of the books—everyday events in familiar surroundings: *Vad Anna fick se* (1954; Eng. tr. *What Anna Saw*, 1964), *Lilla Annas mamma fyller år* (1966; Eng. tr. *Little Anna's Mama Has a Birthday*, 1966), *Niklas röda dag* (1964; Eng. tr. *Nicholas' Red Day*, 1967), *Niklas önskedjur* (1967; Eng. tr. *Nicholas' Favorite Pet*, 1969), and *Mattias bakar kakor* (1968; Eng. tr. *Daniel and the Coconut Cakes*, 1973). In contrast to Beskow, there is less attention to backgrounds, interiors, and details. The pictures are schematic, plain, and naive; the stories, simple and amusing. They are aimed at very young children, as are the popular *Totte* and *Emma* series by Gunilla Wolde (1939–): *Totte går ut* (1969; Eng. tr. *Thomas Goes Out*, 1971 and others), *Emmas dagis* (1976; Eng. tr. *Betsy's First Day at Nursery School*, 1976), with descriptions of common events in a child's life such as going to the doctor, bathing, baking, or playing in the sand. The books of Gunilla Bergström (1942–) about Alfons Åberg deal with situations from the child's familiar environment: *Aja baja Alfons Åberg* (1973; Eng. tr *You're a Sly One, Alfie Atkins*, 1979 and others).

There is a return to backgrounds, rich in detail and in appeal to the imagination, in the colorful works of author-illustrators such as Ulf Löfgren (1931–): *Barnen i vattnet* (1964; Eng. tr. *Children in the Water*, 1966) and *Det underbara trädet* (1969; Eng. tr. *The Wonderful Tree*, 1970). Jan Lööf (1940–) contributed *Bergtrollens nya hem* (1977; The mountain trolls' new home) and *Pelles ficklampa* (1978; Pelle's flashlight). One of the most popular figures of the 1980s is the Wild Baby, in a series written in verse by Barbro Lindgren and illustrated by Eva Eriksson: *Mamman och den vilda bebin* (1980; Eng. tr. *The Wild Baby*, 1981) and its sequels. A major feature of these books is the interaction of text and illustrations; the pictures are no longer mere depictions of the text; they carry a wealth of information and must be "read" and decoded alongside the verbal text.

Beginning in the late 1970s, picturebooks become more fanciful and imaginative; like books for older children, they venture away from everyday life into realms of fantasy and adventure. This trend is evident in such works as *Den farliga resan* (1977; The dangerous journey), by Tove Jansson; *Tummens resa* (1978; Thumb's journey), by Inger and Lasse Sandberg; *Den vilda bebiresan* (1982; Eng. tr. *Wild Baby Goes to Sea*, 1983), by Barbro Lindgren and Eva Eriksson (1949); *Minus och den stora världen* (1985; Eng. tr. *Willie in the Big World*, 1986), by Sven Nordqvist (1946–)—worthy followers of Arosenius's *Kattresan*. The fantastic journey may be suggested as a dream, as in *Kom i min natt, kom i min dröm* (1979; Eng. tr. *Come into My Night, Come into My Dream*, 1981), by Stefan Mählqvist (1943–) and Tord Nygren (1936–), but usually readers are allowed to give free rein to their imagination. The later books by Inger and Lasse Sandberg, *Lilla Nollan* (1985; Little Zero), *Vit och svart och alla de andra* (1986; White, black, and all the others), and *ABCD* (1987) are spirited plays with colors, letters, and numbers, free from didacticism yet filled with practical information and psychological insight.

Lennart Hellsing's illustrated children's verse resulted in picturebooks such as *Den underbara pumpan* (1975; Eng. tr. *The Wonderful Pumpkin*, 1976), *Bananbok* (1975; Banana book), and *Ägget* (1978; The egg). They are brilliant nonsensical abstractions that can be enjoyed by any age group. Sven Nordqvist's series about Festus and Mercury, beginning with *Pannkakstårtan* (1984; Eng. tr. *The Pancake Pie*, 1985), offers the best example of madcap humor and whimsicality. The rich variety and the high quality of Swedish picture books have earned them international acclaim.

RETURN TO IMAGINATIVE ART:
FROM THE LATE 1970S TO THE 1990S

In 1973, Astrid Lindgren published *Bröderna Lejonhjärta* and blazed a trail out of the confinement of socially committed children's literature. Imaginative, romantic, and filled with adventure, it described an alternative world; it dealt with death, if not as a positive experience, at least as a source of less anxiety. The book aroused a storm of criticism; Lindgren was accused of escapism through her use of fantasy and of misleading young readers about existential problems. In retrospect, however, the book stands as a milestone; it initiated a shift in the main trend of Swedish juvenile literature. From the early 1980s, a large number of Swedish books as well as translations of works from around the world reinstated fantasy in Swedish children's literature.

It is noteworthy that fantasy, in spite of Astrid Lindgren's brilliant novels, did not have deep roots in Sweden as it did in the Anglo-Saxon tradition. There is a certain romanticism in the exploration of the past, historically distant or more recent, as in Maria Gripe's later series of *Shadow* books, *Skuggan över stenbänken* (1982; The shadow on the stone bench) and its three sequels; superficially, they have some traits in common with the traditional Gothic novel.

Although dealing with mystery, adventure, and the supernatural, this literature for the young does not follow in the footsteps of Robert Louis Stevenson or Walter Scott. The focus is on the individual; rather than present adventure for its own sake, history is used as a mirror to reflect a contemporary reality. A number of traditional genres are deliberately subverted: the pirate story in *Husbonden* (1985; The master of the house), by Mats Wahl (1945–); the American Indian story in *Jenny från Bluewater* (1982; Jenny from Bluewater), by Stig Ericson (1929–86), a subversive feminist text devoid of all Wild West romanticism; and the robber story in *Ronja Rövardotter* (1981; Eng. tr. *Ronia, the Robber's Daughter*, 1983), by Astrid Lindgren. For all the changes in setting and historical costume— Swedish concessions to fantasy—the books continue the tradition from the realistic 1960s and 1970s; although considerably less didactic, they deal with such familiar themes as the search for identity or conflicts with parents and peers.

Stories concerning a contemporary reality were less "problem-oriented," less bent on misery. In her series about the girl Mimmi, *En ettas dagbok* (1982; The diary of a first-grader) and its sequels, Viveca Sundvall (1944–) portrays a happy, well-balanced child, in harmony with her parents, moderately bright at school, and busy inventing everyday adventures for herself. The books are not idyllic in the *Bullerby* sense; some problems exist, but they are described with distance and humor. At the core of *Dårfinkar och dönickar* (1984; Nuts and no-goods), by Ulf Stark (1944–), there is a serious message, although everyday problems are dealt with in a comical way.

In *Janne min vän* (1985; Eng. tr. *Johnny, My Friend*, 1991), Peter Pohl (1940–) presents a suspense story in which the answer to the mystery is known, or at least may be easily deduced, from the beginning; throughout the book the reader is fed clues that eventually fit like pieces in a jigsaw puzzle. As in Maria Gripe's *Shadow* books and *Dårfinkar och dönickar*, a girl is disguised as a boy.

Janne min vän is a sophisticated multidimensional story about friendship and love, about the family and the gang, about exploitation and abuse—an existential novel of very high quality but with all the necessary components of a good thriller. It also presents a subtle treatment of death, a pervading theme in Pohl's books: assumed murder in *Janne min vän;* suicide in *Vi kallar honom Anna* (1987; Let's call him Anna), and assumed or attempted suicide by a very young girl in *Alltid den där Anette* (1988; Always that Anette).

The first years of the 1990s show a shift in literature for young people toward stories of contemporary life. A good example is *Vinterviken* (1993; Winter bay), by Mats Wahl, which was awarded the prestigious August Prize. On the surface it is a teenage novel with its main theme of quest for identity and its strong social engagement, its depiction of traditional conflicts of parents versus children and the individual versus the gang, and a whole set of issues such as class differences, juvenile delinquency, violence, and sex, including the daring topic of incest. But contrary to earlier teenage fiction, there is less emphasis on the issues than on the protagonist, and the novel presents a stronger artistic unity.

Among the authors of the 1990s, Per Nilsson (1954–) must be mentioned. His novels, informed by self-irony and humor, are written with a clear postmodern orientation and employ temporal paradoxes and metafictitious devices while addressing issues with which young readers can easily identify.

In the works of Peter Pohl and some other contemporary Swedish juvenile authors, there is a clear tendency toward increasing literariness. As in the modernistic novel, these authors demonstrate a complexity of structure and style, intricate time-space relationships, time shifts, and experimental narrative forms, through diaries or first-person and even second-person accounts, alternate endings, and parallel actions. Juvenile books— and to some extent also children's books—evince intertextual relations with frequent allusions to and quotations from world literature.

More important than purely formal experiments, however, is the realization on the part of the authors of juvenile literature that good intentions and burning social issues are no longer the sole criteria of good literature for the young. The focus shifts from pedagogical to literary concerns, not least because of extensive research and competent and informed criticism. Modern Swedish juvenile literature has thus come a long way toward being a significant part of the national literature and the cultural heritage.

Bibliography

ABBREVIATIONS

EDDA   *Edda*. Oslo, 1914–

MS   *Mediaeval Stories*

POS   *A Pageant of Old Scandinavia*

SBR   *Swedish Book Review*. Lampeter, Wales, 1983–

SC   *Scandinavica*. Norwich, U.K., 1962–

SD   *Svenskt diplomatrium*

SFSS   *Samlingar utgivna av svenska fornskriftsällskapet* (Numbers cited in the text refer to the volume numbers supplied in *Fornsvensk bibliografi* and its supplements.)

SGL   *Samling af Sweriges Gamla Lagar*

SMB   *Sveriges medeltida ballader*

SR   *Scandinavian Review* (until 1975, *American-Scandinavian Review*). New York, 1913–

SRS   *Scriptores rerum Sveciacarum*

SS   *Scandinavian Studies*. Madison, Wisconsin, 1911–

WLT   *World Literature Today* (until 1977, *Books Abroad*). Norman, Oklahoma, 1927–

General References

BIBLIOGRAPHIES

Holmbäck, Bure. *About Sweden, 1900–1963: A Bibliographical Outline*. Compiled with the assistance of Ulla-Märta Abrahamson and Mariann Tiblin. Stockholm, 1968. (In *Sweden Illustrated*, vol. 15 [1968], pp. 1–94.)

Josephson, Aksel G. S. *A List of Swedish Books, 1875–1925.* New York: Bonniers, 1927.

Suecana Extranea: Books on Sweden and Swedish Literature in Foreign Languages. Stockholm: Royal Library, 1963–.

Svensk bokförteckning. Årskatalog. The Swedish National Bibliography. Stockholm: Svensk bokhandel, 1913–.

Svensk bokkatalog, 1866 ff. Stockholm: Svenska bokförläggarföreningen, 1878–.

Svensk littreraturhistorisk bibliografi. Uppsala: Svenska litteratursällskapet, 1880–. (In *Samlaren: Tidskrift för Svensk Litteraturhistorisk Forskning,* 1880–).

GENERAL ANTHOLOGIES IN ENGLISH

Ahlberg, Fred. *Masterpieces of Swedish Poetry.* Tujunga, Calif.: Cecil L. Andersen, 1952.

Allwood, Martin S., and Lindsay Lafford. *Swedish Songs and Ballads.* New York: Bonniers, 1950.

Brandberg, Paul. *A Swedish Reader.* London: Athlone Press, 1953.

Fleischer, Frederic. *Seven Swedish Poets.* Malmö: Bo Cavefors, 1963.

Hannay, Carolyn, and J. M. Nosworthy. *Some Swedish Poets.* Stockholm: Swedish Institute, 1958.

Larsen, Hanna Astrup. *Sweden's Best Stories.* New York: American-Scandinavian Foundation and W. W. Norton, 1928.

McLean, Reginald J. *A Book of Swedish Verse.* London: Athlone Press, 1968.

Modern Swedish Short Stories. 1934. Rpt. Plainview, N.Y.: Books for Libraries Press, 1974.

Stork, Charles W. *Anthology of Swedish Lyrics from 1750–1925.* 2d rev. and aug. ed. New York: American-Scandinavian Foundation; London: H. Milford, Oxford University Press, 1930.

———. *Modern Swedish Masterpieces.* New York: E. P. Dutton, 1923.

LITERARY HISTORY

Algulin, Ingemar. *A History of Swedish Literature.* Stockholm: Swedish Institute, 1989.

Ardelius, Lars, and Gunnar Rydström, eds. *Författarnas litteraturhistoria.* 3 vols. Stockholm: Författarförlaget, 1977–78.

Gustafson, Alrik. *A History of Swedish Literature.* Minneapolis: University of Minnesota Press, 1961.

Howitt, William, and Mary Howitt. *The Literature and Romance of Northern Europe.* 2 vols. London: Colburn, 1852.

Lönnroth, Lars, and Sven Delblanc. *Den svenska litteraturen.* 7 vols. Stockholm: Bonniers, 1987–90.

Rossel, Sven H. *A History of Scandinavian Literature, 1870–1980.* Minneapolis: University of Minnesota Press, 1982.

Schück, Henrik, and Karl Warburg. *Illustrerad svensk litteraturhistoria.* Stockholm: Rabén & Sjögren, 1949.

Tigerstedt, E. N. *Ny illustrerad svensk litteraturhistoria.* Stockholm: Rabén & Sjögren, 1967.

Zuck, Virpi, Niels Ingwersen, and Harald S. Naess, eds. *Dictionary of Scandinavian Literature.* Westport, Conn.: Greenwood Press, 1990.

HISTORY AND CIVILIZATION

Koblik, Steven, ed. *Sweden's Development from Poverty to Affluence, 1750–1970.* Minneapolis: University of Minnesota Press, 1975.

Nordstrom, Byron, ed. *The Dictionary of Scandinavian History.* Westport, Conn.: Greenwood Press, 1986.

Scott, Franklin D. *Sweden, the Nation's History.* Carbondale: Southern Illinois University Press, 1988.

Chapter Bibliographies

CHAPTER 1: THE MIDDLE AGES

GENERAL

Fornsvensk bibliografi. Ed. Robert Geete. Stockholm: P. A. Norstedt & Söner, 1903. *Supplement.* Ed. Robert Geete. Stockholm: P. A. Norstedt & Söner, 1919. *Supplement 2.* Ed. Isak Collijn. Uppsala: Almqvist & Wiksell, 1945–48.

Hällristningar och hällmålningar i Sverige [with English summaries]. Ed. Sverker Janson, Erik B. Lundberg, and Ulf Bertilsson. 3d rev. ed. N.p.: Forum, 1989.

Haugen, Einar. *The Scandinavian Languages: An Introduction to Their History.* Cambridge, Mass.: Harvard University Press, 1976.

Hildebrand, Hans Olof H. *Sveriges medeltid: Kulturhistorisk skildring,* 3 vols. 1879–1903. Rpt. Stockholm: Gidlunds, 1983–.

Jansson, Sven B. F. *The Runes of Sweden,* Trans. P. G. Foote. London: Phoenix House, 1962.

Jansson, Sven-Bertil. *Medeltidens rimkrönikor: Studier i funktion, stoff, form* [with a German summary]. Studia litteratum Upsaliensia 8. N.p.: Läromedelsförlagen, 1971.

Kulturhistorisk leksikon for nordisk middelalder. 22 vols. København: Rosenkilde & Bagger and others, 1956–78.

Medieval Scandinavia: An Encyclopedia. Ed. Phillip Pusliano et al. New York: Garland, 1992.

Mitchell, Stephen. *Heroic Sagas and Ballads.* Ithaca, N.Y.: Cornell University Press, 1991.

Roesdahl, Else. *The Vikings.* Trans. Susan M. Margeson and Kirsten Williams. Harmondsworth, England: Allen Lane, Penguin Press, 1991.

Sawyer, P. H. *Kings and Vikings: Scandinavia and Europe, A.D. 700–1100.* London and New York: Routledge, 1982.

Scandinavian Mythology: An Annotated Bibliography. Ed. John Lindow. Garland Folklore Bibliographies 13. New York: Garland, 1988.

Svensk medeltidsforskning idag: En forskningsöversikt. Ed. Göran Dahlbäck. Uppsala: Humanistisk-Samhällsvetenskapliga Forskningsrådet, 1987.

NONANTHOLOGIZED SOURCES AND LITERATURE IN
ENGLISH TRANSLATION

[Adam of Bremen.] *Adami Gesta Hammaburgensis ecclesiae pontificum.* Monumenta Germaniae historica. Scriptores rerum germanicarum 2. Hannover: Hahn, 1876. *History of the Archbishops of Hamburg-Bremen by Adam of Bremen.* Trans. F. J. Tschan. New York: Columbia University Press, 1959.

Beowulf: A Dual-Language Edition. Ed. and trans. Howell D. Chickering Jr. Garden City, N.Y.: Anchor Books, 1977.

Birgitta of Sweden: Life and Selected Revelations. Ed. Marguerite Tjäder Harris, trans. Albert Ryle Kezel, and intro. Tore Nyberg. New York: Paulist Press, 1990.

Diarium Vadstenense: The Memorial Book of Vadstena Abbey. Ed. Claes Gejrot. Acta Universitatis Stockholmensis. Studia Latina Stockholmensia 33. Stockholm: Almqvist & Wiksell, 1988.

Edda: Die Lieder des Codex Regius nebst verwandten Denkmälern. Ed. Gustav Neckel. 5th ed. Hans Kuhn. Heidelberg: Carl Winter, Universitätsverlag, 1983. *The Poetic Edda.* Trans. Lee M. Hollander. 2d ed. 1962. Rpt. Austin: University of Texas Press, 1987. [Includes "The Sayings of Hár" and a translation of "Vǫluspá."]

Jóns saga helga [older version], in *Byskupa sögur. 2. Hólabyskupar.* Ed. Guðni Jónsson. Reykjavík: Íslendingasagnaútgáfan, 1948.

[Jordanes.] *Iordanis Romana et Getica.* Ed. Theodor Mommsen. Monumenta Germaniae historica. Auctores antiquissimi, 5:1. 1882. Rpt. Berlin: Weidmannschen, 1961. *The Gothic History of Jordanes in English Version.* Trans. Charles C. Mierow. 2d ed. Cambridge: Speculum Historiale; New York: Barnes & Noble, 1966.

[*King Alfred's Orosius.*] *Two Voyagers at the Court of King Alfred: The Ventures of Ohthere and Wulfstan, together with the Description of Northern Europe from the Old English Orosius.* Ed. Niels Lund, trans. Christine Fell. York: Sessions, 1984.

[*Konungs skuggsjá.*] *Speculum Regale. Konungs skuggsjá. Kongespeilet.* Ed. Rudolph Keyser, Peter Andreas Munch, and Carl Rikard Unger. Christiania: Carl C. Werner, 1848. *The King's Mirror.* Trans. Laurence Larson. Scandinavian Monographs 3. New York: American-Scandinavian Foundation, 1917; rpt. New York: Twayne, 1973.

Medieval Stories. Ed. Henrik Schück, trans. W. F. Harvey. London: Sands, 1902. [Includes translations of the Old Swedish *Flores and Blancheflor; Duke Frederick; John, the Knight of the Lion; Nameless and Valentine; Karl and Alegast;*

The Journey to Constantinople; Roland; The Seven Wise Masters; Amicus and Amelius.]

A Pageant of Old Scandinavia. Ed. Henry Goddard Leach. 1946. Rpt. Princeton and New York: Princeton University Press for the American-Scandinavian Foundation, 1955. [Includes partial translations of the runic inscriptions at Rök and Gripsholm, the *Russian Primary Chronicle,* Ibn Fadlān's account of the Rus', Adam of Bremen's comments on worship at Uppsala, the life of St. Erik, *Västgötalagen,* and *Gutasaga.*]

[Rimbert.] *Vita Anskarii auctore Rimberto.* Ed. Georg Waitz. Monumenta Germaniae historica. Scriptores rerum germanicarum 55. 1884. Rpt. Hannover: Hahn, 1977. *Ansgar: The Apostle of the North, 801–865.* Trans. Charles H. Robinson. London: Society for the Propagation of the Gospel in Foreign Parts, 1921.

Saga Heiðreks konungs ins vitra. The Saga of King Heidrek the Wise. Ed. and trans. Christopher Tolkien. London: Thomas Nelson & Sons, 1960.

[Saxo Grammaticus.] *Saxonis Gesta Danorum.* Ed. Carl Knabe and Paul Herrmann, rev. ed. Jørgen Olrik and Hans Ræder. 2 vols. Copenhagen: Levin & Munksgaard, 1931–57. *Saxo Grammaticus: The History of the Danes* [Books 1–9]. Trans. Peter Fisher. Totowa, N.J.: Rowman & Littlefield, 1979.

Scandinavian Ballads. Ed. and trans. Sven Rossel. Madison: University of Wisconsin, Department of Scandinavian Studies, 1982.

Snorri Sturluson. *Heimskringla 1–3.* Ed. Bjarni Aðalbjarnarson. Íslenzk fornrit, 26–28. Reykjavík: Hið íslenzka fornritafélag, 1941–51. *Heimskringla: History of the Kings of Norway.* Trans. Lee M. Hollander. 1964. Rpt. Austin: University of Texas Press for the American-Scandinavian Foundation, 1987. [Includes "The Saga of the Ynglings" and "The Saga of the Sons of Magnus."]

Vita Katherine. Facsimile tryck av Bartholomeus Ghotans i Stockholm 1487 tryckta bok. Ed. and trans. Tryggve Lundén. Uppsala: Bokförlaget Pro Veritate, 1981.

Wahlgren, Erik. "A Swedish-Latin Parallel to the *Monachorum.*" *Modern Philology* 36 (1939), 239–45.

Yngvars saga viðforla jämte ett bihang om Ingvarsinskrifterna. Ed. Emil Olson. Samfund til Udgivelse av gammel nordisk Litteratur 39. København: S. L. Møller, 1912. *The Vikings in Russia: Yngvar's Saga and Eymund's Saga.* Trans. Hermann Pálsson and Paul Edwards. Edinburgh: Edinburgh University Press, 1989.

ANTHOLOGIZED SOURCES

Corpus codicum sueciorum medii aevi. Ed. Elias Wessén. 20 vols. København: Munksgaard, 1943–67.

Hymni sequentiae et piae cantiones in regno Sueciae olim usitatae. Ed. Gustaf E. Klemming. 4 vols. Stockholm: P. A. Norstedt & Söners, 1885–87.

Samling af Sweriges Gamla Lagar. Corpus iuris Sueco-Gotorum antiqui. 13 vols. Ed. D.C.J. Schlyter (vols. 1–2 with D.H.S. Colin). Imprint varies: vol. 1, Stockholm: Z. Haeggström; vols. 2–3, Stockholm: P. A. Norstedt & Söner; vols. 4–13, Lund: Gleerups, 1827–77.

Samlingar utgivna av svenska fornskriftsällskapet. Imprint varies: 1844–1921, Stockholm: P. A. Norstedt & Söner; 1923–74, Uppsala : Almqvist & Wiksell; 1974–, Lund: Carl Bloms. [The majority of Old Swedish texts are published in this series; more than 250 fascicles have appeared to date.]

Scriptores rerum Sveciacarum medii aevi. Ed. Erik M. Fant et al. 3 vols. Uppsala: Palmblad, 1818–76.

Småstycken på fornsvenska. Ed. Gustaf E. Klemming. Stockholm: P. A. Norstedt & Söner, 1868–81.

Svenskt diplomatarium. Ed. Joh. Gust. Liljegren et al. Vols. 1– (10 vols. to date). Stockholm: P. A. Norstedt & Söner, 1829–.

Sverges traktater med främmande magter jemte andra dit hörande handlingar. Ed. O. S. Rydberg. [Vols. 1–4 to 1571.] Stockholm: P. A. Norstedt & Söner, 1877–88.

Sveriges medeltida ballader. Ed. Bengt R. Jonsson, Margareta Jerskild, and Sven-Bertil Jansson. Vols. 1– (3 vols. to date). Stockholm: Svenskt Visarkiv and Almqvist & Wiksell, 1983–.

Sveriges runinskrifter. Vols. 1– (15 vols. to date). Stockholm: Kungliga Vitterhets Historie och Antikvitets Akademinens Handlingar, 1900–.

CHAPTER 2: THE REFORMATION AND
SWEDEN'S CENTURY AS A GREAT POWER: 1523–1718

GENERAL

Belfrage, Esbjörn. *1600–talspsalm.* Lund: Gleerup, 1969.

Carlson, Marvin. "Renaissance Theatre in Scandinavia." *Theatre Survey: The American Journal of Theatre History* 14 (1) (1973), 22–54.

Castrén, Gunnar. "Scandinavia's International Baroque Theatre." *Educational Theatre Journal* 28 (1976), 5–34.

———. *Stormaktstidens diktning.* Helsingfors: Helios, 1907.

Hansson, Stina. *Svenskans nytta Sveriges ära: Litteratur och kulturpolitik under 1600–talet.* Göteborg: Litteraturvetenskapliga institutionen vid Göteborgs universitet, 1984.

Johannesson, Kurt. *I polstjärnans tecken: Studier i svensk barock.* Stockholm: Almqvist & Wiksell, 1968.

———. *Svensk retorik: Från Stockholms blodbad till Almedalen.* Stockholm: Norstedt, 1983.

Roberts, Michael. *Gustavus Adolphus: A History of Sweden, 1611–1632.* London, New York, and Toronto: Longmans, Green & Co., 1953, 1958.

Rystad, Göran, ed. *Europe and Scandinavia: Aspects of the Process of Integration in the Seventeenth Century.* Solna, Sweden: Esselte Studium, 1983.

Ståhle, Carl Ivar. *Vers och språk i Vasatidens och stormaktstidens svenska diktning.* Stockholm: Norstedt, 1975.

Wikland, Erik. *Elizabethan Players in Sweden, 1591–92: Facts and Problems.* Stockholm: Almqvist & Wiksell, 1962.

SELECTED WORKS IN ENGLISH

Ahléen, Reinhold, trans. *Poets of the Seventeenth Century: Some Gleanings from the Swedish Parnassus*. San Francisco: Parker, 1932.

MONOGRAPHS AND ARTICLES

Christina, Queen

Atkinson, Jeanette Lee. "Sovereign between Throne and Altar: Queen Christina of Sweden." In *Women Writers of the Seventeenth Century*, ed. Katharine M. Wilson and Frank J. Warnke. Athens: University of Georgia Press, 1989, 405–14.

Johnson, Amandus. "Queen Christina: The First Modern Woman of the Western World." In *American-Swedish Historical Foundation Yearbook*. Philadelphia: American-Swedish Foundation, 1966, 1–9.

Setterwall, Monica. "Queen Christina and Role Playing in Maxim Form." *SS* 57 (1985), 162–73.

Columbus, Samuel

Ekholm, Ragnar. *Samuel Columbus: Bidrag till kännedomen om hans levnad och författarskap*. Uppsala: Almqvist & Wiksell, 1924.

Lucidor, Lasse

Hansson, Stina. *Bröllopslägrets skald och bårens: En studie i Lucidors tillfällesdikt-ning*. Göteborg: Litteraturvetenskapliga institutionen vid Göteborgs universitet, 1975.

Magnus, Johannes and Olaus

Isacson, Kerstin. "A Study of Non-Classical Features in Book XV of Olaus Magnus' Historia de Gentibus Septentrionalibus, 1555." *Humanistica Lovaniensia: Journal of Neo-Latin Studies* 38 (1989), 176–99.

Johannesson, Kurt. *Gotisk renässans: Johannes och Olaus Magnus som politiker och historiker*. Stockholm: Almqvist & Wiksell, 1982.

Petri, Olaus

Bergendoff, C.J.I. *Olaus Petri and the Ecclesiastical Transformation in Sweden*. New York: Macmillan, 1928.

Rudbeck, Olaus

Ekman, Ernst. "Gothic Patriotism and Olof Rudbeck." *Journal of Modern History* 34 (1963), 52–63.

Runius, Johan

von Platen, Magnus. *Johan Runius: En biografi*. Stockholm: Wahlström & Widstrand, 1954.

Spegel, Haquin

Olsson, Bernt. *Guds werk och hwila: Tillkomsthistoria, världsbild, gestaltning*. Stockholm: Natur & Kultur, 1963.

Stiernhielm, Georg

Olsson, Bernt. *Den svenska skalde-konstens fader och andra Stiernhielmstudier.* Lund: Gleerup, 1974.

Wivallius, Lars

Schück, Henrik. *Lars Wivallius, hans lif och dikt.* Uppsala: Skrifter utgivna af Litteratursällskapet, 1893–95.

CHAPTER 3: THE ENLIGHTENMENT AND THE GUSTAVIAN AGE

GENERAL

Anchor, Robert. *The Enlightenment Tradition.* Berkeley: University of California Press, 1967.

Anderson, Matthew Smith. *Europe in the Eighteenth Century, 1713–1789.* New York: Oxford Galaxy, 1966.

Barton, H. Arnold. *Scandinavia in the Revolutionary Era, 1760–1815.* Minneapolis: University of Minnesota Press, 1986.

Byström, Tryggve. *Svenska komedien.* Stockholm: Norstedt, 1981.

Cassirer, Ernst. *The Philosophy of the Enlightenment.* Trans. Fritz C. A. Koelln and James P. Pettegrove. Boston: Beacon Press, 1964.

Frängsmyr, Tore. "The Enlightenment in Sweden." In *The Enlightenment in National Context,* ed. Roy Porter and Mikulas Teich. Cambridge: Cambridge University Press, 1981, 164–75.

Lamm, Martin. *Upplysningens romantik: Den mystiskt sentimentala strömningen i svensk litteratur.* 2 vols. 1918–20. Rpt. Enskede: Hammarström & Åberg, 1981.

Levertin, Oscar. *Från Gustaf III:s dagar.* Stockholm: Bonniers, 1908.

Lindroth, Sten. *Svensk lärdomshistoria: Frihetstiden.* Stockholm: Norstedt, 1975–81.

———. *Svensk lärdomshistoria: Gustavianska tiden.* Stockholm: Norstedt, 1975–81.

Nelson, Walter W. *A Bibliography of Scandinavian Literature between 1760–1820.* Lund: n.p., 1988.

Personne, N. *Svenska teatern: Från Gustaf III:s död till Karl XIV Johans ankomst till Sverige, 1792–1810.* Stockholm: Wahlström & Widstrand, 1914.

———. *Svenska teatern under Gustavianska tidehvarfvet.* Stockhom: Wahlström & Widstrand, 1913.

von Platen, Magnus. *1700-tal: Studier i svensk litteratur.* Stockholm: Natur & Kultur, 1963.

Sahlin, Gunnar. *Författarrollens förändring och det litterära systemet, 1770–1795.* Stockholm: Sahlin, 1989.

Skuncke, Marie-Christine. *Sweden and European Drama, 1772–1796.* Stockholm: Almqvist & Wiksell, 1981.

SELECTED WORKS IN ENGLISH

Bellman, Carl Michael

Britten Austin, Paul, trans. *Fredman's Epistles and Songs.* Stockholm: Reuter, 1977.

————. *Songs.* Stockholm: n.p., 1963.

Lenngren, Anna Maria
Nelson, Philip K., trans. *Anna Maria Lenngren, 1784–1817.* Stockholm: Imprime, 1984.

Linné, Carl von (Linnaeus)
Black, David ed. *Travels.* New York: Scribner, 1979.

Swedenborg, Emanuel
Heaven and Its Wonders and Hell. New York: Swedenborg Foundation, 1931.
Intercourse between the Soul and the Body. Boston: Massachusetts New-Church Union, 1950.

MONOGRAPHS AND ARTICLES

Bellman, Carl Michael
Afzelius, Nils. *Myt och bild: Studier i Bellmans dikt.* Stockholm: Prisma, 1963.
————. *Staden och tiden: Studier i Bellmans dikt.* Stockholm: Norstedt, 1969.
Britten Austin, Paul. *The Life and Songs of Carl Michael Bellman.* New York: American-Scandinavian Foundation, 1967.
Massengale, James. *The Musical-Poetic Method of Carl Michael Bellman.* Uppsala: Almqvist & Wiksell, 1979.

Creutz, Gustaf Philip
Castrén, Gunnar. *Gustaf Philip Creutz.* Stockholm: Natur & Kultur, 1949.

Dalin, Olof
Lamm, Martin. *Olof Dalin: En litteraturhistorisk undersökning af hans verk.* Uppsala: Almqvist & Wiksell, 1908.

Gustav III
Hennings, Beth. *Gustaf III.* Stockholm: Hugo Geber, 1957.

Kellgren, Johan Henrik
Ek, Sverker. *Kellgren: Skalden och kulturkämpen.* 2 vols. Stockholm: Natur & Kultur, 1965–80.

Lenngren, Anna Maria
Warburg, Karl. *Anna Maria Lenngren.* Stockholm: Norstedt, 1887.

Linné, Carl von (Linnaeus)
Broberg, Gunnar. *Carl Linnaeus.* Swedish Portraits. Stockholm: Swedish Institute, 1992.
Frängsmyr, Tore, ed. *Linnaeus: The Man and His Work.* Berkeley, University of California Press, 1983.
Hagberg, Knut. *Carl Linnaeus.* London: Cape, 1952.
Larson, James L. *Reason and Experience: The Representation of Natural Order in the Work of Carl von Linné.* Berkeley: University of California Press, 1971.

Nordenflycht, Hedvig Charlotta

Stålmarck, Torkel. *Hedvig Charlotta Nordenflycht*. Stockholm: Natur & Kultur, 1967.

Oxenstierna, Johan Gabriel

Frykenstedt, Holger. *Johan Gabriel Oxenstierna's* Skördarne: *A Major Swedish Work in the Literary Genre of Thomson's* The Seasons. Uppsala: Almqvist & Wiksell, 1961.

Swedenborg, Emanuel

Bergquist, Lars. *Emanuel Swedenborg*. Swedish Portraits. Uppsala: Swedish Institute, 1986.

Brock, Erland, ed. *Swedenborg and His Influence*. Bryn Athin, Pa.: Academy of the New Church, 1988.

Lindroth, Sten. *Emanuel Swedenborg*. Swedish Men of Science, 1650–1940. Stockholm: Swedish Institute, 1952.

Wallenberg, Jacob

Barker, Steven John. "Wallenberg and His English Contemporaries: A Study in Affinities." Ph.D. dissertation. Seattle: University of Washington, 1980.

Graves, Peter. "Jacob Wallenberg, His Galley, and a Digression on Literary Histories." SBR 2 (1989), 20–24.

CHAPTER 4: THE ROMANTIC PERIOD

GENERAL

Aarseth, Asbjorn. *Romantikken som konstruksjon: Traditionskritiske studier i nordisk litteraturhistorie*. Bergen: Universitetsforlaget, 1985.

Benson, Adolph B. "The English Element in Swedish Romanticism." *SS* 5 (1918–19), 47–71.

———. "A List of English Translations of *Frithiofs Saga*." *Germanic Review* 1 (1926), 142–67.

———. *The Old Norse Element in Swedish Romanticism*. New York: Columbia University Press, 1914.

———. "The Problem of Catholic Sympathies in Swedish Romanticism." In *Studies in Honor of Albert Moray Sturtevant*, ed. L. R. Lind. Lawrence: University Press of Kansas, 1952, 138–61.

Engdahl, Horace. *Den romantiska texten*. Stockholm: Bonniers, 1986.

Gosse, Edmund W. *Studies in the Literature of Northern Europe*. London: C. K. Paul, 1883.

Hustvedt, S. B. *Ballad Books and Ballad Men: Raids and Rescues in Britain, America, and the Scandinavian North since 1800*. Cambridge, Mass.: Harvard University Press, 1930.

Nilsson, Albert. *Svensk romantik*. Lund: Glerups, 1916.

SELECTED WORKS IN ENGLISH

Geijer, Erik Gustaf

Sprigge, Elizabeth, and C. Napier, trans. *Impressions of England*. London: J. Cape, 1932.

Tegnér, Esaias

Bethune, J.E.D., trans. *Axel*. In *Specimens of Swedish and German Poetry*. London, 1948.

Longfellow, Henry Wadsworth. "The Children of the Lord's Supper." In *Poems by Tegnér*. New York: American-Scandinavian Foundation, 1914.

Wallin, Johan Olof

Almqvist, A. W., trans. *The Angel of Death* (with "Biography of the Author"). New York: Gazlay Bros., 1884.

MONOGRAPHS AND ARTICLES

Almqvist, Carl Jonas Love

Blackwell, Marilyn Johns. *C.J.L. Almqvist and Romantic Irony*. Stockholm: Almqvist & Wiksell, 1983.

Romberg, Bertil. *Carl Jonas Love Almqvist*. Boston: Twayne, 1977.

Atterbom, Per Daniel Amadeus

Tykesson, Elisabeth. *Atterbom, en levnadsteckning*. Stockholm: Bonniers, 1954.

Geijer, Erik Gustaf

Landquist, John. *Geijer, en levnadstechning*. Stockholm: Bonniers, 1954.

Spongberg, Viola H. "The Philosophy of Erik Gustaf Geijer." Ph.D. dissertation. New York University, 1945.

Stagnelius, Erik Johan

Böök, Fredrik. *Stagnelius: Liv och dikt*. Stockholm: Bonniers, 1954.

Tegnér, Esaias

Böök, Fredrik. "Esaias Tegnér," SR 14 (1926), 653–59.

Brandes, Georg. "Esaias Tegnér." In *Creative Spirits of the Nineteenth Century*. New York: Thomas Y. Crowell, 1923.

CHAPTER 5: LIBERALISM, REALISM, AND THE MODERN BREAKTHROUGH: 1830–1890

GENERAL

Bredsdorff, Elias. "Moralists *versus* Immoralists: The Great Battle in Scandinavian Literature in the 1880s" SC 8 (1969), 91–111.

Brockett, Oscar G. *History of the Theatre*. Boston: Allyn & Bacon, 1987.

Gosse, Edmund W. *Studies in the Literature of Northern Europe*. London: C. K. Paul, 1883.

Nolin, Bertil, and Peter Forsgren, eds. *The Modern Breakthrough in Scandinavian Literature: Proceedings of the Sixteenth Study Conference of the International Association for Scandinavian Studies*. Göteborg: University of Göteborg, 1988.

SELECTED WORKS IN ENGLISH

Bremer, Fredrika

Milow, Frederick, and Emily Nonnen, trans. *Life, Letters, and Posthumous Works of Fredrika Bremer*. New York: American-Scandinavian Foundation, 1976.

Runeberg, Johan Ludvig

Stork, C. W., trans. *The Tales of Ensign Stål*. New York: American-Scandinavian Foundation; London: Oxford University Press, 1938.

Strindberg, August

Erichsen, N. *Eight Famous Plays*. London: Duckworth; New York: Scribner, 1949.

Faber, Max, trans. *Miss Julie and Other Plays*. London: Heinemann, 1960.

Field, C., trans. *The German Lieutenant and Other Stories*. London: T. W. Laurie; Chicago: A. C. McClurg, 1915.

✓ Schleussner, Elsie, trans. *In Midsummer Days and Other Tales*. London: H. Latimer, 1913.

Sprinchorn, Evert, trans. *Selected Plays*. Minneapolis: University of Minnesota Press, 1986.

MONOGRAPHS AND ARTICLES

Almqvist, Carl Jonas Love

Hemming-Sjöberg, Axel. *A Poet's Tragedy: The Trial of C.J.L. Almqvist*. Trans. E. Classen. London: Allen & Unwin, 1932.

Romberg, Bertil. *Carl Jonas Love Almqvist*. Trans. S. Liden. Boston: Twayne, 1977.

Benedictsson, Victoria

Bjørby, Pål. "Myth and Illusion: The Aesthetics of Self in Victoria Benedictsson's *Pengar*." *Edda* 4 (1985), 209–29.

Moberg, Verne. "Motherhood as Reality for Victoria Benedictsson." *Edda* 5 (1984), 289–300.

Bremer, Fredrika

Anderson, Carl L. "Fredrika Bremer's 'Spirit of the New World.' " *New England Quarterly* 38 (1965), 187–201.

Rooth, Signe. *Fredrika Bremer and America: Her Literary Contacts and Social Impressions*. Chicago: University of Chicago Press, 1953.

Stendahl, Brita K. *The Education of a Self-Made Woman: Fredrika Bremer, 1801–1865*. Lewiston, N.Y.: Edwin Mellen Press, 1994.

Flygare-Carlén, Emilie
Kjellén, Alf. *Emilie Flygare-Karlén: En litteraturhistorisk studie.* Stockholm: Bonniers, 1932.

Geijerstam, Gustaf af
Björkman, Edwin. "Gustaf af Geijerstam." In *Scandinavian Classics* 18. New York: American-Scandinavian Foundation, 1921.

Leffler, Anne Charlotte
Shogren, Melissa Lowe. "The Search for Self-Fulfillment: The Life and Writing of Anne Charlotte Leffler." Ph.D. dissertation, University of Washington, 1984.
Sylvan, Maj. *Anne Charlotte Leffler, en kvinna finner sin väg.* Stockholm: Biblioteksförlaget, 1984.

Runeberg, Johan Ludvig
Nilsson, Kim. "J. L. Runeberg as a Modern Writer: The Evidence of *Julqvällen.*" *SS* 58 (1986), 1–9.
Wretö, Tore. *J. L. Runeberg.* Boston: Twayne, 1980.

Rydberg, Viktor
Holmberg, Olle. *Viktor Rydbergs lyrik.* Stockholm: Bonniers, 1935.
Warburg, Karl. *Viktor Rydberg, hans levnad och diktning.* Stockholm: Bonniers, 1913.

Snoilsky, Carl
Olsson, Henry. *Carl Snoilsky.* Stockholm: Norstedt, 1981.

Strindberg, August
Blackwell, Marilyn J., ed. *Structures of Influence: A Comparative Approach to August Strindberg.* Festschrift to Professor Walter Johnson. Chapel Hill: University of North Carolina Press, 1981.
Carlson, Harry G. *Strindberg and the Poetry of Myth.* Berkeley: University of California Press, 1982.
Cullberg, Johan. *Skaparkriser: Strindbergs inferno och Dagermans.* Stockholm: Natur & Kultur, 1992.
Dahlström, Carl. *Strindberg's Dramatic Expressionism.* Ann Arbor: University of Michigan Press, 1930.
Grant, Vernon W. *Great Abnormals: The Pathological Genius of Kafka, Van Gogh, Strindberg, and Poe.* New York: Hawthorne, 1968.
Johannesson, Eric O. *The Novels of August Strindberg.* Berkeley: University of California Press, 1963.
Johnson, Walter. *August Strindberg.* Boston: Twayne, 1978.
Lagercrantz, Olof. *August Strindberg.* New York: Farrar, Straus, Giroux, 1984.
Lamm, Martin. *August Strindberg.* Trans. and ed. Harry G. Carlson. New York: B. Blom, 1971.
Madsen, Børge Gedsø. *Strindberg's Naturalistic Theatre.* Seattle: University of Washington Press, 1962.

Meyer, Michael. *Strindberg: A Biography*. New York: Random House, 1985.

Robinson, Michael. *Strindberg and Autobiography*. Norwich, England: Norvik Press, 1986.

Sprinchorn, Evert. *Strindberg as Dramatist*. New Haven and London: Yale University Press, 1982.

Steene, Birgitta. *August Strindberg: An Introduction to His Major Works*. Stockholm: Almqvist & Wiksell International; Atlantic Highlands, N.J.: Humanities Press, 1982.

————., ed. *Strindberg and History*. Stockholm: Almqvist & Wiksell International, 1992.

Stockenström, Göran, ed. *Strindberg's Dramaturgy*. Minneapolis: University of Minnesota Press, 1988.

Törnqvist, Egil. *Strindbergian Drama: Themes and Structure*. Stockholm: Almqvist & Wiksell International; Atlantic Highlands, N.J.: Humanities Press, 1982.

CHAPTER 6: INTO THE TWENTIETH CENTURY: 1890–1950

GENERAL

Borland, Harold. *Nietzsche's Influence on Swedish Literature, with Special Reference to Strindberg, Ola Hansson, Heidenstam, and Fröding*. Göteborg: Wettergren & Kerber, 1956.

Furuland, Lars. "Statare" in Swedish Literature (in Swedish with English summary). Stockholm: Tidens Förlag, 1962.

Graves, Peter. "The Collective Novel in Sweden." *SC* 12 (1973), 113–27.

Holmbäck, Bure. "About Sweden, 1900–1963: A Bibliographical Outline." *Sweden Illustrated* 15 (1968), 5–94.

Scobbie, Irene, ed. *Aspects of Modern Swedish Literature*. Norwich, England: Norvik Press, 1988.

Thompson, Laurie. "Heaven or Hell? Pessimism and Fyrtiotalisterna." In *Proceedings of the Conference of Scandinavian Studies in Great Britain and Northern Ireland*. Surrey: University of Surrey Press, 1983, 158–71.

ANTHOLOGIES

Allwood, Martin S., ed. *Modern Swedish Poems*. Rock Island, Ill.: Augustana Book Concern, 1948.

Bly, Robert. *Friends, You Drank Some Darkness: Three Swedish Poets*. Boston: Beacon Press, 1975.

Fleisher, Frederic, trans. and ed. *Eight Swedish Poets*. Malmö: Cavefors, 1969.

Hannay, Carolyn, and J. M. Nosworthy, trans. *Some Swedish Poets*. Stockholm: Swedish Institute, 1958.

Locock, Charles D. *Modern Swedish Poetry*. London: H. and W. Brown, 1936.

SELECTED WORKS IN ENGLISH

Andersson, Dan

Schleef, Carolina, trans. *Charcoal-Burner's Ballad and Other Poems.* New York: Fine Editions Press, 1943.

———. *The Last Night in Paindalen.* New York: C. Schleef, 1958.

Aurell, Tage

Allwood, Martin S., trans. *Rose of Jericho and Other Stories.* Madison: University of Wisconsin Press, 1968.

Bergman, Hjalmar

Johnson, Walter, trans. *Four Plays.* Seattle: University of Washington Press, 1968.

Dagerman, Stig

✓Walford, Naomi, trans. *The Games of Night: Ten Stories and an Autobiographical Piece.* Philadelphia: Lippincott, 1961.

Ekelöf, Gunnar

✓Auden, W. H., and Leif Sjöberg, trans. *Selected Poems.* New York: Pantheon, 1972.

Bly, Robert, and Christina Paulston, trans. *I Do Best Alone at Night.* Washington, D.C.: Charioteer Press, 1977.

———. *Late Arrival on Earth: Selected Poems.* London: Rapp & Carroll, 1967.

Rukeyser, Muriel, and Leif Sjöberg, trans. *Selected Poems.* New York: Twayne, 1967.

Engström, Albert

Borland, H. trans. *Twelve Tales.* London: Harrap, 1949.

Fröding, Gustaf

Stork, C. W., trans. *Selected Poems.* New York: Macmillan, 1916.

Hallström, Per

Fielden, F. J., trans. *Selected Short Stories.* New York: American-Scandinavian Foundation, 1922.

✓ *Heidenstam, Verner von*

Allnutt, A. A., trans. *Five Stories Selected from "The Karolines."* London and New York: Harrap, 1922.

Stork, C. W., trans. *Sweden's Laureate: Selected Poems.* New Haven: Yale University; London: H. Milford, 1919.

Karlfeldt, Erik Axel

Stork, C. W., trans. *Arcadia Borealis: Selected Poems.* Minneapolis: University of Minnesota Press, 1938.

✓ *Lagerkvist, Pär*

Blair, Alan, trans. *The Eternal Smile and Other Stories.* New York: Random House, 1954.

Blair, A., and C. E. Lindin, trans. *The Marriage Feast, and Other Stories.* London: Chatto & Windus, 1955.

Buckman, Thomas R., trans. *Modern Theatre: Seven Plays and an Essay.* Lincoln: University of Nebraska Press, 1966.

✓ *Lagerlöf, Selma*

Field, C., trans. *The Tale of a Manor and Other Sketches.* London: T. W. Laurie, 1922.

Söderberg, Hjalmar

Stork, C. W., trans. *Selected Short Stories.* Princeton: Princeton University Press; New York: American-Scandinavian Foundation, 1935.

Södergran, Edith

Allwood, Martin, trans. *The Collected Poems of Edith Södergran.* Mullsjö: Anglo-American Center, 1980.

Taube, Evert

Asbury, H., trans. *Sea Ballads and Other Songs.* Stockholm: Kings Press, 1940.

MONOGRAPHS AND ARTICLES

Ahlin, Lars

Lundell, Torborg. *Lars Ahlin.* New York: Twayne, 1977.

Aspenström, Werner

Sjöberg, Leif. "Werner Aspenström: A Writer for All Seasons." *SR* 57 (1969), 385–92.

Törnqvist, Egil. "Poet in the Space Age: A Theme in Aspenström's Plays." *SS* 39 (1966), 1–15.

Bergman, Hjalmar

Linder, Erik Hjalmar. *Hjalmar Bergman.* Trans. Catherine Djurklou. Boston: Twayne, 1975.

Sprinchorn, Evert. "Hjalmar Bergman." *Tulane Drama Review* 6:2 (1961), 117–27.

Boye, Karin

Tegen, Gunhild. "Karin Boye in Memoriam." *SR* 30 (1942), 240–43.

Vowles, Richard B. "Ripeness Is All: A Study in Karin Boye's Poetry." *Bulletin of the American-Swedish Institute* (Spring 1952), 3–7.

Dagerman, Stig

Bergmann, S. A. "Blinded by Darkness: A Study of the Novels and Plays of Stig Dagerman." *Delta* 11 (1957), 16–31.

Stig Dagerman. SBR Supplement, 1984.

Thompson, Laurie. *Stig Dagerman.* Boston: Twayne, 1983.

Edfelt, Johannes

Johannes Edfelt. SBR Supplement, 1989.

Ekelöf, Gunnar

Shideler, Ross P. "An Analysis of Gunnar Ekelöf's 'Röster under jorden.'" *SC* 9 (1970), 95–114.

Sjöberg, Leif. *A Reader's Guide to Ekelöf's* A Mölna Elegy. New York: Twayne, 1973.

Thygesen, Erik. *Gunnar Ekelöf's Open-Form Poem:* A Mölna Elegy, *Problems of Genesis, Structure, and Influence.* Uppsala: Acta Universitatis Upsaliensis, 1985.

Ekelund, Vilhelm

Johannesson, Erik O. "Vilhelm Ekelund: Modernism and the Aesthetics of the Aphorism." *SS* 56 (1984), 213–34.

Ferlin, Nils

Vowles, Richard B. "The Poet as Clown and Scapegoat." *The Norseman* 12 (1954), 424–29.

Fridegård, Jan

Graves, Peter. *Jan Fridegård: Lars Hård.* Studies in Swedish Literature 8. Hull, England: University of Hull, 1977.

Fröding, Gustaf

Fleisher, Frederic. "Gustaf Fröding, 1860–1911." *SR* 42 (1954), 303–8.

Flygt, Sten G. "Gustaf Fröding's Conception of Eros." *Germanic Review* 25 (1950), 109–23.

Gullberg, Hjalmar

Vowles, Richard B. "Hjalmar Gullberg: An Ancient and a Modern." *SS* 24 (1952), 111–18.

Gyllensten, Lars

Isaksson, Hans. *Lars Gyllensten.* Boston: Twayne, 1978.

Warme, Lars G. "Lars Gyllensten's *Diarium Spirituale:* The Creative Process as a Novel." *SC* 19 (1980), 165–80.

Hallström, Per

Dahlström, C.E.W.L. "Hallström's Impressionism in *A Secret Idyll.*" *Publications of the Modern Language Association of America* 46 (1931), 930–39.

Hansson, Ola

Brantly, Susan. "Creating an Alternative to Naturalism: Ola Hansson's Assimilation of Nietzsche." *Orbis Litterarum* 42 (1987), 44–57.

Hume, David R. "The First Five Years of Ola Hansson's Literary Exile, 1888–93." In *Facts of Scandinavian Literature.* (*Germanische Forschungsketten* 2.) Lexington, Ky.: Apra Press, 1974, 32–39.

Heidenstam, Verner von

Böök, Fredrik. "Verner von Heidenstam, Author of 'The Charles Men.'" In *Scandinavian Classics* 15. New York: American-Scandinavian Foundation, 1920.

Bibliography

Brantly, Susan, "Heidenstam's *Karolinerna* and the Fin de Siècle." In *Festschrift in Honor of Harald S. Naess,* ed. Faith Ingwersen and Mary Kay Norseng. Columbia, S.C.: Camden House, 1993, 69–77.

Gustafson, Alrik. "Nationalism Reinterpreted: Verner von Heidenstam." In *Six Scandinavian Novelists.* 1940. Rpt. New York: Biblo & Tannen, 1969, 123–76.

Johnson, Eyvind

Orton, Gavin. *Eyvind Johnson.* New York: Twayne, 1972.

Warme, Lars G. "Eyvind Johnson's *Några steg mot tystnaden:* An Apologia." *SS* 49 (1977), 452–63.

Karlfeldt, Erik Axel

Fleisher, Frederic. "The Vagond in the Life and Poetry of Erik Axel Karlfeldt." *SS* 26 (1954), 25–27.

Hildeman, Karl-Ivar. "Erik Axel Karlfeldt: An Evaluation." *SS* 40 (1968), 81–94.

Key, Ellen

Nyström-Hamilton, Louise. *Ellen Key: Her Life and Her Work.* Trans. A.E.B. Fries, intro. H. Ellis. New York and London: Putnam, 1913.

Krusenstjerna, Agnes von

Jones, Llewellyn. "Agnes von Krusenstjerna: A Swedish Proust." *WLT* 23 (1949), 10–14.

Lagerkvist, Pär

Sjöberg, Leif. *Pär Lagerkvist.* New York: Columbia University Press, 1976.

Spector, Robert Donald. *Pär Lagerkvist.* New York: Twayne, 1973.

Warme, Lars G. "Pär Lagerkvist." In *European Writers: The Twentieth Century,* ed. George Stade, vol. 10. New York: Scribner's, 1990, 1677–1702.

Lagerlöf, Selma

Berendsohn, Walter. *Selma Lagerlöf: Her Life and Work.* Adapted from the German by G. F. Timpson, with a preface by Vita Sackville-West. London: Nicholson & Watson, 1931.

Edström, Vivi. *Selma Lagerlöf.* Boston: Twayne, 1984.

Levertin, Oscar

Murdock, Elinor E. "Oscar Levertin: Swedish Critic of French Realism." *Contemporary Literature* 5 (1953), 137–50.

Lindegren, Erik

Ekner, Reidar. "The Artist as the Eye of a Needle." *SS* 42 (1970), 1–13.

Vowles, Richard B. "Sweden's Modern Muse: Exploded Sonnets and Panic Poetry." *Kentucky Foreign Language Quarterly* 2 (1955), 132–40.

Lo-Johansson, Ivar

Ivar Lo-Johansson. *SBR Supplement,* 1991.

Wright, Rochelle. "Dream and Dream Imagery in Ivar Lo-Johansson's Godnatt, jord." *ss* 64 (1992).

Lundkvist, Artur

Eriksson, Magnus. "The Formation of an Artistic Identity: The Young Arthur, Lundkvist." *ss* 66 (1994), 382–99.

Sjöberg, Leif. "An Interview with Artur Lundkvist." *WLT* 50 (1976), 329–36.

Vowles, Richard. "From Pan to Panic: The Poetry of Artur Lundkvist." *New Mexico Quarterly* 22 (1952), 288–96.

Martinson, Harry

Bergman, S. A. "Harry Martinson and Science." *Scandinavian Proceedings* 88 (1966), 99–120.

Johannesson, Eric O. "*Aniara:* Poetry and the Poet in the Modern World." *ss* 32 (1960), 185–202.

Martinson, Moa

Wright, Rochelle. "The Martinsons and Literary History." *ss* 64 (1992), 263–69.

Moberg, Vilhelm

Alexis, Gerhard T. "Sweden to Minnesota: Vilhelm Moberg's Fictional Reconstruction." *American Quarterly* 18 (1966), 81–94.

Holmes, Philip. *Vilhelm Moberg.* Boston: Twayne, 1980.

Johnson, Walter. "Moberg's Emigrants and the Naturalistic Tradition." *ss* 25 (1953), 134–46.

McKnight, Roger. *Moberg's Emigrant Novels and the Journals of Andrew Peterson: A Study of Influence and Parallels.* New York: Arno Press, 1979.

Warme, Lars G. "Vilhelm Moberg." In *European Writers: The Twentieth Century,* ed. George Stade, vol. 11. New York: Scribner's, 1990, 2203–32.

Winther, Sophus K. "Moberg and a New Genre for the Emigrant Novel." *ss* 34 (1962), 170–82.

Sjöberg, Birger

Engblom, Carl J. "Birger Sjöberg." *SR* 47 (1959), 159–63.

Söderberg, Hjalmar

Butt, Wolfgang. *Hjalmar Söderberg:* Martin Bircks ungdom. Studies in Swedish Literature 7. Hull, England: University of Hull, 1976.

Geddes, Tom. *Hjalmar Söderberg:* Doktor Glas. Studies in Swedish Literature 3. Hull, England: University of Hull, 1975.

Lofmark, Carl. *Hjalmar Söderberg:* Historietter. Studies in Swedish Literature 10. England: University of Hull, 1977.

Södergran, Edith

Hird, Gladys. "Edith Södergran: A Pioneer of Finland-Swedish Modernism." *Books from Finland* 12 (1978), 4–7.

Schoolfield, George C. *Edith Södergran: Modernist Poet in Finland.* Westport, Conn.: Greenwood Press, 1984.

Wägner, Elin
Death, Sarah. "The Sleeping Fury: Symbol and Metaphor in Elin Wägner's *Silverforsen.*" SC 24 (1985), 183–95.

CHAPTER 7: LITERATURE AFTER 1950

GENERAL

Algulin, Ingemar. *Contemporary Swedish Prose.* Stockholm: Swedish Institute, 1983.
Bisztray, George. "Documentarism and the Modern Scandinavian Novel." SS 48 (1976), 71–83.
Carlson, Harry G. "Riksteatern: The Sweidsh National Provincial Theatre." *Educational Theatre Journal* 15 (1963), 39–46.
Hilleström, Gustaf. *Swedish Theater during Five Decades.* Stockholm: Swedish Institute, 1963.
Nolin, Bertil. "A Successful Realization of Group Theater in Sweden." SS 43 (1971), 22–34.
Orton, Gavin. "The Swedish Novel Today." SC 15 (1976), 159–70.
Rosengren, Karl Erik. *Sociological Aspects of the Literary System.* Stockholm: Natur & Kultur, 1968.
Schwanbom, Per. "New Directions in the Swedish Theater." SR 6 (1973), 259–67.
Scobbie, Irene, ed. *Aspects of Modern Swedish Literature.* Norwich, England: Norvik Press, 1988.
Sharpe, Eric J. "Myth Reinterpreted: Biblical Themes in Modern Swedish Literature." *AUMLA: Journal of the Australasian Universities Language and Literature Association* 66 (1986), 218–48.
Vowles, Richard B. "Visions and Revisions: The State of Swedish Letters." *Literary Review* 9 (1965), 165–75.
William-Olsson, Magnus. "Contemporary Swedish Poetry." *Talisman* 6 (1991), 72–74.
Wizelius, Ingmar. "New Swedish Fiction." WLT 38 (1964), 128–34.

ANTHOLOGIES

Anderman, Gunilla, ed. *New Swedish Plays.* Chester Springs, Pa.: Dufour Editions, 1993.
Bäckström, Lars, and Göran Palm. *Sweden Writes: Contemporary Poetry and Prose.* Stockholm: Prisma & the Swedish Institute, 1965.
Bruce, Lennart, and Sonja Bruce, eds. and trans. *Speak to Me: Swedish-Language Women Poets.* Flushing, N.Y.: The Spirit that Moves Us Press, 1989.
Fleischer, Frederic, trans. and ed. *Eight Swedish Poets.* Helsinki: Cavefors, 1963.
Fulton, Robin, trans. *Five Swedish Poets.* South Orange, N.J.: Spirit, 1972.

———. *Four Swedish Poets: Lennart Sjögren, Eva Ström, Kjell Espmark, Tomas Tranströmer.* Fredonia, N.Y.: White Pine Press, 1990.

———. *Preparations for Flight and Other Swedish Stories.* London: Forest Books, 1990.

Gustafsson, Lars. *Forays into Swedish Poetry.* Trans. Robert T. Rovinsky. Austin: University of Texas Press, 1978.

Harding, Gunnar, and Anselm Hollo, eds. *Modern Swedish Poetry in Translation.* Minneapolis: University of Minnesota Press, 1979.

Lagerlöf, Karl Erik, ed. *Modern Swedish Prose in Translation.* Minneapolis: University of Minnesota Press, 1980.

Mattias, John, and Göran Printz-Påhlson, trans. *Contemporary Swedish Poetry.* Chicago: Swallow Press, 1980.

Modern Nordic Plays: Sweden. New York: Twayne; Oslo: Universitetsforlaget, 1973.

Wästberg, Per, ed. *An Anthology of Modern Swedish Literature.* Merrick, N.Y.: Cross-Cultural Communications, 1979.

SELECTED WORKS IN ENGLISH

Espmark, Kjell
Fulton, Robin, trans. *Béla Bartók against the Third Reich.* Stockholm: Norstedt, 1985.

Forssell, Lars
Carlson, Harry G., trans. *Five Plays.* San Francisco: Literary Discoveries, 1964.

✓ *Gustafsson, Lars*
Fulton, Robin, trans. *Selected Poems.* New York: New Rivers, 1972.

Harding, Gunnar
Fulton, Robin, trans. *They Killed Sitting Bull and Other Poems.* London: London Magazine Editions, 1973.

Sjöstrand, Östen
Fulton, Robin, trans. *The Hidden Music: Poems.* New York: Oleander, 1975.

———. *Toward the Solitary Star.* Provo, Utah: Brigham Young University Press, 1988.

Sonnevi, Göran
Hogue, Cynthia, and Jan Karlsson et al., trans. *Göran Sonnevi: Poetry in Translation.* Göteborg: Swedish Books, 1982.

On the War: A Bilingual Pamphlet of Poems. Madison, Wis.: Third Coast Press, 1968.

Tranströmer, Tomas
✓ Bly, Robert, et al. *Selected Poems, 1954–1986.* New York: Ecco Press, 1987.

✓ Fulton, Robin, trans. *Collected Poems.* Newcastle-upon-Tyne: Bloodaxe Books, 1987.

MONOGRAPHS AND ARTICLES

Delblanc, Sven

Robinson, Michael. *Sven Delblanc:* Åminne. Studies in Swedish Literature 12. Hull, England: University of Hull, 1981.

Sjöberg, Leif. "Delblanc's *Homunculus:* Some Magical Elements." *Germanic Review* 49 (1974), 105–24.

Vowles, Richard B. "Myth in Sweden: Sven Delblanc's *Homunculus.*" WLT 48 (1977), 20–25.

Ekman, Kerstin

Wright, Rochelle. "Approaches to History in the Works of Kerstin Ekman." SS 63 (1991), 293–304.

———. "Kerstin Ekman: Voice of the Vulnerable." WLT 55 (1981), 204–9.

———. "Kerstin Ekman's Crime Fiction and the 'Crime' of Fiction: *The Devil's Horn.*" SBR 2 (1984), 12–21.

———. "Theme, Imagery, and Narrative Perspective in Kerstin Ekman's *En stad av ljus.*" SS 59 (1987), 1–27.

Enquist, Per Olof

Blackwell, Marilyn Johns. "Enquist's *Legionärerna:* A Plea for the Necessity of Fiction." SC 22 (1983), 129–40.

Shideler, Ross. *Per Olov Enquist, a Critical Study.* Westport, Conn.: Greenwood Press, 1984.

———. "Putting Together the Puzzle in Per Olov Enquist's *Sekonden.*" SS 49 (1977), 311–29.

———. "The Swedish Short Story: Per Olov Enquist." SS 49 (1977), 241–48.

Evander, Per Gunnar

Petherick, Karin. *Per Gunnar Evander.* Boston: Twayne, 1982.

Forssell, Lars

Carlson, Harry G. "Lars Forssell—Poet in the Theater." SS 37 (1965), 31–57.

McKnight, Christina S. "Lars Forssell: The Jester as Conscience." WLT 55 (1981), 210–15.

Gustafsson, Lars

Dubois, Ia. "In Search of an Identity: The Heroic Quest in Lars Gustafsson's Fiction, 1960–1986." SS 67 (1995), 163–80.

Sandstroem, Yvonne L. "The Machine Theme in Some Poems by Lars Gustafsson." SS 44 (1972), 210–23.

Isaksson, Folke

Sjöberg, Leif. "Folke Isaksson." SBR 2 (1989), 44–45.

Jersild, P. C.

P. C. Jersild. SBR Supplement, 1983.

Shideler, Ross. "The Battle for the Self in P. C. Jersild's *En levande själ.*" SS 56 (1984), 256–71.

Bibliography

———. "Dehumanization and the Bureaucracy in Novels by P. C. Jersild." *SC* 23 (1984), 24–38.

———. "P. C. Jersild's *Efter floden* and Human Value(s)." *SC* 27 (1988), 31–43.

Kallifatides, Theodor

Norlen, Paul. "Theodor Kallifatides: An Introduction." *SBR* 2 (1989), 20–24.

Lidman, Sara

Borland, Harold. "Sara Lidman, Novelist and Moralist." *Svensk litteraturtidskrift* 36 (1973), 27–34.

———. "Sara Lidman's Progress: A Critical Survey of Six Novels." *SS* 39 (1967), 97–114.

Lindgren, Torgny

Torgny Lindgren. SBR Supplement, 1985.

Norén, Lars

Neuhauser, Lotta. "The Intoxication of Insight: Notes on Lars Norén." *Theater* 22 (1990–91), 89–92.

Pleijel, Agneta

Thompson, Laurie. "Introducing Agneta Pleijel." *SBR* 8 (1990), 2–4.

Sjöstrand, Östen

Bergsten, Staffan. *Östen Sjöstrand.* New York: Twayne, 1974.

Sandstroem, Yvonne L. "Östen Sjöstrand's Winding Stair." *WLT* 55 (1981), 245–49.

Sundman, Per Olof

Hinchcliffe, Ian. *Per Olof Sundman: Ingenjör Andrées luftfärd.* Studies in Swedish Literature 13. Hull, England: University of Hull, 1982.

McGregor, Rick. *Per Olof Sundman and the Icelandic Sagas: A Study of Narrative Method.* Skrifter utgivna av Litteraturvetenskapliga institutionen vid Göteborgs universitet 26. Göteborg: University of Göteborg, 1994.

Sjöberg, Leif. "Per Olof Sundman: The Writer as a Reasonably Unbiased Observer." *WLT* 47 (1973), 253–60.

Stendahl, Brita. "Per Olof Sundman on the Expedition of Truthtelling." *WLT* 55 (1981), 250–56.

Warme, Lars G. *Per Olof Sundman, Writer of the North.* Westport, Conn.: Greenwood Press, 1984.

———. "Per Olof Sundman and the French New Novel—Influence or Coincidence?" *SS* 50 (1978), 403–13.

Tranströmer, Tomas

Bankier, Joanna. "The Sense of Time in the Poetry of Tomas Tranströmer." Ph.D. dissertation, University of California, Berkeley, 1985.

Rönnerstrand, Torsten. " 'The Frontier between Silence and What Can Be Articulated': On the Idea of Language in Tomas Tranströmer's Poetry." *SC* 29 (1990), 215–32.

Sellin, Eric. "Tomas Tranströmer and the Cosmic Image." *SS* 43 (1971), 241–50.

Steene, Birgitta. "Vision and Reality in the Poetry of Tomas Tranströmer." *SS* 37 (1965), 236–44.

"Tomas Tranströmer: 1990 Neustadt Laureate." *WLT* 64 (1990), 549–604.

Trotzig, Birgitta

Boyer, Regis. *Job mitt ibland oss: En studie över Birgitta Trotzigs verk.* Stockholm and Uppsala: Katolska bokförlaget, 1978.

D'Heurle, Adma. "The Image of Woman in the Fiction of Birgitta Trotzig." *SS* 55 (1983), 371–82.

Tunström, Göran

Göran Tunström. SBR Supplement, 1988.

CHAPTER 8: WOMEN WRITERS

GENERAL

Death, Sarah, and Helena Forsås-Scott, eds. *A Century of Swedish Narrative: Essays in Honor of Karin Petherick.* Norwich, England: Norvik Press, 1994.

Forsås-Scott, Helena. *Textual Liberation: European Feminist Writing in the Twentieth Century.* London: Routledge, 1991. [Chapter on Scandinavia, pp. 39–73.]

Holmquist, Ingrid, and Ebba Witt-Brattström, eds. *Kvinnornas litteraturhistoria,* vol. 2. Stockholm: Författarförlaget, 1983.

Nilsson, Ruth. *Kvinnosyn i Sverige från drottning Kristina till Anna Maria Lenngren.* Lund: CWK Gleerup, 1973.

Nordin Hennel, Ingeborg. *"Ämnar kanske fröken publicera något?" Kvinnligt och manligt i 1880-talets novellistik.* Acta Universitatis Umensis 56. Umeå, 1984.

Ramnefalk, Marie Louise, and Anna Westberg, eds. *Kvinnornas litteraturhistoria.* Stockholm: Författarförlaget, 1981.

Westman Berg, Karin, and Gabrielle Åhmansson, eds. *Mothers—Saviours—Peacemakers: Swedish Women Writers in the Twentieth Century.* Kvinnolitteraturforskning 4. Uppsala: Reprocentralen HSC, 1983.

ANTHOLOGIES

Arkin, Marian, and Barbara Shollar, eds. *Longman Anthology of World Literature by Women, 1875–1975.* New York: Longman, 1989. [Includes pieces by and about Benedictsson, Lagerlöf, Wägner, Södergran, Boye, Solveig von Schoultz and Tove Jansson of Finland, Åkesson, Margareta Ekström.]

Clareus, Ingrid, ed. *Scandinavian Women Writers: An Anthology from the 1880s to the 1980s.* New York: Greenwood Press, 1989.

SELECTED WORKS IN ENGLISH

Södergran, Edith

Katchadourian, Stina, trans. *Love and Solitude: Selected Poems, 1916–1923.* Seattle: Fjord Press, 1985.

McDuff, David, trans. *Complete Poems*. Newcastle-upon-Tyne: Bloodaxe Books, 1984.

MONOGRAPHS AND ARTICLES

Benedictsson, Victoria
Bjørby, Pål. "The Study of a Vision in the Authorship of Victoria Benedictsson." Ph.D. dissertation. University of Minnesota, 1983.
Moberg, Verne. "Truth against Syphilis: Victoria Benedictsson's Remedy for a Dreaded Disease." *Edda* (1983), 31–44.

Brenner, Sophia Elisabeth
Kaminsky, Amy. "Nearly New Clarions: Sor Juana de la Cruz Pays Homage to a Swedish Woman Poet." In *In the Feminine Mode*, ed. Noël Vallis and Carol Maier. London and Cranbury, N.J.: Bucknell University Press, 1990, 31–53.

Elgström, Anna Lenah
Register, Cheri. "Consuming Flames/Illuminating Starlight: Feminist Pacifist Themes in a Short Story by Anna Lenah Elgström." In *Mothers—Saviours—Peacemakers*, 75–105.

Horn, Agneta
Mitchell, Stephen A. *Job in Female Garb: Studies on the Autobiography of Agneta Horn*. Skrifter utgivna av Litteraturvetenskapliga institutionen vid Göteborgs universitet 14. Göteborg: University of Göteborg, 1985.

Key, Ellen
Lundell, Torborg. "Ellen Key and Swedish Feminist Views on Motherhood." *SS* 56 (1984), 351–69.
Register, Cheri. "Motherhood at Center: Ellen Key's Social Vision." *Women's Studies International Forum* 5 (6) (1982), 599–610.

Lagerlöf, Selma
Register, Cheri. "The Sacrificial Hera: Selma Lagerlöf's *The Treasure* as a Feminist Myth." In *Mothers—Saviours—Peacemakers*, 29–73.

Wägner, Elin
Death, Sarah. "Sexual Politics and the Defeat of Sisterhood in Elin Wägner's *Släkten Jerneploogs framgång*." In *Mothers—Saviours—Peacemakers*, 125–44.

CHAPTER 9: LITERATURE FOR CHILDREN AND YOUNG PEOPLE

Cott, Jonathan. "The Happy Childhoods of Pippi Longstocking and Astrid Lindgren." In his *Pipers at the Gate of Dawn: The Wisdom of Children's Literature*. New York: Random House, 1983, 135–58.
Culture for Children. Stockholm: Swedish Institute for Children's Books, 1982.
Edström, Vivi. *Astrid Lindgren*. Stockholm: Swedish Institute, 1987.

————. *Barnbokens form*. Göteborg: Gothia, 1982.

Lundqvist, Ulla. "Some Portraits of Teenagers in Modern Junior Novels in Sweden." In *The Portrayal of the Child in Children's Literature: Proceedings of the Sixth Conference of the IRSCL 1983,* ed. Denise Escarpit. München, New York, London, Paris: Saur, 1985, 117–24.

Mählqvist, Stefan. "Children's Books in the Kingdom of Sweden." In *Printed for Children*. München, New York, London, Paris: Saur, 1978, 383–90.

Metcalf, Eva-Maria. *Astrid Lindgren*. Twayne's World Author Series 851. New York: Twayne, 1995.

Ørvig, Mary. *Children's Books in Sweden, 1945–1970: A Survey*. Wien: Austrian Children's Book Club, 1973.

————. "A Collage: Eight Women Who Write Books in Swedish for Children." In *Crosscurrents of Criticism,* ed. Paul Heins. Boston: Horn Book, 1977, 248–60.

The Contributors

Susan Brantly is a professor of Scandinavian studies at the University of Wisconsin-Madison. She is the author of *The Life and Writings of Laura Marholm*.

James Larson is a professor of Scandinavian at the University of California, Berkeley. His books include *Reason and Experience: The Representation of Natural Order in the Work of Carl von Linné*; *Songs of Something Else*; *Renaissance of the Goths*; and *Interpreting Nature: The Science of Living Form from Linnaeus to Kant*.

James Massengale is a professor of Scandinavian literature at the University of California, Los Angeles. He is the author of *The Musical-Poetic Method of Carl Michael Bellman*; *Systerligt förente*; and *Analytical Song Index for Bellman's Poetry*. He is coeditor and music commentator for several editions of Bellman's works.

Stephen A. Mitchell is a professor of Scandinavian folklore at Harvard University, curator of the Milman Parry Collection of Oral Literature, and coeditor of its series, *The Milman Parry Studies in Oral Tradition*. His publications include *Job in Female Garb: Studies on the Autobiography of Agneta Horn* and *Heroic Sagas and Ballads*.

Maria Nikolajeva has a doctorate in literature from Stockholm University, where she is a teacher and researcher. Her books include *The Magic Code: The Use of Magical Pattern in Fantasy for Children* and *Selma Lagerlöf ur ryskt perspektiv*.

Bertil Nolin is an associate professor in the Department of Literature at the University of Göteborg. He was visiting professor at the University of Chicago in 1968–70 and at the University of Washington in 1987 and 1988. His research has focused on the Modern Breakthrough and Swedish theater studies: *Den gode europén*; *Georg Brandes*; *The Modern Breakthrough in Scandinavian Literature*,

1871–1905 (ed.); *Lorensbergsteatern, 1916–1934* (ed.); and *Kulturradikalismen: Det moderna genombrottets andra fas.*

Cheri Register has a doctorate in Scandinavian languages and literatures from the University of Chicago. Her books include *Kvinnokamp och litteratur i U.S.A. och Sverige*; *Mothers—Saviours—Peacemakers: Swedish Women Writers in the Twentieth Century*; *Living with Chronic Illness: Days of Patience and Passion*; and *"Are Those Kids Yours?" American Families with Children Adopted from Other Countries.*

Birgitta Steene was a professor of comparative and Scandinavian literature at the University of Washington from 1973 to 1990 and professor in the Department of Theatre and Cinema at Stockholm University from 1990 to 1993. She has published books on Ingmar Bergman and August Strindberg and is the author of numerous scholarly articles on Scandinavian and comparative literature and film.

Lars G. Warme holds degrees from the University of Lund, Sweden, and the University of California, Berkeley. He is an associate professor in the Department of Scandinavian Languages and Literature at the University of Washington. He has published a book on Per Olof Sundman and a number of articles.

Rochelle Wright is a professor of Scandinavian literature at the University of Illinois, Urbana. She is the coauthor of *Danish Emigrant Ballads and Songs* and the translator of novels by Ivar Lo-Johansson.

Index

Index   550

Index

Index

Index

In A History of Scandinavian Literatures series

Volume 1
A History of Danish Literature
Edited by Sven H. Rossel

Volume 2
A History of Norwegian Literature
Edited by Harald S. Naess

Volume 3
A History of Swedish Literature
Edited by Lars G. Warme